Emergency Remote Teaching and Beyond

Julian Chen

Editor

Emergency Remote Teaching and Beyond

Voices from World Language Teachers
and Researchers

 Springer

Editor
Julian Chen (iD)
School of Education
Curtin University
Perth, WA, Australia

ISBN 978-3-030-84066-2   ISBN 978-3-030-84067-9   (eBook)
https://doi.org/10.1007/978-3-030-84067-9

This Springer imprint is published by the registered company Springer Nature Switzerland AG
The registered company address is: Gewerbestrasse 11, 6330 Cham, Switzerland

Preface

It is hard to believe that more than a year has passed since the eerie pandemic turned the entire world upside down and derailed every aspect of our normal lives. Just when we thought, hoped and naively predicted that this global crisis would have abated by now, little did we know that the second, third and N^{th} waves of the coronavirus outbreak would still be looming over our world. While I am writing this editorial at this very moment, regrettably, the threat of unforeseen coronavirus mutations is haunting us relentlessly, dimming and delaying a promising post-COVID recovery. One cannot help but wonder when we will get back to normal, free from social distancing and communicating from behind a face mask.

No one can predict what the future holds and how long the crisis will continue to disrupt the equilibrium of the social-emotional learning and well-being of all the stakeholders in the education sector. The devastating COVID-19 has drastically altered the landscape of in-class teaching and learning, forcing language educators into crisis teaching almost overnight. While online courses generally take considerable time and effort to prepare before the rollout, the abrupt switch to crisis teaching has prevented this 'luxury'. It rushed teachers, unprepared and in a state of shock, into remote teaching in order to battle the crisis brought about by the coronavirus pandemic (Zimmerman, 2020). In fact, Hodges et al. (2020) coined the term 'emergency remote teaching' (ERT), to capture this chaotic phenomenon in the wake of COVID-19. This sets the stage for this edited volume, since all the inclusive chapters are based on the ERT phenomenon, and cover the salient aspects of crisis teaching associated with language pedagogy and research.

While COVID-19 has affected all students, ERT may even be more problematic for the social and emotional learning aspects of our language learners. Although ERT allows them to continue their studies amid the global pandemic, it also undermines opportunities for social connections and peer and teacher support, since '[t]he screen makes the students feel more anonymous and isolated' (Richards, 2020). Furthermore, our language learners have to not only tackle the challenging demands of academic learning, but also the linguistic and cultural barriers to participation that were already an issue prior to the pandemic, but which have been exacerbated by ERT. Let us not forget that socioeconomically disadvantaged students may have difficulty accessing (stable) broadband internet and the devices required for ERT, such as smartphones or laptops, thus aggravating inequality and the digital divide that already exists in technology-deprived contexts (Porumbescu, 2020).

By the same token, not all language teachers are well-equipped and comfortable with teaching remotely, and much less so when they have unstable internet connections or outdated devices, which only add to their frustration and anxiety (McMurtrie, 2020). For those unfamiliar with or downplaying remote teaching, ERT might have initially as appeared to be an 'easier' or 'lighter' alternative to face-to-face teaching conducted in a physical class; after all, surely all the online teachers needed to do was to copy what was done in class in the online space? Voilà! Problem solved! Little did they realise that remaining online constantly while juggling technical glitches, virtual class management, and students' online engagement and performance is actually more stressful and time consuming, particularly for teachers who were new to remote teaching. Consequently, ERT took a toll on teachers' well-being and mental health (Schaffhauser, 2020; Tate, 2020) – the list can go on.

The question that remains is how language teachers, particularly online teaching novices, countered the inevitable threat posed by ERT and turned the tables. Specifically, what adaptive strategies and resilient innovations did they employ to overcome the challenges of ERT? How did this experience translate into their teacher identity, professional development and future teaching practices? Similarly, researchers were only able to gather data remotely during the lockdown, an inevitable constraint that sabotaged their original research plans that were geared towards a physical setting. What contingency plans did they develop, and how would these drastic changes impact on their research designs and outputs? To play devil's advocate, has ERT also 'pushed' them to reinvigorate their research agendas and to explore uncharted waters via methodologies that may unearth more virgin research terrains? Above all, what lessons can we all learn from these world language teachers and researchers in the current climate and in the post-COVID-19 era?

Exploratory and inclusive in nature, this edited volume aims to examine the ERT phenomenon in more depth and to provide a platform for language practitioners and researchers to share their compelling stories about stepping outside of their comfort zones and charting their remote teaching and research trajectories. With regard to pedagogy, it spotlights how those teachers who were novices in online teaching revamped their existing teaching practices, (re)learned the technical skills needed for online delivery, reflected on the initial setbacks, reinforced their resilience and professionalism, and reimagined new identities as capable online teachers. In terms of research, it promotes the 'teacher as researcher' agenda, showcasing how researchers systematically documented their use of technology, their critical reflections on their achievements and the pitfalls in collecting data remotely, and evaluated the participants' attitudes towards this drastic change. More importantly, this collection shows how researchers can capitalise on creative research design, data collection and analysis that can only be accomplished in a fully online environment.

Readership

Given its well-rounded scope that accommodates diverse educational settings and target languages in the global context, as well as innovative research agendas and approaches, this collection speaks to a wider audience. It is tailored to language practitioners across the world, as well as to curriculum designers, teacher trainers and online educators who have been affected by ERT and are eager to learn from the best practices and strategies shared by the contributors in this volume. It also appeals to tertiary academics, researchers and students in the fields of language education, applied linguistics and distance learning, who would benefit from creative research designs and viable data collection approaches that transcend social distancing. Readers will also find the pedagogical and research implications applicable to their own contexts, thus paving the way for online pedagogy and research beyond the pandemic.

Overall, this timely volume can serve as a practical guide for language educators who are involved in or are preparing for future distance or blended learning. The well-documented and concrete research plans in the curated chapters will also be beneficial for scholars involved in research regarding technology-enhanced language learning (TELL) or mobile assisted language learning (MALL). Academics and (under)graduate students can also use this collection as a main text or as a resource in courses related to educational technology and computer-assisted language teaching (CALL).

Features

This eclectic collection features the following aspects that differentiate it from its counterparts:

1. *A timely and urgent agenda:*
   The global pandemic has affected all the stakeholders in language education and beyond. In this volume, teachers and researchers from across the world share their vivid stories and context-responsive strategies while pinpointing caveats in addressing burning issues in crisis teaching. Not only do their cases resonate with other like-minded readers, the lessons drawn from their first-hand ERT experiences are also valuable and transferrable to the readers' own teaching/research contexts.

2. *Global perspectives*:
   This volume transcends geopolitical and spatiotemporal boundaries. It showcases a rich variety of target languages spoken around the world such as Arabic, Bangla, French, Finnish, Spanish, English, Japanese, Vietnamese and Bahasa Indonesia. It also reports on what is currently happening in ERT practices in both developing and developed countries, with a focus on under-explored contexts

such as Puerto Rico, Kazakhstan, the Philippines, Ukraine, Colombia and Bangladesh. Thus, it whets the international appetite.

3. *Diverse educational settings and topics*:

The curated chapters in this edited volume encompass culturally/linguistically diverse backgrounds and teaching/research at various educational settings, ranging from K-12 to university, and from the urban to remote regions. Specifically, it zeros in on low socioeconomic contexts in which access to the internet and facilities that are integral to remote teaching and learning are not available. Therefore, a true representation of what is occurring in the pandemic world has been attempted. Numerous contemporary topics are also tailored to the various needs and interests of all the affected stakeholders, such as online teaching practicum, online professional development, auto- and virtual ethnography, case studies and mixed methods research.

4. *A balance of research and practice*:

This well-rounded collection of both pedagogical and research pieces is welcomed by teachers and researchers alike. Both seasoned and emerging researchers and classroom teachers have joined forces to share their ERT trajectories and to shed light on innovative approaches to remote teaching and research. For example, how do practitioners utilise digital technologies to conduct online mentoring, modify study-abroad programmes and build virtual communities? Similarly, how do researchers think creatively to conduct ERT research from afar, such as social media research? This contributes to the pool of resources and handbooks for courses related to language-teaching methodologies, research methods in applied linguistics and technology-enhanced instruction.

5. *Accessible language and concrete examples*:

Given the practical orientation of the book, the language and structure are reader-friendly, first-person voice and easy to follow. This work intends to engage pre- and in-service language teachers, as well as novice researchers who prefer a more accessible guide to a dry academic piece. While the chapters in the second half of the book are research-driven, there are ample illustrative examples and well-detailed implementation plans to enable readers to replicate these studies on their own. Each chapter begins with a clear roadmap that highlights the essence of its contents, and ends with food for thought that suggests the implications for future language teaching and research beyond ERT.

Rigour

Admittedly, curating a large collection of 24 unique chapters and interweaving them seamlessly was no easy task for a single editor. To my pleasant surprise, the original call for chapters was enthusiastically answered by 85 submissions from around the world! This fervent expression of interest showed that this urgent topic resonated with the world's language teachers and researchers who had been deeply impacted by crisis teaching, and were eager to share what actually happened in their own ERT practices, the challenges they encountered and the lessons learned, and how we all can grow as more resilient, creative and forward-thinking language educators during and after the pandemic.

Despite being intrigued by the wealth of the 85 topics that were submitted in the initial pool, I was fully aware that a more stringent approach was needed to streamline the volume by carefully selecting chapters that shared the same theme and were more suitable for the readership. After finalising the chapter selection, I conducted my own editorial screening to provide feedback and suggestions for each chapter's author(s) and to invite them to revise their chapters. Knowing that the contributors would benefit greatly from 'pearls of wisdom' from their peers, I decided to undertake the second round of internal blind review. That is, authors working in the same thematic category (for example, *Case Study Research*) were invited to provide feedback in a blind peer review in which, reciprocally, they would receive feedback from their peer reviewers. This added another layer of quality assurance to each chapter, and enabled the contributors to not only include useful peer feedback when refining their chapters, but also be inspired by and learn from their colleagues' work. All the revised chapters were then sent to Springer's external review before the final round of revision.

This iterative, co-constructive and rigorous process further epitomises how a virtual community of practice can be built remotely in the context of a pandemic.

Structure

As expressed in the title, this edited volume balances research and practice. Language practitioners and researchers across continents have joined forces to share their stories and insights, while candidly highlighting the unforeseen challenges and caveats in ERT. Twenty-four of the selected chapters are thoughtfully categorised into *Teacher Voice* – geared more towards practitioners dealing with all aspects of crisis teaching and learning, and *Researcher Corner* – delving more into innovative research designs and approaches triggered by ERT. Chapters in both parts are also thematically organised around context-responsive, pedagogy-oriented and research-informed topics that concern all the stakeholders.

Each chapter contains the following key sections:

1. *An abstract* summarises the essence of the chapter.
2. *Highlights* foreground the key chapter takeaways for the readers.
3. *The main body* presents the context of the chapter, provides a synthesised review of the literature (or theoretical framework), methodology (or research design), data presentation and discussion, implications, and a conclusion.
4. *Food for thought* offers hands-on recommendations and directions in advancing language teaching and research beyond ERT.
5. *A summary table* (in 'Teacher Voice') summarises the features of digital tools or online platforms mentioned in the chapter when available.

Final Remark

Although a dark cloud still hangs over us, every cloud has a silver lining. The DNA of this volume is to champion world language teaching and research and to celebrate all the fantastic works we have accomplished during ERT, paving the way for more sustainable and innovative pedagogy and research in the post-COVID era.

Perth, Australia   Julian Chen
May 2021

References

Hodges, C., Moore, S., Lockee, B., Trust, T., & Bond, A. (2020, March 27). The difference between emergency remote teaching and online learning. *Educause Review*. https://er.educause.edu/articles/2020/3/the-difference-between-emergency-remote-teaching-and-online-learning

McMurtrie, B. (2020, April 6). Students without laptops, instructors without internet: How struggling colleges move online during Covid-19. *The Chronicle of Higher Education*. https://www.chronicle.com/article/Students-Without-Laptops/248436/#.XoyH2pMlmFU.email

Porumbescu, G. (2020, March 18). The digital divide leaves millions at a disadvantage during the coronavirus pandemic. *The Conversation*. https://theconversation.com/the-digital-divide-leaves-millions-at-a-disadvantage-during-the-coronavirus-pandemic-133608

Richards, E. (2020, May 24). Coronavirus' online school is hard enough: What if you're still learning to speak English? *USA Today*. https://www.usatoday.com/in-depth/news/education/2020/05/14/coronavirus-online-classes-school-closures-esl-students-learn-english/5178145002/

Schaffhauser, D. (2020, June 6). Educators feeling stressed, anxious, overwhelmed and capable. *THE Journal*. https://thejournal.com/articles/2020/06/02/survey-teachers-feeling-stressed-anxious-overwhelmed-and-capable.aspx?admgarea=News1

Tate, E. (2020, April 16). For educators, being 'always-on' during COVID-19 can lead to burnout. *EdSurge*. https://www.edsurge.com/news/2020-04-16-for-educators-an-always-on-mentality-during-covid-19-can-lead-to-burnout

Zimmerman, J. (2020, March 10). Coronavirus and the Great Online-Learning Experiment. *The Chronicle of Higher Education*. https://www.chronicle.com/article/coronavirus-and-the-great-online-learning-experiment/

Editor's Notes

To ease readers into this volume, my editor's notes below serve as a reading guide that spotlights the essence of each chapter, whilst weaving together salient themes and take-away lessons across the 24 curated chapters. I hope readers will find pearls of wisdom in these vivid, first-hand ERT stories, shared by world language educators and scholars amid the global pandemic that hit us all hard in the beginning of 2020.

Teacher Voice

This volume starts by making language educators' voices heard (loudly and clearly) from the *stakeholder perspectives*. Setting the stage for the entire volume, the first two chapters open a window for us to examine what is actually happening in global crisis teaching and how the impacted stakeholders perceive its repercussions for the ecology of classroom teaching, teachers' well-being and local infrastructure that have been challenged by ERT.

In Chapter "Language Teaching in Times of COVID-19: The Emotional Rollercoaster of Lockdown", ***Christine Appel*** and ***Jackie Robbins*** take us back to when the global lockdown began in March 2020 and how language teachers and students located in Catalunya, Spain, as well as in other parts of the world, coped with this sudden and drastic shift to remote teaching. Drawn from the responses from online teachers (n=64) and students (n=307), their large-scale survey results reveal an area that is relatively overlooked in the literature, namely teacher emotion research. The authors also point out how programme coordinators can support language teachers more effectively by considering their emotional states and well-being, which subsequently affect the students. This consideration would help coordinators to make informed decisions regarding empowering staff during their on-going professional development, not only during the lockdown but also in the post-COVID stage. Chapter "Infrastructure, Literacy and Communication: The Challenges of Emergency Remote Teaching in a University in Japan", by ***Todd***

James Allen, re-examines the status quo in Japan regarding how the higher education sector copes with ERT. As an expatriate academic teaching English at a
Japanese university, he candidly reveals the stark mismatch between our stereotype
of the 'technology giant' and, surprisingly, Japan's lack of technological capacity to
implement crisis teaching. Through the lens of his critical observation and evaluation, we witness how stakeholders (university academics, administrators and students) struggled with the rapid shift to ERT from classroom teaching due to the
deficient IT infrastructure and literacy, coupled with inadequate communication and
support. Stress, confusion and anxiety were exacerbated in the aftermath of
ERT. Nonetheless, both chapters also shed light on the opportunities that ERT provides for trialling various new digital tools and fostering technology literacy in
online language teaching and learning.

One of the most talked about aspects in the context of ERT, *online professional
development and virtual community of practice,* is also highlighted in Teacher
Voice. Three compelling and heartfelt stories shared by English teachers and professors in Indonesia and Columbia remind us of who we are as adaptable and endeav-
ouring language-teaching professionals. In Chapter "Teachers' Instructions and
Online Professional Development During Emergency Remote Teaching in
Indonesia", *Hanna Sundari, Susianti Rosalina* and *Lalu Handi Rizal* recount how
they sought all forms of professional development (PD) opportunities in the wake of
the pandemic. Despite teaching in different settings (university and high school),
they initiated online PD webinars and activities, while sharing resources with other
fellow teachers in order to help them upskill their online teaching. High levels of
creativity and online engagement permeated their virtual communities of practice,
supported by multimodal technologies such as social media (WhatsApp, Instagram
and Facebook), ICT-based platforms (*PembaTIK*) and digital games (Kahoot! and
Quizizz). Similarly, Chapter "Surviving ERT: How an Online Professional Learning
Community Empowered Teachers During the Covid-19 School Lockdown in
Indonesia" illustrates that Indonesian English teachers were at the forefront with
their PD when facing challenges in ERT! *Maya Defianty, Kate Wilson* and *Dadan*
portray how a professional group of Indonesian English teachers built a tight-knit
community of practice via WhatsApp. It is impressive to see that members of this
supportive community joined forces in publishing practitioner-oriented outputs in
order to disseminate and share them with fellow teachers who were in urgent need
of best practices in ERT. They are definitely a force to be reckoned with.

Alignment with this PD movement and building virtual communities is also evidenced in Latin America. In Chapter "Transforming from Off-liners to On-liners:
Voices from Foreign Language Professors in Colombia", *Kathleen A. Corrales* and
Lourdes Rey-Paba make a strong case for a group of university professors in
Colombia who rose to the occasion in ERT despite their lack of experience in online
teaching. Through a supportive and empathetic online PD program, they unlearned
and relearned pedagogical, technological and affective aspects of remote teaching
while capitalising on a wide variety of digital tools, such as Google Classroom,
ShowMore and Flipgrid, to facilitate remote teaching and optimise student learning.
Most importantly, both authors draw our attention to the challenges commonly

faced in a developing country, such as no or unstable access to the internet, or limited electronical devices being available in remote regions, which aggravated the challenges associated with remote teaching and learning during the most difficult of times.

Another salient theme integral to ERT is *teacher identity and agency*. Chapter "Emergency Remote Teaching in the Kazakhstan Context: Deprofessionalization of Teacher Identity" opens our eyes to how ERT played out in another context that is less explored in the literature, Kazakhstan, a post-Soviet developing country. Readers can only imagine the hurdles and barriers Kazakh teachers and students have experienced during this difficult time given the limited resources, and the unrealistic expectations of and lack of support from the parents and governments. By employing grounded theory and co-constructed positionality, **Kamila Kozhabayeva** and **Nettie Boivin** equitably reveal the multifaceted complexities of geopolitical, institutional and sociocultural tensions in Kazakhstan, which further jeopardised teachers' emotions, well-being and identities during the pandemic. Despite all the constraints and difficulties, readers will find solace in some of the Kazakh teachers' proactive approaches in exploring various technological and pedagogical solutions to resolve issues. There is no doubt that more teacher PD training in ICT and open communication will play a paramount role in '(re)professionalising' teacher identity and efficacy. By adopting the interesting lens of employability capital, in Chapter "Vietnamese Pre-service Teachers' Perceived Development of Employability Capital in Synchronous Learning Amidst the Pandemic", **Ngoc Tung Vu**, **Hoa Hoang** and **Thao Nguyen** focus on how pre-service English teachers in Vietnam perceived their employability during synchronised online learning (SOL) triggered by COVID-19. Surprisingly, their survey results indicated the strong career aspirations of these pre-service teachers, which were linked positively to their psychological, social and cultural capitals. This positive finding also brings a breath of fresh air to ERT, as these Vietnamese teacher trainees capitalised on SOL to strengthen their employability capital (for example, their job-related knowledge and skills), thus promoting greater investment in their identity capital for future career pursuits beyond ERT.

One of the most frequently asked questions amidst the pandemic was how language teaching practicum or study exchange programmes broke through the global lockdowns and border closures. We find some innovative solutions to *online practicum and virtual study programmes* in the next two chapters. Chapter "The Adaptation of Action Research into Online Practicum in Unprecedented Times: Opportunities and Constraints", by **Müzeyyen Nazlı Güngör**, reveals how an initial English language teacher education (IELTE) programme in Turkey beat the odds by using online action research as a model, supported by technology-enhanced pedagogy, to continue the practicum remotely in the wake of COVID-19. We see how student teachers were still able to analyse live-streamed and video-based lesson materials, and to observe their mentor teachers' remote teaching, debrief with their supervisors via Skype or WhatsApp calls, reflect critically on their own online lesson plans, and carefully evaluate the appropriate digital tools, such as Educandy and Animaker, to engage online learning. This sheds a positive light on the future implementation of online practicum when facing a crisis such as COVID-19. In a similar vein, in Chapter "French Language Studies in New Caledonia despite COVID-19: The Emergency Response Move from In-Country to Virtual Program", **Beate Mueller** and **Susan Oguro** share an inspiring story about how they turned a 3-week intensive programme for Australian students to study French in New Caledonia into a virtual study-abroad programme in response to the global lockdowns. Programme coordinators and teachers were able to recoup and creatively morph the programme in the remote-teaching space while ensuring that the ethos of the study-abroad programme, which was an immersive cultural experience, was safeguarded. This was made possible via a synergy of the best practices in viable online platforms (such as Zoom and Facebook Messenger) and multimodal tools (such as LearningApps.Org) to enable transformative collaboration, to build a virtual community to enhance the teachers' presence and interactions, and to include local experts in New Caledonia to maximise the rich target culture/history experience. This is another vivid example of language teachers' adaptability, resilience and innovation to combat the challenges posed by ERT.

The final three chapters in Teacher Voice shift the lens back to *language learners* and the *adaptive pedagogy* that was developed to serve them during the unprecedented times. In Chapter "Implications of a Sudden Shift Online: The Experiences of English Education Students' Studying Online for the First-Time During COVID-19 Pandemic in Japan", **Jean Kim** echoes Chapter "Infrastructure, Literacy and Communication: The Challenges of Emergency Remote Teaching in a University in Japan" (**Todd Allen**) that online education and infrastructure in Japan surprisingly lag behind other developed countries. The abrupt shift to ERT has consequently derailed the long-held teacher-centred, classroom-based instruction, leaving both Japanese teachers and students unprepared for remote crisis teaching that demands IT literacy skills and student-driven pedagogy. Despite their initially negative attitudes towards ERT, Japanese EFL students were pleasantly surprised to learn that both their English proficiency and IT skills had improved in leaps and bounds due to their teacher's sound understanding of technology-enhanced pedagogy (community of inquiry) to optimise teaching, and the social and cognitive presence in online education. The next chapter tells a compelling story about how crisis teaching unfolded in the Philippines. Similar to the ERT phenomenon in other developing countries such as Colombia (Chapter "Transforming from Off-Liners to On-Liners: Voices from Foreign Language Professors in Colombia") and Kazakhstan (Chapter "Emergency Remote Teaching in the Kazakhstan Context: Deprofessionalization of Teacher Identity"), Chapter "Online Instruction as a New Learning Territory for a Filipinized Critical Language Pedagogy: From the Era of Pandemic Onward" uncovers that ERT also magnified the underlying issue of unequal access to IT technology and resources in the current Philippine education system. Despite difficulties with infrastructure, **Juland Dayo Salayo** innovatively adopted critical language pedagogy and user-friendly platforms such as Google Meet and Zoom to overcome the barriers while promoting online engagement. His high school students were able to voice their critical views and raise awareness of social conscience during ERT, leading to their action plans to address real-world issues such as 'equal rights to education and social justice' and 'youth, women and senior citizens'.

The final chapter, "Fostering Interaction and Motivation in EFL Live Virtual Classes at University", highlights the great extent to which digital tools can be utilised to support EFL university students in Argentina amid ERT, arguing that learners' motivation and interactions with their peers, content materials and instructors should not be compromised during crisis teaching. Informed by the self-determination theory and strategies for promoting learner motivation, *Ana Cecilia Cad, Claudia Alejandra Spataro* and *Paul Alexis Carrera* demonstrate how these essential elements can be integrated into online course design, sustained by both synchronous and asynchronous tools such as Educaplay and Quizizz.

These inspiring cases are strong evidence that language teachers could still transform student learning via adaptive pedagogy and viable technology, even during the pandemic.

Researcher Corner

The second half of this volume directs our attention to how language researchers around the world tapped into innovative ways of gathering and analysing data remotely, or put their own spin on standard research designs during the global lockdowns. The first four chapters usher us into a fascinating domain that has attracted growing attention in the fields of applied linguistics and language education, namely *ethnographic research*. Here we see two unique types of ethnography, *autoethnography and virtual ethnography,* spawned from ERT during these unprecedented times.

In Chapter "Teacher Emotion in Emergency Online Teaching: Ecstasies and Agonies", *Maggie McAlinden* and *Toni Dobinson* transport us back to where it all started when COVID-19 hit us hard at the beginning of 2020. By employing autoethnography as a research approach, both authors provide candid verbatim accounts of grappling with ERT and its impact on teacher emotion, anxiety and well-being, thus unveiling 'the elephant in the room' that deserves more research attention in the literature (also see Chapters "Language Teaching in Times of COVID-19: The Emotional Rollercoaster of Lockdown" and "Emergency Remote Teaching in the Kazakhstan Context: Deprofessionalization of Teacher Identity"). The hallmark of ethnography, thick description, is strengthened by the emotional appraisal and multimodal semiotic analyses of rich data, triangulated from their real-time session recordings, side chats and unit evaluation reports. Their great sense of humour and critical reflections are a breath of fresh air that helped them to battle and transcend ERT. Credit also goes to the authors' two lovely pets, Arizona the cat and Yallah the beagle, making the reading even more enjoyable. Following suit, *Katherine Morales, Gabriel Romaguera* and *Edward Contreras* conducted autoethnographic research as a trio to paint a fuller picture of how ERT takes place in Puerto Rico, a US territory that had been ravaged by hurricanes and earthquakes, followed by the global pandemic. Their heartfelt thick descriptions shed light on the hurdles in crisis teaching, which are exacerbated by poor IT infrastructure (see Chapters "Infrastructure, Literacy and Communication: The Challenges of Emergency Remote Teaching in a University in Japan" and "Implications of a Sudden Shift Online: The Experiences of English Education Students' Studying Online for the First-Time During COVID-19 Pandemic in Japan" for cases in Japan) and unequal access to the internet, similar to the situations observed in other developing countries (see Chapters "Transforming from Off-Liners to On-Liners: Voices from Foreign Language Professors in Colombia", "Emergency Remote Teaching in the Kazakhstan Context: Deprofessionalization of Teacher Identity" and "Online Instruction as a New Learning Territory for a Filipinized Critical Language Pedagogy: From the Era of Pandemic Onward"). Despite all the challenges, their reflective autoethnographies helped them to make educated decisions when adapting pedagogy and evaluating technology that allowed for remote teaching and learning in their specific context considering the low socioeconomic realities and needs of the students.

The next two chapters take a step further in illuminating how virtual (online) ethnographic research could be conducted during the pandemic. Chapter ""I Will Teach from the Heart": Teachers' Beliefs and Practices During an Emergency Remote Language Pedagogy in a Heritage Language School During the COVID-19 Lockdown" explores the linguistic and cultural dimensions of a Finnish-immigrant, community-run heritage school in Canada by focusing on how volunteer teachers made sense of their ERT practices shaped by the teachers' beliefs, experiences, and collaborations with the parents and the community. *Anu Muhonen* demonstrates how she gathered virtual ethnographic data from her field notes on observing remote Finnish language classes, teacher reflections documented via Padlet, casual discussions and interviews. While ERT may pose challenges, we witness another successful case in this chapter, as the teachers established a strong bond with the parents and the Finnish community in order to continue supporting their heritage students. Remote teaching also brought this tight-knit heritage community closer, fostered teachers' ERT practices and developed new beliefs about community-driven, learner-oriented remote-teaching pedagogy. By the same ethnographic token, Chapter "Emergency Remote Teaching (ERT) or Surveillance? Panopticism and Higher Education in Bangladesh" presents a compelling case of students' voices and reactions to ERT in the higher education sector in Bangladesh, another developing country that was impacted severely by the global pandemic due to the inadequate IT infrastructure and resources. By adopting a virtual ethnographic approach, *Shaila Sultana* illustrates how she remotely shadowed and observed the first-hand online activities and posts made by Bangladeshi university students on various Facebook pages. The rich multimodal data, peppered with English, Bangla, Hindi, emoticons and symbols, was analysed using the transglossic framework. Given her online immersive engagement, she was able to pin down the metaphorical panopticism by unearthing the frustrations, emotions and anxieties the students experienced due to the surveillance imposed by the authorities during ERT.

In the absence of face-to-face peer contact, it is vital to discover both the positive and the negative impacts of social media on teachers' experiences during the pandemic crisis, and how they developed the resilience to not only survive, but thrive. However, little research has attempted to explore the wealth of social media data involving language teachers during ERT, and few attempts to investigate the discursive practices of online professional development communities have been made to determine how social media use alleviates teachers' affective, cognitive and socioemotional challenges. This motivated the inclusion of *social media research* in this volume.

In Chapter "The Generative Affects of Social Media Scroll-Back Interviews: In Conversation with Spanish as a World Language Teachers During the COVID-19 Lockdown in Australia", **Danielle H. Heinrichs** employs an innovative remote data collection approach, namely social media scroll-back interviews, to examine the affective aspects of Spanish language teachers in Australia during the global lockdowns. Rather than following a standard interview protocol, she creatively tapped into the teachers' Facebook posts, timeline activities and screen sharing as a mechanism to untangle the entanglements of their affects due to ERT. The author rightly shows that the social media scroll-back method opens up a new avenue for researchers to bypass social distancing, thus indicating its potential merit in remote research. Chapter "Peer Capacity Building in Emergency Remote Teaching: Informal Language Teacher Professional Development on Twitter" illustrates how ERT research can be conducted remotely using another popular social media platform, Twitter. By undertaking a document analysis of original tweets generated by various professional teacher communities connected through hashtags (#), **Karin Vogt** discovered nuanced dimensions in peer-capacity building among language teachers in Germany in the wake of COVID-19. Despite the well-intentioned online community building to support teachers' professional development during ERT, topical tweet discussions focused primarily on pedagogical aspects such as digital tools, thus leaving teachers' emotions as the elephant in the room (also see Chapters "Language Teaching in Times of COVID-19: The Emotional Rollercoaster of Lockdown", "Emergency Remote Teaching in the Kazakhstan Context: Deprofessionalization of Teacher Identity" and "Teacher Emotion in Emergency Online Teaching: Ecstasies and Agonies"). Again, this chapter foregrounds the relevance and viability of social media research that opens our eyes to uncharted territory.

The following three chapters bring us back to one of the most popular research designs in social sciences and applied linguistics, *case study research*. Chapter "Individual and Institutional Responses to the Exigency of Online Teaching: A Case Study from Qatar", by **Mick King** and **Sedigh (Sid) Mohammadi**, presents a solid case of EFL college teachers' experiences of and reactions to ERT in Qatar, another unique context that deserves more research attention. Exploratory and interpretive in nature, the case study design is strengthened by the rich data gathered from multiple sources, ranging from documents (official emails sent by the administration) and surveys to focus group interviews with the teachers and management team throughout the pandemic. By adopting a thematic analysis of the triangulated data, the authors' findings reveal salient themes regarding how EFL teachers reacted to ERT such as resilience, self-efficacy, professional development (Virtual Academy), collegiality and administrative support (Virtual Hub). These best practices can also be transferrable to other similar settings.

Chapter "Pedagogical Insights into Emergency Remote Teaching: A Case Study of a Virtual Collaboration Project in the Turkish and Hungarian Pre-service Teacher Education Context" illuminates another interesting case in a telecollaboration project between Turkish and Hungarian pre-service EFL teacher programmes during the pandemic. This unique setting amid the crisis justifies the case selection criteria in this chapter. By employing an exploratory case study approach, *Işıl Günseli Kaçar* and *Imre Fekete* illustrate the implementation of pre-project planning, suitable online assessments, the selection of digital tools, viable mentoring supervision, and mutual engagement in project tasks in virtual exchanges. Despite social distancing preventing face-to-face connections in students' lives during the pandemic, the telecollaboration project shortened the virtual distance while offering both cohorts a gateway to co-construct new knowledge with their counterparts in technology-enhanced pedagogy and intercultural competence. Both the teacher researchers and the students were empowered and gained new understanding via this fruitful virtual exchange project amid the pandemic. Chapter "A Multi-case Study of English Language Teachers in Vietnam in Emergency Remote Teaching Mediated by Technologies: A Sociocultural Perspective" takes us to Vietnam, and explores the ERT practices and beliefs of eight English language teachers with Vietnamese or English as an L1. Motivated by sociocultural theory, *Hanh Dinh* and *Thu Dao* adopt a multi-case study design to paint a fuller picture of the similarities and differences in the experiences of these EFL teachers within and across ERT settings. Their robust thematic analysis of teacher interviews (via Zoom) and authentic teaching materials reveal that ERT, albeit disruptive and challenging, has 'pushed' these teachers to self-regulate and re-construct their knowledge, approaches and strategies to engage in remote teaching, mediated by reflective and revamped pedagogy and (a)synchronous digital platforms. These successful case studies prove that the sky is the limit.

As our world is becoming more complex, multifaceted and sometimes confusing, particularly during the global pandemic, relying on a single research method or approach, be it quantitative or qualitative, might not capture a holistic picture of the phenomenon being investigated. Hence, the final three chapters foreground the designs of *mixed methods research,* another popular type of research that is embraced by scholars across disciplines.

Chapter "Exploring EFL Teachers' Technological Pedagogical Content Knowledge and Student Engagement in an Emergency Remote Teaching Context" examines how EFL teachers' technological pedagogical content knowledge (TPACK), informed by sociocultural theory, determined student engagement (SE) in a Saudi Arabian university during ERT. By adopting an explanatory sequential mixed methods design, **Dian N. Marissa** and **Wedad Allahji** show how they gathered quantitative data (TPACK and SE questionnaires) that further informed the purposeful selection of participants in qualitative data (Zoom interviews and online artefacts and activities documented in Google Classroom), followed by rigorous data analyses such as a normality check and using Dedoose software to locate conflicting evidence. The findings highlight three key elements in teachers' pedagogical competence that eased the teachers' path into ERT and sustained SE, namely reflexivity, adaptability and responsiveness. The authors' study sets a viable benchmark for how rigorous mixed methods research can be conducted remotely.

Chapter "Listening to Student Voice to Improve the Quality of Emergency Remote Teaching" shifts the focus back to our students. Using students' voices as a conceptual framework, **Olga Yashenkova** examines how 549 EFL students at a Ukrainian university perceived their ERT experiences and the implications of using their voices to make a difference in current and future education. Unlike Chapter "Exploring EFL Teachers' Technological Pedagogical Content Knowledge and Student Engagement in an Emergency Remote Teaching Context", a convergent mixed-methods design was adopted and triangulated from multiple data sources such as e-learning and institutional surveys, interviews, an authentic task and student feedback. The rich qualitative and quantitative data merge to reveal illuminative themes, indicating that Ukrainian students are ready and willing to embrace remote learning despite the constraints of poor internet access, the lack of soft skills, IT literacy and the teachers' attention to individual needs. These students' voices are definitely valued and heard loudly, and can hopefully be fed back into a transformation of language education in Ukraine.

The last but definitely not the least crucial chapter that concludes this volume presents a large-scale mixed methods study conducted in the European Union (EU) during the pandemic. **Ágnes Pál** and **Rita Koris** touch on a thought-provoking topic that every language teacher would like to know more about: How do we select viable alternative assessments in the context of ERT? In this regard, 177 university educators in the EU who were involved in the field of language for specific purposes (LSP) provided their perspectives of the types of assessment that are suitable for crisis teaching. By adopting a convergent mixed methods design (see Chapter "Listening to Student Voice to Improve the Quality of Emergency Remote Teaching"), the authors collected quantitative data by surveying these teachers about their experiences with 29 alternative assessments, with attention being paid to higher-order thinking skills (HOTs) according to Bloom's taxonomy, ranging from cloze or multiple-choice tests to telecollaborative projects or portfolios. Based on the survey results, they selected 12 teachers to take part in semi-structured interviews. It is noteworthy that, overall, LSP teachers welcomed assessments that tapped into learners' HOTs, and considered them to be more effective and suitable for remote and blended learning in the future. Chapter "LSP Teacher Perspectives on Alternative Assessment Practices at European Universities Amid the COVID-19 Crisis and Beyond" fittingly concludes this volume on a positive note.

Endnote

These 24 inspiring, heartfelt and compelling stories are evidence that teachers and researchers alike can still rise to the occasion during crises; that is, the global pandemic has forced us to teach and research outside the box, to upskill and to grow under pressure. Every crisis presents a great opportunity, and I rest my case in this edition.

Acknowledgements

To all the teachers and researchers who have unwaveringly conquered ERT and turned crisis into opportunity with compassion, creativity, resilience and humanity in language teaching and research, you are beating the odds by making a difference in students' social-emotional learning, and by pushing the research envelope even during the most difficult of times. Kudos to you all!

To all my contributors who saw the merit and potential of this edited volume in its early form and took a leap of faith with me to embark on this challenging but rewarding journey, this project would not come to fruition without your expertise and innovations that have inspired our fellow teachers and researchers around the world. I am humbled by and deeply indebted to your professional commitment and dedication.

To J. E., thank you for unconditionally supporting and fervently believing in me.

Contents

Part I
Teacher Voice: Stakeholder Perspectives

Language Teaching in Times of COVID-19: The Emotional Rollercoaster of Lockdown

Christine Appel and Jackie Robbins

Highlights

Teacher emotions and well-being need to be taken into account in teacher development programmes both in the short and the long term.

Continuous professional development fosters increased levels of confidence so that teachers can adapt more effectively to new teaching contexts.

Detailed course protocols are essential aids for teachers to deal with unforeseen circumstances/crises.

1 Introduction

The COVID-19 pandemic declared in the first months of 2020 has given rise to far-reaching changes around the globe and this has been no different in the world of education. By the end of March 2020, many countries had implemented or were in the process of implementing radical measures to control the spread of this highly-infectious and fast-spreading disease and one of these was to move education online. This shift to emergency remote education has meant that a good proportion of students have been able to continue learning, albeit within a landscape of social injustice, inequity and the digital divide (Bozkurt et al., 2020, p. 1). In addition to this, teachers were under pressure to adapt curricula to remote learning environments, often with minimal if any previous experience. What is more, regardless of the level of preparedness of teachers and students, "the impact from the stress and grief people have experienced in a short period of time will impact us long after this pandemic has ended" (Salas, 2020). As Schleicher (2020, p. 7) posits, "The ongoing

C. Appel (✉) · J. Robbins
Universitat Oberta de Catalunya, Barcelona, Spain
e-mail: mappel@uoc.edu; jrobbins@uoc.edu

© The Author(s), under exclusive license to Springer Nature
Switzerland AG 2021
J. Chen (ed.), *Emergency Remote Teaching and Beyond*,
https://doi.org/10.1007/978-3-030-84067-9_1

3

Covid-19 crisis has been, and will continue to be, both a massive challenge and a learning experience for the global education community."

The aim of this report is to understand how the pandemic and the lockdown that it brought about affected teachers of English as a foreign language working at the Universitat Oberta de Catalunya (UOC). The UOC was one of the world's first fully online universities and was set up in 1995 to provide distance higher education in Catalan. From its origin, the UOC established agreements with other universities and public educational institutions in Catalonia to hire members of their staff part-time. This set-up meant that online teaching skills and competences could be cascaded back into those other institutions. With time, the UOC has attracted part-time teachers from other parts of Spain and the rest of the world. Since part-time language teachers at the UOC teach both online at the UOC and also on regular courses at other educational institutions, this had to be taken into account at the onset of the March-June 2020 lockdown when making decisions about the measures to support our teaching staff. Not only were our team of teachers facing the consequences of confinement in their homes, working in close proximity with partners and children, having family members directly affected by illness or job loss, some teachers contracted COVID-19. What is more, along with the rest of society, teachers around the world were fearful and anxious about contracting the virus. In Spain and Catalonia in particular, they were suffering from a lack of physical exercise and coping with the harsh lockdown measures imposed there; for example, children were not allowed out of their homes, adults could only leave home once a day for grocery shopping, and dog walking was limited to no farther than 100 metres from home. These measures were especially hard on those with no outdoor spaces at home and the effect on physical and psychological well-being was felt by all. Teachers in particular were also facing a challenging situation in their main jobs by either having to transition to online teaching, from one day to the next, or in some cases, losing their jobs.

The work here was motivated by our wish to understand better the struggles our teachers were facing, within the framework of their work for our institution and outside of it, under the extreme circumstances imposed on the society in Spain that was confined to their homes from March 14th to May 2nd 2020, when lockdown restrictions were gradually eased in a process that lasted till the end of June.

2 Online Learning Before the COVID-19 Crisis

Prior to the COVID-19 health crisis, remote teaching was taking place in the context of distance education, and online education had been a growing area of interest for research. Three lines of inquiry are pertinent in the context of the COVID-19 situation: firstly, the changing roles of teachers, secondly, emotions in online learning, and thirdly, training teachers in digital competences.

In the field of language learning and teaching, the situation before the COVID-19 emergency situation was one which had incorporated the communicative approach into foreign language classrooms first and then the task-based approach transformed teaching practices and the roles of teachers and learners alike. From the 1980s, thanks to the premises proposed by the communicative approach, teachers began to assume their current role of facilitator or mediator of learning, with students acting as negotiators and interactors who give as well as take (Nunan, 1989). This changing terminology is an indication of how teaching roles have changed too in online learning contexts. Warschauer and Healey (1998) and Bax (2003) noted the shift in the role of the online language teacher from "provider of knowledge" (Bax uses the term "monitor") to one of "facilitator of learning". Harms et al. (2006), established a correlation between the facilitator role and the teacher's need to promote co-presence to help students feel less distant from the learning environment. To them, constructing a learning community is considered beneficial as it fosters good group rapport and encourages participation. Alberth (2011) also emphasised the fact that teachers' facilitation skills are a crucial part of online language learning. As part of their in-service formative training of faculty members in instructional conversation, Meskill and Sadykova (2011) found one of the challenges their participants (teachers who are moving into online teaching environments) faced was the change of pedagogical approach. Specifically, they had to transition from more teacher-centred to more learner-centred teaching, with a consequential change in the role of the teacher to "guide", "helper" and "mentor". In a similar vein, in Moore and Kearsley's (1996) view of distance learning, teachers and other stakeholders are part of the same system and cannot function without the others. That is, the teacher "humanises the learning environment, facilitates and encourages interaction, organises and presents information, and provides feedback" (Compton, 2009, p. 87). As Williams et al. (2015, p. 34) noted:

> Sometimes we need to be in the role of the controller or director and at other times we need to become a facilitator or participant. However, a role we never relinquish is that of group leader, and one of our principal responsibilities remains to manage and develop the group of learners we work with (Harmer, 2011). As teachers, we will typically be the central focus in our classrooms and one most likely to affect the classroom atmosphere and group dynamics.

Teachers' attitudes towards technology and developing new identities provide important justifications for professional development for online language teachers. In this sense, Comas-Quinn (2011) claimed that teachers in the past may have moved to online teaching contexts through an inherent interest in technology; however, more recently, teachers are being required to teach online and as a result may not have such positive attitudes and this is even more true with the COVID-19 situation. Comas-Quinn considers professional development programmes to be essential, both in practical issues but also in the affordances which technology can offer and insists that teachers and institutions need to invest "time, effort and commitment" (Comas-Quinn, 2011, p. 221). However, due to the almost overnight change of circumstances caused by the COVID-19 crisis, there was simply no time for anybody in education to prepare and many teachers had to learn new skills just hours before they were faced with new tools and teaching methods. In a study on how teaching practice was remodelled during the COVID-19 crisis, Littlejohn

(2020, p. 61) noted the need for training and suggested that "Rather than providing courses and training, educators' professional development is likely to be more effective integrated within their everyday practice." We find this is certainly the case in the Centre for Modern Languages at the UOC. The extensive experience gained as a fully online centre has, over the years, led us to the conclusion that ongoing and experiential professional development is vital: technology is constantly changing and teachers need to update their skills in the context(s) they are working in to be as effective as possible.

3   Teacher Emotions

The COVID-19 crisis has forced many teachers into emergency remote teaching, often without any prior training. At the same time, they have had to deal with the impact the health crisis has had on their personal lives. It is therefore of paramount concern to understand the impact of COVID-19 on teachers' emotions. Along this line, research in the area of education increasingly considers teaching to be "an emotional-laden process" (Gkonou et al., 2020, p. 1). However, research focusing on teachers' emotions is limited. Sutton and Wheatley (2003) pointed out that more research in teacher emotions is required and also the need for this research to go beyond beliefs and identity. Fifteen years later, Mercer (2018) expresses the concern that teachers are still being left out of the area of research of the psychology of learning which has mainly focused on the learners, and urges for this imbalance to be re-addressed. She also argues that teachers' needs and their professional well-being need to be brought (back) to the research agenda.

A number of studies have explicitly examined the interconnections between teacher and learner emotions, engagement, motivation and autonomy; see for example Skinner and Belmont (1993), Little (1995), Hargreaves (2000), Frenzel et al. (2009), Mifsud (2011), and Becker et al. (2014). It therefore follows that if teacher and student emotions are interconnected, we must not overlook teachers when it comes to considering the emotional impact of specific learning situations. What is more, teachers' psychologies and professional well-being have been shown to be connected to the quality of their teaching as well as student performance (Caprara et al., 2006; Day & Gu, 2010; Klusmann et al., 2008). Long before the COVID-19 situation arose, researchers were already acknowledging that teachers are increasingly under enormous stress: there are record rates of burnout and teachers are leaving the profession (e.g., Hong, 2010; Macdonald, 1999). One of the causes of stress in teachers can be dealing with changes beyond their control. Tran et al. (2017) identified four types of response to a change in research policy which relate to participants' emotional experiences and emergent identities: there are enthusiastic accommodators, who welcome change and embrace new possibilities, pressured supporters, who accept change, albeit somewhat reluctantly, losing heart followers, who gradually lose faith in the system, but go along with change anyway and discontented performers, who are openly against change. The findings of this study showed that career stage, qualification and area of specialisation do not have a clear impact on the emotional reactions of the lecturers, but rather these stem from the interplay between the individual beliefs and goals of the academic staff and the changes taking place.

4   The Impact of Lockdown on Teacher Emotions

It is important to note the distinction between research which examines teacher emotions and wellness in general, and work which explores emotions in response to emergency situations. Several studies have already reported on the impact that COVID-19 has had on education. For example, Bozkurt et al. (2020) suggest that the current practices are best defined as emergency remote education. As the authors argue, emergency remote education differs from previously existing distance education approaches such as online learning, principally due to the fact that it is not optional, but rather an obligation imposed by circumstances, and that all those involved are undergoing "trauma, psychological pressure and anxiety" (2020, p. 3). The writers report on cases from 31 countries, revealing many similarities such as the fact that while technology is already incorporated into existing educational policies, several studies highlight the lack of digital competences in a significant number of teachers (e.g. in Spain: Rodríguez et al., 2018; Rodríguez García et al. 2019; Fernández Batanero & Rodríguez Martín, 2017). Bozkurt et al. (2020) go on to link this lack of digital competences among teaching staff, as well as their students and families, with increasing levels of anxiety and stress during the COVID-19 crisis. They claim that there is a need for training and support across teachers' professional communities and urge school leaders and academic management to provide this support to teachers. Finally, linking to the central role of emotions in a period of crisis, they advocate for a pedagogy of "care, affection and empathy" (Bozkurt et al., 2020, p.4).

A number of papers are appearing now investigating how teachers experienced the first stages of the COVID-19 emergency situation. For example, MacIntyre et al. (2020) examined teacher stress and their coping responses during the confinement period in the spring of 2020 and point out that results of studies such as these should inform future responses in education to cope with educational reform, or work-intensive periods and that skills to cope should be part of pre- and in-service teacher development programmes. Similarly, Schleicher (2020) argued that the disruption caused by the COVID-19 emergency situation and the transformations that it brought about will long outlive the crisis.

5   Objectives of the Study

We set out to explore the impact that the March-June 2020 lockdown which was implemented as a result of the COVID-19 situation had on a group of language teachers working at the UOC, a fully online university based in Spain. We were guided by the following questions.

1. *How did the teachers experience the March-June 2020 lockdown?*

   (a) *How were teachers' emotional states affected?*
   (b) *How were teachers affected in their regular online work at the UOC?*
   (c) *How was their face-to-face teaching affected?*
   (d) *To what extent did teachers feel their needs for support were met?*

2. *How were the teachers' online students affected?*
3. *What actions did these teachers' coordinators undertake?*

While the focus of this report is the teachers, we also collected information about these teachers' online students and the teachers' coordinators in order to obtain a broader picture of their context. The information elicited from students and coordinators is related to these teachers.

6   Context and Participants

Our report centres on teachers working at the Centre for Modern Languages within the Universitat Oberta de Catalunya (UOC), which is a fully online institution. In March 2020, the COVID-19 health crisis led to a full lockdown in Spain from 14th March which was gradually relaxed from the middle of May onwards until the end of June 2020, when freedom of movement was restored. However, educational institutions remained closed and teachers were required to set up emergency remote teaching until the end of June. The UOC is a fully-online institution and therefore, our courses continued throughout this period without any changes, but the impact of the health crisis was still felt by students and teachers. This report focuses on the effects the crisis had on a group of 66 language teachers, 64 of whom work part-time as English as a foreign language teachers. The other two participants are researchers, who coordinate English courses at the UOC. In addition, we also report on the impact of the crisis on the teachers' students.

The language teachers at the UOC come from a wide variety of backgrounds, both geographically and academically. Of the total number of teachers, 62.5% of those surveyed are based in Catalonia, 10.9% are based in other parts of Spain, and the remaining 26.6% are based in other countries around the world. The teachers at our fully-online institution work part-time but they also work in other face-to-face teaching institutions. Figure 1 shows the type of institutions the teachers work in for their other jobs.

Fig. 1 Types of institutions UOC language teachers also work for

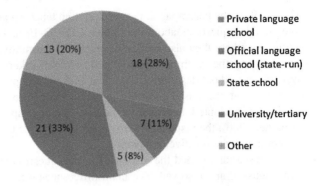

- Private language school
- Official language school (state-run)
- State school
- University/tertiary
- Other

13 (20%) 18 (28%) 21 (33%) 7 (11%) 5 (8%)

Of the 64 teachers who took part in the survey, 85% had been teaching languages for a period of 10 years or more, 14% had been working between 5 and 10 years and 1.5% of the teachers had been teaching languages for under five years. Additionally, 20% of the teachers surveyed have been working with the UOC for 10 years or more, 25% have been working for 5-10 years and the remaining 54% have been working at the UOC for under five years. 62% of the teachers were female, 36% were male and 1.5% of the teachers preferred not to indicate their gender. Of the 64 teachers, 61 were working on the B2 English programme and the remaining three were working on other levels.

The two coordinators, who are also the authors of this paper, are full-time lecturers at the UOC, in charge of the instructional design, training programme for new teachers and overall coordination. They were both female foreigners that had been working in Catalonia for 15 and over 25 years in the field of language education.

Students in the UOC are typically adult students aged 24-55, who combine work with study and family duties. There were 307 students in the B2 English programme who responded to the survey.

7   Procedures

We present the results of a voluntary questionnaire sent to a group of online language teachers in June 2020. The questionnaire was designed to understand the personal and professional effects of the lockdown implemented during the second semester of 2020–2021 as a result of the COVID-19 crisis. The questionnaire combines closed and open questions and in addition to a short section about the teachers' background, it consisted of two main sections:

- The impact of COVID-19 on teaching at the UOC, and
- The impact of COVID-19 on other teaching commitments.

The questionnaire consisted of 33 questions which were organised into three sections. The first section of the questionnaire focused on collecting background data about the participants. Section two of the questionnaire asked about the impact

COVID-19 on the participants' part-time online teaching at our institution. Section three included questions about the impact COVID-19 had on teachers at the other institutions where they also work. We opted for a combination of closed and open questions, together with questions which included Likert-scale options to choose from. We carried out descriptive statistical analysis and prepared charts to report on the results from the closed questions in the questionnaire and for the open response questions, we adopted an inductive thematic analysis approach (Fereday & Muir-Cochrane, 2006): the responses were coded by two researchers initially in terms of whether they were positive or negative.

Each researcher coded the responses to one question each and any differences were discussed and resolved. The main differences were in how to code a neutral effect reported by teachers in their comments with negative language, as in the case of "I had to...". The researchers agreed to code these instances as negative because from the teachers' perspective, these changes were imposed on them.

In addition, a short survey was sent to these teachers' online students which consisted of two questions. The first asked students to rate on a scale of 1 to 5 the degree to which the COVID-19 situation had affected their level of dedication to the subject and the second was an open question inviting the participants to add any particular comments they felt were pertinent.

The course coordinators and authors of this paper were faced with a number of decisions at the beginning of the lockdown period in March 2020 and implemented certain actions in response to the situation, such as increasing the degree of flexibility for submission deadlines. More details are provided in the final section of the Findings below, where we will also reflect on the rationale behind each of these actions.

8   Findings

8.1   How Were Teachers' Emotional States Affected?

We asked teachers whether their emotional state had been affected during the semester on a scale of 1-5, where 1 indicated "not at all" and 5 "extremely". The results are presented in Fig. 2.

As we can observe in Fig. 2, very few teachers indicated that their emotional state had not been affected at all (2% of teachers in Spain and 6% of teachers in the rest of the world). In fact, we find that the vast majority of teachers were affected, either somewhat, quite a lot, or extremely. The trends we can observe for teachers in Spain and in the rest of the world are similar, although our results do seem to indicate a higher intensity of impact on teachers' emotions in Spain.

In addition to asking teachers about the extent to which COVID-19 had affected them emotionally, we also invited them to share anything else about the impact the situation had had on them and their work. This question generated a range of

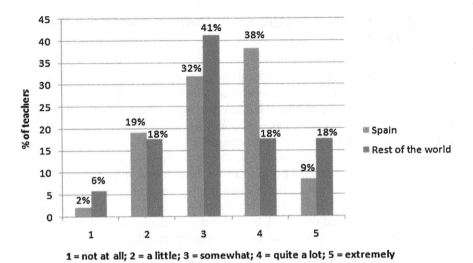

1 = not at all; 2 = a little; 3 = somewhat; 4 = quite a lot; 5 = extremely

Fig. 2 Impact of COVID-19 crisis on teachers' emotional states in Spain and Rest of the world

responses in terms of the positive and negative effects of the situation, but most of the answers seemed to focus on the negative ones. Teachers made reference to their feelings of anxiety for themselves and their learners. For example, one teacher wrote "My daughter is a nurse and was working in Barcelona hospital - on the front line - so, I was extremely worried about her which, at times, took my focus away from work", while another teacher explained "Psychologically, it's been hard for me and my students. We've all had some kind of anxiety and/or depression". Several other teachers commented on their feelings of sadness and loneliness. One teacher wrote "it's all still very sad and scary" and another explained "On my solitude, on my work - I felt overwhelmed with everything I had to do", to the sheer physical and mental exhaustion they had experienced. One teacher elaborated "being able to cope mentally with the situation was a constant struggle" and another wrote "I get overtired of working in front of a screen all day!". These perceptions were particularly exacerbated because they were work-ing from home, sharing their workspace with their families. In this sense, one teacher said that "Concentration was another issue because teaching other people and making sure they receive the appropriate information was difficult, especially if all the other members of your family share the same space." The issue of staying focused was referred to by another teacher who said "it was difficult to maintain a "work head" on".

On the other hand, several teachers pointed out the opportunities that had emerged; one teacher admitted "I'm shattered! However, it has been a great learning experience", while another suggested that the COVID-19 context "should be seen as an opportunity to improve and change those things which weren't working at school".

8.2   How Were Teachers Affected in Their Regular Online Work at The UOC?

We asked teachers whether the COVID-19 situation had affected their online teaching work at the UOC. 48% of the teachers said it had not, 25% said it had in a negative way, while 27% reported that the effect had been positive. Teachers were also invited to reply to an optional open question describing their experience. These comments were coded as positive/neutral/negative. Of the 62 comments, 27 (43%) were negative, 10 (16%) were neutral and 25 (40%) were positive.

The negative comments tended to focus on the logistical implications brought about by confinement. One teacher reported that the impact had been negative for her students and wrote "They had people ill at home, more work, children at home… as a result they delivered their work late". Another teacher referred to the issue of multi-tasking and how that affected her work. She reported that:

> juggling with all the personal and family duties (looking after a baby, cooking, learning, etc.) at the same time I had to work at home was extremely complicated, mainly because I did not have enough time to finish everything I was supposed to do.

Several teachers reported in more neutral terms the impact on their online work. One teacher explained that the experience had led to "just different things to take into account" while another explained "The topic of COVID has replaced other work-related topics in our content". Several teachers referred to how the way they communicated with students changed. One noted that "The new situation affected the way I communicated with my students at the UOC. I needed to be more patient and understanding with the personal situations students were involved in", and another found "a tighter relationship with the students which was an interesting dynamic."

On the other hand, some teachers were more positive when describing the effect on their online work. The main themes that emerged from the teachers' positive responses related to the flexibility offered for organising their own and their students' work. One teacher explained that "The COVID-19 situation affected my work at the UOC in a positive way because I've had more time to organise myself. I've had less time pressure and more flexibility. Consequently, I think I have worked in a more relaxed way." Another teacher noted "I had more time to give personalised feedback and the contributions of the students were more accurate." Another teacher found that "The flexibilisation of rules and deadlines have had a positive effect. A caring, affectionate classroom environment was the result."

8.3   How Was Teachers' Face-to-Face Teaching Affected?

We asked teachers how much the COVID-19 situation had affected their main job outside the UOC on a scale from 1 to 5 where 1 was "not at all" and 5 was "a lot". A total of 77% of the teachers answered 4 or 5. When we asked teachers if their workload had been affected, 70% reported they had worked more hours, 16% reported they had worked fewer hours and 14% reported no change.

When asked what specifically they had to change in their main jobs, the main theme that emerged from the data was the inclusion of synchronous sessions (55 comments), of which 15 were about methodology, and 40 were about tools (22 mentioned Zoom, 12 Meet, and 6 Skype.) Table 1 in the appendix summarises the tools teachers mentioned using during the lockdown period. The rest of the topics that came up were about their increased workload (11), one-to-one synchronous meetings with students (10), redefining course plans (7), and producing video-recordings (4). All these comments were also rated as positive, neutral or negative. Only 2% of the comments were positive, 50% were expressed in a neutral manner and 48% were negative. For example, one teacher described the changes as: "More zoom meetings. Radically more organization, which continues, substantially more support for students, complete restructuring of the program for the coming year, etc etc etc. It's been a lot and continues to be." This comment seems to sum up the over-all impression from the teachers surveyed.

We were also interested in finding out teachers' views on how much their online teaching experience at the UOC had helped them deal with changes in their other work. The majority of the teachers (73%) answered yes to this question, with only 13% of teachers answering no, and the remaining 14% answered that it was not applicable (mainly due to the interruption of teaching in their main job places). A comment by another teacher illustrates the ways in which their online experience had helped them: "Over the years, I have understood that online communication needs to be clear, concise and consistently supportive. This helps with dealing with students who are not used to learning online. I have developed patience over the years!"

The feeling of confidence in the use of technology and, online teaching in general surfaced positively as can be perceived in this teacher's comment: "I felt comfortable and confident using the computer to teach my regular face-to-face lessons. I had more resources to face technical difficulties. I was able to give more detailed feedback on their writing assignments." This confidence was also expressed in relation to the use of technology, "Being used to using all kinds of online tools, even though they're not necessarily the ones you use in other contexts." This confidence transpires in the responses to the question of whether they thought the changes they had introduced in their main jobs worked, with 28 positive answers, 10 neutral and 9 negatives. The negative answers included responses from primary school teachers who thought that teaching children online is more difficult. There were also frustrations over the cancellation of end-of-course assessments of their students, and concern that "Students often did not have adequate technology or internet access. High attrition rate locally."

The following positive answer illustrates the spirit of most of the positive answers from teachers:

> I wouldn't be overly confident saying that with the primary kids, but with the teens - yes. They have actually been brilliant and the 2-to-1 speaking sessions have worked really well. They have spoken more online than they usually do in class. It is something that we are considering continuing with even if we can go back into the classroom.

Overall, teachers in this study seem to have found their previous experience in the UOC extremely useful for dealing with the change to emergency remote teaching in their other face-to-face work. This does not deter from the fact that teachers still struggled, particularly in terms of how to solve assessment issues which arose from the COVID-19 situation.

8.4   To What Extent Did Teachers Feel Their Needs for Support Were Met?

When asked whether teachers felt they had received enough support for their UOC teaching, 89% of them said yes, nobody said no, and 11% said this was not applicable. When we analysed the teachers' comments about support, again, the majority of comments were positive (24), although there were 4 negative comments and 6 neutral responses. The positive comments varied in terms of content: some highlighted the fact that they felt well-supported by their course coordinators. For example, one teacher wrote "I've always had a quick response from the coordinators" and another noted "There was always a friendly response to any questions teachers asked, maybe even more friendly than usual which was nice". However, there were several comments which were more negative. One teacher felt that "Support and flexibility was mainly student-focussed" and another wrote "I would like to see more consistent messaging about flexibility in grading deadlines during a pandemic". The neutral comments consisted of teachers expressing that they had not felt the need for extra support.

On the other hand, we also asked teachers if they had needed any other type of support in their other jobs. 62% of the teachers reported that they had not needed any other support, whereas 38% of teachers indicated that they would have liked more support. When we asked teachers to specify the type of extra support they felt they had needed, just under half of the comments (44% of these) indicated that teachers felt they needed more training in the use of specific tools. For example, one teacher wrote that they would have liked "Training in tools and assessment", while another wrote "access to materials, more teacher training". Other areas where teachers identified as requiring additional support were more stable work conditions, technical equipment, faster reaction times from their superiors and flexibility. In this sense, one teacher wrote "more flexibility to meet the deadlines and more empathy with the situation, as we were all struggling at various levels to juggle everything at the same time."

In general, our findings seem to show that while teachers felt they had enough support for their online work at the UOC during the health crisis, they identified several areas where more support would have been welcome for their work in the other institutions where the shift from face-to-face teaching to ERT had taken place. Specifically, the area where they indicated that additional support was needed most was in training in the use of specific tools.

8.5 How Were the Teachers' Online Students Affected?

We also sent a short survey to the B2 programme students and asked them how much COVID-19 had affected their participation in the subject where 1 = not at all and 5 = a lot. Figure 3 shows the results.

As can be observed in Fig. 3, 10% of the students reported that the health crisis had affected their participation in the course a lot while 17% of students reported no change at all. The majority of students reported it had had some or quite a lot of impact on their participation. We also invited students to comment on how the COVID-19 crisis had affected their work during the course. We analysed the 40 comments from students and found 20 were positive in terms of the effect on their work, while 20 were negative. For example, five comments from students noted the issues they struggled with in terms of balancing their work, study and family commitments. One student wrote "I was especially affected because I'm a mother of two children and run a small family business and the situation meant I struggled to cope with everything". Six students mentioned that being health workers meant

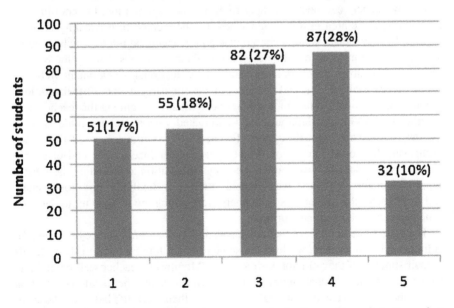

Fig. 3 How much did COVID-19 affect your participation in this subject?

they found it difficult to study due to having to work longer hours. In this respect though, one student noted "Great collaboration from my teacher for offering me flexibility, bearing in mind that I was particularly affected due to my job (I'm a doctor)". Nineteen students expressed their appreciation of the extra support they had received from their teachers. One student wrote "Thanks to the teaching staff of this subject because I had problems during the course and they helped me throughout." Another student noted the flexibility and said "Good flexibility to deal with the situation." Finally, some of the students were closely affected by the situation through their work or family issues, as noted by several teachers and reported in the section above about how teachers' online teaching was affected. One student explained:

> I work in the health industry and was therefore affected, but each day I found time to for the subject. I have to say that above all, I had had a teacher who helped motivate me because they were always there when anyone asked questions.

8.6   What Actions Did These Teachers' Coordinators Undertake?

The course coordinators implemented certain actions in response to the situation. The teachers surveyed are all members of an online staffroom, which includes several channels of communication. One of these is an asynchronous discussion forum where all teachers can post and reply to each other at any time; the coordinators created a specific area in this forum where teachers could post teaching ideas or share links to webinars about technological and pedagogical issues which could be helpful in the transition to online teaching in their other jobs. During the March-June 2020 lockdown, teachers shared links to professional development webinars and suggestions about tools and resources they were using in their other institutions in this space. In order to facilitate synchronous interaction among the teachers and coordinators, a Google Hangout chat was created where teachers could keep in contact and provide mutual support. Teachers and coordinators used this space exclusively for social interaction. Finally, the regular face-to-face end of course meeting was replaced by two online meetings. In addition to providing these extra support channels, the course was adapted in terms of flexibility, both for teachers and learners, so that if teachers or learners were struggling to keep up to date, we validated extended deadlines for both.

The main issue of concern that arose was finding the right balance between providing support to teachers while at the same time not forcing them to share details of their situation if they did not wish to do so. Monitoring teacher well-being in an online environment is challenging at the best of times, but the lockdown situation compounded this as teachers struggled to manage their work-life balance. The asynchronous nature of the communication channels employed meant that the coordinators were able to be in as much or as little contact as each teacher needed.

Synchronous meetings with teachers were discarded during the lockdown period, given the overload of synchronous teaching that the majority of teachers were subjected to in their main jobs.

Overall, the coordinators prioritised maintaining the normal running of the course insofar as this was feasible in the circumstances. It was our belief that teachers would be reassured by a calm approach from the coordinators and would pass this on to students. However, behind the scenes the coordinators were monitoring the staff room posts and classrooms for any signs of undue stress and stepping in to offer extra support whenever necessary. In this way, being more present than usual in the teachers' virtual staff room and ensuring that the tone of all of our messages to teachers were written with a sense of "care, affection and empathy" (Bozkurt et al., 2020, p. 4) were part of the strategies we adopted during the pandemic. Finally, in our role as mediators between students and teachers, an important aspect was reminding students that teachers were also being affected in different ways by the crisis.

9   Discussion

Our findings have shown that teachers in this study experienced the March-June 2020 lockdown in different ways. Teachers were affected at a personal level and experienced hardship as part of the society they belong to, but while the circumstances were adverse, we found that many teachers in their professional capacity were able to generate solutions and the resulting sense of empowerment led to positive emotions.

The vast majority of teachers (98% of teachers in Spain and 94% of teachers in the rest of the world) reported being affected by the pandemic. Of those, 47% in Spain and 36% in the rest of the world reported being affected a lot or extremely, which reflects that teachers suffered the consequences of the crisis. There seems to be a slightly higher impact on teachers in Spain than on those in the rest of the world. This may be related to the stronger measures implemented in Spain although the small scale of our study means it is not possible to draw firm conclusions. In teachers' online work, they experienced added stress, and this was evident in their comments. The sources of this stress were mainly from the lockdown situation in general, the added workload in their main jobs which interfered with their regular online teaching, and to a certain extent, dealing with anxious students.

On the whole, we have seen that teachers rolled with the changes in their main jobs (one of our teachers actually used that expression) and in this sense, a large proportion of our teachers could be classified as "enthusiastic adopters" (Tran et al., 2017); not only did they deal with the challenges that they were presented with, but many of them identified opportunities, explored new ways of working and implemented these successfully. The difficulties they experienced revolved mainly around heavier workloads, the need to redesign courses, and an excessive use of synchronous sessions to substitute their face-to-face teaching.

The support received in the UOC was well received by teachers who appreciated in particular the additional channels of communication and the flexibility offered when necessary. As regards to the support received in their main jobs, nearly 70% of our teachers reported that they did not need any, but where they did, it tended to involve training in tools they were having to use for the first time. This can be explained by the fact that just over 70% agreed that their experience working at the UOC helped them transition to new ways of working in their main jobs.

Students were also affected, and this had a knock-on effect on teachers who were already finding themselves under stress, experiencing anxiety but the added responsibility of dealing with students who were in precisely the same situation meant that they had to put their needs aside to address their students' needs. From the students' comments, students were very appreciative of the flexibility and empathy shown by their teachers, which resonates with what Bozkurt et al. (2020, p. 4) refer to as a "pedagogy of care, affection and empathy" needed in times of trauma and highly stressful situations. Similarly, the teachers appreciated the additional support mechanisms introduced by the coordinators and made special mention of the increased level of interpersonal communication during the course.

The nature of online courses requires thorough forward planning for a wide array of situations and every aspect of the educational experience needs to be structured, explicit and transparent so that processes and protocols are readily available and clear to everybody involved. This involves elaborating detailed teachers' guides, student and teacher activity guidelines and course plans; in times of crisis, these "rule books" provide a support framework for coordinators, teachers and students alike. These processes were instrumental for the coordinators in ensuring that the course ran in a "business-as-usual" manner.

10   Conclusions

Despite this highly stressful situation, having had the training and experience in the use of the technologies together with the methodology in the UOC meant that the teachers who took part in the survey had the necessary confidence to transfer their knowledge to different environments, situations and target learners when forced to shift to ERT in their face-to-face teaching. Our main conclusion is that pre- and in-service professional development plays a crucial role in teachers' ability to incorporate technology in their face-to-face teaching. What is also evident is that when coordinating online teachers, it is crucial to provide regular support as they carry out their work.

From the teachers' comments, it is clear that emotions were high, but while these could be negative at times, many teachers were able to put a positive spin on the situation. For future actions, we believe teacher professional development programmes in the use of technologies are paramount and teachers' well-being should form an integral part of these. More research into the emotional support systems which might be put in place in the long term would be an interesting area for future research.

Many areas of our lives have changed forever, and the field of education is no exception. Regardless of whether institutions go back to the way they were prior to the COVID-19 health crisis, because policy changes are inevitably slow, teachers and learners have now tried new ways of working and have been able to experience firsthand the affordances that technology has to offer. Subsequent conversations with teachers have revealed that they are being called upon by their colleagues in their other jobs to provide technical and pedagogical support, and thus becoming the driving force behind more long-term change. Looking into this is a promising line of future investigation.

11   Food for Thought: Beyond ERT

11.1   Implications for Course Coordinators

Course coordinators need to explore and make use of the range of different communication channels available to stay in touch with teachers. They also need to think carefully about deepening the relationships among teams of teachers and between the teachers and the coordinators. In this way, feelings of isolation can be minimised with obvious benefits to teachers and their students.

11.2   Implications for Language Teaching Design

One of the main causes for the increase of workload in those institutions where ERT took place was the long hours dedicated to synchronous communication which left them physically and emotionally drained. We feel that the excessive use of synchronous sessions was misled. More teacher-led group sessions do not compensate for the lack of closeness and simply overburden the teacher. Training in the how, what for and when synchronous sessions are the right choice is an urgent need for the future. We would recommend teachers to invest some of their time in designing learning amongst students that does not require the presence of the teacher. It is a question of striking the right balance of teacher-led and student-student small group/pair-work, which is recorded or reported on in different formats.

11.3 *Effects on Teachers (and Learners)*

We cannot underestimate the potential long-term effects of this experience on teachers and learners and we believe it will be important to monitor well-being of all those involved in the educational experience. There will be an adjustment period, and this will parallel the grieving process: for lost loved ones, for lost social experiences, for lost educational opportunities, for lost jobs, etc. On a more positive note, the experience teachers and learners have had incorporating technology into their educational contexts is opening up exciting new possibilities for the future of education and a long-awaited paradigm shift towards learner-centred approaches.

Appendix

Table 1 Tools used by teachers for emergency remote teaching

Digital tools/ platform	Links	Description
Zoom	https://zoom.us/	Videoconferencing and online chat services through a cloud-based peer-to-peer software platform.
Google Meet	https://meet.google.com	Free Videoconference tool which is part of Google Workspace. It hosts secure video meetings right from Gmail or Google calendar.
Skype	https://www.skype.com/	Free Videoconference tool owned by Microsoft. Users may transmit text, video, audio and images.
Microsoft Teams	https://www.microsoft.com/ en/microsoft-teams/free	Communication platform developed by Microsoft which offers workspace chat and videoconferencing, file storage, and application integration
WhastApp	https://www.whatsapp.com/	WhatsApp is a freeware, cross-platform messaging and Voice over IP service owned by Facebook, Inc. to send text messages and voice messages, make voice and video calls, and share images, documents, user locations, and other media.
Blackboard Collaborate	https://www.blackboard. com/en-eu/teaching- learning/collaboration-web- conferencing/ blackboard-collaborate	Browser-based web conferencing with screen sharing and whiteboarding, developed by Blackboard Inc.
Webex	https://www.webex.com/	Secure app that allows to host video conferences with HD video, audio and screen sharing and connect instantly with team messaging, secure file-sharing and whiteboarding.

References

Alberth, A. (2011). Critical success factors in online language learning. *TEFLIN Journal, 22*(1), 16–33. https://doi.org/10.15639/teflinjournal.v22i1/16-33

Bax, S. (2003). CALL—past, present and future. *System, 31*(1), 13–28. https://doi.org/10.1016/S0346-251X(02)00071-4

Becker, E. S., Goetz, T., Morger, V., & Ranellucci, J. (2014). The importance of teachers' emotions and instructional behavior for their students' emotions–An experience sampling analysis. *Teaching and Teacher Education, 43*, 15–26. https://doi.org/10.1016/j.tate.2014.05.002

Bozkurt, A., Jung, I., Xiao, J., Vladimirschi, V., Schuwer, R., Egorov, G., ... Rodes, V. (2020). A global outlook to the interruption of education due to COVID-19 Pandemic: Navigating in a time of uncertainty and crisis. *Asian Journal of Distance Education, 15*(1), 1–126. https://zenodo.org/record/3878572

Caprara, G. V., Barbaranelli, C., Steca, P., & Malone, P. S. (2006). Teachers' self-efficacy beliefs as determinants of job satisfaction and students' academic achievement: A study at the school level. *Journal of School Psychology, 44*(6), 473–490. https://doi.org/10.1016/j.jsp.2006.09.001

Comas-Quinn, A. (2011). Learning to teach online or learning to become an online teacher: An exploration of teachers' experiences in a blended learning course. *ReCALL, 23*(3), 218–232. https://doi.org/10.1017/S0958344011000152

Compton, L. K. L. (2009). Preparing language teachers to teach language online: a look at skills, roles, and responsibilities. *Computer Assisted Language Learning, 22*(1), 73–99. https://doi.org/10.1080/09588220802613831

Day, C., & Gu, Q. (2010). *The new lives of teachers*. Routledge.

Fereday, J., & Muir-Cochrane, E. (2006). Demonstrating rigor using thematic analysis: A hybrid approach of inductive and deductive coding and theme development. *International Journal of Qualitative Methods*, 80–92. https://doi.org/10.1177/160940690600500107

Fernández Batanero, J. M., & Rodríguez Martín, A. (2017). TIC y diversidad funcional: conocimiento del profesorado. *EJIHPE. European Journal of Investigation in Health, Psychology and Education, 7*(3), 157–175.https://doi.org/10.30552/ejihpe.v7i3.204

Frenzel, A. C., Goetz, T., Lüdtke, O., Pekrun, R., & Sutton, R. E. (2009). Emotional transmission in the classroom: exploring the relationship between teacher and student enjoyment. *Journal of Educational Psychology, 101*(3), 705–716. https://doi.org/10.1037/a0014695

Gkonou, C., Dewaele, J. M., & King, J. (2020). Introduction to the emotional roller coaster of language teaching. In C. Gkonou, J. M. Dewaele, & J. King (Eds.), *The emotional rollercoaster of language teaching* (pp. 1–12). Multilingual Matters.

Hargreaves, A. (2000). Mixed emotions: Teachers' perceptions of their interactions with students. *Teaching and teacher education, 16*(8), 811–826. https://doi.org/10.1016/S0742-051X(00)00028-7

Harmer, J. (2011). *The practice of English language teaching* (4th ed.). Pearson Longman.

Harms, C. M., Niederhauser, D. S., Davis, N. E., Roblyer, M. D., & Gilbert, S. B. (2006). Educating educators for virtual schooling: Communicating roles and responsibilities. *The ElectronicJournal of Communication, 16*(1–2), 17–24. http://www.cios.org/www/ejcmain.htm

Hong, J. Y. (2010). Pre-service and beginning teachers' professional identity and its relation to dropping out of the profession. *Teaching and Teacher Education, 26*(8), 1530–1543. https://doi.org/10.1016/j.tate.2010.06.003

Klusmann, U., Kunter, M., Trautwein, U., Lüdtke, O., & Baumert, J. (2008). Teachers' occupational well-being and quality of instruction: The important role of self-regulatory patterns. *Journal of Educational Psychology, 100*(3), 702–715. https://doi.org/10.1037/0022-0663.100.3.702

Little, D. (1995). Learning as dialogue: The dependence of learner autonomy on teacher autonomy. *System, 23*(2), 175–181. https://doi.org/10.1016/0346-251X(95)00006-6

Littlejohn, A. (2020). Seeking and sending signals: Remodelling teaching practice during the Covid-19 crisis. *Contemporary Issues in Education, 40*(1), 56–62. https://doi.org/10.46786/ac20.8253

MacIntyre, P. D., Gregersen, T., & Mercer, S. (2020). Language teachers' coping strategies during the Covid-19 conversion to online teaching: Correlations with stress, wellbeing and negative emotions. *System, 94*, 1–13. https://doi.org/10.1016/j.system.2020.102352

Macdonald, D. (1999). Teacher attrition: A review of literature. *Teaching and Teacher Education, 15*(8), 835–848. https://doi.org/10.1016/S0742-051X(99)00031-1

Mercer, S. (2018). Psychology for language learning: Spare a thought for the teacher. *Language Teaching, 51*(4), 504–525. https://doi.org/10.1017/S0261444817000258

Meskill, C., & Sadykova, G. (2011). Introducing EFL faculty to online instructional conversations. *ReCALL, 23*(3), 200–217. https://doi.org/10.1017/S0958344011000140

Mifsud, M. (2011). *The relationship of teachers' and students' motivation in ELT in Malta: a mixed methods study* (Doctoral dissertation, University of Nottingham). Retrieved from: http://eprints.nottingham.ac.uk/12983/1/555348.pdf

Moore, M., & Kearsley, G. (1996). *Distance education: A systems view*. Wadsworth Publishing Company.

Nunan, D. (1989). *Designing tasks for the communicative classroom*. Cambridge University Press.

Rodríguez, A. M., Cáceres, M. P., & Alonso, S. (2018). La competencia digital del futuro docente: análisis bibliométrico de la productividad científica indexada en Scopus. *International Journal of Educational Research and Innovation. IJERI, 10*, 317–333.

Rodríguez García, A. M., Trujillo Torres, J. M., & Sánchez Rodríguez, J. (2019). Impacto de la productividad científica sobre competencia digital de los futuros docentes: aproximación bibliométrica en Scopus y Web of Science. *Revista Complutense de Educación, 30*(2), 623–646. https://doi.org/10.5209/RCED.58862

Salas, M. J. (2020, April 9). The COVID-19 Crisis is a trauma pandemic in the making. *PsychCentral*. https://psychcentral.com/blog/the-covid-19-crisis-is-a-trauma-pandemic-in-the-making/

Schleicher, A. (2020). Education disrupted - Education rebuilt. Spotlight: Quality education for all during Covid-19 crisis. OECD/Hundred Research Report #011. https://hundred-cdn.s3.amazonaws.com/uploads/report/file/15/hundred_spotlight_covid-19_digital.pdf

Skinner, E. A., & Belmont, M. J. (1993). Motivation in the classroom: Reciprocal effects of teacher behavior and student engagement across the school year. *Journal of educational psychology, 85*(4), 571–581. https://doi.org/10.1037/0022-0663.85.4.571

Sutton, R. E., & Wheatley, K. F. (2003). Teachers' emotions and teaching: A review of the literature and directions for future research. *Educational Psychology Review, 15*(4), 327–358. https://doi.org/10.1023/A:1026131715856

Tran, A., Burns, A., & Ollerhead, S. (2017). ELT lecturers' experiences of a new research policy: Exploring emotion and academic identity. *System, 67*, 65–76. https://doi.org/10.1016/j.system.2017.04.014

Warschauer, M., & Healey, D. (1998). Computers and language learning: An overview. *Language teaching, 31*(2), 57–71. https://doi.org/10.1017/S0261444800012970

Williams, M., Mercer, S., & Ryan, S. (2015). *Exploring psychology in language learning and teaching*. Oxford University Press.

Infrastructure, Literacy and Communication: The Challenges of Emergency Remote Teaching in a University in Japan

Todd James Allen

Highlights

- While the Japanese Ministry of Education has encouraged the use of technology in the classroom, students in Japan still do not have adequate IT skills.
- The COVID-19 crisis has highlighted a deficit in technology infrastructure and literacy in the university context.
- Communication barriers between stakeholders (students, teachers and administration staff) created stress and anxiety, usually not experienced in face-to-face class formats. However, this led to the creation of online support communities, assisting with a variety of issues faced in the virtual classroom.
- The COVID-19 crisis has given teachers the opportunity to "modernise" their teaching practices by experimenting with and implementing various forms of technology in their language classrooms.
- Universities should invest in technology-related resources (e.g., learning management systems) and promote IT literacy among teachers and students.

1 Introduction

The world we currently live in has been dramatically changed and impacted due to COVID-19, an infectious disease that was first discovered in December 2019 (WHO, 2020). This disease has since influenced our lives in many ways, including the way in which we interact with other people. The crisis has also significantly impacted the global economy, and many people around the world find themselves without work or a means to provide for themselves and their families. In addition,

T. J. Allen (✉)
Kansai University, Osaka, Japan
e-mail: tjallen@kansai-u.ac.jp

© The Author(s), under exclusive license to Springer Nature Switzerland AG 2021
J. Chen (ed.), *Emergency Remote Teaching and Beyond*,
https://doi.org/10.1007/978-3-030-84067-9_2

COVID-19 has affected education systems in various countries, including the higher education sector. This includes teaching, research, all levels of study and student mobility. Not only are campuses experiencing negative changes, many institutions have also seen a downturn in study abroad programs as borders around the world are locked down in an attempt to manage the spread of COVID-19.

As a response to this crisis, universities have sought to mitigate the dangers of this virus by implementing emergency remote teaching (ERT). ERT is the impermanent alteration to the delivery of teaching and learning to an online format due to a crisis (Hodges et al., 2020; Nae, 2020). This is somewhat different from other terms used interchangeably to describe non-face-to-face teaching, such as online learning or distance education. In this sense, Hodges et al. (2020) accurately describes the context in which educators currently find themselves in the higher education sector:

> ...many of the online learning experiences that instructors will be able to offer their students will not be fully featured or necessarily well planned, and there's a high probability for suboptimal implementation. We need to recognize that everyone will be doing the best they can, trying to take just the essentials with them as they make a mad dash during the emergency. Thus, the distinction is important between the normal, everyday type of effective online instruction and that which we are doing in a hurry with bare minimum resources and scant time: emergency remote teaching. (p. 4)

This chapter discusses the above-mentioned issues surrounding ERT in the Japanese context. Firstly in this chapter, I review the literature that has investigated ERT in section two. In section three, I explore teaching in Japan in general, and in section four I describe my experiences of language instruction in the current context of ERT. In section five, I discuss the challenges of remote teaching, with a particular focus on the stakeholders at my university. Specifically, I examine how the university has responded and assisted during this crisis, and how teachers and students have adapted to this last-minute change to teaching and learning online. I also discuss these three stakeholders in the context of the availability of IT infrastructure, stakeholders' IT literacy and the communication issues arising from university directions and expectations. Lastly, I offer my final thoughts on ERT in the Japanese context, and discuss the lessons learned from this experience.

2   ERT

The implementation of ERT is a new reality for some institutions, teachers and students in various countries around the world. As a result, a small number of recent studies and reports have discussed how ERT has been implemented in various countries and contexts. In this section, I discuss both academic sources and other reports on ERT to contextualise the reality of teaching various language subjects in Japan during the COVID-19 crisis.

2.1   University Support

In a *Japan Times* article from April 2020, the authors described how parents in Japan have reacted to the current crisis in terms of their children's education. While parents and guardians had great concern for their children's academic welfare during the COVID-19 crisis as they were unable to attend school, online education has yet to be adopted and has failed to gain popularity ("Japan keen to accelerate remote education", 2020).

Notwithstanding the central government's keen interest to adopt and fast-track technology in the classroom, local governments have remained unwilling. In addition, there have been a number of factors affecting the successful implementation of online education in Japanese schools. These include delays in distributing devices such as laptops and tablets, as well as developing networks and internet accessibility points in these schools. As similar issues were being faced by university students (in particular, the lack of applicable devices to access online content for classes), universities in Japan subsidised online classes by offering financial assistance to students ("Universities in Japan try to soften blow", 2020). Table 1 shows examples of the amount of funding being offered to students at various universities in Japan.

Other universities offered delays and extensions to deadlines for fees, or offered a reduction in tuition payments to assist students in their transition to ERT. In addition, a number of universities offered financial assistance to those students living away from home, including international students who were facing difficulties in finding work.[1]

Table 1 University funding for students in Japan

(Examples)

University	Amount of funding
Meiji Gakuin University	50,000 Yen ($664 AUD)
Tokai University	10,000 Yen ($133 AUD)
Kanagawa University	50,000 Yen ($664 AUD)

---

[1] https://www.kansai-u.ac.jp/ja/about/pr/news/2020/06/post_5043.html Kansai University offered various financial support options for students. Information about additional initiatives from government agencies can be found here: https://www.mext.go.jp/a_menu/koutou/ryugaku/1405561_00007.htm

2.2   Teaching and Learning in an ERT Environment

While university administrators announced that there would not be a drop in educational standards, students, parents and stakeholders were hesitant about ERT. Although educators were working to ensure that their students were well supported, there was and continues to be a misconception in terms of comparing ERT with traditional face-to-face teaching or other forms of planned online learning and teaching. Instead there should be clear messaging from the university to the various stakeholders that ERT should not be compared to other forms of teaching during a crisis. Hodges et al. (2020) explained that the:

> primary objective in these circumstances is not to re-create a robust educational ecosystem but rather to provide temporary access to instruction and instructional supports in a manner that is quick to set up and is reliably available during an emergency or crisis. (p. 7)

That is, ERT is only a temporary solution to a difficult situation and is not meant to replicate or replace face-to-face instruction or planned online teaching. Hodges et al. (2020) also pointed out how ERT has been successfully applied in other countries during times of crisis such as war (see for example, Davies, 2010) or natural disasters, where various distance educational models were implemented such as radio and other forms of blended learning technologies (Hodges et al., 2020).

Examining past-crisis examples of ERT implementation demonstrates that teachers need to find creative solutions to the challenge of moving classes online quickly (Hodges, et al., 2020; Head et al., 2002). In addition, teachers and students need to be flexible (Zhang et al., 2020) and adapt to unpredictable circumstances as seen during this crisis (e.g., the first, second and third waves of the virus, the various lockdowns and legal limitations, and the various expectations of ERT).

University IT departments and other support teams are also vital during an ERT situation. However, these departments are often not able to support teachers and students in their usual ways (Hodges et al., 2020). In a normal situation, these departments may be able to offer faculty and students support with various online learning tools (e.g., LMS) and may even help with the management of classrooms (through the use of teaching assistants). Hodges et al. (2020) noted that support in a crisis-free environment includes "full-course design support, professional development opportunities, content development, learning management system training and support, and multimedia creation in partnership with faculty experts" (p. 8). As teachers have varying levels of IT literacy (discussed later in Sects. 5.2 and 5.3), Hodges et al. (2020) explained that:

> ERT requires that faculty take more control of the course design, development, and implementation process. With the expectation of rapid development of online teaching and learning events and the large number of faculty in need of support, faculty development and support teams must find ways to meet the institutional need to provide instructional continuity while helping faculty develop skills to work and teach in an online environment. (p. 8)

In other words, designing, implementing and teaching online courses may be left up to individual teachers, with support departments offering minimal help at various times. As a way forward, universities need to consider how they will offer support during these times (Hodges et al., 2020) and rethink ways to better assist staff in the future for dealing with crises and ERT (Trust & Whalen, 2020; Green et al., 2020). If universities fail to do so, they may leave both faculty and students at risk of being isolated and left behind unless other measures organically form among those stakeholders to alleviate such problems.

3   Language Teaching in the Japanese University Context

Foreign educators moving to Japan to teach English has a long history, beginning in the 1600s (Ike, 1995). Although English has been taught in Japan for quite some time, Japanese students still struggle to acquire high levels of proficiency due to the differences in pronunciation, syntax and word order (e.g., omission of pronouns, particles and plural forms) (Dougill, 2008). The Ministry of Education, Culture, Sports, Science and Technology (MEXT), a government department that directs and governs education policy in Japan has stated that:

> With the progress of globalization in the economy and in society, it is essential that our children acquire communication skills in English, which has become a common international language, in order for living in the 21st century. This has become an extremely important issue both in terms of the future of our children and the further development of Japan as a nation. (MEXT, 2002)

This statement suggests that the MEXT realises the significance of English language education in Japan, and thus universities have responded to this policy by implementing various English language programs and support (Allen, 2019) and encouraging study abroad among their students. For example, in the university and faculty where I teach, students undertake four years of language study (English and Chinese majors, and minors in German, French, Spanish, Russian and Korean). During this time, they focus on developing language skills such as reading, writing, listening and speaking. In their second year of study, students travel abroad and attend a foreign university for one year, learning English language skills (listening, reading, writing and speaking) and their other language minor (if applicable). Students also study other related subjects such as intercultural communication and linguistics. Once they return from their study abroad, students specialise in a particular area such as intercultural communication, foreign language education, translation and interpreting, area studies or language analysis.

To teach English language skills at universities in Japan, typically staff are required to have a Master's degree in applied linguistics, education or other related area. PhDs in similar fields are looked upon favourably, and open doors to tenured positions. Usually, if foreign staff have a Master's degree, they are employed on a five-year contract. Once these contracts expire, teachers are required to find alternative positions elsewhere and cannot return to the same university for one year. Tenured staff on the other hand are required to teach, research, obtain grants, work on various committees and publish. Contract staff do not have these stipulations in place but are able to research and publish as well. Both tenured and contract staff often work at other universities in part-time positions to supplement their incomes. Tenured staff teach 7–8 *koma*[2] per week, while contracted full-time teachers are expected to teach up to 10 *koma* per week.

Teachers in the faculty I belong to are also expected to teach classes in other faculties. For example, staff members teach in the faculty of literature, economics, engineering, sociology and information science. These courses are typically labelled "general English" classes, where students learn basic communication in English as well as other academic skills (e.g., critical thinking). These classes typically follow the communicative language teaching approach (e.g., Richards, 2005; Littlewood, 2014) and encourage students to work collaboratively in developing their English language skills. However, as these students do not major in English or other related subjects such as linguistics (i.e., they major in other subjects in different faculties), motivation and interest are often much lower when compared to other students who major in foreign languages.

4 Language Teaching and ERT in the Japanese Context

As a tenured member of faculty at the university, I am expected to teach five classes (or *koma*) in the spring semester and seven classes (or *koma*) in the fall semester. In the spring (2020) semester, I taught two general English courses (advanced reading and writing) to two non-linguistic faculties and one listening and speaking class to students majoring in a foreign language (e.g. English). In addition, I coordinated the first-year academic writing course in our faculty, where I taught two classes to students majoring in a foreign language. The semester is typically 15-weeks in duration; however, due to COVID-19, the semester was shortened to give teachers time to move to an ERT format. Instead, the duration of the semester was 13 weeks.

While moving to ERT has been a necessity to remain safe, there have been several mainstream news and academic articles written about the positive and negative aspects of working from home in regard to resources and access (e.g., Webb, 2020). These challenges also relate to teachers' experiences at universities. For example, positive aspects include avoiding the risks of contracting coronavirus; more time for personal activities as you are not commuting between the office, classroom and home; and more time to spend with family. However, the articles also point out a number of negative aspects. For example, Webb (2020) noted that:

> The sudden transition to working from home, coupled with the compact size of most Japanese houses and apartments, means that most people don't have a home office setup, and not having a dedicated room, or even desk, strictly for work-related activities, which was the top complaint among the survey respondents... (para. 10)

This has also increased pressures on worker's mental health and home lives. A number of people responded to the survey in Webb's (2020) article claiming that working at home all day and being isolated in a single room has led to increased mental stress. In

---

[2]A *koma* is typically a 90-minute class in Japan.

addition to these negative consequences of working from home, minority communities are also facing significant impacts on their day-to-day lives because of closures to institutions, schools and universities (Aguilera & Nightengale-Lee, 2020). Furthermore, at my university, teachers are working from home and caring for small children at the same time, attempting to balance both parental and vocational responsibilities.

4.1 Description of Courses and Online Teaching

In a face-to-face and non-COVID-19 setting, classes typically run for 90 minutes and are structured around explicit instruction and activities focused on various language skills. Students develop a routine around this particular structure. However, for online learning in an ERT context, classes followed the structure outlined in Fig. 1. In addition, class times were shortened to 45–60 minutes to reduce the negative effects of prolonged screen time, which were implemented by the teacher. By altering class times and structure, I used both synchronous and asynchronous approaches in all lessons.

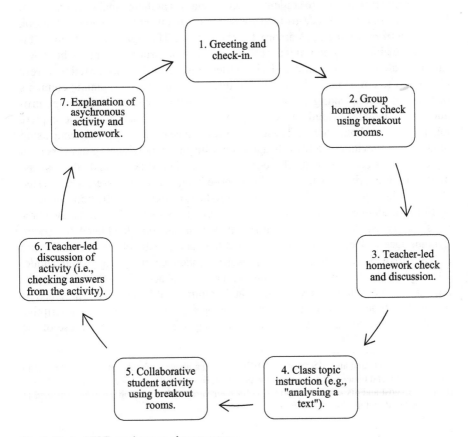

Fig. 1 Typical ERT synchronous class structure

Classes were also structured in a way to include as much social interaction as possible between students to encourage both their language skills development (listening and speaking) and support their psychological and emotional wellbeing (Kim, 2021, see Chapter "Implications of a Sudden Shift Online: The Experiences of English Education Students' Studying Online for the First-Time During COVID-19 Pandemic in Japan" in this volume). As mentioned above, teachers facilitated two general English classes from different faculties, using a synchronous format. The university's learning management system (LMS[3]) allowed students to attend Zoom classes, which were recorded and distributed at the end of each class.

In these classes, students would listen to instructions from the teacher and complete activities individually and as a group using the breakout room function. In addition, as this course focused on reading and writing, students were prescribed readings and activities from the textbook (*Reading Explorer 3*, Cengage) that developed their grammatical and vocabulary knowledge. Students were also asked to complete writing activities such as responding to particular questions in paragraph format using Google Forms via the LMS.

In the listening and speaking course, classes were also structured around a synchronous format, where students attended classes at their usual time on Zoom. In a similar manner to face-to-face classes, students used the assigned textbook (*Contemporary Topics 2*, Pearson) for the course. Through this textbook, students were able to register and access online content through the publisher ('My English Lab'), such as audio and video files studied in the class. Students were also asked to collaboratively respond to questions about the pragmatic elements of listening and speaking through the LMS asynchronously. To encourage production of language, students were given a number of activities to complete together in breakout rooms. These activities focused on developing and using pragmatic behaviours such as disagreeing with or acknowledging conversation topics, as a listener. Students also completed a number of exams and other assessment items (e.g., presentations) similar to those in face-to-face classes, which tested students' abilities in vocabulary, language production and pragmatic knowledge.

In the academic writing course, classes were also structured around a synchronous format. Students attended classes at their usual time facilitated by Zoom. Echoing face-to-face classes, students used the course textbook (*Focus on Writing 3*, Pearson), which uses the process approach to academic writing (e.g., Akinwamide, 2012). Students were expected to complete a number of activities to build their writing skills and develop their vocabulary and grammatical knowledge. These activities guided students to write three types of paragraphs: (1) narrative, (2) descriptive and (3) opinion. Students worked collaboratively together through the use of the

---

[3] The university created an LMS prior to COVID-19 crisis; however, faculty seldom used it due to the complexity and unnecessary nature of the platform. However, during the crisis, faculty adopted the LMS to host and disseminate information for their various classes. Students were expected to review material on the LMS for each of their classes.

breakout room function on Zoom (to complete homework assignments and read aloud their writing), as well as asynchronously on the LMS. Students completed a number of assessment items, which focused on testing students' grammar and vocabulary knowledge, their metalanguage about academic writing and their production of actual texts.

4.2 Activities and Assessments

In a typical (non-COVID-19) university context, students need to complete assessment items to pass their courses. The size, weight and number of these assessment items are determined by the coordinator of the course. However, due to the move to ERT, my university mandated that each course needed to offer students several assessment items as a way to reduce the weighting of each item overall. This gave students a number of opportunities to succeed in their courses in the event that they faced technical issues and were unable to complete an assessment item on time. As a result, the following activities and assessments were implemented in each of the classes.

In the general English courses, students completed a number of assessment items, which included exam format and written-type assignments.[4] For examination format assessments, students completed exams and quizzes on Zoom, with their cameras turned on, to ensure that they were not using other devices or their notes to look up answers, chat to others to find the answer, or have someone else complete the test.[5] These exams were created through Google Forms (see Fig. 2), an application that allows students to enter their personal information and complete various types of questions such as closed responses (i.e., multiple choice) and short and long format questions (e.g., paragraph length), which are then downloadable through Google Drive.

Students were given sufficient time to complete each exam, depending on the number of question items. For other written types of assessment items, students were asked to produce written paragraphs. These were then assessed across criteria, on topics related to discussion questions from the textbook. These were also delivered and completed via Google Forms.

---

[4]LMS assessment items were time and date restricted for security reasons. This also includes assessment items made available through Google Forms and Google Drive.

[5]It should be pointed out here that there were no assurances that students did not engage in academic misconduct. However, the Zoom camera was used as way to monitor students as much as possible. Creating time limits for exams were an effective strategy in keeping students on task as well as using 'randomiser' functions that create the same questions for students but order them differently. In addition, lowering the value/weight of each assessment item mitigated the potential impact of academic misconduct on their overall grade. Moreover, if students could not turn their camera on for various reasons, then they were not forced to.

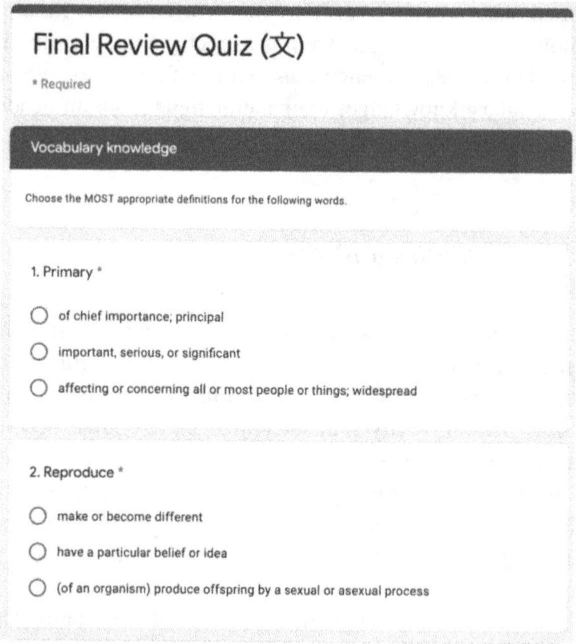

Fig. 2 General English
course exam vocabulary
section example (Google
Forms)

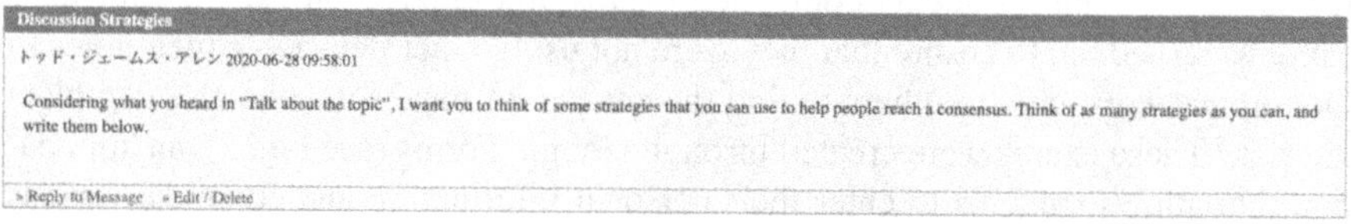

Final Review Quiz (文)

* Required

Vocabulary knowledge

Choose the MOST appropriate definitions for the following words.

1. Primary *

○ of chief importance; principal

○ important, serious, or significant

○ affecting or concerning all or most people or things; widespread

2. Reproduce *

○ make or become different

○ have a particular belief or idea

○ (of an organism) produce offspring by a sexual or asexual process

Discussion Strategies

トッド・ジェームス・アレン 2020-06-28 09:58:01

Considering what you heard in "Talk about the topic", I want you to think of some strategies that you can use to help people reach a consensus. Think of as many strategies as you can, and write them below.

» Reply to Message   » Edit / Delete

Fig. 3 Discussion strategies activity example (discussion forum posted to the university LMS)

For the listening and speaking course, students also completed a number of assessment items throughout the semester, which included exams and presentation tasks. For exams, a combination of Google Forms, the university's LMS and the textbook online resources site were used. Students were given ample time to navigate the different platforms, as well as complete the exams. Students also needed to complete these exams on Zoom with their cameras turned on to avoid academic misconduct. As students needed to produce presentations, they uploaded these videos to YouTube and emailed the link to me. If students were unable to do this (for various reasons such as privacy concerns), they could send the file directly to me via email or upload them to the shared class folder on Google Drive. To assess participation, students were asked to complete online discussion activities (asynchronously) together, which focused on particular pragmatic features of listening and speaking (shown in Fig. 3).

For the academic writing classes, students completed a number of written assessments in addition to quizzes and exams, conducted in similar ways to other courses. To encourage students to write in a collaborative way, they were given a space on

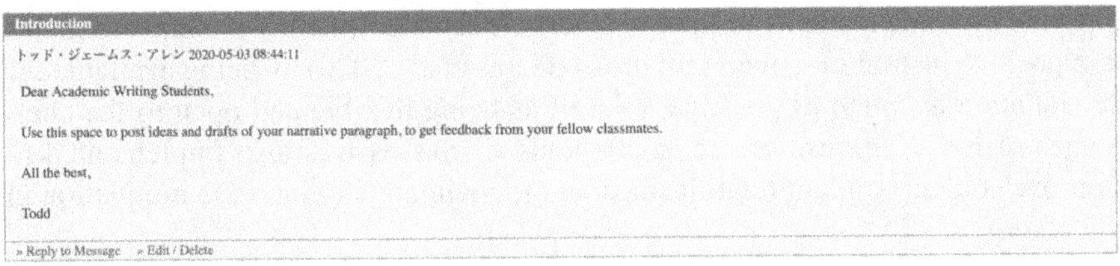
Introduction

トッド・ジェームス・アレン 2020-05-03 08:44:11

Dear Academic Writing Students,

Use this space to post ideas and drafts of your narrative paragraph, to get feedback from your fellow classmates.

All the best,

Todd

» Reply to Message » Edit / Delete

Fig. 4 Collaborative writing example (unstructured) (discussion forum posted to the university LMS)

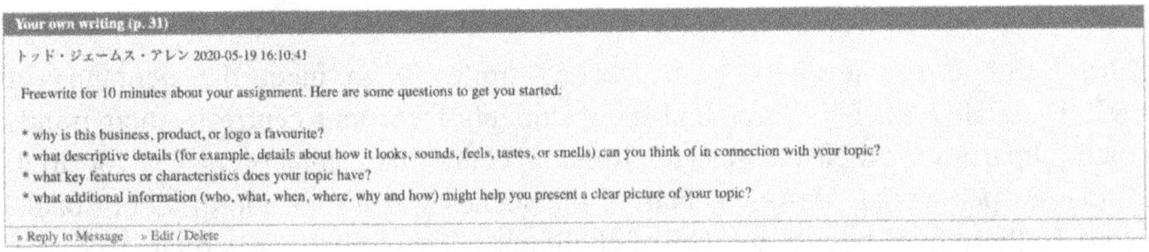
Your own writing (p. 31)

トッド・ジェームス・アレン 2020-05-19 16:10:41

Freewrite for 10 minutes about your assignment. Here are some questions to get you started:

* why is this business, product, or logo a favourite?
* what descriptive details (for example, details about how it looks, sounds, feels, tastes, or smells) can you think of in connection with your topic?
* what key features or characteristics does your topic have?
* what additional information (who, what, when, where, why and how) might help you present a clear picture of your topic?

» Reply to Message » Edit / Delete

Fig. 5 Collaborative writing example (structured) (discussion forum posted to the university LMS)

the university LMS to share ideas and thoughts about their writing assignments (see Fig. 4). While this was made available to students, they did not engage well with the collaborative writing spaces. A number of students viewed the writing space, but none of them engaged in the activity.

However, students did engage well with other activities posted on the university LMS that were more structured (often taken directly from the textbook) and could directly benefit them when producing their paragraph assessment item. For example, all students responded to the activity in Fig. 5.

For written assessments, students used their own devices and relevant software to complete their tasks. The university uses Microsoft products, and students have access to these applications for free (e.g., Microsoft Word). Before the first assessment item was submitted, I explained how to set up the software to ensure students knew how to use it. For example, students were taught how to change the dictionary from Japanese to English on a Microsoft Word document, how to accurately format the paragraph following American Psychological Association (APA) conventions, including font type and size. For exams, like the other courses, Google Forms was used, with students working under the same exam conditions. In terms of assessing written assignments, students uploaded their writing to the university LMS, and the texts were downloaded and reviewed using Microsoft Word track-changes and assessed against a criterion.

While each of the assessment items discussed above were implemented in a way to ensure students could complete all tasks on time with as much support as possible (with the teacher often spending more time on class preparation than face to face classes), some students did not complete all assessment items. This could be because some students may have lost interest or motivation during the semester or may have felt overwhelmed by the number of hours spent online (as was reported by some students to their teachers). This is despite my attempts to maintain positive instructor–student relations (Gares et al., 2020) by being available for consultation as much as possible, as well as being flexible and open to the challenges of ERT. The use of breakout rooms in classes was also implemented to improve student–student relationships and to maintain and increase motivation in the class.

5   The Challenges of ERT in the Japanese Context

During this crisis, teachers have worked tirelessly to meet the demands of ERT. Dedicated teachers have had their students front and centre in their minds when preparing for their classes (for some teachers this means preparing for up to 20 classes per week). However, behind the scenes and the facade of Zoom backgrounds, there have been a number of challenges. These challenges relate to the IT infrastructure available to both teachers and students. In addition, IT literacy has also been a challenging factor in the delivery of ERT. In particular, teachers have needed to dedicate time to teach not only their subject area but also how to use particular forms of technology (e.g., computer compatibility) and software (e.g., Microsoft Word). These challenges are made worse due to the difficulties in communicating particular expectations as well as language proficiency in Japanese by both tenured and contract teachers.

5.1   Digital Infrastructure at the University

Prior to the COVID-19 crisis, most universities around the world had incorporated elements of online learning with the use of interactive LMSs such as Blackboard or Moodle. In addition, some of these universities also have large IT departments ready to assist course designers, teachers and students in times of difficulty (Hodges et al., 2020). These online environments are relatively stable and user friendly, enabling both designers and users to freely navigate the systems. However, in most Japanese universities this is not the case, and it has been a challenge for ERT during the COVID-19 pandemic. The LMS used in my university, while stable, was difficult to navigate and use for both educators and students. In addition, the LMS was not visually appealing, which may deter or demotivate teachers and students (Grant-Smith et al., 2019).

In general, the LMS had basic features such as the ability to create various quizzes, to control the time and the number of attempts that a user could access the material, upload content and assessment items, and engage with each other using bulletin boards. Furthermore, designers are able to upload material such as PowerPoint slides, class notes and other content required for each class. However, compared with other LMSs available on the market, the current LMS was difficult to use as it required specialist terminology and an understanding of basic coding. Also, the LMS featured both English and Japanese language versions. However, the translations of particular phrases in Japanese to English were not always accurate or complete. In some instances, messages on pages vanished when changing the language setting to English.

Due to the difficulty in using the LMS, a number of teachers and instructors decided to use it cautiously. Instead, teachers often redirected their students to other services available through Google, Dropbox and Microsoft. While this was permitted by the university, these external services were not supported by the IT centre on campus (except for Dropbox).

Besides the issues with the appearance and functionality of the LMS, in the first few days of remote teaching, students and teachers found themselves unable to connect to the university's online services at various times. This was due to service congestion, whereby a large amount of internet traffic was attempting to access the LMS at the same time, leading to a collapse of the system. While IT staff were quick to intervene and rectify the problem by increasing bandwidth, both teachers and students experienced anxiety and stress by not being able to attend classes on time or access needed material.

5.2   *Information Technology Literacy and Resources*

Japan is often stereotyped as a technologically advanced country as neon signs and talking robots seem to confuse foreign residents and tourists alike. However, Japan is lagging behind other countries such as China and Korea (Sawa, 2020; Kim, 2021, see Chapter "Implications of a Sudden Shift Online: The Experiences of English Education Students' Studying Online for the First-Time During COVID-19 Pandemic in Japan" in this volume) in terms of technology use and development. In relation to education, as a relatively new teacher in Japan, I quickly discovered that when compared to students in other countries (such as Australia), digital literacy remains low. This has also been identified in previous literature (Milliner & Cote, 2016; Cote & Milliner, 2017). The MEXT has acknowledged the deficit in digital literacy in young people (MEXT, 2002) and has mandated the inclusion of IT education in school curriculums and tertiary institutions. However, in 2015 "the Organization for Economic Co-operation and Development OECD... released a statement on the literacy of Japanese youth, noting that 25% (age 16–29) lack basic computer skills" (Cote & Milliner, 2017, p. 127). One such reason for this deficit in computer literacy may be because schools and tertiary institutions are not responding to the MEXT's demands quickly enough.

Students in Japan (like most students around the world) are adept in the use of smartphone technology and the various applications associated with them (Ohashi, 2019; Wang, 2020). However, using educational applications (e.g., LMS) and devices (e.g., Laptop) for class work was a challenge for some students. More specifically, some students struggled with the transition to remote education as some did not have access to a device that could be used effectively for class activities (e.g., using a smartphone on Zoom). This also created a divide between those who had the financial resources to purchase suitable equipment and those who might not have been able to. Furthermore, some students also did not have access to a reliable internet connection[6] and were relying on their smartphones to complete class activities remotely.

Some teachers also found themselves in similar positions. Language teachers in Japanese universities use a range of resources in the classroom in a pandemic-free context. Resources such as audio, video and textbooks are used to complement various types of activities in language classrooms. To facilitate classes in an ERT context, some teachers found themselves without enough IT experience or expertise to move these activities and resources online or even to develop materials for students to access and use on the LMS. As a temporary solution, publishers gave teachers access to online versions of the textbook to assist teachers in moving such activities to an ERT format. This also gave teachers the ability to share resources with students without having to spend a lot of time making materials from scratch for online classes.

As reported in some mainstream news articles (e.g., Webb, 2020), teachers also found that while working from home had a number of advantages, there were also a number of disadvantages. Most teachers were not immediately equipped with home offices and prepared for the transition to ERT. Often times, teachers had to contend with other family members such as children and pets while conducting classes online. This in turn led to additional mental stress on teachers in an already stressful situation, as well as distracting students at various times. In addition, some financial resources (e.g., personal teaching funds) were not able to be used for purchasing equipment to establish a home office. Instead, teachers (both contract and tenured) had to use their own money to establish suitable spaces for ERT in their homes.

5.3   Communication

Working in a different country brings with it many challenges such as cultural and linguistic barriers, which have been well-researched in the literature from various perspectives (e.g., Zhang & Peltokorpi, 2016; Bodycott & Walker, 2000). However, in an ERT context in Japan, these issues can also arise, particularly when information is provided to teachers in Japanese and they lack the appropriate language and cultural abilities to fully understand the directions.

Teachers in the current context have many reasons for coming to and remaining in Japan (such as family, a passion for teaching English, research interests). While most have the ability to use the Japanese language for day-to-day life, some find it difficult to read and understand directives written formally by universities. At the beginning of the semester, the university established a list of directives and expectations for teachers to follow in designing their classes. These directives included:

---

[6] Some telecommunication companies in Japan offered free data or reduced rates for students to access the internet through their mobile devices. For example see: https://mainichi.jp/english/articles/20200404/p2a/00m/0na/009000c

- The types of class formats permitted to be used for classes (e.g., synchronous, asynchronous or 'on demand[7]');
- How to contact students and how to approach the first few weeks of teaching;
- How to re-establish classes due to the move to ERT (i.e., changes to assessment ratios);
- Managing attendance;
- Creating classes that are seen as "equivalent to face-to-face classes"; however, teachers needed to avoid placing a heavy burden on students (i.e., doing too much online and pacing the students appropriately);
- Managing students' privacy, avoiding additional costs for students (i.e., having them buy hardware and software), and being flexible with classwork and assessment;
- Protocols for students to submit their assessments.

However, as these directives and expectations were first written and sent in Japanese, this led to some difficulty in understanding what was actually required by teachers, adding further stress, anxiety and confusion during an already challenging time. Once university management realised this issue, instructions were re-written in English, but were still at times confusing as they were often ambiguous and unclear. For example, for those teachers who could read and understand both English and Japanese, there were some discrepancies between both versions.

Furthermore, the university also included directions on the types of applications that could be used in the delivery of classes, such as the university LMS, Dropbox and Zoom. In addition, the university gave some instruction on how to use these applications; however, they were typically introductory guides from the particular company that developed them, or very brief overviews. This led to further stress and isolation amongst teachers (see for example Trust & Whalen, 2020; Green et al., 2020), as they could not fully operate the various hardware and software required for their teaching (as discussed in Sect. 5.2). Figure 6 illustrates the trends for the search term "Zoom使い方" ('How to use Zoom') in Japan. This demonstrates that people were searching for ways to learn more about how they could use Zoom effectively, particularly in the months of May, April and June. While this graph includes people across all professions, it does highlight people's needs to learn more about the software. This would include teachers wanting to know how to use the software and deal with students who struggled to use it.

To address these challenges, however, an online community organically formed by a number of Japanese and non-Japanese professors (tenured, contract and part-time), who were experienced in facilitating online learning prior to the COVID-19 crisis. This community grew to over fifty teachers who corresponded mainly through email. In these email exchanges, teachers discussed troubleshooting with various technologies, as well as clarifying issues surrounding the

---

[7] 'On demand' (a word from the Japanese オンデマンド) classes are a form of teaching at the current university where teachers upload lecture videos and other class content for students to access and complete in their own time.

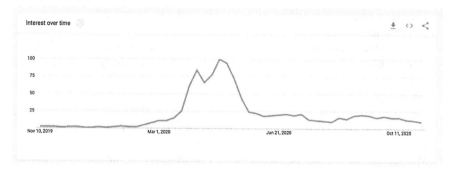

Fig. 6 Google Trends ("Zoomの使い方" 'how to use Zoom') in Japan

university's expectations and directives. Other discussion topics related to ERT included:

- Pedagogical questions and ideas for classes (i.e., how to go about structuring classes);
- Sharing ideas about exams and other assessment items (which applications are best to use or sharing actual data to be used in classes);
- Exchanging tips to manage online learning and teaching fatigue;
- Translating directives from administrative departments;
- General day-to-day information, such as scheduling.

In addition to the email exchanges, some workshops were held online to help teachers become familiar with Zoom and the university's LMS. As some instruction was given officially by the university, the workshops focused on practical experiences of the LMS and Zoom features. This again gave teachers opportunities to experience these applications and ask questions about particular areas of confusion. While this was sufficient for the majority of teachers, there were instances where less IT-skilled and experienced teachers struggled. As a result, separated and more customised workshops for less-skilled teachers would have been more appropriate and useful, as the less-skilled teachers often slowed down the momentum of the workshop, and with time limitations, facilitators were unable to cover more advanced features of these platforms.

Lastly, the communication between students and teachers was also problematic at times during the use of ERT. The first semester in Japanese universities typically begins in April and is usually a time for teachers to meet their students and build positive relationships for the year ahead. As there were no opportunities to meet face-to-face, teachers relied heavily on Zoom and other applications to build a strong rapport with their students. For some teachers and students though, this was a challenging feature of ERT. At times when students did not attend classes or did not submit particular assessment items on time, teachers attempted to contact them. There were a number of instances where students failed to respond to the teachers' attempts to contact them, which created further stress and anxiety for both parties. Teachers felt that they needed to be flexible, but also fair to other students who had submitted assessment items on time. Once students missed one or two assessment items, motivation decreased, which led to further missed submissions and possibly isolation and despair. This then became challenging for teachers as they tried to ensure that students were managing remote learning as well as they could.

6 Conclusion

In this chapter, I have attempted to offer some insight into the current COVID-19 crisis in the context of ERT in Japan. I have discussed my experiences as a language teacher in Japan, highlighting the challenges faced by both instructors and students. While the above sections have focused on some of the challenging aspects of ERT, several positive aspects have also emerged from this experience that can be drawn on for future use in the language classroom. These positive aspects have also been explored in recent literature (i.e., Ando, 2020). For example, one aspect is the learning of new skills by both teachers and students. Another aspect is the need to develop stable and secure IT infrastructure on campuses. Furthermore, another positive aspect involves teachers and their ability to now "modernise" their methods of teaching by experimenting with and increasing their use of technology in the classroom. A limitation of this chapter though is that it offers only one person's experience of ERT and the COVID-19 crisis in Japan. Further reflection, introspection and examination of this crisis in terms of all stakeholders' experiences should be pursued in the future.

Finally, at the time of writing this chapter, classes had returned to a face-to-face format for teachers who did not have known underlying health conditions. For preventative measures against COVID-19, teachers and students were expected to participate in COVID-safe measures such as social distancing, wearing masks and cleaning facilities regularly. As typical classes (pre-COVID-19) were interactive and used discussion activities, in the current context, this has become difficult to facilitate due to implementing COVID-safe measures (e.g., social distancing). As a result, blended learning (e.g., Hrastinski, 2019) activities were implemented as a means to encourage students to discuss various topics covered in class time asynchronously. As students were familiar with online tools such as Google Forms/Docs and the university's LMS, tasks have been set each week for them to complete online. These typically include questions aiming to develop students' critical thinking skills that are also explored later in class. However, teachers who remained working from home did report some difficulty in engaging students. Some teachers reported that class attendance and participation had been low as students were split between classes online and face-to-face. While these issues have arisen, teachers and students are continuing to work together to complete their studies in a safe and successful way during this unprecedented time.

7 Food for Thought

This crisis has forced both teachers and students to confront technology and applications that they normally would not engage with. As a result, both students and teachers have now developed skills that are intrinsically and extrinsically valuable. That is, by adopting technology in the classroom, students and teachers can now continue to develop their skills and use them in the future. When discussing ERT with students, most of them were positive towards ERT (see also Kim, 2021, Chapter "Implications of a Sudden Shift Online: The Experiences of English Education Students' Studying Online for the First-Time During COVID-19 Pandemic in Japan" in this volume). Some students remarked that while ERT was not ideal, it did give them the opportunity to develop new skills, which they could use for their future studies or vocations. Teachers too remarked that they could continue to use these skills in class, which also gave them the confidence to try to implement other IT-related activities in the classroom. This has also been explored in recently published studies (e.g., Raaper & Brown, 2020). Teachers should continue to experiment with other technologies in the classroom. In addition, they should collaborate with other teachers to raise IT literacy in their schools or faculties, and encourage awareness and use of technologies in the classroom.

As a teacher of listening, speaking, academic writing and general English classes, this crisis has given me the chance to experiment with various applications, and "modernise" and update my teaching practices in the classroom. For example, as quizzes and exams were recently uploaded to a digital format, this has resulted in two positive outcomes. Firstly, it has allowed me to recycle material more effectively. As these exams and quizzes have been set up in a way that makes questions completely random, they can be reused without the worry of academic misconduct. Moreover, as the results are stored on the system, grading is completed automatically, saving further time in the semester. In addition, keeping track of students' grades has also become easier as results can be downloaded and imported into a spreadsheet automatically, or the LMS can store students' grades in the 'gradebook' feature. Students too benefit from this feature as they are able to obtain their results immediately upon completion and download and review incorrect answers at the same time. Teachers should plan and implement realistic IT objectives into their classrooms in similar ways. That is, decide what elements of teaching should be moved to an online platform (e.g., assessment items) and determine the success of the implementation over time.

Acknowledgements I wish to thank Dr Julian Chen for his guidance and assistance with this chapter. I also wish to express my sincere thanks to my students for being understanding and adaptable during this very challenging time.

Appendix

Overview of learning approach and technology type

Approach	Tool	Activity types (Examples)
Synchronous	Zoom	Checking in with students; going through homework; explicit instruction (i.e., writing topic sentences); exam assessments; student skills development (in groups completing activities together). These classes were supported by the use of PowerPoint slides to structure the class and show resources for learning.
Asynchronous	University LMS	Discussion questions; presentation-type and written assessments; PowerPoint slides and Zoom recording uploaded; assessment results and feedback.
Synchronous and Asynchronous	YouTube	Uploading presentation-type assessments (e.g., presentations).
	Google Drive	Used as a repository for resources (e.g., returning feedback to students). Linked through the university LMS.
	Google Forms	Used to facilitate discussion questions, writing-type assessments and other forms of assessment (e.g., vocabulary quizzes). Linked through the university LMS

References

Allen, T. J. (2019). Facilitating graduate student and faculty member writing groups: Experiences from a university in Japan. *Higher Education Research & Development, 38*(3), 435–449.

Aguilera, E., & Nightengale-Lee, B. (2020). Emergency remote teaching across urban and rural contexts: Perspectives on educational equity. *Information and Learning Sciences, 121*(5/6), 471–478.

Akinwamide, T. K. (2012). The influence of process approach on English as second language students' performances in essay writing. *English Language Teaching, 5*(3), 16–29.

Ando, S. (2020). University teaching and learning in a time of social distancing: A sociocultural perspective. *Journal of Human Behavior in the Social Environment,* 1–14.

Bodycott, P., & Walker, A. (2000). Teaching abroad: Lessons learned about inter-cultural understanding for teachers in higher education. *Teaching in Higher Education, 5*(1), 79–94.

Cote, T. J., & Milliner, B. (2017). Preparing Japanese students' digital literacy for study abroad: Is more training needed? *JALT CALL Journal, 13*(3), 187–197.

Davies, L. (2010). *Understanding education's role in fragility: Synthesis of four situational analyses of education and fragility: Afghanistan, Bosnia and Herzegovina, Cambodia, Liberia* (Report for INEE). UNESCO.

Dougill, J. (2008). Japan and English as an alien language. *English Today, 24*(1), 18.

Gares, S. L., Kariuki, J. K., & Rempel, B. P. (2020). Community matters: Student–instructor relationships foster student motivation and engagement in an emergency remote teaching environment. *Journal of Chemical Education, 97*(9), 3332–3335.

Grant-Smith, D., Donnet, T., Macaulay, J., & Chapman, R. (2019). Principles and practices for enhanced visual design in virtual learning environments: Do looks matter in student engagement? In M. Boboc & S. Koç (Eds.), *Student-centered virtual learning environments in higher education* (pp. 103–133). IGI Global.

Green, J. K., Burrow, M. S., & Carvalho, L. (2020). Designing for transition: Supporting teachers and students cope with emergency remote education. *Postdigital Science and Education,* 1–17.

Head, J. T., Lockee, B. B., & Oliver, K. M. (2002). Method, media, and mode: Clarifying the discussion of distance education effectiveness. *Quarterly Review of Distance Education, 3*(3), 261–268.

Hodges, C., Moore, S., Lockee, B. B., Trust, T., & Bond, A. (2020). The difference between emergency remote teaching and online learning. *Educause Review, 27, 1–12.*

Hrastinski, S. (2019). What do we mean by blended learning? *TechTrends, 63*(5), 564–569.

Ike, M. (1995). A historical review of English in Japan (1600–1880). *World Englishes, 14*(1), 3–11.

Japan keen to accelerate remote education amid virus spread. (2020, April 6). *Japan Times* https://www.japantimes.co.jp/news/2020/04/06/national/japan-remote-education-coronavirus/

Kim, J. (2021). Implications of a sudden shift online: The experiences of English education students' studying online for the first-time during COVID-19 pandemic in Japan. In J. Chen (Ed.), *Emergency remote teaching and beyond: Voices from world language teachers and researchers* (pp. 193–214). Springer.

Littlewood, W. (2014). Communication-oriented language teaching: Where are we now? Where do we go from here? *Language Teaching, 47*(3), 349.

Milliner, B., & Cote, T. (2016). Adoption and application of CMS: Crucial steps for an effective e-learning component. *International Journal of Computer-Assisted Language Learning and Teaching (ijcallt), 6*(3), 54–67.

Ministry of Education, Culture, Sports, Science and Technology (MEXT). (2002). *Developing a strategic plan to cultivate "Japanese with English abilities."* Retrieved from http://www.mext.go.jp/english/news/2002/07/020901.htm

Nae, N. (2020). Online learning during the pandemic: Where does Japan stand? *Euromentor Journal, 11*(2), 7–24.

Ohashi, L. (2019). *Using digital technology for autonomous, out-of-class English language learning: The influence of teacher support at a Japanese university* (Doctoral thesis, Charles Sturt University, New South Wales, Australia). Retrieved from https://researchoutput.csu.edu.au/en/publications/using-digital-technology-for-autonomous-out-of-class-english-lang

Raaper, R., & Brown, C. (2020). The Covid-19 pandemic and the dissolution of the university campus: Implications for student support practice. *Journal of Professional Capital and Community, 5*(3/4), 343–349.

Richards, J. C. (2005). *Communicative language teaching today.* SEAMEO Regional Language Center.

Sawa, T. (2020, August 6). *Japan lags in AI use and internet literacy.* https://www.japantimes.co.jp/opinion/2019/08/06/commentary/japan-commentary/japan-lags-ai-use-internet-literacy/

Trust, T., & Whalen, J. (2020). Should teachers be trained in emergency remote teaching? Lessons learned from the COVID-19 pandemic. *Journal of Technology and Teacher Education, 28*(2), 189–199.

Universities in Japan try to soften blow from pandemic with internet subsidies, scholarships and tuition cuts. (2020 April 25). *Japan Times* https://www.japantimes.co.jp/news/2020/04/25/national/universities-japan-coronavirus-internet-subsidies-scholarships-tuition-cuts/

Wang, M. (2020). The emergency remote learning process of Japanese university EFL students in a global topics course. *THT Journal: The Journal of Teachers Helping Teachers, 8*(1), 64–84.

Webb, A. (2020, April 28). We really weren't ready to work from home. *Japan Times.* https://www.japantimes.co.jp/opinion/2020/04/28/commentary/world-commentary/really-werent-ready-work-home/

World Health Organization. (2020). Coronavirus disease 2019 (COVID-19): situation report, 72.

Zhang, H., Yan, Y., & Gronseth, S. L. (2020). Adding flexibility to curriculum: A practical guide for student-directed assessment. In Ferdig, R.E., Baumgartner, E., Hartshorne, R., Kaplan-Rakowski, R., & Mouza, C (Eds.), *Teaching, technology, and teacher education during the COVID-19 pandemic: Stories from the field* (pp. 113-118). Association for the Advancement of Computing in Education (AACE). Retrieved June 15, 2020 from https://www.learntechlib.org/p/216903/

Zhang, L. E., & Peltokorpi, V. (2016). Multifaceted effects of host country language proficiency in expatriate cross-cultural adjustments: A qualitative study in China. *The International Journal of Human Resource Management, 27*(13), 1448–1469.

Part II
Teacher Voice: Online Professional Development and Virtual Community of Practice

Teachers' Instructions and Online Professional Development During Emergency Remote Teaching in Indonesia

Hanna Sundari, Susianti Rosalina, and Lalu Handi Rizal

Highlights

- The rapid change from traditional face-to-face classes into ERT brings about a new digital system of teaching and learning to unprepared teachers, students, and parents.
- Adaptations to this new teaching and learning system, using various technological devices, are used to maintain teacher professional teaching services. This leads to a techno-pedagogical revolution.
- Despite the challenges experienced during ERT, teachers have a great opportunity to immensely increase and professionally develop their capacity in teaching and technology.
- The TPD practices are in the form of government initiatives, teacher forums, online workshops/webinars, and membership in professional networked learning communities.

1 Introduction

The outbreak of the coronavirus in Wuhan, China, increased by 13-fold in 2 weeks and was quickly declared a global pandemic by the World Health Organization (Cucinotta & Vanelli, 2020; WHO, 2020). The pandemic has significantly

H. Sundari (✉)
Universitas Indraprasta PGRI, Jakarta, Indonesia

S. Rosalina
SMAN 1 Bogor, Bogor, West Java, Indonesia

L. H. Rizal
SMP PGRI 3, Jakarta, Indonesia

© The Author(s), under exclusive license to Springer Nature
Switzerland AG 2021
J. Chen (ed.), *Emergency Remote Teaching and Beyond*,
https://doi.org/10.1007/978-3-030-84067-9_3

45

influenced the health, economy, education, religion, and social psychology sectors (Megatsari et al., 2020). According to Viner et al. (2020), the pandemic led to the closure of public schools in over 107 countries, thereby forcing 862 million children and young people to study from home. This population includes 60 million children in Indonesia as the country with the fourth-largest population of children in the world (UNICEF, 2020). Therefore, the government rapidly changed the traditional face-to-face (FtF) to emergency remote teaching (ERT) due to the unpreparedness of the teachers (Bozkurt & Sharma, 2020).

Although this process is commonly viewed as online learning or distance education, ERT comes with specific features in objectives and implementation. For instance, it is a temporary teaching system used as a realistic solution during a global pandemic. Hodges et al. (2020) described this system as follows:

> ... a temporary shift of instructional delivery to an alternate delivery mode due to crisis circumstances. It involves the use of fully remote teaching solutions for instruction or education that would otherwise be delivered face-to-face or as blended or hybrid courses..... There are many examples of other countries responding to school and university closures in a time of crisis by implementing models such as mobile learning, radio, blended learning, or other solutions that are contextually more feasible. (p.5)

After the spread of Covid-19 throughout Indonesia and the government restrictions on large-scale social gathering in the middle of March 2020, most schools/ universities, particularly those in the red zone[1], were temporarily shut down. This also forced people to stay at home and carry out their various daily activities virtually. The policy of school closure was supposed to be applied for two weeks, however, this was not the case as some teachers went through various shifting schedules while students were mandated to study from home. These regulations led to the use of the remote teaching system (ERT) by teachers and students to carry out educational activities. For teachers, this changing system needs more demands in teaching and technology. Furthermore, compared to FtF class, online or offline remote teaching takes different learning materials, activities/tasks, and assessment, hence, new approaches and strategies are vital and necessary. Besides that, teacher competence in the use of technology is significantly behind innovation, especially in the Indonesian context. Therefore, undertaking teacher professional development (TPD) activities becomes indispensable to overcome the inconsistencies associated with the ERT system.

This chapter describes teaching and learning during ERT and TPD activities from three different perspectives, namely a university (Hanna), senior (Susi), and junior (Rizal) high school teachers experienced in ERT while establishing the practices of TPD by engaging in myriad activities and programs. Overall, Sect. 1 of this chapter tries to raise and discuss the issues associated with emergency remote teaching on both local and national scales. It also provides the ERT praxis taken from teachers teaching contexts and experiences. In Sect. 2, this chapter reviews the issues concerning ERT implementation in Indonesia in the areas of challenges and

---

[1] https://corona.jakarta.go.id/en

adaptation. Section 3 discusses TPD programs and activities endorsed by the Indonesian government and explores the practices of community-based TPD and other online TPD activities during ERT. Furthermore, this chapter narrates the three EFL teachers' TPD activities to anticipate the changing circumstances and maintain teaching service and professional growth. In the final section, food for thought is provided to determine the strategies used by teachers to manage their online instructions between challenges and opportunities.

2 Teaching and Learning During ERT in the Indonesian Context

In response to the COVID-19 pandemic, the Indonesian government mandated the closure of schools in mid-March 2020 and implemented the study from a home model, popularly known as *Belajar dari Rumah* (BDR). The government also implemented the work from home strategy to limit interactions between people and enforced physical/social distancing to curb the spread of virus transmission. Therefore, teachers and students were compelled to apply online and offline learning devices to facilitate remote teaching in which their parents accompany the students during learning activities. Consequently, teachers, students, and parents have a great responsibility to succeed in this process. Therefore, they need to prepare, involve, and manage daily remote teaching activities, as informed in the guidance of BDR during the Covid-19 crisis issued by the Ministry of Education and Culture (MoEC), as shown in Table 1.

Table 1 The Roles of Teacher, Student, and Parents in ERT (MoEC, 2020)

Teacher	Student	Parents
Facilitate online and offline remote teaching. Create a communication system between teacher, student, and parent. Design lesson plan based on student needs. Select tasks and the submission. Use coursebooks, modules, and learning materials, with the use of television and radio as media.	Prepare a learning kit and set a comfortable place to learn. Make regular communication with teachers. Read and understand the school timetable and purposes. Actively participate in learning and discussion. Complete all learning tasks and assignments, submit a photo when necessary. Communicate difficulties and constraints to the parents (if any) Write a learning plan.	Build communication with school staff and discuss learning/lesson plan with the teacher Prepare a learning plan. Ensure the student actively participate in learning and monitor daily progress. Discuss the constraints during the BDR with the teacher. Set a comfortable and safe learning place/room/facility for the student.

The change in the educational system significantly affected the teaching and learning activity in students' daily life. At this level, teachers had to redesign their learning materials, reselect activities, and re-examine types of assessment suitable to the learning devices, curriculum demands, and student needs. When the school and students fail to afford technological devices applicable to online learning, teachers should provide alternative solutions. Therefore, students are immediately forced to become digital/remote learners that use gadgets for learning, and not only for communication and entertainment. Meanwhile, parents are also asked to work from home, therefore, they also tend to assist their children in carrying out their various learning activities (Alifia et al., 2020).

2.1 Challenges in Teaching and Learning in Early ERT

This section provides an overview of the strategies adopted by the three EFL teachers (Rizal, Susi, and Hanna) in handling and managing their classes in the early ERT. Before the Covid-19/pandemic and ERT, education in Indonesia had already faced many problems, such as inadequate infrastructure, poor teacher competence, national curriculum, etc. This is in addition to the stereotype between public and private schools and the stigma between those within and outside Java Island, which have led to inequality among schools, teachers, students, and the quality of education at the national scale. According to a Rizal that teaches in a private junior high school in a sub-urban area, most students in this type of school are poorly motivated and low-self-regulated. Furthermore, this category of students are low-performing learners, hence the teachers need greater effort and attention to manage teaching.

In the early months of ERT, the teachers and students experienced many difficulties and constraints due to either technological competencies or internet infrastructure. Rizal stated that the school was ready to carry out paper-based tests for students in grades 7, 8, and 9 as an exam week on the day before the announcement of school closure in mid-March. The examination was then shifted into an online system using Google Classroom (https://classroom.google.com/) and Google Forms (https://docs.google.com/forms/), with WhatsApp (https://www.whatsapp.com/) used for communication lines, as shown in Fig. 1. Meanwhile, the paper tests are still stored in 33 stacks of envelopes to date.

For teaching and learning practice, Rizal kept thinking of the right ways to deliver the teaching materials and adjust the format to be more accessible and friendly for the students. This led to the application of multiple learning platforms for the classes, using Google Classroom, WhatsApp mobile application, and sometimes Zoom videoconferencing (https://zoom.us/). Furthermore, text messages and voice notes through WhatsApp Groups were used to provide school timetables and make class announcements. Meanwhile, material distribution and task submission were uploaded to Google Classroom and Forms. A synchronous

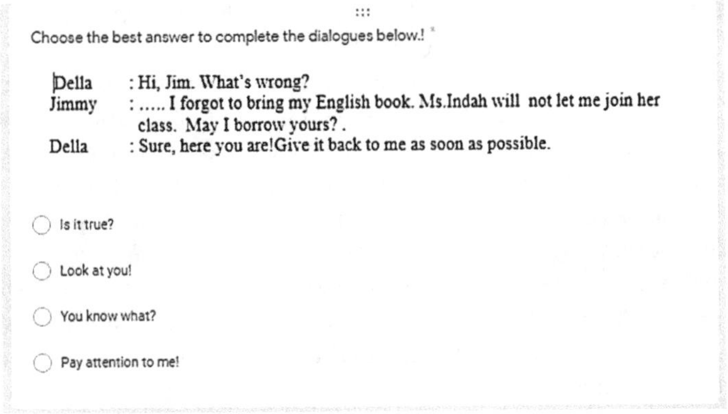

:::

Choose the best answer to complete the dialogues below.!

    Della   : Hi, Jim. What's wrong?
    Jimmy   : ..... I forgot to bring my English book. Ms.Indah will not let me join her
                class. May I borrow yours? .
    Della   : Sure, here you are!Give it back to me as soon as possible.

◯ Is it true?

◯ Look at you!

◯ You know what?

◯ Pay attention to me!

Fig. 1 Rizal's English Test using Google Forms

session using Zoom was often used. Rizal hosted video conferences outside the school timetables to keep in touch with the students. It was a non-obligatory program because not all students and parents were able to join. The family backgrounds and economic conditions are some of the factors capable of hindering students' abilities to access online learning. Some students did not have cell phones or notebooks. In a few cases, a cell phone was used for all family members. Additionally, Rizal complained that internet expenses increased up to 250% higher on bills because working, teaching, and learning online required much connectivity. This category of teachers was obliged to work from home, usually for eight to ten working hours on normal days, and during ERT, they had to carry out tasks more than 16 hours a day.

Similarly, Hanna, a faculty member at a private university in Jakarta, stated that early ERT was filled with confusion and uncertainty. Hanna's students were unable to afford learning through videoconferencing and expressed their unwillingness and objection to its usage. Therefore, teaching via WhatsApp, which is cheaper and affordable, was a more realistic option for them. Finally, the use of WhatsApp helped in conducting interactive synchronous sessions, meanwhile Google Classroom was for material distribution and submission until the end of the semester. Moreover, Hanna revealed the use of a swift instructional design, including content material similar to FtF classes for online and virtual learning activities.

Conversely, Susi teaches English at a senior high school in the urban area in Bogor, which was equipped with computers and an online system before the pandemic. According to Susi, teachers had to join ICT training two years ago to apply technological devices/tools for teaching, with the final examination carried out using a computer-based test. Additionally, the school also developed an e-learning platform. However, as the policy of ERT forced them to conduct online learning, the platform was unable to accommodate all students due to limited capacity. Therefore, in the meantime, Susi decided to use several other platforms, such as video conferencing or messenger applications. Other online resources were also selected to help

Susi in the teaching process, such as YouTube channels and electronic schoolbooks (*buku sekolah elektronik*/BSE) published by MoEC.

Access to learning tools, school infrastructure, and internet connection are factors inhibiting the delivery of online learning (Alifia et al., 2020; Churiyah et al., 2020; Lie et al., 2020). Schools in rural areas, such as those in mountainous regions, have limited or zero opportunities to carry out online learning. Therefore, teachers in these regions need to provide other solutions such as home visits. Rizal mentioned that teachers prepared copied modular worksheets of lesson materials for students that were unable to afford online learning and testing systems. They were also allowed to take offline tests at school with the application of health protocols. Schools in rural areas with high internet access and more fortunate students still faced similar problems.

Technology illiteracy was the next enemy because most teachers lacked preparation and readiness to carry out online learning using technology devices or tools (Atmojo & Nugroho, 2020; Lie et al., 2020). Hanna admitted not to have ever heard of Zoom, Cisco WebEx (https://www.webex.com/video-conferencing), or video-conferencing before the ERT. Furthermore, despite blending teaching with technology in FtF classes before the pandemic, Hanna found it difficult to use a full online learning system and manage full online remote learning.

Students' participation and submission were another issues in early ERT. Hanna informed that not all students always had an attempt in synchronous sessions, and the submission of the assignments was relatively low due to various reasons. Therefore, Hanna tried to redesign lesson materials and worksheets for a self-study activity and provide immediate feedback on synchronous sessions. These were part of her strategies to maintain teaching and motivate students to participate in the session actively. However, sometimes it seemed that the process failed to work as expected.

In summary, the Indonesian context learning inequalities occurred as inhibiting factors of teaching and educating students before the inception of ERT. However, it is noteworthy that the sudden ERT and crises bring the long-existing inequalities to a higher level. This leads to many challenges as follows:

- Educational technology infrastructure (devices, tools, internet access).
- Teacher factors (technological knowledge and competence, ICT experience, and exposure).
- Student factors (technology availability and literacy, motivation, participation).
- Support system (parents, government, community of practices).

Most teachers and students were not ready to embrace the digital system. Additionally, remote teaching relied heavily on smartphones or laptops, thereby leading to teachers' screen fatigue and burnouts. Confusion and uncertainty with unclear written instructions and heavy academic assignments failed to motivate the students, thereby leading to stress and anxiety.

2.2   Adaptions in Teaching, Technology, and Policy

This sub-section portrays the strategies used by EFL teachers in adapting to new teaching situations using technology due to the rapid change, which requires immediate and accurate responses. This change which led to a shift in the teaching system using technological devices, needs specific competence and skills. Teaching management and interaction in a virtual learning environment is not similar to the FtF classroom. However, due to the pandemic, some teachers have no alternative option to adopt the new teaching era. Moorhouse (2020) stated that "courses were designed for the face-to-face classroom, therefore, tutors need to adapt suitable online instruction process" (p. 1).

Long before the pandemic, Susi thought that blended learning would give extra time and effort for lesson preparation and create more burden on students. Despite Susi's experience and exposure to ICT training before ERT, she did not consider technology as an essential and vital in classroom teaching. However, the ERT system has conversely replaced Susi's traditional meetings into full online learning through video conferencing, messenger application, blogging, and school e-learning platform, called *Smansa Digi*[2] which helped Susi to deliver instructions, information, and assignments. During initial implementation on early ERT, this e-learning platform failed to meet user expectations due to under capacity, eventually, after some time it was upgraded and succeeded in facilitating online teaching needs. Consequently, the enactments of digital technologies in all activities made Susi realize the emergence of a techno-pedagogical revolution during the pandemic. The remote teaching in this emergency drove Susi and most teachers to use technology devices and improve technological competencies (Fig. 2).

In July, at the beginning of the new school year 2020/2021, the MoEC launched regulations and policy to adjust the impact of the Covid-19 pandemic on teaching and learning practices. The Decree of the Minister of Education and Culture Number 719/P/2020 was issued to provide Guidelines for Implementing the Curriculum at Educational Units in Special Conditions, known as the emergency curriculum for early childhood, elementary, and secondary levels. Therefore, schools and teachers were allowed to flexibly choose to keep implementing the national curriculum, make simplification thereto, or create a situated curriculum. With this regulation, every school that undergoes a special situation has the ability to adjust its curriculum to suit the students.

Governed by the regulation, Rizal described that several teachers contributed to the curriculum preparation of the DKI Jakarta emergency development team. Rizal reported that teachers need to have made some adjustments, including reducing basic competencies on their syllabus ahead of the new school year 2020/2021. For example, in teaching English, Rizal decided to reduce the basic competencies from fourteen to only five. In fact, Rizal added that the reduced competencies took a prolonged period to redesign the syllabus and operationalize it into lesson plans.

---

[2] http://www.sman1bogor.sch.id/site/

Fig. 2 Susi's
communication via
WhatsApp (sending blog
link)

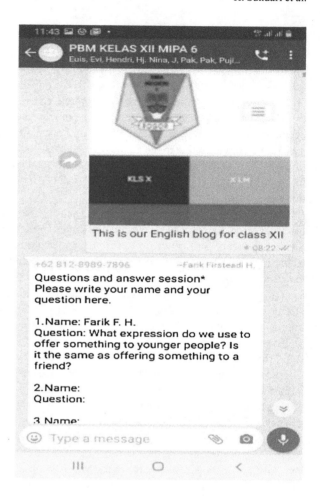

Furthermore, Rizal and teachers dedicated more effort and preparation to adopting the process. Fortunately, the MoEC has also allocated US$532 million (Rp.7.2 trillion) as social assistance in the form of phone credits and internet data packages from September to December 2020 for students and teachers conducting ERT[3] that demands high internet access.

With the start of the new semester around late August or early September 2020, some universities established LMS to manage their remote teaching. However, Hanna's university LMS was frequently unreliable to support teaching because of the heavy traffic and overloaded capacity. Therefore, Hanna anticipated the teaching process by preparing the content materials in formats such as PowerPoint slides and PDF with Google Classroom and WhatsApp to manage the material distribution.

---

[3] https://www.thejakartapost.com/news/2020/08/27/ministry-provides-rp-7-2-trillion-in-phone-credit-data-packages-to-support-distance-learning.html

During this semester, synchronous Zoom sessions are conducted only with students' approval. However, some students from outside Jakarta preferred to manage ERT from their hometown, which had limited access to internet connection. Therefore, having no attempts to join the course sessions, late submission, and demanding extensions became common.

3   Teacher Professional Development (TPD) in Indonesian Context

This unprecedented situation and the ERT policy exposed the teachers to significant challenges in new teaching practices that highly exploit technology. However, it has been a blessing in disguise because it is a great opportunity to accelerate teacher professional development, particularly in technological competence. According to Lie et al. (2020):

> For countries like Indonesia, the pandemic has provided rare momentum to initiate strategic change and opened doors to jumpstarting technology access for students in impoverished schools particularly in remote regions... it also entails continuing improvement of teachers' capacity and changed professional practice.... (p.825)

Teachers need to undertake personal and professional growth throughout their career because teaching is a profession. According to John Cotton Dana 'Those that dare to teach must never cease to learn,' therefore, teachers need to build their occupational role development, including self-awareness, from time to time (Bubb & Earley, 2007). Given the importance of teacher professional development, Borko et al. (2010) emphasized that 'for schools to offer more powerful learning opportunities to students, more powerful learning opportunities need to be provided to teachers' (2010, p. 548). The ERT policy that forces mostly online environments provides ample opportunities for teachers to learn and develop their professional capacities in many areas based on their interest, goal, and need through myriad development activities.

3.1   Teacher Professional Development Prior to the ERT

The growth of teacher professional development in Indonesia has evolved from government regulation to the reality of needs, practices, and challenges. The Ministry of Administrative and Bureaucratic Reform of the Republic of Indonesia formally issued a regulation Number 16/2009 which declared that the teachers' continuing professional development need to cover three activities, namely self-development, scientific publication, and innovative work (Permen PAN RB, 2009). These activities comprise attending government-mandated training and collective teacher events, publishing research articles or textbooks, and creating innovative tools or artwork to support learning and teaching. The TPD activities are organized by either government initiatives or the professional community. Alternatively, the teachers need to engage in self-initiated TPD activities.

Base on the literature online learning community has positively affected teachers' professional capacity building and the process of shared knowledge (Sari, 2012). However, a combination of face-to-face and online learning is a suggestive TPD activity for Indonesian teachers (A. Widodo & Riandi, 2013). Widodo and Allamnakhrah (2020) stated that the professional learning community (PLC) project is a networked PLC that contributes to shifting the teacher's professional identity from a curriculum deliverer to a curriculum developer. Despite its benefits and merits, either full online or blended PD projects need to consider the disparities of PD needs for teachers in urban and rural schools (Soebari & Aldridge, 2016). This is because teachers in rural schools struggle with class sizes, student discipline, and inadequate infrastructure (Soebari & Aldridge, 2016). Teachers have the ability to empower themselves to be local facilitators in order to share best teaching practices for those in the rural community (Harjanto et al., 2018).

At primary school levels, EFL teachers stated that their attention and needs on professional development in language proficiency and pedagogical skills. Zein (2017) specifically reported that the needs of primary EFL teachers focused on improving speaking consisting of pronunciation, L1 utilization, and classroom instruction. In terms of pedagogical skills, the teachers need more assistance to enhance their performance on classroom management, language skill integration, error correction, feedback provision, lesson planning, and material selection and adaptation.

A mixed-method study developed by Cirocki and Farrell (2019) investigated the perceptions of 250 EFL teachers from secondary schools in three provinces in Indonesia. The study found that TPD can be used as a school-based learning system, an academic undertaking process, a professional pursuit outside the school environment, and a government scheme and self-directed learning process. In the past 12 months, they engaged in sixteen types of CPD activities, including informal dialogue, attending 1-day ELT workshops, participating in performance appraisal, attending ELT conferences and seminars, and conducting classroom research. Meanwhile, teachers rarely participated in ELT webinars and the act of reading professional literature.

Indonesian EFL teachers defined PD as becoming a professional technique at the university levels by developing pedagogical knowledge skills and practices in line with *Tridarma* as a pillars of higher education containing teaching, research, and community service (Hartono, 2016). The university teachers expressed that their PD activities cover five major areas, namely 1) attending seminars, conferences, and workshops, 2) writing scholarly articles, conducting research and having publications, 3) joining a professional organization, 4) reading, finding, and developing teaching methods, and 5) becoming a coach, adjudicator, examiner and a teacher trainer. Despite the numerous PD activities undertaken by the teachers, they also revealed some difficulties and challenges. For instance, the lack of institutional and financial support due to professional development programs, heavy teaching load, and lack of information are some of the factors that hinder their PD programs (Hartono, 2016).

Specifically, this chapter comprises three EFL teachers. They revealed that engaging in teacher development activities has been part of their professional job long before the pandemic changed FtF seminars and training. Susi and Rizal are now pursuing their master's degree in English language teaching because they continually develop and enlarge their teaching capacity in any circumstance. Hanna started the visitation of at least three seminars or workshops in and outside the city. It was sometimes an international conference on another island where Hanna had to fly and spend a lot of time and money. Therefore, joining the online PD program is not new because, before the pandemic, Hanna had already registered in many paid-online and offline TEFL courses and received certificates as a token of appreciation. Since then, Hanna has engaged in some free digital educational platforms for educators, such as Canvas Network (https://www.canvas.net/), FutureLearn (www.futurelearn.com/), and Cambridge Assessment English (https://www.cambridgeassessment.org.uk/). However, in one year, Hanna was only able to complete one course, while others expired due to inability to complete due to some constraints, such as different time zone, lack of time management, and many more.

3.2   Government initiatives PD Programs in ERT setting

As a response to ERT and the emergency curriculum, the national government, through the MoEC and local government, initiated numerous programs to build teachers' knowledge and skills in conducting online instruction. These training and webinar series enabled teachers to prepare lesson materials and execute and design online assessments to fit students. For example, 86-hour training managed by LPPPTK KPTK (Institute for Development and Empowerment of Educators and Education Personnel) offered sessions on designing online tests and developing online assessment and evaluation[4].

Hanna registered in some webinar series on the strategies needed to create interactive content materials and the process needed to utilize Moodle (https://moodle.org/) and Edmodo (https://new.edmodo.com/) in LMS SPADA organized by Directorate of Learning and Student Affairs, Directorate General of Higher Education, Ministry of Education and Culture[5]. The webinar series presented various free-to-choose topics and skills. The sessions were conducted through Cisco WebEx videoconferencing and failed to exceed 1000 participant-teachers. Due to

---

[4] https://kptk.or.id/profil-lembaga

[5] https://spada.kemdikbud.go.id/

many participants in rooms, the process was streamed live on YouTube Channel SPADA INDONESIA.

Apart from one-day webinar series, SIMPATIK (*Sistem Informasi Manajemen Pelatihan berbasis TIK*) ICT-based Training Management Information System released continued training program called *PembaTIK* (ICT-based teaching)[6]. *PembaTIK* is a teacher ICT competency improvement program that refers to the UNESCO framework for enhancing the competence of teachers. It covers four levels, namely technology literacy, knowledge implementation, knowledge creation, and knowledge sharing. This program aims to strengthen teachers' digital and technological competence. The final stage is selecting 30 teacher-participants to be the ambassador of *Rumah Belajar* (Learning House) managed by the Minister of Education and Culture.

As an enthusiastic teacher, Susi chronologically narrated her involvement in *the PembaTIK* program 2020, with selections and training carried out from April to October 2020. Susi started the program in April 2020, downloaded the self-study coursebook, and participated in the online course with 71.492 teachers. She received certificate level one after passing the test and uploaded video documentation and testimony on how technology is beneficial for teaching and learning. This encouraged Susi to create a YouTube Channel and make several videos, which enabled her to bag a certificate level 2. Course level three then required Susi to create another learning content video, as shown in Fig. 3. This time, Susi chose to make a video on the use of Present Perfect Tense. Making videos activated Susi's creativity and skill in writing scripts, recording and editing videos. At last, Susi was able to pass the level 3 test and received a certificate, although she was not one of the thirty selected

Fig. 3 Susi's Video for PembaTIK

[6] https://simpatik.belajar.kemdikbud.go.id//user/pembatik_2020

ambassadors of *Rumah Belajar*. Despite not being selected as an ambassador, Susi acquired valuable knowledge and skill in ICT and teaching and learning, which improved self-regulation and study. Teachers recently need these types of development activities to overcome teaching situations. Indeed, online programs for teacher professional development should respond and access local needs (Treacy et al., 2002).

3.3   Teacher Forums and Associations

Several decades ago, teacher forums and communities were established, with authorization from Education and Culture Office in each city/district throughout Indonesia. They are two forms of forums, namely *Kelompok Kerja Guru* (Teacher Working Group) and *Musyawarah Guru Mata Pelajaran* (Subject Teacher Deliberation). *Kelompok Kerja Guru* is a forum for professional activities for elementary school/Madrasah teachers at the cluster or sub-district level. Meanwhile, *Musyawarah Guru Mata Pelajaran* is a forum for professional activities of subject teachers at secondary schools located in one region/district/city cluster and serves as a means of communicating, learning, and exchanging ideas and experiences to improve teacher performance as practitioners/actors of changes in classroom learning orientation[7]. Wenger et al. (2002) defined this process as 'communities of practices in which groups of people share a common concern, set of problems, or passion on a topic, to deepen their knowledge and expertise in this area by interacting on an ongoing basis.' (p.4). Although teachers do not work together every day in the same schools, they discuss teaching situations, help each other and find value in their interaction.

Susi and Rizal have been members of MGMP *Bahasa Inggris* at their districts, with both stating that the monthly meetings used to hold a face-to-face session discussed the latest issues and government educational policy. However, this pandemic did not deter their activities rather it provided more virtual meetings to maintain communication and interaction, thereby allowing them to share information on emergency curriculum, educational programs, and its technical guidance in special conditions. This also enabled all teachers and school staff in the district to have similar perceptions on the strategies needed to implement teaching contexts. They admitted that joining this forum helped them gain the latest information related to the government regulations and seminars or workshops specifically for English teachers.

Susi's engagement with learning communities increased when the ERT was launched. Currently, Susi is a member of modern education from VCT alumni and Sadar IGI. The first is a community for the alumni-teachers that took part in a virtual coordinator training (VCT) in which she joined a couple of years ago and knew

---

[7] http://yfatyr.blogspot.com/2017/08/pengertian-fungsi-dan-tujuan-organisasi.html

features on Google for teaching and Quizizz (https://quizizz.com/) for testing. In VCT alumni, they extended the learning activities by maintaining communication and sharing information among members. It allowed Susi to acquire and share information on online seminars deal with technology and the policy and regulations related to education and teaching. Meanwhile, IGI (*Ikatan Guru Indonesia*), or Indonesian Teachers Association, is a professional teacher organization authorized by the government in 2009. Its purpose is to facilitate teachers to transform themselves as a driving force for the nation independently. Meanwhile, Sadar IGI is a virtual-based community, through a WhatsApp Group, for the IGI members to share knowledge and information through text, videos, or links, commonly dealt with the technology used for teaching. For example, a member of Sadar IGI posted a set of links on making content materials in Office 355/365, editing video with a cell phone, and making a recording using Apowersoft (www.apowersoft.com) and FastStone (www.faststone.org). Another post was an invitation to a webinar session entitled 'teaching through educational radio.' Radio is used as an alternative media for teaching due to the underdevelopment of infrastructure in Indonesia. Therefore, such programs enable teachers to apply educational radio sounds as a realistic solution.

3.4   Online Networks and Communities

After the government implemented the social/physical distancing policy and school shutdown in Indonesia, seminars, workshops, and conferences were rarely conducted in school/campus halls. However, information and invitations are easily found in social media, such as Instagram (www.instagram.com) and Facebook (www.facebook.com). The faculty member or community actively hosted numerous webinar series, virtual talks, live discussions, online public lectures, round table discussions, online classes, and other learning activities to improve knowledge and upgrade skills. Online TPD programs tend to reach wider audiences from different cities, islands, or even countries that FtF or in-site unaffordable by other programs. They offered many advantages for the participants (Treacy et al., 2002), as follows:

- Increased access to meet the individual learning goal
- Experience with the use of technology
- Use of rich multimedia resources and new technologies
- Anytime, anyplace learning
- Ability to meet special needs
- Collaborative learning opportunities
- Direct impact on classroom practices
- New opportunities for follow-up

Hanna engaged in various online TPD activities during the ERT and worked from the home process. To acquire more knowledge, Hanna started following Instagram accounts that post and share information related to webinars, such as

@eltseminarinfo and *@publikasiilmiah*, as shown in Fig. 4. Hanna further realized that there were tons of online workshops and webinars with numerous themes and topics on education and teaching during the pandemic, with research related to other ELT issues. Some of them were free, while others asked for registration fees. Hanna was happy to be able to participate in many online seminars and webinars without much effort and struggles on travel and equipment. At the beginning of ERT, she joined regular series of virtual talks managed by the Indonesian Extensive Reading Association (IERA) called vERtual Talk. It was a 2-hour talk through Zoom and Live on Facebook scheduled every Saturday morning or afternoon promoting issues and practices of extensive reading, particularly in the Indonesian context. Some professional experts and well-recognized scholars in the field were also invited to be speakers to provide valuable knowledge and insights. They keep conducting virtual talks until today, although Hanna followed up the 6th Number and registered in many webinars with various topics, such as Kahoot! (https://kahoot.it/), Elsevier's (www.elsevier.com), British Council (https://www.britishcouncil.org/) and TEFLIN webinar series.

However, Hanna was aware of the need to be more focused on developing the right teaching and research techniques to achieve the right online teaching style,

Fig. 4 Instagram accounts followed by Hanna

research knowledge, and writing skills at a more global level. Furthermore, Hanna thought that her current research competence and academic writing competence were inadequate for the wider international level of publication. Therefore, Hanna attended virtual workshop series entitled 'systemic functional linguistics (SFL) in critical academic writing' for four meetings facilitated by an Indonesian well-recognized expert as the lead speaker and decided to be a member of the SFL Community: Post-Hallidayan. The same speaker presented virtual workshops discussing instructional design for virtual classes and design-based research for research and publication organized by the Indonesian Community of Educational Action Researchers (ICEAR), in which Hanna finally decided to be a member. Hanna also joined *Perkumpulan Peneliti dan Penulis Ilmu Sosial* (Association of Indonesian Social Science Researchers and Writers) based in West Java.

Overall, Hanna participated in three learning communities that managed several virtual workshops that served teachers and lecturers, particularly in health and social studies. The learning communities organized one or a series of virtual workshops with specific topics. Furthermore, the members were able to freely choose the session they wanted to join and paid the fee for submission. At first, Hanna imagined the session would be two to three hours of a listening session with many slides from the expert speaker. However, it was a one-day workshop with virtual zoom conferencing from morning to afternoon, and participants were free to respond and ask questions. This was a synchronous interactive session between the expert and the online participants.

From July to October 2020, Hanna intensively joined various virtual workshops specifically in research, writing, and publication and sometimes felt overwhelmed with the large daily information. However, some were very valuable and applicable in recent teaching situations, while others needed more time. In September 2020, one of the communities initiated collaborative research among the members to build groups of three to five people guided and supervised by an expert through virtual workshops. Publishing article in reputable indexed journals became the goal of the collaboration and supervision. Therefore, having been involved in collaborative research in the community, Hanna learned a lot of things from the teammates in constructive dialogue or conversation. Some of these attributes include thinking as a researcher and managing research procedures.

In Hanna's group communities, the activities were mostly to offer online thematic webinar sessions, participate in live events, and provide encouragement. Hanna was tagged 'a lurker', a silent reader that rarely posted comments or shared content but kept looking at the latest information to obtain benefits from an expert leader. According to Macià & García (2016), Hanna still took advantage of the community through peripheral participation. Above all, these communities met Hanna's specific TPD needs and goals. Voluntary participation in a networked community with a specific domain, as a bottom-up PD activity, immensely benefits teachers in many ways. Wenger et al. (2002) explained that the communities of practices value the members twofold by improving the experience of work and fostering professional development. In short-time value, member-teachers acquire access to expertise, help with challenges, expand skills, and enhance professional reputation and identity. In the long-term, it values the members in expanding skills and expertise as well as in enhancing professional reputation and identity.

4   Food to Thought: Beyond ERT

The policy of ERT with emergency curriculum and all its consequences are similar to a two-sided coin for teachers, with various challenges and opportunities. Within several months, this new teaching and learning system accelerated teachers in teaching management and technology compare to normal days, which would take years to encounter. Sandars et al. (2020) stated that due the rapid migration of online learning, teachers are able to anticipate their online classes with optimization of multimodality learning and simplification on their instruction.

- Optimize the potential of multimodality learning
  Multimodality refers to the variety of modes to deliver a piece of information and interactivity between the different modes either separately or fully integrated (Guichon et al., 2016). Teachers are able to provide more meaningful online remote learning. For example, creating short functional texts such as flyers or posters using Canva (https://www.canva.com), a digital storytelling that brings some affective and technological outcomes (Wu & Chen, 2020) using plotagon (https://www.plotagon.com), Kinemaster (https://www.kinemaster.com/) and Animaker (https://www.animaker.com/) for creating learning live-action videos.
- Simplify the instructions
  Initially, speaking or listening to the blank wall appeared strange to both teachers and students. Boredom and screen fatigue demotivate students to participate in online learning actively. Therefore, teachers have to look at the students' perspectives when designing materials and learning activities. Teachers have the ability to break down learning into small, sequenced activities with a single objective each time. Providing sequential written instruction is helpful to students, especially in asynchronous mode, which lacks non-verbal communication and oral interaction.
- Maintain communication with the students
  Not all students have the ability to afford high teaching technology due to the poor internet access, technology devices, and other constraints. When the students experience many difficulties in carrying out online learning, teachers need to maintain communication with the students. Besides giving lectures or issuing assignments, teachers can do a random home visit or send regular text messages to provide personal and mental support to the students.

Despite the challenges and adaptation to the new teaching system, it is great momentum for teachers to professionally develop their teaching skills to fit the current education needs. In any circumstances, a teacher is a lifelong learner, therefore, learning to teach becomes a routine. Furthermore, undertaking formal courses or participating in virtual informal learning communities immensely increases teachers' teaching skills and performance. Sometimes the implications of PD practices are not directly and immediately seen on teaching practices and students' achievement, therefore patience and perseverance are highly required.

Acknowledgments The authors are grateful to Dr. Julian Chen and the reviewers for their constructive comments and valuable guidance to improve the quality of this chapter.

Appendix

The summary of digital tools/platforms

Digital Tools/ platform	Links	Description
Google Classroom	https://classroom.google. com/	Google Classroom is a free web service developed by Google for schools, which aims to simplify create, distribute, and grade assignments to streamline the process of sharing files between teachers and students.
Google Forms	https://docs.google.com/ forms/	Google Forms is a survey administration software included in the Google Docs Editors software suite and used to collect information from users through surveys.
WhatsApp	https://www.whatsapp. com/	WhatsApp Messenger, or simply WhatsApp, is an American freeware, cross-platform messaging and Voice over IP service owned by Facebook, Inc. It is used to send text and voice messages, make voice and video calls, and share images, documents, user locations, and other media.
Zoom video conferencing	https://zoom.us/	Zoom Video Communications, Inc. is an American communications technology used to provide videotelephony and online chat services through a cloud-based peer-to-peer software platform for teleconferencing, telecommuting, distance education, and social relations.
Cisco WebEx video conferencing	https://www.webex.com/ video-conferencing	Webex Meetings lets you host online meetings with HD video, audio and screen sharing.
Canvas Network	https://www.canvas.net/	The Canvas Network offers free online courses and classes from the world's leading universities.
FutureLearn	http://www.futurelearn. com/	FutureLearn is a digital education platform used as a Massive Open Online Course learning platform.
Cambridge Assessment English	https://www. cambridgeassessment. org.uk/	Cambridge Assessment English, or Cambridge English, is the biggest of three main exam boards forming Cambridge Assessment, a non-teaching department of the University of Cambridge.
Moodle	https://moodle.org/	Moodle is a free and open-source learning management system written in PHP and distributed under the GNU General Public License.

Digital Tools/ platform	Links	Description
Edmodo	https://new.edmodo.com/	Edmodo is an educational technology company offering a communication, collaboration, and coaching platform to enables teachers to share content, distribute quizzes, assignments, and manage communication with students, colleagues, and parents.
Quizizz	https://quizizz.com/	Quizizz is a creativity software that can be used in class, group works, pre-test review, exams, unit test and impromptu tests.
Apowersoft	http://www.apowersoft.com	Online Screen Recorder allows you to capture any screen activity with audio in one click and share your recording to web immediately.
FastStone	http://www.faststone.org	FastStone Image Viewer is an image viewer and organizer for Microsoft Windows, provided free of charge for personal and educational use, including basic image editing tools.
Kahoot!	https://kahoot.it/	Kahoot! is a game-based learning platform, used as educational technology in schools and other educational institutions.
Google Meet	https://meet.google.com/	Google Meet is a video-communication service developed by Google. It is one of two apps that constitute the replacement for Google Hangouts, the other being Google Chat.
Google Drive	https://drive.google.com/	Google Drive is a file storage and synchronization service allowing users to store files on their servers, synchronize files across devices, and share files.
Canva	www.canva.com/	Canva is a graphic design platform, used to create social media graphics, presentations, posters, documents and other visual content including templates for users to use.
Plotagon	www.plotagon.com/	Plotagon is a free animation app that makes your stories come to life.
kinemaster	www.kinemaster.com/	KineMaster provides a wide range of video editing functions, including transition effects, text and handwriting overlays, video and image layers, up to four additional audio tracks, detailed volume envelope control, and more.
Animaker	www.animaker.com/	Animaker is an online do-it-yourself (#DIY) animation video maker that brings studio quality presentations within everyone's reach.

References

Alifia, U., Barasa, A. R., Bima, L., Pramana, R. P., Revina, S., & Tresnatri, F. A. (2020). Learning from home: Portrait of teaching and learning inequalities in times of the covid-19 pandemic. *Smeru Research Note, 1*(1), 1–8.

Atmojo, A. E. P., & Nugroho, A. (2020). EFL classes must go online! teaching activities and challenges during COVID-19 pandemic in Indonesia. *Register Journal, 13*(1), 49–76. https://doi.org/10.18326/rgt.v13i1.49-76

Borko, H., Jacobs, J., & Koellner, K. (2010). Contemporary approaches to teacher professional development. In P. Peterson, E. Baker, & B. McGaw (Eds.), *International Encyclopedia of Education* (Vol. 7, pp. 548–556). Oxford: Elsevier.

Bozkurt, A., & Sharma, R. C. (2020). Emergency remote teaching in a time of global crisis due to CoronaVirus pandemic. *Asian Journal of Distance Education, 15*(1), 1–6. Retrieved from http://asianjde.org/ojs/index.php/AsianJDE/article/view/447

Bubb, S., & Earley, P. (2007). *Leading and managing continuing professional development* (2nd ed.). Paul Chapman Publishing.

Churiyah, M., Sholikhan, S., Filianti, F., & Sakdiyyah, D. A. (2020). Indonesia education readiness conducting distance learning in covid-19 pandemic situation. *International Journal of Multicultural and Multireligious Understanding, 7*(6), 491. https://doi.org/10.18415/ijmmu.v7i6.1833

Cirocki, A., & Farrell, T. S. C. (2019). Professional development of secondary school EFL teachers: Voices from Indonesia. *System, 85*, 102111. https://doi.org/10.1016/j.system.2019.102111

Cucinotta, D., & Vanelli, M. (2020). WHO declares COVID-19 a pandemic. *Acta Biomed, 91*(1), 157–160.

Guichon, N., Cohen, C., Guichon, N., Multimodality, C. C., Farr, C., & Routledge, L. T. (2016). Multimodality and CALL. In F. Farr & L. Murray (Eds.), *The Routledge handbook of language learning and technology* (pp. 509–521).

Harjanto, I., Lie, A., Wihardini, D., Pryor, L., & Wilson, M. (2018). Community-based teacher professional development in remote areas in Indonesia. *Journal of Education for Teaching, 44*(2), 212–231. https://doi.org/10.1080/02607476.2017.1415515

Hartono, R. (2016). *Indonesian EFL Teachers' Perceptions and Experiences of Professional Development.* Retrieved from https://search-proquest-com.ezproxy3.library.arizona.edu/docview/1793408228?pq-origsite=primo

Hodges, C., Moore, S., Lockee, B., Trust, T., & Bond, A. (2020). The difference between emergency remote teaching and online learning. *Educause Review, 7.* Retrieved from https://er.educause.edu/articles/2020/3/the-difference-between-emergency-remote-teaching-and-online-learning

Kementerian Pendidikan dan Kebudayaan [MoEC]. (2020). *Pedoman Pelaksanaan Belajar Dari Rumah Selama Darurat Bencana Covid-19 di Indonesia: Surat Edaran Sekretaris Jenderal No. 15 Tahun 2020* [Guidelines for the Implementation of Learning From Home During the Covid-19 Disaster Emergency in Indonesia: Secretary]. Jakarta.

Lie, A., Tamah, S. M., Gozali, I., Triwidayati, K. R., Utami, T. S. D., & Jemadi, F. (2020). Secondary school language teachers' online learning engagement during the Covid-19 pandemic in Indonesia. *Journal of Information Technology Education: Reseach, 19*(January 2008), 803–832. https://doi.org/10.28945/4626

Macià, M., & García, I. (2016). Informal online communities and networks as a source of teacher professional development: A review. *Teaching and Teacher Education, 55*, 291–307. https://doi.org/10.1016/j.tate.2016.01.021

Megatsari, H., Laksono, A. D., Ibad, M., Herwanto, Y. T., Sarweni, K. P., Geno, R. A. P., & Nugraheni, E. (2020). The community psychosocial burden during the COVID-19 pandemic in Indonesia. *Heliyon, 6*(10). https://doi.org/10.1016/j.heliyon.2020.e05136

Moorhouse, B. L. (2020). Adaptations to a face-to-face initial teacher education course 'forced' online due to the COVID-19 pandemic. *Journal of Education for Teaching.* https://doi.org/10.1080/02607476.2020.1755205

Permen PAN RB. (2009). *the Regulation of the Ministry of Administrative and Bureaucratic Reform of the Republic of Indonesia number 16 year 2009 about Teacher Functional Position and Its Credits.*

Sandars, J., Correia, R., Dankbaar, M., de Jong, P., Goh, P. S., Hege, I., ... Pusic, M. (2020). Twelve tips for rapidly migrating to online learning during the COVID-19 pandemic. *MedEdPublish, 9*(1), 1–14. https://doi.org/10.15694/mep.2020.000082.1

Sari, E. R. (2012). Online learning community: A case study of teacher professional development in Indonesia. *Intercultural Education, 23*(1), 63–72. https://doi.org/10.1080/1467598 6.2012.664755

Soebari, T., & Aldridge, J. M. (2016). Investigating the differential effectiveness of a teacher professional development programme for rural and urban classrooms in Indonesia. *Teacher Development, 20*(5), 701–722. https://doi.org/10.1080/13664530.2016.1185031

Treacy, B., Kleiman, G., & Peterson, K. (2002). Successful online professional development. *Learning & Leading with Technology, 30*(1), 42–47. Retrieved from http://community.mdec-gateway.org/olms/data/resource/1686/SuccessfulOnlinePD_.pdf

UNICEF. (2020). *Situasi anak di Indonesia 2020 – Tren, Peluang, dan Tantangan Dalam memenuhi Hak-Hak Anak.* [The situation of children in Indonesia 2020 – Trends, Opportunities and Challenges in Fulfilling Children's Rights]. Jakarta

Viner, R. M., Russell, S. J., Croker, H., Packer, J., Ward, J., Stansfield, C., ... Booy, R. (2020). School closure and management practices during coronavirus outbreaks including COVID-19: A rapid systematic review. *The Lancet Child and Adolescent Health, 4*(5), 397–404. https://doi.org/10.1016/S2352-4642(20)30095-X

Wenger, E., McDormett, R., & Snyder, W. M. (2002). *Cultivating communities of practice.* Harvard Business School Press.

WHO. (2020). *Coronavirus disease (COVID-19) weekly epidemiological update.* https://doi.org/10.1097/jcn.0000000000000710

Widodo, A., & Riandi. (2013). Dual-mode teacher professional development: Challenges and re-visioning future TPD in Indonesia. *Teacher Development, 17*(3), 380–392. https://doi.org/1 0.1080/13664530.2013.813757

Widodo, H. P., & Allamnakhrah, A. (2020). The impact of a blended professional learning community on teacher educators' professional identity: Towards sustainable teacher professional development. *Journal of Education for Teaching, 46*(3), 408–410. https://doi.org/10.108 0/02607476.2020.1761249

Wu, J., & Chen, V. D. (2020). A systematic review of educational digital storytelling. *Computers & Education.* https://doi.org/10.1016/j.compedu.2019.103786

Zein, M. S. (2017). Professional development needs of primary EFL teachers: Perspectives of teachers and teacher educators. *Professional Development in Education, 43*, 293–313. https://doi.org/10.1080/19415257.2016.1156013

Surviving ERT: How an Online Professional Learning Community Empowered Teachers During the Covid-19 School Lockdown in Indonesia

Maya Defianty, Kate Wilson, and Dadan

Highlights

This virtual online community contributed substantially to teachers' practice and well-being during ERT because:

- It was already a vibrant network when the pandemic hit
- It was a trusted source of just-in-time information about teaching strategies, technology and education policy during the crisis
- It was a source of "positive energy", motivation and inspiration
- Information could be shared with colleagues beyond the virtual community
- It helped to strengthen teachers' professional identity

1 Introduction

The sudden impact of Covid-19 in early 2020 reverberated across the world. In Indonesia, as in numerous other countries, schools were locked down at a day or two's notice, and teachers were thrown into teaching remotely with little or no preparation. This initial period of ERT (Emergency Remote Teaching) (Hodges et al.,

M. Defianty
UIN Syarif Hidayatullah, Tangerang, Indonesia
e-mail: maya.defianty@uinjkt.ac.id

K. Wilson (✉)
University of Canberra, Canberra, Australia
e-mail: kate.wilson@canberra.edu.au

Dadan
Bandung Independent School, Bandung, Indonesia

J. Chen (ed.), *Emergency Remote Teaching and Beyond*,
https://doi.org/10.1007/978-3-030-84067-9_4

2020) called upon teachers to put into practice a range of digital literacies in ways which had hardly been imagined previously.

Indonesia, in some ways, was in a good position to launch ERT. The country has a high rate of internet penetration in comparison with many developing countries, and one of the highest rates of smartphone users in the world, with the number of smartphone users in 2020 estimated to be 81.87 million (Statistica, 2020a, b). The uptake of social media has been exponential: for example, in 2013, Indonesia already had 64 million active Facebook users (Patahuddin & Logan, 2019), and that number has now more than doubled to reach 140 million (Statistica, 2020a, b). The country is also rated highly as an innovator in education, well above the OECD average (Vincent-Lancrin, 2019). Nevertheless, although Indonesia has a rapidly emerging middle class, about 10% of the population still live below the poverty line (The World Bank, 2020), and the country's economy has been hard hit by the pandemic. So access to digital devices and internet subscriptions is still challenging for many students, particularly in remote areas.

Despite the enormous interest in digital participation and many rapid social changes, Indonesia retains many traditional values. It has a generally collectivist culture, valuing social harmony, collaboration, conformity and politeness, rather than individual competitiveness. It is important to show respect for elders and those in senior positions, and so the role of the leader or manager is likely to be very significant in Indonesia (Sriwindono & Yahya, 2012). In addition, the culture of education still tends to be didactic rather than interactive, and teachers may lack awareness of active pedagogy and higher-order learning (OECD/ADB, 2015). This tradition is evident in formal professional learning communities such as MGMP (Musyawarah Guru Mata Pelajaran - Panel of secondary school subject teachers) and/or KKG (Kelompok Kerja Guru -Primary teachers working group). However, some studies document that these two professional learning communities have not yet been successful in building a cohesive community that empowers teachers (see for example, Dimyati, 2018; Sianipar, 2019). In fact, members consider their participation as an obligation to fullfil instead of a community to meet their personal needs (Trilaksono et al., 2019).

It was in this social context that Komunitas Guru Pembaru[1] (KGP) was launched. KGP is an informal professional online community for language teachers in Indonesia, established in 2018. In contrast to the government's formal professional learning community for teachers, KGP is online, member-driven and entirely voluntary. This chapter explores the role of KGP during the early months of ERT. Using a qualitative research methodology, we conducted two focus groups and ten individual interviews via Zoom, in order to listen to the teachers' authentic voices as they reflected on how KGP had supported them in coping with the shock of transitioning to ERT during the early days of the Covid-19 pandemic. We also analysed members' interaction in the WhatsApp group (hereafter, WAG), which formed the platform for the virtual community, from the beginning of the school lockdown (March 15, 2020) to end of the semester (May 30, 2020).

---

[1] We use pseudonyms throughout this chapter to protect the participants' identity.

We begin with a brief review of the literature on virtual professional communities for teachers, followed by a detailed description of KGP. Next, we will hear teachers' voices as they talk about their experience of participating in KGP during the period of ERT. Finally, we discuss the lessons that can be learned from the case study. We argue that a virtual professional community can be a valuable means of "future-proofing" teachers against crises such as ERT by building their repertoire of teaching strategies and strengthening their identity as creative and committed professionals.

2   What Does the Literature Tell Us About Virtual Professional Communities?

Professional development is a crucial factor in building resilient, innovative education systems, yet traditional approaches to professional development have often been criticised as lacking in relevance to individual teachers, and for taking a top-down approach which can be resisted by teachers (eg. Kennedy, 2016; Patahuddin, 2013). As Krutka, Carpenter and Trust (2016, p. 156) put it, "Conventional approaches are often rooted in hierarchical structures that de-skill teachers from their intellectual work, treat them as passive recipients of mandates, and fail to engage them as pedagogical experts." By contrast, informal online professional communities in which teachers participate voluntarily may play an important role in building teachers' skills and knowledge. They are arguably well-placed to fulfil what Patahuddin and Logan (2019) present as the five key characteristics of their Effective Professional Development framework: they can be on-going, collaborative, student-oriented, focused on PCK (Pedagogical Content Knowledge), and relevant to teachers and their contexts.

Since the rapid rise of social media, teachers across the world have eagerly taken up opportunities for informal online learning in many forms. Many teachers have developed their own Personal Learning Networks (also known as Professional Learning Networks) (PLNs) (See, for example, Krutka et al., 2016; Tour, 2017; Trust & Horrocks, 2017). As individual teachers, they actively search out weblinks and may participate in multiple groups on Twitter, Facebook, Instagram and numerous other platforms. In the ELT (English Language Teaching) online world, open sites such as *Dave's ESL Café* and the British Council's *TeachingEnglish* have become increasingly widely used. Information in the modern world is freely and easily available, and the internet has made it possible for individuals to interact freely across time and space. Indeed, during the Covid-19 pandemic it was often easier to communicate across the world than with your local colleagues.

In contrast to these open sites, online professional communities are characterised by more intimate relationships and may have a closed membership (Macià & García, 2016). An online professional community is defined by Duncan-Howell (2010, p. 326) as "any form of electronic communication which provides for the opportunity for on-line synchronous/asynchronous two-way communication between an individual and their peers, and to which the individual has some commitment and professional involvement over a period of time."

A recent review paper of 52 empirical studies investigating online teacher communities found that a common feature of all such communities was ongoing professional interaction characterised by "shared values, respect, trust and supportive leadership" (Lantz-Andersson et al., 2018). The studies showed that members valued their online community as a rich source of information, as well as for the emotional and professional support they received from their peers. The community was also able to filter, or "curate" new ideas for teaching, and members relied on each other to be discerning in what they shared. In addition, Macià and García (2016), in an earlier review of research into teacher professional communities, found that clear purpose, and the collaborative production of artefacts held the group together.

Individuals participate in virtual professional communities in various ways. Not all members are necessarily active participants. In fact, the majority may participate simply as "lurkers" (Macià & García, 2016) - observing, but not usually contributing comments or sharing ideas. Lave and Wenger (1991), in their seminal work on communities of practice, talked about this kind of behaviour as "peripheral participation". Other activities can be sharing, chatting, commenting and co-constructing (Prestridge, 2019). Based on semi-structured interviews with 15 expert teachers in five western nations, Prestridge (2019) identified four categories of participation in teachers' online professional learning: *info-consumers* seek out new information to build their own knowledge; *info-networkers* seek out new knowledge in order to share it with others, but do not contribute much of their own; *self-seeking contributors* contribute ideas, questions and experience in order to seek feedback or help; and *vocationalists,* who are driven by a sense of altruism, participate actively in the hope of promoting the good of the profession. Macià and García (2016) identified the role of moderator as having a key influence on the success and operation of the community, though this role varied greatly in the various studies they reviewed.

Despite the rapid increase in the rate of participation in virtual communities of practice among teachers, the benefits of such groups have yet to be established both in terms of teachers' changing practices and student development (Lantz-Andersson et al., 2018; Macià & García, 2016). Nevertheless, teacher professional development through collaboration with peers has been shown to contribute to student achievement, particularly where teachers have high self-efficacy (Moolenaar et al., 2012), and a study of teachers' use of PLNs found that almost all of the 732 participants reported modifying their teaching practices, while a quarter changed their view of teaching as a result of their PLN (Krutka et al., 2016). Furthermore, the participants in informal online learning communities are there by choice, and, as Kennedy (2016) reminds us, teachers' willingness to learn is a necessary condition for professional learning to succeed.

In the Indonesian context, the government has established several learning communities such as MGMP and KKG. These communities were developed based on the region and/or learning subject. Nonetheless, Sianipar (2019) and Dimyati (2018) argued that these communities have not yet become a space for teachers to improve their teaching competence. One of the conspicuous reasons is because these communities were not built by teachers themselves, and it is compulsory for teachers to enrol; thus, teachers' participation may be purely due to fulfilling their obligation instead of satisfying their needs (Dimyati, 2018; Sianipar, 2019; Trilaksono et al., 2019).

Studies on professional learning communities in Indonesia have mostly focused on how to establish a PLC and the role of the leader in the PLC. Although these studies provide useful information about the field, there is a need to learn more about the role of PLCs, especially in the face of a crisis such as the pandemic. The experience in Indonesia can also shed light on the role of PLCs in other countries, especially those in the developing world.

As Patahuddin et al. (2020) point out, most research on teachers' online communities has been carried out in developed countries. This chapter hopes to redress this balance to some extent by presenting a case study of a virtual online community of English teachers in Indonesia. We will listen to their voices as they reflect on how the community supported them during the first months of the pandemic lockdown, providing just-in-time information and motivational support as they adjusted to ERT.

3 What Is KGP?

KGP is a WhatsApp group whose members are mostly English language teachers. The community was initiated in 2008 when a group of English language teachers were participating in a professional development program. The main purpose of the program was to develop teachers' innovation and creativity; at the time, such information was not readily available for teachers in Indonesia. The program itself ended in 2012; however, members still kept in touch, and even published several books together on creative language teaching.

The WhatsApp group itself was launched in 2018, and the participants in the original professional development program were invited to become members. The moderator, who was also the initiator of the original professional development program, stated that the aim of the community is to connect, learn, share, collaborate, inspire, and empower teachers professionally. Members may post information related to English Language Teaching (ELT) including teaching strategies, government policy on education, and information about seminars, workshops and webinars about ELT. The moderator informed the group that it is not permissable for members to post materials related to religion and politics, and other contributions that could be offensive for others. When occasionally members breach this rule, he contacts them individually and politely advises them that their postings are not appropriate.

Commonly, members join the group based on peer invitation. Since membership is free and open, any member can leave the group at any time, and any teacher can become a member regardless of his or her level of experience or place of residency. However, WhatsApp has a limit of 256 in any group. All the members have equal opportunities to share, respond, and comment on any information shared in the group, provided that they comply with the rules of the group; however, not all members actively participate in the group. Many remain silent, although this cannot be an indication that they have not made use of the information shared in the group.

The moderator stated that, to date, there have not been any members leaving the group. This suggests that members consider there are distinct professional and/or personal benefits from belonging to the group.

Every day, early in the morning, the moderator posts a greeting to participants, and this is often followed by an exchange of friendly greetings, and postings relating to language teaching, for example, useful strategies for opening an online class. This commonly leads to further comments, questions and suggestions, with new topics being initiated by members as well as by the moderator. Sometimes, the moderator and members of the group congratulate each other for small achievements they make in their career.

KGP members have also been responsible for collaborating on the publication of a number of books on practical issues relating to ELT, some of which can also be applicable to other subject areas. These publications have been widely distributed at minimal cost to teachers across Indonesia.

4   How Did We Gather Data About KGP?

As teacher researchers, we were keen to learn how KGP supported teachers in the early days of ERT. We set out to elicit teachers' views as they reflected on the community interaction during that period. We issued an invitation to participate on the WhatsApp group itself. Ten teachers (five men, five women) quickly volunteered, and we were able to conduct two semi-structured focus groups, each with five participants and lasting 2 h in duration, and an individual interview of 1 h with each of the ten participants. Because of the restrictions on face-to-face contact during the coronavirus pandemic, these interviews and focus groups were conducted on Zoom. The invitation explained the research project and assured volunteers that personal information would not be used, and the project would be reported using pseudonyms. All volunteers signed a consent form before the data was collected.

The volunteers were all secondary school English teachers. Most participants were located in various parts of West Java, one was in Kalimantan, and one taught in West Papua. The data was collected in June/July 2020 at the end of the first 3 months of ERT.

The focus groups and interviews were conducted in English as all the respondents were English teachers and they were keen for the opportunity to use their language skills for an authentic purpose. The sessions were recorded, transcribed and coded using an Excel spreadsheet. Using a reiterative process of coding and categorising, adapted from Creswell (2005), themes from the data were gradually distilled.

The interview data was triangulated with a similar thematic analysis of the WhatsApp group (WAG) chat between the beginning of the school lockdown (March 15, 2020) to end of the semester (May 30, 2020).

5 What Did We Learn from Listening to the Teachers' Voices?

Three main themes emerged from the data: first, the powerfully positive views of the teachers; second, the benefits that they reaped in terms of sharing information; and finally, the affective support they gained from the online community during this challenging period.

5.1 Positive Responses

The teachers all voiced enthusiastic support when asked about KGP. For example,

- *It's definitely a really excellent resource for me. (Annie, Focus Group (FG)2, 1.41)*
- *This is one of the groups that I haven't deleted any of the chat because it is very useful for me... First thing I look at in the morning. (Ian, FG1, 1:32)*
- *I am so lucky to be part of a group like that! (Alfred: AS 0:42).*
- *I'm really thankful for all the knowledge that has been set with the great teachers in [KGP]. (Austin, FG1, 1:36)*

Data from the WAG chat echoed this enthusiasm: participants commented that the WAG is "cool", "the most beneficial group" and "up-to-date" (Extract 9/5/20, 11/4/20, 13/4/20, 14/5/20).

5.2 KGP as Source of Practical and Applicable Information About ELT

The most prominent reason that most participants gave for remaining with the group was that **they valued the knowledge and information** they gained, whether it be about educational technology, teaching strategies, webinars, or government policy. As Annie said, she loved the *brain food* (Annie 00:44), and as Cassandra said, *it's really broadened my knowledge* (Cassandra, 0:39). They felt that sharing information was particularly important during the pandemic in helping teachers deal with the new challenges they faced. As Isaac said,

- *Actually, this pandemic has proven that we really need this group. Many of my fellow teachers did not know what to do. Uh, they only asked through WhatsApp how to do the task and then we found that there are many ways we can use (Isaac, 00:31)*

Especially at the beginning of the Covid-19 lockdown when students began to study from home, members were seeking and sharing information about the government's policies on how to teach online; how to use national television as a learning tool; and how to write students' report cards during ERT. The teachers valued the fact that the ideas and strategies they learned from KGP were immediately relevant to their needs, and were appropriate to their own context in the Indonesian education system. Harry, for instance, explained that KGP helped him not only with teaching strategies, but also how to deal with administrative challenges in his school:

- *For example, many pandemic topics, we get many topics from the webinar [links] and it helps me a lot as well, so it helps how to handle the students, and schools' policies for example in a pandemic situation. (Harry, FG1 1:39)*

Results of the study showed that information shared in the group was dominated by **the use of educational technology**, especially for English language teaching. Members of the group were particularly interested in selecting media for virtual classes as a replacement for face to face learning. Data from the WAG chat showed that Zoom was the most discussed educational technology at the beginning of ERT. The discussion included how to install Zoom [eg. Extract 21/3/20], available features in Zoom such as breakout rooms [Extract 29/3/20] and the whiteboard [Extract 10/4/20]. These extracts implied that KGP supported teachers' learning progression, from not knowing anything about an app to finding out how to put the app to the maximum use. Interestingly, data from the WAG chat also showed that sometimes the moderator of the group invited the members to participate in a simulation prior to applying the educational technology with their students. For example, he offered to try out Edpuzzle with the participants in a Zoom meeting [Extract 1/4/20]. Furthermore, some members also reported on their experience of applying the educational technology being discussed in the group [Extract 1/4/20]. Some participants also received individual coaching from the moderator, as revealed from the interview data:

- *Sometimes I use Google Meetings. I'm learning from [the moderator] the way how to use it. We sometimes have a private chat how to use certain technology in order to ease myself and my students to use it. (Daisy, FG2 00:12)*

Most importantly, the participants reported, KGP provided interesting **strategies for teaching**, using technology appropriate for ERT. Some examples:

1. Alfred had learned a progressive strategy for presenting a writing assignment to his students on his class WhatsApp chat group. First, working synchronously, he sent them a photo. Then he had the students brainstorm vocabulary in response to the photo. The next step was for the students to suggest sentences created from the vocabulary, and finally to submit paragraphs – all done in the class WhatsApp group (Alfred 00:15).
2. Austin had prompted a discussion on the KGP WhatsApp group by asking how others coped with the problem of silent students in online discussions. His peers suggested that it was better to call on individual students by name to respond:

- *In a normal classroom in a face-to-face classroom, you would elicit answers from everybody and make sure that everybody gets a turn. How does that work online? Some students volunteer and some students remain very quiet. (Austin, FG1 0:51)*

3. Daisy explained that one of the strategies that she had learned from KGP was to ask her students to video record a book review, and then upload it to her personal Youtube channel. In this way, they practiced all four communicative skills: reading, writing, speaking and also listening, when they peer-assessed each others' videos. The results were impressive! Daisy explained that there was a very high attendance rate in her English class during ERT, because she was inspired by KGP to use many varied strategies and sources to keep her students engaged:

- *They like to stay in my class, because I always take out some ideas, inspired by [the KGP moderator], and many kinds of sources like providing them with enjoyable learning (Daisy, 00:05).*

4. Another KGP member shared how he used WhatsApp as a means of teaching reading. On the WAG chat, he included verbatim the online worksheets he had sent his students. The students were asked to audio-record their answers and submit the recordings via WhatsApp. At the end of his posting, he complained that he was now overwhelmed because he had to assess 120 individual recordings on WhatsApp. A rich discussion followed on the WAG chat [Extract 14/5/20].

The WAG chat also included frequent **links to webinars**, which became a particularly popular form of professional learning in the ERT context. Previously, teachers needed to travel when they wanted to join or participate in a seminar or conference, and this can be time consuming and costly for teachers. During ERT, seminars, workshops, and conferences were conducted online; thus, teachers had more opportunities to participate regardless of their location. Data from the WAG chat showed that besides sharing information about the availability of webinars, the WAG members also frequently discussed the webinar content within the group [eg. Extract 11/4/20].

The teachers commented that the information on KGP was **practical, convenient and easy to access.** As Harry and Annie explained,

- *It helps me a lot... very fast to get (Harry, FG1, 1:39)*
- *In KGP you can find the resource directly instead of looking in your laptop and googling it (Annie, 00:47)*
- *I'm not really keen to listen to educational theory I prefer to listen to 'how you teach this' using particular methodology or some kinds of game, so it's more technical and applicable in the classroom. Only listening to theory blah..blah.. blah.. it's kinda boring. (Austin, 00:42)*

Several participants also mentioned that postings in the Group are always relevant: unlike other groups they belonged to, there were no jokes, and no religious or political proselytising.

Nevertheless, **the quantity of information was sometimes confusing**, and sometimes members were overwhelmed. They tended to pick out only the information that was particularly relevant to them. As Austin and Cassandra said,

- *However, there are many information that always been shared in the group. So sometimes I lost focus. And since I have lots of other WhatsApp groups, so, you know, I tend to be like confused myself with everything. (Austin, 00.35)*
- *Sometimes it's just confused me, but I read some that interest me (Cassandra, 00:39)*

The moderator tried to address this problem by creating a well-catalogued archive which members could access online.

It was not clear to what extent the rich information presented on KGP actually affected **student learning**. Most of the participants gave practical examples of how their teaching had been enriched by strategies they had learned on KGP. However, two of the participants admitted that they enjoyed reading the information, but were not able to apply it extensively in their practice. Cassandra, who was very positive about the possibilities of ERT, felt she was learning a great deal from KGP, but was still cautious about applying new ideas with her large classes:

- *... what's good about it is that all of people in [KGP] are people who want to grow and become a better practitioner, and it motivates me to be better also, but ... I don't really apply the tools being discussed. I need to keep it one step at a time. (Cassandra 00:43)*

For Rachel, it was hard to practice new ideas because of peer pressure from other teachers in her school:

- *I want to say frankly, when there is an idea of using another media, for example Instagram.... there will be, you know what kind of gossip, or rumours in the teachers' room. (Rachel 00:18)*

In addition, during the pandemic, the participants' ability to apply innovative strategies was limited by poor internet connections, the relatively high cost of internet subscriptions, and students' lack of access to devices. Although the teachers had used a wide variety of educational technology for teaching in their classrooms previously, during ERT they all had to resort principally to WhatsApp as the only cheap and accessible way of reaching their students during the lockdown. As Isaac said,

- *Actually I tried to apply Google Classroom, but it's a great challenge for me because actually the condition of the place I teach is in the remote place where it is not easy to find signal. ... So I only use the WhatsApp because every student has WhatsApp. (Isaac FG1 1:27).*

Data from the WAG chat highlighted the same issue. One of the members explained that he was still unable to decide the best apps for teaching as most of his students could only afford internet data for WhatsApp. This posting was confirmed by several other teachers in the group [Extract 26-27/3/20].

On the other hand, six of the ten participants not only applied the information and strategies they had learned from KGP in their own practice, but also about shared it with other teachers in their schools and district. Ian and Daisy, for instance, recounted:

- *[KGP] introduces you to the method and strategies for teaching, so at least I transfer it to other teachers and it's quite fast to get it, the information from the [KGP] group relating to technology. ... The last one for example I used Quipper.[2] So, I tried to adapt it to students, and probably some teachers could not use it, but at least I could transfer or help them to use that technological thing. So it helps a lot. (Harry FG1, 1:39)*
- *I have told all I have from [KGP] to all my friends, all my colleagues, and I have implemented in my internal MGMP [local professional development group], and my school. I told them to do this and that, using ideas from [KGP] (Daisy 00:36)*

5.3   KGP as a Source of Affective Support During the Crisis

In addition to the information that they received, all the respondents agreed that there were strong affective reasons for belonging to the Group which were even more important during the challenging first months of the pandemic.

The respondents agreed that they valued the Group as a **source of support, inspiration, energy and motivation** to develop professionally. Alfred explained,

- *This group is supportive. I told you that this is not only shared about the information, but also share the positive energy. Yeah, the positive energy. ... it's just given me a positive energy and make me curious. (Alfred 0:42).*

They were inspired by the experiences of others in the group to try out new strategies. As Ian said,

- *If he or she can do, I can do it too. (Ian 00:30)*

In particular, the participants frequently mentioned the role of the moderator and his inclusive style in inspiring and motivating them:

- *[The moderator] always says great things in early morning. Early morning. Yeah, they say hi, at four or three a.m..... I feel that I'm part of them. I feel that they respect me as the participant on the group (Alfred 00:47)*

Others explained that belonging to the Group made them feel **less isolated**. Ian, for instance, explained:

- *We here in [a remote area], at first that I thought I'm alone. I mean, I try to apply some kind of tools, but other teachers said it's unuseful because we live in remote area, something like that. But in the Pandemic, so we are forced to do, we must apply them. (Ian FG1, 1:32)*

---

[2] Quipper is a web-based learning tool that provides various different practice lessons and tests

The teachers who participated were all clearly dedicated and committed teachers, and they enjoyed linking up with others who are passionate about teaching. They described the Group as warm, welcoming and non-judgemental. For example,

• *They are all so welcoming, including [the moderator] is very good ... they are never blame someone, so we can talk freely. (Alfred, 0:42).*

By contrast, their own colleagues were sometimes less professional:

• *My school did not pay attention whether the teacher teach their students or not. They just aware of the score of the students that should be collected on time. (Rachel, FG2 1:10)*

The participants also talked about the **contribution of KGP to their professional identity**. An interesting comment on the WAG was that teachers enjoyed participating because there were few opportunities to use their English language skills during the pandemic:

• *Soooo glad to have your recording and to listen to your voice. In somehow it renew my spirit that I have partners to practice my English. In these 2 months I haven't practiced English a lot. By responding to your questions, I have chances to speak up. [WAG 14/5/20]*

Also, by participating in the group, teachers learned about certificates that they could gain and webinars that they could attend, and they were able to share their learnings with local colleagues. In some cases, Group members were invited to become keynote speakers in professional development sessions in their respective districts. They also had the opportunity to participate in creating the KGP publications, and this was also a boost to their careers and their identity as committed teachers. As Daisy put it,

• *[The moderator] is one of the inspirators. He provided me with some kinds of ideas related to technology, and also helped me how to write about teaching with technology. [The Group provided] a world of information, and new friends, ... and many more. That's why it improves my life, improves my teaching capacity, and improves my quality as a teacher. [Daisy 00:36]*

6   What Can We Learn from This Virtual Professional Community of Teachers?

The teachers in this case study made it clear that KGP was **already a vibrant network** of trusted colleagues when the pandemic hit. As previous studies have also found, the participants valued the virtual professional group community both for the rich information they could find there and for the emotional support it provided (Lantz-Andersson et al., 2018; Macià & García, 2016). Both of these factors became particularly important when teachers were suddenly faced with the challenges of teaching/learning from home and the feelings of isolation that were common across the world as social distancing was enforced.

In the crisis of ERT, teachers needed **just-in-time information, tips and strategies** that were relevant to the sudden change to remote teaching. Teachers across Indonesia were facing similar challenges: many were struggling to teach 12 classes of 35 students/class; many of their students had no access to devices, and others could not afford the expense of using their internet subscription to access Google Classroom or other internet platforms; many of their students were having to communicate on their parents' smartphones which were only available in the evening. All the teachers were struggling to catch up with new government regulations as they came out during the pandemic and all were dealing with the issue of cheating – they could not be sure that the students were submitting their own work. The teachers were struggling with issues such as how to keep their students engaged when learning from home, and how to meet the demands of the curriculum in this difficult time. All these issues and more could be discussed on the WhatsApp group, and while solutions were not always easily come-by, the teachers at least felt that they had the support of the group.

Arguably, much of the information provided on KGP could have been located by the teachers themselves through Google searches. However, the WhatsApp Group, and particularly the moderator himself, performed an **important function in filtering or "curating"** (Lantz-Andersson et al., 2018) content that was relevant to the teachers. This meant that highly relevant information came to the teachers at the time when they needed it, in an accessible form right onto their smartphones. And it came from trusted peers who really understood the problems they were facing.

Of course, not all the teaching strategies and tips could be put into practice, so it is hard to evaluate the effect of the KGP on actual teaching practice, let alone on student learning. As mentioned above, two of the teachers explained that it was too difficult for them to implement much change in their teaching. However, the other teachers gave multiple examples of how they had introduced innovations into their practice as a result of KGP. Although these innovations were at the level of teaching strategies, or the application of a new technological tool, they were characterised by an interactive and communicative approach to language learning - a shift away from the didactic tradition of education in Indonesia.

In terms of their interaction in the group, the members participated in different ways, reflecting the roles described by Prestridge (2019). Some of the participants could be categorised as "**Info-consumers**": like Cassandra, they were happy to read and learn from the information, but rarely participated in the conversations. Others, like Ian, both posted comments online, and also shared information from the Group with colleagues in their own schools: they could be categorised as "**info-networkers**". Others, like Austin, could be categorised as "**self-seekers**" – they shared information in order to get feedback on their ideas, or to get answers to questions that they posted. Importantly the moderator of the group is clearly a "**vocationalist**" (Prestridge, 2019). His motivation is to sustain and enrich the profession by ensuring the productivity and continuity of the KGP group and fostering student-centred, communicative language teaching. This spirit of altruism, passion for student learning, and willingness to share and support each other permeated the whole group as a result of his leadership.

The role of the moderator was crucial, as Macià and García (2016) also found. The teachers all spoke about the moderator with great warmth and respect, not just as an administrator for the group, but also as a mentor, coach and motivator. His altruism and dedication were key to the productivity and continuity of the group. He maintained the group's cohesion and engagement by posting friendly greetings, involving various participants by name, for example, "Good morning, Pak Harry. How are you this morning?". He was able to select information and teaching tips as he was familiar with the teachers' own contexts. He also monitored postings and immediately advised anyone who posted off-topic comments that they were not appropriate. Importantly, as an Indonesian himself and a practising senior school teacher, he understands the sociocultural context of the members. For example, he was sensitive to the teachers' preferred learning style: Indonesia is predominantly an oral culture and he was aware that the Group members did not want to read lengthy documents such as research articles. As Austin pointed out, he preferred to listen, and to focus on practical tips rather than theory. The moderator also used friendly, informal language to engage and motivate the participants. The exchanges were rich in code-switching which contributed to the informality as well as the solidarity of the community (Holmes & Wilson, 2017). He understood, too, how to help the participants advance in their own careers, by being able to access certificates from webinars, by being keynote speaker in a webinar, and by participating in publishing. He was generous in enabling multiple group members to contribute to the community's publications and in distributing leadership by encouraging members to participate in the WAG. His role in the group was consistent, friendly, modest and always positive and encouraging.

Participation in the group, embedded in the Indonesian context, inevitably **reflected Indonesian cultural norms**. Although Prestridge's (2019) proposed system of categorising participants in online communities of practice could be applied to KGP, the Indonesian participants in this case study reflected very different values to Prestridge's respondents. Prestridge identified themes of competition, compliancy and curiosity, but, although the Indonesian participants were certainly curious, and keen to learn, the ethos in the group was clearly more of collaboration than of competition and more concerned with innovation than with compliancy. The members also showed great respect for the moderator. Indonesia has a long-standing tradition of showing respect for leaders (Sriwindono & Yahya, 2012) and the moderator of KGP took on this role with dedication and modesty, providing a foundation for the culture of collaboration and mutual respect among the participants. In proposing ideas, the members seemed to be genuinely interested in sharing, rather than self-promotion, as appeared to be the case with some of Prestridge's participants. On the other hand, it could be argued that there was little critical reflection on the ideas raised in the WAG: perhaps this could also be attributed to the sociocultural context, as critical reflection in Indonesia can be taken as criticism of the person posting the idea rather than a reflection on the idea itself. Not surprisingly, the members of the group conformed to the unspoken rules of politeness fundamental to Indonesian culture.

Finally, the group members obviously thought there were benefits in participating in the group – not just in learning new teaching strategies, but also social benefits of associating with a like-minded and supportive group of peers, and in building their professional status, through sharing and collaborating with others.

7 Conclusion

The community of practice which has developed in KGP demonstrates all five of the characteristics in Patahuddin and Logan's (2019) framework for Effective Professional Development:

(i) it is **on-going** – the Group has been sustained over a period of time, and was already running well and consistently when the switch to ERT occurred

(ii) it is **collaborative** – although the group is sustained mainly by the moderator, the participants feel able to share freely and openly and to co-construct solutions to problems.

(iii) it is **student-oriented** – the teachers in this study demonstrated amazing dedication to helping their students to learn, some even visiting their students' homes if they were unable to access the internet

(iv) it **focuses on PCK** (Pedagogical Content Knowledge – knowledge about teaching with reference to the particular subject area), and particularly **on TPACK** (technology for teaching)

(v) it is highly **relevant to the teachers' contexts** and needs – especially when the challenge of ERT arose.

Importantly, KGP was already well-established before the pandemic hit. It was already a thriving, supportive, collaborative group of like-minded teachers who enjoyed daily interaction about teaching. The information, strategies and inspiration arrived on their smartphones every morning – they did not have to spend time trawling the internet to find solutions to their problems. They knew they had a trusted, inclusive community of fellow teachers who were sharing the same challenges in the face of the coronavirus lockdown. So, when the need for ERT arose, KGP was able to respond to the teachers' contexts and needs on a "just-in-time" basis with information and strategies to deal with the challenges they faced.

8 Food for Thought

This case study shows how a vibrant virtual community of teachers was able to support a each other during the first months of ERT. Importantly, the Group had already established a pattern of "professional interaction characterised by shared values, respect, trust and supportive leadership" (Lantz-Andersson et al., 2018).

Key features of the virtual community were:

- on-going, regular and frequent interaction
- culturally appropriate, friendly and supportive interaction
- dedicated and consistent leadership
- relevant content for teachers' contexts and concerns
- rich, practical and just-in-time information.

Teachers should consider establishing similar informal communities of like-minded professionals, in order to "future-proof" themselves against uncertain times ahead. Through mutual support, and by sharing ideas and information, the teachers in this online professional learning community were able to survive – and thrive – through the difficult times of Emergency Remote Teaching.

Appendices

Appendix 1

Screenshot Sample from WhatsApp Group Conversation

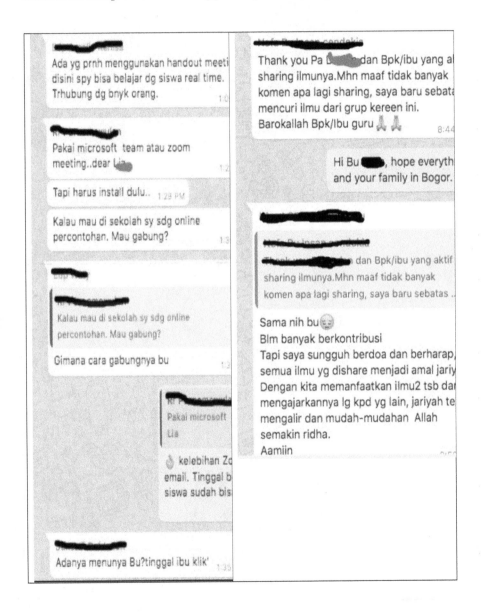

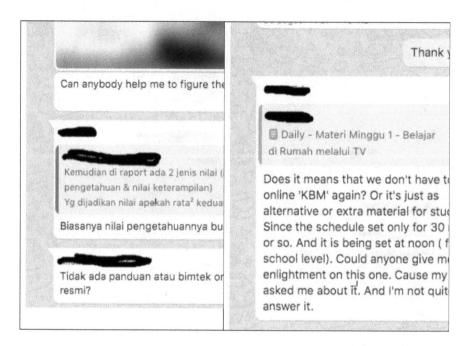

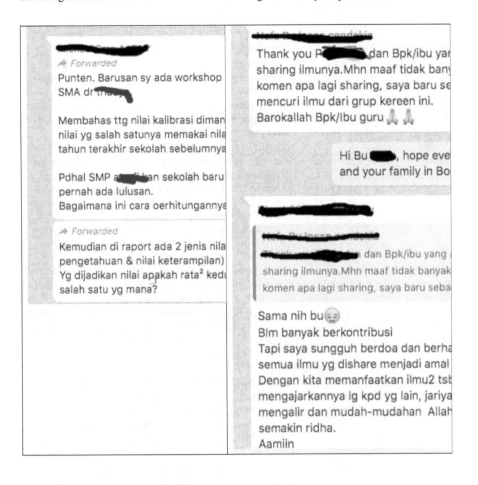

Appendix 2: Educational Technology Mentioned by the Participants in the Research

Platform/ Application	Weblink	Comments
WhatsApp	https://www. whatsapp. com/?lang=en	WhatsApp is an application that enables users to interact via messages, voice calls and video calls. The application also makes it easy for users to send photos, videos, files and voice notes. Although WhatsApp was not created as an educational technology, many teachers make use of this application as means of teaching as it can be used in groups and with low internet connection. Most importantly, it allows synchronous learning, although teachers may not be able to recognize each participating student in the group

(continued)

Platform/ Application	Weblink	Comments
Dave's ESL Café	https://www.eslcafe.com/	This website was created to share free ESL learning resources, and thus has become a 'meeting place' for ELT practitioners
British Council's teaching English	https://learnenglish.britishcouncil.org/	This platform provides educational resources that can be used for learning English, graded from elementary to higher education
Zoom	https://zoom.us/	Zoom can be considered as an icon for COVID-19 as before the pandemic hit, it had not gained much attention. In Indonesia, zoom is used as a substitute for the face to face classroom. Teachers can explain and show learning materials and record the meeting for later use. Besides teleconferencing, the platform provides a breakout room facility which enables teachers to put learners into groups, and an interactive whiteboard for teaching
Google meetings	https://meet.google.com/	Google meet enables members to have synchronous video communication. Teachers (and students) are able to share files and video throughout the learning session. It also enables participants to send messages throughout the session
YouTube channel	https://youtube.com	YouTube is a platform that focuses on videos and events. For educational purposes, teachers can set up a password-protected YouTube channel to upload their own and their students' videos
Instagram	https://www.instagram.com/	Instagram enables users to post pictures, posters, and videos to communicate with other users. This has prompted some teachers to use the media for teaching
Google classroom	https://edu.google.com/products/classroom/	Google classroom is a free web-based service that enables teachers to manage the class online. The website is literally a classroom which is online; teachers are able to collect students' assignments, provide feedback, trace students' progress, and upload assignment and learning materials. Thus, it is not surprising that the platform has become one of the most prefered platforms for teachers during the pandemic in Indonesia
Quipper	https://www.quipper.com/id/	Quipper is an online learning management system that provides services such as e-learning, coaching, tutoring, and assessment. The services can be different in different countries. In Indonesia, the platform has gained popularity because it prepares learners for the national examination as one of its services
Edpuzzle	https://edpuzzle.com/	Edpuzzle is a learning platform that can be used for language learning. Teachers who prefer to deliver their lesson through videos will find Edpuzzle very convenient. The platform links to several websites which commonly use video learning resources such as YouTube, Khan Academy, National Geographic, TED Talks, Veritasium, Numberphile, and Crash Course. Teachers can also make their own videos. The platform enables teachers to manage the video to suit their own context

References

Dimyati, A. (2018). *Pengaruh professional learning community terhadap pengembangan profesi guru pada madrasah aliyah negeri di provinsi Lampung.* Universitas Islam Negeri Radin Intan Lampung.

Duncan-Howell, J. (2010). Teachers making connections: Online communities as a source of professional learning. *British Journal of Educational Technology, 41*(2), 324–340. https://doi.org/10.1111/j.1467-8535.2009.00953.x

Hodges, C., Moore, S., Lockee, B., Trust, T., & Bond, A. (2020, March). The difference between emergency remote teaching and online learning. *Educause Review, 27*, 2020. https://er.educause.edu/articles/2020/3/the-difference-between-emergency-remote-teaching-and-online-learning

Holmes, J., & Wilson, N. (2017). *An introduction to sociolinguistics* (5th ed.). Routledge.

Kennedy, M. M. (2016). How does professional development improve teaching? *Review of Educational Research, 86*(4), 945–980. https://doi.org/10.3102/0034654315626800

Krutka, D. G., Carpenter, J. P., & Trust, T. (2016). Elements of engagement: A model of teacher interactions via professional learning networks. *Journal of Digital Learning in Teacher Education, 32*(4), 150–158. https://doi.org/10.1080/21532974.2016.1206492

Lantz-Andersson, A., Lundin, M., & Selwyn, N. (2018). Twenty years of online teacher communities: A systematic review of formally-organized and informally-developed professional learning groups. *Teaching and Teacher Education, 75*, 302–315. https://doi.org/10.1016/j.tate.2018.07.008

Lave, J., & Wenger, E. (1991). *Situated learning: Legitimate peripheral participation.* Cambridge University Press.

Macià, M., & García, I. (2016). Informal online communities and networks as a source of teacher professional development: A review. *Teaching and Teacher Education, 55*, 291–307. https://doi.org/10.1016/j.tate.2016.01.021

Moolenaar, N. M., Sleegers, P. J. C., & Daly, A. J. (2012). Teaming up: Linking collaboration networks, collective efficacy and student achievement. *Teaching and Teacher Education, 28*, 251–262. https://doi.org/10.1016/j.tate.2011.10.001

OECD/ADB. (2015). *Education in Indonesia: Rising to the challenge.* https://doi.org/10.1787/9789264230750-en

Patahuddin, S. M. (2013). Mathematics teacher professional development in and through internet use: reflections on an ethnographic study. *Mathematics Education Research Journal 25*(4), 503–521.

Patahuddin, S. M., & Logan, T. (2019). Facebook as a mechanism for informal teacher professional learning in Indonesia. *Teacher Development, 23*(1), 101–120. https://doi.org/10.1080/13664530.2018.152478

Patahuddin, S. M., Rokhmah, S., & Lowrie, T. (2020). Indonesian mathematics teachers' and educators' perspectives on social media platforms: The case of educational Facebook groups. *The Asia-Pacific Education Researcher.* https://doi-org.ezproxy.canberra.edu.au/10.1007/s40299-020-00503-3

Prestridge, S. (2019). Categorising teachers' use of social media for their professional learning: A self-generating professional learning paradigm. *Computers and Education, 129*, 143–158. https://doi.org/10.1016/j.compedu.2018.11.003

Sianipar, G. W. (2019). *Implementasi PLC (Professional Learning Community) di Sekolah Dasar Gagas Ceria Bandung.* A thesis. Indonesia University of Indonesia.

Sriwindono, H., & Yahya, S. (2012). Toward modeling the effects of cultural dimension on ICT acceptance in Indonesia. *Procedia, Social and Behavioral Sciences, 65*, 833–838. https://doi.org/10.1016/j.sbspro.2012.11.207

Statistica. (2020a). *Leading countries based on Facebook audience size as of July 2020.* https://www.statista.com/statistics/268136/top-15-countries-based-on-number-of-facebook-users/ Accessed 12 Oct 2020.

Statistica. (2020b). *Number of smartphone users by country as of September 2019.* https://www. statista.com/statistics/748053/worldwide-top-countries-smartphone-users/ Accessed 12 Oct 2020.

The World Bank. (2020). *The World Bank in Indonesia.* https://www.worldbank.org/en/country/ indonesia/overview, Accessed 17 Oct 2020.

Tour, E. (2017). Teachers' self-initiated professional learning through personal learning networks. *Technology, Pedagogy and Education, 26*(2), 179–192. https://doi.org/10.108 0/1475939X.2016.1196236

Trilaksono, T., Purusottama, A., Misbach, I. A., & Prasetya, I. H. (2019). Leadership change design: A professional learning community (PLC) project in eastern Indonesia. *International Journal of Evaluation and Research in Education (IJERE), 8*(1). https://doi.org/10.11591/ijere. v8i1.15662

Trust, T., & Horrocks, B. (2017). "I never feel alone in my classroom": Teacher professional growth within a blended community of practice. *Professional Development in Education, 43*(4), 645–665. https://doi.org/10.1080/19415257.2016.1233507

Trust, T., Krutka, D., & Carpenter, J. (2016). "Together we are better": Professional learning networks for teachers. *Computers and Education, 102*, 15–34. https://doi.org/10.1016/j. compedu.2016.06.007

Vincent-Lancrin, S., et al. (2019). Indonesia. In Vincent-Lancrin, S. et al., (Eds) *Measuring Innovation in Education 2019: What Has Changed in the Classroom?* Paris: OECD Publishing. https://doi.org/10.1787/a588d3ad-en

Transforming from Off-Liners to On-Liners: Voices from Foreign Language Professors in Colombia

Kathleen A. Corrales and Lourdes Rey-Paba

Highlights

- The COVID-19 pandemic had an unexpected positive outcome on both formal and informal teacher development in our foreign language faculty.
- Teachers reported that they learned pedagogical aspects necessary to the online teaching situation such as learning how to use technological teaching tools, adapting their teaching methods to the new reality, having contingency plans, and developing an awareness for the need for clarity in instructions and communication with students.
- Teachers' development resulting from the transition to online teaching fostered a more "humane" and compassionate view of the teaching-learning situation during the crisis.
- The crisis brought about a synergy among faculty where they were able to learn from others and also about themselves.

1 Introduction

With the spread of COVID-19 to Latin America, higher education institutions were forced to transition to emergency remote teaching (ERT) (Hodges et al., 2020) in a short period of time, shaking the foundations of teaching and of professional development around the region. Coupled with this, pre-pandemic research shows that teaching online differs vastly from teaching face-to-face (Elliott et al., 2015) and that traditional types of teaching do not seem to translate well to online education (Shelton & Saltsman, 2005). This research also has demonstrated that one of the

K. A. Corrales (✉) · L. Rey-Paba
Universidad del Norte, Barranquilla, Colombia
e-mail: kwade@uninorte.edu.co

© The Author(s), under exclusive license to Springer Nature
Switzerland AG 2021
J. Chen (ed.), *Emergency Remote Teaching and Beyond*,
https://doi.org/10.1007/978-3-030-84067-9_5

biggest challenges in this shift is to help teachers embrace the new possibilities of online teaching (Montelongo, 2019). However, during the COVID-19 pandemic, the shift was not voluntary but rather, as Watson Todd (2020) defines it, a "power-coercive unplanned innovation" (p. 4), which, according to Lamie's ideas of educational innovation (2005 as cited in Watson Todd, 2020), is very likely to be unsuccessful. Therefore, professional development (PD) became essential to prepare teachers for the new teaching-learning environment to transform this forced, unplanned innovation into something successful.

In the field of education, professional development has been defined from different perspectives. Generally, it can be understood as "processes through which teachers learn to learn, learn to teach, and improve their pedagogical, innovation, and research skills in the development of their teaching, extension, and research activities" (Velasquez-Torres et al., 2017, p. 2). Diaz Maggioli (2003) emphasizes that PD is "an evolving process of professional self-disclosure, reflection, and growth" (p. 1). Thus, in this paper, we use the term PD to not only address the process of teacher learning but also the resulting teacher growth.

Other authors emphasize the fact that PD should be systematically planned in order to develop teachers' skills, knowledge, and expertise (Avidov-Ungar & Herscu, 2019), and, as a result, improve teaching practices (Darling-Hammond et al., 2017). A key element to successful professional development implies a strong commitment by teachers to the process (Diaz Maggioli, 2004) and the understanding that it not only involves pedagogical and professional aspects but also social and personal dimensions (Cárdenas et al., 2011).

The literature shows different categories for professional development activities. For instance, Caffarella and Zinn (1999) classify them into three types: "(1) self-directed learning experiences; (2) formal professional development programs; and (3) organizational development strategies" (p. 242). For these authors, self-directed PD involves teachers, on their own, carrying out activities that are planned, implemented, and evaluated. Thus, teacher learning "takes place as a result of preparing class materials, teaching classes, designing new courses, revising curriculum, supervising dissertations, conducting research, and being involved in service functions" (p. 242). The second type of PD described by these authors are formal programs that can focus on teaching or more "academic" aspects such as scholarship and research. The purpose of the last type, organizational development, is to effect change in the institution as a whole rather than individual change. Within these overarching categories, PD can also be classified according to the type of activities that teachers pursue. From Herman's (2012) classification of effective PD activities for shifting from face-to-face to online courses, four categories can be highlighted: (1) self-teaching, (2) peer mentoring, (3) face-to-face or online workshops, and (4) collaborative course design. In the case of self-teaching, professors autonomously use different resources (e.g., books, online seminars, videos) to learn. Peer mentoring can refer to faculty members who support their colleagues either formally (i.e., appointed and trained by the institution) or informally (i.e., offering their expertise voluntarily). Face-to-face or online workshops include a one-time training or a series of activities involving lectures or hands-on work. Finally, collaborative course design refers to working together with colleagues to create new courses or adjust existing ones.

Within these types of professional development activities, authors have highlighted specific topics that are essential to include when preparing teachers to move to online teaching. The first aspect relates to raising teacher awareness about the different modalities of online teaching and the challenges each of these poses (Ragan & Schroeder, 2014) since there has been a lack of diffusion about what these modalities are (Hodges et al., 2020). These authors have listed these modalities as: "distance learning, distributed learning, blended learning, online learning, mobile learning, and others" (para. 5). Contributing to the confusion is the advent of the new modality beginning during the 2020 pandemic: emergency remote teaching. A second dimension includes helping teachers use technological tools effectively to organize course content, teach asynchronous and synchronous lessons, facilitate interaction, and assess learning (Baran et al., 2011; Barry, 2019; Herie, 2005). This means that teachers need not only to learn about education tech tools but also how to successfully integrate them into their practice. A third area includes helping teachers see that their role goes beyond the content that they teach. Whereas students of this generation have been termed as "digital natives," many of them have not used technology in their formal educational experience. Thus, part of teacher PD is to learn how to provide students with the necessary support so they can learn through online tools (Watson & Pecchioni, 2011).

The worldwide transformation from offline to online teaching and learning seems to not be just a temporary response to the crisis but rather a far-reaching paradigm shift of institutions as this may be the only safe option of continuing to provide education in the short-term, or it may become the new norm in the long-term. Furthermore, as Watson Todd (2020) posits, "the suddenness of the shift to online learning means that the relevance of previous research investigating moves to online learning is unclear" (p. 5). Thus, the profound effect of emergency online teaching needs to be fully explored and understood to make appropriate decisions for the future of education. Since the teacher is central to this process, including their perspectives in the research of online learning is essential. Therefore, this chapter highlights the voices of professors as they move out of their offline comfort zone and transition to online teaching.

This chapter focuses on the professional development of a group of foreign language professors during their shift to ERT. First, we describe the context where these teachers work and the PD they experienced during this time. In the next section, we report on the areas that teachers consider they learned, including their perspectives and examples of their solutions to the challenges they faced as they worked at the frontline of ERT. Finally, we conclude with a reflection on what this process has entailed for us, as teachers and as an institution, and we offer suggestions about what comes next in terms of professional development during future crisis situations.

2   Our Case

This chapter is based on the experience of a group of foreign language professors at a private university in Colombia which serves approximately 16,000 students. The Department of Foreign Languages is in charge of the development of communicative competence in foreign languages (English, German, French, and Portuguese). There are approximately 80 faculty members, which include tenured and non-tenured full-time faculty as well as adjunct professors. The campus began working from home on March 16, 2020, after the first identified positive cases of COVID-19 in the country, and allotted 2 weeks to prepare for remote teaching. We began ERT on March 30, 2020, and, at the time of this chapter, continue teaching online.

In order to better understand the context that this chapter reports on, it is important to acknowledge several particular conditions that are inherent to Colombia as a "developing" country that have impacted the smooth transition to more technology-based teaching modalities. These challenges include a lack of dependable electrical and internet service, limited or no access to internet and cellphone signals in some remote areas, and precarious economic conditions of some students. Therefore, the transformation to and the integration of technology has historically been difficult in Colombia (González & Campins, 2016), affecting both teachers and students, especially during the COVID-19 crisis.

Emergency remote teaching, for our particular context, was conceived as a combination of synchronous and asynchronous sessions with the balance of these two decided by each academic department. In our department, classes meet 4 h a week, so it was decided that a minimum of 2 h would be synchronous lessons while the other two consisted of independent work which teachers would review and give feedback on. Consequently, ERT teaching was a total change for us. Teachers not only had to figure out how to teach live online but also had to design activities and material that were sufficiently clear for students to be able to do them on their own.

As stated above, our institution had only 2 weeks to transition to the remote education modality. At our university, while teachers have been integrating technology in the classroom, emphasis had traditionally been placed on face-to-face education; therefore, when confronted with this emergency, many of our foreign language faculty lacked conceptual and practical knowledge of online course design and delivery. Therefore, the institution scrambled to offer professional development sessions to meet the needs of the professors. After a thorough literature review, the institution offered different types of professional development which focused on the topics suggested for successful online courses. The types of PD, according to Herman (2012), were mentoring, workshops given synchronously and asynchronously, and collaborative course design. It was also clear that some teachers were involved in autonomous PD, where they looked for solutions to their particular problems and employed trial-and-error in the classroom to learn. In relation to the topics, the PD related to: (1) learning about different technological tools available for both synchronous and asynchronous classes and how to integrate them into the teaching-learning process, (2) understanding the different online teaching modalities (i.e.,

ERT vs. virtual vs. blended), and (3) helping teachers and their students deal with emotional needs during this time.

One additional element relates to the support of the university's Center of Teacher Excellence (CEDU) that offered a face-to-face and synchronous mandatory campus-wide training on the institutional technological platforms to be used. These training sessions were recorded and made available for professors to consult at their leisure. After this initial session, the CEDU offered optional workshops on other essential aspects of teaching online such as course organization, lesson planning, and assessment design. The CEDU also assigned one mentor to each academic department who supported faculty with technical issues.

In spite of these general institutional PD opportunities, some professors felt insufficiently prepared to face the challenge of teaching *languages* online, so the Department of Foreign Languages implemented a series of PD initiatives to support its faculty. These included collaborative lesson planning, weekly synchronous small-group faculty meetings, and teacher WhatsApp groups, all aimed at working together to share concerns, solutions to challenges, and pertinent tools and websites for class use. During this time, besides the institutional PD opportunities, some professors actively contributed to the professional development of their less tech savvy colleagues by making tutorials on educational tech tools, giving formal specialized webinars and workshops about online teaching, and providing concrete examples of effective language learning and teaching, material design, and assessment for remote learning. The institution formally recognized these teachers by asking their colleagues to nominate those who supported them the most. This information was consolidated and an award was given to the 15 who received the most votes. Furthermore, the Department of Foreign Languages also placed special attention on the emotional effect the crisis was having on students and teachers. For example, one professor gave a workshop on how to support emotionally struggling students. These initiatives not only addressed students' needs but also those of teachers, especially faculty who lived alone, through special informal events including "coffee time," "movie night," or "cooking lessons."

3   What We Found

An unexpected positive result of the transition to ERT relates to the fact that the crisis boosted teacher professional development, even if it was unplanned and harried. Most of what we have heard in the educational field and through social media is about the negative aspects of the pandemic where parents, teachers, and students argue about the effectiveness of the online shift. Thus, we felt it was necessary to highlight the voices of the professors about what exactly they have learned during this time.

The participating teachers are all faculty of the Department of Foreign Languages and teach either English, German, French, or Portuguese. Each of them holds a Master's degree or higher and have a minimum of 3–20 years of experience at the university-level. As mentioned earlier, these teachers are a mixture of tenured, non-tenured, adjunct, Colombian and international professors. In terms of their experience with online education, some had taken online courses, but the vast majority had not taught online in the past. For a general picture of the demographics of the faculty, see Table 1 below.

In order to explore our teachers' PD during the shift, we asked all the faculty of the department to write two short reflections on what they learned, once after the first week of ERT and again at the end of the 8-week process (i.e., when the semester finished) in order to gather qualitative comments. Out of the 85 professors invited to participate, 71 responded. We reviewed their responses, identified keywords, and coded the answers into nine different categories (see Table 2) using content analysis (Elo et al., 2014). Then, these keywords were used to identify representative quotations to illustrate the teachers' perceptions about their PD. In this chapter, their quotations are marked by the letter R to indicate response and number of the participant (e.g., R49).

Interestingly, when reviewing these nine categories that represented what teachers had learned during the ERT process, three main themes became clear. Table 2 is organized by the frequency of the responses of the categories identified and also relates them to the main themes that emerged. The first corresponds to the transformation of teacher pedagogy as a response to the online teaching situation such as

Table 1 Demographics of participating professors

Biological sex		Language program				Nationality	
Female	Male	English	French	German	Portuguese	Colombian	International
54%	46%	88%	4%	2%	6%	79%	21%

Table 2 Main areas learned

#	Theme	Areas of learning	Reflection 1	Reflection 2	Total
1	Teacher pedagogy	Technological skills and teaching tools	15	48	63
2	Teacher pedagogy	Teaching method	10	21	31
3	Humane approach	Flexibility	9	10	19
4	Learning from others and about themselves	Self-learning	7	11	18
5	Humane approach	Empathy	10	7	17
6	Learning from others and about themselves	Learning community	9	3	12
7	Humane approach	Support to students	4	7	11
8	Teacher pedagogy	Contingency plans	6	3	9
9	Teacher pedagogy	Awareness of the need for clarity of instruction/communication	5	1	6

technological skills and teaching tools (#1), teaching methods (#2), contingency plans (#8), and an awareness for the need for clarity in instructions and communication (#9). The second aspect refers to the development of a more "humane" and compassionate view of the teaching-learning situation during the crisis. Attitudes such as flexibility (#3) and empathy (#5) brought about a need to support students (#7). Finally, the third theme revealed the creation of an organic learning community with their colleagues (#6) and a deeper knowledge about themselves, both professionally and personally (#4).

3.1 Teacher Pedagogy

The following categories refer to the changes that teachers had to make in their teaching due to the transition to ERT. These include aspects related to technology, methodology, and communication in the classroom.

3.1.1 Technology Skills and Teaching Tools

Unsurprisingly, technological skills and teaching tools was the area that the professors expressed they learned the most, which makes sense since during the transition to ERT classes, technology was essential for this change. This can be seen in the following statement:

> Virtual tools are not new and some of us were already using them, but it was not an institutional policy. Each professor used them as they wished. I was also using some, but they were not at the core of my teaching. Now I have learned many technological tools that I didn't take into account before because of the strong emphasis on face-to-face teaching. (R95)

During the past 15 years, institutions have been promoting the use of learning management systems such as Blackboard, Canvas, and Moodle, to mention a few. While some institutions were more ahead than others, over that period of time, professors in our context started to integrate these and other technological tools into their classrooms with different levels of success. However, the imposed shift to ERT made this integration compulsory, forcing professors to discover new tools to widen the array of technological options they could successfully use. Many teachers saw this move to ERT as a professional development opportunity as one professor expressed:

> The new skills learned…have caused a huge leap in my life as an English teacher. I have started a new phase full of new technological and pedagogical learning. (R51)

In terms of educational technology, professors stated that they learned to use new platforms (Blackboard Collaborate Ultra (BBCU), Google Meet, Zoom, and Microsoft Teams), apps, other software, and Google extensions. It is important to mention that each professor developed their skills at their own pace; some cited very complex technical developments while others mentioned very basic knowledge such as "becoming an expert in PowerPoint" (R128). Some voices of the teachers include:

> I learned about Google Meet, which I hadn't known. I started to mess around with Google Classroom, which I knew but had never used as a teacher. (R20)

> I learned to use Zoom, in general, and share my screen. I learned what worked and didn't work in Zoom; for example, it is better to share a YouTube link rather than play it for them. I learned to use Flipgrid and more functions of Kahoot. (R126)

Among the most cited apps, teachers reported using Jamboard, Mentimeter, Liveworksheets, Nearpod, Pear Deck, and ShowMore as a way to make the classes more engaging, encourage interaction, and provide students with the opportunity to reflect on their learning process. Figure 1 demonstrates how Jamboard was used as an "exit ticket" for students to carry out a reflection.

Some teachers also created virtual offices using Bitmoji to visually organize their classrooms and give students a sense of being in a physical room (see Fig. 2). Additionally, professors stated the need to create faster communication channels. Many decided on opening WhatsApp groups with their students and implementing clear rules of engagement.

> In the Portuguese program, we always use WhatsApp. We create the group in the first week of classes, establish communication rules. It's an excellent tool that allows students to learn in an informal way. (R53)

Fig. 1 Sample Jamboard exit ticket

Fig. 2 Sample Bitmoji virtual classroom

3.1.2 Teaching Method

While the overwhelming learning for the professors in the shift from face-to-face to online classes related to technological skills and teaching tools, another very important result refers to the pedagogical adjustments teachers made during this transition. As one teacher stated, "there is a big difference between a remote and a face-to-face class, especially in relation to teaching a foreign language" (R53). This is particularly significant given the fact that language teaching implies the development of the four skills (reading, writing, listening, and speaking) as well as grammar, vocabulary, and culture. Therefore, this category encompasses a wide variety of aspects ranging from planning to delivery to assessment.

In terms of planning a lesson, professors identified that this process takes longer than that for face-to-face contexts because they were new to this modality, and, therefore, had to adjust most elements of the lesson to the new reality. This implied that teachers had to take into account the types of activities that would be the most effective in the synchronous and asynchronous moments, the time students need in order to complete tasks, the promotion of effective interaction, among others. One professor succinctly summarized some of these areas when he said:

> I learned that due to the difficulties of monitoring tasks online, pace and timing are really difficult to get right, and clear visual and aural feedback on all answers to a task is particularly important in a virtual setting. ICQs [instruction checking questions] are of course essential for checking understanding of tasks and when dealing with MFP [meaning, form, and pronunciation], CCQs [concept checking questions] and eliciting are also important. But I find calling directly on students helps with this. (R22)

Some technology-based strategies that teachers used to overcome these challenges included using Pear Deck, Jamboard, and Flipgrid as a way to create more

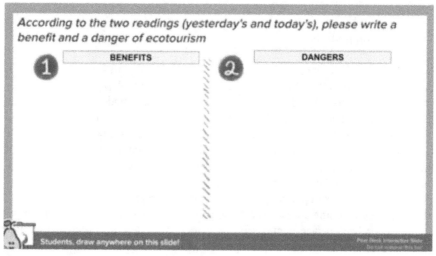

Fig. 3 Sample Pear Deck interactive slides

teacher-student and student-student interaction (see Fig. 3). This change was implemented because during class delivery, teachers realized that student participation was limited. For instance, some teachers wrote that they used Flipgrid portfolio activities, where students had to record a series of videos on assigned topics, watch a minimum of two peers' videos, and record video comments. Another teacher designed Flipgrid warm-ups to compel students to speak during every class. To foster student engagement and participation, another strategy that several teachers employed was to divide their class into two or three groups and teach each group the same content separately. This allowed the teacher to have more time with each student for instruction and feedback. Similarly, teachers used breakout groups when using BBCU and Zoom or created separate Google Meet sessions (where they would participate intermittently).

Furthermore, professors acknowledged some benefits of the online modality related to their teaching method. ERT pushed them to delve more deeply into students' needs and interests as a crucial element to be taken into account when selecting topics and designing activities and material since "it is necessary to think about each pedagogical event from the student's perspective, needs, and interests" (R115) to help "them be more active" (R72). Additionally, many cited that formative assessment was favored since giving personal feedback on students' written and oral production seemed to be easier with this modality. For example, some professors asked students to record their answers using Vocaroo (vocaroo.com) and would give individual feedback through this same tool. Google Classroom and Google Docs were also very helpful to provide students with feedback on their written work, especially through the suggestions mode.

Finally, other professors indicated that ERT allowed them to use alternative forms of assessment rather than traditional written tests. Teachers experienced a paradigm shift towards creating performance, skills-based tests instead of traditional multiple-choice, fill-in-the-blanks-type evaluations. Several teachers said that they had students read a text, watch a video, or listen to an audio text and respond to questions or record their answers. These oral and written responses allowed teachers to evaluate both the development of language skills and structure (vocabulary and grammar) and the attainment of the learning outcomes.

3.1.3   Contingency Plans

This category has emerged from a local challenge. As mentioned earlier, in our context, electricity and internet services are not fully reliable, affecting class delivery. Both teachers and students have reported connection problems and unplanned power outages. For this reason, a normal factor of ERT in this context is to have contingency plans in mind. Teacher 59 summarized what many others stated: "I learned that we need to have a plan B and C in case there are problems at the moment of the synchronic class. We have to understand that we could have problems in this modality" (R59).

These difficulties can manifest themselves in different ways; for example, students enter and leave the synchronous class because of the quality of internet connection, students are unable to attend class at all, or the teacher cannot deliver their class because of lack of electricity. This has caused teachers to innovate the way they teach. For example, some of the teachers maintained synchronous communication with their students through WhatsApp during a power outage. Others created self-explanatory videos, material, and guides so students could work independently and ask questions to the professor via a chat function. In spite of teacher and student creative solutions to this lack of stable service, this aspect caused a lot of frustration among them, so a significant lesson learned was patience. As one teacher wrote:

"we really must have patience and be able to adapt to unforeseen change. Expect the unexpected always" (R121).

3.1.4 Awareness of the Need for Clarity of Instruction and Communication

ERT also made teachers aware of the need for clarity when giving instructions and for continuous contact with their students. Face-to-face classes allow teachers to read the body language of their students; however, in online settings, and especially where students are loath to turn on their cameras, this does not occur. Thus, professors were required to use strategies to check students' understanding of what was expected from them. After being "bombarded" with many questions, one teacher wrote that she "learned that instructions have to be clear, more than ever, but in this process our students need to become independent learners if they want to be successful. Autonomy must be fostered, too" (R39). This comment relates both to asynchronous classes and to times when electricity or internet connection is interrupted.

Another aspect that teachers have noticed is that keeping fluent communication with students can be difficult. Teachers mentioned that students in class often do not respond to questions, answer emails, and/or turn on cameras and microphones, leaving professors with few ways to keep in touch with them. For this reason, teachers have become creative with their approach to communicating with students. Many have created WhatsApp groups, used social media, have contacted students' academic department directors, and have even called students directly on their cell phones in order to find out how they are doing. One teacher believes that: "it is very important to stay in contact with each of the students and provide timely feedback on their work as during these circumstances. This is the only way to keep in touch with them" (R87).

3.2 Humane Approach

The aforementioned areas related more to the pedagogical aspects of teaching in ERT. Now we turn to the three categories of ERT that teachers indicated having learned that relate to what we have termed "humane." To clarify this term, we refer to "humane" as the acknowledgement that particular aspects of human nature permeate the teaching-learning process, and, therefore, classroom decisions evidence this fact.

3.2.1 Flexibility

The first aspect refers to flexibility with students in terms of acknowledging the limitations that some of them had with access to the internet and computers and how this affected completion of assignments and class participation. Many teachers cited that they were flexible with both how students turned in their assignments and the due date as well as offering extra opportunities for students to complete in-class presentations or other work. In fact, the institution adjusted the student handbook to waive the attendance requirement. One example of this flexibility was allowing students to turn in assignments using whatever form was possible (e.g., WhatsApp, Google Drive, etc.) even though the LMS of the institution is Blackboard. A teacher summarized this idea when she said: "I learned that a teacher needs to be flexible with students with both connection issues and the deadline for assignments" (R88).

3.2.2 Empathy

Very connected to the idea of flexibility is that teachers learned to be more empathetic with students as they recognized the shared challenges that both faced. These challenges were not only tied to technological issues but also to personal and emotional aspects. Because of the pandemic, many families of the students were affected financially, causing students to be unsure as to whether they would be able to continue their studies the next semester. Also, because of the health crisis, some students and teachers became sick or lost members of their families or worried about the possibility of contracting the virus. This impacted the mental and emotional health of the whole academic community, which, in turn, affected performance in class. All these factors led teachers to develop a feeling of solidarity and compassion for their students. One teacher said: "I have learned that flexibility and empathy are very important in this process. We're all facing new situations, and some students tend to feel stressed and frustrated" (R48).

One of the strategies that many teachers used was to not ignore the crisis situation but, conversely, to open up opportunities for students to express their feelings during class. Some teachers allowed 10 min at the beginning or end of some sessions for students to talk about how they were coping, and others took advantage of writing or speaking assignments and geared the topic toward issues related to the pandemic (e.g., life of a young adult in lockdown; comparison of university life between 2019 and 2020). The benefits of exploring the challenges of the crisis in class were summarized by one professor: "I learned this week that the most important aspect of this amazing job is the human part. Giving students an opportunity to share their feelings and emotions was a great professional and personal experience" (R63). Furthermore, this showed professors that students highly valued this time and expressed that the language class became a moment in which they could address these topics, quite different from what occurred in their other discipline courses. The majority of teachers' reflections demonstrated that rather than complaining about their students (which teachers often do), they displayed a newfound growth of respect and care towards their students. This can be seen in the following statement: "Our students this semester went through something new and stressful during a socially stressful time. Truly, you must respect the students that made great academic efforts while there were so many things happening in their lives" (R99).

3.2.3 Support to Students

The last "humane" aspect that teachers reported relates to acknowledging their role in supporting students at different levels: academic, technical, emotional, and even economic. In terms of academic support, teachers saw the need to offer extra office and class hours for those students who needed more guidance. For instance, some professors scheduled short individual meetings outside of class time with students every 3 or 4 weeks. This time was informal and could be used however the students wanted: to just talk and get to know each other better or to ask course-related questions. During these meetings, the professors stated that they listened attentively much more than they talked. Tied to the academic support teachers gave their students is the technical support which focused on helping students learn how to learn in the online modality and use the educational tech tools. One teacher reflected: "These young people are not 'digital natives' but rather 'social media natives', and in this situation, it makes it necessary to teach them these skills, too" (R138). One unexpected response mentioned by several teachers was associated with offering students economic support to provide them with the internet service required to attend the classes, which was one of the major difficulties encountered by some students.

All of the strategies mentioned above resulted in students feeling at ease in the class not only as students but also as human beings. One particular professor said that because she had many first-semester and several international students, she knew they felt they were "missing out on what should have been a 'bigger' and more complete experience!" She also added that she learned "new ways to make sure they feel special even though they are not having the semester they envisioned" (R51).

3.3 Learning from Others and About Themselves

In this last theme, we highlight both the cooperative learning that teachers experienced as a community that was collectively facing a huge challenge as well as professors' self-learning, professional and personal, resulting from their own struggles in coping with ERT.

3.3.1   Learning Community: Support and Learning from Others

This category addresses the collective learning process teachers experienced during the crisis situation. Although isolated physically, many teachers emphasized feeling part of a community and supported by their peers and leaders not only in terms of educational tech tools but also in sharing successful strategies and materials. Much of this emerged spontaneously in the whole- and small-group faculty meetings when some of the professors aired their concerns. This motivated some teachers to take the initiative to make tutorials, design materials, offer webinars, and give individual support to help their colleagues. One teacher highlighted this in his response: "I learned that I have an amazing team supporting us, our leaders, collaborators that are very committed, and a group of creative teachers that have faced the crisis under high levels of tension and adversity with their best effort" (R70). This support could also be seen through the organic creation of several teacher WhatsApp groups which served as a way to keep professors connected and share not only concerns and successes related to classes but also the promotion of social activities. In the social aspect, many teachers met online to celebrate their colleagues' birthdays, to make brownies and watch movies together, and to have trivia nights.

Related to the academic aspect, teachers shared tutorials that they created of different educational tech tools, they asked and answered questions about technology (e.g., how to use Jamboard with Google Classroom), they reminded each other about institutional events and dates (e.g., grade due dates), and they shared academic articles about aspects related to ERT. This feeling of community and camaraderie allowed teachers to realize that they were "together in spite of the physical distance and that together, [they were] capable of supporting each other to face the new challenges [they] have been struggling with" (R66) and that "this boosted [their] capacity to respond to change" (R127). In general terms, the pandemic had a positive impact on consolidating a community, even between professors who had not met in person before.

3.3.2   Learning About Oneself

The shift from face-to-face to ERT also permitted teachers to learn aspects about themselves, both professionally and personally. Of the 141 teacher responses, only one was negative. The rest showed the positive attitude that teachers adopted towards this new challenge. Many embraced the shift towards ERT as an opportunity to develop themselves professionally although some mentioned that at the beginning they were anxious. One teacher expressed this idea by saying: "It was a great experience. At the beginning, it was not that easy but little by little, I learned how to use technology and this allowed me to complement and improve my teaching skills" (R93). Others recognized that the struggles they experienced were actually a moment for professional learning, as one stated: "I learned that although sometimes technical tools do not work appropriately, it is all part of learning and professional growth and that I will succeed" (R3).

In terms of personal gains, teachers pointed out that ERT allowed them to become aware of some personal qualities that they had not acknowledged before. Attitudes such as resilience, tolerance, "capacity to value what was essential in life…[and] the conviction of the need to move on with our educational mission" (R102) were reported. Another insight teachers expressed related to the importance of the work-life balance that is often touted and rarely put into practice. They realized that it was necessary to take care of themselves both physically and mentally during this time. One teacher wrote:

> We should think in terms of our students' benefits but also in our own welfare as teachers, too. The balance between personal and professional responsibilities. For many teachers, this topic is a challenge due to family circumstances and we need to bear this in mind when we create our work schedules and decide on our workload. (R117)

4 Conclusion

This has not been the first nor will it be the last crisis in history. Humankind has and will continue to endure health, economic, and social challenges that will bring about new ideas. Therefore, it is important to look for the *silver lining* from the health crisis of 2020. In our experience with the COVID-19 pandemic, in spite of the uncertainty and terrible events around the world, we were able to observe the positive outcome of both formal and informal teacher development in our faculty and their learning through the transition to the remote teaching modality.

When teachers were given the opportunity to reflect back on their experiences and learning during this shift, the overwhelming majority viewed ERT as a moment of growth in spite of the challenges they faced. They developed as both educators and as human beings. In the educational field, they learned how to plan, deliver, and assess student learning in an online context. This knowledge, especially with regards to educational tech tools and skills, is something that even when we return to the face-to-face modality, will contribute to more interactive and engaging classes. As humans, teachers became more understanding of what both they and their students were going through both personally and academically. This opened the door to more flexible and empathetic environments that favor learning. Another positive aspect was the fact that teachers came together as a community, and instead of having rivalries and guarding their ideas, they openly shared their expertise, insights, and even their pitfalls, all with the ultimate purpose of teaching successful emergency remote classes.

5   Food for Thought: Beyond ERT

This crisis has impacted higher education profoundly, causing institutions to rethink their whole educational model, their professional development plans for their faculty, and even the allocation of resources. While we believe that face-to-face classes are not going to disappear, as the result of the experience that institutions have gained, designing and offering virtual, hybrid, and online courses has become an achievable goal. Moreover, because of the pandemic, the negative perception of online courses (i.e., that they are of lesser quality; students do not actually learn) has changed, opening a new world of educational possibilities. In our particular case, before ERT, moving to online education was not a goal for the short-term but rather something we were planning for in 5–10 years. Now, this has changed. Based on our experience and what we have learned during the crisis, we have started to transition some of our programs to 100% online, especially courses for students who are completing an internship or are already working.

We believe that this "new norm" will require professional development programs to adjust to the new characteristics of the teaching-learning situation. This adaptation will not only involve pre- but also in-service education and should be broad enough so teachers can successfully perform in different teaching modalities. The PD itself should be a model of this transformation by offering a mixture of face-to-face, online, and blended opportunities. Also, the PD should not only focus on the technical aspects but also include other essential areas such as how to support students both emotionally and academically, how to foster engaging online environments, how to create learning communities with peers, how to pursue autonomous professional development, and other areas that will result from a worldwide discussion on the topic. This development should also raise teachers' awareness and allow them to reflect on the gains that they have made. Our department has decided to include all of the elements mentioned above in our professional development programs as a way to provide teachers with the necessary tools to adapt their teaching to the uncertainties of the future. Nevertheless, it is essential that PD continue to evolve to include the results of the research on the effects of ERT that are just beginning to be published.

We would like to conclude this chapter with the voices of two of our professors who have wisely encapsulated what most of the other teachers believe:

> We should not undervalue the value of virtual programs. This teaching modality works, depending on the tools used and the effort put forth [by teachers and students]. (R137)

> Despite the fact that remote teaching is a complex process, it is clear that traditional education has gained a new and valuable element: an infinite array of online options and tools that are available. (R141)

Now professional development will need to adapt and "catch-up" with the experience that teachers have gained through ERT to face the unexpected challenges that will surely emerge in the future.

Appendix

The following table is a summary of the educational tech tools mentioned in this chapter.

Technology	Description	Link to Website (when available)
Blackboard	Learning Management System	https://www.blackboard.com/teaching-learning/learning-management
Canvas	Learning Management System	https://www.instructure.com/canvas
Moodle	Learning Management System	https://moodle.org/
Google Classroom	Part of the Google Workspace. A type of LMS where teachers can create an online classroom, manage material, and create assignments	https://workspace.google.com/
Blackboard Collaborate Ultra	Part of the Blackboard LMS. Used for synchronous delivery of classes	n/a
Google Meet	Part of the Google Workspace. Used for synchronous delivery of classes	https://meet.google.com/
Zoom	Used for synchronous delivery of classes	https://zoom.us/
Microsoft Teams	A collaboration platform by Microsoft. Can be used for synchronous delivery of classes	https://www.microsoft.com/en-us/microsoft-teams/group-chat-software
Jamboard	Part of the Google Workspace. Form of digital whiteboard	https://workspace.google.com/products/jamboard/
Mentimeter	Tool to make interactive presentations	https://www.mentimeter.com/
Nearpod	Tool to make interactive lessons, videos, and formative assessments. Can be used with Google Slides	https://nearpod.com/
Liveworksheets	Tool to create interactive worksheets	https://www.liveworksheets.com/
Pear Deck	Add-on for Google Slides. Create interactive questions, formative assessments, reflection moments to presentations in Google Slides	https://www.peardeck.com/googleslides
ShowMore	Tool to record computer screen and audio into video	https://showmore.com/
Kahoot	Tool to create learning games	https://kahoot.com/schools-u/
Vacaroo	Tool that allows for voice recording	https://vocaroo.com/
Flipgrid	Tool to create and share short videos and facilitate video discussions	https://info.flipgrid.com/
Bitmoji	Tool to create an emoji and to make a bimoji classroom	https://www.bitmoji.com/

References

Avidov-Ungar, O., & Herscu, O. (2019). Formal professional development as perceived by teachers in different professional life periods. *Professional Development in Education*. https://doi.org/10.1080/19415257.2019.1647271

Baran, E., Correia, A. P., & Thompson, A. (2011). Transforming online teaching practice: Critical analysis of the literature on the roles and competencies of online teachers. *Distance Education, 32*(3), 421–439. https://doi.org/10.1080/01587919.2011.610293

Berry, S. (2019). Professional development for online faculty: Instructors' perspectives on cultivating technical, pedagogical and content knowledge in a distance program. *Journal of Computing in Higher Education, 31*, 121–136. https://doi.org/10.1007/s12528-018-9194-0

Caffarella, R. S., & Zinn, L. F. (1999). Professional development for faculty: A conceptual framework of barriers and supports. *Innovative Higher Education, 23*(4), 241–254. https://doi.org/10.1023/A:1022978806131

Cárdenas, M., Del Campo, R., & Nieto, M. (2011). El programa de desarrollo profesional docente PROFILE: Experiencias, reflexiones e implicaciones para el contexto Colombiano [The teacher professional development program PROFILE: Experiences, reflections, and implications for the Colombian context]. In J. Bastidas & G. Muñoz (Eds.), *Fundamentos para el desarrollo profesional de los profesores de inglés [fundamentals of the professional development of English teachers]* (pp. 135–167). Universidad de Nariño.

Darling-Hammond, L., Hyler, M. E., & Gardner, M. (2017). *Effective teacher professional development*. Learning Policy Institute. Retrieved October 15, 2020 from https://learningpolicyinstitute.org/product/effective-teacher-professional-development-report

Diaz Maggioli, G. H. (2003). *Professional development for language teachers (EDO-FL-03-03)*. ERIC. https://citeseerx.ist.psu.edu/viewdoc/download?doi=10.1.1.134.245&rep=rep1&type=pdf

Diaz Maggioli, G. H. (2004). *Teacher-centered professional development*. ASCD.

Elliott, M., Rhoades, N., Jackson, C. M., & Mandernach, B. J. (2015). Professional development: Designing initiatives to meet the needs of online faculty. *Journal of Educators Online, 12*(1), 160–188. (EJ1051031). ERIC. https://files.eric.ed.gov/fulltext/EJ1051031.pdf

Elo, S., Kaarianinen, M., Kanste, O., Polkki, R., Utriainen, K., & Kyngas, H. (2014). Qualitative content analysis: A focus on trustworthiness. *Journal of Mixed Methods Research, 1*(2), 112–133.

González, F. D., & Campins, B. B. (2016). La transferencia de tecnología en universidades Colombianas [The transfer of technology at Colombian universities]. *Economía y Desarrollo, 157*(2), 182–198. http://scielo.sld.cu/pdf/eyd/v157n2/eyd13216.pdf

Herie, M. (2005). Theoretical perspectives in online pedagogy. *Journal of Technology in Human Services, 23*(1–2), 29–52. https://doi.org/10.1300/J017v23n01_03

Herman, J. H. (2012). Faculty development programs: The frequency and variety of professional development programs available to online instructors. *Journal of Asynchronous Learning Networks, 16*(5), 87–106. (EJ1000093). ERIC. https://files.eric.ed.gov/fulltext/EJ1000093.pdf

Hodges, C., Moore, S., Lockee, B., Trust, T., & Bond, A. (2020). The difference between emergency remote teaching and online learning. *EDUCAUSE review*. Retrieved May 21, 2020 from https://er.educause.edu/articles/2020/3/the-difference-between-emergency-remote-teaching-and-online-learning

Montelongo, R. (2019). Less than/more than: Issues associated with high-impact online teaching and learning. *Administrative Issues Journal: Connecting Education, Practice, and Research, 9*(1), 68–79. https://doi.org/10.5929/9.1.5

Ragan, L. C., & Schroeder, R. (2014). Supporting faculty success in online learning: Requirements for individual and institutional leadership. In M. G. Moore (Ed.), *Leading the e-learning transformation of higher education: Meeting the challenges of technology and distance education* (pp. 108–131). Stylus Publishing.

Shelton, K., & Saltsman, G. (2005). *An administrator's guide to online education*. Information Age Publishing.

Velásquez-Torres, A., Palacios Sánchez, L., Denegri Flores, J., Lizcano López, E. C., Garzón-Díaz, K., Carreño Durán, C., ... Martín Saavedra, J. S. (2017). Desarrollo profesoral: Oportunidades y desafíos en la Universidad del Rosario. Mesa de trabajo Docencia de excelencia formación profesoral [Professional development: Opportunities and challenges at the Universidad del Rosario. Work group: Teaching excellence-professional development]. *Reflexiones Pedagógicas URosario, 10*, 1–8. Retrieved September 12, 2020 from https://editorial.urosario.edu.co/pageflip/acceso-abierto/reflexiones-pedagogicas-10.pdf

Watson, J. A., & Pecchioni, L. L. (2011). Digital natives and digital media in the college classroom: Assignment design and impacts on student learning. *Educational Media International, 48*(4), 307–320. https://doi.org/10.1080/09523987.2011.632278

Watson Todd, R. (2020). Teachers' perceptions of the shift from the classroom to online teaching. *International Journal of TESOL Studies, 2*(2), 4–16. https://doi.org/10.46451/ijts.2020.09.02

Part III
Teacher Voice: Teacher Identity and Agency

Emergency Remote Teaching in the Kazakhstan Context: Deprofessionalization of Teacher Identity

Kamila Kozhabayeva and Nettie Boivin

Highlights

- ERT caused teachers, even those who did not use of technology in lessons, to reevaluate the range of opportunities that applications, platforms and websites offer.
- Administrative communication lacked clear guidelines causing teachers in schools to become more independent and flexible in their approach to pedagogy during ERT.
- Complaints from parents had hindered the learning process as administration had to make re-corrections and accommodations for parents thus muting teachers' voices.
- ERT also empowered younger teachers to take initiative and search for non-conventional solutions in overcoming teaching issues.

1 ERT Kazakhstan Teacher Experience

The COVID-19 pandemic, which has affected 210 countries, is not the first global pandemic. However, it is the first to shut down schools and halt business and international travel. The national lockdown in Kazakhstan, similar to other countries globally, that took place during the first few months of the pandemic was unprecedented and forced teachers and students to implement emergency remote teaching

K. Kozhabayeva
LangLab Language School, Nur-Sultan (Astana), Kazakhstan
e-mail: kamila.kozhabayeva@alumni.nu.edu.kz

N. Boivin (✉)
Jyvaskyla University, Jyväskylä, Finland
e-mail: nettie.l.boivin@jyu.fi

J. Chen (ed.), *Emergency Remote Teaching and Beyond*,
https://doi.org/10.1007/978-3-030-84067-9_6

(ERT) (Hodges et al., 2020). Moving instruction online could enable flexibility of teaching and learning; however, in this instance, the speed with which the move happened was staggering and unprecedented. Unlike online pedagogy, emergency remote training forces teachers to suddenly switch student modes of social interactive learning. Emergency remote teaching occurs typically without any training (Hodges et al., 2020). Prior research has investigated teachers' reactions to the switch from in-person to online pedagogy, finding that they often resist changing their pedagogical approaches to integrate ICTs into their practice (Finley & Hartman, 2004; Garrison & Anderson, 2000; Pajo & Wallace, 2001). The main reasons for this resistance are lack of training, lack of support, and time pressures (Redmond, 2011, p.1055). The present report builds on this previous work with a focus on how the sudden switch to ERT affected the identity of teachers in Kazakhstan. Particular focus will be in terms of cultural and structural institutional identity, lack of resources and lack of communication as intersecting factors creating a feeling of deprofessionalization (Silova, 2009; Kassymova et al., 2020), a term that we will unpack below.

The sudden, unprepared shift of pedagogical mode from face-to-face to online created an extra burden for teachers, especially those in bureaucratic educational institutions in Central Asian countries such as Kazakhstan (Silova, 2009; Kassymova et al., 2020; Vaughan, 2020). A number of intersecting tensions – institutional, socio-cultural and historical – created additional challenges in ERT pedagogy for Kazakhstan teachers, including a paradigm shift in how they communicated with their students in online discussions and in how they designed online courses to initiate the act of learning (Redmond, 2011, p. 1058). Moreover, during the pandemic, the government provided little or no instruction for teachers and changed modes of assessment without consulting them. Therefore, the intersecting issues, which should be mentioned included lack of access to internet and resources, rural issues with resources; inconsistencies in a lack of appreciation for the constraints of ERT; communication and resources, which impacted and deprofessionalized teachers' identity.

This chapter provides a report from teacher qualitative interview data with seven teachers of different ages, from different regions and with different experiences. The lessons learnt from their narratives will benefit policymakers by underscoring the extent to which digital pedagogy is not equivalent to ERT, as well as the need for communication, flexibility and patience (Hodges et al., 2020; Earle, 2002). ERT teaching difference from online pedagogy. It is not just a matter of students using a different mode; it entails a wholesale reshaping of the understanding of learning. In the specific context of the application of ERT in Kazakhstan, this chapter explores which areas in current teaching practices need to be revamped, what types of online skills need to be relearned for ERT, what reflections and lessons learnt can be taken from initial setbacks, and how teachers can reimage their new forced online teacher identity. We recommend practical solutions to the issues of teacher identity, resources, communication, and regional and digital divides by addressing these questions: *(1) What factors affected teacher identity during ERT? (2) To what extent do uncertainty and rapid changes deprofessionialize teachers' sense of self?*

2   Educational Context in Kazakhstan

Kazakhstan is a trilingual, developing post-Soviet country. The educational context is one where government and administrative stakeholders expect to create an education system with standards equal to those of schools in the West. However, Kazakhstan education is still embedded in post-Soviet traditions (Zogla, 2006), and all decision-making with regards to curriculum, content, testing and assessment is made and communicated in accordance with a top-down model (Shamshidinova et al., 2014). One of the key aspects of Soviet and now post-Soviet education institutions is the bureaucratic, top-down control curriculum and expected pedagogical approach and outcomes which impact teachers sense of their professional identity (Shamshidinova et al., 2014; Zogla, 2006). Therefore, teachers have little autonomy over pedagogical choices (Shamshidinova et al., 2014). The culture in the local society has strong expectation that the teachers are regarded as responsible for a child's success or failure, and they experience significant pressure both from parents (to ensure that their children succeed) and from education administrators (to produce effective student testing results) Fimyar, & Kurakbayev, 2016).

2.1   Kazakhstan Context of Pedagogy vs Teaching Online

For countries with a teacher-centered and strongly hierarchical educational culture, such as Kazakhstan, online learning carries a stigma of being lower quality than face-to-face learning, despite research showing otherwise (Kerimbayev et al., 2016). Culturally, traditional attitudes towards teaching online is negative as opposed to face-to-face teaching. Fraillon et al. (2020) also investigated Kazakhstan and other country teachers' general attitudes to the use of technology in the classroom. In their report, more than two-thirds of teachers had at least 5 years of experience in using ICT during lessons or in their preparation. However, the majority of the teachers in the survey stated that they lacked confidence regarding the use of online discussions, online collaboration and learning management systems, and were therefore not well prepared for the use of technology in their classes. Other research has indicated that teacher self-efficacy (Bandura, 1997) regarding their technological ability deprofessionalized their teacher identity and influenced computer use in the classroom (Hatlevik & Hatlevik, 2018; Nikolopoulou & Gialamas, 2016). The development of teachers' expertise in ICT-related teaching and learning has been identified as an important variable in enabling their use of ICT and the teaching and learning of ICT-related skills (Lawrence & Tar, 2018). Confidence required familiarity with resources, which in some regions of Kazakhstan were unavailable.

Furthermore, online pedagogy (not ERT) consists of nine dimensions including: modality, pacing, student–instructor ratio, pedagogy, instructor role online, student role online, online communication synchrony, the role of online assessments, and sources of feedback (Hodges et al., 2020, p. 4). This approach recognizes learning as both a social and a cognitive process, not merely a matter of information trans-mission. For the effective design of a course of study, it is important that teachers, parents and administrators understand the purposes and roles of the different media and how people learn with them (Neyland, 2011). Realizing that online pedagogy is not just a quick fix of shifting online but requires time, planning, training and resources is relevant during ERT. Therefore, we will investigate not only the resources used but also the teachers' understanding of what is needed to move classes fully online in an effective manner. ERT forces teachers to utilize a different modality for teaching and learning interaction. Unlike online pedgagoy ERT is quick without time for preparation or assessment of teaching needs. Consequently, for teachers who come from a teacher-centered context their identity shifts. Kazakhstani teachers are traditionally used to having enough time to prepare mate-rials for student's learning. These aspects diminish teacher identity of being knowl-edgeable, completely in control of the class and all aspects during the lessons. Therefore, the move to ERT that is online diminished teachers' status and identity it deprofessionalizes them (Kerimbayev et al., 2016; Silova, 2009).

2.2   Prior Kazakhstani Teacher Views of Technology

A quantitative global study by Fraillon et al. (2020) investigated the attitudes of teachers and policymakers to teaching utilizing technology, in several countries including Kazakhstan. The results showed that a majority of teachers in Kazakhstan found that there were not enough resources, Internet bandwidth, computers for les-sons, software resources, or sufficiently powerful computers and IT equipment. This is in line with the work of local academics who studied ungraded schools. They found that modern computer equipment and the necessary technical support was unavailable in ungraded schools (one-room rural schools where all students learn together) and that teachers had not been prepared for its use (Kerimbayev et al., 2016). Moreover, due to the distance from other population centers and localities, and a lack of integration with other educational, scientific and public organizations, ungraded schools lacked basic technological resources (Kerimbayev et al., 2016). Therefore, access to resources, as much as attitudes to online teaching, is a factor in effective ERT.

2.3   The Urban–Rural Divide

Another challenge for some teachers forced into ERT was in rural areas there was a lack of infrastructure and resources as well as basic man power. Teachers dealt with students from the ungraded schools, secondary schools with a small contingent of students combined class-sets and a specific form of training sessions. Today, ungraded schools represent 70% of schools in Kazakhstan and are found mainly in rural areas (Kerimbayev et al., 2016, p. 444). Teachers at these schools had little experience or training in creating new online materials. The central authorities did not allow schools to choose texts, which were rarely updated (Burkhalter & Shegebayev, 2012, p. 64). Therefore, the Governments national edict of forcing a lockdown and causing teachers onto ERT created a situation of digital divide (Kamila can you find a source to cite). Those teachers in urban centers had more access to internet connection, resources and materials. Therefore, for teachers in rural areas the put on greater pressure and challenges that effected their ability to produce expected learning outcomes (Shamshidinova et al., 2014). Research has highlighted that most local teachers did not venture outside the chosen texts and rarely create or find material that better suited the needs of their students (Yakavets et al., 2017; Nikolopoulou, & Gialamas, 2016).

2.4   Aspects Deprofessionalization of Teachers

2.4.1   Bureacratic Institutional Structures

The post-Soviet education institutional structure remains anchored in a hierarchical framework that devalues teacher autonomy through a myriad of bureaucratic regulations (Bridges, 2014; Silova, 2009). An example of this is was the introduction of bonuses and performance-based pay. This system was designed "for disciplining and punishing teachers" (Steiner-Khamsi et al., 2006, p. 230), who are expected to meet standards set out by the National Education Department regardless of whether this is feasible with the resources available. Teachers are given very little freedom to apply their pedagogy creatively. This stems from initial teacher training, which is heavily situated in learning concepts with little consideration of their practical application. As Yakavets et al. (2017) noted, "theory is presented without much connection to practice. Teachers' professional knowledge is mediated by academic staff in a largely didactic style with little or no critical engagement or exploration of implications for practice" (p. 606). Furthermore, teachers in Kazakhstan are rewarded or punished according to their students' progress. The reward or punishment system is a throw-back to the old Soviet system as a means of motivating teachers to reach expected educational outcomes (national and international testing and assessment). There is a pervasive fear of failure and penalties for non-conformity that cannot help but shape students' performance and attitudes (Burkhalter & Shegebayev, 2012, p. 67). The bureaucratic nature of this education system and its lack of creative collaboration becomes more evident when an emergency forces teachers into a position where they must think critically and creatively. During the COVID pandemic, these issues were even more pronounced for those teaching in rural areas. **Therefore, aspects that impact deprofessionalization of teachers include institutional support and expectations, community expectations and expected communication from teachers.**

The aim of the study was to investigate aspects during ERT that impacted on teachers identity. More specifically, the study investigated teachers' beliefs in relation to two questions: *(1) What factors affected teacher identity in respect of well-being and mental health during the shift online? (2) To what extent do uncertainty and rapid changes impact teachers' sense of self?*

3 Methodology

This report used grounded theory (Glaser, 1992) and co-constructed positionality (Charmaz, 2011) to understand and unpack the ERT experience and its meanings for the participants. The methodological underpinnings focused on how the participants constructed meaning concerning the area of inquiry (Glaser, 1992). As we discussed above, the aim was to elicit lessons learnt from their ERT teaching experience during the COVID pandemic.

Recruitment of volunteer participants initiated with contacting of one gatekeeper who worked at the school. The gatekeeper informally invited their colleagues to participate. In addition, we published a post on Instagram that invited teachers from schools who worked during the spring term online to participate in a study on the experiences of teachers. The post stated that participation was expected to be confidential and that all interested individuals will be given further more detailed information. Eventually, three participants volunteered through social media and four participants came forward after being contacted by the other three participants. However, with increased workload of teachers had throughout the data collection process, three interested individuals had to withdraw from the study, as they did not have enough time to answer the open-ended questions. Therefore, we decided to employ as many convenient tools of communication as possible as long as they are helpful and help participants plan their time efficiently. The platforms used were WhatsApp video and audio chats, WhatsApp and Telegram voice messages, face to face interviews and phone calls. These were all utilized after gaining informed consent from the participants. We had to accommodate the needs of teachers as participants living in rural areas. This was due to the unstable internet connection in rural areas. WhatsApp voice calls kept crashing, thus voice messages became a more effective data collection method. This method of landline and computer voice messages was available to the majority of participants. It was also more convenient as they could answer the questions any time and at the pace they preferred. The recruitment post on Instagram was shared by teachers in their WhatsApp chats, which include people from different cities. We managed to find at least one representative from each area of Kazakhstan. In some cases, the participant who has already taken part in the study asked us if they could invite someone they know from another city because they thought we were interested in collecting narratives from different oblasts (administrative regions similar to provinces or states), so the participants themselves helped us receive a more holistic picture.

Table 1 Participants

ID	City, oblast	Subjects taught	Grades taught	Work experience (years)	Age	Means of communicating with participants
P1	Central, urban	Primary school (all subjects)	1–2	29	52	Face to face, Telegram audio messages, WhatsApp call
P2	North, urban	English, Chemistry	1–11	14	38	WhatsApp audio messages, phone call
P3	Central, urban	Chemistry, Biology	5–10	37	59	Phone call, Telegram audio messages
P4	Central, urban	English literature	8–10	2	23	WhatsApp video call, WhatsApp audio messages
P5	West, rural	English	1–11	5	28	WhatsApp video call, WhatsApp audio messages
P6	South, rural	English	7	2	23	Telegram audio messages
P7	Central, urban	English	8	1.5	26	Phone call

All seven participants are women; they range in age from 23 to 59, but most are middle-aged (see Table 1). All regions of Kazakhstan are represented (North, South, East, West and Central). The subjects taught by the participants include sciences, primary school subjects and languages (English). Most of the teachers work at the secondary school level. Each interview was conducted in the language, location and method of the participant's choice, and all the participants volunteered to take part; they provided informed consent and were free to withdraw from the report at any time. General Data Protection regulations regarding data protection and privacy were adhered throughout the research process. Data privacy was maintained by pseudonymizing the names of the participants, schools and regions.

To collect the data, we carried out qualitative interviews around the themes of resources, communication, time, professional identity and technology. Because of the COVID restrictions, there were no face-to-face interviews; instead, we used FaceTime, Skype and digital social media tools such as WhatsApp. In line with our co-constructivist perspective, we confirmed with the participants all inferences taken from the data.

The data were analyzed utilizing De Fina's (2009) interactional approach to narrative analysis, looking at the "befores and afters" of how the participants positioned themselves (Bamberg, 2011). The questions in the interviews were thematic, asking what participants to discuss the types of constraints occurred in teaching online which included but not limited to issues with communication, technology, resources and guidance from administrators. These areas of issues with ERT, were analyzed comparatively from the teacher's responses to highlight patterns. These patterns formed small story narratives, which were extracted from the interviews. We analyzed the narratives from reflections of aspects around issues in ERT that impacted teacher identity. These also informed our analysis of the lessons learnt.

However, as we analyzed the reflections and interview narratives we continued to clarify our inferences with the participants. Finally, we discussed with the participants what they would change for future ERT, what lessons they learned and what is needed for ERT to be more effective.

4   Findings

4.1   Access to the Internet and Other Resources

One of the main issues revealed in the teacher narratives was the lack of consistency in the resources used. Each state schools used different types of tools to organize an apprenticeship. As previous research noted, there was a variety in types of platforms utilized. Most of them used Google Classroom, Zoom, Google Meet, Google Hangouts and EduPage, and the MoE organized the main subject lessons for all grades on government TV channels (Kerimbayev et al., 2016, p. 450). However, our participants used Kundelik, a platform for students to upload their homework. Notably, not all participants had equal access to resources. So while some teachers did not feel the impact of ERT context others were forced to utilize any modality they could find themselves. Some (P1, P3, P4, P5 and P7) reported having to buy audio and video materials with their own money.

Our findings also highlighted the view of IT resources corroborating the conclusion of Fraillon et al. (2020) that "Older teachers felt less confident in using ICT and teachers who used ICT more frequently for teaching were more confident about using ICT" (pp. 179–180). As stated previously, familiarity is a prerequisite of confidence in the use of ICT. All the participants mentioned their fear or unease in relation to using new programs or websites. P1 described how many teachers who are also parents resorted to learning from their own children in order to teach:

> If it wasn't for my children, I would not have succeeded with saving all data ... my children helped me figure out new ways to save the materials I needed. It was very stressful and discouraging when I finally learned how to use Zoom and then we were forbidden to use it ... some random strangers entering the video chats and showing porn videos. I did not feel safe. I did not feel stability and confidence in what we all were doing.

The issue is a lack of the home resources and familiarity illustrated their need to practice becoming more proficient in digital technology. Teachers do not make a lot of money and do not always have computers at home. Therefore, teachers from the teacher-centered context of Kazakhstan were put into a situation of lack of access to resources at home and lack of familiarity with new modalities. Nevertheless, six of the participants of most understood the importance of technology during COVID. Six out of seven agreed that the pandemic had helped them to understand the importance of technologies and had introduced them to websites and applications that they could use to improve their routine work. For example, P2 and P4 shared multiple platforms that they found to save time checking homework and explaining topics.

Another issue with resources that arose during the pandemic but was rarely discussed is how to assess students. Although technology was already being used to support teaching and learning, the assessment aspect tends to be underdeveloped (Timmis et al., 2016). P4, a teacher who is also a class supervisor (within a mentorship system that has continued in the Kazakhstan educational system since the dissolution of the USSR), expressed concern that because students were not observed while completing their assignments, some teachers suspected them of cheating or using other sources. In response, they increased the amount of homework to help "minimize the damage technologies have done." Assessment became an issue as teachers grading is tied to children's future aspirations. Good grades directly connect to the status of the school and administration views them as a reflection of how good teachers are performing (Bridges, 2014). Thus, during ERT education officials changed how and when students were to be assessed without consulting teachers. This directly impacts the deprofessionalization of teachers as they had no control yet were expected to produce the assessment outcomes. Moreover, computer assessment is not traditionally a large component in Kazakhstan schools. In Kazakhstan, fewer than half of teachers were found to endorse the use of ICT in teaching and learning (Fraillon et al., 2020, p. 183). Our findings echoed this but with greater severity. Teachers complained that "students did not take the tasks seriously, as they initially thought that they could find answers online and copy and paste them to send to a teacher" (P3). Therefore, teachers had to contest with parental expectations, government expectations and students lack of interest in computerized expectations. Statements of this kind were made by the urban teachers in this report, who have better access to the Internet and online resources. Now we will consider the additional difficulties for rural teachers.

4.2 Rural Resource Issues

One of our main findings with the rural schools was a lack of communication and a lack of leadership awareness concerning the availability of resources for rural areas. The administration did not seem to understand that there were schools with no access to the Internet that were obliged to send homework to students via the post office. The fact was that many teachers are not familiar with or had no access to specific online programs for ungraded schools. The addition into the curriculum of online pedagogy did nothing to provide them with resources or time to prepare. Additionally, access to the Internet and online resources varied greatly between rural and urban areas. Therefore, simply asking teachers to move their practice online diminished their professional identity. There is a great deal more to online pedagogy and understanding of online teaching platforms than just knowing a mode of transmitting learning. P3, a teacher with 37 years of experience who lived and worked in a small village, said that the Internet had not been (and still was not) working in the village. To submit their assignments via WhatsApp, students had to walk to the single location with a comparatively steady signal. P3 clarified the situation:

> Here, having any Zoom calls or uploading homework to a server was never an option, so we knew we had to use messengers to communicate. I take pictures of the home tasks that I develop and send them to my students. I cannot even blame them in case they do not do them because there are families with four children and only one phone, so they have to make a schedule of phone usage.

A teacher (P6) from a slightly larger village with a better Internet connection, said that "this distance learning was like hell." In addition to the instability of the Internet connection, teachers had to deal with students' home Internet access as a recurring excuse for not doing homework.

In this report, when we discussed resources, we mainly referred to access to the Internet, which in some regions of Kazakhstan was minimal due to the cost and the national digital infrastructure. Therefore, the Ministry of Educations' declaration that all schools move online during the pandemic simply overlooked many parts of the country (Nurmaganbetova, 2020). As mentioned, some teachers ended up sending lesson materials to students on paper via the postal system. Others used WhatsApp, one phone per family, and this ultimately became the main mode of transmitting lessons and homework in rural regions, as P6 explained:

> I think the method with mailing homework to students was ignored by teachers. At least from what I witnessed. This simply did not make sense. At the time of strict quarantine, teachers were advised to go to the post office and mail the materials. We [P6 and colleagues] decided to use WhatsApp messenger.

This narrative illustrated how teachers were forced into the position of being problem-solvers. However, they had to solve problems that they had never encountered and were not prepared for. This impacted their feeling of confidence as stated above the situation was 'hell'. This feeling by the rural teachers impacts and deprofessionalizes their identity. In this case, teachers formed a group and collectively created solutions to their Internet and resource issues. However, there was another, even more fundamental issue that created stress for teachers: basic consistent communication and support for administration.

4.3 Lack of Communication and Institutional Support

All the participants stated that they received no definite information from the administration of their schools about whether they would have to switch to ERT (or that the information did not arrive until the last minute). There was a lack of clear communication from the MoE and from regional administrators. The officials would not clarify how students were to be assessed or when this would occur. Additionally, the government changed the assessment outcomes due to parental pressure. The confusion around assessment and curriculum was also due to uncertainty as to how long the lockdown would last and the extent to which it would interfere with regular face-to-face lessons. As P1 stated, in a view that was echoed by other participants:

I doubt they knew what to do themselves, the situation was chaotic. It was especially egregious for those teachers who had little or no computer skills. Or no computers. It seemed like suddenly our work and professionalism was dependent on something we do not have, so we felt helpless.

This 'feeling helpless' was an emotion echoed by many of the participants. Teachers who culturally work in a teacher-centered environment were suddenly left feeling helpless which impacted them and deprofessionalized their identity in the eyes of the parents. This feeling of confusion and helplessness lead teachers to seek out solutions by communicating with their peers. Shortly after the lockdown was announced, educators started discussions in unofficial group chats to share their plans and strategies for teaching in the new conditions. WhatsApp chats became (and remain) a helpful social media platform for teachers in Kazakhstan to share their concerns, ask for help and advice, and exchange websites and other digital teaching resources that might be helpful during ERT. Thus, teachers united to create a larger pedagogical network, adding their colleagues and acquaintances to the chat groups, and creating a snowball effect. As P3 explained, "Colleagues helped each other, the situation was critical, especially for us, older people, we were extra nervous."

Some of the nervousness was due to the confusion created by the national response. The national educational platform froze due to the exceedingly high number of users, and then numerous hackers attacked the online Zoom platform. Consequently, teachers were banned from using these platforms, leaving individuals to make their own decisions about what platforms they should use instead. These authoritarian directives without consultation with teachers, especially those in rural contexts, impede teachers from presenting themselves as confident in control teachers. This creates an environment surrounded by confusion where community stakeholders begin to view teachers as less in control. P7 characterized this as "a situation when schools were thrown into a fire," as all the websites and platforms became overloaded and teachers struggled to learn how to use new ones. Yet, P4 described feeling guilty for sharing new sources with colleagues:

I learned this new website for automatic homework checking, and another one for video calls with a whiteboard. Colleagues didn't want to learn one more – it was too much information for them, so I felt like I was annoying everyone with this new knowledge, and I stopped bragging about helpful websites.

The other teachers were torn between utilizing the new technology and doing it as they had before as there was little guidance by top officials as to the length or expectations. In part, as stated earlier, this confusion was due to top-down decision-making on most aspects of education (including pedagogy, assessment and curriculum). However, teachers were not only wrestling with new online pedagogical knowledge. In addition, teachers in certain regions did not have access to basic resources, forcing them to use their own money to purchase simple teaching resources, as several of our participants confirmed.

There was a lack of consultation of teachers in the ERT process. The lack of support and communication by administrators and government officials was compounded by community and parental communication.

4.4   Issues on Communication Impacting Teacher Identity

Communication around the shift to ERT caused confusion and frustration, not only with teachers but with families. The lack of clarity by the government created a ripple effect. First, the continual shifts in how ERT would impact students modes of learning, assessment and learning outcomes caused parents to become anxious. Testing and ranking of students and schools plays a crucial role in future employment. Students attending a good school have a better chance of obtaining a place at a good University and getting a good job. Therefore, the disruption in the school process for parents and teachers connects to future rewards. Kazakhstani teachers, who are usually the ones to disseminate the policies and knowledge to the families, were bypassed by unexpected statements made on national television about the academic year.

A notable difficulty was the lack of communication between main stakeholders and teachers. Six of our seven participants reported that parents complained about the difficulties they faced when their children had to report from home. Communication of this type included complaints to teachers and the administration, open conflict, threats to call the MoE, calls to city education departments and/or the MoE, boycotts of deadlines, and blaming the teachers. P1 shared a traumatic experience:

> Had multiple cases when parents called and yelled at me because they didn't know how to figure out websites and assignments, they accused me of being a bad teacher. I felt like I was failing. Some parents threatened me, saying that they have acquaintances in the Ministry and they can push some buttons. They mostly were frustrated with the fact they had to spend time helping their children, that their Internet connection was bad, and they blamed it on me … I felt exhausted … it's just too much of a stress.

Our findings make acutely clear what other researchers have characterized as "deprofessionalization" associated with teacher overload and ambiguity in relation to work (Goodson & Hargreaves, 1996, p. 18). Parents expressed their frustration by contacting both teachers and the administration to claim that "teachers don't deserve their salaries because they [parents] do the teachers' job, explaining topics and helping children with home assignments" (P2). Some even blamed teachers for a slow Internet connection:

> One parent recorded a lesson on a platform … the picture kept glitching. The parent posted it on the Internet to reveal "the quality of the lessons." Later, it turned out that the rest of the students in the class had a good connection and heard the teacher perfectly. But still I had an unpleasant conversation with the administration and had a panic attack.

In response to the volume of calls from parents, the education administration in various cities forbade teachers from setting deadlines for assignments during the spring term, which led to even greater challenges and workload for teachers. The removal of deadlines had a negative impact on student focus and comprehension of new topics. It also presented obstacles to discipline and time management. P1 reported several cases when, despite the restrictions and quarantine, teachers were required to go to students' houses. Although our participants stated that the administration had helped them with training in using websites, they reported that it did not support them when parents complained. This lack of support undermined their teaching methods (P1, P4, P6 and P7). As P3 put it:

> I just didn't know what else I had to do not to cause more complaints from parents, because it seemed that they blamed teachers for everything. Administration also said their traditional words – that we had to do our work right.

The teachers reported a larger workload, as receiving assignments by mail or messenger at all times led to irregular working hours. Six participants claimed that their working hours had been extended and that they had to stay online around the clock. Moreover, two participants revealed that they felt fear and guilt if they could not reply immediately to messages from parents or students. ERT deprofessionalized their identity, as they were expected to be in touch at all times: "Personal boundaries are being blurred, you receive homework 24/7" (P7). P2 explained:

> If I went to school to teach at least twice a week, I could have a smaller workload, not 24/7. Plus, teachers had to create and adapt sources to the students with special needs, because some of mine require more detailed instructions, so I actually needed to go through the lesson preparation stage twice.

The increase in online and social media (WhatsApp) meetings was detrimental to teachers' ability to separate their work from their free time. Thus, it created a situation where there were no boundaries between work and life, as P3 and P1 observed:

> My phone is always hot because I get notifications every 10 minutes. Children keep asking questions about homework or they send their homework and I can never say it is my off-work time. If I don't answer, then they won't do the homework.
> Parents think that we do not do our work as we do not physically go to school, so they think we have to answer their calls or messages right away.

Our data also show the influence of parents in modifying ERT requirements, with deadlines for homework and even some types of assignments (such as speaking and listening for English lessons) being abolished in response to their calls. This made teachers feel ignored and dispirited: "The requirements multiply, but no facilities for teachers and students are being developed" (P7). For parents in Kazakhstan, the legacy of the traditional knowledge-based approach remains at the forefront of the discussion about the purpose of education (Fimyar & Kurakbayev, 2016, p. 93).

Similarly, our findings emphasize how significant it was for teachers not to be included in the process of decision-making. All the participants reported that they did not support most of the guidelines and instructions they were given. P2 admitted feeling demotivated, as "they [the MoE] don't know how it works in practice, they have assumptions but they don't ask us. But we could really help!". This implies

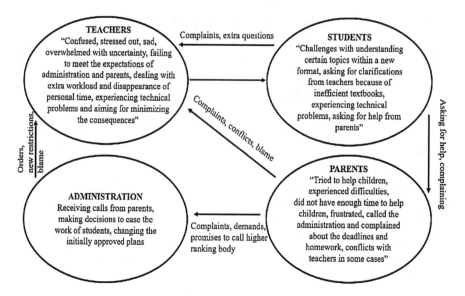

Fig. 1 Roles of communication in teacher deprofessionalization

that the measures teachers were being asked to take were unrealistic or inapplicable in certain teaching contexts. Figure 1 illustrates how the communication, assumptions and expectations from different stakeholders created extra challenges and stress, leading to teachers feeling deprofessionalized, but also how such a situation can be avoided in future with appropriate planning.

5   Discussion

Over the past decade, Kazakhstan has made tremendous strides towards adapting its education institutions to connect to multilingual and digital competences, with training and development of digital technology in some of its school systems. However, as discussed above, there is a difference between online pedagogy and ERT. ERT requires not only training and resources for teachers prior to an emergency. This understanding was lacking on the part of administrators and community stakeholders therefore an issue, which due to the punitive nature of the Soviet education system impacted teachers identity. Another issue Kazakhstan faces was that digital resources are not available in all regions for families, communities or, more importantly, for teachers. It is not realistic in this context simply to dictate that all teaching must take place online; resources must be in place for teachers who do not have Internet access. Therefore, the digital divide in Kazakhstan between well-resourced urban areas and under-resourced ungraded schools (that often have multiple grades in a single classroom and have no running water) creates additional stress and emotional burdens.

Furthermore, in the Kazakhstan institutional education structure, it is essential to teachers' identity that they project authority. A shift onto an unfamiliar platform with little training or experience has the effect of deprofessionalizing teachers' identity, causing them to lose their sense of worth in their ability to meet administration and community expectations. This created a lower self-efficacy (Bandura, 1997) Yet, redefining professional identity and teaching practices takes time. Without training, many instructors try to replicate existing course design and pedagogical practices when they move from face-to-face teaching to blended or online teaching (Redmond, 2011, p.1051). There were positive unexpected pedagogical moments that occurred during ERT teaching. One was the online collaborative community teachers created on WhatsApp. This provided a means to share ideas, practices and resources. Another was due to everyone being in lockdown opened a space for teachers to have more practical freedom with their practices. This occurred due to necessity rather than planned national policy. Finally, the inherent hierarchical education system was upended, allowing for younger teachers with digital expertise to have voice to train older teachers and provide their knowledge. However, the majority of recommendations from the evidence in this report focus on how not to deprofessionalize teachers if ERT occurs again.

6   Conclusion

The narratives from all seven teachers who participated in this report indicate that their sense of self-efficacy plummeted due to their poor access to ICT and lack of skill in using it. Their narratives illustrated how some teachers felt relatively empowered while those who were uncertain about digital technology felt "less experienced and less skilled" (P4 and P7) in the eyes of their colleagues. Moreover, emotional stress was generated from the pressure exerted by both parents and the administration. The evidence from the narratives discussing resources, access to and training on digital platforms, and communication throughout the pandemic illustrated how the stress created by these factors may have had a negative and emotional effect on teacher identity. As Meloncon (2007) argued, "If educators are changing teaching places, they need to redefine themselves in light of the change in landscape" (pp. 37–38). The abovementioned considerations are evidence of how lack of resources, inconsistent and unclear communication with all stakeholders, and unrealistic expected outcomes affect teacher identity in the form of deprofessionalization, and this evidence should be disseminated to policymakers. The recommendations from the teachers and the researchers highlight the need for governments, administrators and community stakeholders to communicate the challenges of ERT, to train and prepare proactively for future pandemics, and to create multilevel solutions that enable teachers to continue being professional and avoid feeling undervalued. Pandemics are expected to become more common, and therefore governments should prepare effective, realistic and flexible alternative pedagogical plans.

However, implementing the recommendations will require planning, collaboration with stakeholders, and open-minded flexibility in creating national ERT policies.

7 Food for Thought

7.1 *Understanding ERT vs Online Context*

Our first recommendation is to **raise awareness of the differences between online pedagogy and ERT**, as well as of the roles that administration, government and the community play in making ERT successful. Videos and radio podcasts and newspaper stories should be disseminated in advance of a future pandemic in order to communicate the fact that moving onto an online platform is not a simple matter of switching teaching modes. In addition, comparing international experiences of the difficulties that teachers and families have faced during the COVID episode of ERT will illustrate the realities of the situation and help to avoid negative and stressful teacher–stakeholder communication. It is hoped that such awareness-raising will enable administrators, teachers and caregivers (including parents, extended families and community members) to be more flexible in their expectations of learning and assessment outcomes.

7.2 *Communication and Realistic Expectations*

Our second recommendation lies at the intersection of communication and realistic expectations on the part of administrators, policymakers and families: **make administrators, governmental officials and community stakeholders aware of the challenges of online ERT**, which too often remain invisible. Specifically, a video of a day in the life of a teacher during COVID should be uploaded onto social media and online platforms, as well as broadcast on television. A clear visual depiction of the multitude of tasks, the excessive emails and texts from parents, administrators and students, and the challenges of planning, designing, and delivering an online class will help to raise awareness of the extra work teachers have been doing – especially if a clock is visible in the corner of the screen. A companion video should focus on the particular challenges and lack of resources faced by rural educators. The videos could be filmed on a phone as the teacher visually illustrates a daily interaction and overall teaching process that occurred during the pandemic. This visual evidence can then be used to alert government officials to the need to create alternative resources, such as a series of subject-specific television and radio lessons for use during a future period of ERT. It is important that administrators consult teachers in the creation of these resources to ensure that they are authentic, context-specific learning tools.

7.3 Throw Away Learning Outcomes

Our third recommendation concerns **flexibility in expectations of meeting curriculum learning outcomes**. Evaluation of learning during ERT should be focused more on the context, input and process elements than on the product (learning). Note that we are not advocating no evaluation of whether or not learning has occurred or to what extent it has occurred; we are simply emphasizing that the most critical elements to evaluate during a crisis are the urgency of ERT and everything that is required to make it happen in a short time frame. This is slowly being recognized, as a few institutions have announced a change from letter grades to a pass/fail system during ERT (Hodges et al. 2020: 8).

7.4 Plan, Plan and Back-Up Plan

Involve Teachers in Strategy Planning

As was suggested to us in interviews, teachers recommended "establish[ing] a mechanism that allows teachers to play an active role in planning the strategies of ERT," such as "a hotline for teachers that will both provide professional help and accept suggestions and/or complaints about the strategies implemented." (P2). Such a mechanism would ensure that policymakers take the voices of practitioners into account.

Improve Access to Devices and Internet

P3 suggested "establishing a system that would help families with financial problems borrow or buy gadgets to be able to report from home, as many students had to share one smartphone with several siblings." P2 and P4 reported that "schools borrowed PC computers and laptops from school computer science [departments], but there were only a limited number available." An initiative that P4 "considered effective was asking for help from local businessmen." One example is the project run by the Rotary Club Astana, which collected used smartphones, tablets and laptops to give to students in need.

Although finding ways to collect devices is useful, a backup strategy is still required for the case where none can be obtained. For rural areas, making more use of pre-recorded lessons on television and radio would help with the lack of devices. Even the schools which managed to secure sponsorship from local businesses to help students and teachers purchase portable Wi-Fi routers encountered further problems: in most cases, only the first month of the data package was paid for. All our participants agreed that "teachers and students should be provided with an Internet connection, so that everybody has an equally efficient connection." People living in rural areas continue to struggle with extremely low and unstable connections, despite numerous complaints submitted to the relevant government department.

Provide Appropriate Storage for Digital Resources

In school, most teachers rely on physical textbooks and discs containing audio and video materials. However, ERT put them in a position where they had to work from home with no digital resources. Many purchased digital resources themselves without ever being reimbursed for the expense. P2, P4 and P7 suggested "establishing a platform where all Kazakhstani teachers could access teaching resources." The platform, which could be purchased by the MoE, would provide consistency and access to resources. It could include space for teachers to share their experience, ideas and knowledge of websites and applications they find useful. P2 emphasized that this "would especially assist in adapting lessons and learning resources for the needs of students with special needs."

Appendix

Digital Teaching Resources

Digital Tools/ platform	Links	Description
WhatsApp	https://www.whatsapp.com/	An instant messenger that is the most popular in Kazakhstan. We used text and voice messages, video and audio calls function
Telegram	https://telegram.org/	Telegram is a freeware, cross-platform, cloud-based instant messaging software and application service. Telegram messages are heavily encrypted and can self-destruct. This messenger is considered as the safest one. We also used voice and video calls and voice messages
FaceTime	https://apps.apple.com/us/app/facetime/id1110145091	FaceTime is a proprietary videotelephony product developed by Apple Inc. FaceTime is available on supported iOS mobile devices. FaceTime video calls were used when there were connection problems and the speed of the internet was not enough for WhatsApp video calls
Skype	https://www.skype.com/en/	Skype specializes in providing video chat and voice calls between computers, tablets, mobile devices. We used it for the users who wanted to use their computers and not phones

References

Bamberg, M. G. W. (2011). *The Acquisition of Narratives: Learning to use language.* De Gruyter.

Bandura, A. (1997). *Self-efficacy: The exercise of control.* W. H. Freeman.

Bridges, D. (Ed.). (2014). *Education reform and internationalisation: The case of school reform in Kazakhstan.* Cambridge University Press.

Burkhalter, N., & Shegebayev, M. R. (2012). Critical thinking as culture: Teaching post-soviet teachers in Kazakhstan. *International Review of Education, 58*(1), 55–72.

Charmaz, K. (2011). A constructivist grounded theory analysis of losing and regaining a valued self. In F. J. Wertz, K. Charmaz, L. J. McMullen, et al. (Eds.), *Five ways of doing qualitative analysis: Phenomenological psychology, grounded theory, discourse analysis, narrative research, and intuitive inquiry* (1st ed., pp. 165–204). Guilford.

De Fina, A. (2009). Narratives in interview – The case of accounts: For an interactional approach to narrative genres. *Narrative Inquiry, 19*(2), 233–258.

Earle, R. S. (2002). The integration of instructional technology into public education: Promises and challenges. *Educational Technology, 42*(1), 5–13.

Fimyar, O., & Kurakbayev, K. (2016). "Soviet" in teachers' memories and professional beliefs in Kazakhstan: Points for reflection for reformers, international consultants and practitioners. *International Journal of Qualitative Studies in Education, 29*(1), 86–103.

Finley, L., & Hartman, D. (2004). Institutional change and resistance: Teacher preparatory faculty and technology integration. *Journal of Technology and Teacher Education, 12*(3), 319–337.

Fraillon, J., Ainley, J., Schulz, W., Friedman, T., & Duckworth, D. (2020). *Preparing for life in a digital world.* Springer International Publishing.

Garrison, D. R., & Anderson, T. (2000). Transforming and enhancing university teaching: Stronger and weaker technological influences. In T. Evans & D. Nation (Eds.), *Changing university teaching: Reflections on creating educational technologies* (pp. 24–32). Kogan Page.

Glaser, B. G. (1992). *Basics of grounded theory analysis.* Sociology Press.

Goodson, I. E., & Hargreaves, A. (Eds.). (1996). *Teachers' professional lives.* Routledge.

Hatlevik, I. K., & Hatlevik, O. E. (2018). Examining the relationship between teachers' ICT self-efficacy for educational purposes, collegial collaboration, lack of facilitation and the use of ICT in teaching practice. *Frontiers in Psychology, 9,* 935. https://doi.org/10.3389/fpsyg.2018.00935

Hodges, C., Moore, S., Lockee, B., Trust, T., & Bond, A. (2020). The difference between emergency remote teaching and online learning. *Educause Review, 27.* Retrieved from https://medicine.hofstra.edu/pdf/faculty/facdev/facdev-article.pdf

Kassymova, G. K., Lavrinenko, S. V., Kraynova, E. R., Gasanova, R. R., Kamenskaya, E. N., Kosov, A. V., & Gorelova, I. V. (2020). Modern concepts and archetypes of the management in education: Psychological, social and economical aspects. *Bulletin of the National Academy of Sciences of the Republic of Kazakhstan, 2*(384), 194–204.

Kerimbayev, N., Akramova, A., & Suleimenova, J. (2016). E-learning for ungraded schools of Kazakhstan: Experience, implementation, and innovation. *Education and Information Technologies, 21*(2), 443–451.

Lawrence, J. E., & Tar, U. A. (2018). Factors that influence teachers' adoption and integration of ICT in teaching/learning process. *Educational Media International, 55*(1), 79–105.

Meloncon, L. (2007). Exploring electronic landscapes: Technical communication, online learning, and instructor preparedness. *Technical Communication Quarterly, 16*(1), 31–53.

Neyland, E. (2011). Integrating online learning in NSW secondary schools: Three schools' perspectives on ICT adoption. *Australian Journal of Educational Technology, 27*(1), 152–173.

Nikolopoulou, K., & Gialamas, V. (2016). Barriers to ICT use in high schools: Greek teachers' perceptions. *Journal of Computers in Education, 3*(1), 59–75.

Nurmaganbetova, Z. (2020, March 31). *Kazakh pupils to attend online test classes Apr 1.* Kazinform. https://www.inform.kz/en/kazakh-pupils-to-attend-online-test-classes-apr-1_a3631674

Pajo, K., & Wallace, C. (2001). Barriers to the uptake of web-based technology by university teachers. *Journal of Distance Education, 16*(1), 70–84.

Redmond, P. (2011). *From face-to-face teaching to online teaching: Pedagogical transitions* [Conference paper]. ASCILITE 2011: 28th Annual Conference of the Australasian Society for Computers in Learning in Tertiary Education: Changing Demands, Changing Directions, Hobart, 4–7 December. https://eprints.usq.edu.au/20400/2/Redmond_ascilite_2011_PV.pdf

Shamshidinova, K., Ayubayeva, N., & Bridges, D. (2014). Implementing radical change: Nazarbayev intellectual schools as agents of change. In D. Bridges (Ed.), *Educational reform and internationalisation: The case of school reform in Kazakhstan* (pp. 71–82). Cambridge University Press.

Silova, I. (2009). The crisis of the post-Soviet teaching profession in the Caucasus and Central Asia. *Research in Comparative and International Education, 4*(4), 366–383.

Steiner-Khamsi, G., Silova, I., & Johnson, E. M. (2006). Neoliberalism liberally applied: Educational policy borrowing in Central Asia. In J. Ozga, T. Seddon, & T. S. Popkewitz (Eds.), *Education research and policy: Steering the knowledge-based economy* (pp. 217–245). Routledge.

Timmis, S., Broadfoot, P., Sutherland, R., & Oldfield, A. (2016). Rethinking assessment in a digital age: Opportunities, challenges and risks. *British Educational Research Journal, 42*(3), 454–476.

Vaughan, S. (2020). Exploring teachers' experiences of action research. *London Review of Education, 18*(3), 408–422.

Yakavets, N., Bridges, D., & Shamatov, D. (2017). On constructs and the construction of teachers' professional knowledge in a post-Soviet context. *Journal of Education for Teaching, 43*(5), 594–615.

Zogla, I. (2006). Leading educators' relearning in a post-Soviet country. *Theory Into Practice, 45*(2), 133–142.

Vietnamese Pre-service Teachers' Perceived Development of Employability Capital in Synchronous Learning Amidst the Pandemic

Ngoc Tung Vu, Hoa Hoang, and Thao Nguyen

Highlights

- SL, adopted as the primary teaching and learning method during social distancing and university shutdowns, is an engaging platform, but PSTs have never experienced using it to gain employability capital;
- PSTs' genders and years of college experience impact the construction of employability capital differently when they are exposed to platforms such as Zoom or Skype;
- Given the COVID-19 pandemic, SL can provide English-majoring PSTs with both career opportunities and challenges;
- SL continues to play a significant role in English language teacher education programs under globally pressing conditions, thus stakeholders should join hands to support students career aspirations and achievement success;

1 Our Initial Thoughts

The key goal of HE is not only to develop students subject learning, but also to enhance their future employability. These dual aims contribute to students' competitive advantages in their chosen fields of employment. These goals are consistent with the long-held missions of HE institutions around the world, who have

N. T. Vu (✉)
The University at Albany, SUNY, Albany, NY, USA

VNU University of Languages and International Studies, Hanoi, Vietnam
e-mail: thaonguyentt.hnue@gmail.com

H. Hoang · T. Nguyen
VNU University of Languages and International Studies, Hanoi, Vietnam

J. Chen (ed.), *Emergency Remote Teaching and Beyond*,
https://doi.org/10.1007/978-3-030-84067-9_7

133

determined that employability constitutes a primary dimension to assess institutional quality (McCowan, 2015). Since the world is embracing flexibility and mobility, the landscape of the international workforce should be able to foster "flexible employment contracts, multi employers, lateral job moves and multi career changes" (Clarke, 2018, p. 8). Also, the landscape of multilingualism and multiculturalism should fully allow global employees to fill job vacancies that fit HE graduates personal, educational, and professional goals. Similarly, the Revolution 4.0 has imposed an essential requirement for college graduates to demonstrate digital competence in search of employability.

In the context of HE, university students are believed to be exceedingly active in enhancing their employability, thus they adapt well to changing market dynamics. It is evident that PSTs no longer passively rely on their HE institutions' resources to gain employability skills. Instead, they fully engage themselves in what is readily available to them. For example, standardized university syllabi emphasize language competence development, information technology, and communication skills which are equally vital for graduates' employability. However, the global COVID-19 pandemic, with social distancing and university shutdowns, put everything on halt and created a huge challenge for their learning.

Working in Northern Vietnam, we found it would be very convenient to start exploring PSTs' narratives in terms of how they perceived the impacts of SL given the COVID-19 pandemic, which caused a shift away from face-to-face instruction and likely influenced their construction and development of employability capital. As discussed earlier, no general form of online education has been developed in Vietnam, and the nationwide deployment of SL during the university shutdowns and school closures was unprecedented. In this chapter, SL refers to the kind of learning in which "the instructor and the students in the course engage with the course content and each other at the same time, but from different locations [with the help of] live classes or meetings" (University of Waterloo, 2020). Social distancing and school shutdowns caused by the escalation of COVID-19 prevented HE students, including teacher trainees at the undergraduate level, from employing various traditionally face-to-face techniques to maximize their learning outcomes for their professional readiness. It is clear that the outbreak of the pandemic disrupted not only HE institutions' educational strategies and implementations, but also hardened HE students' schedules of study and work. As reported by the United Nations, many HE institutions around the world simply decided to delay teaching and learning activities because they had no desire to implement the commonly known SL or even asynchronously online learning – recorded lectures or online platforms (United Nations, 2020). However, Vietnam was very quick to adopt online teaching and learning, also known as emergency remote learning (Hodge, 2020; Milman, 2020), which is specific to SL via Zoom, Skype, or Google Meet (Van-Khanh, 2020). This form of SL used to be very unfamiliar to Vietnamese HE students in comparison to conventional face-to-face teaching and learning (Van-Khanh, 2020). In addition to the transition to SL, Vietnamese HE students in their final (third and fourth) years were prevented from participating in various academic programs, especially their teaching practicum or other forms of internship and extra-curricular activities. This may have truly accelerated their fears when imagining their future work positions. However, SL digital learning platforms (such as E-courses for language, disciplinary, and interdisciplinary learning to name a few) are immensely rich in terms of academic and non-academic learning experiences. Therefore, if students can be guided to make use of those experiences, their development may remain on track.

In this chapter, we aim to outline our observations of how Vietnamese HE students, specifically English-major pre-service teachers (PSTs) in their final years, self-reflected on their employability capital accumulation at the time of extensive exposure to SL in light of the global COVID-19 pandemic. We focused on the students in their final years of college because their personal commitment and career identities are believed to be impacted by SL. Pedagogical implications on how to successfully integrate technology and make SL more engaging and meaningful, specifically in English-major teacher education programs, are provided in response. The PSTs in their final years appeared to be insecure about their employment prospects caused by the global pandemic. We are under the impression that SL is more accessible and complimentary to learners, regardless of their backgrounds. Besides unexpected conditions, SL has become a preferred choice for global educators and learners because it can eliminate their issues related to geographical distance (including travel-related restrictions). The COVID-19 impacts on education are remnants for which PSTs will be responsible for when they enter their teaching professions. Our work was designed with implications in mind for in-service teachers' professional development programs, which aim to provide continuous learning opportunities. As a limitation, we do not highlight the pros and cons of SL due to its novel existence, but we do emphasize the critical shift in employability capital under the opportunities and constraints of SL, which students have been largely unfamiliar with.

2   How Can "Employability" Be Defined?

The global employment landscape has triggered the need for HE institutions to focus on developing students' discipline-specific knowledge and employability skills so that they can become, and remain, highly employed (Pham & Jackson, 2020). On the other hand, the Australian Department of Education, Science, and Training (2019) details employability competence to include communication, teamwork, problem-solving, initiative and enterprise, planning and organization, self-management, learning and technology literacy.

In addition to the aforementioned definitions, employability has also been seen under the perspective of "*a lifelong career.*" However, employability has recently been viewed as graduates' *adaptability* to change (Fugate et al., 2004). Therefore, graduates should have "career management skills" (Bridgstock, 2009). Evidently, to develop career management skills, graduates need to hold positive attitudes and behaviors. Furthermore, Holmes (2001) broadens the list of employability skills by combining graduates' forms of competence (i.e., personal identities that reflect on their lived experiences). This explains why Holmes (2001) encourages future research to include individuals of particular identities, values, and actions when it comes to explaining employability skills.

3 Tomlinson's (2017) Employability Capital

3.1 Human Capital

According to Tomlinson (2017), human capital refers to the link between graduates' knowledge acquired from formal training and the skills needed for their work settings. Based on this definition, disciplinary knowledge and skills are undeniably important, but do not adequately guarantee graduates' employability. HE graduates also need to develop various other skills (i.e., job searching, CV designing, interview skills) in order to develop human capital. From our instructional experiences, knowledge development continues to be fully possible through SL. Generally speaking, teacher educators and classroom teachers are still likely to develop relevant learning material and instruction while teaching digitally to meet PSTs' diverse needs.

3.2 Social Capital

Social capital is useful to graduates to navigate the job market. This element usually refers to building networks and interpersonal relationships with other people, as well as their awareness of what employment should look like. Social capital enhances students' human capital to meet the requirements of the labor market. From our personal views, the increasing use of SL (as part of emergency remote learning is helpful for students or fresh graduates to better expand their networks on numerous social-networking platforms. Therefore, educators of PSTs can show them how to use reliable sources to deepen their social circles.

3.3 Cultural Capital

Cultural capital is defined as an understanding of cultural values, behaviors, and personalities that align with the goals of graduates' desired careers. First defined by Bourdieu (1986), and then re-modeled by Tomlinson (2017), cultural capital allows potential employees to investigate and integrate some of the core cultural values of their future work settings. This form of capital also assists individuals to realize that work contexts possess unique cultural values and diversity that one needs to accept.

Culture can be greatly fostered in learning communities that are facilitated by online platforms. We are confident that SL is a community of practice where students that hold different cultural backgrounds and competencies can equally contribute to their learning and that of others. Active and passive students may struggle in different ways to engage in learning by sharing their perspectives or questions. Thus, SL potentially tackles some existing challenges, including unequal voices in the classroom and flexibility to facilitate personal growth and academic development. Inspired by Vu (2020b), constructivist learning is likely useful in SL to develop PSTs' cultural capital and intercultural competence.

3.4 Identity Capital

Career identity focuses on graduates' investments to build their distinctive identity for employability. The job market highly requires future employees to develop competence and interest in their intended professions. Therefore, graduates' interactions with others and their engagement in work contexts contributes to the development of their self-image and commitment to specific careers (Jackson, 2016). Understanding the role of identity capital allows graduates to work towards personal values and goals, as well as evaluate their suitability for specific professions. In line with their cultural capital growth, identity may be attribute to their levels of engagement and contributions in learning communities. SL critically inspires students to consider sharing their perspectives and to ask many questions without fear of being negatively judged or discriminated against. In a new technology-mediated world, students' identities are of paramount importance in the sense that they need to know who they are and how they can express their identity in an effective manner. Graduates who struggle to realize their identity can be placed in an inferior position, thus limiting their employability in socio-culturally rich working settings.

3.5 Psychological Capital

Fugate et al. (2004) finds psychological capital to be one's adaptability and resilience to handle changes and challenges in their profession. Brown et al. (2012) exemplifies psychological capital as a measure for graduates' risks in the job market, such as job instability or job redundancy. Graduates' high levels of flexibility, self-efficacy, and self-control help to overcome work pressure and withstand difficult conditions to achieve promising outcomes in their careers. Given the prominence of Emergency Remote Teaching and diverse forms of SL, students have increasingly stronger autonomy and agency to pave their way to academic success. Students require flexibility and critical thinking to maintain their psychological well-being and address possible mental disabilities.

4   What Have We Found Related to Our Work?

It is clear that PSTs can develop employability skills multiple in different ways. For example, together with their formal university training, PSTs can take additional courses on soft-skills or IT skills, and they can enrich their experiences with part-time teaching jobs. In addition to increasing their awareness of their beliefs, feelings, motivations, and pedagogical knowledge that drives their job performance, PSTs should also increase their self-efficacy. Colson et al. (2017) proved that colleagues need to adequately support PSTs, especially in the early stages of their careers, to strengthen their self-efficacy (Moulding et al., 2014). This is particularly necessary in teaching settings where students' backgrounds are very diverse. Coupled with a sound understanding of their internal selves, teachers should actively engage in exploring their students' cultural backgrounds while supporting their academic achievement, which has been shown by Vu (2020a, b) in the context of Vietnamese HE prior to the COVID-19 pandemic. Although they had a small sample of participating teachers, Vu (2020a) demonstrates that online training can benefit teachers to develop agency because of traditional geographical constraints between PSTs and teacher educators. Furthermore, Vu (2020b) points out that teachers' cultural knowledge and comprehension further expands when constructivist learning is incorporated.

However, due to social distancing and university shutdowns, the COVID-19 pandemic appears to have created huge challenges for all education programs, including teacher education and professional development programs. In conventional teacher education programs, students are usually trained with content knowledge specific to their major, teaching methodology, and educational psychology. Although, across developing countries, this training typically never occurs through online learning (either synchronous or asynchronous online learning). Growing concerns are shared by teachers in areas severely affected by COVID-19, where synchronous teaching and learning is employed on different platforms, such as Zoom, as it is replacing traditional face-to-face teaching and learning. This way of teaching and learning is very unfamiliar to most students in general, and teacher trainees in particular. Therefore, as PSTs were left with inadequate training for SL, which has been adopted due to COVID-19, it is meaningful to explore how they capitalize on their employability for their future careers during this unprecedented pandemic.

SL offers both students and teachers a number of advantages, such as real-time discussions, learning and assessment. However, in the context of HE in Vietnam, experience with SL is very limited due to Vietnam's low-equipped infrastructure, as well as socio-cultural acceptance. There is a body of literature that indicates a pedagogical weakness concerning SL (Le et al., 2013; Hodge, 2020). According to Hodge (2020), online education delivery is less effective than traditional face-to-face education. Similarly, Le et al. (2013) argue that online teaching and learning, including SL, "mainly stop at the level of using technology" and "no pedagogical strategy has been made specifically for Vietnam's higher education context yet"

(p. 240). On the contrary, the flexibility of SL proves to be essential for developing graduates' employability skills (Australian Flexible Learning Framework, 2009; Singh & Singh, 2017).

In Vietnam, the successful and timely adoption of SL during the COVID-19 outbreak has led many educators to emphasize the essence of SL facilitation in training the future workforce. Many educators and students have appreciated their first-hand experience in SL (Van-Khanh, 2020), and it is even reported that further adoption of SL in formal training is already planned. However, for English-major teacher education in Vietnam, there are still contrasting opinions about SL. Some have expressed concerns regarding the quality of teaching and learning throughout COVID-19 online learning due to its alienation to both teachers and students in Vietnam (Van-Khanh, 2020). Specifically, for final-year students, not only were their internships and practicum interrupted, but their scheduled transitions into the workforce were also delayed. Needless to say, these experiences are extremely crucial for them to obtain the discipline-specific knowledge and work-related skills they need for future employment, which SL cannot fully replace.

The current literature on SL's impacts on English major PSTs' employability capital in HE is still under preliminary research. This is especially true in terms of how PSTs in their final years of college may perceive employability capital differently, which directly shapes their professional knowledge, network property, teaching identities, psychological well-beings, and career-related decisions. We personally participated in SL as required by our schools. Therefore, our discussion is centered around exploring our observed PSTs' engagement. To unpack our participants' multifaceted reflections, we will focus on two aspects. First, we emphasize the statistical values of self-rated employability capital. Secondly, we focus on understanding PSTs' opinions of SL and its impact on them by examining their responses to interview questions.

5 Our Work's Engaging Method

Participation in SL, given the challenging time of the COVID-19 pandemic, affected our PSTs' perceived development of employability, including their career decisions and their learning experiences that shaped their future teaching identities. During social distancing, they were primarily engaged in Zoom meetings to complete their courses. Exams were still physically administered on campus at the conclusion of their courses. Flexible class participation was required, but they could utilize class recordings with permission from their instructors to review lessons at a later time.

To seek the answers to our questions, our sequential explanatory work included both survey questionnaires and interviews to inform our contextual educational concerns as teacher educators, given PSTs' recognition of changing capital in response to their participation in SL, which they seem to be unfamiliar with (Yin, 2009, p. 18). Our collected data primarily reflects our understanding and interpretation of Tomlinson's (2017) framework of employability, which we used to design the survey questionnaire before developing the interview protocol to validate PSTs' insights and generalize how SL impacts their job-related intentions and successes related to employability. We conducted random choice sampling, which was limited to the university where three of us were working at the time of research. PSTs participated in our study on a voluntary basis, meaning that their course completion was not decided by their participation in research. After consultation with experts in the field, we piloted a survey with 10 students to ensure the importance, inclusion, and comprehension of the questions. The survey (Link to the Vietnamese version of the English originality: https://forms.gle/8ZfhccGap69RqFdv6) included (1) *Demographic Information* which was used to gather PSTs' personal backgrounds, including gender and year of study, and (2) The *Employability Capital Questionnaire* to measure the PSTs' self-rated employability capital levels.

The Employability Capital Questionnaire consists of 29 five-point scale questions, ranging from *Strongly Disagree* (1) to *Strongly Agree* (5). The scale includes Identity Capital (6 items), Social Capital (5 items), Cultural Capital (8 items), Human Capital (5 items), and Psychological Capital (5 items). We processed the data using SPSS version 20. Based on Tomlinson's employability framework, five forms of capital were quantitatively analyzed in a separate manner. To ensure the reliability of the survey, we used the Cronbach's alpha ($\alpha = .941$), with each alpha value being .876, .749, .890, .898, and .873, respectively. The alpha levels showed that the overall instrument and specific sub-scales were effective and should be fully considered for data collection and analysis. Based on the survey responses received following distribution, we were able to use 168 out of the 250 responses which were considered complete, meaning that they did not leave any questions blank. Of the 168 students, 12.5% were male and 87.5% were female. In addition, 60% were third-year students and 40% were fourth-year students. The first author was responsible for the statistical analysis and the other authors designed the interview protocol.

A group of 10 out of the 168 PSTs were invited to the semi-structured interviews. This enabled us to develop our insights by including PSTs' explanations and examples of reflections on the underlying opportunities and potential challenges in terms of SL. To inform our insights correctly, the second and third authors interviewed the participants, and the third author transcribed the interview data before meeting to finalize the qualitative evidence. We will name the interviewees P for student participants, with a number to distinguish between one and another (P1, P2, P3, and so on).

6 Our Work's Valuable Findings

In this section, we disclose the findings which we observed from two sources of data. After revealing the statistical results on PSTs' perceived employability capital, we continue to develop our understanding by considering their process behind their survey ratings and unfold other interesting insights about their thoughts regarding how SL might impact their construction of employability capital.

We found that our PSTs were very positive about their employability capital while, to differing extents, still struggled with the impacts of COVID-19, and their positive attitude motivated them to enact a different form of learning from their usual preferences. We observed that their confidence was placed most on psychological capital ($M = 3.630$) and human capital ($M = 3.278$). Social capital and identity capital yielded the lowest confidence. In stark contrast to popular belief of Asian culture, participants were least confident in cultural capital, which we were eager to find potential causes in the interviews.

Not only did we see the degrees of teacher trainees' capital, but we also managed to unfold new insights about the impact of students' genders and years of schooling on their employability capital. In terms of gender, it was surprising that cultural capital was very different between male students and female students. Female PSTs responded more positively to their capital than their male counterparts ($t(166) = 0.213$, $p < 0.05$). In support of this emerging evidence, Xu and Jaggars (2013) shared a similar observation. However, it was contrast to what Tsai (2006) found, in a country with Confucian cultural heritage like Vietnam, females tend to be "passive, submissive and subservient" in their societies (Tsai, 2006, p. 473).

Between years of schooling, only psychological capital appeared to be impacted differently. We can conclude that the younger students felt more optimistic than the older students in terms of psychological capital growth given the exposure to SL during COVID-19. It can be explained that the former students may feel relaxed as they have more time to prepare for their career in case of prolonged challenges in relation to the new form of learning ($t(166) = 0.755$, $p < 0.05$). Similarly, Xu and Jaggars (2013) also suggest that younger students learn more effectively than older students in digital-assisted learning environments.

Interviews with the PSTs revealed that their perceptions of their employability capital amidst COVID-19 were generally optimistic. Almost all of the interviewees agreed that the transition was timely in regards to inclusive learning environments, where a few of them found themselves more comfortable in making their voices heard. For example, the use of flipped learning, which refers to prioritizing active learning during class time by assigning students lecture materials and presentations to be viewed at home or outside of class, allows students some required preparation, such as reading materials and even lecture presentations to be viewed beforehand, allows to benefit from teachers' resources and their exploration of knowledge within their fields of interest. Zoom meetings can facilitate engaging discussions, with students' utmost equitable voices to be heard. Similar to the perspectives of Luo et al. (2017), it is clear that digital-assisted and face-to-face forms of learning are likely to produce equal impacts as a venue to grow employability, even when threatened by the prolonged effects of COVID-19. For example, fully integrated synchronous learning provided students with an imagined identity as an English teacher able to manage many different instructional platforms (P3). Asynchronous learning, although less integrated than synchronous learning, trained student to become a flexible teacher in response to uncommon situations (P6). Asynchronous online learning required them to stay committed, as they are theoretically expected, to independent learning.

I was not surprised at the university's decision concerning online learning. I think it was a vital decision … [T]he lecturers created such a great atmosphere that we found no difference compared with face-to-face learning. Online learning encouraged me to study harder and to be more responsible for my own learning. And you know this could happen in the future, so I felt prepared. Maybe I need to teach online after graduating. Who knows? (P3)

[M]y sense of adaptability has been much improved. I was actually trained to be active in response to the unexpected incidents. (P6)

The same two participants (P3 & P6) also discovered that they benefitted psychologically, which we found was comprehensively aligned with the numerical data (in the beginning of this section). However, this considerably contrasts from our expectations in terms of their personal identities as teachers due to foreseeable obstacles caused by COVID-19. We argue that COVID-19 began at a point of time when the new generations of teachers should have been concerned with their dynamically changing identities, under which they may need to apply a wide assortment of culturally responsive pedagogies. This important insight is a basis to be further explored in the interviews, including uncovering participants' thinking and planning, which has also been questioned by Moulding et al. (2014). Furthermore, our quantitative data findings support that the relatively equal values of social, cultural, and identity can be seen as interconnected. This is a good direction for research in this field, as advised by Pham et al. (2019). However, we were primarily motivated to explore the low level of human capital. While we assumed it would be the highest ranked value among the five forms of capital, the interviews offer promising fresh insights.

We found that having access to SL during COVID-19 greatly enhanced PSTs' confidence in a way that they increased their understanding about who they are and who they want to become. However, despite their obvious confidence being boosted within this tentative period, they were worried about the global pandemic. PSTs needed to test their abilities to react to presenting obstacles, as well as other unimaginable incidents in the future. Learning experiences during this challenging time were unforgettable for the PSTs, as they positively shaped their teaching identities. Their positive increases in psychological capital were a direct consequence of their growth within their majors. For example, internet platforms offered free advice on where to find informative online sources. PSTs' career and social development improved significantly, especially given their access to supplementary subjects (e.g., *Translating and Interpreting, International Studies* and *Educational Management*). Before the pandemic, universities tended to integrate these courses into teacher education programs because they wanted to encourage PSTs to expand their professional identities and cultural communities. The following is what we have heard from the PSTs:

Synchronous online learning offered me some more space to understand myself and explore my strengths and weaknesses. I realized that I had to be responsible for my own learning, believing that some actions need[ed] to be taken. Because I was in this critical time, I need[ed] to keep myself self-motivated and open to what may happen in the future. That's why I feel I need to be always prepared. If I am to be an English teacher, I might need to teach online. Who knows? (P3)

Although I haven't decided yet what career path to take, I have tried to integrate this [discipline-specific] knowledge in order to achieve access in some part-time jobs, such as tutoring, event organizing. (P4)

In recognition that PSTs' employability can benefit from developing social capital, cultural capital, and identity capital, SL was found to be the primary factor that informed their rapports with peers. To develop social capital, they mentioned that:

In the time of online learning, many of the assessment tasks were changed, which required us to work more online. Therefore, we, my group mates and I, texted and chatted all the time. So I feel we have become closer to each other. (P3)

Besides social capital, Tomlinson (2017) recommends that graduates should understand their cultural capital (such as values, behaviors, and personalities) in order to immerse themselves in their future workplaces, hence maximizing graduates' career prospects. To explore the growth of cultural capital given limited physical interactions, participants still expected to be given a fair sense of their future working environments (e.g., language centers, higher education institutions, K-12 schools), regardless of the delivery mode. Even after a period of suspended online learning, PSTs were aware that online delivery will become more popular, even after the COVID-19 pandemic, from partial to complete transition to synchronous online learning due to its operational cost reduction and the convenience to learners from diverse backgrounds. These back-and-forth movements present an opportunity for PSTs to familiarize themselves with future career-related challenges to practice adaptability, similar to pre-service teachers having to adapt to newer forms of learning that they struggle with early on (Vu, 2020b). One convincing reflection was that:

[SL], with certain Zoom or Skype technology, encouraged me to study more and to become more responsible for my own learning. And you know this can happen in the future, so I feel prepared. Maybe I need to teach virtually after graduating. Who knows? (P3)

According to Jackson (2016), identity capital refers to graduates' self-image and their unique features that help them define their strengths and weaknesses to formulate their sense of self and who they want to become. Thus, they can mediate their future success in the workforce. Based on these arguments, we believe it is important to recognize that the PSTs shared what they actually gained during mandated social distancing and the implementation of SL. A majority of interviewees admitted that they learned to become who they are and what they need to do in pursuit of their career prospects. Third-year teacher trainees, although having no serious thought about their teaching careers, still considered how this global crisis could trigger technologically-purposeful changes within their careers. Otherwise, they considered themselves as inferior players in their communities of practice. This point is supported by Vu (2020a). One student participant discussed that:

I used to consider English as a doorway to go abroad or to make friends with foreigners, so I decided to choose this university for that naked reason ... I have been trying many different types of jobs, such as tutoring, teaching assistant, translating and interpreting... During the time I learned remotely, I spent more time working on my own and I feel a sudden urge to work something else. (P1)

Meanwhile, one student was happy that their exposure to optional courses motivated them to explore additional employment options besides being an English teacher.

> With what I have been trained for, after graduation, I can work for a range of firms, all of which sounds very appealing to me. Also, I am attracted by the fact that there is non-traditional content and tasks, from the discipline-specific knowledge to creative assessments. (P2)

When it comes to human capital, it was observed that online learning was a powerful way to help students develop many skills, such as collaborating, presenting, and IT.

> Online learning helps boost my IT skills a lot, [...] like searching for information, or using google drive, word processing software such as Word, Excel, PowerPoint. Moreover, my teamwork skills are also improved. (P9)

Interviewees reported that they needed to be actively engaged in other forms of learning, such as university events or clubs, which were temporarily virtual, to help themselves avoid the unnecessary burden of stress as a result of physical isolation. Our findings suggested they were likely to rely on extra-curricular activities or short-term courses to learn soft skills, such as communication and teamwork. We also found that the PSTs' sense of adaptability significantly improved, thus positively contributing to their future teaching roles. A few others also worked part-time as tutors or teaching assistants in commercial language centers as a way to utilize their English language competence and to support their monthly expenses. While some students above indicated positive aspects of their engagement in SL, a few others were discouraged because of their unmet expectations of online learning compared to traditional learning. For example, besides poor internet connection (P2 & P7), another student participant thought that SL was not effective due to health-related effects caused by long hours using smart devices. This led him to believe that in order to become an effective online teacher and instructor, he needed to consider a wide range of issues so that his students would not be poorly affected as he suffered. He said that:

> I don't like working with computers, but during the time I learned online, I had to use it all day long .... I believe my health was badly affected, especially my eyes. I always felt tired. (P4)

Another student also shared concerns regarding SL in relation to his readiness to prepare for participation in online learning. For example, he was worried about how to take effective notes from the lectures in a virtual classroom, or how to manage time for different tasks and assignments. Therefore, without willingness and adaptability from both English teachers and students, their relationships may be ruptured, which then triggers failure to succeed. Some argued that:

> Vietnam education is not yet accustomed to online learning, so both lecturers and students were confused, especially with the bulky administration and logistics concerning online learning. (P6).

It was hard to concentrate on the lecture when I learned online. I confessed that sometimes I was cooking while still learning online. (P9)

Finally, SL urged PSTs to reshape their learning habits so that all of the afore-mentioned worries they shared were gradually solved:

My learning habit[s] changed in the time of online learning (P3)

This is believed to be the earliest signal of PSTs' adaptability to the unprecedented learning experience.

7   Our Work's Valuable Contribution

Based on what we observed from the survey results and interviews with the PSTs, we are able to reveal several insights. Beginning with psychological capital, we recognized that the PSTs felt privileged to have increased their sense of confidence through synchronous online learning. In addition to their acceptance of a new platform of learning, they happily found new insights into teaching, shaping them as well-educated educators and interdisciplinary instructors. Within their own space to access endless online resources and online academic advising, they improved their knowledge within their English-major discipline and other social fields. Hence, they were in favor of these learning opportunities and had positive feelings, beliefs, and motivations towards their experiences. We interpret that the global pandemic required us all to personally reflect more than ever. Thus, in addition to holding sufficient knowledge and skills on educational pedagogies, as suggested by Shulman (1986), and technological skills, as suggested by Rienties et al. (2012), they should also hold strong entrepreneurial skills (Adeyemo, 2009). Those who have sufficient entrepreneurial skills are competent at having "self-belief, boldness, tenacity, passionate, empathy, readiness to take expert advice, desire for immediate result, visionary, and ability to recognize opportunity" (Salgado-banda, 2005, as cited in Adeyemo, 2009, p. 59). From another perspective, Colson et al. (2017) mentions that teacher beliefs can shape their behaviors, meaning that they will be willing to engage in various other supporting areas of knowledge to make their future classes more engaging and motivating.

In response to the transition to SL given the COVID-19 pandemic, we realized that PSTs closely considered how to actively develop their social networks. That is, this transition represented a typical crisis that prevented them from physically participating in their communities. Without taking any social action, it is likely that they will fail to seek their desired careers. Although students did not claim growth of their social networks in the present situational constraints, experiential learning, as proposed by Yip et al. (2019), can close social inequalities among students and welcome students' voices regardless of how teaching and learning are mediated (i.e., offline or online). While a few students noticed that they needed to be critical thinkers to approach this compulsory change, a few others were challenged to adapt to this new learning culture – which was stimulated by online learning rather than traditional face-to-face learning. Students faced challenges which might be caused by their lack of initial experiences and hands-on skills in online learning. Therefore, they felt that their reach of future careers was threatened regardless of the fact that they were found to competently utilize other forms of capital to fuel their weaker capital.

We come to recognize that PSTs' motivations can shape their identities, meaning that motivations inform their decisions. Among PSTs in Vietnam, besides their peers or colleagues, families have more tendencies to get involved in planning for their children's future careers within Asian culture. Also, in light of the virtual interactions, the support of social networking sites works effectively to greatly improve people's lives. Several communication tools have been developed to make up for the negative impacts of the pandemic. Exploration via digital platforms, plus work-from-home requirements, can provide PSTs with more time and effort to maximize their flexibility and creativity. Accompanied by these positive changes, we strongly believe that education will reach a new era of innovation and success. As the pandemic accelerates, and is not expected to resume to normal conditions in the near future, the promotion of SL was similarly adopted to facilitate the continuation of learning for the sake of PSTs' competence which combines knowledge and skills. We also discovered that as they virtually attended their lecturers, they learned to conduct synchronous online instruction effectively. They can also apply this to their part-time job roles, which are performed remotely as teachers and students. As English language education is primarily facilitated in online environments during the current times, PSTs can search for domestic or overseas part-time jobs to gain introductory experience in (a)synchronous online teaching, which can help to develop their competence for their careers.

Since we imagine extended development of SL to take place around the world as COVID-19 remains prominent, SL and accompanied learning activities are popular options for those who are comfortable with these newly adopted preferences. This finding is relevant to Sekiguchi (2012) and Tran et al. (2019), who showed that part-time jobs contribute to PSTs' work-related learning, with particular regards to specialized teaching knowledge and skills. Because Tran et al. (2019) add that the part-time jobs can help PSTs develop their social networks, human capital, and quickly adapt to their future work cultures, it can be beneficial to also further explore the other forms of capital. Also, because of the dominant use of face-to-face learning in Vietnam, PSTs should be increasingly aware of their future students' willingness and adaptability to succeed in online learning (Dang, 2010; Ha & Lam, 2010; Humphreys & Wyatt, 2014).

8   Our Concluding Remarks

Our work explored English-major PSTs' self-perceptions on their experience of the transition to SL in a wake of the pandemic outbreak. According to Tomlinson's (2017) framework of employability capital, five forms of capital are intertwined and mutually impacted. Firstly, it was observed that psychological capital was rated the highest, while human capital was the lowest, but all forms were generally rated positively. These rating values mean that the PSTs were very positive about the transition to synchronous online learning, particularly with its impact on their employability capital. Also, consistent with the previous literature (Pham et al., 2019), it was seen that social, cultural, and identity capital tended to be closely interactive, with those ratings being relatively similar. In the context of Vietnamese education, where this study took place, the adoption of SL was unexpected, but greatly benefitted HE English-major PSTs to develop their (non-)academic competencies, social networks, cultural recognition, professional identities, and psychological motivations.

Our work holds multiple limitations. Since we decided to cover a small educational context that was relevant to our experiences and we were familiar with the students, it is necessary that we continue to explore other settings across Vietnam. Therefore, we suggest that future studies are carried out in a broader and more longitudinal manner to allow English-major teacher trainees to fully engage in this form of learning, and to closely examine their formation of each capital type and the inextricable relationships between forms of capital. The most significant observation, as confirmed by Pham et al. (2019), was about the relationship between social capital, cultural capital and identity capital, but this observation needs to be validated by more quantitative and qualitative data.

9   Food for Thought

- SL should be prioritized in a balanced manner for teacher education programs, as a means to help PSTs' survive the world's competitive teaching industries.
- SL can be considered an alternative to face-to-face teaching conventions and still be effective to develop PSTs' employability capital.
- SL can support PSTs' development of professional competence, unlock their restricted social networks, build their sense of acculturation, strengthen psychological well-being, and inform their personal and professional identities;
- SL can enable PSTs to adapt to the foreseeable challenges for their future jobs by critically and flexibly thinking about solutions rather than accepting the problem itself.

Appendix A: Digital Platforms

Digital platforms	How they are embedded in the study?
Zoom (https://zoom.us)	Zoom is a product of an American communication enterprise, which offers tools that assist multiple purposes. For education specifically, video chat and online text services make it suitable for synchronous online learning
Google Docs (https://docs.google.com)	Google Docs is a free-of-charge service provided by Google, which is a online word processor which can be accessed and updated online in a convenient fashion for users wishing to collaborate on a shared file
Kahoot! (https://kahoot.it)	Kahoot! Is a game-based platform that supports educational activities and can serve a large number of students at the same time. Multiple-choice quizzes can be utilized via web browser or device app (e.g., laptops, smart phones or tablets)
Skype (https://www.skype.com/en/)	Similar to Zoom, Skype is a telecommunication application to be used by computers, laptops, tablets or smart phones, which fully supports synchronous online teaching and learning by enabling telecommunications (including calls or texts) between learners regardless of their geographical locations

References

Adeyemo, S. A. (2009). Understanding and acquisition of entrepreneurial skills: A pedagogy re-orientation for classroom teacher in Science education. *Journal of Turkish Science Education, 6*(3), 57–65.

Australia Department of Education, Science, and Training. (2019). *Science, technology, engineering and mathematics: Australia's future.* https://www.chiefscientist.gov.au/2014/09/professor-chubb-releases-science-technology-engineering-and-mathematics-australiasfuture. Accessed 10 Jan 2019.

Australian Flexible Learning Framework. (2009). *The impact of E-learning on employability skills: Final report.* Australian Government: Department of Education, Employment and Workplace Relation.

Bourdieu, R. (1986). Forms of capital. In J. G. Richardson (Ed.), *Handbook of theory and research for the sociology of education* (pp. 241–259). Greenwood Press.

Bridgstock, R. (2009). The graduate attributes we've overlooked: Enhancing graduate employability through career management skills. *Higher Education Research & Development, 28*(1), 31–44. https://doi.org/10.1090/07294360802444347

Brown, A., Bimrose, J., Barnes, S.-A., & Hughes, D. (2012). The role of career adaptabilities for mid-career changers. *Journal of Vocational Behavior, 80*(3), 754–761. https://doi.org/10.1060/j.jvb.2012.01.003

Clarke, M. (2018). Rethinking graduate employability: The role of capital, individual attributes and context. *Studies in Higher Education, 43*(11), 1923–1937. https://doi.org/10.1080/0307507 9.2017.1294152

Colson, T., et al. (2017). Pre-service teachers and self-efficacy: A study in contrast. *Discourse and Communication for Sustainable Education, 8*(2), 66–76. https://doi.org/10.1515/dcse-2017-0016

Dang, T. T. (2010). Learner autonomy in EFL studies in Vietnam: A discussion from a sociocultural perspective. *English Language Teaching, 3*(2), 3–9. https://eric.ed.gov/?id=EJ1081573

Fugate, M., Kinicki, A. J., & Ashforth, B. E. (2004). Employability: A psycho-social construct, its dimensions, and applications. *Journal of Vocational Behavior, 65*(1), 14–38. https://doi.org/10.1017/j.jvb.2003.10.005

Ha, N. T., & Lam, H. T. G. (2010). How to foster learner autonomy in country studies at the faculty of English—Hanoi National University of Education? *VNU Journal of Science, Foreign Languages, 26*, 239–245.

Hodge, R. (2020). *Using zoom while working from home? Here are the privacy risks to watch out for*. CNET, 2 April. https://www.cnet.com/news/using-zoom-while-working-from-home-here-are-the-privacy-risks-to-watch-out-for/. Accessed 28 Aug 2020.

Holmes, L. (2001). Reconsidering graduate employability: The 'graduate identity' approach. *Quality in Higher Education, 7*(2), 111–119.

Humphreys, G., & Wyatt, M. (2014). Helping Vietnamese university learners to become more autonomous. *ELT Journal, 68*(1), 52–63. https://doi.org/10.1093/elt/cct056

Jackson, D. (2016). Re-conceptualising graduate employability: The importance of pre-professional identity. *Higher Education Research & Development, 35*(5), 925–939. https://doi.org/10.1080/07294360.2016.1139551

Le, L. D., Tran, H. V., & Hunder, A. (2013). Developing active collaborative e-learning framework for Vietnam's higher education context. In M. Ciusi & M. Augie (Eds.), *Proceedings of the 12th European conference on e-Learning ECEL 2013* (Vol. 1, pp. 240–249).

Luo, T., Hubbard, L., Franklin, T., & Moore, D. R. (2017). Preparing teacher candidates for virtual field placements via an exposure to K-12 online teaching. *Journal of Information Technology Education: Research, 16*, 1–14. https://digitalcommons.odu.edu/stemps_fac_pubs/24

McCowan, T. (2015). Should universities promote employability? *Theory and Research in Education, 13*(3), 267–285. https://doi.org/10.1177/1477878515598060

Milman, N. B. (2020). *Pandemic pedagogy*. Phi Delta Kappan.

Moulding, L. R., Stewart, P. W., & Dunmeyer, M. L. (2014). Pre-service teachers' sense of efficacy: Relationship to academic ability, student teaching placement characteristics, and mentor support. *Teaching and Teacher Education, 41*, 60–66. https://doi.org/10.1016/j.tate.2014.03.007

Pham, T., & Jackson, D. (2020). The need to develop graduate employability for a globalized world. In T. L. H. Nghia, T. Pham, M. Tomlinson, K. Medica, & C. D. Thompson (Eds.), *Developing and utilizing employability capitals: Graduates' strategies across labour markets* (1st ed., pp. 21–40). Routledge.

Pham, T., Tomlinson, M., & Thompson, C. (2019). Forms of capital and agency as mediations in negotiating employability of international graduate migrants. *Globalization, Societies and Education, 17*(3), 394–405. https://doi.org/10.1080/14767724.2019.1583091

Rienties, B., Brouwer, N. M., & Lygo-Baker, S. (2012). The effects of online professional development on higher education teachers' beliefs and intentions towards learning facilitation and technology. *Teacher and Teacher Education, 29*(1), 122–131. https://doi.org/10.1016/j.tate.2012.09.002

Salgado-Banda, H. (2005). Entrepreneurship and economic growth: An empirical analysis. *Journal of Developmental Entrepreneurship, 12*, 3–29.

Sekiguchi, T. (2012). Part-time work experience of university students and their career development. *Japan Labor Review, 9*(3), 5–29.

Shulman, L. S. (1986). Those who understand: Knowledge growth in teaching. *Educational Researcher, 15*(2), 4–14. https://doi.org/10.2307/1175860

Singh, A., & Singh, L. B. (2017). E-learning for employability skills: Students perspective. *Procedia Computer Science, 122*, 400–406. https://doi.org/10.1016/j.procs.2017.11.386

Tomlinson, M. (2017). Forms of graduate capital and their relationship to graduate employability. *Education & Training, 59*(4), 338–352. https://doi.org/10.1108/ET-05-2016-0090

Tran, L. H. N., Phuong, H. Y., & Tran, L. K. H. (2019). The contribution of part-time work experience to pre-service teachers' development of graduate employability. In I. E. Strohschen & K. Lewis (Eds.), *Competence-based and social-situational approaches for facilitating learning in higher education*. IGI Global.

Tsai, C. T. L. (2006). The influence of Confucianism on women's leisure in Taiwan. *Leisure Studies, 25*(4), 469–476. https://doi.org/10.1080/02614360600898177

United Nations. (2020). *Policy brief: Education during COVID-19 and beyond*. United Nations.

University of Waterloo. (2020). *Synchronous and asynchronous online learning*. Retrieved from: https://uwaterloo.ca/centre-for-teaching-excellence/teachingresources/teaching-tips/teaching-tips-inclusive-instructional-practices/synchronous-and-asynchronous-online-learning

Van-Khanh. (2020). *Triển khai đào tạo trực tuyến thời dịch Covid-19, đâu mới là khó khăn thực sự đối với trường đại học?* [What are the challenges when it comes to online learning in COVID-19 pandemic?]. http://ttvn.toquoc.vn/trien-khai-dao-tao-truc-tuyen-thoi-dich-covid-19-dau-moi-la-kho-khan-thuc-su-doi-voi-truong-dai-hoc-20200410175703031.htm. Accessed 30 Aug 2020.

Vu, N. T. (2020a). Examining teacher agency among teacher educators: An action research in Vietnam. *Australian Journal of Teacher Education, 45*(7). https://doi.org/10.1422/ajte.2020v45n7.6

Vu, N. T. (2020b). A case study of constructivist learning and intercultural communicative competence in English-majoring pre-service teachers. *The Journal of English as an International Language, 15*(2), 52–76.

Xu, D., & Jaggaers, S. S. (2013). *Adaptability to online learning: Differences across types of students and academic subject areas*. CCRC Working Paper, 54. https://ccrc.tc.columbia.edu/publications/adaptability-to-online-learning.html.

Yin, R. K. (2009). *Case study research: Design and methods* (4th ed.). Thousand Oaks.

Yip, S., Fung, J., & Chu, J. (2019). *Grassroot students need quality, business-school corporation learning activities – Impact study of experiential learning activities*. http://www.hkpri.org.hk/en/research/detail/impact-study-experiential-learning

Part IV
Teacher Voice: Online Practicum and Virtual Study Program

The Adaptation of Action Research into Online Practicum in Unprecedented Times: Opportunities and Constraints

Müzeyyen Nazlı Güngör

Highlights

- Explain the importance and the nature of action research to student-teachers (STs). Encourage them to work with different mentors to enrich their online teaching practices.
- Motivate STs through weekly interactive tasks, regular online meetings, and multiple feedback in pandemic times. Channel their energy into their professional development through predetermined goals in practicum.
- Encourage STs to teach different age groups with the guidance of their mentors in online platforms. This will be a wonderful experience in terms of live teaching experiences.
- Share your local studies and reflections in online platforms, i.e., online conferences, webinars and publicise them. In these hard times, sharing and reflecting on local experiences are getting more and more valuable.

1 Introduction

In times of a global lockdown, with the closure of schools and universities, the rapid move from face-to-face to online education entailed challenges for teachers, supervisors, and professional development providers (Flores & Gago, 2020; Kidd & Murray, 2020; van der Spoel et al., 2020). Specifically, this has presented considerable hardship in initial English language teacher education (IELTE) (Allen et al., 2020; Quezada et al., 2020) since supervisors, student-teachers (STs), and mentors were asked to adapt to the "new normal" with little pedagogical or technological

M. N. Güngör (✉)
Gazi University, Ankara, Turkey
e-mail: nazlidemirbas@gazi.edu.tr

© The Author(s), under exclusive license to Springer Nature
Switzerland AG 2021
J. Chen (ed.), *Emergency Remote Teaching and Beyond*,
https://doi.org/10.1007/978-3-030-84067-9_8

guidance. Among the courses being offered in IELTE programmes, practicum is one of the most negatively affected ones due to its content, requirements, and tasks that STs had to fulfil in real atmosphere but could not do so due to the rapid move in COVID-19 times (Flores & Gago, 2020). Council of Higher Education (CoHE), in collaboration with the Ministry of National Education (MoNE), in Turkey issued emergency guidance early in lockdown, suggesting changing requirements for the practicum and leaving supervisors and mentors to generate alternative online learning-teaching experiences and online assessment ways for STs. Accordingly, it was reported that STs would be evaluated solely for their performances in schools between February 3 to March 13, 2020 (the pre-pandemic term) by supervisors in collaboration with mentors, and that supervisors could teach the practicum content (a)synchronously and assess STs in projects and tasks to complete the practicum (CoHE, 2020 issue no: 75850160-104.01.07.01-E25557 date: 07.04.2020). In other words, there was a clear need for understanding learning-teaching experiences in online practicum in Turkey as well as internationally (Allen et al., 2020; Carrillo & Flores, 2020; van der Spoel et al., 2020).

On the one hand, practicum needs to be completed under these unprecedented conditions, but on the other hand, there is limited emphasis for supervisors, STs, and mentors by CoHE on how to transfer practicum component online as is the case in England (Kidd & Murray, 2020) and elsewhere. As a result, the situation has become increasingly challenging and brought about many constraints in practice for four stakeholders: students, mentors, STs and supervisors in the process. First, students living in rural areas hardly have the chance to attend online lessons and do the assignments due to the lack of technical support, low family income, and low computer literacy levels. Second, mentors experience problems about technology, strategies to motivate students, effective lesson delivery, assessment, and feedback due to similar reasons. Third, STs can neither observe face-to-face classroom atmosphere nor teach language skills or components to students as expected of them in the pre-pandemic situation. Fourth, supervisors were left to give quick but meaningful and functional decisions to continue the practicum online with no specific guidance.

Since action research (AR) is considered to be one of the methodological approaches for professional development through research and systematic self-study (Burns, 2010; Gilliland, 2018), STs' engagement in the action research can be characterized as an opportunity in which they can activate their pedagogical knowledge, reflect on their teaching practice, and increase their awareness and creativity in finding solutions to the challenges experienced in practicum schools in these unprecedented times. As Kidd and Murray (2020) emphasized, teaching practicum has become a "design science" that needs to be adapted into the changing teaching contexts. Based on a study conducted in 2020 ERT pandemic term, this chapter hence aims to introduce the integration of action research into online practicum component to remedy the needs of STs, mentors, and supervisors in lockdown. To this end, the chapter first gives brief information about the components of practicum in IELTE in Turkey. Next, the action research design is presented in three steps:

local needs and constraints, the study with data and reflections, and sample lesson plans with future implementations.

2   The Practicum in IELTE Programmes and in Turkey

A practicum, which functions as a bridge between pedagogical courses offered in IELTE and the real world of teachers and students in a classroom, is a loaded component of IELTE programmes and includes supervised teaching, teaching experience with systematic observation, and gaining familiarity with a particular teaching context (Gilliland, 2018; Richards & Farrell, 2011). Participants in the practicum in IELTE are university-based supervisors, STs, mentors, and students in the real atmosphere (Bailey, 2006; Gebhard, 2009). The practicum enables STs to:

- gain practical classroom teaching experience,
- apply theory and teaching ideas from previous course work,
- discover from observing experienced teachers,
- enhance lesson-planning skills,
- gain skills in selecting, adapting, and developing original course materials,
- expand awareness of how to set their own goals related to improving their teaching,
- question, articulate, and reflect on their own teaching and learning philosophies,
- see their teaching differently by learning how to make their own informed teaching decisions through systematic observation and exploration of their own and others' teaching. (Gebhard, 2009, p.251)

IELTE programmes in Turkey follow the concurrent model for all levels of education. According to this model, STs receive subject training, pedagogical subjects and a certain amount of practicum credit during their four-year undergraduate studies. These programmes educate STs for primary, secondary and tertiary levels. In the first academic term of the fourth-year, STs are obliged to attend a 6-h practicum weekly and observe the real classroom atmosphere systematically, and document the observations in line with the tasks assigned by the supervisors regularly. In the second academic term, STs are expected to design their own lesson plans and apply them in real contexts four times, minimum. STs receive feedback from mentors on their teaching practices at schools. In post-observation conferences that are held after the weekly practicum, STs and supervisors gather for feedback and reflection purposes on the teaching practice.

There are varied roles of participants in the practicum (Bailey, 2006). To specify, mentors who are frequently paired with a group of 4 STs serve as the role model and pedagogical tutor for STs. They evaluate STs' lesson plans, observe teaching performances and give feedback afterwards. Supervisors represent the IELTE programme. They help STs link the theory (the pedagogical knowledge they gain in IELTE) and practice (their teaching performances) in the real classroom atmosphere, give feedback on STs' lesson plans and teaching performances in the practicum school, and reflect on their practice teaching performance by discussing their strengths and weaknesses. STs are required to observe real classes regularly, negotiate teaching and learning procedures with mentors, prepare lesson plans, perform their teaching to the real students in the practicum school, and attend the post-observation conferences with their supervisors weekly.

2.1 Components of Practicum

2.1.1 Pedagogical Reasoning, Lesson Planning, Practice Teaching and Assessment

The overall evaluation criteria for STs' practicum in Turkey are based on four primary elements: subject matter knowledge, pedagogical content knowledge, lesson planning skills, and assessment practices (uod.meb.gov.tr). STs are expected to integrate the subject matter and pedagogical content knowledge into the lesson plan appropriately, write up the aims and objectives comprehensively, develop age-appropriate materials, choose alternative assessment techniques in line with the target behaviours, and relate the subject to the previous and following lessons.

Studies suggest that STs are primarily concerned about issues related to selecting the objectives and matching them to the assessment strategy, teaching the content, motivating students, designing and adapting age-appropriate materials, and addressing to diverse students' needs and interests in the practicum classroom (Mutton et al., 2011; Kola, 2019; Swennen et al., 2004). As these studies reveal, STs' concerns point to the importance and necessity of pedagogical reasoning in the practicum. Pedagogical reasoning is composed of a cyclical process in which STs reflect their beliefs and assumptions about the nature of teaching and learning, their understanding of the content of the lesson, their learners' and their own roles in the class, and the methodology they plan to implement (Nilsson, 2009; Richards & Farrell, 2011). One way to develop pedagogical reasoning is to provide STs to engage in the lesson planning practice in practicum in IELTE (Kola, 2019; Mutton et al., 2011; Pang, 2016).

A lesson plan is a complex and dynamic process in which teachers critically become aware of the classroom context in several ways. Firstly, it is a clear classroom guide in which teachers transform the pedagogical and theoretical knowledge (teaching and learning theories, teaching methodology, language teaching skills, the proficiency of students, the focus and content of the lesson, teachers' beliefs about effective teaching) into practice through a set of stages (warm-up, pre-, while, and post teaching) and activities addressing to the needs, ages, and interests of students. Secondly, it is a road map in which they make decisions on the aims and objectives, solve problems about the process and product of planning, and build their confidence by ensuring that the necessary content has been covered. Thirdly, it is a reflective tool in which teachers question themselves and students in each minute of the lesson (Kola, 2019; Pang, 2016; Purgason, 2014; Richards & Farrell, 2011). Following this line of reasoning, lesson planning has a range of functions and aims in the practicum, activating teachers' cognitive and conceptual processes.

Lesson planning is considered as a three-stage process (Purgason, 2014; Richards & Farrell, 2011). The first one is "developing the plan" process in which teachers make decisions before class. Although there are various lesson plan formats, an effective lesson plan depends on several factors such as the lesson content, teachers' subject matter and pedagogical content knowledge, students' learning styles, ages, levels, and the class size. STs both become familiar with the curriculum and materials, and consider aims, objectives, activities, sequencing, timing, grouping, and resources in this process. The second one is "conducting the lesson plan" process. This can be shaped by many unpredictable factors such as task effectiveness, language focus, language support, grouping, interest, sequencing, transitions, pacing, difficulty, student understanding, and student behaviour. The third process is "evaluating the lesson plan" in which the teacher reflects on the students' reactions, and successful and less successful parts of the lesson.

2.2 The Need for Action Research in Practicum in ERT Times

Encouraging STs to reflect on their own teaching performances is viewed as an important part of the teaching practice experience (Richards & Farrell, 2011; Yangın-Ekşi & Güngör, 2018). There are several reasons for this. Reflection offers newer perspectives, deepens STs' understandings of teaching and lesson planning skills, and gives STs greater confidence as a future teacher. In practicum, although several ways are listed for STs' self-reflection such as keeping narrations, video/audio recordings, critical incidents, action research has been closely related to reflection in recent studies due to its interactive, reflective, inquiry-based, research informed, and cyclical nature (Burns, 2010; Gilliland, 2018; Kola, 2019).

Embracing the action and research in its nature, action research is a small-scale teacher-conducted classroom research that has been used as a means of self-reflective enquiry (Carr & Kemmis, 1986), and so, as a vehicle for professional development (Burns, 2010) in teacher education. It is based on the view that teachers become the explorer of their own teaching context by planning, acting, systematically observing, collecting data, identifying the problem or the gap, developing new ideas, intervening, reflecting on the whole process, and re-planning for solution and improvement (Burns, 2010; Richards & Farrell, 2011). Recent studies on the use of action research in IELTE have shown that action, reflection and research serve various purposes such as addressing and finding solutions to particular problems in specific teaching situations (Gilliland, 2018; Güngör, 2016), facilitating the individual-professional development of STs (Crawword-Garret et al., 2015), enhancing research skills (Kola, 2019), developing STs' lesson planning skills in practicum (Kola, 2019; Pang, 2016; Yangın-Ekşi & Güngör, 2018), and deepening their own theories of practice (Gilliland, 2018; Güngör, 2016; Kola, 2019).

With these aforementioned situational constraints, the need for new learning experiences in practicum, and requirements of the practicum in mind, this study employs cyclical action research design by Kemmis and McTaggrat (1988). It is used as a small-scale research project that ended in remedial effective lesson plans in online practicum classes in an IELTE programme during the COVID-19 pandemic. The aims of using action research are to help STs improve and transform their pedagogical content knowledge into practice via lesson plans, to create opportunities for STs to interact, socialize and exchange information with mentors who are teaching online, to raise their awareness of these mentors' remote teaching experiences with diverse student populations in rural and urban Turkey, to encourage STs to engage in research and the use of ICT, and to develop their decision making, problem solving, and creative thinking skills in IELTE.

3   The Setting

Realities and constraints of the situation were determined upon the interviews with mentors and STs in the system, and the analysis of the official practicum conduct document (CoHE, 2020). As both the supervisor and the researcher of this study, I discovered that constraints were related to disequilibrium between the emergent lockdown situation across the nation and the official practicum requirements. Similar to the constraints stated in Carrillo and Flores (2020), they were threefold: (a) the social, cultural, and economic background of students in terms of access to the Internet, MoNE digital sources, task completion, and interaction with peers and the teacher, (b) mentors' first time remote English language teaching experiences on the "Educational Informatics Network" (EBA) online teaching platform suggested by the MoNE in Turkey, c) the social and economic background of STs in terms of the access to technology, academic resources, and the Internet for task completion. In addition, as la Velle et al. (2020) stated, the lockdown and remote teaching increased STs' time for reading, researching and reflecting. Given these realities and limitations, the necessity to develop lesson plans that would comply with practicum requirements and that would help mentors who teach English remotely was clearly explained to STs at the beginning. The stages of developing lesson plans were negotiated among three stakeholders (STs, mentors, and me). For this purpose, I informed STs and mentors about the online practicum process in lockdown and emphasised the importance of collaboration, interaction, and feedback in developing lesson plans through stages. All in all, STs and mentors all agreed to follow the online practicum format based on the cyclical action research model by Kemmis and McTraggart (1988). In this way, STs preceded with the action research phases at the beginning of April (the official beginning of the online practicum in Turkey) as a small-scale intervention to address the constraints and issues aforementioned.

3.1 Participants

The participants of the study are two groups. The first group consists of seven fourth-year STs in an ELT programme of a large university in central Anatolia in Turkey. Four of them were male while three of them were female. Their ages ranged between 22 and 24. They were taught subject matter courses (advanced reading, writing, listening, speaking, translation, English literature), pedagogical content knowledge (teaching English to young learners, teaching language skills, materials preparation, language acquisition, approaches and methods in ELT), pedagogical knowledge (classroom management, testing and evaluation, educational philosophy, educational technology) and general knowledge courses (history, Turkish, community service) in the four-year long IELTE programme. These STs were assigned at the beginning of the term by the head of the programme randomly. It had been only 2 weeks since STs attended the practicum when the COVID-19 broke out. These STs applied the cyclical action research model to plan the two online lessons assigned by their supervisor. Each of these plans lasted 1 month due to the cyclical nature of the model. Totally, STs developed two lesson plans for online practicum classes in 2 months.

The second group consists of seven mentors who were teaching English to different age groups (primary, secondary, and high school students) in socioeconomically different parts of Turkey: Ankara (private and state schools), Hatay (village), Tokat (village), and Sakarya (city center). In addition to the two official mentors (in Ankara), I invited five more to contribute to this study. And, they voluntarily agreed to be a part of this study, sending the signed and scanned consent forms on Camscanner via e-mail. When the MoNE announced that the remote teaching in state schools in Turkey would be carried out on a voluntary basis, these mentors volunteered to teach remotely to their own students. Private schools also asked their teachers to teach online.

4 The Suggested Action Research for the Online Practicum

This study is exploratory and employs a qualitative approach. Kemmis and McTggart's (1988) cyclical action research model is employed by STs in the online practicum. Accordingly, STs in this study followed four main phases: planning, action, observation, and reflection.

Phase 1: Planning
In the first week, STs employed non-observation method in data collection process to determine the realities and constraints before them. The aim in this stage was to deepen STs' knowledge about how mentors viewed remote teaching experiences, how students perceived remote learning experiences, and how parents were involved in this process. To this end, they used open-ended interview questions and

classroom documents as data collection techniques. The interview questions prepared in collaboration with the supervisor and the STs were as follows:

- What are the constraints that mentors experience in remote teaching in lockdown?
- What are the constraints that students experience in remote learning in lockdown?
- What are the needs of mentors in remote teaching in lockdown?
- What are the needs of students in remote learning in lockdown?

They interviewed their mentors and students via Skype or Whatsapp calls twice (in April and May). STs then analysed the lesson plans and digital course materials these mentors used in online teaching. The aim of integrating mentors, students, parents and the two data collection techniques was to ensure triangulation for credibility concerns (Burns, 2010). STs analysed the responses to determine the deficiencies in remote learning and teaching process in detail. Then, they met on Skype with their supervisor to discuss the data in detail and to specify the aspects of the lesson plan they would prepare. This group meeting allowed STs to enrich their knowledge about online teaching and learning experiences (students' socioeconomic and sociocultural status, mentors' teaching styles and beliefs) in state schools, to start thinking critically about the stages of an online lesson with students (how to start, continue, and end the lesson online, what motivational strategies to use, how to do tasks collaboratively and give feedback online), and to understand the functions of digital materials (videos, PPT slides, songs) and applications being used (see Table 3 in Appendix).

4.1   Results of the Online Interviews: Constraints and Needs in ERT Times

From Mentors' Perspective

The constraints mentors experienced are at the same time found to be sources of their needs; therefore, they are categorized under three main themes in relation to their needs (see Table 1).

Online language teaching was the first time experience for most mentors. With the sudden launch of the remote teaching decision by the MoNE, mentors at first had difficulty in understanding the system, transferring their teaching skills into the online platform EBA (eba.gov.tr), and preparing lesson plans and activities for the appropriate age groups. When they started teaching online, their needs and problems were detailed and varied. To specify, some students closed their webcams, watched outside, ate food in front of the camera, or asked to go to the restroom to take their teachers' attention. Not only did this situation reduce their motivation and attention, it caused classroom management problem too. Then, the teacher was in need of choosing the most effective activities and tools that could attract students' attention in the given time, which raised another problem for teachers. Most of them searched websites for teaching materials that would keep students' interaction and

Table 1 Constraints and needs experienced by mentors in online education

Constraints	Needs
Online language teaching experience (first time experience for most mentors)	How to motivate students How to manage online classes How to use activities for interaction and collaboration How to prepare and use online age appropriate teaching materials How to assess students online How to give feedback online
Time limitation	How to increase students' participation How to choose and use the most effective teaching techniques How to give effective feedback How to provide comprehensible input How to decide on the effectiveness of language skills to be practiced
Technical support	Frequent internet connection problems The lack of in-service training for the online programmes the MoNE advised How to maintain interaction among students

collaboration going on; however, choosing and using the most appropriate ones were not easy. Although students were excluded from the mainstream grading system due to the socioeconomic limitations and health problems in the pandemic term, teachers wanted to check whether the learning had really taken place or not. For this purpose, how to assess students in online platforms was among the needs they stated in the interviews. Since no assessment went without feedback, they complained about the limited course hours for effective feedback. This was an important issue for most students because in this feedback giving process they felt like they were face to face at school with their teachers. So, teachers needed to spend time as effectively as possible. However, this was not possible most of the time.

While teachers were struggling to keep students' attention and teach the topic, they were at the same time trying to give turns to students for participation. They reported that due to the limited time (an English class lasted 30 min) it was hard to provide students with equal participation opportunities. While some students could answer the teacher's questions, the rest of the class had to listen to him, which also affected silent students' attention negatively. Most of the time, teachers could teach limited reading and writing, and listening skills, but had problems with speaking skills. Indeed, this resulted from several factors. First, speaking requires comprehensible input, realistic and achievable aims, interaction, appropriacy and authenticity (Lazaraton, 2014). Finding speaking activities that were suitable to these requirements was problematic. Second, since students had anxiety in front of the cameras, teachers thought that it would be better to assign collaborative speaking activities. However, organizing pair/group work activities for collaboration took much time in classes, which resulted in more timing problems and ended up with desperation.

The Internet connection and technical background were among the reasons why teachers experienced constraints so much. Most teachers were new to teaching on EBA. Similar to the case in the Netherlands (van der Spoel, 2020), there was an absence of in-service teacher training for this in Turkey too. So, when teachers had any problem in the online lesson, they spent much time to understand and solve the problem.

From Students' Perspective

Issues raised in the interviews with students and parents (Table 2) were not different from teachers' in several ways. They are even related to each other's. The biggest constrains of the students were socioeconomic inequalities due to the family income, the place where they live (rural vs urban), the number of siblings in the family, and family expectations of students. Most families could not buy computers or mobile phones to their children due to the low income. In this case, some students used their parents' phones for online classes. However, when their parents were at work, they could not attend the classes. Moreover, there were some frozen moments in the synchronous teaching due to the Internet connection. This negatively affected the adaptation process of students into the system.

Since students could not get adapted to the platform properly, some of them were unwilling to answer the questions in the lesson. Some opened windows, watched outside, ate. In some houses with more than one child, other siblings came into the room suddenly or shouted at home. Students could not see each other at the same time because of the Internet connection problem. When they wanted to answer for the second time, they could not because of the time limitation. These problems caused students to believe that interaction in the online class was not real. Since students could not maintain interaction among themselves, their motivation reduced.

As seen in Tables 1 and 2, mentors' and students' constraints and needs were interrelated. This lengthened the adaptation process into the online education system for both groups in lockdown.

Phase 2: Acting

In the second phase, STs determined the problems mentioned in the interviews and analysis. Next, they started doing research on how to overcome these problems

Table 2 Constraints and needs experienced by students

Constraints	Needs
Technical problems	Lack of technical equipment (computers, mobile phones, etc.) Internet connection Online learning and teaching platforms Adaptation to this platform
Motivation	Unwillingness Shyness Interference
Practising language skills online	Unreal interaction Limitations of the platform Timing (course hours)

through effective lesson plans with online sources and peer feedback. They used the websites below to find alternative ideas:

- Teaching English – British Council (https://www.teachingenglish.org.uk),
- ELT Forum (https://americanenglish.state.gov/forum),
- Pearson Education (https://tr.pearson.com/tr.html),
- One Stop English (https://www.onestopenglish.com),
- NatGeo Webinars (https://webinars.eltngl.com),
- and TESOL Resource Center (https://www.tesol.org/connect/tesol-resource-center)

The lesson plan template STs used for planning lessons was downloadable on this link https://www.teachingenglish.org.uk/sites/teacheng/files/teaching-kids-my-sea-creature-lesson-plan.pdf. This sample was important to inform the STs about the lesson plan components. A new folder was set up on Google Drive and the link was shared with the participants (see Fig. 1). This enabled all to upload, download, or comment on the documents on the Drive folder, and to track each other's activities. STs sent their lesson plans as first drafts to their mentors and the supervisor on Google Drive. By using the "*add a comment*" option on the document, the supervisor gave instant and detailed feedback on the objectives, planning phases, appropriateness of online materials, and the language item and functions they focused. Mentors also checked the effectiveness of the solutions STs developed for their needs. STs revised their lesson plans based on the online multiple feedback and submitted their final versions through a common Gmail account - opened solely for this study - to the supervisor as midterm take-home examination. The supervisor kept all the drafts and finalized versions on a separate Drive folder as a portfolio of each ST. Some of the sample finalized lesson plans can be found at https://drive.

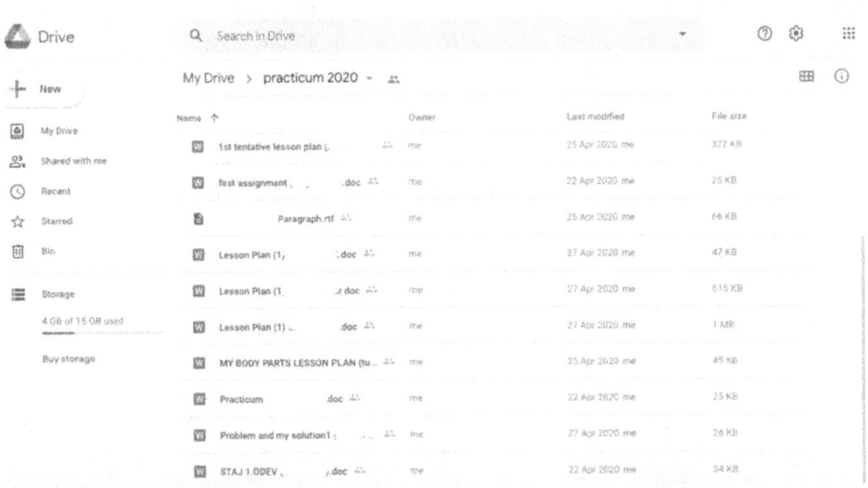

Fig. 1 Google Drive folder for ERT Practicum 2020 as of April 27, 2020 (STs' names were removed from the documents for ethical reasons)

google.com/drive/folders/1hcmSomVbh4BxrsDReDDHtIOE8WsDBxEQ?u
sp=sharing

Phase 3: Observing

In the third week, mentors applied lesson plans in their classes and shared their observations with STs afterwards. Since only mentors were allowed to teach in classes, STs could not participate in the lesson delivery part actively. Thus, mentors informed STs about the successful and less successful parts of their lesson plans upon their actual experience via WhatsApp calls. Next, the supervisor held a meeting on Skype with STs to allow them to reflect on their experiences and give feedback on their final submissions. The focus of this meeting was lesson introduction, delivery and conclusion, online materials, and digital tools STs used as remedy.

Phase 4: Reflecting

In the fourth week, STs were asked to write their reflections on their experiences in both cycles and self-evaluate themselves on the lesson plans they developed. Then, they submitted their written reflections to their supervisor on the Drive folder. STs revised the whole process they spent and reflected on the challenges, their solutions, and further steps they needed to take. In addition to the written reflections, another Skype meeting was held to elaborate on their written answers for deeper and multiple discussion of the process they went through in this first cycle of action research. The focus of the meeting was on lesson plan components, their own solution, content of the feedback they got from mentors, and their role as researchers. This gave them the opportunity to deepen their understanding of the importance of action research study in distance education system in unprecedented times. This was the end of the first round of action research cycle and the beginning of the second action research cycle in the online practicum class. STs followed the same steps with same goals in the second round for another month. They focused on a different problem this time and developed a new remedial lesson plan. Throughout the first and second cycles, a WhatsApp group was set to fasten the communication and the spread of the announcements between the supervisor and STs (Fig. 2).

4.2 Student-Teachers' Reflections on the AR Study

Burns (2010) highlights the necessity of reflection in AR studies, so the reflections of STs are introduced in three dimensions below: reflecting on the research process, on beliefs and values, and on feelings and experiences to deepen our understanding in STs' AR process with mentors and students. Although reflection on practice is also suggested in AR studies, it is embedded into the lesson planning process and presented in the "reflection on research process" part below since STs were not able to apply those remedial lesson plans themselves online. This can be considered a limitation of the study.

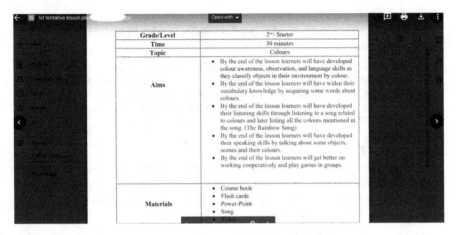

Grade/Level	2ⁿᵈ / Starter
Time	30 minutes
Topic	Colours
Aims	• By the end of the lesson learners will have developed colour awareness, observation, and language skills as they classify objects in their environment by colour. • By the end of the lesson learners will have widen their vocabulary knowledge by acquiring some words about colours. • By the end of the lesson learners will have developed their listening skills through listening to a song related to colours and later listing all the colours mentioned in the song. (The Rainbow Song) • By the end of the lesson learners will have developed their speaking skills by talking about some objects, scenes and their colours. • By the end of the lesson learners will get better on working cooperatively and play games in groups.
Materials	• Course book • Flash cards • Power-Point • Song • Video

Fig. 2 A sample lesson plan to be commented on as of April 27

Reflections on the Research Process

The first dimension focused on how STs used the data to prepare their lesson plans, how the interviews with mentors and students affected STs' choice and use of target language skills and online activities in lesson plans, and how all this process helped them extend their view of research.

> In this process, preparing a lesson plan was easier than I guessed thanks to the help and support of my mentor… Interviews with and feedback by my mentor showed me that some students could not use computers without the assistance of their parents… So, I changed the game activity. (ST1)

> I understood that distance education was certainly different from face to face education. The data I collected via interviews showed me mentors' challenges such as evaluating and motivating students in online classes. With research and weekly tasks, I shared the responsibility of my mentor. Also, this collaboration and task helped me enrich my repertoire of digital tools… I became a part of the online education (ST2).

> I think that my problem-solving skills are developed in this AR study. The feedback while preparing the lesson plans and after the finalized lesson plans lowered the feeling of being distant… I was so happy to have learnt that my mentor used digital activities designed by me… Interviews and this process helped me develop my writing skill that is generally neglected at school. (ST6)

Reflections on Beliefs and Values

The second dimension captured STs' beliefs and values about online teaching and AR experiences in practicum, how these beliefs affected their choice, and how AR research deepened their beliefs and values in English language teaching online.

> Interviewing English teachers to learn about their problems in distance education, I found out that developing speaking skills of students was difficult in online atmosphere and that some students did not have the Internet connection at home. To overcome this, I planned telephone calls to engage them in the learning process through one-to-one calls. Although we couldn't have the chance for real practicum experience, this model [AR] showed us realities about ERT. (ST2).

AR process helped me broaden my horizons about constructing a lesson plan. Writing a lesson plan to remedy teachers' and students' challenges in collaboration with mentors was the best thing that we could do in this ERT. (ST3).

I believe that contacting with each other and collaborating with mentor were rewarding because we learnt a lot about developing online teaching materials. Contacting students, learning about their socioeconomic status, and understanding their neighbourhood via interviews were invaluable to me because this helped me understand realities about the new generation. (ST6)

Reflections on Feelings and Experiences

In the third dimension, STs' personal feelings and emotions were revealed through reflection questions such as how their personal feelings contributed to the way they did AR, what personal reactions were given to the changes that resulted from practical actions, and how negative reactions triggered new ideas.

This process was difficult and new for all of us because we were in lockdown and away from the real atmosphere... I felt desperate at first and sought solutions for the problems mentioned in the interviews. Finding a way to communicate with these students was very important for me. Taking feedback from my mentor was also very helpful to understand which activities worked or not. (ST2)

I think it was a good experience to design remedial lesson plans under these conditions... Before this, we did not know much about problems mentors and students experienced. So, it was productive for me to find solutions, adapt online activities to the target group, and write a lesson plan. (ST3)

At first, it was hard and tough for me to prepare a lesson plan with suggestions... However, within time, trying to understand mentors and students, seeking solutions, and suggesting alternatives developed my empathy skills (ST4).

5   Discussion and Conclusion

This chapter has provided an evidence-based perspective on what worked in a practicum class in unprecedented times. As Carrillo and Flores (2020) emphasize, it is significant to understand the potential and use of online practices in such ERT times. In this respect, this chapter has gone beyond the ERT practices and focused on the instructional design and planning, the characteristics, processes, outcomes and reflections, and implications of online action research transformation into the practicum content. It is my hope that this AR study will continue to be a piece of the adaptation process in the new normal on the part of all stakeholders.

Supervisors were expected to give quick but meaningful and functional decisions to continue the practicum at the beginning of ERT times (Kidd & Murray, 2020). Through this AR study, I found the chance to transform practicum content to match the emergent needs of mentors, STs, students, and supervisors. During the pandemic, it became clearer that effective learning could be facilitated through community, creativity, and connectivity via technology (Kalloo et al., 2020). Similarly, this study gave the participants to communicate with each other any time, solve problems through creativity and collaboration in lesson plans, and keep connectivity through useful web links, applications, and social media platforms. To exemplify, lesson plans were more intensely examined via multiple feedback from supervisors and mentors thanks to "*add a comment*" option on Google Drive. Instant online meetings in each AR cycle (task assignment, systematic observation, feedback, and final revision) on Zoom / Skype removed the pressured, formal and long intervals in post teaching conferences between supervisors and STs, and provided interaction between STs, mentors, and the supervisor. The deadlines were also flexible enough for STs to think, make choices, and prepare tasks.

As a limitation of the study, STs could not perform lesson plans in online platforms in ERT times. Mentors applied the final version of these plans themselves, and gave feedback to STs about the details of the plan. Nevertheless, STs felt sense of belonging, achievement and usefulness when they got feedback from mentors about how their own lesson plans worked (or not) in online classes (Ax et al., 2008). STs continued learning about teaching practice from a different perspective.

Notably, studies have made it clear that an effective online teaching and learning is closely related to the development of social, teaching, cognitive, and student presences (Carrillo & Flores, 2020; Darling-Hammond & Hyler, 2020). In this study, STs perceived AR as a bridge to keep close cooperation, collaboration, and problem solving among the stakeholders. The adaptation of AR into online practicum content was contextualized in an ELT programme in ERT times, personalized through regular feedback to each ST's lesson plan targeting each mentor's diversified needs, social due to the multiple mutual interactions in AR cycles, formative with reference to the research and learning-teaching process details, and integrated through formal and informal ways of learning in interviews, tasks and online meetings. Although the context was online, the communication and the participants' commitment to the tasks, problems, and content were real.

This chapter has clarified that further attention should be paid to various areas. First, more research needs to be carried out to understand how the different nature of online education (e.g., the use of ICT skills, online assessment practices, digital inequalities, contextual factors) in ERT times and beyond affects/shapes STs', mentors' and supervisors' roles, identities, and competences. This will enrich our understanding of how their beliefs and practices mediate the online practicum process. The practicum component in online education can be revised in light of these studies. Second, we need to seek alternatives to minimise the socioeconomic and digital inequalities experienced by students, mentors, STs and supervisors, and to maximize collaboration and participation opportunities in online education through international projects. Third, more focus is needed on pedagogical approaches and online practicum experiences to enrich the online content of practicum in teacher education programmes. STs should be allowed to observe online lessons and apply their own lesson plans on the national online education platforms in collaboration with mentors. Specifically, the nature of practicum tasks should include the integration of ICT (Kola, 2019; van der Spoel et al., 2020), alternative assessment practices, problem-based scenarios (Darling-Hammond & Hyler, 2020), and inquiry-based learning. Acknowledging and addressing to mentors' and students' diversified needs in various online contexts will contribute to our deeper understanding, planning, and enacting online practices in practicum.

6 Food for Thought

In conclusion, I share the alternative practicum ideas to apply in ERT and beyond for all stakeholders as follows:

- In the online practicum context, you may use a workbook developed for the practicum component and published as an outcome of ILTERG (Erasmus+ KA203) project in Turkey (Akcan & Güngör, 2018). It is based on 28 novice EFL teachers' critical incidents experienced in real teaching atmosphere in Turkey and Poland, and followed by five or six discussion questions in each incident. A new pedagogical theme such as material development, classroom management, teaching and learning issues, sociocultural diversity is handled in each incident.
- These incidents and the follow-up questions will help you and your STs think, understand, compare and contrast own learning-teaching context, develop their own solutions, and discuss them in online practicum hours. This will provide invaluable source for understanding similar and new contextualized teaching and learning practices, and challenges from the perspectives of Turkish and Polish novice teachers in rural and urban parts of these countries. Each week, an incident can be studied.
- If needed, additional readings related to the theme in the incident may be assigned to STs so that they can deepen their knowledge on it and gain multiple perspectives on the incident. You may even conduct classroom research on how these incidents affect/change/shape your STs' understanding of the teaching profession, and their evolving identities.
- Some live-streamed and video-recorded lessons, and sample lesson plans and activities for ERT and online education are shared free on different websites that were also used in this study. They can be adapted as a complimentary material to the workbook, or as a separate teaching material.
- Encourage STs to collaborate with their counterparts in their own and different countries via teachers', teacher associations', or supervisors' groups on social media such as Twitter, Facebook, Instagram. This will develop their empathy skills, keep them updated, enrich teaching ideas, and contribute to future teaching competences.
- The lockdown process may help us transform negative situations into positive. Various projects and help campaigns can be organized with the help of online practicum opportunities (Donitsa-Schmidt & Ramot, 2020). Supervisors may assign STs to teach online with the guidance of their mentors in online platforms during the online practicum component. For this, STs may be asked to teach family members or friends in the neighbourhood, or students with low-income

families who cannot support their children with the necessary technical and pedagogical support at home. These teaching practices can be recorded and sent to mentors and supervisors for feedback, evaluation, and reflection. It will both support children pedagogically and contribute to online teaching experiences of STs.

- Supervisors may assign STs to attend webinars organized by teacher associations, institutions, or leading actors in education. STs may be asked to write a summary and a reflection of these webinars, and discuss how to adapt the ideas into local contexts in online practicum meetings.
- There are different types of AR (Burns, 2010): participatory, collaborative, exploratory, so on. Supervisors may focus on any one of them and guide STs to carry out such small-scale studies to engage them in the continuing collaboration, interaction and learning process.

Acknowledgements I would like to express my gratitude to Dr. Julian Chen for the insightful feedback on the chapter. I also thank my wonderful practicum group for their willingness, dedication, and cooperation in hard times.

Appendix

Table 3 Features of commonly used applications by STs in teaching English online

Applications	Weblink	Comments
Quizizz	https://quizizz.com/	Quizizz can be used in class for group works, pre-test review, exams, unit test and impromptu tests. Teachers can view individual student progress and whole-class data, which is great for assessing student learning. Participants can join from any device with web browser and use iPhone and Android applications
Prezi	https://prezi.com	Prezi is a presentation software in which you can show relationships between the big picture and fine details
Animaker	https://www.animaker.com/	Animaker is an online do-it-yourself animation and live action video maker. English teachers can use their own productions for storytelling in teaching English
Educandy	https://www.educandy.com/	Educandy is a Web 2.0 tool that helps teachers create interactive learning games and engaging activities in minutes. They can be used on individual computers, tablets via the Educandy app and on interactive whiteboard
Padlet	https://tr.padlet.com/	Padlet is a Web 2.0 tool that helps teachers and students collaborate, reflect, and share links and pictures in a secure location
Tekhnologic	https://tekhnologic.wordpress.com/	Tekhnologic is a blog of an EFL teacher in Japan. He shares some successful and less successful activities from his own perspective

References

Akcan, S., & Güngör, M. N. (2018). *A workbook for prospective language teachers: Challenges from diverse classroom contexts.* Boğaziçi University. Downloadable from https://06384ab7-ed9a-4847-847f-b486f916eb48.filesusr.com/ugd/00f379_ed94d4e70fdb4583b767b2a-b8c2861df.pdf

Allen, J., Rowan, L., & Singh, P. (2020). Editorial: Teaching and teacher education in the time of COVID-19. *Asia-Pacific Journal of Teacher Education, 48*(3), 233–236. https://doi.org/10.108 0/1359866X.2020.1752051

Ax, J., Ponte, P., & Brouwer, N. (2008). Action research in initial teacher education: An explorative study. *Educational Action Research, 16*(1), 55–72. https://doi.org/10.1080/09650790701833105

Bailey, K. M. (2006). *Language teacher supervision: A case-based approach.* Cambridge University Press.

Burns, A. (2010). *Doing action research in English language teaching: A guide for practitioners.* Routledge.

Carr, W., & Kemmis, S. (1986). *Becoming critical: Knowing through action research.* The Falmer Press.

Carrillo, C., & Flores, M. A. (2020). COVID-19 and teacher education: A literature review of online teaching and learning practices. *European Journal of Teacher Education, 43*(4), 466–487. https://doi.org/10.1080/02619768.2020.1821184

Council of Higher Education [Yükseköğretim Kurulu]. (2020, April 7). *Teaching practicum* [Öğretmenlik Uygulamaları]. https://www.turkiye.gov.tr/yok-ebys

Crawford-Garrett, K., Anderson, S., Grayson, A., & Suter, C. (2015). Transformational practice: Critical teacher research in pre-service teacher education. *Educational Action Research, 23*(4), 479–496. https://doi.org/10.1080/09650792.2015.1019902

Darling-Hammond, L., & Hyler, M. E. (2020). Preparing educators for the time of COVID ... and beyond. *European Journal of Teacher Education, 43*(4), 457–465. https://doi.org/10.108 0/02619768.2020.1816961

Donitsa-Schmidt, S., & Ramot, R. (2020). Opportunities and challenges: Teacher education in Israel in the Covid-19 pandemic. *Journal of Education for Teaching*, 2–10. https://doi.org/1 0.1080/02607476.2020.1799708

Educational Informatics Network [Eğitim bilişim ağı]. (2020, April 15). www.eba.gov.tr

Flores, M. A., & Gago, M. (2020). Teacher education in times of COVID-19 pandemic in Portugal: National, institutional and pedagogical responses. *Journal of Education for Teaching*, 2–10. https://doi.org/10.1080/02607476.2020.1799709

Forum (English Teaching Forum). (2020, November 2). https://americanenglish.state.gov/forum

Gebhard, J. G. (2009). The practicum. In A. Burns & J. C. Richards (Eds.), *The Cambridge guide to second language teacher education* (pp. 250–258). Cambridge University Press.

Gilliland, B. (2018). Teacher research during an international practicum. *ELT Journal, 72*(3), 260–273. https://doi.org/10.1093/elt/ccx054

Güngör, M. N. (2016). Turkish pre-service teachers' reflective practices in teaching English to young learners. *Australian Journal of Teacher Education, 41*(2), 9.

Kemmis, S., & McTaggart, R. (1988). *The action research planner* (3rd ed.). Deakin University Press.

Kidd, W., & Murray, J. (2020). The COVID-19 pandemic and its effects on teacher education in England: How teacher educators moved practicum learning online. *European Journal of Teacher Education, 43*(4), 542–558. https://doi.org/10.1080/02619768.2020.1820480

Kola, M. (2019). Pre-service teachers' action research: Technology education lesson planning in a South African University. *Educational Action Research.* https://doi.org/10.1080/0965079 2.2019.1686043

Kalloo, R. C., Mitchell, B., & Kamalodeen, V. J. (2020). Responding to the COVID-19 pandemic in Trinidad and Tobago: challenges and opportunities for teacher education. *Journal of Education for Teaching, 46*(4), 452–462.

la Velle, L., Newman, S., Montgomery, C., & Hyatt, D. (2020). Initial teacher education in England and the COVID-19 pandemic: Challenges and opportunities. *Journal of Education for Teaching*. https://doi.org/10.1080/02607476.2020.1803051

Lazaraton, A. (2014). Second language speaking. In M. Celce-Murcia, D. M. Brinton, & M. A. Snow (Eds.), *Teaching English as a second or foreign language* (pp. 106–120). National Geographic Learning & Heinle Cengage Learning.

Ministry of National Education (MoNE). (2020, October 5). *Student-Teacher Evaluation System.* http://uod.meb.gov.tr

Mutton, T., Hagger, H., & Burn, K. (2011). Learning to plan, planning to learn: The developing expertise of beginning teachers. *Teachers and Teaching, 17*(4), 399–416. https://doi.org/10.1080/13540602.2011.580516

National Geographic Learning. (November 2, 2020). https://webinars.eltngl.com/

Nilsson, P. (2009). From lesson plan to new comprehension: Exploring student teachers' pedagogical reasoning in learning about teaching. *European Journal of Teacher Education, 32*(3), 239–258. https://doi.org/10.1080/02619760802553048

One Stop English. (November 2, 2020). https://www.onestopenglish.com/

Pang, M. (2016). Companion guidelines for lesson planning: A planning template and a lesson pro forma. *ELT Journal, 70*(4), 444–454. https://doi.org/10.1093/elt/ccw053

Pearson Education. (November 2, 2020). https://tr.pearson.com/tr.html

Purgason, K. B. (2014). Lesson planning in second/foreign language teaching. In M. Celce-Murcia, D. M. Brinton, & M. A. Snow (Eds.), *Teaching English as a second or foreign language* (pp. 362–379). National Geographic Learning & Heinle Cengage Learning.

Quezada, R. L., Talbot, C., & Quezada-Parker, K. B. (2020). From bricks and mortar to remote teaching: A teacher education programme's response to COVID-19. *Journal of Education for Teaching*. https://doi.org/10.1080/02607476.2020.1801330

Richards, J. C., & Farrell, T. S. C. (2011). *Practice teaching: A reflective approach.* Cambridge University Press.

Swennen, A., Jörg, T., & Korthagen, F. (2004). Studying student teachers' concerns, combining image-based and more traditional research techniques. *European Journal of Teacher Education, 27*(3), 265–283.

Teaching English British Council. (2020, November 2). https://www.teachingenglish.org.uk/

TESOL International Association. (November 2, 2020). TESOL Resource Center. https://www.tesol.org/connect/tesol-resource-center

van der Spoel, I., Noroozi, O., Schuurink, E., & van Ginkel, S. (2020). Teachers' online teaching expectations and experiences during the COVID-19 pandemic in the Netherlands. *European Journal of Teacher Education, 43*(4), 623–638. https://doi.org/10.1080/02619768.2020.1821185

Yangın Ekşi, G., & Güngör, M. N. (2018). Exploring the use of narratives to understand pre-service teachers' practicum experiences from a sociocultural perspective. *Australian Journal of Teacher Education, 43*(4), 9.

French Language Studies in New Caledonia Despite COVID-19: The Emergency Response Move from In-Country to Virtual Program

Beate Mueller and Susan Oguro

Highlights

- An international short-term language course was transformed into a virtual program for university students in times of a global pandemic.
- A sense of community amongst learners and teachers in online language teaching programs was achieved with the help of online platforms, multiple communication channels, and informal language.
- Online immersive cultural experiences were ensured through cultural experts, authentic materials, and interactions with local students.

1 Introduction

Triggered by the COVID-19 pandemic and international border closures in Australia from March 2020 onwards, previous student mobility programs came to a rapid halt. The move by higher education institutions to online delivery at short notice, described as 'online triage' (Gacs et al., 2020) was unprecedented and highly disruptive (Crawford et al., 2020). As all universities worldwide, we at the University of Technology Sydney (UTS) were faced with the immediate challenge to move teaching online including providing programs for students who had previously travelled internationally to experience the languages and cultures of other countries.

This chapter presents a case study of the swift design and delivery of an online synchronous French language course by a language college in New Caledonia for Australian students from UTS. The French language college in Noumea, New Caledonia is the Centre de Rencontres et d'Echanges Internationaux du Pacifique

B. Mueller · S. Oguro (✉)
University of Technology Sydney, Ultimo, Australia
e-mail: beate.mueller@uts.edu.au; susan.oguro@uts.edu.au

J. Chen (ed.), *Emergency Remote Teaching and Beyond*,
https://doi.org/10.1007/978-3-030-84067-9_9

173

(CREIPAC) and affiliated with the Université de Nouvelle Calédonie. In past years, students from UTS travelled to New Caledonia for a 3-week immersive and intensive French language program including homestay opportunities and cultural activities. In order to provide our students with similar opportunities for learning French language and cultural facets of New Caledonia, an intensive 3-week course was created in July 2020 with 2 h of synchronous online classes delivered by CREIPAC teachers every morning supplemented by a variety of blended and cultural activities. Eight UTS students participated in two language classes of each four students on a B1 and B2 level. While we are not involved in the teaching of the French classes, we coordinate a subject students take at UTS that prepares them for the international program and guides them through a range of reflective activities and assessments to maximise the learning afforded by the language course so they can receive academic credit for the short-term program.

This chapter explores how five of the CREIPAC staff members adapted to the emergency online delivery of their previously face-to-face (f2f) delivered language program, their experiences and perspectives in facilitating learning, building relationships and interacting online, and effectively immersing students into the cultures of New Caledonia. The teachers' experiences are supplemented by the students' evaluations of the interventions. Overall, three questions guided this project:

- How did the teachers respond to the need for online delivery in response to the COVID restrictions?
- How did the teachers build an online community?
- How did the teachers create immersive linguistic and cultural experiences and how did students evaluate their impact?

Through the data collected, a key finding was the teachers' focus on establishing and maintaining community and creating immersive experiences, relevant for all kinds of teaching but particularly for language and culture programs. Additionally, their use of language, learning activities, and multimedia platforms will also be presented in the findings section.

To provide theoretical framing to interpret the experiences of students and teachers in our study, the following review of literature from the fields of teacher professional practice and virtual/online teaching will provide an overview of currents trends.

2 Theoretical Background

2.1 Requirements of Online Language Teaching

In the field of language teaching, there has been ongoing expansion over the past decade in online delivery (Hall & Knox, 2009; Shelley et al., 2013) and like all content areas, online and blended teaching has presented challenges to language teachers (Shelley et al., 2013). Baran et al. (2013) warn against trying to replicate face-to-face (f2f) practices when teaching online, while Thomas and Thorpe (2019) argue that the ability to create collaborative, transformative online learning processes is largely dependent on the course facilitator's presence and their pedagogical expertise, not just the adoption of the latest technological tool. In this sense, Collie and Martin (2016) stress the importance of the teacher's emotional, behaviour and cognitive adaptability for effective teaching. However, these new skills and demands do not automatically develop and not all teachers find it easy to cope with the change of moving from f2f to online delivery (De Paepe et al., 2019; Mendieta & Barkhuizen, 2020; Shelley et al., 2013). The assumption that a teacher who is good at teaching in a f2f class can easily teach in this new medium is a common myth (Compton, 2009). Tudini (2018) expands on the multitasking skills required by language teachers to balance synchronous instruction, interaction opportunities, monitoring students, while also understanding linguistic and intercultural concepts. Thus, teachers become producers of media resources, workflow managers and online tutors (Bañados, 2006) which can put additional strain on their ability to deliver courses successfully.

Not only does technology impact on teacher practices, Comas-Quinn et al. (2012) point out that the adoption of technology-mediated teaching approaches has subverted the traditional roles of teachers and the kinds of relationships that develop between teachers and learners. This can change the perception learners have of the teacher and challenge the identity of the teacher themselves, which can be unsettling and demanding. Shelley et al. (2013) point out that this shift may also evoke emotions which teachers might find difficult to regulate, and as Mendieta and Barkhuizen (2020) argue, can impact on a teacher's sense of ownership in relation to their technical abilities. Faced with many unknowns and the readjustment of their own roles and identity in the classroom, teachers might employ specific strategies to overcome these issues which are relevant to teaching any cohort. These include building a collaborative community of inquiry and a strong sense of belonging of all group members which will be explored in the following.

2.2 Community Building in Online Language Teaching

Community is a key consideration in all teaching and in online delivery the development of social presence in communities of language learners is crucial to maintain a sense of connectedness (Lomicka, 2020). It has long been established in foreign language pedagogy that building a sense of community and belonging in f2f classroom contexts is essential to support learning (González-Lloret, 2020) and it can be argued that this is even more crucial in online modes where interaction is not physically possible (Du et al., 2010; Lomicka, 2020). In investigating this group of teachers' experiences of suddenly delivering a French language program online, 'teaching presence' (Richardson et al., 2015) is particularly significant in understanding how effective online learning communities can be created. Teaching presence is also referred to by some scholars as 'instructor presence' and research has shown the value students place on teachers who are responsive to their needs (Hodges & Forrest Cowan, 2012; Sheridan & Kelly, 2010) and where the instructor projects him−/herself as a real person (Richardson et al., 2015). A sense of community also facilitates language learners' sense of security, and willingness to participate, interact and engage with the teacher and other students (Lomicka, 2020).

Interactivity is seen as a key feature of online learning that can contribute positively to students' sense of belonging and their confidence to express themselves and with others in the target language. The value of interactivity and the need to create this emotional connection when facilitating learning in online environments is a feature of Salmon's (2011) model of teaching and learning online which identifies learner needs and the support teachers can provide to achieve higher levels of interactivity. She argues that learners' motivation can be enhanced by the choices of technologies a teacher chooses and emphasises the use of activities to address learners' needs for socialisation and connectedness. The intersection of technology plus pedagogy is again foregrounded and the necessity for teachers to learn how to integrate both. Additionally, teachers have to be able to then personalise these strategies and technologies for individual students and adapt them to different language levels and specific requirements of the program. While online learning can often include synchronous interactions and communication with instructors and peers, it also provides for asynchronous learning in which space and time are not barriers (Means et al., 2014). These benefits are often obtained at a cost, as the online mode may also result in reduced opportunities for student-to-teacher and student-to-student interactions and communication if not blended and scaffolded sufficiently. As a focus point of this study, the strategies and platforms that teachers used to establish and maintain their presence and a sense of community in their emergency response teaching and how teachers and students perceived these shifts will be further discussed in the data findings section.

2.3 Cultural Immersion in Online Teaching

Where traditional international programs offer the invaluable opportunity for students to immerse themselves in the languages and cultures of the host country, the lack of this possibility in online programs is often perceived as one of the biggest drawbacks of online programs. To overcome this, virtual exchanges (VE) are an innovative practice in international education designed to bridge this gap and still contribute to globally competent students (O'Dowd, 2018; O'Dowd & Lewis, 2016). VE is defined as the engagement of groups of students in online intercultural interaction and collaboration with students from other cultural contexts or geographical locations as an integrated part of course work and under the guidance of educators and/or expert facilitators (O'Dowd & Lewis, 2016).

However, Garcés and O'Dowd (2020) remind us that virtual exchange is not the same as virtual learning. In contrast to many forms of virtual learning, which are based on the transfer of information through video lectures and online content, VE uses collaborative, student-centred approaches where intercultural understandings and knowledge are constructed through learner-to-learner interaction. On the positive side, VE has been found to have positive impact on students' linguistic, intercultural development, and digital competencies (De Wit, 2016; Garcés & O'Dowd, 2020). However, Richardson reminds us that many VE programs 'reflect the face-to-face assumption that if students interact with those different to themselves, they (the students) will somehow be transformed by the experience. We know that this is not the case, so a very careful design of online learning activities is essential' (Richardson, 2016, pp. 123–124).

With appropriate curriculum implementation and opportunities for students to interact and co-construct knowledge online with peers internationally, VE has been shown to be effective for developing intercultural competence (Guth & Helm, 2017). As part of their intercultural learning, students' ways of thinking about themselves and others and their behaviours can be transformed (Mueller, 2021). New capabilities, often referred to as transferable or generic skills, however, can also be acquired in classroom settings and online learning experiences, provided that students have to overcome challenges to adjustments and meaningfully engage with others in project- or problem-based learning (Mueller & Oguro, 2021). Further, O'Dowd (2019) links linguistic skills to employment in the digital age. Many challenges of emergency online learning and the cultural interventions that students experienced triggered the development of these transferable skills, that students might also need in their future workplaces, and we will look at them in the section below.

While our program was not an exchange program, elements of VE were incorporated into the program CREIPAC developed for our students. We will examine two cultural interventions created by the program directors that facilitate exchanges between students and local experts to provide the UTS students opportunities to meaningfully engage with others in French as a key component of intercultural learning. Students further reflect on these experiences by linking them to transferable learning outcomes and employability development.

3   Methodology and Participants

The study design adopted a case-study approach exploring our three questions through various semi-structured interview prompts based on the literature and features of emergency and online learning under investigation. With approval from the university's research ethics committee, we interviewed the first two participants together (one teacher and the program director) and then each of the three main teachers individually approximately 1 month after the program finished. These in-depth interviews lasted between 45 and 80 min and were recorded. The primary motivation was to give teachers a voice and understand how they saw their changing role and adaptation of teaching activities in the emergency response teaching

Table 1 Teacher profiles

Teacher pseudonym	Age bracket	Years as French teachers	Years at CREIPAC	Language level taught in program
Amelie	30–40	10	4	B1
Philippa	40–50	20	3	B2
Bianca	40–50	N/A	4	N/A (coordinator)
Emma	40–50	23	2	B1
Rebecca	30–40	19	8	B2

because listening 'to teachers' stories of practice can contribute to our understanding of how teachers construct emerging language teaching contexts' (Mendieta & Barkhuizen, 2020, p. 180). A summary of the teacher participant profiles is in Table 1.

In addition to the teacher participants, all eight students were also invited to participate in interviews and three of them accepted. Student interviews took between 45 and 60 min and the question prompts covered the same categories as the teacher questions, but from the students' evaluation perspective. All students were undergraduate and aged 20–25. They had been learning French for between 3 and 5 years and were upper intermediate level.

The data analysis followed Hancock and Algozzine's (2006) qualitative content analysis stage model for case study research. Though the research and interview questions were set, we wanted to leave room for a grounded approach in finding reoccurring and salient new categories. These categories were determined after several rounds of data analysis and interpretation. Although we only had a handful of interviews, we were able to identify patterns among the teachers, between teachers and the research literature and between teachers and students. Drawing on the review of research literature, we found recurring notions in the teachers' initial reactions and subsequent innovations and adaptations, how they built a community in the online classroom and the cultural interventions they created.

4 Pedagogical Interventions

4.1 Initial Responses and Adaptability

New, unfamiliar, and potentially uncomfortable teaching demands, as those resulting from the COVID-19 situation, can create emotional and behavioural responses in teachers which impact on their ability to adjust to the circumstances, engage with learners, and support the achievement of learning outcomes. According to Collie and Martin (2016), adaptability is crucial to teachers' work and entails being able to emotionally, behaviourally and cognitively respond to and manage these changes in everyday circumstances, and particularly in 'emergency' teaching contexts.

When asked for their initial reactions to the need to teach online, the teachers expressed reactions ranging from apprehension to enthusiastically seizing the opportunity. Two staff members admitted that they were initially cautious and somewhat overwhelmed about the prospect of moving to teach fully online in a short time frame, but also to adjust to our program requirements and creating a new curriculum that included cultural immersion activities. They described it as a task they *'have to do'*, adjusting to *'the unknown'*, and as *'feeling stressed'* as increased preparation and organisation was necessary. They also anticipated issues with internet connectivity and felt it could potentially negatively impact on the engagement with students and building of relationships. Other teachers with more experience in online teaching did not express such strong reactions. They shared their worries around the impact of unstable internet connections for effectively teaching especially in lower-level classes, but as they previously taught online, they saw this as an opportunity to test new tools and platforms. Teaching in a location with connections to smaller offshore islands, online teaching already existed in New Caledonia.

It was interesting to note that several teachers mentioned that they perceived the shift to online teaching and the necessity to explore different platforms and technologies as a natural part of their lifelong learning as teachers and professional development. They expressed a sense of normalcy in adapting to technologies such as: *'it's always been available, and I have always used it'* (Emma). Some even showed excitement at being able to explore new ways of teaching and wanting to enhance their online teaching practices: *'we need this kind of thing [pandemic] to put it into practice (Philippa)'*; *'it generated more interest in me to learn about new teaching technologies'* (Emma); *'I was quite happy ...to try to see how it can work with different levels and to test different tools for real'* (Emma).

While teachers' initial reactions to the emergency differed, all mentioned that the experience overall was very *'enriching and interesting'* (Emma), that they were *'happily surprised'* (Amelie) how well it worked and enjoyed teaching this course. This suggests they were able to transform their initial fears or excitement and use cognitive and behavioural strategies, such as creativity, flexibility, and collaboration to deal with unforeseen issues and to identify new approaches and pedagogical methods to fit the circumstances and learners. The teachers express this as not only being a part of their professional identity, but also of their personality: *'I'm quite resilient, I could work anywhere'* (Emma). Overcoming issues of restrictive internet connectivity for their initially chosen platform (Skype), they quickly moved to use Zoom and familiarised themselves with its functions, in so doing demonstrating their behavioural and cognitive ability to learn and change initial plans (Collie & Martin, 2016). For this group of teachers, their needs and desire for innovation and change was embraced as a natural part of lifelong learning. Their embracing of personal and professional development might also be due to the experience of this group of women that had undergone extensive changes in their lives, including changing careers, moving to new countries, and adapting to new lifestyles.

4.2 Building Relationships and Engaging with Students Online

This section explores teachers' strategies and feelings around meaningfully connecting with students, in building strong relationships with them and creating a sense of belonging in the online classroom. Building a community and a sense of belonging is essential for any group-based learning activity, and while it might be initially more challenging online, it can be done successfully (Hampel & Stickler, 2015). In our study, all teachers acknowledged that it is important to them to connect with students in creating a trusting atmosphere. The teachers described previous in-person classroom teaching as tangible experiences, being able to '*breathe them*', '*feeling information sinking in*', perceiving physical responses and overhearing conversations which are important feedback mechanisms for teachers to know students' progress and understandings. Physical presence, the ability to feel the energy when students talk over each other was also mentioned by Blum (2020) as a feature that contribute to making sense of interactions in a classroom. However, all our teachers thought that the online classroom offered many of these aspects at least visually, and they felt similar levels of connectedness with not much difference between how they connect with students in the classroom or online. They attributed this mostly to the small group sizes that allowed them to get to know the students on a more personal level and to be less formal with them. The teachers referred to our students as '*disciplined*' in this regard emphasising that they followed the rules that were initially given, and all tried to engage with all materials and tasks. This was further linked to command and functionality of technology as also stressed by Salmon (2011). Several teachers mentioned that a stable internet connection, turning on their cameras and microphones, and general digital competencies contribute to building good relationships.

In getting to know their students better, all teachers included personalised approaches to students to talk about their lives, experiences, and opinions, showing them that they listened and retained the information. One teacher mentions that she paid particular attention to students' personalities and individual qualities to achieve this. Several teachers agreed that much about building relationships online depends also on the students' personalities and openness of sharing as well as their level of language command with more proficient language users naturally able to share more personal insights and be more spontaneous and interactive. This illustrates the importance of the concepts of 'social presence' and 'teacher presence' as theorised within the Community of Inquiry framework (Garrison et al., 1999) and as a key to facilitating online community and supporting learning (Lomicka, 2020).

4.2.1 Communication Platforms

Numerous online platforms are now at teachers' disposal to facilitate communication with and between learners in online learning contexts. Specific strategies that our teachers developed in response to teaching the classes remotely include the use of additional social media platforms for communication which also facilitated less formal interactions. Gacs et al. (2020) remind us that 'a community atmosphere and personal connections have to be carefully crafted in online environments' (p. 382) especially when visual means are missing. Although the teachers had 2 h of synchronous teaching daily where they saw students in the online classroom, the additional media platforms needed more cautious use to really connect with students, especially because of the added hurdle of communicating through a foreign language.

Emma acknowledged that *'it's important as a group to get to know each other outside the classroom to get a sense of community'* which in f2f teaching would happen informally during break times or after classes. One of the teachers reported using Facebook messenger to connect with her cohort. First, it was used as an emergency response during the first class where the internet connection did not allow for much synchronous teaching time. They instantly discussed the issue on Messenger where students suggested alternatives to Skype. Through an authentic situation and the use of instant messaging the group connected and bonded using French to solve the problem. The teacher explained that this way of communicating on smartphones was much faster and more informal and allowed for further relationship building and discussions after class. She felt that she bonded faster with this cohort than with f2f cohorts because of the more informal way of sharing personal insights through social media. Another example included following up on a personal matter one student had raised during class time. Using social media communication platforms, the teacher could connect with the individual student in an informal and personalised way and extend her presence beyond class time and place restrictions (Means et al., 2014).

Our findings around communication platforms support Dixon's (2010) research which found that learners are more engaged in online programs when multiple communication channels are used. It also echoes Guillén et al. (2020) findings that Zoom fatigue can be prevented through the use of additional mobile technologies. Students' evaluations show that they enjoyed using informal channels in addition to the already informal Zoom classes. Students welcomed teachers using additional communication platforms to supplement traditional emails. They felt this made teachers more approachable and that they could continue their language learning beyond the structured class time.

4.2.2 Informal Communication

Another strategy identified which was often undertaken less consciously is teachers' reports of being more informal with the online students compared to larger f2f groups in classrooms settings where they normally establish more of a professional distance. All teachers reported using the personal pronoun 'tu' and first names as opposed to the formal 'vous' and encouraged students to do the same. Several teachers mention that this choice is not necessarily deliberate but comes from a less formal working atmosphere in the language school (as opposed to working at a university) and due to the small group size where classroom management or discipline was unnecessary. Using informal language could bridge the gap created by communicating through computer screens. Reflecting on her status, one teacher acknowledged that she adopted a more informal approach with this group without losing her authority, because the group was small and disciplined. She did not think a similar approach could be used in a f2f classroom though. The more individualised approach also enables teachers to continuously ask students for feedback and their input on content and methods.

Lomicka (2020) argues that it is important for teachers to be authentic in the classroom and that students value when teachers share something of themselves, including their own interests and stories. Gacs et al. (2020) echo this sentiment: 'many students enjoy seeing the human side, which includes mistakes and even intrusions from real life' (p. 388). Indeed, our students, though they were all surprised about the relaxed atmosphere, welcomed the informal approach and believed this contributed to relationship building and in making the learning more enjoyable. Students acknowledge this specifically, comparing this experience to the similarly "laid back" atmosphere in Australia as opposed to their study experiences in France and Canada where they perceived the teaching approach as more formal.

4.3   Innovations and Adaptation Strategies

In terms of changes to their normal approach, the program directors needed to create a new curriculum that took into account the absence of f2f opportunities and the requirements of our university to immerse students into language and culture learning to acquire knowledge and transferable skills for use beyond the language classroom context. This process led to a number of innovations by CREIPAC with regard to communication processes, teaching modes and platforms, content, and teaching and learning activities. These new approaches are introduced here with a focus on the integration of cultural immersion activities. Each teacher faced the challenge of incorporating this into their daily teaching and to find suitable platforms and methods for their cohort.

4.3.1 Blended Learning and Multimodal Approach

In their emergency response, the move to blended learning options was a logical step for the teachers in this course. Two teachers mentioned how they immediately switched to a blended learning approach embracing the opportunities that this posed for their cohorts. Having all files and documents in a single place to access for teaching enabled easy sharing of them with students. Teachers adopted a system where they sent students homework or post-class activities, so students could prepare for the following day and dive deeper into the content matter. Homework was also shared via the Zoom chat during class and other platforms such as shared folders, email, LearningApps.org, and Facebook Messenger after class which allowed students to further follow up and access the information after class ended. Through the same channels, student submitted their homework tasks and received feedback daily. The teachers describe this as an extension of the immersion from the normal class hours where students would normally log out and go about their life in their home setting. Instead, through blended learning and connections through communication platforms, they continued being immersed in French and learnt more about New Caledonia in their own time similar to what might happen if students were in-country.

Teachers in both levels of French classes commented that the blended learning modes helped them to individualise their teaching, to give responsibility to students in their learning process and to involve them more into the actual teaching time as they would present homework tasks they prepared beforehand. The multimodal approach was kept during class times too, making use of Zoom features such as screen sharing for slides and videos, the annotation whiteboard for joint and group activities, and the chat for vocabulary listings and questions. Another benefit that the multimodal teaching afforded was the distribution and personalisation of assessments. For listening and speaking tasks, teachers usually had to find different classrooms to assess students individually, whereas here they could meet students privately in breakout rooms and send them different audio links for their listening tasks, therefore avoiding the inconvenience of rigid exam supervision and room bookings. Students also had to asynchronously prepare presentations alone and with other students. These types of project-based learning activities are considered especially suitable for online learning (Link & Li, 2018) and in this case required higher levels of language use, collaboration, and regulation of emotional and behavioural processes by the students.

Students perceived the blended learning approach very positively and reported finding it easy to adjust to the new ways of accessing their language course. One student mentioned that it was much easier to stay engaged during classes as the interactivity kept them more engaged than in f2f classes where they often drift off. This was partially attributed to the interactivity possible through the small class size. They saw the ability to access different platforms synchronously as advantageous to help with understanding the subject matter, looking up vocabulary or accessing information.

4.3.2   Immersion Activities

One of the main drawbacks of an online program could be the lack of immersion into the languages and cultures of New Caledonia as the course is usually held in-country. As mentioned above, culture learning does not automatically happen in a language classroom or by being in another country. The teachers thought that physical presence in the country opens many more immersion opportunities after and in-between classes; however, they also critically acknowledge that students can be in the country without interacting with locals, instead merely observing local cultures. Interactions during breaks from class with other school staff, or with the students' homestay families are important opportunities that would usually help to develop their cultural understandings. In response, the program directors for the online program developed two innovative activities to creatively incorporate virtual immersion and exposing students to different cultural arenas of New Caledonia by facilitating contact with other students and locals. As all the teachers had moved to New Caledonia later in their lives, they felt the need to bring students together with various local community members to share others' experiences and insights.

Culture Experts
The first innovation included structuring each week around a cultural topic that an expert was invited to talk about and that many learning activities during the week aimed to prepare for linguistically. All teachers wanted to give students as much specifically New Caledonian vocabulary as possible to familiarise them with the local vernacular. The talks were described as linking 'the past with the present and future' and help students draw connections to their own situations with a critical view on various contemporary issues. As Emma commented: *'we showed them the beautiful things about New Caledonia, but also the plastic pollution'*. For the online program, the focus of each talk was as follows:

- An expert in the history of New Caledonia presented an overview of the country's rich pre- and post-colonial history and also spoke about contemporary issues such as the independence referendum. Classes were enriched by introducing essential vocabulary and grammatical points beforehand and giving students additional talking points and documents on the history after the class.
- The second expert introduced environmental aspects of New Caledonia's unique location and situation and discussed topics such as maritime life, and issues of pollution and degradation. In a f2f setting, students would see these aspects on tours of the islands and surrounding waters, but in the online mode, they viewed videos and were provided materials by the expert and the Tourism board and were then able to ask questions to engage with these aspects and reflect on their home environments further.
- The third expert was an Indigenous (Kanak) artist, musician and storyteller who was invited to read his creation tales and play a traditional flute. Preparation activities included videos to introduce students to the local Kanak dialects and vernacular and introduce Kanak voices on the referendum and post-colonialism (Image 1).

Image 1

Screenshot of Learning Apps page created to scaffold learning activities on Kanak culture and vocabulary.

Apart from the preparation materials and activities, the expert visits were then used to reflect on aspects of environmental issues, interculturality, and post-colonialism in Australia. Students had the opportunity to ask questions and voiced their views and knowledge on similar aspects in their home country but also assumptions they might have had on New Caledonia and its relationship to France and Australia. Where initially the teachers felt that students did not have much knowledge of New Caledonia, they felt that the three expert visits not only enhanced their cultural knowledge, but also filled the gaps they could themselves not deliver and to give students more encounters with other community members to make the experience more authentic, interactive, and as enriching as possible.

Another strategy to bring a New Caledonian experience to the students was for the teachers to relate their own experiences of moving to New Caledonia and adjusting to local cultures. One teacher shared her experience of living with Kanak communities on a small island and another shared her perspective of being excluded from the independence referendum and the various views on this. While using storytelling methods, key grammar and vocabulary learning were focussed on to enhance comprehension. The teachers found students to be engaged with these experiences, asking many questions, and reflecting on their own life journeys. Through these interactive sessions, the students as well as teachers and experts were able to receive insights into each other's experiences and lives showing that various interactions with different people/instructors can enhance learning on both sides.

Although the students acknowledged that not physically being in New Caledonia was not ideal, they did not see it as a major disadvantage for their cultural learning.

Travelling on their own and especially in times of a pandemic was not something they were willing to do, which made this online program a preferred option. They also mentioned affordability and accessibility as advantages, in times of a crises or border restrictions. Further, they found such a program to be an ideal way to distract from the negative emotional impact of pandemic restrictions and efficiently using their winter semester break to engage in learning something new. Students reacted very positively to the cultural experts, acknowledging the increased learning and feeling of immersion to one of Australia's closest neighbours. It inspired them to travel to New Caledonia once borders re-open and left them broadening their understanding of Francophone countries and other cultures in the Pacific region.

More significantly in terms of intercultural reflection, all students mentioned that the cultural activities triggered their thinking about their own society and its issues. They all admitted their knowledge gaps about environmental issues and reconciliation with Indigenous peoples in Australia. One student explained how they became aware of the lack of inclusion of Indigenous aspects in Australia. However, this notion was challenged by the French teachers who felt Australia to be more progressive with its Indigenous reconciliation efforts compare to New Caledonia. The cultural talks and reflection activities suggested that students developed their cultural competence further by 'practicing critical reflexivity, awareness of one's own culture and the ability to identify existing cultural bias' (Hyett et al., 2019, p. 390).

Interactions with Local Students

Enabling direct contact with residents of the host country enables authentic language use and contributes to 'diversifying geographically, culturally, and identity-wise their target-language community' (Guillén et al., 2020, p. 321). The emergency situation posed by COVID-19 also provided an opportunity to more intentionally connect with users of other languages virtually (Guillén et al., 2020) and helps to connect people affected by similar isolation processes and restrictions. Building on this, an additional immersive activity was introduced to purposely facilitate contact with other French speakers in two sessions during which the UTS students virtually "met" one-on-one with students from the Université de la Nouvelle-Calédonie (UNC). The UNC students were training to become French language teachers and therefore the reciprocity of the encounters in terms of language teaching and learning could be ensured. Students on both sides prepared a set of questions ranging from questions about the other's families, studies, jobs, travels, and future plans. The UNC students shared with UTS students' images or videos of New Caledonia, and their favourite food and music. The second meeting was more spontaneous where students were encouraged to freely interact with each other. This offered more opportunities for students to explore aspects of interest and to share experiences of the pandemic. Teachers observed these sessions and offered assistance.

Students reported these activities to be very valuable and effective in applying their language skills with peers. They found these meetings gave them unique insights into the life of students in New Caledonia and to hear about their personal circumstances, aspirations, and experiences. One student reported on how they exchanged aspects of multicultural life in their countries and how they took advantage of it. Another reported how different perceptions of living away from one's family to study and work intersected and at times clashed. Reflecting on the status of language learning, one student found Australia's approach to language education very lacking compared to New Caledonia as the students she interacted with were all at least trilingual. However, the student also mentioned a new appreciation of the opportunities in Australia including not needing to move away to pursue study or work opportunities. These insights show that this activity and the subsequent reflection on it challenged students' initial perceptions and triggered self-reflection, two important aspects of critical cultural competence development (Hyett et al., 2019).

5   Discussion and Recommendations

The teachers' initial reactions to moving to online teaching under pandemic-enforced restrictions surprised us, and we found ourselves being corrected on our initial assumptions. Where it took us a few weeks to adjust our own teaching to the new online world, these teachers had already experience in online teaching and instantly adapted their teaching methods. These teachers in a small island nation showed us that online teaching had been a part of their teaching and mindset for years already and that language teachers have to adjust to new circumstances all the time embracing new opportunities. CREIPAC's innovative approach to incorporating cultural immersion through bringing experts and students into the online classroom effectively helped students engage with the culture topics, practice their language skills, and to feel like they have been immersed and experienced various New Caledonian cultural facets.

Being asked for which recommendations a teacher would give others or what they would do differently, they stated that the blended learning approach requires more consistent preparation of pre- and post-class activities and also the increased and consistent testing of knowledge. In order to build communities online, they recommend teachers listening and stepping back so students can engage more with each other, rather than a teacher-centred approach. An initial "practice run" where the digital tools and platforms will be explained (in English) and clear instructions on classroom etiquette were further mentioned.

Students agreed that taking the class time seriously, preparing for classes, doing homework, and actively collaborating during class all helped them to get more out of the program. Overcoming one's fears of interacting in another language online takes as much effort as f2f but can ultimately bring the same learning outcomes and engagement in classes.

6 Food for Thought: Beyond ERT

From our years of experience in student mobility programs, virtual and online programs never seemed possible or were marked as second-class experiences. Through the interviews with teachers and students we learnt that both groups were way more open to emergency remote learning and teaching than we expected. In fact, none of our participants mentioned that any part of the program felt like a makeshift solution but were well planned and executed. Although Hodges et al. (2020) make the point that learning evaluations in ERT should not be focus due to the short period of time that was provided to develop materials, our study shows that this can be done very successfully with a high level of success and satisfaction for faculty, instructors, and students.

Emergency remote teaching is often perceived as temporary and the return to f2f is seen as inevitable (Hodges et al., 2020); however, the success of this program shows that learning can continue in two forms and online immersive programs may thrive if we learn from the initial emergency response and develop sound curricula for future cohorts (Goertler & Gacs, 2018). The fact that a new group of students has already enrolled into the program half a year after the initial online program, shows that they have already embraced online immersive learning and are more than willing to continue to participate in this more accessible and sustainable program. Though technology is an integral part, a well-developed curriculum and pedagogical practices are the key to the success (González-Lloret, 2020).

As a form of immersive language and culture learning, a scaffolded approach with preparation activities and guided reflection opportunities throughout and after the program remains important so that students can maximise the many learning outcomes afforded by an online language and culture program.

Digital Tools Used

Digital platforms	Methodological use
Zoom (whiteboard, annotations, breakout rooms, chat)	For synchronous learning activities: whiteboard and annotations for grammar learning; breakout rooms for collaboration, chat function for vocabulary and sharing of links
Facebook Messenger	Informal chats after class and for questions on the materials and homework
Email	For homework submissions and feedback
YouTube	To present authentic videos of cultural and language aspects
LearningApps.org	Creation of a sequence of activities such as gap filling, matching, texts, video, and audio

References

Bañados, E. (2006). A blended-learning pedagogical model for teaching and learning EFL successfully through an online interactive multimedia environment. *CALICO Journal, 23*(3), 533–550. https://doi.org/10.1558/cj.v23i3.533-550

Baran, E., Correia, A. P., & Thompson, A. D. (2013). Tracing successful online teaching in higher education: Voices of exemplary online teachers. *Teachers College Record, 115*(3), 41.

Blum, S. (2020). Why we're exhausted by Zoom. *Inside Higher Education.* https://www.insidehighered.com/advice/2020/04/22/professor-explores-why-zoom-classes-deplete-her-energy-opinion

Collie, R. J., & Martin, A. J. (2016). Adaptability: An important capacity for effective teachers. *Educational Practice and Theory, 38*(1), 27–39. https://doi.org/10.7459/ept/38.1.03

Comas-Quinn, A., de los Arcos, B., & Mardomingo, R. (2012). Virtual learning environments (VLEs) for distance language learning: Shifting tutor roles in a contested space for interaction. *Computer Assisted Language Learning, 25*(2), 129–143. https://doi.org/10.1080/0958822 1.2011.636055

Compton, L. K. L. (2009). Preparing language teachers to teach language online: A look at skills, roles, and responsibilities. *Computer Assisted Language Learning, 22*(1), 73–99. https://doi.org/10.1080/09588220802613831

Crawford, J., Butler-Henderson, K., Rudolp, J., Malkawi, B., Glowatz, M., Burton, R., Magni, P. A., & Lam, S. (2020). COVID-19: 20 countries' higher education intra-period digital pedagogy responses. *Journal of Applied Learning & Teaching, 3*(1), 9–28. https://doi.org/10.37074/jalt.2020.3.1.7

De Paepe, L., Zhu, C., & Depryck, K. (2019). Development and implementation of online Dutch L2 courses in adult education: Educators' and providers' perceptions of constraints and critical success factors. *Innovation in Language Learning and Teaching, 13*(3), 277–291. https://doi.org/10.1080/17501229.2018.1462369

De Wit, H. (2016). Internationalisation and the role of online intercultural exchange. In R. O'Dowd & T. Lewis (Eds.), *Online intercultural exchange: Policy, pedagogy, practice* (pp. 192–208). Routledge.

Dixon, M. (2010). Creating effective student engagement in online courses: What do students find engaging? *Journal of the Scholarship of Teaching and Learning, 10*, 1–13.

Du, J., Liu, Y., & Brown, R. L. (2010). The key elements of online learning communities. In H. H. Yang & S. C. Y. Yuen (Eds.), *Handbook of research on practices and outcomes in e-learning: Issues and trends* (pp. 119–132). IGI Global. https://doi.org/10.4018/978-1-60566-788-1

Gacs, A., Goertler, S., & Spasova, S. (2020). Planned online language education versus crisis-prompted online language teaching: Lessons for the future. *Foreign Language Annals, 53*(2), 380–392. https://doi.org/10.1111/flan.12460

Garcés, P., & O'Dowd, R. (2020). Upscaling virtual exchange in university education: Moving from innovative classroom practice to regional governmental policy. *Journal of Studies in International Education.* https://doi.org/10.1177/1028315320932323

Garrison, D. R., Anderson, T., & Archer, W. (1999). Critical inquiry in a text-based environment: Computer conferencing in higher education model. *The Internet and Higher Education, 2*(2–3), 87–105. https://doi.org/10.1016/S1096-7516(00)00016-6

Goertler, S., & Gacs, A. (2018). Assessment in online German: Assessment methods and results. *Die Unterrichtspraxis/Teaching German, 51*, 156–174. https://doi.org/10.1111/tger.12071

González-Lloret, M. (2020). Collaborative tasks for online language teaching. *Foreign Language Annals, 53*(2), 260–269. https://doi.org/10.1111/flan.12466

Guillén, G., Sawin, T., & Avineri, N. (2020). Zooming out of the crisis: Language and human collaboration. *Foreign Language Annals, 53*(2), 320–328. https://doi.org/10.1111/flan.12459

Guth, S., & Helm, F. (2017). *SUNY COIL Stevens initiative assessment.* http://coil.suny.edu/sites/default/files/2018-01/SUNY%20COIL%20Stevens%20Initiative%20Assessment.pdf

Hall, D., & Knox, J. (2009). Issues in the education of TESOL teachers by distance education. *Distance Education, 30*(1), 63–85. https://doi.org/10.1080/01587910902845964

Hampel, R., & Stickler, U. (Eds.). (2015). *Developing online language teaching: Research-based pedagogies and reflective practices.* Palgrave.

Hancock, D. R., & Algozzine, R. (2006). *Doing case study research: A practical guide for beginning researchers.* Teachers College Press.

Hodges, C. B., & Forrest Cowan, S. (2012). Preservice teachers' views of instructor presence in online courses. *Journal of Digital Learning in Teacher Education, 28*(4), 139–145.

Hodges, C., Moore, S., Lockee, B., Trust, T., & Bond, A. (2020). The difference between emergency remote teaching and online learning. *Educause Review, 27.* https://er.educause.edu/articles/2020/3/the-difference-between-emergency-remote-teaching-and-online-learning

Hyett, N., Lee, K. M., Knevel, R., Fortune, T., Yau, M. K., & Borkovic, S. (2019). Trialing virtual intercultural learning with Australian and Hong Kong allied health students to improve cultural competency. *Journal of Studies in International Education, 23*(3), 389–406. https://doi.org/10.1177/1028315318786442

Link, S., & Li, J. (Eds.). (2018). *Assessment across online language education.* Equinox.

Lomicka, L. (2020). Creating and sustaining virtual language communities. *Foreign Language Annals, 53*(2), 306–313. https://doi.org/10.1111/flan.12456

Means, B., Bakia, M., & Murphy, R. (2014). *Learning online: What research tells us about whether, when and how.* Routledge.

Mendieta, J., & Barkhuizen, G. (2020). Blended language learning in the Colombian context: A narrative inquiry of teacher ownership of curriculum change. *Computer Assisted Language Learning, 33*(3), 176–196. https://doi.org/10.1080/09588221.2018.1553888

Mueller, B. (2021). It's all in the mind: Developing new ways of thinking and acting during a semester abroad: An australian case study. In E. Mikulec, S. Potempa, & K. P. Imman (Eds.), *Education abroad: Learning environments in a global context* (pp. 19–37). Information Age Publishing.

Mueller, B., & Oguro, S. (2021). Closing the gap: Facilitating employability development in international internship subjects. In S. Ferns, A. Rowe, & K. Zegwaard (Eds.), *Theories, practices and research in work-integrated learning in Australia: Enhancing employability capabilities for a sustainable future* (pp. 191–200). Routledge.

O'Dowd, R. (2018). From telecollaboration to virtual exchange: State-of-the-art and the role of UNICollaboration in moving forward. *Journal of Virtual Exchange, 1,* 1–23. https://doi.org/10.14705/rpnet.2018.jve.1

O'Dowd, R. (2019). A transnational model of virtual exchange for global citizenship education. *Language Teaching,* 1–14. https://doi.org/10.1017/S0261444819000077

O'Dowd, R., & Lewis, T. (Eds.). (2016). *Online intercultural exchange: Policy, pedagogy, practice.* Routledge.

Richardson, S. (2016). *Cosmopolitan learning for a global era.* Routledge.

Richardson, J. C., Koehler, A. A., Besser, E. D., Caskurlu, S., Lim, J., & Mueller, C. M. (2015). Conceptualizing and investigating instructor presence in online learning environments. *The International Review of Research in Open and Distributed Learning, 16*(3), 256–297. https://doi.org/10.19173/irrodl.v16i3.2123

Salmon, G. (2011). *Moderating: The key to teaching and learning online.* Taylor & Francis.

Shelley, M., Murphy, L., & White, C. (2013). Language teacher development in a narrative frame: The transition from classroom to distance and blended settings. *System, 41*(3), 560–574. https://doi.org/10.1016/j.system.2013.06.002

Sheridan, K., & Kelly, M. A. (2010). The indicators of instructor presence that are important to students in online courses. *MERLOT Journal of Online Learning and Teaching, 6*(4), 767–779.

Thomas, G., & Thorpe, S. (2019). Enhancing the facilitation of online groups in higher education: A review of the literature on face-to-face and online group-facilitation. *Interactive Learning Environments, 27*(1), 62–71. https://doi.org/10.1080/10494820.2018.1451897

Tudini, V. (2018). Interactivity in the teaching and learning of foreign languages: What it means for resourcing and delivery of online and blended programmes. *The Language Learning Journal, 46*(2), 132–145. https://doi.org/10.1080/09571736.2014.994183

Part V
Teacher Voice: Language Learners and Adaptive Pedagogy

Implications of a Sudden Shift Online: The Experiences of English Education Students' Studying Online for the First-Time During COVID-19 Pandemic in Japan

Jean Kim

Highlights

- How pandemic-initiated online EFL courses were developed and facilitated to accommodate and support novice students in higher education.
- Shifting attitudes towards learning English online from negative to positive.
- Implications for providing guidance for educators in the development and/or maintenance of online EFL courses.

1 Background Information

Online education has had rapid growth internationally, and the use of technology in online education can be seen as a common practice worldwide. More than 28% of tertiary-level students are enrolled in online courses in higher education (Budhai & Williams, 2016). Universities appear to increasingly offer online courses as it seems to be cost-effective to facilitate and increase student enrolment (Driscoll et al., 2012).

On the contrary, there appears to be a lack of technology use in teaching practice in Japan (O'Donoghue, 2020). In February 2020, the Japanese government confirmed the COVID-19 outbreak and locked down schools nationwide and online education became the only remaining medium of teaching (Allen, 2021, chapter "Infrastructure, Literacy and Communication: The Challenges of Emergency Remote Teaching in a University in Japan" in this volume). Although Japan used to be a leading country in technology development, the implementation of online education in Japan lags behind other OECD countries (Luu, 2020). The pandemic situation has created a huge and sudden shift from face-to-face and teacher-centred

J. Kim (✉)
University of Canterbury, Christchurch, New Zealand
e-mail: jean.kim@canterbury.ac.nz

© The Author(s), under exclusive license to Springer Nature
Switzerland AG 2021
J. Chen (ed.), *Emergency Remote Teaching and Beyond*,
https://doi.org/10.1007/978-3-030-84067-9_10

classroom interactions to online interactions on digital platforms across educational sectors (Obe & Okutsu, 2020; also see chapter "Infrastructure, Literacy and Communication: The Challenges of Emergency Remote Teaching in a University in Japan" in this volume). To date, the use of technology, desktops or laptops in particular, in daily life has not yet reached the current global standard (McCarty et al., 2017); for example, university students tend not to bring their own laptop or tablet to classes, and courses still appear to be paper-based and textbook-oriented in higher education.

English is categorised as a foreign language in Japan. That is, English is not a medium of communication in day-to-day interactions. Students may not always view how speaking English fits into the context of their lives, but they go through the process of passing English exams to enhance possible future career options. This has led students to mainly focus on vocabulary and grammar features that are demonstrated by teachers. Within this teacher-centred instruction, learning tasks and materials are not always related to relevant real-life contexts (McCarty et al., 2017).

This chapter aims to explore how pandemic-initiated online education has impacted teaching and learning English as a foreign language in a tertiary educational context in Japan. The chapter investigates students' experiences of their first-time online learning and their feelings about satisfaction, advantages, and challenges of studying these online English courses. The chapter sheds light on the sudden shift from classroom education to online education in a tertiary setting and hopes to suggest research-informed implications for the initial and immediate development of EFL courses to support educators and teachers who wish to facilitate courses online. Given the importance of the immediate development of online courses, the Community of Inquiry (CoI) framework has proved to be a useful tool to facilitate courses. In the following section, the CoI and the relevant studies are reviewed.

2 Review of the Related Studies on Online Education

2.1 Community of Inquiry (CoI)

The CoI theory can be seen as a useful tool to design, facilitate and evaluate online education (Garrison et al., 1999; Garrison & Cleveland-Innes, 2005; Holbeck & Hartman, 2018; Shea & Bidjerano, 2009). This framework can guide teachers when they develop and facilitate courses online in higher education. There are three core elements; teaching presence, social presence, and cognitive presence, that need to be integrated into the online community in order to promote successful learning for students (Garrison et al., 1999; Shea & Bidjerano, 2009).

Teaching presence is defined as designing, organising, and facilitating courses (Garrison & Cleveland-Innes, 2005; Holbeck & Hartman, 2018), and direct instruction (Garrison, 2019; Kilis & Yildirim, 2019). It is identified as a key factor in enhancing and developing learners' sense of belonging to the online community; social presence (Shea & Bidjerano, 2009). Through successful teaching and social presence, learners are able to critically think and reflect on learning; cognitive presence. Therefore, teaching presence influences the integration of the core elements that foster the development of social and cognitive presence (Garrison & Cleveland-Innes, 2005; Hay et al., 2004; Wu & Hiltz, 2004).

To promote teaching presence, the role of the teacher is crucial (Preisman, 2014; Worley & Tesdell, 2009) in that it affects learner performance and course satisfaction (McFarland & Hamilton, 2005). In online settings, students value the teacher's performance as a determinant of learning success (Brocato et al., 2015). Teachers need to consider setting topics related to real-life experiences, assigning regular activities for both individuals and groups during the course, fostering a safe environment through friendly behaviour, and providing immediate feedback (Kilis & Yildirim, 2019).

Social presence is defined as "the ability to project one's self and establish personal and purposeful relationships" (Garrison, 2019, p. 63) that enables students to develop a sense of belonging amongst themselves and leads to deep learning, helping to fundamentally achieve students' educational goals (Garrison & Cleveland-Innes, 2005). There are three aspects of social presence: emotional expression, open communication, and group cohesion (Garrison et al., 1999; Kilis & Yildirim, 2019). Emotional expression can be seen as a positive factor in the development of social presence (Garrison et al., 1999). When students share personal information and express their emotions during online courses, it increases their engagement in the online community, thereby reducing their feelings of social isolation. This enables students to have open communication with classmates, become mutually aware of each other, and voluntarily participate in group discussions in threaded discussion forums. Students' collaboration through critical discourse positively affects learners' achievement (Holbeck & Hartman, 2018). Assigning group projects, a form of collaboration, promotes group cohesion that enhances the development of social presence (Cunningham & Bergstrom, 2020).

Cognitive presence can be seen as the most significant element in the framework (Akyol & Garrison, 2008). Cognitive presence is defined as the confirmation stage of learning for students when exploring and integrating knowledge to solve problems through a reflective mechanism (Garrison, 2019). As online courses progress, students start recognising problems and become curious to solve them. They explore contents and integrate them into a wider setting to synthesise, reflect on the problems, and think critically to solve the problems (Kilis & Yildirim, 2019). There are some teaching strategies for promoting cognitive presence: addressing real-life topics (Kilis & Yildirim, 2019), facilitating asynchronous discussion (Garrison & Cleveland-Innes, 2005), and facilitating interactions between teacher-student, content-student, student-student (Garrison & Cleveland-Innes, 2005). Taking the chosen framework into consideration, I will explore how these strategies affect and influence the development and progression of online teaching in higher education in the following section.

2.2 Factors Affecting Online Learning

Well-designed online courses with appropriate pedagogy are likely to provide effective learning environments that are equivalent to outcomes from face-to-face courses (Driscoll et al., 2012). In fact, the online setting has the benefits of providing a virtual space to archive teaching materials and offers flexibility for students to gain access to the archived files (McFarland & Hamilton, 2005). Accessible teaching materials and effective course delivery increases student engagement that supports the development of social presence (Holbeck & Hartman, 2018). When course topics are related to real-life experiences, students display self-disclosure and are willing to foster a collaborative learning environment (Kilis & Yildirim, 2019). This enables students to become motivated to fully participate in communications and group collaboration online (Garrison, 2019) both of which increase students' satisfaction (McFarland & Hamilton, 2005).

Student satisfaction is identified as the most influential factor in determining the success of online courses (Thurmond et al., 2002). In online settings, students value interactions with teachers and peers that foster both teaching and social presence (Mohd Khalid & Quick, 2016). Through these interactions, both students and teachers are likely to achieve their goals in online education (Bolliger & Wasilik, 2009), and become satisfied with outcomes.

The use of video conferencing is an effective tool to increase co-presence in a virtual environment (Kozar, 2016) and promote teacher-student and student-student interactions in an online environment (Maher, 2020). This also enables teachers to gain access to external professionals to provide focused information in their teaching context (Maher, 2020). With its flexibility in time and space, teachers are able to virtually take students to an overseas location, to some extent. There is, however, a lack of research on the use of video conferencing in English language education during the pandemic (Maher, 2020).

Using Zoom's breakout rooms facilitates student-student interactions (Cunningham & Bergstrom, 2020). When participating in group discussions in breakout rooms, students have an opportunity to gain a deeper understanding of topics and compare their own opinions/thoughts with others, thereby leading to increased feelings of intimacy (Logan et al., 2002). Consequently, students are encouraged to actively participate in the course and develop group cohesion.

Collaborating work on the threaded discussion forum is claimed to both reduce learner anxiety and increase a willingness to communicate in online learning (Logan et al., 2002). In a teacher-centred and open classroom environment, students may become unwilling to actively participate in discussions, whereas students may feel less intimidated by an online medium. Through asynchronous communication in threaded discussion forums, students have an equal opportunity to post their thoughts and reflections, respond to each other in a safe environment (Clark-Ibáñez & Scott, 2008). This results in the student displaying self-disclosure and promoting student engagement to the online group (Logan et al., 2002).

Due to the flexibility of online learning, students are able to take advantage of a student-centred learning environment by taking classes anywhere at a convenient time therefore avoiding the time pressures of commuting. Students tend to become self-driven and take a spontaneous and more responsible position for their study which enhances learner autonomy (Logan et al., 2002). Under online circumstances, students are likely to focus more on the content of the course and therefore have more opportunities to voice their views and reflections to enhance their learning (Logan et al., 2002).

Although former studies articulate benefits and advantages, there are some identified challenges in online education. A lack of students' experience in prior online courses can be identified as a hindering factor in students' satisfaction (McFarland & Hamilton, 2005). Students in a face-to-face environment appear to view interactions with teachers and peers as an important factor in their study and value a real-time and in-person discussion when seeking answers. In this regard, in student-centred instruction, feelings of learning through group collaboration are reported to be lower than actual learning. Often, novice students who have not been exposed to an active learning environment are unable to accurately evaluate their *actual* learning (Deslauriers et al., 2019). While students in student-centred settings outperform the teacher-centred setting in their studies, their perception of learning appears to be low. In addition, some passive students often report that discussion with peers in both online and face-to-face contexts does not help with their learning in a student-centred environment as they have greater value of direct instruction from teachers (Deslauriers et al., 2019).

As with face-to-face instruction, if students do not develop a sense of belonging to an online community they may harvest feelings of loneliness and isolation (Bowers & Kumar, 2015) which impedes satisfaction and performance (McFarland & Hamilton, 2005). Research claimed collaborative activities in threaded discussion forums as a positive factor in developing social and cognitive presence (Clark-Ibáñez & Scott, 2008; Garrison & Cleveland-Innes, 2005), whereas, other research suggested that posting a non-anonymous task online may increase learner anxiety (Gruber & Bauer, 2020). Some passive students may not be willing to publicise their thoughts and reflections in threaded discussion forums that hinders active participation in collaborative activities.

3   The Raised Questions to Understand This Unprecedented Phenomenon

In line with the background information and the identified influential factors from the relevant literature, some questions are raised to explore and investigate a sudden shift online in the Japanese context:

1. What are the students' experiences of pandemic-initiated online English language courses?

2. Are the students satisfied with their first-time English language learning online, or otherwise?
3. What are the advantages and challenges for the students when immediately learning English language courses online?

4   Description of Teaching Context and Student Profile

This chapter focused on three graduate General English courses[1] with 53 students that I facilitated in my university during semester 1, 2020. Prior to COVID-19, these courses were facilitated as traditional face-to-face classes on campus, but due to the nationwide lockdown, the course delivery changed to an online format. The courses are non-mandatory but are voluntarily chosen by students from diverse faculties and age groups. The teaching context is English Medium Instruction (EMI) in a module focused on learning EFL. The structure of the courses was framed by the CoI and a communicative task-based approach.

Both the pre- and post-course questionnaires were administrated online and were assigned on Manaba.[2] The students were asked to complete the pre-course questionnaire in reference to the course in which they were enrolled and 47 students, out of 53, completed the questionnaire. As a result, the topics of the courses were selected: English for daily life, English for study, English for travelling, and English for work. Based on these topics, I produced real-life contextual materials in English and posted them on Manaba prior to the courses. The post-course questionnaire asked the students about their experiences of, and feelings about first-time online education, including course contents and delivery (teaching presence), student engagement and collaborative work (social presence), satisfaction and achievement (cognitive presence), and making suggestions to overcome identified challenges. The questionnaire contained 82 questions: 64 with a 5-point Likert scale, ranging from 1: strongly disagree to 5: strongly agree, six multiple choices, and 12 open-ended questions (see Fig. 1). Forty-three students completed the post-course questionnaire. During the course, students' participation, three English writing tasks, and the presentation on course reflection were examined to determine the students' final grade. Table 1 shows the completion of each task.

The courses were only delivered online instruction and were delivered using both Manaba and Zoom. Manaba was the hub of course information that enabled the teacher to post teaching materials and resources and to facilitate text-based communications between the teacher-student(s) and student-student. Zoom was used to facilitate synchronous class interactions for 90 min once a week. In the first Zoom webinar, I welcomed all students and introduced the course contents, objectives, assignments, and assessments. The students were invited to introduce themselves

---

[1] All the courses accommodated multi-level students from beginner to intermediate level.

[2] Manaba is an online learning management system (LMS) in the study university.

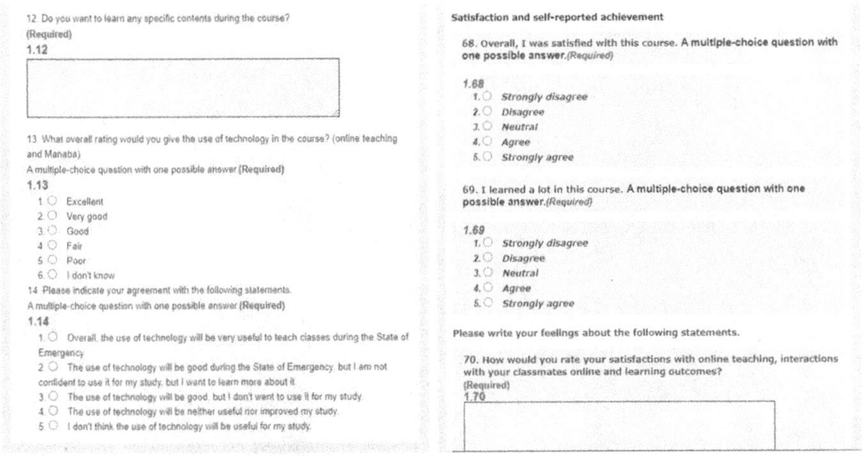
12 Do you want to learn any specific contents during the course?
(Required)
1.12

13 What overall rating would you give the use of technology in the course? (online teaching and Manaba)
A multiple-choice question with one possible answer (Required)
1.13
1. Excellent
2. Very good
3. Good
4. Fair
5. Poor
6. I don't know

14 Please indicate your agreement with the following statements.
A multiple-choice question with one possible answer (Required)
1.14
1. Overall, the use of technology will be very useful to teach classes during the State of Emergency
2. The use of technology will be good during the State of Emergency, but I am not confident to use it for my study, but I want to learn more about it
3. The use of technology will be good, but I don't want to use it for my study
4. The use of technology will be neither useful nor improved my study
5. I don't think the use of technology will be useful for my study

Satisfaction and self-reported achievement

68. Overall, I was satisfied with this course. A multiple-choice question with one possible answer.(Required)

1.68
1. Strongly disagree
2. Disagree
3. Neutral
4. Agree
5. Strongly agree

69. I learned a lot in this course. A multiple-choice question with one possible answer.(Required)

1.69
1. Strongly disagree
2. Disagree
3. Neutral
4. Agree
5. Strongly agree

Please write your feelings about the following statements.

70. How would you rate your satisfactions with online teaching, interactions with your classmates online and learning outcomes?
(Required)
1.70

Fig. 1 Screenshot of the pre- and post-questionnaire

Table 1 Number of completion of each task

Task	Number of completion	Percentage
Course enrolment	53	100%
Pre-course questionnaire (Pre-Q)	47	88.7%
Writing task 1 (WT1)– Teaching presence	52	98.1%
Writing task 2 (WT2)– Social presence	43	81.1%
Writing task 3 (WT3)– Cognitive presence	44	83.0%
Presentation (P)– Course evaluation	47	88.7%
Post-course questionnaire (Post-Q)	43	81.1%

and ask questions about the teacher, classmates, course contents, and process. Collaborative activities of both a personal and analytical discussion were assigned on a threaded discussion board on Manaba during the courses. The thread discussion allowed students to post their answers to the questions and comment on their peers' responses (see Fig. 2). Students were also encouraged to share their knowledge and experiences during a real-time class on Zoom and applied their learning to regular activities. Diverse English speakers,[3] mainly from New Zealand, were invited to the real-time class fortnightly via Zoom. This provided more opportunities for students to implement their learning in a realistic situation online. The teacher monitored and gave suggestions when necessary.

[3] Across the course, seven English speakers (ESOL teachers) were invited to attend at different times; every fortnight, an ESOL teacher was invited to the three courses. Four of them were in New Zealand, two in Japan, and one in Hong Kong.

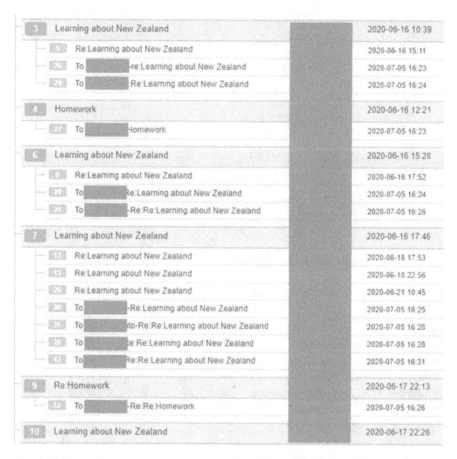

Fig. 2 Screenshot of analytical discussion task on thread discussion board with students' names deleted

The live class sessions via Zoom lasted for 90 min per week for a duration of 13 weeks.[4] During the live class, the students were paired or grouped and assigned in breakout rooms to work collaboratively. Students shared their experiences, knowledge, and thoughts on the topic for 5 min, and changed breakout rooms to talk with a different group of students. The teacher attended a different breakout room to monitor the students' interactions and provided feedback on their work. Posting students' work on an asynchronous discussion board; a thread discussion on Manaba, was used to identify indicators for the development and maintenance of social, cognitive, and teaching presence (Kilis & Yildirim, 2019). Based on the course topics, discussion questions were designed and required students to present their ideas and reflections on a weekly basis. Both the teacher and peer-students

---

[4] Prior to COVID-19, classes last for 90 min per week for a duration of 15 weeks in a face-to-face setting.

commented on students' posts. This enabled students to assure an understanding of the contents and build a sense of membership in the online community. Initially, I asked students discussion questions to share their experiences or ideas of the week's topic (e.g., If/When you met a foreigner who asked you for help in English at the train station, what would/did you say and do?) to get to know each other. Later, evaluative and analytical questions were asked to develop critical thinking skills (e.g. Looking at the educational systems in New Zealand and Japan, which educational system would bring better outcomes?).

In order to gain a deeper understanding of pandemic-initiated online EFL courses in my university in Japan, I examined 53 students and their work for 13 weeks over three English courses. Pre- and post-course questionnaires, students' reflective writings on Manaba, and the final exam were conducted to collect data, and thematic analysis (Vaismoradi et al., 2013) was employed to analyse the data. In the following section, results regarding students' experience of the pandemic-initiated online course, satisfaction, and benefits and challenges of online learning are addressed with students' quotes from the post-course questionnaire to illustrate their voices and reflections regarding English courses online.

5 Findings

5.1 Shift from Negative to Positive in Online Learning

Overall, despite negative thoughts about online lectures prior to the courses, the majority of students reported having positive experiences of the EFL courses as it was seen to significantly enhance their English language proficiency. Figure 3 shows the result of questions about the use of digital tools, students' feelings about progress, and outcomes from the post-course questionnaire.

A lack of both pedagogical understanding and technological skills caused the students to have negative feelings about online learning (WT1). All the students indicated their negative feelings about online learning before the course started. In Japan, traditional, text book-oriented, and face-to-face settings are still common practice in educational settings (Obe & Okutsu, 2020). This causes the students lack of ability in using technology in their study and exposure to online education. The study university informed the teaching staff that there were many students who did not have either a desktop or a laptop. According to the post-course questionnaire (Post-Q), the majority of the students owned (95.3%) and used (81.4%) either a desktop or laptop in addition to a smartphone in their study. In contrary to the literature, only two students reported having only a smartphone to use in their study. Figure 4 shows the number of digital devices owned and used in students' study.

Although the ratio of access to digital devices is relatively high, some students reported feeling anxious about using a digital device for their study: "*I was anxious because I'm not good at using a computer. So if I used it I would break it*", and "*I*

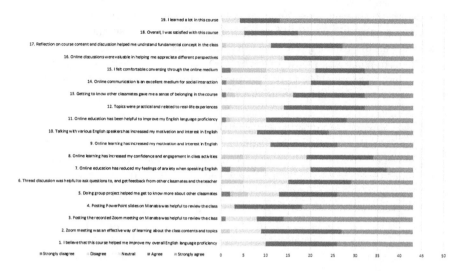

Fig. 3 Students' reported feelings about satisfaction and achievement in the present study

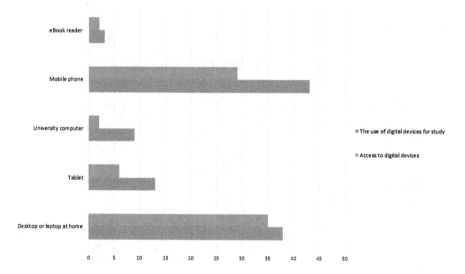

Fig. 4 Access to digital devices and the use of digital devices for study

used Zoom for the first-time so I was nervous because I don't know how to use it"* (Post-Q).

Due to traditional classroom teaching being common practice in Japan, many students reported valuing face-to-face classroom teaching more as they believed that learning takes place through interactions in person. In the Pre-Q, almost all the students reported similar answers to these quotes: *"I don't like online very much. You have to meet your classmates in person to understand them"*, and *"I felt uneasy about studying alone at home"*. As the students outlined their lack of experience and understanding of online learning, they reported having negative attitudes towards the first-time pandemic-initiated online courses.

As the courses progressed, the students' negative feelings gradually changed to being positive. Students reported that both accessing materials on Manaba and participating in Zoom meetings were easier than expected. This led students to find the online classroom setting was similar to face-to-face teaching. One student reflected on the development of social presence a couple of weeks after the course started by stating that *"I feel connected, but I don't know why"* (WT1). Four weeks later, the students posted their positive feelings about attending a real-time class on Zoom: *"Online classes are more fun and practical than I thought"*, and *"My worry disappeared immediately"* (WT2). Even a student who did not have a desktop/laptop expressed; *"Now I understand I don't need to use a computer. I can study online on my smartphone.....The class on Zoom can do many exciting things that can only be online"* (WT2). The lack of online learning experience made most of the students anxious (90.7%), but in reality, the students have found that online education is affordable and has more potential.

The use of Manaba is reported to be an important factor in getting easy access to both course materials and recorded webinars before, during, and after the course. All class materials were produced as PowerPoint slides and Word documents, uploaded on Manaba before the semester started. Many students mentioned that *"the PowerPoint materials were very easy to read. I thought the important parts were written concisely, and it was easy to review when doing tasks"* (WT1). Each webinar on Zoom was recorded and the link posted on Manaba. This enabled the students to watch the recorded webinar again at their convenience. Initially, 81.4% of the students revisited the recordings to gain a deeper understanding of the class' contents, then posted their thoughts on this, such as; *"Watching the recorded webinar is very useful to study English"* (WT1).

Facilitating a real-time class via Zoom weekly was found to be successfully supportive in student learning and engagement online. Zoom was reported to be easy to use and facilitated teacher-students and student-student interactions similar to taking classes in person. This was verified in the students' posts on Manaba: *"I think online is a good idea. It was easy to talk to people. I like Zoom"* (WT1), *"it made me feel like I had met them without having to meet them in person"* (WT2), and *"I can't experience such experience in face-to-face because I can always see the faces of my classmates and understand their expressions and reactions online"* (Post-Q).

Through Zoom interactions, the students were able to be immersed in the target language and culture in daily life circumstances in New Zealand. This helped them build their English language competence by practising spontaneous communication with native English speakers. Every fortnight, various ESOL teachers, mainly from New Zealand, were invited to the class. The students had an opportunity to ask questions about the topic of the week. During the classes with the guest teachers, there were two occasions when the guest teacher's family took part in class and naturally talked about their house. The students valued this experience in the Post-Q by stating that *"It was great to see a guest teacher's home environment. Her mother and her dog suddenly joined the class and we had a chance to talk with them. I can understand their lifestyle in New Zealand. It was a great experience"*. Getting more access to native English speakers helped the majority of students (81.4%) gain confidence and become more motivated to speak in English.

> English course online is so fun. Because I can try to speak in English and know culture of New Zealand. The guest teachers and the teacher are so kind and friendly. I enjoyed talking with them. I love the class.
>
> I can't communicate much in other classes. I'm so happy to talk to the guest teachers. I wanted to be able to speak more English after taking this class. I look forward to every Tuesday.

Group interactions in a breakout room are reported as both a positive factor by the 67.4% of the students and a negative factor by some passive students (32.6%). From the positive response group, students reported having more opportunities to speak in English and understanding common thoughts of the peers that assured them about learning and helped them gain more insight into the topic. These students expressed that *"Group discussion [was the best]. Each student's questions were unique. I liked debating in a group discussion with different people every week"* (Post-Q), and *"When we are solving a given problem together in a breakout room, we can talk about it and find out what we don't understand and solve it together"* (Post-Q). This also provided an opportunity for some students at a lower level to gain clarification about uncertain elements from either classmates or the teacher in a small group setting. One student noted that *"During group discussions, we spoke in both English and Japanese. Through this, I could double-check with the group members, and made me assured that I understood the content"* (Post-Q). Group discussion in a breakout room provided students peer-support by speaking in both English and Japanese to clarify and gain a deeper understanding of the class contents.

There are, however, some students who negatively commented about the breakout room activities. As the classes consisted of multi-levelled and multi-aged groups of students from diverse faculties, some of the passive students did not feel comfortable talking with classmates outside of their peer groups. In Japan, it is the cultural norm for students who are older than them, senior, and students who are younger, junior, instead of calling by name. Although the students learned the cultural norms in English-speaking countries, i.e. New Zealand, and were encouraged to practise New Zealand cultural norms during the class activities, they appeared to practise the Japanese culture. In the Post-Q, the students in this group highlighted that: *"Everybody was in different age groups. This made me reluctant to speak with each other"*, and *"I was a little nervous in the group discussion because we've never met"*. A lack of student-centred strategies was also revealed: *"In a group discussion, no one was taking a leading role. It was difficult to manage the discussion"*.

Posting a writing task in English on Manaba increased learner anxiety for the passive students. With a lack of either English language proficiency or student-centred strategies, these students appeared to not be eager to post their thoughts or reflections in the threaded discussion forum where everybody can easily gain access. Four students described that: *"I don't feel comfortable because I am not good at*

English. I think that making a mistake is scary" (WT2), and "*It's embarrassing if someone sees my wrong answer*" (WT2).

However, the majority of the students, 49 out of 53, valued posting answers, thoughts, and reflections in the forum positively. They viewed this as a learning curve and appreciated a different way of thinking, exchanging diverse ideas and opinions, and gaining a general view of the topics.

5.2 Students' Feelings About Satisfaction, Advantages and Challenges

The first-time online learning experience has led students to appreciate advantages and challenges of both online and traditional face-to-face learning. Many students (88.4%) emphasised having positive and productive experiences during COVID-19 online learning. They came to realise their achievements in improving both technological skills and English language proficiency. In this regard, several students expressed their feelings about achievement: "*I was surprised because I didn't expect to be able to take classes online like I do now*" (Post-Q), and "*I wasn't very good at using the computer, but the online classes gave me more opportunities to use the computer and I got used to it*" (Post-Q). About 62% of the students reported changing their perceptions of online education from negative to positive as one student stated; "*I used to think that face-to-face interaction was the only way to go, but now we can usually do it online, so I think we're in an era where we can respond to different situations*" (Post-Q).

Through the process of actually learning and experiencing, students identified some advantages of online learning. Firstly, taking a course at the students' convenience and own pace is reported to be an advantage. Many students came to realise that "*I found it convenient to take classes easily at home*" (Post-Q). Some students who had long commutes to school highlighted; "*I could use my commuting time as study time, so I could study hard*" (Post-Q). One of the students reported in her presentation that she used to spend 2–3 h for commuting before COVID-19. Since online learning was implemented, she was able to focus more on her study and felt her English level improved from a beginner to an intermediate level during the semester. The second advantage is developing learner autonomy. Due to the nature of student-centred pedagogy, some students have become responsible for their study. Some students noted that "*I was able to manage my time and was able to study myself. I was able to secure more study time than before*" (post-Q). The third advantage is that when students study autonomously, they are likely to become more reflective about their learning. One student articulated her experience of online learning in her presentation:

> The good thing about this online course for me was the close connection between my classes and my personal life, it means that I have the advantage of being able to return to my private life as soon as the class is over. It also means that I can think in English after the classes. Through this I have developed my English skills. When I was in the classroom, it

was difficult for me to make the connection between my classes and my personal life. Since the online classes study I have become more active in learning English.

Online medium instruction reduced learner anxiety in an EFL context. Some students expressed that they were able to perform better when giving a presentation online than in face-to-face lessons, and speak more fluently. This is supported by 53.5% of the students saying that "*online classes reduced anxiety because I wasn't nervous when talking to the monitor*" (Post-Q). Some introverted students valued online learning by saying that "*if it's embarrassing to ask the teacher, I can ask privately in chat*" (Post-Q). Although all students believed that learning takes place through face-to-face interactions in a classroom environment at the beginning, they appeared to appreciate learner autonomy and becoming more reflective. A student stated in the Post-Q that "*In the classroom, I can ask my friends right away what I don't understand, and maybe I'm not learning in return. Online is an environment where you work on your own, so I think you'll learn more*".

It was clear that students initial negative perceptions of online learning developed over the semester to be more positive. In a traditional classroom environment, it would be difficult to have various English speakers. A student highlighted that; "*I felt that the only way to connect with foreign countries and Japan is through online tools*" (Post-Q). When the students had more opportunities to be engaged with English speakers, they appeared to study hard to actively participate in conversations. A student reported that "*I've studied English a lot. I was able to show that by speaking in English I've learned so far when the guest teacher came to visit, I was able to communicate effectively*" (Post-Q). Such online interactions enabled some students to become motivated to learn English and develop learner autonomy and deliberately prepare for the next meeting with another English speaker. Another student said that "*To express my opinion, I did a lot of research to make sure my opinion was well expressed*" (Post-Q).

In the Post-Q, many students reported that Zoom is the most effective tool for learning English online. Students came to realise that it is easy to gain access to native English speakers using Zoom. A student emphasised that:

> In Japan, it is difficult to hire ALTs (assistant language teachers), but online enables us to talk with many native speakers. As long as Wi-Fi access is available, online learning is very beneficial.

Many students valued having a different guest speaker fortnightly during the courses. This led the students to become more motivated to speak in English, build confidence when meeting with new English speakers, and enhance their speaking skills.

On the contrary, some challenges of online learning were also identified. A lack of computer skills and poor Wi-Fi environment at home impeded online learning. During the semester, two students had to leave the Zoom meeting and come back because they were unable to connect to the audio system. Also, a few students who could not attend the Zoom webinar because of a Wi-Fi breakdown. This resulted in feelings of frustration about online learning and was expressed in comments such as; "*I like Zoom, but I can't do anything when my computer freezes*" (Post-Q).

Taking a class in a home environment is also identified as a challenge in online learning. Often individual life environments, for example, family voices, dogs and train sounds, were exposed during the real-time classes on Zoom. Some students noted that *"there are more temptations around me at home, like my smartphone is around me, I can play games easily"* (P).

The third challenge is being lonely and becoming fatigued. Although online learning reduces learner anxiety when speaking English, two students expressed that *"even though I can see each other's faces in the online class, it's lonely to take classes at home"* (Post-Q), and *"it's sad that I can only speak to the screen"* (Post-Q). Another student commented that *"in online, it is necessary to always overly act in order to avoid making the speakers feel sad. It was good, but also very tiring looking at the monitor like that"* (P). In this regard, some students explained that *"although you can get to know classmates to some extent online, I find it difficult to expand my circle"* (Post-Q). To summarise challenges of online learning, one of the students made a clear statement of her feelings about her first-time online learning:

> I found technology to be very useful. However, I was able to realise that I was grateful for the face-to-face classes that I had taken for granted before. In the online class, we had to go through the assignments without understanding them, and there were inevitably parts of the class that we didn't understand. Without meeting the teacher in person, there were things I couldn't understand, so I thought the face-to-face class was better. (Post-Q)

Considering the worries and anxieties that the students initially felt, they reported that they were satisfied and significantly learned from the pandemic-initiated online English courses. This led some outperforming students to develop learner autonomy and feel that they were learning more online than in face-to-face. The 88.4% of the students reported being satisfied with the first-time online English courses. The majority of students valued getting easy access to course information and teaching materials on Manaba at their convenience. Also, the majority of students reported having a real-time class on Zoom was effective in online medium instruction in the EFL context. Overall, 65.1% of the students reported that they learned more from online learning, whereas 34.9% of the students reported learning more from face-to-face classroom settings. Although the majority of students indicated that they were satisfied with and learned more in the course, some students pointed out their preference for traditional classroom settings.

6   Lessons Learned

The findings in this chapter demonstrate that the well-designed and well-facilitated online English courses shifted most students' attitudes from negative to positive thoughts early on. Due to lack of students' prior experience with online learning, initially, the majority of the students indicated their preference for face-to-face teaching rather than online. Before the start of the semester, most students reported an increase in anxiety. In Japan, a teacher-centred classroom environment is seen as a common practice. That is, students often rely on their teacher to foster a learning environment, rather than co-constructing the learning environment. In this regard, students perceive a higher level of learning and satisfaction (cognitive presence) when they recognise a high level of teaching presence.

Teachers need to take this into account when designing and facilitating courses to accommodate novice students online. All the teaching materials and instructions were uploaded and structured on Manaba prior to the courses in order to reduce learner anxiety. Cunningham and Bergstorm's study (2020) revealed that with accessible and clearly structured courses, students can easily find course materials and follow instructional guidelines to enhance online learning. Doing this may provide a learning environment equivalent to the traditional classroom which enabled the students to feel satisfied with the pandemic-initiated online English courses.

Manaba is also reported to be a useful tool as a resource room for sharing students' thoughts and reflections through treaded discussion forums. The online resource room brought benefits for both teachers and students due to its flexibility and time efficiency. When the students came to realise the ease of access to class materials, they appreciated they had more time and could focus more on their studies. Under such circumstances, students became self-driven and developed learner autonomy. From this point, the students were engaged with the course contents (teaching presence) and started posting and sharing their thoughts logically as the students viewed online as an intimate environment that enhanced the development of a sense of belonging to the online community (social presence). They then became motivated to actively participate in group communications on threaded discussion forums, focus on the tasks and voice their views (cognitive presence).

The majority of students highlighted that posting their thoughts and reflections, and commenting on peers' posts on Manaba were identified as beneficial factors. These students confirmed that through such collaboration their level of understanding of the topic increased by reading and commenting on others' posts and made them appreciate and understand different views. As previous research has demonstrated, the nature of a student-centred environment online made the students feel they were learning more online than face-to-face (Clark-Ibáñez & Scott, 2008), and they were satisfied with the online courses (McFarland & Hamilton, 2005).

Regardless of reported significant benefits of group collaboration work online, some passive students with a lack of English language proficiency reported feeling anxious when posting their reflections on a threaded discussion board where all classmates could read and comment. This impeded these students' active participation in collaborative work during the course. The students in this group reported they valued teacher-centred instruction in face-to-face classroom settings as they believed that real education cannot be achieved through peer-to-peer collaboration.

Facilitating a real-time class on Zoom is reported to be user friendly and a useful tool in the EFL context online. The use of audio and video supports gives the sense of a real person and promotes social presence. This was revealed in the Post-Q in that the Zoom webinar enables the students to see their names and faces which reduces learner anxiety in an online environment. During real-time classes on Zoom, students feel as if they are interacting with a teacher and classmates in person. Through these activities, student engagement and teacher-student connections can be built that assist students to develop a sense of belonging to the online community and raise student satisfaction. This results in students becoming motivated to study and fully participating in group collaboration. In addition, teacher-students real-time class interactions via Zoom increased student satisfaction, with even passive students being able to actively interact and communicate with the teacher and peers through text-chat (Cunningham et al., 2010). There are, however, some students who preferred traditional teaching and reported that although the class using Zoom provided the same effect as a face-to-face class in a real classroom, they were unable to expand their social circle.

The majority of students' attitudes towards online English courses changed from negative to positive. As a former study (McFarland & Hamilton, 2005) identified, almost all the students reported to be satisfied with talking with diverse native English speakers during the courses that they would be otherwise limited to having in higher education in the Japanese EFL context. The use of Zoom enables teachers and students to virtually visit English speaking countries while having conversations with native English speakers, which is not limited to any time or venue constraints. In response to Maher's study (2020), this chapter can confirm that the use of video conferencing is proven to be an effective tool for providing a diverse experience of speaking with native English speakers in EFL education.

Group discussion in a breakout room is shown as both a positive factor reported by the majority of the students and a negative factor by some passive students. As the literature demonstrates (Cunningham & Bergstrom, 2020), the majority of the students value a group discussion as they can work collaboratively to solve problems and assure their understanding of the topic to enhance their learning. These students reported that discussion in a breakout room led to them gaining a deeper understanding of the topic (cognitive presence) and developing group cohesion (social presence). As a result, the students were encouraged to actively participate in an intimate environment and built a sense of belonging to the online community. In contrast, some passive students stated group discussion in a breakout room as a negative factor. These students appeared to be introverted and Japanese cultural-oriented so they were reluctant to initiate a discussion with multi-aged classmates from diverse faculties. These students may not appreciate that learning literally takes place in the process of group collaboration to solve problems while working on their own.

Feelings of loneliness and isolation are pointed out as negative factors in online education. In this chapter, findings show that students who are familiar with face-to-face classroom pedagogy reported feeling lonely and isolated in online lectures. These students reported difficulty in developing a sense of belonging to an online community, and they were not willing to spontaneously participate in classes. In addition, they replied that they preferred not to talk to the monitor and felt the fatigue easily. Consequently, these students may not feel satisfied with online lectures nor achieve their learning goals.

7 Final Remarks

Considering students' initial negative attitudes towards online learning, none of the students reported to be unsatisfied upon the completion of online learning. With a lack of prior exposure to a student-centred environment online, the students appeared to be unable to accurately evaluate their feelings about satisfaction with active engagement. Overall, my students' reported feelings about pandemic-initiated online learning as largely positive, although some students remarked on the challenges of the first-time online English courses. It does appear that the online English courses offer more potential, through meeting with diverse native English speakers and observing their real lives overseas rather than watching video resources online during the real-time classes. This is reported to be the most effective factor in the EFL context online in the chapter. Also, in a student-centred environment online, my students tend to have become self-driven and able to focus more on their studies. Through this experience, students may not be willing to go back to *the old style* of learning (Yamamoto, 2020) in Japan. This current situation presents the opportunity to be a catalyst for future hybrid learning environments, which would incorporate traditional face-to-face and online learning contexts.

8 Food for Thought

The chosen framework (CoI) is proven to be a useful tool to design and facilitate courses online, especially for those who are considering moving away from face-to-face learning and deliver courses online in higher education. The framework guides a course instructor to gain a deeper understanding of an online environment and how to effectively facilitate courses that enable students to shift their attitudes from negative to positive. This chapter highlights a significant relationship between teaching, social presence and satisfaction. Providing easy and flexible access to related materials, building connections between student-teacher and student-student have reduced learner anxiety and increased group cohesion. This resulted in students feeling a sense of achievement and satisfaction in their first-time online learning experience. The focus of the chapter is to immediately facilitate English courses online and enhance the first-time online students' English language proficiency, but much of what we learn through these findings may be applied to SL/EFL contexts in any educational setting. Through the pandemic-initiated online English courses, my students had the chance to interact with diverse English speakers, they developed both computer skills and learner autonomy, and were able to acknowledge the advantages and challenges of face-to-face and online learning. The accuracy of the students' achievement is not the focus of this chapter; however, it would be valuable to investigate students' progress in the future in online teaching and research (Table 2).

Table 2 Features of the tools used in the chapter

Tool	Usage
Manaba (online learning management system)	Virtual space to archive teaching materials and recorded webinars Administrating Pre- and Post-course questionnaire Collaborating between students on personal and analytical discussions on thread board Assigning reflective writing tasks Providing feedback and comments on students' work Posting questions, class news, and thoughts/reflections
Zoom (video conferencing)	Organising and recording real-time class Facilitating interactions between teacher-student and student-student Gaining access to diverse English speakers outside of Japan Facilitating group discussion in a breakout room Communicating with students through text-chat

Acknowledgement I would like to acknowledge my students for their willingness to participate in the study and to share their ERT experience during the COVID-19 pandemic. I also wish to express my gratitude to Dr. Julian Chen for his on-going support and assistance with this chapter.

References

Akyol, Z., & Garrison, D. (2008). The development of a community of inquiry over time in an online course: Understanding the progression and integration of social, cognitive and teaching presence. *Journal of Asynchronous Learning Networks, 12*(3–4), 3–22.

Allen, T. J. (2021). Infrastructure, literacy and communication: The challenges of emergency remote teaching in a university in Japan. In J. Chen (Ed.), *Emergency remote teaching and beyond: Voices from world language teachers and researchers* (pp. 23–42). Springer.

Bolliger, D. U., & Wasilik, O. (2009). Factors influencing faculty satisfaction with online teaching and learning in higher education. *Distance Education, 30*(1), 103–116. https://doi.org/10.1080/01587910902845949

Bowers, J., & Kumar, P. (2015). Students' perceptions of teaching and social presence: A comparative analysis of face-to-face and online learning environments. *International Journal of Web-Based Learning and Teaching Technologies, 10*(1), 27–44. https://doi.org/10.4018/ijwltt.2015010103

Brocato, B. R., Bonanno, A., & Ulbig, S. (2015). Student perceptions and instructional evaluations: A multivariate analysis of online and face-to-face classroom settings. *Education and Information Technologies, 20*(1), 37–55. https://doi.org/10.1007/s10639-013-9268-6

Budhai, S. S., & Williams, M. (2016). Teaching presence in online courses: Practical applications, co-facilitation, and technology integration. *The Journal of Effective Teaching, 16*(3), 76–84.

Clark-Ibáñez, M., & Scott, L. (2008). Learning to teach online. *Teaching Sociology, 36*(1), 34–41. https://doi.org/10.1177/0092055X0803600105

Cunningham, U., & Bergstrom, A. (2020). Reimaging learning in a language education course thrust online: Social constructivism in times of social isolation. In R. E. Ferdig, E. Baumgartner, R. Hartshorne, R. Kaplan-Rakowski, & C. Mouza (Eds.), *Teaching, technology, and teacher education during the COVID-19 pandemic: Stories from the field* (pp. 449–456). AACE-Association for the Advancement of Computing in Education. https://www.learntechlib.org/p/216903/

Cunningham, U., Beers Fägersten, K., & Holmsten, E. (2010). "Can you hear me, Hanoi?" Compensatory mechanisms employed in synchronous net-based English language learning. *International Review of Research in Open and Distance Learning, 11*(1), 161–177. https://doi.org/10.19173/irrodl.v11i1.774

Deslauriers, L., McCarty, L. S., Miller, K., Callaghan, K., & Kestin, G. (2019). Measuring actual learning versus feeling of learning in response to being actively engaged in the classroom. *Proceedings of the National Academy of Sciences, 116*(39), 19251–19257. https://doi.org/10.1073/pnas.1821936116

Driscoll, A., Jicha, K., Hunt, A. N., Tichavsky, L., & Thompson, G. (2012). Can online courses deliver in-class results? A comparison of student performance and satisfaction in an online versus a face-to-face introductory sociology course. *Teaching Sociology, 40*(4), 312–331. https://doi.org/10.1177/0092055X12446624

Garrison, D. (2019). Online community of inquiry review: Social, cognitive, and teaching presence issues. *Online Learning, 11*(1), 61–72. https://doi.org/10.24059/olj.v11i1.1737

Garrison, D., & Cleveland-Innes, M. (2005). Facilitating cognitive presence in online learning: Interaction is not enough. *American Journal of Distance Education, 19*(3), 133–148. https://doi.org/10.1207/s15389286ajde1903_2

Garrison, D., Anderson, T., & Archer, W. (1999). Critical inquiry in a text-based environment: Computer conferencing in higher education. *The Internet and Higher Education, 2*(2), 87–105. https://doi.org/10.1016/S1096-7516(00)00016-6

Gruber, A., & Bauer, E. (2020). Fostering interaction in synchronous online class sessions with foreign language learners. In R. E. Ferdig, E. Baumgartner, R. Hartshorne, R. Kaplan-Rakowski, & C. Mouza (Eds.), *Teaching, technology, and teacher education during the COVID-19 pandemic: Stories from the field* (pp. 175–178). AACE-Association for the Advancement of Computing in Education. https://www.learntechlib.org/p/216903/

Hay, A., Hodgkinson, M., Peltier, J. W., & Drago, W. A. (2004). Interaction and virtual learning. *Strategic Change, 13*(4), 193–204. https://doi.org/10.1002/jsc.679

Holbeck, R., & Hartman, J. (2018). Efficient strategies for maximizing online student satisfaction: Applying technologies to increase cognitive presence, social presence, and teaching presence. *Journal of Educators Online, 15*(3). https://doi.org/10.9743/jeo.2018.15.3.6

Kilis, S., & Yildirim, Z. (2019). Posting patterns of students' social presence, cognitive presence, and teaching presence in online learning. *Online Learning Journal, 23*(2), 179–195. https://doi.org/10.24059/olj.v23i2.1460

Kozar, O. (2016). Perceptions of webcam use by experienced online teachers and learners: A seeming disconnect between research and practice. *Computer Assisted Language Learning, 29*(4), 800–810. https://doi.org/10.1080/09588221.2015.1061021

Logan, E., Augustyniak, R., & Rees, A. (2002). Distance education as different education: A student-centered investigation of distance learning experience. *Journal of Education for Library and Information Science, 43*(1), 32–42. https://doi.org/10.2307/40323985

Luu, H. (2020, May 18). COVID-19 and university life in Japan. *Izanau*. Retrieved from https://izanau.com/article/view/coronavirus-universities-in-japan

Maher, D. (2020). Video conferencing to support online teaching and learning. In R. E. Ferdig, E. Baumgartner, R. Hartshorne, R. Kaplan-Rakowski, & C. Mouza (Eds.), *Teaching, technology, and teacher education during the COVID-19 pandemic: Stories from the field* (pp. 91–96). AACE-Association for the Advancement of Computing in Education. https://www.learntechlib.org/p/216903/

McCarty, S., Satō, T., & Obari, H. (2017). *Implementing mobile language learning technologies in Japan*. Springer.

McFarland, D., & Hamilton, D. (2005). Factors affecting student performance and satisfaction: Online versus traditional course delivery. *Journal of Computer Information Systems, 46*(2), 25–32. https://doi.org/10.1080/08874417.2006.11645880

Mohd Khalid, M. N., & Quick, D. (2016). Teaching presence influencing online students' course satisfaction at an institution of higher education. *International Education Studies, 9*(3), 62–70. https://doi.org/10.5539/ies.v9n3p62

O'Donoghue, J. J. (2020, April 21). In era of COVID-19, a shift to digital forms of teaching in Japan: Teachers are having to re-imagine their roles entirely amid school closures. *The Japan Times*. Retrieved from https://www.japantimes.co.jp/news/2020/04/21/national/traditional-to-digital-teaching-coronavirus/#.Xs9Fp2gzbIU

Obe, M., & Okutsu, A. (2020, March 9). Coronavirus forces Japan schools to grapple with online education. *Nikkei Asian review*. Retrieved from https://asia.nikkei.com/Business/Technology/Coronavirus-forces-Japan-schools-to-grapple-with-online-education

Preisman, K. A. (2014). Teaching presence in online education: From the instructor's point of view. *Online Learning, 18*(3), 1–16. https://doi.org/10.24059/olj.v18i3.446

Shea, P., & Bidjerano, T. (2009). Community of inquiry as a theoretical framework to foster "epistemic engagement" and "cognitive presence" in online education. *Computers & Education, 52*(3), 543–553. https://doi.org/10.1016/j.compedu.2008.10.007

Thurmond, V. A., Wambach, K., Connors, H. R., & Frey, B. B. (2002). Evaluation of student satisfaction: Determining the impact of a web-based environment by controlling for student characteristics. *American Journal of Distance Education, 16*(3), 169–190. https://doi.org/10.1207/S15389286AJDE1603_4

Vaismoradi, M., Turunen, H., & Bondas, T. (2013). Content analysis and thematic analysis: Implications for conducting a qualitative descriptive study. *Nursing & Health Sciences, 15*(3), 398–405. https://doi.org/10.1111/nhs.12048

Worley, W. L., & Tesdell, L. S. (2009). Instructor time and effort in online and face-to-face teaching: Lessons learned. *IEEE Transactions on Professional Communication, 52*(2), 138–151. https://doi.org/10.1109/TPC.2009.2017990

Wu, D., & Hiltz, S. R. (2004). Predicting learning from asynchronous online discussions. *Journal of Asynchronous Learning Network, 8*(2), 139–152. https://doi.org/10.1142/S1609945104000115

Yamamoto, S. (2020, June 16). Coronavirus crisis shows Japan lagging in online education. *NHK World Correspondent*. Retrieved from https://www3.nhk.or.jp/nhkworld/en/news/backstories/1137/

Online Instruction as a New Learning Territory for a Filipinized Critical Language Pedagogy: From the Era of Pandemic Onward

Juland Dayo Salayo

Highlights

- Philippine education has been affected by the COVID-19 pandemic causing the learners' unequal access and opportunity to remote learning.
- While the tenets of the country's Department of Education highlight the significance of 'criticality,' its concept faces difficulties in concretizing its practical purpose to the clientele.
- Technology and language learning support the learners' critical thinking through active online engagement guided by more authentic instructional and teaching materials that raised their social consciousness through online participatory approach.
- Through critical language pedagogy, the learners developed their voices, proving that they have read the world more than just reading the word.

1 Introduction

The COVID-19 pandemic has drastically changed the lens of Philippine education at all levels. Those changes, like the shift of instructions from the traditional face to face to virtual mode, initially gained controversies involving the attitude and competence of the teachers, and the students. As a developing country, the Philippines is primarily and generally unprepared in remote instructions. Among those directly affected are those in the government schools that do not have a strong internet connection and do not even have gadgets for an online learning modality. Aida Yuvienco mentioned in an interview by GovInsider that only 26% of the government schools

J. D. Salayo (✉)
University of Santo Tomas, Manila, The Philippines
e-mail: jdsalayo@ust.edu.ph

© The Author(s), under exclusive license to Springer Nature
Switzerland AG 2021
J. Chen (ed.), *Emergency Remote Teaching and Beyond*,
https://doi.org/10.1007/978-3-030-84067-9_11

have internet connection (Basu, 2020). While the national and local government, which are supported by the private and non-government sectors, have exerted extra efforts to make education accessible to all, such access generally remains exclusive to those who are privileged and fortunate. Hence, the gap between the rich and the poor remains even wider. I would say that most of the marginalized and oppressed students in far-flung areas experience this the way they endure problems on their electricity connection and other basic needs connected to learning engagement. In the same interview with Yuvienco, she emphasized that at least 5000 public schools do not even have access to electricity (Basu, 2020). In effect, this reality has worsened their even poorer economic condition.

On my end, I still consider myself fortunate to be with a private comprehensive university which can provide for the needs of our students in any form of emergency like the COVID-19 pandemic because of their Learning Management System (LMS) being used by both teachers and students long before the pandemic hit the country and the world. Besides, my students are also economically fortunate to have easy access to remote learning. But looking at the broader kaleidoscope of the present health crisis, it has undoubtedly broadened the gap between the rich and the poor regarding their right to education. Moreover, this pandemic has created a bigger and stronger wall that divides fortunate and less fortunate learners. As an honest assessment, the issue here is not about the rich and the poor because all of them are victims of this great oppressor, the virus. Hence, the present condition has given birth not just to the so-called new normal, but rather, the learning oppression becomes unlikely normal. While we look at the darker side of this reality, this learning oppression can also give way to an initial move to cause the learners to think radically if their right to education is equally and justly offered and received. Because of these beleaguered experiences, the cognitive revolution to understand the societal problem that affects every breath becomes a way for them to think even more critically. In the end, the condition paves a way to produce an even stronger voice to read the world, not just the word.

This chapter focuses on the condition, significance and implication of critical pedagogy in language teaching to provide learners an arena for voice production needed for them to become community builders. This pandemic allowed me to design student-centered lessons and activities that allow the learners to use the English language in building active and socially-relevant language learning in both synchronous and asynchronous sessions. In this case, critical language pedagogy (CLP) is concretized by providing student-centered classroom instructions by initially promoting negotiations and agreements to defeat the burden caused by the pandemic through online participatory approach. Similarly, dialogic engagements allow them to experience democratic and emancipated learning as they listen to everyone's story, problem and ideas; hence, they even learn how to value authentic knowledge from everyone and to provide solutions to the presented challenges. Through participatory approach, CLP helps students to become more active learning participants as they understand themselves as members of the community and their roles to play in defining democracy and equity through effective language use.

The first part of this chapter presents the condition of the Philippine education and the use and challenges of CLP as a classroom approach in the country during pandemic. It is followed by the discussion of pandemic as a form of learning oppression and at the same time, the opportunity for acknowledging the impact of CLP in making the language learning more meaningful. Finally, the practical employment of CLP using participatory approach is emphasized through the learners' critical engagements to social issues integrated with technology.

1.1 'Filipinization' of the Philippine Critical Pedagogy in the Basic Education

As a high school teacher, I always make sure that my actions and decisions are guided by the Department of Education's (DepEd) mission and vision to shape the learners' critical thinking skills. Through these, achieving the ultimate goal of critical literacy, emancipation, and social justice for the learners to serve as nation builders can be materialized. When carefully reading the DepEd's mission, vision, and significant features, I am happy to note that the critical features are highlighted, which shows its responsiveness to the learners' needs. To cite, the mission states that the Department of Education's (DepEd) primary task is *"to protect and promote the right of every Filipino to quality, equitable, culture-based, and complete basic education.* Similarly, DepEd envisions that every Filipinos would *"enable them to realize their full potential and contribute meaningfully to building the nation"* (Department of Education, n.d.).

Understanding how the country's education system remains committed to its goal of serving its clienteles, I am fascinated by how the government values every member of the community's equal participation in building a stronger nation through accessible education. Despite my respect for the effusive statements of the role of the Department of Education, I constantly asked if these highly constructed statements of responsibilities and maxims are translated into what they ought to achieve in transforming lives. With the spirit of an individual's capacity, knowledge and skills, values, and aspirations, education becomes a cradle of life-long learning in empowering the learners through the support of all the stakeholders. In the end, everyone in the society will benefit from this collaborative and cooperative approach to achieve the common goal of social change. This mission and vision is every teacher's framework to concretize our oath to the learners, the country, and God.

Hence, DepEd's general goals adhere to the important principles, which center on the curriculum and the learners, as prescribed by the Republic Act No. 10533 in pursuit of the K to 12 programs. Some of these goals include learner-centered, inclusive, relevant and appropriate, research-based, culture-sensitive, contextualized and global, constructive, inquiry-based, reflective, collaborative, differentiated, and integrative instructions. Hence, the K to 12 program features the target learners to achieve the following skills to become critical thinkers: information, media and technology skills; learning and innovation skills; communication skills; and life, and career skills (Department of Education, 2019).

Before the implementation of the K to 12 program in the basic education curriculum, the Philippine government has already made various academic and legal support to promote equality, emancipation, and social justice. Some of those are Education for All 2015 Acceleration, Alternative Learning System (ALS), Special Education (SpEd) Program, Indigenous Peoples' Education, and Mother Tongue-Based Multilingual Education (MTB-MLE), among others. All of these aim to respect individualities, differences, and identities necessary to encourage the production of the learners' voices in building a stronger nation and in increasing learners' participation rate to formal education through local knowledge and skills in addressing their needs for literacy development (Department of Education, 2009, 2011; World Education Forum, 2015). In the end, they all shared common goal of shaping critical approach in teaching to materialize both the mission and vision of the Philippine education.

1.2 Challenges of Critical Pedagogy

Despite those government efforts to produce a just, democratic and accessible education for all, there is still a severe presence of internalized oppression in Philippine education. For example, problems on discrimination, violence, racism, political pressure, and stereotyping still appear in the classroom instructions and the instructional and assessments tools. Mostly, the victims include women, LGBTQI+, poor, and indigenous people. Unfortunately, Philippine education's oppression problem is worsened by language-based oppression like the use of unfavorable and demeaning terminologies. The country also has a long history of oppression, especially on women, despite the country's reputable international standing toward women's empowerment (Asean Today, 2019) caused by colonization and dictatorship. With these, Philippine education deserves to have a serious inclusion of critical pedagogy that will construct citizens who have high regard to social equality, democracy, and transformation in the vortex of globalization and internationalization (Monroy-Adarlo, 2016). Therefore, more than the educational goal of developing skills needed to help learners be globally competitive in the marketplace, classroom instructions must develop them into critical, creative, logical and analytical thinkers. These are open and reflective to understand and value others by equally treating as they share their voices necessary to build community (Baluran & Pido, 2017). With these academic, legal, and philosophical frames, I am deeply influenced by Viola's (2009) encouragement to produce "filipinized" critical pedagogy. Accordingly, this does not settle on reflection alone, but most importantly, to concretize the call to change the course of understanding the world by employing both theories and practices that bring democracy, peace, and equality.

1.3   The Language and Its Role in Critical Pedagogy

Unfortunately, critical pedagogy, as an approach, is not widely acknowledged in language teaching in the Filipino context because of the cultural conservatism as it claimed to be true among Asians as passive and reticent (Kumaravadivelu, 2010). Indeed, language classrooms highly focus on language structures and rules than achieving the social functions of the language. As a result, this reality threatens the full implementation of shaping student-centeredness.

Influenced by the works and minds of critical thinkers from Paulo Freire and other modern-day advocates of criticality in education and instruction, I am coming from reflective teaching accounts during the height of the COVID-19 pandemic on how revolutionary [language] learning establishes power and social justice. This is by understanding if the role of education is justly served to the learners, giving them opportunities for participation and allowing them to recognize power relation (Richardson, 2001). It is essential to understand that learning activists do not learn in social isolation. Instead, they often learn from one another by networking and observing the actions and strategies to become more skilled (Ollis, 2012). Critical and anti-oppressive pedagogy must then take a decisive role in directing the learners towards identity shaping and, in the end, a social reconstruction (Baudu, 2012; Tuman, 1998). Besides, it is also worthy of considering language as a tool in strengthening their voice through awareness and participation to configure social, cultural, economic, political, and historical statuses. The reform of pedagogy in the name of a higher level of critical thinking must be a priority in the language class-room as a form of social resistance by making the program, i.e., the curriculum and instruction, more contemporary, more politically aware, and more critical. Thus, teaching English must be labeled as the best way of enfranchising, liberating, enabling, and empowering those who will make the future (Tuman, 1998) as there are reflective numbers of studies and literature. They become the source of more critical language pedagogy features as a discipline, a philosophy and a movement for whatever purpose.

Having this Freirean ideology through critical language pedagogy, the problems in the society such as injustice, oppression, discrimination, marginalization, and similar social occurrences are recognized by the ESL learners. With an emphasis on the use of language, CLP helps develop such power and political ideologies needed to address such social inconsistencies and deficiencies through revolutionary deliv-ery of the language pedagogy with a greater purpose of going beyond the common understanding of the merely communicative discipline, but rather, an avenue of pro-cessing democracy and social reforms initiated by the empowered language learn-ers. This shows the presence of politics and power necessary to attain the goal of social transformation successfully.

Hence, this approach solidifies the student-centeredness in the teaching-learning processes. The students are the heart of learning since they tend to be dynamic members of the learning community. In the end, the process allows them to think provocatively and reflectively by engaging themselves in any sociopolitical issues and activities. With these opportunities, they would undoubtedly enjoy academic freedom while enjoying their rights and power in education and decision making. These rights afforded to them may not necessarily mean a way of disempowering the teachers. Rather, these enhance their role as they create every possibility, power, and equality present in their authentically designed classroom tasks. As teachers pose problems that invite students to engage positively and produce new knowledge, they become learners in their own rights. Providing clarity to this scenario, teachers and students appear to be in an equal learning arena. Hence, critical reflection and action break the gap between social and educational theory and classroom and community practices.

2   The Pandemic as a Form of Learning Oppression

On top of this condition, pandemic becomes a form of learning oppression that limits our students' rights and opportunities toward education, especially in a community like the Philippines. Indeed, most learners have lost their voices in acquiring and producing the much needed authentic knowledge. With those inevitable effects of the pandemic, our government has immediately responded to protect us from a more severe impact by making policies and precautionary measures. Sad to say, significant government agencies and even private academic institutions have failed to listen to the clamours of the ordinary teachers and students' voices as substantial elements in framing responses to the shift of the learning modality. Our students, who are considered the center of the educational processes, are not even consulted to determine their needs and demands. The school administrations and their consultants drastically created policies on their own. Hence, the skeletal force of those guidelines and policies are highly influenced by their power instead of the learners'.

In these cases, equal opportunity among the schools' stakeholders becomes problematic as the powerful control the systems entirely without looking at how significant the others are in designing better guidelines, programs, and policies. As a result, the learners' needs and demands are at risk in no way that they are not justly consulted in understanding them during the pandemic. After all, they are our measurement of learning successes.

2.1   The Pandemic Opportunities to Social Learning and Understanding

True enough, most of students are helpless to get access to equal instructions. Surprisingly, it appears that their discriminated and oppressed encounters from the influential figures in the academe have become their means to concerted critical pedagogy in their language classroom. Most of them freely discussed society's realities that silenced them during the pandemic. The imposed lockdown in Metro Manila and eventually in the nearby provinces to the rest of the country has initially boxed the learners to substantial learning exposure and engagement in the typical classroom settings. Like many Filipinos, homes and workplaces become one where students have barely seen the wall that divides their schools and their families.

Many of my students suffered from different forms of anxiety, which appeared in many stories and social media posts. Others even claimed to have depression. While I merely relied on social media, I assume that these are but the expected consequences of this world crisis. But again, the limited movement and engagement of my students in language learning have even proved their sense of social knowledge and understanding of the reality of their community. While its discussions that raise social awareness and relevance are not typically observed among them, perhaps of their age and interests, they have started to talk about specific societal issues that directly and indirectly affect them. Most of them do not only speak about class suspensions, but the justifications of this academic decision have been explored. More to that is their serious discussion on the government education system's readiness to provide their needs for them to survive in this learning challenges. The decision of the administration is now observed and becomes critical to them like the instant remote instructions, the quality of learning they would gain and the quality of engagement they have with the teachers and their fellow learners. In effect, social media platforms become their territory to dissect the related issues to this learning modality. Some of those online trending issues are the call to education freeze and the total suspension of all academic activities to prioritize every family's economic condition, health, and security. On a positive note, the Philippine educational institutions remain tough in continuing the learning in the midst of pandemic.

Similarly, my senior high school students are now critical to talk about food security and agricultural resiliency during the pandemic. They have started to care about the poor who have suffered from the scarcity of the basic needs in these difficult times. Some of them discussed the Philippines' health status and its readiness to provide care and protection to the millions of Filipinos, especially those affected by the virus. Interestingly, most of them even researched the health department's budget and how this possibly responds to the healthcare condition. On top of these is their active discussion on government officials' alleged corruption issues as a hindrance to the public services. Problematizing these anomalies and malpractices in the government, they have begun to think of the marginalized sectors, especially the poor students and their families: how they engage and survive in remote learning, how they equally receive their rights to education, how they survive the day with enough food on their table, how they fight the virus with enough protection and information, and how they continue their access to the world while living in isolation and physical distancing. True enough, their voices have started to grow bigger and louder to know and tell the truth that affects their lives.

These changes in the beliefs and attitudes of the students are greatly attributed to their language learning through their proper, careful and effective use of language as they discussed those socially-relevant issues that worsen the pandemic condition.

Evidences appear through citations and references of the issues as proofs of their academic discourse. Likewise, the degree of their participations has been strengthened by critical questioning, and by providing solutions to the issues presented. These are all evident in their written works, online discussion fora, and classroom discussions. Hence, their voices are all heard and become authentic source of information in doing and refining their classroom works.

3   Critical Pedagogy and Language Learning

3.1   *Academic Writing and Pandemic Issues: Learning the World More than Learning the Word*

Due to this pandemic, our institution has implemented two-hour synchronous and asynchronous sessions in a week. Before the sessions, we designed the course sites with the needed materials like the following: course information folder containing course and course site description, online house rules, and weekly expectations. We also have additional folders for a course outline, teacher's information folder, and consultation hours that further provide our learners extra time for clarifications. Learning module folders are also created to give students a guide to know their weekly learning standards and competences, learning materials, assessments and rubrics, links, and materials for synchronous and asynchronous sessions and consultation periods. In case my students cannot attend the synchronous class because of their poor internet connection and other technical problems, they are provided with teacher-prepared learning packets that serve as their guide to monitor their learning. Similarly, they are also provided with a copy of the recorded online class for their reference in their own pace. These teachers' efforts become our means to narrow or limit the possibility of inequality and injustices. Giving justice to our students, we adopted the Department of Education's Most Essential Learning Competencies (MELCs) in response to time challenges. The government and private schools both employ virtual and modular approaches to serve their clienteles justly.

Interestingly, a virtual language classroom appears to be a perfect venue for creating multiple voices that inspire subjectivities. In my academic writing class, we primarily use the Blackboard Learning System. It encourages the production of their voices through some of its useful features like Discussion Board, Active Collaboration and Integration, Group Management, Social Learning, and SafeAssign. We also have access to other relevant institutional course tools like Microsoft Team, Zoom, Cloud Campus, and Google Meet. Using these course tools, my students showed their hunger for learning due to the pandemic's learning oppression. These are manifested by their stand on different issues that oppressed them, including economic, agricultural, health resiliency, and education readiness. Discussing these issues as materials for learning, the process proves that the learners do not just learn the grammar structures, characteristics and features of academic writing, but more importantly, they understand the real condition of the world. Technology, in this case, has fully supported the critical pedagogy and critical learning because language learners, being digital natives, are more engaged in virtual mode using different news sites and apps that are helpful in their learning acquisition. Hence, their understanding of the world appear in most classroom activities, such as classroom interactions and writing like journals and reflections.

3.2   Online Participatory Approach Toward Dialogic, Democratic, and Collaborative Academic Writing

The prewriting stage is considered crucial in establishing well-crafted academic writing. This stage is initialized and strengthened by dialogic, democratic, and collaborative online discussions in this pandemic. Several social issues are raised, brainstormed, and justified, like suspensions of classes and different social events and gatherings, readiness and flexibility of education system, food security and sustainability of agriculture, the strength of public health, the essential public services and transparency of the government amid a health crisis.

With those problems raised by my students, I thought of a participatory approach in executing the lessons in academic writing. Through this approach, my students would able to solve their problems in relation to their social world guided by the language of academic writing. With their engagement and intervention with the pandemic issues, they could think and offer authentic solutions through their outputs. In this case, they are empowered in such a way that they make their own decision and action as they intensify their language literacy through writing.

Similarly, dialogic and democratic online group discussions are showed by thoroughly penetrating the nature and impact of the social problems, understanding and questioning the government imposed precautionary measures, and providing self-formulated and authentic solutions to the identified social issues. These features of critical pedagogy are highly shown by the use of the learners' first language (L1) during the pre-writing stage. Mostly, private schools in the Philippines implement the "English-Only Policy" (EOP). Still, most of the time, those schools or even the classroom-based language policy ends up miserably because others would instead observe silently rather than participate. This silence becomes an outlet of my students who are afraid of others' possible judgment if they commit grammatical mistakes. While many classroom teachers remain skeptical on the role and impact of L1 in L2 learning, Vygotsky's sociocultural theory of learning supports the use of L1 (Harun et al., 2014). The first language, as a cultural artefact, serves as a regulatory tool in L2 learning. Indeed, it connects their learning and the social world; hence, their active participation in the second language classroom discourse can be empowered by their L1. Through this, empowerment is also supported by their agency and identity as language learners.

In my class, I highly encourage using English as a second language as it is the heart of the subject I teach in support to the school's "English-Only Policy". However, the learners' home language still functions especially in the early stages of writing. For instance, in one of the highlights of the lessons in Academic Writing when I discussed writing a Position Paper, I asked them to reflect on the present condition of the country and the world concerning COVID-19 pandemic. To establish the academic value of the discourse, I encouraged them to read both local and international articles and watch news programs that highlight the pandemic. These were all parts of their homework prior to the discussion proper. During the discussion and the pre-writing stage of the position paper writing, the class was divided into smaller groups to prepare the topic to be discussed in their paper as their output using Blackboard Collaboration for at least 30 min. This activity gave them opportunity to share the gathered materials about COVID-19 and their reflections about it, including their personal, family and community experiences during the preliminary part of the lockdown.

During the small group discussion (breakout session), I observed that most of my students discussed and brainstormed using Filipino or Taglish (a mix of Tagalog and English). These codeswitching and code-mixing are dominantly used not just in academic institution, but the rest of the country. In this case, I felt how they were incredibly connected to their community by discussing national and local issues that directly and indirectly affect them. After the pre-writing stage, they engaged themselves into group writing using google editing for an hour. Looking into their final output, I can say that they successfully create cohesive position paper using the rubric I personally prepared (focus/clarity of the position, organization and structure, argument and support/evidence for position, and mechanics of writing). Aside from quantitative remarks, I also consider qualitative feedback guided by the provided rubric. There are indeed more inputs or authentic knowledge that they produced and shared. This is because of their connection to the language's cultural impact and how they connect themselves to the topic being discussed. In this case, I can directly say that the effective and cohesive output of my students are supported by the use of technology and students' use of their L1 in an L2 class as a source of power to understand and speak the truth about pandemic that affect both instructions and learning.

The following were excerpted from their recorded conversations:

Excerpt 1: Financial Support of the Government to the Poorest of the Poor Filipinos

Student A: *May ayuda na ba from the government?* (Is there already a financial aid from the government?)
Student B: *Feeling ko wala pa lahat?* (I think not everyone has received that yet.)
Student A: *Dami na nagrereklamo. Look at the news.* (There are a lot of Filipinos who are complaining now.)
Student B: *What can you expect? Normal na 'yan sa gobyerno natin, inutil.* (It's the government, so inutile!)

Student C:	Kawawa talaga yung mga mahihirap sa ... yung mga hinuli. (I pity the condition of the poor ... They were arrested.) (About the mass demonstration happened during the lockdown in the north of Metro Manila initiated by the poor community sectors.)
Student B:	Yes, wala na nga makain, hinuli pa. (Yes, they don't even have food, and yet they were arrested.)
Student A:	Kase nga wala silang social distancing... (I think they did not observe social distancing.)
Student B:	Oh common, they have nothing on their tables, walang trabaho, walang kita. Natural magagalit sila sa gobyeno. (... no jobs, no salary. They will naturally get angry at the government.)

The excerpt conversations, taken from their small group discussion using Blackboard Collaboration and Zoom, allow them to express their knowledge as a product of their social interactions in various online discussions. They cannot merely absorb pandemic stories. Still, they feel that they need to engage in relevant social media platforms like Facebook and Twitter. Using their home language appears in the recorded conversations, they created identities and agency as members of a bigger community affected by the pandemic. They need to speak to produce a more potent and transformative voice representing student and youth sectors in their little ways.

Additionally, their participation has become a platform for interrogation of power that deals with the officials' insensitivity to handle the increasing number of confirmed affected patients. They also joined the public clamors toward the health secretary's resignation because of his incompetence and corruption in the agencies under his office.

Excerpt 2: On the Public Clamor Toward the Resignation of the Health Secretary

Student 1:	Until now, wala naman nababago. Bagot na ako sa sitwasyon natin. (Until now, nothing has really changed. I'm getting bored with the situation.)
Student 2:	Lahat naman tayo. Do we have any choice? (Everybody does.)
Student 1:	I dunno. Pero sa nakikita ko, walang silbi si Duque (the Health secretary). (I think Duque is useless.)
All:	Tama hahahaha. (True hahahaha.)
Student 3:	Oo nga. Dapat magresign na sya. Dami nang galit. (Yes, he should resign. Many are already upset.)
Student 4:	Kapal lang ng mukha. (Shameless.)
Student 1:	Agree.
Student 2:	The president should consider a better health practitioner for the position. Dami naman d'yan. (There are plenty who can really do his job.)
Student 1:	I think may mga suggestions naman ang ibang agencies like the Senate. (I think there are already suggestions from other agencies like the Senate.)

In the end, the use of L1 in a dialogic and democratic discourse exemplifies a solid structure of empowering multiple voices in an ESL classroom as the development of students' voice should be about moving from a model of practice concerned with 'efficiency and hierarchical modes of accountability characterized by metaphors of wholeness, reflection and inquiry and collaboration and congeniality (Rodduck & Flutter 2004, cited in Bain, 2010).

Likewise, it is interesting to highlight that when the topic provokes and promotes social relevance, students engaged more in the discussions and activities. They can even produce unexpected insights that are not customarily observed during their typical classroom instructions. For example, when I asked them to write their stand on "the no-touch policy" with the president (this was among the initial policies that the government proposed during the first few weeks of the lockdown), most of them have rich arguments expressing both their support and opposition to it. For those who have supported the policy, the stands were supported by legal arguments being the head of state, leader of national government, and commander in chief. For instance, Fig. 1 stressed that the president needs to remain healthy to lead the country, especially in this most trying time. Additionally, Fig. 2 cited the president's age, who is now 74 years old and vulnerable to the disease. Hence, it is a must to ensure the president's safety as mandated by the Philippine constitution.

While other students support the policy, they cannot avoid suggesting that the government or the president implements other equally significant actions. This is to ensure the security of the people like improving public sanitation and strict implementation of home quarantine and social distancing. In Fig. 3, it was emphasized that protecting the president should also be extended to the people around him and generally, the public. Still emphasizing the age of the president, Fig. 4 added the public sanitation to intensify the public safety against the virus.

On the other hand, while some of my students understand the legal protocols that protect the president, most of them are critical to handle the issue. Indeed, one of my students stated that this policy is self-serving that prioritizes his family more than his country. Some believe that this "no-touch policy" with the president may be detrimental to the effectiveness of the basic services he needs to offer to the Filipino people. Indeed, most of my students expressed that the president has the oath to serve the country, the people, and the constitution like the emphasis given in Figs. 5 and 6. Therefore, protection to be given to the president must also be extended to

3/10/20, 6:02 PM   •••

As the Head of the State and Government, the President possesses control over all the offices and departments of the Philippines. With this amount of responsibility, his travels, conferences and meetings are inevitable which risks the President's health, which is essential to prioritize in times of outbreaks. His authority is needed in order to implement strategies and plans in dealing with the outbreak.

Reply | Show Replies (1)

Fig. 1 Student A's response to the online blackboard forum. Retrieved November 25, 2020, from https://ust.blackboard.com/ultra/courses/_106945_1/engagement/discussion/_2922876_1?view= discussions&courseId=_106945_1. Screenshot by author (University of Santo, 2020).

3/10/20, 4:24 PM

The Word Health organization reported that approximately 78% COVID-19 patients are aged 30-69 years old. It is understandable that we should take into account the overall health status of the president, considering that he is 74 years old. But, WHO said that all ages can be infected by the said disease. It is stated in the 1987 Constitution that the public should be informed of the state of the president's health. Carmel Abao, an Ateneo de Manila Univrsity political science professor, discussed that the state of the president's health is a national security concern. She emphasized that our countrymen deserve a fully-functioning presidency. The transparency about his health should be relayed to the public, because he is the highest form of authority in the country. Yet, this is considered as a privilege. As of now, the most plausible action to be taken is the suspension of classes. Sanitation withi the Metro is a must. The government should coordinate with different health sectors to create another precautionary measure for the community.

Reply | Show Replies (1)

Fig. 2 Student B's response to the online blackboard forum. Retrieved November 25, 2020, from https://ust.blackboard.com/ultra/courses/_106945_1/engagement/discussion/_2922876_1?view= discussions&courseId=_106945_1. Screenshot by author (University of Santo, 2020)

3/10/20, 4:47 PM

Upon reading the news about the 'No touch' policy implemented by the Presidential Security Group (PSG) due to the threat of Covid-19, it made me think how about other people around him other than his family. I understand the intentions of this policy and the importance of a president in a country since these past few days the cases just keep on rising and this became a major threat not only to the public and also to the president, but I think this policy would be much better if they will also include everyone even around the president like the staff and also the general public. Because I think this would be a good platform to spread more caution and awareness to everyone, also this may lessen the continuous increase of infected people. It would be much better if this policy would cover everyone since anyone can be infected by the Covid-19, and it is a threat to everyone and not only to the president.

Reply | Show Replies (1)

Fig. 3 Student C's response to the online blackboard forum. Retrieved November 25, 2020, from https://ust.blackboard.com/ultra/courses/_106945_1/engagement/discussion/_2922876_1?view= discussions&courseId=_106945_1. Screenshot by author (University of Santo Tomas, 2020).

3/11/20, 10:04 AM

The number of COVID-19 patients has increased as of March 11 and the DOH has confirmed that there are a total of 33 individuals who are confirmed to be infected. With that being said, our president is known for having flights from Manila to Davao or he goes to events where people would be in contact with him. For me, I think this policy is necessary for presidents especially that he is 74 years old and he is highly vulnerable to the disease. I think that the government should be sanitizing public areas, giving out masks and providing sanitizers around since there are still people that are required to go to work and they can be the next one infected.

Reply | Show Replies (1)

Fig. 4 Student D's response to the online blackboard forum. Retrieved November 25, 2020, from https://ust.blackboard.com/ultra/courses/_106945_1/engagement/discussion/_2922876_1?view= discussions&courseId=_106945_1. Screenshot by author (University of Santo Tomas, 2020).

3/10/20, 2:16 PM

Shouldn't the President dedicate his whole life to the people no matter the consequences? "...Preserve and defend its Constitution, execute its laws, do justice to every man, and consecrate myself to the service of the Nation." taken from Constitution of the Philippines, art. 7, sec. 5. The President of the Philippines, Rodrigo Duterte, is responsible for the safety and protection of our country, not just himself, and his family. This "no-policy" policy that is recently implemented seems to be a really selfish move by the president, because it only highlights the protection of himself. I understand that prevention is better than cure since the President is part of the elderly age group, and he is more vulnerable to the deadliness of this disease, but the declaration of this policy shows that the President considers his life more valuable than the life of his people.

Reply | Show Replies (1)

Fig. 5 Student E's response to the online blackboard forum. Retrieved November 25, 2020, from https://ust.blackboard.com/ultra/courses/_106945_1/engagement/discussion/2922876_1?view=di scussions&courseId=_106945_1. Screenshot by author (University of Santo Tomas, 2020).

3/10/20, 2:06 PM

As a Filipino citizen, I understand how important the president is to the whole nation however, according to the World Health Organization, the virus can spread from one person to another through small droplets from the mouth or nose when an infected person coughs or sneezes. This is why there is a need for people to maintain social distance. Considering Duterte's role in the country and his age, he is highly susceptible to COVID-19 but the no-touch policy sounds a bit selfish because instead of prioritizing the Filipinos, they are focusing only in a single person. The government's decisions should benefit the majority of the citizens and not just a part of it. Instead of implementing a no-touch policy, the government should look into other matters that would really benefit the whole country like the lack of testing kits for COVID-19.

Reply | Show Replies (1)

Fig. 6 Student F's response to the online blackboard forum. Retrieved November 25, 2020, from https://ust.blackboard.com/ultra/courses/_106945_1/engagement/discussion/_2922876_1?view= discussions&courseId=_106945_1. Screenshot by author (University of Santo Tomas, 2020).

every Filipino through social distancing, home quarantine, and other health protocols.

The students' active engagement from their classroom interactions, breakout sessions, and discussion fora has further helped them create different social actions, projects, and programs in proposal writing. Several themes were identified showing how they penetrate social problems and issues during the pandemic that affect them as community members. Similarly, their proposals have shown that several themes empower everyone's voices as significant components of building a stronger community. Through these proposals, the students have proven that more than reading and writing the word, it is more powerful to read and write the world. After reading all their proposals, I categorized them by themes. Some of the constructs involved equal rights to education, sustainability to fitness, health and sanitation, food security and agricultural resiliency, equal access to common services, women and senior citizens, support to the transportation sectors, and LGBTQIA+ group.

Interestingly, they have discussed clearly how these proposals would be implemented. On top of their proposals is the community's role, similar to other sectors, supporting the pandemic's most affected sectors. It proves that every member of

Table 1 Thematic summary of students' proposals

Identified problems	Proposed Activities/Projects	Implementation
1. Equal Rights to Education and Social Justice	*"Knowledge is the Key"*	Virtual or modular instructions
	"THE MORE YOU KNOW, THE BETTER: A Healthcare Teaching Project"	Partnership with the local government units for monitoring, administration, and supervision
	"Kalinangan sa Barangay" (Cultivation in Villages)	
	"ALAM PINOY: Know Your Risk and Know Your Status" (Filipino Knowledge)	Empowering non-government organizations (NGO's)
	"Gadgets for All"	Virtual or distant consultations
	"Disconnecting the line is disconnecting learning."	
2. Sustaining Fitness, Health, and Sanitation	*"Health on Wheels: Caravan on a Medical Mission"*	Partnership with the local government units and rural health units for monitoring, administration, and supervision
	"Plants vs. Zumba"	
	"Brain Maps: A Modern Take on Mental Health"	
	"howrYOU: an innovative application for teenagers who self-harm."	Empowering non-government organizations (NGO's)
	"Breakfast is served: A Feeding Program to Fight against Malnutrition."	Virtual or modular physical activities
	"Bangon Bata: Accessible Healthcare to Street Children" (*"Stand Children*)	Virtual or distant consultations
	"Think Blue"	
3. Food Security and Agricultural Resiliency	*"Healthy Wealthy Deli: A Culinary Community Workshop"*	Partnership with both government and non-government organizations
	"Public On-site Greenhouse Implementation (POGI)"	Promoting urban farming
	"Urban Gardening"	Virtual or modular training (webinar)
4. Equal Access to Public Services	*"#SanaAll: Basic Health Services Access to Low-lying Areas in The Philippines"* (#IWishEverybodyCould)	Partnership with both government and non-government agencies
	"Project GRAB (Generating Resources for Access to hospital Beds): A Program Solution for the Lack of Hospital Beds in Metro Manila."	Creation of internet applications for monitoring and supervision of the basic services, especially the recipients
	"Helping Hands Ready to Reach Out"	
	"Ayuda Time!: From Class A to E" (Time to Help: From Class A to E)	

(continued)

Table 1 (continued)

Identified problems	Proposed Activities/Projects	Implementation
5. Youth, Women and Senior Citizens	*"Urban YOUth : YOUth Serving Youth"*	Partnership with both government and non-government agencies Creation of more accessible hotlines for youth, women, and Senior citizens' concerns online or modular engagements and consultations with the experts
	"LifeBoost for Kids: A Perspective for the Young Minds"	
	"Hotline: Saving Women"	
	"ENGAGE!: Giving The Life Back to the Elderly Generation"	
	"Kahit Maputi na ang Buhok Ko" (Despite our Old Age)	
6. Transportation Sector	*"Know the Aid for the Pain"*	Partnership with government and non-government organizations
7. LGBTAQ+ Condition	*"Balay Kulay Center For All Colors"* (Rainbow House Center for All)	Partnership with government and non-government organizations Online and distant consultations

society's voices and significance can shape a better place if everyone equally participates and whose voices are heard and acted upon. Despite this health crisis, students believe that virtual engagement and implementation can work successfully. It becomes the new mode of community understanding. The table below shows the summary of the students' output with an emphasis on empowered voice and critical stand (Table 1).

These identified themes from the students' output appear to be the "filipinized" critical pedagogy in teaching the language. Every proposal clearly shows what the people, especially the marginalized and the oppressed, need to do to survive the pandemic. These proposals have all started with the students' reflection and end with their authentic action. Indeed, these proposals show that power and transformation can be achieved through community involvement and partnerships. With the authenticity of the voice from the learners, supported by their connection to their community, the presented output achieved cohesiveness and coherence.

Very importantly, the success of their work which is manifested in both synchronous and asynchronous tasks are also supported by the teacher's assessment style that construct criticality in language learning. Primarily, there is a rubric used to assess every activity, but students' voice should be presented already in this stage. This can be done through negotiation and agreement in such a way that I presented the elements that an academic writing should possess; on the other hand, students also contributed in constructing the rubric such as the level of argument and position. In assessing their works, I highly observed both teachers' and peers' feedbacking focusing on their writing mechanics to maintain the academic value of their work. In the end, I allotted space for their inquiry about my feedback. Online discussion and consultations followed in case there are groups with questions or clarifications.

4   Conclusion

True enough, nobody can stop one from learning even at the height of any form of disaster or crisis. Like any form of oppression, the more people experience the pains of either human or non-human tyranny, the more effort they exert to look for any possible way to crush the oppressive elements that caused their miserable life. In the beginning, when the Philippine government, through the Department of Education, has implemented different precautions to sustain learning during a pandemic, everything was rejected. Every mind has various dogmas, every mouth has other verses, and every heart has different concerns. However, while the issue of remote teaching is still under argument because of its perceived oppressive effect that divides the privileged and the underprivileged, the impact of the health crisis has also made way for the learners to become more radical in problematizing the present condition, in social engagement, and in providing more feasible programs and policies that would address this global pandemic. While I see and experience how marginalized students suffer enormously from the unjust effect of COVID-19, I still believe that everyone is a victim with different degrees. But on the brighter side, this learning oppression has created a more aggressive instructional approach. This effect directs the learners to a more meaningful and substantial language learning as critical language pedagogy is highly observed in English class.

Among those shreds of evidence is the dialogic and democratic involvement in the virtual discussions using Blackboard and Google Meet by giving their authentic insights in producing better and stronger knowledge necessary in the discipline. Similarly, this situation has encouraged the use and application of truth-based instructions by highlighting and dissecting social issues that directly and indirectly affect their lives. My engagement with CLP during pandemic is, indeed, intensified by participatory approach that allows my students understand the reality of today's world. Hence, problematizing pandemic issues also allow them to offer self-constructed solutions that empower them through language learning. This approach is supported in dialogic and collaborative online discussions that further shape democratic language learning. Allow me to emphasize the power of L1 in L2 learning because, in the Philippines, the learners' first language is not commonly considered a language resource. As a matter of fact, most Filipino teachers in English look at it as an impediment to L2 learning. Another exciting feature of CLP in my class is their first language producing different but rich ideas that contribute effectively in producing their final output. Finally, every learner proposed other social actions to continuously extend support and care to the various societal sectors, especially the marginalized, oppressed and discriminated making the instructions more ethical.

The issue of instructional materials and resources is also among those that further gives color to the criticality of language teaching. Primarily, there is an unavailability of the textbooks, manuals and other instructional materials that support critical pedagogy in language teaching. This experience shows that our school system is not yet ready to employ critical teaching and learning; nevertheless, our cultural conservatism remains powerful to find newer and fiercer formula in language teaching and learning. Additionally, the lack of those materials has also forced us to look into locally available resources that help my students engage actively. For instance, we consider the daily news, editorials, commentaries and personal stories and experiences that provoked their thinking to be more radical in assessing issues that affect our lives during the pandemic. Since news websites are just a click away, they become the most accessible means for us to understand the society. This reality appears to be a very advantageous practice because it highlights the truth-based feature of critical pedagogy in raising consciousness.

5   Food for Thought

Virtual teaching and learning is definitely challenging especially for the Filipinos and perhaps in other developing countries and regions whose technology and internet service are not responsive to the demands of language education today. However, learning must continue despite all those struggles; otherwise, we will simply worsen the condition of learning oppression.

To my fellow language teachers who believe that language is more than just a structure, but a means of empowering the learners especially during the pandemic, I ask you all to join me in my journey in looking for all possible ways to provide the needs of our students. In times characterized by limitations and boundaries, online platforms become effective avenue of discovering more of our students' potentials in letting them engage with the world to know themselves fully and to concretize their role in creating dialogic, democratic and ethical territory where voices are humanely treated. In my engagement to language teaching, I have the following online platforms with specific features that allows an even louder students' voices (Table 2).

Table 2 Suggested online platforms and their relevant features

Online platform	Relevant features that encourage students' voice
Blackboard/Cloud Campus	Blackboard is compatible across devices Breakout Rooms allow the students to engage in small group discussion initiating brainstorming and knowledge facilitation and production Blackboard Forum allows students to freely give their feedback, reactions, comments and suggestions to the given topic Group Management supports small group collaborative and cooperative discussion SafeAssign supports students to produce authentic knowledge as it traces plagiarized contents from the submitted written output
Google Meet	Google Meet is also compatible to all devices Students can use chatbox to participate in case they cannot have problem with their audio Students can easily share screen when presenting their outputs
Zoom	Zoom is also compatible to all devices Breakout Rooms help students engage in small group discussions Students can freely share their screen when presenting their output Polls are available to let participants engage in an online polls Chatbox can also be used in case students cannot use their audio

Hopefully, this reflective account will direct language educators and researchers to investigate critical language pedagogy during and even after the pandemic. It is good to carefully scrutinize the essential elements in language instructions to trace how language develops power among the learners as future nation-builders.

References

Asean Today. (2019). *The continued oppression of Filipino women*. Retrieved from https://www.aseantoday.com/2017/02/the-continued-oppression-of-filipino-women/

Bain, J. (2010). Integrating student voice: Assessment for empowerment. *Practitioner Research in Higher Education, 4*(1), 14–19.

Baluran, C. A., & Pido, R. G. (2017). The oppressive classroom: Student construction of subjectivities. *Asia Pacific Journal of Multidisciplinary Research, 5*(3), 80–86.

Basu, M. (2020). *The Philippines gets serious about connecting its schools: Interview with Aida Yuvienco, tech chief of the federal Department of Education*. GovInside. Retrieved from https://govinsider.asia/innovation/the-philippines-gets-serious-about-connecting-its-schools/

Baudu, C. (2012). *Anti-oppressive education through English language arts: A recollection journey*. (Doctoral dissertation). University of Regina.

Department of Education, Republic of the Philippines. (2009). *Inclusive Education as strategy for increasing participation rate of children (DepEd Order 72, s. 2009)*. Retrieved from http://www.deped.gov.ph/2009/07/06/do-72-s-2009-inclusive-education-as-strategy-for-increasing-participation-rate-of-children/

Department of Education, Republic of the Philippines. (2011). *Adopting the national indigenous peoples (IP) education policy framework (DepEd Order 62, s. 2011)*. Retrieved from https://www.deped.gov.ph/2011/08/08/do-62-s-2011-adopting-the-national-indigenous-peoples-ip-education-policy-framework/

Department of Education, Republic of the Philippines. (2019). *Policy guidelines on the K to 12 basic education program (DepEd Order 021, s. 2019)*. Retrieved from https://www.deped.gov.ph/wp-content/uploads/2019/08/DO_s2019_021.pdf

Department of Education, Republic of the Philippines (n.d.). *Mission, vision, core values, and mandate*. Retrieved from https://www.deped.gov.ph/about-deped/vision-mission-core-values-and-mandate/

Harun, H., Massari, N., & Puteh Behak, F. (2014). Use of L1 as a mediational tool for understanding tense/aspect marking in English: An application of concept-based instruction. *Elsevier/Procedia: Social and Behavioral Sciences, 134*(2014), 134–139. https://doi.org/10.1016/j.sbspro.2014.04.231

Kumaravadivelu, B. (2010). Problematizing cultural stereotypes in TESOL. In B. Kumaravadivelu (Ed.). *TESOL Quarterly (The Forum), 37*(4), 709–719. https://doi.org/10.2307/3588219

Monroy-Adarlo, G. (2016). (Re)framing citizenship education in the Philippines: A twenty-first century imperative. *The Good Society, 25*(2–3), 256–288. https://doi.org/10.5325/goodsociety.25.2-3.0256

Ollis, T. (2012). *A critical pedagogy of embodied education: Learning to become an activist*. Palgrave Macmillan.

Richardson, S. E. (2001). *Positioning student voice in the classroom: The postmodern era*. (Doctoral dissertation). Virginia Polytechnic Institute and State University.

Tuman, M. C. (1998). *Language and limits: Resisting reform in English studies*. State University Press.

University of Santo Tomas. (2020). *UST Cloud Campus* (Screenshot by author). https://ust.blackboard.com/ultra/institution-page

Viola, M. (2009). The filipinization of critical pedagogy: Widening the scope of critical educational theory. *Journal for Critical Education Policy, 7*(1), 1–28.

World Education Forum. (2015). *Education for all 2015 National Review Report: Philippines, 2015*. UNESDOC Digital Library.

Fostering Interaction and Motivation in EFL Live Virtual Classes at University

Ana Cecilia Cad ⓘ, Claudia Alejandra Spataro, and Paul Alexis Carrera

Highlights

- Digital tools, such as Educaplay, Quizizz and Breakouts, can be used to foster different types of interactions among instructor, learner and content.
- Digital tools combined with different modes of interaction can motivate EFL students in large classes.
- These tools can be used synchronously and asynchronously in ERT contexts and beyond.

1 Introduction

The coronavirus pandemic has had a strong impact on every sphere of our lives and education is no exception to this. Born in the context of a worldwide pandemic, Emergency Remote Teaching (ERT) emerged as an attempt to minimize the temporary disruption of the formal educational system (Hodges et al., 2020). Its implementation was supposed to be short-lived; however, its use has been extended beyond original estimations, and everything seems to indicate that it is here to stay. Several institutions of higher education have been challenged to adapt themselves to this new situation with unprecedented speed and little time for preparation. Even when some institutions already offered online learning, i.e., learning which takes place via the Internet (Dudeney & Hockly, 2012), very few were ready to move their entire face-to-face courses online due to lockdown.

Interestingly, the difference between online learning and learning online was soon documented in the literature. Hodges et al. (2020) introduced the term ERT,

A. C. Cad (✉) · C. A. Spataro · P. A. Carrera
Facultad de Lenguas, Universidad Nacional de Córdoba, Córdoba, Argentina
e-mail: anaceciliacad@unc.edu.ar; claudia.spataro@unc.edu.ar; paul.carrera@unc.edu.ar

© The Author(s), under exclusive license to Springer Nature Switzerland AG 2021
J. Chen (ed.), *Emergency Remote Teaching and Beyond*,
https://doi.org/10.1007/978-3-030-84067-9_12

which quickly became familiar among educators all over the world, to refer to "the type of instruction being delivered in these pressing circumstances" (n.p.). This form of instruction, planned in haste and with little preparation and resources, marks a sharp contrast with online learning, which has long aided education and ELT for almost three decades in the form of distance learning, blended learning and mobile learning (Dudeney & Hockly, 2012). In fact, Oskoz and Smith (2020) refer to "online teaching vs teaching online" to express this opposition between e-learning and ERT. Despite the pressure and time constraints, in a few weeks, teachers managed to learn to use virtual classrooms, digital tools and online resources to accommodate to this new form of teaching.

This chapter outlines the main lessons we have learned from the use of digital tools to foster interaction and motivation in live sessions for EFL undergraduate students in a teacher training/ translation university programme in Argentina in times of ERT and, at the same time, it offers and invites reflection on what avenues may lie ahead. Due to lockdown, the undergraduate course English Language was taught on a fully remote basis through a virtual classroom on Moodle and optional weekly online sessions on Google Meet for about 100 students. Considering that learning a language is a social collaborative process, it was important to foster meaningful interaction to pave the way for EFL learning in these live sessions. To achieve this goal, we drew on research by Moore (1989) which shows that meaningful integration of modes of interaction can improve learning outcomes (Keaton & Gilbert, 2020; Moore & Anderson, 2003). Making use of the various online resources available for ELT (Peachey, 2017; Dudeney & Hockly, 2012), we combined online resources, games and tools, such as Educaplay, Quizizz and Genial.ly, to create online lessons that fostered student-teacher-content interaction. Deci and Ryan's (2000) self-determination theory in online education and Dörnyei and Csizér's (1998) strategies for motivating language learners were also considered in the design and implementation of the online activities.

This chapter describes some of the online activities that we designed and used in our live sessions as well as their gains, challenges and setbacks. Students' feedback from the online chat and a Google questionnaire are also presented. Although these activities have helped students engage in online sessions, they can also be used in face-to-face lessons, or in virtual classrooms for blended or distance learning. The ideas shared below will hopefully help inspire TESOL and CALL researchers to use digital tools to create interactive and motivating online and face-to-face lessons.

2   Interaction and Motivation in Online Learning

For the design of our online activities, we used Educaplay, Quizizz and Genial.ly to create engaging and interactive online meetings for almost 100 EFL students on Meet. The two main areas of research that guided our study were types of interaction and motivation.

2.1   Types of Interaction

The process of learning and producing a language is both intrapersonal and interpersonal. It is intrapersonal as individual mental processes are involved in the production of language; it is also interpersonal as language is learned through interaction with others (Pellergrino & Hilton, 2012). In online language learning, a key concern is how to "arouse and maintain in (…) learners a desire to interact online" (White, 2003, p. 55) since interaction plays an important role in promoting motivation, collaboration and co-construction of knowledge. Jonassen (1988) defines interactivity in Computer-mediated communication (CMC) as "an activity between two organisms and with a computer-based application, involving the learner in a true dialog" (p. 160).

Referring to distance education, Moore (1989) describes three categories of interactivity: student-instructor, student-student, and student-content (in Moore & Anderson, 2003). Each category can be further subdivided to account for the specific character of an interaction; that is, where it occurs, who initiates it, and in what time frame it is achieved (Moore & Kearsley, 1996). Although these classifications have been applied specifically to distance learning, we have adopted them as a guide for the use of digital resources that foster interaction in ERT since, as is documented in the literature, learning outcomes increase when these types of interaction are meaningfully integrated (Bernard et al., 2009). As an added advantage, the implementation of these tools can be extended beyond ERT to meet the needs of diverse educational contexts.

In student-instructor interaction, the instructional design and selection of learning activities influence the quality and quantity of interaction taking place in live sessions and in other educational settings (Moore & Anderson, 2003). When it comes to instructional design, adequate planning of the way instructions are given is paramount to make an efficient use of time. In turn, the development of activities can be based on two main concepts: maximizing and providing alternative forms of interaction. Following Thatch and Murphy (1995), student-instructor interaction can be promoted by a. establishing learning outcomes/ objectives; b. providing timely, useful feedback; c. facilitating information presentation; d. monitoring and evaluating student progress; e. facilitating learning activities; f. facilitating discussions; and g. determining learning needs and preferences.

Student-student interaction "forces learners to construct or formulate an idea in a deeper sense" (Moore & Anderson, 2003, p. 134). When students can establish meaningful interactions among each other, the interactants' interest and motivation increase as they are engaged in a process where a positive response is expected and constant feedback is exchanged. Langer (1989, 1997) compares this state of high cognitive involvement to a state of mindfulness that has three important characteristics: the ongoing creation of new categories, the openness to new information, and the realization that more than one perspective is possible. Thus, building and sustaining this type of interaction is relevant for ERT and beyond.

Student-content interaction is dependent upon the use of media alternatives or multimedia. Sims (1997) proposes the term *multimedia* which consists of "media (text, audio, visual), technology (computers) and the products (education, games, information)" (p. 158). As this type of interaction can be constructed by means of media, technology and products, it can be fostered in live sessions as well as in other educational environments. Sims also created a taxonomy to describe forms of interactivity. For the purpose of this chapter, we will focus on *object, linear, support, update, construct, reflexive, and nonimmersive contextual interactivity.* Although this theory focuses on the system and not on the learner (Domagk et al., 2010), it provides key concepts to describe how interaction is constructed and sustained by means of digital resources.

Object interactivity entails the activation of objects by clicking buttons and icons. When the users click on an object, there is some form of audio-visual response. In *linear interactivity*, users are able to move backwards and forwards "through a predetermined linear sequence of instructional material" (Sims, 1997, pp. 162–163). *Support interactivity* refers to the users' options to receive support and to access tutorials. *Update interactivity* consists of a computer presenting or generating content to which the learner must respond. In *construct interactivity*, the learner is required to complete different tasks or operations to achieve a specific goal. In this type of interaction, the learner is immersed in real-world actions. *Reflective interactivity* allows a student to enter a response and to compare his/her responses with other users. One benefit of this type of interactivity is that learners "can reflect on their response and make their own judgment as to its accuracy or correctness" (Sims, 1997, p. 165). Finally, in *nonimmersive contextual interactivity*, a virtual training environment integrates and extends different interactive levels. In this type of interactivity, learners are transported into a microworld which "models their existing work environment, and the tasks they undertake reflect those of the work experience" (p. 167). Digital resources can be used to create and engage the students in these forms of interactivity (Fig. 1).

Each type of interactivity, student-instructor, student-student and student-content, can be analyzed in terms of where it occurs, who initiates it and in what time frame interaction is achieved. Interactions can happen in private, as is the case of emailing, or in a live conference; they can be started by the instructor or by the student and they can occur synchronously or asynchronously.

The different concepts presented regarding interactivity have been drawn from the field of computer sciences, specifically application development, and the field of

object   linear   support   update

Fig. 1 Types of student-content interactivity with digital tools

distance learning. We have used these concepts as thinking tools to facilitate the description of the practices that we have carried out during ERT, which are mainly characterized as synchronous in nature. We hope that the use of tools from other fields that we have made in our research and practice can become a springboard for considering other potential uses of similar practices beyond ERT.

2.2 *Motivation*

Motivation is key to students' success in language learning as this drive will help students accomplish their goals. Even when most scholars acknowledge the importance of motivation, this is an abstract concept that defies definition (Lamb et al., 2019). We adhere to Dornyei & Otto (1998) definition of motivation in second language learning as "the dynamically changing cumulative arousal in a person that initiates, directs, coordinates, amplifies, terminates, and evaluates the cognitive and motor processes whereby initial wishes and desires are selected, prioritized, operationalized and (successfully or unsuccessfully) acted out" (p. 65). This definition embodies the intrinsic notion that motivation is a process rather than a product. Such process perspective is important to understand that teachers should work to keep students motivated all throughout the class.

Different authors have explored the topic of motivation and its impact on second language learning. Dornyei (2001) and Dornyei & Cizere (1998) propose specific classroom strategies to help generate and maintain students' motivation that have been successfully implemented in foreign language learning (Muñoz et al., 2020; Cuccinota, 2019). Motivational strategies help to generate positive student attitudes towards language learning, and they also help to sustain and protect motivation. Although these strategies were put into practice in the context of a brick-and-mortar classroom, some of them are still valid for online settings: creating a learner-friendly atmosphere and clear instructions, promoting students' autonomy and their interrelation with other peers, and establishing clear goals.

Apart from these strategies, Ryan and Deci's (1985, 2000, 2017) self-determination theory (SDT) of motivation is also relevant since it paves the way for the analysis of motivation in an online environment (Bovermann & Bastiaens, 2020). SDT is based on the idea that people within a community are motivated to grow and develop influenced by three innate and universal needs: *relatedness, autonomy* and *competence.*

(a) *Relatedness*: learners need to experience a sense of belonging, social meaning and value.
(b) *Autonomy*: students need to develop a sense of control of their own behaviours and goals. This aspect will play a critical role in helping people achieve their self-determination.
(c) *Competence*: people need to perceive tasks as an achievable challenge and, in turn, these tasks will lead to the attainment of goals that are of personal value.

SDT leads to the exploration of situated motivation in relation to learners' autonomy. According to this theory, it is important that the environmental conditions in which students are immersed support the individual's need for autonomy, competence and relatedness as these three factors can contribute to boosting students' intrinsic motivation (Ryan & Deci, 2000). When students are not self-motivated, they tend to derive motivation extrinsically, mostly from high grades or teacher's praise.

Addressing the difference in types of motivation has important pedagogical implications since teachers can tailor their instruction to help students see the relevance of the tasks they perform. For example, in order to appeal to extrinsically motivated learners, it is important to explain the rationale behind each task, craft relevant instructional activities that respond to students' personal interests and present clear deadlines and directives (Hartnett, 2016).

Structuring the learning environment is key to the development of students' linguistic competence and their needs of belonging. To this end, online environments should be scaffolded structures that include explicit instructions, detailed information, clear criteria for assessment, expected goals and course objectives, proper timely feedback, and options for comments and suggestions (Hartnett, 2016). Tasks should be optimally challenging for learners to experience a feeling of self-determination. The learning atmosphere should also reflect teachers' involvement in the construction process. If students can perceive the time invested, the attention devoted to detail, the teacher's respect and relatedness during exchanges, they will feel supported to learn and their motivation will most likely be boosted.

Creating a learner-friendly environment that fosters learners' competence, a sense of autonomy and relatedness is crucial to keep them motivated. Exploring motivation in online settings is important since it plays a key role in determining what, when and how students learn (Ryan and Deci, 2000). It may also determine students' level of engagement and achievement in a course. Understanding motivation in these unprecedented circumstances, in which diverse social factors, personal experiences and access to technology are at play, may help draw some pedagogical implications for teaching and learning during emergency remote teaching and beyond.

3   Context of Implementation

Following the main tenets on modes of interaction and motivation in online environments outlined in Sect. 2, we have used Educaplay, Genial.ly and Quizizz to design online activities for our students at a teacher training/ translator university programme in Argentina during the Covid-19 lockdown period. Most of our students are aged between 18 and 20, they are all native speakers of Spanish and they are starting their first year at university. As the program is run by a state university, one of the main challenges we face is the high student-teacher ratio since we usually have around 100 students in our classes.

Our course is taught from April to October, and its main aim is to help students develop their proficiency in English as a Foreign Language (EFL) at a B1 level. This is done through different content units that focus on the development of the four macro skills as well as vocabulary and use of English. The content units are *Technology and Telecommunications, Housing, Money and Shopping* and *Food and Health.* In 2020, we did not have the chance to meet our students face-to-face as the beginning of the school year coincided with the beginning of the lockdown. The course was taught on a fully remote basis through a virtual classroom on Moodle and optional weekly online sessions through videoconference on Google Meet for groups of about 100 students. The main aim of the live sessions was to offer students a synchronous form of communication with their teachers and classmates and to help students develop the language skills and review content material, vocabulary and use of English studied in the virtual classroom the week before. Considering the problem of digital technologies in low resource contexts (Hockly 2013) and that ERT has marked what Oskoz and Smith (2020) have referred to as "digital divide", the live sessions were optional since not all the students had good Internet connection. To encourage students to attend and take part in these optional sessions, we designed online lessons using digital tools that helped us combine different modes of interaction and boost motivation.

4   Digital Tools to Foster Interaction and Motivation

This section focuses on the description of three main digital tools and on practical ways in which they can be implemented in the online or face to face class to foster interaction and motivation. The tools' main strengths and weaknesses are outlined based on our own experience in the live sessions. We have also included students' views on the tools collected from the chat on Google Meet and an informal survey conducted at the end of the course with Google forms.

4.1   Educaplay (https://www.educaplay.com)

4.1.1   Description

Educaplay is an educational games generator that allows teachers to create and access multimedia activities (*Educaplay*, 2020). The platform offers free and premium accounts. In both cases, users can design and save multimedia activities and create groups with students and colleagues. Moreover, activities can be shared on Google Classroom and Microsoft Teams, and exported to any virtual platform with SCROM or LTI like Moodle, Canvas or Blackboard (*Educaplay*, 2020).

There are 16 types of activities available, and they range from common activities available on other platforms, like gap-filling, matching and multiple-choice/

Fig. 2 Types of activities with Educaplay

true-false quiz, to more innovative activities like riddle, map quiz, alphabet game, memory game, wordsearch puzzle, crossword and word and letter unscrambler (Fig. 2). Educaplay also offers the possibility of designing activities with audios and videos through the dialogue game, dictation and video quiz.

> **Student's Comment 1**
> I really enjoyed the dynamic of these games, for me they were a way to practice and make things clearer for me.

Without much knowledge of ICT, it is possible to create self-check multimedia activities with Educaplay. Users have to specify the country, school year and course for which the activity is intended. Each activity is accompanied by a video tutorial and a specific guide to help users improve the quality and reliability of the activity they are designing. Once created, the multimedia activities can be shared through links and embedded codes so that students can try them asynchronously or synchronously by means of a "challenge" with a temporary code.

4.1.2 Implementation

Educaplay has a great potential as its 16 types of activities can be designed and tailored for students of different ages, needs and contexts. In our particular context, we mainly implemented this digital tool to help our students revise and consolidate key lexical items, such as phrasal verbs, idioms, set expressions and collocations.

For example, we used the memory game (memotest) and the crossword to design activities with phrasal verbs and pictures. The gap-filling and multiple-choice quiz were used for collocations and set expressions, and the alphabet game proved very useful to combine different types of lexical items.

Student's Comment 2
Believe or not, I have learned A LOT from this kind of games, someway the content has stick in my memory, thanks.

Apart from fostering vocabulary learning, these activities combine different forms of student-content interaction, namely object, linear, support and update interactivity (Sims, 1997). This enabled us to offer students a chance to interact with the activities on their own and to change the usual teacher-student interaction of the live session. Indeed, when we announced before the session that there was a game coming, students showed great enthusiasm by quickly joining and participating in the activities. We had discovered that students' attention and participation increased if we presented them with a sequence of different types of online activities. This could be attributed to the novelty factor of the activities which, from the students' perspective, became fun rather than just a tool to revise content. From the teachers' perspective the activities became an opportunity to give students an active role in the online sessions. To make the most of this digital tool, we usually combined some revision notes with the games designed with Educaplay. For example, for our session on the topic "Problems around house" related to the course unit on *Housing*, we first used some visual aids to help students revise some collocations (torn carpet, dripping tap, leaking roof, etc.), and we then asked them to play a memotest with pictures and sentences (Fig. 3). Next, we revised some key phrasal verbs related to doing up a derelict house, and we asked students to complete a multiple-choice quiz with these verbs. Finally, we asked students to complete a video quiz with a Youtube video on home refurbishing.

Student-student interaction and their motivation through competition were also encouraged in our live sessions thanks to the score system and "challenges" (Fig. 4).

Fig. 3 Memory game or memotest

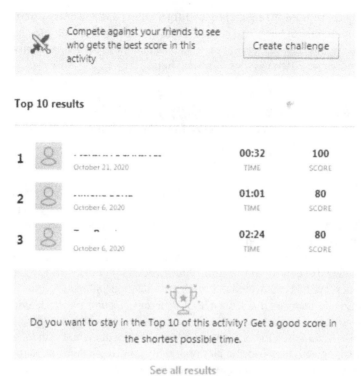

Fig. 4 Competition and challenges with Educaplay

We shared the pin and the link of the "challenge" through the chat box on Google Meet so that students could play remotely on their computers or mobiles. Students got immediate feedback upon completing the activity, and those who received the best scores in the shortest time appeared in the "Top 10 results". The possibility of completing the activities synchronously in the form of competition proved very effective (and enjoyable) among students:

Student's Comment 3
It makes you think hard because you know that you have a time limit and also makes you see what vocabulary you have to study more. It's great for reviewing key vocabulary.

One main drawback of Educaplay that was mentioned by the students, but not noticed by the teachers, was related to the limited number of attempts made available to users. The guide in Educaplay suggests 5 or 10 attempts depending on the nature of the game; however, students noticed that this was a bit discouraging and hard:

Student's Comment 4
I don't like that it has a certain number of tries. If you make 5 or 10 mistakes you can't play anymore ☹. But competition is fun :p

4.1.3 Beyond

The possibility of designing various types of activities that can be implemented synchronously and asynchronously makes Educaplay a useful tool for ERT and beyond. If the class is taught online through online conferencing as we did, the pin number and the link of the activity can be shared through the chat box. If it is taught in the traditional classroom, the teacher can share them through a projector or on the board for students to play the game on their mobiles. Teachers can also design activities for students to complete at their own time and pace. This could be done by sharing the links to the activities through the virtual classrooms, blogs, QR codes or forums. As activities are saved specifying the country, school year and course, the bank of activities on Educaplay is quite varied and extensive. Teachers do not need a username to browse and try the different activities on the catalog which can be useful and suitable for their students. Exploring this digital tool and implementing its activities in the classroom can be an enriching and motivating experience for students in different educational contexts.

4.2 Breakouts *(by Genial.ly https://www.genial.ly/)*

4.2.1 Description

Genial.ly is an online platform that offers the opportunity to design all kinds of interactive content (Fig. 5). By clicking on gamification, users can access breakouts templates. Digital Breakouts are a multi-player activity in which players have to escape different rooms generally in a limited time. To accomplish the task, students have to solve the riddles or puzzles present in each room to obtain a clue. When the participants have gathered all the clues, they can unlock the padlock and escape the room.

Breakouts are an interesting option for the foreign language class. In order to solve each riddle, students need to interact and cooperate to co-construct knowledge; thus, they can purposefully produce language in a meaningful context. This design principle aligns with SDT while promoting different levels of interaction. Breakouts help create a sense of relatedness while fostering autonomy and competence. At the same time, each riddle promotes different interactions since students have to manipulate content and negotiate meaning to solve each task.

Fig. 5 Different templates offered by Genial.ly

4.2.2 Implementation

To promote meaningful learning, digital breakouts must be planned taking into consideration the type of learning that needs to be fostered and the point in the development of the course in which the task will be implemented. Breakouts can be used during a diagnostic or revision stage, or as an instance of formative assessment. The breakout described in this chapter was designed to review a content unit on *Technology and Telecommunications*. The main objectives of this breakout were to check students' understanding of the class material, and to review specific contents and key expressions and vocabulary before the first term test. With that in mind, riddles were selected to correspond to different pedagogical objectives (Guigon et al., 2018). It is important that the main goals and objectives of the breakout are defined before constructing the riddles to organize them into coherent pedagogical tasks.

Student's Comment 5
I wanted to answer everything right to open the padlock quickly.

This breakout was crafted on a free Genial.ly template that included an introduction, four rooms and a reward. In the introduction section, students were presented with the main learning objectives of the breakout. Sharing learning goals and objectives with our students promoted instructor-student interaction as students were aware of teacher's expectations, and they could act in accordance to that. Each room challenged students to solve five to three riddles relying on their content knowledge, their language proficiency and their critical thinking skills. Each room may be considered to be a level (Guigon et al., 2018); thus, all the rooms can be conceived and arranged in terms of cognitive and linguistic difficulty, requiring solving one level before accessing the next one. In the reward stage, we promoted reflection on aspects dealt with in the breakout so that students could become more aware of their learning process.

Student's Comment 6
This breakout made think about the content of the text in a playful manner.

These tasks promoted the development of autonomy and competence, which are key to boosting students' motivation. Initially, however, we took the active role of introducing the activity and explaining how students should navigate the learning environment to succeed in unlocking the room. Each challenge was read aloud and answers were welcomed. Sometimes, when students could not agree on the right answer, we provided them with extra oral cues that helped them take a well-informed decision. After a challenging prompt, there was a debriefing moment for students to further explore all the options available to them and clear any doubts. Then, in our role as facilitators, we prompted student-content interaction by encouraging students to review their class material when they were struggling to solve a task. We also gave them time to re-read a particular text or review vocabulary. In this way, we sought to enhance their critical thinking and their autonomy. Student-student and instructor-student interactions were fostered not only by inviting students to activate their microphones, but also by asking them to write and share their contributions through the Google Meet chat. Even when students were quickly able to identify the right answer to solve each puzzle, they were asked to justify their choices. Sometimes, one student could not provide a fully-fledged answer, and other students were invited to contribute. Thus, providing a justification became the outcome of collaborative work. An interesting feature of breakouts is the variety of activities present in their design. Each room presents a riddle whose layout differs from the rest. This variety contributes to enhancing students' motivation and sense of alertness and caters for diverse learning styles. Different elements provided by the platform can be used as prompts: images, videos, questions and, light and shadows.

Another appealing feature for students is their possibility of having immediate access to feedback (Fig. 6), which fulfills a two-fold purpose. Firstly, it has an impact on motivation since students get immediate information on their performance, which may later inform their decisions regarding their learning process. Secondly, it fosters student-instruction interaction, which can lead to tailor-made instruction that adjusts to meet students' learning needs.

Unlocking the breakroom is a motivational hook for students to pursue the task until the end. Rewards are obtained if students managed to successfully navigate each room. These scattered rewards help to maintain motivation at an optimal level (Fig. 7). Getting rewards along the way can enhance students' confidence in their own skills and, in turn, this has an impact on their learning autonomy. Thus, both elements contribute to boosting students' self-determination.

Fig. 6 Fourth room: immediate feedback

Fig. 7 Numbers and locks

According to our students, digital breakouts present one major drawback: lack of competition. It seems that our students wish to see whether they are solving the task better than their classmates. However, although Genial.ly does not offer the possibility for students to challenge one another, we believe it can provide an opportunity to discuss the role of competition with our students.

> **Student's Comment 7**
> I wish we could compete against our classmates. It's more fun that way.

Upon completing a breakout, we would hold a debriefing session to promote teacher-student interaction. At this stage, the instructor often took the opportunity to clarify concepts or welcome students' questions.

4.2.3 Beyond

Taking into account the main characteristics of breakouts, we believe that they are an excellent teaching and learning tool for virtual sessions and we think that they can be adapted to different types of educational contexts. If educators have access to a computer lab or students have access to mobile phones, breakouts can be implemented in the regular class setting as long as there is a reasonably good Internet connection in the room. Through shareable links or iframes, breakouts can also be shared with students, or they can be embedded in a virtual learning environment; however, if they are assigned to be completed asynchronously, the collaborative aspect may be lost. The flexibility breakouts offer allows teachers to embed different media, design appealing layouts and create activities that suit students' needs and learning styles. In addition, revision and formative assessment activities can be constructed in an engaging way. We believe that through the process of negotiation and collaboration afforded by breakouts, students can further develop their language skills while learning about content units. All in all, we consider that this resource has endless possibilities for virtual and traditional classrooms.

4.3   Quizizz (*https://quizizz.com/admin*)

4.3.1   Description

Quizizz is an educational application created in 2015 by Antik Gupta and Deepak Joy Cheenath which allows teachers to create "student-paced formative assessments in a fun and engaging way for students of all ages" (Quizizz, 2019, para.1). This tool offers the possibility of creating a quiz or a lesson. For a quiz, tutors can choose from different testing options: open-ended, fill-in- the-blanks, multiple choice, poll and checkbox activities (Fig. 8). In the case of lessons, slides are incorporated transforming the Quizizz into a presentation which can be combined with evaluation to allow the tutor to introduce any of the testing options offered by the quiz. In our live session, Quizizz was implemented to assess students' progress in the topics they were expected to study and practice on their own.

Fig. 8 Types of activities with Quizizz

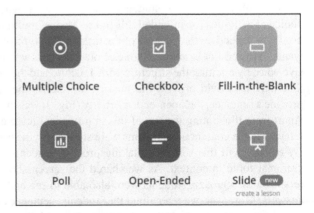

4.3.2 Implementation

Based on its characteristics, Quizizz can be implemented in different educational settings to revise, practice and evaluate a variety of topics. Considering the ERT context, our main concern was to teach grammar in use in a way that could foster motivation and encourage students to participate. We discovered that, by playing Quizizz in the live sessions, it was possible to change the way learners engaged in meaningful interactions with us and with the course content. As students started to participate in the activities, they came to see each activity as an interesting challenge they had to face. This way of presenting activities meant a significant and positive change in the class atmosphere as the students discovered that they were no longer having a receptive role in the live sessions by providing just a one-word answer (yes, no). Thus, the implementation of this app has been an ally in the process of finding ways to promote students' motivation and interaction.

Using Quizizz, we discovered that we could create interactive and engaging live sessions if we followed three stages: *before*, *during* and *after* the quiz. Before the quiz, the students were told how the app was used, what they needed to access the game, what problems they might encounter and possible solutions, and what learning objectives they were expected to achieve. This was an important part of the process as students needed to be familiar with the tool to get fully engaged with the content presented. The presentation of activities in a scaffolded manner was key to building students' motivation and preparing the ground for interaction to take place. As we were aware that the more problems students encountered, the less likely they would be to start interacting with the content, we took time to anticipate the possible problems that might arise during the implementation of the quiz. Engaging in this analysis contributed to optimizing the instructional time and students' involvement in the task. In turn, increasing students' involvement in the task served as a motivational hook to maintain students' expectations high and avoid distractions (Ryan & Deci, 2000). By explaining the rationale behind the completion of a task, the learner starts working towards the process of becoming an autonomous learner.

While playing the quiz, students can be presented with different activities. The choice of activities (open-ended, fill-in-the-blanks, multiple choice, poll and checkbox) will depend on the purpose of the task and the type of interaction the instructor wants to foster. For example, in one of our sessions, we intended to review the passive voice by eliciting the structure with a picture and the beginning of a sentence so that students would provide the missing words. As the students were required to provide a sentence, the open-ended activity (Fig. 9) was the most appropriate option. Apart from illustrating the use of this grammatical feature, the sentences had to be relevant to the content unit students were studying at the time: *Money and Shopping*. By engaging in this sentence-making process, students were able to practise the grammar topic in context. As we shared the screen showing the answers and the report on the Quizizz, students were also able to see and analyse their classmates' answers. Moreover, we read aloud the students' sentences and provided individualized feedback from which the other learners could also profit. In this way, the students were engaged in student-content interaction, more specifically in reflective

Fig. 9 Open ended
activity with Quizizz

interactivity. They feel a sense of self-achievement. Thus, the learning outcomes were two-fold: students learned by doing and by being exposed to their classmates' feedback. From the point of view of motivation, providing immediate feedback enhances students' motivation and sense of alertness. The students who leave the virtual session with the feeling of having learned the topic are more likely to attend the next meeting as they feel a sense of self-achievement that is not only measured metaphorically in terms of huge amounts of gold -given by Quizizz- but also by a number of meaningful learning experiences. Both, giving students praise for their production and receiving rewards contribute to the development of students' extrinsic motivation.

Student's Comment 8
I like it because it's funny and it motivates you to participate.

In another session, we faced the challenge of helping students practice *Key-word transformation sentence*. In this type of exercise, students are asked to rephrase a given sentence using a key-word. Given the degree of linguistic complexity of this exercise, we used Quizizz to pursue the following pedagogical outcomes: diagnosing students' progress and helping them practice and reflect on the purpose of this exercise. We started our online class by asking students to solve a multiple-choice exercise (Fig. 10). This type of exercise served the purpose of helping students develop their analytical skills to pinpoint why some of the options were not appropriate for a given context, and why a given option was the right choice. This purpose was achieved by means of student-content interaction and teacher-student interaction. The former was initiated by Quizizz as it presented the three options under time constraint (*update, object and construct interaction* (Sims, 1997)), and the latter was created when the teachers gave feedback to the students once the tasks had been completed. These were the first steps students took towards the development of autonomy and confidence. Students realized that they were not only being offered motivating features, but they were also being presented with challenging situations they had to solve to move on to the following stage. We believe that such fostering of autonomy, confidence and task-engagement led to enhanced motivation among our students.

Student's Comment 9

I like the adrenaline, and it was really useful to get some feedback at the moment. It was easy and fast.

Multiple-choice activity

Fill-in-the-blanks activity   Open ended activity

Fig. 10 Types of activities to teach Key-word transformation sentences

We continued our online activity on the passive voice by providing learners with fill-in-the-blanks activities (Fig. 10). As students were expected to provide an answer by typing a limited number of words under time-constraint, they soon discovered the highly structured nature of this exercise. Thus, Quizizz served our pedagogical purpose of placing linguistic awareness into focus by means of student-content interaction (*update, object and construct interaction*). In turn, teacher-student interaction was enhanced as more instances of feedback were provided. Given the increased complexity of the task, students' engagement was also positively affected. As the degree of complexity increased, students realized that they were able to complete more challenging tasks, making the learning process more appealing.

Student's Comment 10

I really enjoyed the last few quizzes especially. Having to type out the answers is a great way to receive better and more personalized feedback.

As students' motivation was enhanced through the use of different types of activities, and individualized and group feedback, their degree of confidence and autonomy increased significantly, so much so that they were able to face their biggest challenge: rewriting the first sentence by means of an open-ended activity. At this point, students' degree of interaction reached its climax as the amount of content produced was greater and the type of feedback provided was more detailed.

Figure 10 also shows the results of the interaction initiated by the app; these results were then used to give immediate and individualized feedback to the learners. This individualized feedback turned out to be beneficial for the whole group as this was an instance of co-construction of knowledge. Presenting students with challenging tasks, as was the case of this open-ended activity, can nurture the feeling of self-determination which is a key component in the development of motivation.

Student's Comment 11
I like that Paul [instructor] can read our answers while we do it.

After the activity was completed, we included a slide inviting students to ask questions about the course content, or about some other aspects regarding course procedures, such as the date when course exam results would be available. An advantage of including a slide after the last activity was completed was that students knew at which point of the virtual sessions they would be able to build a different type of teacher-student interaction. This was a type of interaction initiated by students asking questions and making comments, with teachers then responding to such questions. This is another example of the way in which Quizizz can serve the purpose of constructing and enhancing interactivity in the classroom. By being given the possibility of asking questions and clearing up doubts, students can develop autonomy and confidence, both of these being motivating features in the construction of students' self-determination.

4.3.3 Beyond

Considering its main characteristics, Quizizz can be an excellent teaching and learning tool for virtual sessions and beyond as it can be adapted to different types of educational settings. Should teachers wish to introduce this tool into traditional classrooms, i.e. face-to-face meetings, they will need a computer with internet connection, a screen to project the answers, and devices with internet connection for students to log into the quiz. If instructors want to introduce this tool in their virtual learning environments, it is possible to assign the Quizizz for homework so that students can work at their own pace. It is important to consider that implementation of this digital tool in face-to-face educational settings can foster motivation and interactivity in similar ways. However, given that some contextual elements (such as instant feedback from the teacher or the student's answers) are not present in educational platforms, interaction and motivation may be jeopardized if the Quizizz is assigned for homework.

5   Conclusion

The Covid-19 pandemic has changed our lives and forced teaching to move online in an untested and unprecedented way. Educators felt challenged in this unexpected situation in which video conferencing software and digital resources became teachers' instruction tools. Traditional ways of delivering a class were also challenged pushing teachers to reinvent themselves and their teaching. Students were also deeply affected as their learning strategies and forms of study were also altered. In this context, motivating students, engaging them, and getting them enthusiastic about working online seemed an impossible endeavor. However, with the help of the digital resources outlined in this chapter, we discovered that this was not an impossible task. The large number of options available through Educaplay, Genial.ly and Quizizz helped us create interactive and engaging live sessions to almost 100 EFL students at university. Our students showed great enthusiasm when playing live vocabulary and grammar games through "challenges" and live quizzes, and when checking the winners displayed in leaderboards. Getting the clues to unlock rooms and solving riddles made them active participants in the online lessons. Moreover, the variety of templates and options in the question banks also helped us to design activities that suited our teaching methods and purposes. Indeed, as presented in this chapter and summarized in the "food for thought" section below, Educaplay, Genial. ly and Quizizz have been great aids to make our remote lessons interactive and engaging, and we will probably continue using these tools in our lessons in the future.

During ERT, many educators may have "discovered that you can also teach effectively online, despite the technical challenges" (Rayan, 2016, p.31) and our teaching experience has been no exception. The practice of reflecting upon our teaching practices and sharing them with colleagues has been an invaluable opportunity for us, especially in these challenging times. We believe that the outbreak of this pandemic and the resulting sanitary crisis have triggered an unprecedented degree of collaboration among teachers. Immersed in this context, we celebrate being part of a community that works towards a common goal: helping our students learn in meaningful and engaging ways.

6   Food for Thought

The following are some useful tips to consider when using Educaplay, Breakouts and Quizizz in the online classes and beyond (Fig. 11).

Digital tool	Strengths	Weaknesses
Educaplay https://www.educaplay.com/	✓ 16 types of activities ✓ Highly engaging tools: memory game, ABC game ✓ "Challenges" to play with the class synchronously ✓ Teacher-friendly tool with tutorial and "help" option to test and improve the activity ✓ Top 10 results displayed for each activity ✓ Catalog with filters (type of activity, course, rating, age and area of knowledge) to find ready-to-use activities	▪ Limited number of activities for Google Classroom, Microsoft Teams or any LMS with basic plan accounts ▪ Advanced settings like privacy and display of correct answers available only for premium accounts
Breakouts by Genial.ly https://www.genial.ly/	✓ Easy set up. ✓ Variety of templates that offer enough flexibility to add more rooms or riddles to suit the level of difficulty or time constrains of different type of sessions. ✓ Flexible design that can be adapted to suit different types of educational contexts.	▪ Breakout design could be time consuming. ▪ Lack of opportunities to establish challenges.
Quizziz https://quizizz.com/	✓ 5 types of activities apart from the slide tool ✓ Highly engaging tool: open-ended ✓ "Live modes" to play with the class synchronously ✓ Asynchronously learning through the "assign homework" option ✓ Online reports for each participant and question ✓ Teacher-friendly tool	▪ Time constraints to do the activities ▪ Limited deadline for basic plan accounts

Fig. 11 Advantages and disadvantages of Educaplay, Breakouts and Quizizz

References

Bernard, R., Abrami, P., Borokhovski, E., Wade, A., Tamim, R. M., Surkes, M., & Clement Bethel, E. (2009). A meta-analysis of three types of interaction treatments in distance education. *Review of Educational Research, 79*(3), 1,243–1,289.

Bovermann, K., & Bastiaens, T. (2020). Towards a motivational design? Connecting gamification user types and online learning activities. *RPTEL, 15*, 1. https://doi.org/10.1186/s41039-019-0121-4

Cucinotta, G. (2019). Teachers' perception of motivational c classroom: An empirical study on Italian FL and L2 teachers. *Educazione Linguistica Language Education, 7*(3), 447–472. https://10.30687/ELLE/2280-6792/2018/03/006

Deci, E. L., & Ryan, R. M. (1985). *Intrinsic motivation and self-determination in human behavior.* Plenum Press.

Domagk, S., Schwartz, R. N., & Plass, J. L. (2010). Interactivity in multimedia learning: An integrated model. *Computers in Human Behavior, 26*(5), 1024–1033. https://doi.org/10.1016/j.chb.2010.03.003

Dornyei, Z. (2001). *Motivational strategies in the language classroom.* Cambridge University Press. https://doi.org/10.1017/CBO9780511667343

Dörnyei, Z., & Csizér, K. (1998). Ten commandments for motivating language learners: Results of an empirical study. *Language Teaching Research, 2*(3), 203–229.

Dornyei, Z., & Otto, I. (1998). Motivation in action: A process model of L2 motivation. *Working Papers in Applied Linguistics, 4*, 43–69.

Dudeney, G., & Hockly, N. (2012). ICT in ELT: How did we get there and where are we going? *ELT Journal, 66*(4), 533–542.

Educaplay [Educational Software]. (2020). https://www.educaplay.com/

Genial.ly. [Educational Software]. (2020). https://www.genial.ly/

Guigon, G., Humeau, J., & Vermeulen, M. (2018). A model to design learning escape games: SEGAM. *Proceedings of the 10th international conference on computer supported education,* Portugal. https://doi.org/10.5220/0006665501910197.

Hartnett, M. (2016). *Motivation in online education.* Springer.

Hockly, N. (2013). Digital technologies in low-resource ELT contexts. *ELT Journal, 68*(1), 79–84.

Hodges, C. Moore, S. Lockee, B. Trust, T. & Bond, A. (2020). The difference between remote teaching and online learning. *EDUCAUSE Review.* https://er.educause.edu/articles/2020/3/the-difference-between-emergency-remote-teaching-and-online-learning

Jonassen, D. H., Grabinger, R. S., & Wilson, B. G. (1988). Structuring knowledge for expert system solutions: Defining and limiting the problem domain. *Performance + Instruction, 27*(9), 24–28. https://doi.org/10.1002/pfi.4170270912

Keaton, W., & Gilbert, A. (2020). Successful online learning: What does learner interaction with peers, instructors and parents look like? *Journal of Online Learning Research, 6*, 129–154.

Lamb, M., Czizér, K., Henry, A., & Ryan, S. (Eds.). (2019). *The Palgrave handbook of motivation for language learning.* Palgrave Macmillan.

Langer, E. J. (1989). *Mindfulness.* Addison-Wesley.

Langer, E. J. (1997). *The power of mindful learning.* Addison Wesley.

Moore, M. (1989). Three types of interaction. *American Journal of Distance Education, 3*(2), 1–6.

Moore, M., & Anderson, W. (2003). *Handbook of distance education.* Lawrence Erlbaum Associates.

Moore, M., & Kearsley, G. (1996). *Distance education: A systems view.* Wadsworth.

Muñoz, R., Ramirez, M., & Gaviria, S. (2020). Strategies to enhance or maintain motivation in learning a foreign language. *Profile: Issues in Teachers' Professional Development, 22*(1), 175–188. https://doi.org/10.15446/profile.v22n1.73733

Oskoz, A., & Smith, B. (2020). Unprecedented times. *CALICO Journal, 37*(2).

Peachey, N. (2017). *Digital tools for teachers.* PeacheyPublications.com.

Pellegrino, J. W., & Hilton, M. (Eds.). (2012). *Education for life and work: Developing transferable knowledge and skills in the 21st century*. National Academies Press.

Quizizz. (2019). *What is Quizizz*. Help Center. https://support.quizizz.com/hc/en-us/articles/203610052-What-is-Quizizz-

Rayan, A. (2016). One on one: Interview with Nicky Hockly. *The Journal of English Language Teaching (India), 58*(6), 31–36.

Ryan, R. M., & Deci, E. L. (2000). Self-determination theory and the facilitation of intrinsicmotivation, social development, and well-being. *American Psychologist, 55*(1), 68–78. https://doi.org/10.1037/0003-066X.55.1.68

Ryan, R. M., & Deci, E. L. (2017). *Self-determination theory: Basic psychological needs in motivativation, development and wellness*. The Guilford Press.

Sims, R. (1997). Interactivity: A forgotten art? *Computers in Human Behavior, 13*(2), 157–180.

Thatch, E., & Murphy, K. (1995). Competencies for distance education professionals. *Educational Technology Research and Development, 43*(1), 57–79.

White, C. (2003). *Language learning in distance education*. Cambridge University Press.

Part VI
Researcher Corner: Auto- and Virtual Ethnographic Research

Teacher Emotion in Emergency Online Teaching: Ecstasies and Agonies

Maggie McAlinden and Toni Dobinson

Highlights

- Online teaching as a site of intense emotions
- Storytelling, playfulness, and personalisation
- Same pedagogies, different responses
- Online research and creative methodologies

1 Introduction

Shall we Zoom, Collaborate, WebEx or none of these? Where once students who decided to study their university courses fully online did so for many reasons, such as convenience, the COVID-19 disruptions in March 2020 brought students who had signed up to be face-to-face students into the online domain overnight. This introduced intense emotions into the online classroom. Students and teachers had not made a choice to be there and, in some cases, were not prepared for this new mode. This was also at a time when teachers and students were physically distanced, as well as virtually isolated, and this created an opportunity for storytelling, playfulness and greater personalisation in the virtual classroom.

In this auto-ethnographic study we aimed to explore our emotional responses to the sudden shift to online learning. We sought to retrospectively understand the emotions that arose during the study period. During regular communication with

M. McAlinden (✉)
Edith Cowan University, Mount Lawley, Australia
e-mail: m.mcalinden@ecu.edu.au

T. Dobinson
Curtin University, Perth, Australia
e-mail: t.dobinson@curtin.edu.au

© The Author(s), under exclusive license to Springer Nature
Switzerland AG 2021
J. Chen (ed.), *Emergency Remote Teaching and Beyond*,
https://doi.org/10.1007/978-3-030-84067-9_13

each other during the lockdown, we realised that we were having very intense, yet very different, emotional experiences so we decided to focus on this, and see what we could learn. We used a retrospective auto-ethnographic research design, emotional appraisal theory, and multimodal analysis as tools for analysis. The main ethical concerns of the study were related to risks to the reputation of the teacher-researchers by exposing the ecstasies and agonies of their lived experiences through the publication of the findings. Ethics was granted to use the retrospective data captured via the Learning Management System (LMS).

We begin by explaining our approach to emotion in this chapter against the backdrop of isolation and distance issues in online learning and teaching. We then illustrate how multimodal features of synchronous technologies can enhance feelings of intimacy. This is followed by an explanation of our research design. Our findings are presented in the form of two stories, one of ecstasy and the other of agony. Both focus on how the presence and absence of student interaction and student evaluations affected the two teacher-researchers. We finish with reflections and implications for teaching.

1.1 Emotion Words

The word *emotion* is in crisis in the research world (Dixon, 2012) because its nature, purpose and existence is in constant dispute. This means that experts cannot agree on what it means (McAlinden, 2018). Luckily, most language teachers have experience explaining the word emotion and the different types of emotions that have names in English such as happy, sad and angry. In this chapter, we use the term emotion to refer to evaluative judgments about our discursively constructed, and subjectively experienced emotions, including bodily feelings. The word feeling is often used equivocally with the word emotion in everyday use so in this chapter we use both these terms interchangeably. In Western educational research, emotion is often researched and defined from a positivist ontological perspective wherein emotions are studied as subjective dependent variables (McAlinden, 2014). From this perspective, emotions come from within; they are 'intra-psychological functions' (Salvatore & Venuleo, 2008, p. 34) and are researched as 'private components' of an individual, separated from social and cultural contexts (Zembylas, 2008, p. 73). Boler (1999), however, argued that emotion is not only personal and psychological but also social and cultural. Feelings of isolation and distance, therefore, seen from this perspective, are attributed to, and experienced via, the inner personality of the individual, and social interaction.

1.2   Epistemic and Pedagogic Emotion

While there has been a recent resurgence of interest in emotion in language educa-tion (Agudo & de Dios, 2018; Cuéllar & Oxford, 2018; White, 2018), there remains little attention to teacher emotion in language education (McAlinden, 2014, 2018). Moreover, the research methods and approaches used are predominately cognitive, with emotion often being dismissed as having no epistemic value (Ahmed, 1998, Pérez-Sedeño et al., 2019). It has been argued that emotion is not worthy of research, either as a research subject or method (Boler, 1999). Following Ahmed (1998), Boler (1999) and Benesch (2018), we argue that emotions are agentic; they tell us about the world; they do things in the world, as well as being inside our heads. In this chapter, we view emotion, as a basis of empathy (McAlinden, 2014), worthy not only as a subject of inquiry, but also as epistemic and pedagogic.

1.3   Teacher Emotion

How teachers feel, and what they believe about emotion in relation to their work and identity, influences their practice and the quality of their lives in profound ways (Benesch, 2017/2018; Boler, 1999; Cowie, 2011; Cuéllar, & Oxford, 2018; Demetriou, 2018; Hargreaves, 1998). Research into language teacher emotion labour for example shows the pressure teachers are often under to express positive emotions while suppressing negative ones (Benesch, 2017). This pressure to feel, or to not feel, certain emotions can affect teaching practices as well as teachers' long-term wellbeing. It may manifest as cynicism, or as a decrease in the teachers' capac-ity to care and empathise with students (McAlinden, 2018). Despite this, most research into online teaching still focusses almost exclusively on learners (Martin et al., 2020) with very little research looking at teacher emotion (Nyanjom & Naylor, 2020). In this study, we pay attention to teacher emotion as a small step towards changing the prevailing attitudes towards negative emotions and because there is so little focus on teacher emotion in research into online teaching and learning.

1.3.1   Emotion in Online Teaching

The affective aspects of teaching, such as emotion labour, are very likely to be pres-ent in online teaching and have a negative effect on teaching and teacher wellbeing (Nyanjom & Naylor, 2020). Online teaching can create feelings of distance and isolation for teachers (Hawkins et al., 2012). These feelings can impact on teachers' capacity to relate to their students in virtual spaces which has been shown to have an adverse impact on learning (Sato et al., 2017). Computer mediated communica-tion also makes it harder to express and understand emotion (Riordan, 2017). However, research has found that incorporating live video, audio, cameras and microphones, text chat and other modalities into online teaching can improve communication between teachers and students and reduce feelings of isolation and distance (Rudd & Rudd, 2014, Yamagata-Lynch, 2014). Research also suggests that intentional play and storytelling can have a positive effect in online teaching and learning. Play is defined by Gray (2013) as meeting the following criteria: it is self-chosen, self-directed, intrinsically motivated, guided by mental rules but also creative, imaginative and conducted in an alert, active, non-stressed frame of mind. Play is vital to good mental health and personal development from birth through to adult hood (Winnicott, 1971). Playfulness has been associated with positive emotion and effective adult learning (Tanis, 2012). Play can be "a place of rest for the human individual engaged in the perpetual human task of keeping inner and outer reality separate yet interrelated" (Winnicott, 1971, p. 2). Online play involves the sharing of ideas, questions, thoughts, views (Gilmore & Warren, 2007) as well as teasing, joking and bantering. The vehicle for this play is often the side text chat where new topics can be introduced spontaneously (Ugoretz, 2005) and small stories created (Kim, 2015).

Small stories are everyday conversational narratives of personal experience that can be regarded as "unrehearsed renderings of events close to the time of the telling". They contain "hesitations, unfinished thoughts, interruptions, and often contradictions" (Ochs & Capps, 2002, p. 56). Small stories are not narratives with coherent temporal orderings of events and a plot line, a beginning, a middle, and an end, they go beyond this to explore living narratives as "a hallmark of the human condition" (p. 57). They are less practised, less contrived, less coherent, more ubiquitous but central to ordinary social encounters. Personalised storytelling can break down cultural, linguistic and social barriers (Allen & Doherty, 2004). The side text chat plays a key role in storytelling and is also a conduit for support and increased intimacy.

Online interactive chat has been shown to heighten intimacy (Chen & Dobinson, 2020; Cleveland-Innes & Campbell, 2012; Gilmore & Warren, 2007; Lehtonen et al., 2008). Educational intimacy has been used to talk about the powerful role relationships play in learning environments (Uttamchandani, 2020) including friendship (Takeuchi, 2016). Side text chat enables students to carry out their own private, personal discussions through 'multiple feeds' while the lecturer is speaking. This can help rapport building (Yamagata-Lynch, 2014). Text chat can also reduce teacher administration as peers take on facilitating roles without interrupting the flow of the discourse (Garrison, 2009). Some students and teachers feel irritated by the text chat function, however, because it can distract from lecturer input with off-topic banter (Chen & Dobinson, 2020, p. 134).

In summary, teacher emotion is pedagogy, not an add-on to pedagogy. Isolation and distance in online settings are expected and can be mediated through intentional personalisation including storytelling and play, with intimacy often created through teacher personalisation and online side text chat. Emotion is also central to auto-ethnographic and narrative research methodologies. These beliefs are integral to our research design as outlined below.

2 Research Design

We designed a study to retrospectively explore and reflect on the emotions that arose in our teaching during the COVID-19 pandemic. We wondered what had led to our very different experiences, especially as we were both experienced online teachers. We wanted to use a methodology that enabled the direct sharing of personal thoughts and feelings and which viewed emotion as an epistemic tool, so we followed an interpretivist auto-ethnographic narrative research approach.

2.1 Data Collection

We used data from recordings of synchronous online classes and discussion board posts from one class of 25 domestic onshore undergraduate students studying a bachelor's degree with an Australian university and one class of 71 international offshore students studying a master's degree with an Australian university in Vietnam. We also used data from the anonymous routine unit evaluations.

2.2 Interpretive Auto-Ethnography: A Way of Performing Experience

Auto-ethnography is a means by which researchers can create stories through their emotional life experiences (Kim, 2015; Pérez-Sedeño et al., 2019). Our stories are told through the prism of our experiences, emotions, seemingly inconsequential observations and suppositions (Custer, 2014). Using 'meaning-making processes' which frame and narrate (Shim, 2018, p. 1), we attempted to make visible the emotions that arose through our teaching research. In this tradition, there is no distinction between performance and text; what we say and what we speak of are inseparable. We used retrospective auto-ethnography to tell stories. These are emotional stories that are not always permitted to be told. They are based on detailed recollections of brief, but critical events (Hammersley & Atkinson, 2007) that arose during a period of transition to emergency remote teaching.

2.3 Data Analysis

2.3.1 Reflexivity: A Way of Being

In our research, data were interpreted, and meaning negotiated, through a critical reflexive process that allowed ideas to form and settle enough for them to be interpreted by readers. We acknowledge and embrace the potential of the uncertainty and instability of meaning in language. There are no final findings, and we draw no conclusions, just a rendering of meaning via a subjective process constrained by time and other limitations common to all research. Reflexivity (Fortune & Mair, 2011) encouraged us to be present in our research but we strived to avoid narcissism and egoism in our auto-ethnography. Questioning what we think, and what we believe about our emotional experiences, and how we represented these, was an essential part of this process.

2.3.2   Appraisal Theory: A Way of Evaluating Emotions

Psychological Appraisal Theory (Martin & White, 2005) was used to capture and interpret emotional instances and reactions. Feelings, defined as subjective psychological phenomena that are noticed through bodily feelings, are central to the core subsystem of appraisal theory, which includes emotional expression, reaction, and evaluation (appraisal) (Castro & Tenorio, 2020, p. 309). Central to evaluation is *valence* and *arousal*. Valence refers to the judgment of emotions as positive or negative while arousal relates to the intensity attributed to the emotions and feelings which arise (Scherer, 1999).

2.3.3   Multimodal Semiotics: A Way of Revealing

Every sign reveals something about the world (ideational meaning), positions the audience or participants in the interaction in relation to someone or something (interpersonal meaning) and creates a structured text (textual meaning). If we are dealing with text which is multimodal then we need to investigate how all of these meanings are accomplished in the various modes. These modes include words, pictures, sounds, colour, image, gesture, gaze, camera position, perspective, lighting effects and posture. These come together to create a multimodal experience (Kress & van Leeuwen, 2006; O'Halloran, 2004).

3   Narrative Inquiry: Many Ways of Seeing

Jeong Hee Kim (2015, p. 3) uses the metaphor of the kaleidoscope to characterise the nature of narrative inquiry. When we look through a kaleidoscope, our perspective is constantly shifting and changing. The instability and inconstancy of language and human perception is central to narrative inquiry, but we need to hold still to allow the image to form and settle. No two people will see the same thing through a kaleidoscope, so our interpretations of ecstasies and agonies are individual (Richardson & St Pierre, 2008, p.477); "what something means to individuals is dependent on the discourses available to them". The stories told here are ours to tell from within our own views of reality and specific time (Richardson & St Pierre, 2008, p. 477). They are what Van Maanen (2011) calls *confessional tales* and Kim calls (2015) *confessional reflexivity* - reflexive accounts of our experiences as participant teacher-researchers.

4 Research Questions

We created a glimpse of our experiences through reflexive writing. Drawing on our recollections, and weaving in the voices of the students, we wondered:

- What were the teacher emotions in the situation of urgency created by COVID-19 transitions to online learning?
- How did these play out in our online teaching experiences?
- How did isolation and distance manifest itself in the virtual setting?

We acknowledge that in using reflexive writing we will become the subject of our own enquiry (Wiesner, 2020) and that our observations are subjective. We narrate what we experienced while being mindful that "truth is indeed an impossible prey to catch" (Freeman, 2015, p. 919).

5 Findings

In this section we briefly outline the LMS and learning tools we both used while teaching then we share our teaching stories using pseudonyms (Figs. 1, 2, 3 and 4) and colour codes (Fig. 5) to de-identify students.

The e-Learning Platform The units of study described in this chapter were built from a copy of the fully online version of the same units with reduced content and housed within a managed-hosted Learning Management System (LMS) provided by our universities. This system is easily navigated using tabs, learning modules, an orientation bar, and a left panel where users can access all items in the unit. It includes a synchronous collaborative online teaching extension application which has interactive features, including two-way, audio-visual communication, application and desktop sharing, virtual whiteboard, polling, text chat, and breakout rooms. The learning materials were organised into sequential modules, but students were able to access them simultaneously using a table of contents.

5.1 Toni's Teaching Story

This is my story of teaching an onshore unit of study called *Language and Diversity* to third and fourth-year undergraduate students in the Bachelor of Education course at an Australian university over 14 weeks. My story is one of ecstasy ☺ unlike my colleague, Maggie, whose teaching story is told after mine. By ecstasy I do not mean a state of trance-like elation but more a feeling of happiness. Students started the unit in Semester One February 24 to June 5, 2020. All of them, except two, were between the ages of 20 and 30 years old and all were local, either Australian born or resident in Western Australia for a good part of their schooling. Three students were of Indian, Lebanese and Turkish background originally but all three spoke fluent English. In Week Six of their course (March 30), they were forced to move online to a virtual classroom due to COVID-19 disruptions to face-to-face classes. There were 25 students in the class, including five students enrolled in the online version of the class. Moving online was no disruption for these latter students except that they would no longer have recordings of face-to-face workshops. Students in both modes could also access live virtual chat sessions to ask questions about assessments and content.

For me, the teacher-researcher, and the 20 students who had imagined sitting together for 12 weeks in the middle of the afternoon in a classroom with furniture configured into small groups, chatting in a relaxed way, the move to working and studying from home was impactful. I no longer had hard copies of materials to accompany digital PowerPoint slides. I could not 'nip' upstairs at the last minute for more resources. Aside from these physical changes, I also had anxieties about losing the 'intimacy' and 'safety' of the conventional classroom, releasing my control over events that might arise in the new online mode, limiting my capacity to 'perform' well in this mode and forfeiting my access to in-person technological assistance 8 am to 7 pm every day. My home study comprises a secondhand desk rescued from someone's front lawn during a recycling collection week and a fold up table from a local hardware store. Both of these are awash with papers, sticky notes, bottles of perfume, books, sunglasses, business cards, a lock of my 23-year-old son's hair and my son's cat, Arizona. With this cacophony of 'mess', things have never felt quite under control at home and so I have always delivered live virtual classroom sessions from campus. How would the students and I adapt to the new learning environment? Would they complain? Would my teaching evaluations suffer?

Overall, despite my feelings of anxiety and frustration, the 6 weeks of online delivery, using a synchronous platform used by my university for real time interactions, were a time to grow, both for me and the students. A number of points of intimacy were discovered, challenging research which has associated online learning with virtual distance and isolation (Akarasriworn & Ku, 2013; Gedera et al., 2015). This intimacy fostered relationship building and personalisation which amplified my feelings of ecstasy as the teacher.

5.1.1 Relationship Building- Concern for Well-Being

The first, second and last virtual classroom interactive live sessions in the series of six sessions were particularly focused on the students', and my, wellbeing. Talk centered around adjustment to the new COVID-19 pandemic situation and all of our emotional states. I was very aware that the students might be feeling very disoriented with the new mode they were forced to adopt and the associated physical and

#	Time	Discussant	Blackboard Collaborate recording of interaction
1	00:31	Toni	How are you going with your ...oh Tandy is joining now...How are you going with your sort of new reality of everything being online...you managing okay? What about you Bob?
2	00:43	Bob	erm ...It's not too bad ...
3	00:46	Toni	Hmmm (nodding her head and sucking her lips in)
4	00:47	Bob	You know ...it's kinda how it is
5	00:48	Toni	(laughing ..inaudible)...yeah it's kinda like ...suck it up baby ...
6	00:53	Bob	yeah ...it's just weird trying to ...you know ...talk to people cos like you know I've got a dungeons and dragons group
7	01:02	Toni	Oh ...have you?
8	01:03	Bob	And my friends
9	01:03	Toni	(Inaudible overlap)
10	01:04	Bob	we've all sort of like had to play online which is like a weird experience but ... like you eventually get used to it
11	01:12	Toni	Aaah ...I actually thought you did do that online as well as ...as playing it face to face (I look away to the side quite a bit in this bit. I look a bit uneasy)...Ok ...I must ...I'm a bit behind the times ...Yeah ...erm the only issue I have... and I'll just point that out now as obviously this is happening in my house and as you can see my husband's massive record collection behind me... erm ...just worry about people coming behind me ...coming across behind me like erm I don't know ...(laughing and leaning right forward into camera) in their under pants or something....just slightly worried about (look around behind me and left and right) or the cat or something ... so if that happened just carry on like you haven't noticed ..(laughing)

Fig. 1 Audiovisual interaction

virtual isolation. I based this assumption, rightly or wrongly, on my own feelings of disorientation, disbelief and apprehension with the new physically distanced norm and the sudden switch to online learning halfway through a face-to-face unit of study. In the first online workshop I made a point of asking students about their well-being. Throughout the synchronous virtual classroom sessions, I strived to flatten power relations by admitting gaps in my knowledge, owning up to anxieties and creating a virtual community of practice (Cleveland- Innes & Campbell, 2012; Lehtonen et al., 2008). Figure 1 is an example of this.

This interchange with Bob was captured in the audio text not in the side text chat. Both the student and I had our microphones turned on. I had my camera on, but the student did not. Once more students arrived in the room, Bob turned his microphone off and used only text chat. What was most distinctive about this interactive event was that this was probably the only time I had ever spoken to Bob one on one. He had existed in the background in face-to-face mode but he suddenly moved to centre stage in the virtual classroom, reinforcing the ideas of those who claim that virtual space can enhance intimacy between participants (Chen & Dobinson, 2020; Gilmore & Warren, 2007). As Turkle (1995) suggested, Bob had constructed a second self for himself in the virtual environment; transforming in terms of personal feelings, beliefs, values and meaning perspectives. Individuals interacting in virtual environments "become authors not only of text but of themselves, constructing new selves through social interaction" (Turkle, 1995, p. 12). Participants may transform in terms of personal feelings, beliefs and values or meaning perspectives. In the case of Bob, he became more real to me in the online space than he ever was face-to-face. I felt a certain sense of exhilaration with this new development.

My body language in the video recording of the workshop indicates I was feeling slightly uneasy with this personal exchange with Bob who had hitherto escaped my attention. I move around in my seat adjusting my gaze from side to side and avoid looking directly at the camera while admitting I had not really understood how Dungeons and Dragons works ('I actually thought you did do that online'). Asking him about his personal circumstances, I was unconsciously (or not so unconsciously) co-constructing opportunities for me to receive support and acceptance from the student in my new chaotic context. By acknowledging that things might be out of control in my own teaching space I gave students license to have things out of control in their learning spaces. I also made it okay to feel anxious about this.

In the first virtual classroom session students talked about their changed circumstances and their reactions to these circumstances in the side text chat. I asked questions and made comments on video and they replied or talked amongst themselves in the side text chat. This is highlighted in Fig. 2 which is a printable transcript of the side text chat with the video chat on my part inserted.

WEBVTT

00:01:50.000 --> 00:01:50.900
<v Jenny>Sorry if i drop out, I am isolating on the farm and have very limited reception

Video: Toni: Oh you're isolating on a farm Jenny ...that sounds exciting ...(laughing) ...or maybe not ...yeah good idea

00:02:03.000 --> 00:02:03.900
<v Jenny>My home yeah

Video: Toni: Yeah...I did think about that cos I've got a holiday home down in Denmark and I was thinking well... If I've got to be isolated ...I may as well isolate down there...However on Tuesday night it was announced that you couldn't do that so it's going to remain empty I'm afraid...

00:03:49.000 --> 00:03:49.900
<v Brenda>omg so true

00:03:56.000 --> 00:03:56.900
<v Jenny>Agreed!

00:04:04.000 --> 00:04:04.900
<v Brenda>im still in my pjs

00:04:07.000 --> 00:04:07.900
<v Brenda>so bad

00:04:33.000 --> 00:04:33.900
<v Andrew>so blah

00:04:56.000 --> 00:04:56.900
<v Amelia>WE CAN DO THIS!

00:04:57.000 --> 00:04:57.900
<v Andrew>thats what it feels like I mean hahah

00:05:17.000 --> 00:05:17.900
<v Brenda>☺

Fig. 2 Audiovisual discussion with side text chat

Jenny talked about her new situation of being isolated on a farm. Brenda injected humour by confessing to being in her pyjamas in class, a new norm. Andrew reiterated feeling bad ('blah') about the COVID situation. Amelia tried to build team spirit and support by exclaiming, in block capitals, 'WE CAN DO THIS'. The overall feeling was one of community, intimacy and connection between the teacher and the students, the students and the students. This feeling transferred into positive energy for me.

Students did not turn their cameras on throughout the entire six virtual workshops but there was widespread use of multimodal ways of expressing happiness and sadness such as ☺ or ^^^, sms textese such as "omg", WTF, blanked out letters e.g. piece of s***, new words e.g. "so blah" and abbreviations e.g. pjs. Students also described their physical responses linguistically e.g. "oof". In the absence of non-verbal cues and other text-based communication, emojis and emoticons were used to build rapport by conveying positive emotion and increasing intimacy (Riordan, 2017). I also used video and audio to express emotions (Vu & Fadde, 2013).

I consciously tried to create more intimacy using my personal workspace in the camera shots. Rather than using a green screen, I left photographs of loved ones, room deodorisers, records and CDs spilling out of shelves. Shopping bags and mess were left dumped on the desks and I adjusted the angle of my screen and camera so that my son's big orange cat, Arizona, was often in view. As the weeks wore on Arizona moved from a back row, to very up close, to finally sitting on my knee, as can be seen in Fig. 3. This made me feel as though I was sitting on my couch with my cat at the end of the day and instilled me with feelings of contentment and, indeed, ecstasy. At the same time, my gaze moved from sideways to more direct, my physical distance from the camera went from medium to close and the viewpoint of the audience shifted from oblique to slightly more horizontal. This showed how my desire to be close to the students unconsciously translated into my physical actions. My attention to my appearance also changed. I began wearing full make-up and ended with no makeup at all. This mirrored the workshop dynamics; originally distant/self-conscious/more formal and finally closer and more casual. Movement was key to the video function (Baldry & Thibault, 2006). Arizona moved from one position to another, stepping on the keyboard as she got braver. She became so much a part of the virtual community that students exclaimed in the side text chat for the final week, "It's the cat. She's behind you again… just waiting". Movement thus

Fig. 3 Sharing my teaching workspace with Arizona

#	Time	Discussant	Blackboard Collaborate recording of interaction
1	19:09	Toni	Now the next one …everyone should remember this, so I am expecting a few things in that side chat for this one …What is a 'complement return'? …Oh, Tandy has just joined
2	19:32	Tandy	Sorry Toni it totally slipped my mind and then I looked at the time and I was like AAgh!!!
3	19:39	Toni	Never mind we're just doing revision that's all
4	19:42	Andrew	When you use the uno reverse card! (text chat)
5	19:44	Tandy	Okay …thank you
6	19:46	Toni	You're welcome...
7	20:00	Toni	…Andrew's saying when you use the uno reverse card …. That's a very good metaphor Andrew...I'm glad you are here and not off having a cup of tea like last week …(laughing)
8	20:11	Brenda	Hahahaha (text chat)

Fig. 4 An example of student playfulness

engaged the students and punctuated what might have been long sessions of inactivity.

5.1.2 Personalisation – Playfulness and Storytelling

In my teaching story we laughed a lot which made me feel good. Students played with responses in the side text, and responded to my, and other students', banter. Reactions were not audible but were indicated by text which said: "hahaha" or "HAHA" after someone's response. In one two-hour session I counted 11 instances ranging from "haha" to "hahahaha", sometimes in block capitals and sometimes written "ahah". This linguistic play was central to building the intimacy that provided ecstasy over the 6 weeks and was typical of online chat (Gilmore & Warren, 2007). Andrew, in particular, added to my positive emotional experience by keeping us laughing with his teasing and bantering.

The side text chat facilitated playfulness and allowed a permanent record to be kept of the banter. This meant that I could return to Andrew's response to my question: 'What is a compliment return?' after being interrupted by Tandy's late arrival into the virtual room. Andrew's witty response ("When you use the uno reverse card!") in the side text chat might have been overlooked in a face-to-face classroom situation. Having a visual record of the interaction allowed me to return to acknowledge his contribution and to feel good knowing I had acknowledged everyone's contribution. The text chat also created more opportunities for the telling of small stories (Kim, 2015). These stories (often only one line) unfolded each week from the students and me, bringing theoretical concepts divorced from everyday realities into sharper focus. Input from students' lived realities made the discussions feel real and genuinely captivating for me rather than the sometimes negative feeling I had had of just going through the motions each time. I felt a genuine desire to connect

04:56·Toni:··if·I·do·seem·a·little·bit·out·of·kilter·today·I·just·had·…I·don't·know·but·every·other· encounter· I've· had· this· week· …I've· been· walking· a· lot· so· …people· seem· to· have· become· incredibly·friendly·around·the·streets·…they·don't·come·near·you·but·they·at·least·talk·to·you·…· How·you·going?·..you·know·…but·today·I·decided·to·do·a·quick·Coles·run·…just·before·doing· this·session·…and·I·have·to·say·I·encountered·two·of·the·most·alarming·kind·of·COVID·rages·…if· you·like·…I've·had·so·far·..I·don't·know·if·you've·encountered·this·but·at·the·erm·checkout·…you· know·how·you·have·to·do·your·own·bags·now·…put·stuff·in·the·bags·…you·know·I·had·quite·a·lot· of·bags·worth·…I·was·going·as·fast·as·I·could·and·this·chap·…I·don't·know·…he·must·have·been· in·his·late·60s·…maybe·early·70s·starting·commenting·…saying·you·know·…something·like·erm· Well·if·you·could·just·get·a·move·on··I·would·be·able·to·get·through·here·…I·went·Oh·sorry·I·can't· go·any·faster·I'm·just·packing·as·fast·as·I·can·and·then·he·said·well·if·you·just·stop·faffing·around· and·get·them·in·…and·I·was·like·puffs·air·out·excuse·me·…so·I·said·would·you·mind·not·being·so· rude·and·then·he·said·well·would·you·mind·just·getting·a·f…king·move·on·…so·I·was·like·Oh·ok· …so·I·just·silently·went·as·slow·as·I·could·…feeling·very·threatened·by·this·point·and·then·I· thought·what·can·I·say·at·the·end·so·I·turned·around·and·said·to·him·…well·all·I·can·hope·is·that· the·virus·gets·you·and·I·just·walked·off·and·then·I·thought·Oh·dear·he's·probably·going·to·wait·for· me·in·the·car·park.¶

Fig. 5 Toni's small story

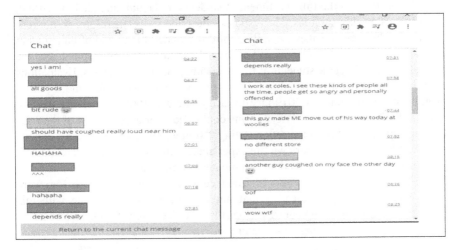

Fig. 6 Student small stories in the text chat in response to my small audio story

with the students each week and to get to know more about them. I would start the session with my own small story, setting the scene for students to follow. Stories were usually related to the themes or topics of the unit e.g. pragmatic behaviours across cultures but sometimes not. Figure 5 is an example of such a story.

Students responded to this story by showing empathy for my situation, advising me on how I might have responded and then proceeding to respond to my story with small stories of their own as seen in Fig. 6. The same colours denote the same individual students.

As can be seen in the side text chat, student blue gives a truncated but powerful two-word response to my story with the words 'bit rude' accompanied by a sad faced emoji. Student yellow takes up my story and adds a rejoinder at which students blue and orange laugh (HAHAHA, ^^^, hahaha). Student green is then inspired to add his or her own personalised small story about experiences working at Coles supermarket to which students orange and yellow add their own small stories, firstly about 'a guy' encountered in Woolworths (Woolies) supermarket and secondly about another 'guy' coughing in another setting. The latter is followed by a smiley face emoji and written vocalisation of the student's distaste for what he/she had experienced ('oof'). These stories are received by student orange with an expression of surprise (WOW) and an expletive in textese (WTF). All of this shows students' engagement with my story and how they seized the opportunity to add their own small stories in response. After these exchanges, we deconstructed their stories to imagine how they might have played out with different participants in the same setting or different cultural settings, based on knowledge from the unit. These individual stories may not have received airtime in a face-to-face classroom setting and were key to building intimacy and making me feel uplifted and motivated to do my best to help the students in this new teaching setting.

Only one third of the full enrollment of students in the unit attended the virtual, synchronous weekly sessions. The responses described here, therefore, do not represent the whole class. Likewise, only a third responded to the end of unit student evaluations. Anonymity prevents us knowing if the students who responded to the evaluation were the same students as those attending the virtual classes. Evaluations were, however, as positive in online mode as previously in face-to-face mode (100% overall satisfaction rate for 2019 face-to-face mode and 100% overall satisfaction rate for 2020 hybrid mode). Two students confirmed their appreciation of the relationship building and personalisation stating: "Toni was willing to share her experiences"; "she incorporates her own life experiences …to make it real and relatable". Significantly, however, one student commented: "I am just sad we had to move to online classes because of COVID-19. The face-to-face experiences with Toni were much more engaging", indicating that not all students were in tune with this approach and corroborating our suspicions that one size cannot fit all. This observation forms the basis for Maggie's teaching story.

5.2   Maggie's Teaching Story

My story focusses on my experience of teaching a group of 71 international postgraduate students enrolled in an offshore Master of TESOL unit. The unit is usually delivered face-to-face in Vietnam over a ten day period. During the COVID-19 shutdown in March 2020, it was delivered synchronously over four days. During this same teaching period, I also transitioned two onshore postgraduate units to synchronous online delivery and carried on with one other fully online postgraduate unit. At the time, I was under pressure but, unlike Toni, I was not worried about transitioning

Fig. 7 Screenshot of introduction to unit

my onshore face-to-face units to a synchronous online unit as I had built a good relationship with the onshore students and was confident in my ability to use technology to teach online. However, from the start, I was worried about transitioning the offshore unit due to the high numbers of students, their capacity to use the technology, the intensive delivery mode and the stability of the internet connection in Vietnam. I was not concerned about students' ability to use and communicate in English. The students in Vietnam usually had no major issues communicating with me or each other in English (Fig. 7).

5.2.1 Personalising

Computer mediated communication makes it harder to express and understand emotion (Riordan, 2017). When I teach online, I include a range of ways to emotionally engage students. One strategy is to use images, text, emojis, and emoticons like ☺ to break down barriers. This includes the use of personal welcome messages with photos of me and my pets as seen below (Fig. 8).

I always include a profile photo in the LMS, ask students to add photos to their profiles and include images and texts that make students feel welcome (Fig. 9).

I also provide multiple means for students to interact multimodally. I encourage the use of cameras and microphones. I also hold synchronous collaborative sessions to build rapport with students and answer questions. Like Rudd & Rudd, (2014), I have learned that live video, chat and the use of cameras and microphones can significantly reduce psychological distance and virtual isolation. I also use small breakout groups during collaborative sessions and pace the session to allow time for interaction (Vu & Fadde, 2013). I used these strategies on all the units I taught during the COVID-19 shutdown, including the offshore online unit that I focus on in this chapter.

What to do first?

If you have never studied with ECU before, first complete the Orientation for Online students in the Unit Menu.

The Participation Activities are designed to activate your prior knowledge and to encourage you to start thinking about tl content. You should do this activity first - there are no wrong or right answers. When you have completed it, post it to yo group Discussion area and to the main Discussion Forum on Blackboard (don't attach as a file).

You need to join your group each day to discuss the learning activities - go to the Groups area to see which group you ar allocated to. You can set up your own collaborate sessions, have your own private discussions and share files in your groups. Your lecturer will visit each group discussion and can join a group collaborate session if needed.

Finally, if you are studying this unit online, don't feel sad or guilty (like my beagle Yallah below) if you can't complete everything - just do what you can - we all work at different paces!

Fig. 8 Using personal photos to build intimacy

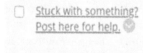 If you need help with anything, post here to get help from your classmates or lecturer.

Fig. 9 Making students feel welcome

5.2.2 Worries

I taught the offshore unit fully online over 4 days, with two sessions a day, one from 9.00 to 12.30 and then a second from 1.30 to 4.30. This schedule was set because students were English language teachers who were working full-time and were taking time off work to study, so it was not possible to extend the teaching period. From the moment I agreed to teach the unit fully online over a shortened teaching period I was really worried about the effect that this would have on learning and teaching. I knew from teaching the unit face-to-face in Vietnam that the internet connectivity was unreliable and inconsistent and that bandwidths were insufficient for live streaming. I was also concerned ☹ about how I would be able to build rapport with so many students over such a short and intensive study period. Looking back at the week when all this started, I recall feeling really stressed and working long hours to get the unit ready after just a week's notice.

5.2.3 Agonies and Urgency

The English word agony, meaning intense physical or emotional pain, derives from the old French *agonie* which referred to the struggle before death (Peters, 2004). The notion of struggle and of bodily suffering fits with my evaluation of the emotions that arose for me when I was teaching the unit. The agonies included, not only my emotional response to the lack of evidence of student engagement and feedback in particular, but also, the physical and psychological effects that I experienced when I had to prepare and teach a face-to-face unit intensively online with very little time to get ready. For me, this agony was related to an overwhelming sense of urgency that emerged before the teaching began and to the many small urgencies and agonies that arose before, during and after the teaching period. The word urgency phonologically and semantically evokes the word emergency although etymologically they are unrelated. This first small story, written in the present, recalls and evokes this urgency.

5.2.4 The Computer and My Cat

I am working quickly and intensively. Emails filling up my bottomless inbox. Typing, reading, searching, copying, pasting, clicking and dragging virtual objects endlessly in a state of intense concentration. The fingertips on my right hand frozen and tingling as if they need a glove to cover them. My toes just reaching the wooden floor, my hands moving over the keyboard as if they have some mission that I have not been informed of. I stop momentarily as I notice cat who is cleaning herself on the chair opposite my desk. The quiet tinkling of her collar as she licks herself and shakes her head gets my attention. I stop what I am doing and notice the ache in my back and neck and the pangs of hunger in my stomach. Time to get up.

5.2.5 Preparing, Smiling and Worrying

At this early stage I was worried that the students would not have a good experience: their internet connection would not be sufficient, they would lack sufficient bandwidth to download resources or stream the audiovisual resources, and they would struggle to navigate the LMS. The unit was not designed to be delivered so intensively and there was no time to redesign it. I revised assessment instructions, re-organised the modules, re-wrote the unit plan, modified the resources and the learning management system. I recommended that we do a trial before the teaching period started, so we did. On the Friday before session one, I sent an email to the ten students who had agreed to the trial. I used a smiley face emoji ☺ and informal expression to build rapport. I enjoyed the trial and it seemed to go well. So, I relaxed a bit (Fig. 10).

Dear students,

Thanks for participating in our online trial of LAN6271. Please be ready to start at 9am sharp your ti if you have a camera that might be needed too. I will send an announcement at 9am with the instructi

Fingers crossed this works and we can learn together as planned ☺.

See you all tomorrow.

Maggie

Fig. 10 Smiley emoji to reduce distance

5.2.6 Agonies Emerge

As I review the recordings of the collaborative sessions one to eight, I recall how, from day one, my worries became a reality when I saw how few students were interacting. Fifty-two students logged into the collaborative session on day one, but only eight participated in the chat and polls. I was very negatively affected by the low numbers of students interacting and found it dispiriting. I knew that if I was feeling so bad, the students were probably feeling worse. Unlike Toni's students, my students were very reluctant to speak, they were unable to turn their cameras and mics on, and very few responded to the attempts I made to build rapport and encourage interaction. This made it very hard for me to remain engaged during the collaborative sessions as I seemed to be communicating into a void. I saw students leave and enter the room multiple times and saw very few responses from students. Even though there were posts on the discussion forum over the whole day, these were mainly to complete tasks that had been set. The low interaction and engagement with students in the collaborative session really affected my sense of intimacy, connection and engagement. I felt tired and drained at the end of each session and it was a strain to communicate with so little response from students. It was really hard not to feel defeated.

In response to the low interaction in session one, I created a simple survey and sent an announcement (Fig. 11).

I really wanted to know how students were getting on and if there were any barriers to interacting that I might be able to address. Only 12 students initially responded to this survey, so I raised my concerns during the next synchronous session, as you can see in Fig. 12, there was no response from students.

Students did not ask any questions or comment when I raised my concerns with them. Despite the lack of response in the synchronous session, more students responded to the survey after this session. These responses indicated the urgency that they were feeling, although some were coping better than others. Of the 23 responses, 12 were feeling fine or had mixed feelings while 11 expressed pressure and stress. The message that I heard was that it was "too much" and "impossible" for them to keep up as illustrated in the survey comments below (Fig. 13). These responses also indicated that the students who responded had no issues expressing

Are you ok? Tell me how your learning experience is going:

Short answers are recommended. You have 250 characters left

Submit

Fig. 11 Screenshot of poll

Maggie: "I·think·that·there·might·be·too·much·to·do·each·day…that·might·be·something·we·need·to·talk·about·is·to·reduce·the·load·in·terms·of·the·activities·for·you·to·do·erm·and·maybe·reduce·the·number·of·recordings·as·well·(6.44·note·no·responses·in·chat)·and·perhaps·you·can·post·some·questions·now·in·chat?·(6.51·no·response).·I·also·did·suggest·that·you·can·use·collaborate·to·meet·with·each·other·online·as·that·can·be·really·helpful·and·please·contact·me·if·you·want·to·meet·on·collaborate·to·discuss·any·issues·you·are·having.¶

Fig. 12 Discussing my worries with students

I am having a difficult time to keep up with the readings and activities with much interference from my children at home during the corona pandemic. Without collaboration session, I feel a bit nervous when others talk about assignment and due date.

Dear Dr. Maggie, I think the workload is too much with us. I haven't finished all. I feel worry about the assignment so can you please give me a map of neccessary things we need to do to meet your requirements.

Fig. 13 Students are feeling overwhelmed

themselves and communicating with me in English, but with no response from the majority of students, I was unable to determine if language was an issue for those who were not responding.

While this poll did not explain why students were not interacting, it did show that at least half of those who responded were feeling overwhelmed. In the next session we discussed the issues they were having in more detail and we agreed to reduce the number of activities and the number of collaborate sessions. I really thought that this was the main issue. I felt a sense of relief from these exchanges with at least some of the students; their responses seemed genuine to me and I felt that some degree of intimacy was being expressed via the honest responses I received.

5.2.7 So Many Questions About the Assessments!

On day one session two, some students had asked questions about the assessments. I recall reminding students where the assessment guidelines and resources were and asking them to post questions about the assessments on the discussion forum. I felt disappointed that students were not asking questions about the content or attempting to interact with each other much and I discussed this with them. From the retrospective analysis, I saw that during the synchronous sessions, students were not asking me questions about the content, instead most of the questions were about the assessments. I remember feeling bad and thinking was my only value to answer students' questions about the assessments, as illustrated in Appendix 2? Moreover, I was responding to the same questions in the virtual classroom, in emails, on the discussion board, and in the live chat platform. I responded to every question but also encouraged students to reply to each other if they knew an answer.

5.2.8 Text-Based Communicating with Students

Language may have been a barrier for the students, but there was no way of addressing this other than the usual accommodations I would make when communicating with students who were not familiar with Australian English. In my text-based communication with students, I purposely used a simple and concise style. My announcements were clear and polite, but looking back, they may have lacked the friendliness that I usually express when communicating with students via email. For example, in the email announcement on day one, there are many directives with few softeners apart from some simple politeness markers like "can I" and "try to".

On reflection, I think that the students were probably confused about what to do a lot of the time and that they had significant time constraints. Like me, they had had this situation thrust upon them and were no doubt juggling much more than their studies. Although I made a lot of changes to address students' needs during the study period, the constraints were many, including poor internet connectivity, absenteeism (many were working), the new learning platform, and the intensity of the study period. There was a marked lack of banter and play in the interactions that did occur. However, the retrospective analysis of the text interaction indicated some degree of positive engagement and intimacy. At the end of the later sessions, for example, some students thanked me and used the heart emoji ♥to express their feelings. Students responded and interacted in the side text chat and also helped each other (see Appendix 1). This was common in most of the later sessions, which made me feel a bit more positive and less worried as teaching continued.

5.2.9 Not a Happy Ending

The agony ☹ that I experienced arose again after teaching ended, as illustrated in the small story that follows. When the study period ended, I was eager to see the students' evaluations and feedback. I knew that the results for the offshore online unit would not be great, but I was hoping that the effort I had made would be appreciated and that students would understand that we were all under enormous pressure and stress. This final small story recollects that experience.

5.2.10 My Heart Sinks

I read the evaluation comments for the offshore unit and my heart starts to sink. I read and re-read some comments and the bad feelings grow in intensity. My stomach flips over and over as I process the words. I revisit these comments in my mind again and again over a few days and gradually, I start to consider their content as well as how they make me feel. I talk to my family and friends. We talk about the ethics of anonymity and I realise that in addition to feeling really disappointed about the low satisfaction rates, despite all my effort, being unable to respond to individual comments that I felt to be unfair and untrue was even more agonising.

The satisfaction rates from my other two onshore units that transitioned to online in 2020 were very high. I had a 100% satisfaction rate in one, 91% in the other, and 83% for the online unit which had not transitioned. I knew that the satisfaction rate from the offshore unit would not be as high as it had been in 2019 when I had taught it face-to-face in Vietnam (91% with a 98% response rate n = 56). However, I was unprepared for the 30% satisfaction rate (92% response rate n = 69). I was shocked and made even more upset by the comments, especially given the efforts I had made to respond to students' questions:

> *I feel like the teacher is too busy to answer students' questions.*

Comments like these hit me like a punch to the stomach. There were clearly issues with the connection and many students mentioned this, but this did not make me feel any better at the time:

> *I feel disappointed about this course. The connection was not good, therefore, I spent most of time on self-study rather than learning with the instructors. I prefer traditional learning due to the fact that I feel more inspired with this approach.*

Many of the students had felt overwhelmed even though I had significantly reduced the number of tasks:

> *There are so many learning activities, slides, videos and materials to view that make me overwhelmed.*

Of course, there were positive and reasonable comments:

> *My experience was great, lessons were easily to follow, and all my questions about lessons were answered. Moreover, I can watch recordings from the lesson as many times as I need, and I could save time on travelling. I was happy about this online learning.*

I barely noticed the positive comments when I first looked at the evaluations and saw the very low overall satisfaction rate. As I reflect on my experience by writing this chapter, I recall the feeling of agony when I first read the evaluation comments. Looking at them months later I can recall the very intense and negative feelings that arose, but the feelings now are far less intense, and I view them as less unpleasant. As I finish writing this chapter, I feel relief, but also some trepidation about sharing this story. Reflecting on the emotions that arose, and experiencing new ones, has been cathartic and looking at the data has helped me to understand how the urgency of the situation, the poor connectivity, and students' unfamiliarity with online learning, probably all contributed to the agonies. Looking back, I needed to dramatically reduce the unit content because of the length of the study period, and the time students had to study. I needed to help students navigate the LMS to reduce their anxiety, and I needed to take the connectivity issues in Vietnam into account more. Fortunately, I was able to use what I learned from this experience to redesign and teach another offshore online unit on the same course in June 2020. My experience was more positive ☺. Students seemed much calmer and less stressed. However, I am yet to review the evaluations, so I am unable to say if the students had a better experience.

6 Implications, Strategies and Suggestions

Following Sarah Ahmed (1998) we, as teacher-researchers, argue that emotions are agentic; they do things in the world. Moreover, there is intrinsic value in paying attention to the emotions that arise in online learning and teaching. We think that emotion is in pedagogy, in relationships and, of course, in our interactions with technology and learners. We use these unusual times to ask that teachers and researchers question why emotion is largely ignored in educational research and why space cannot be made for alternative approaches more often. Feminist, reflective, subjective research approaches (Kim, 2015; Pérez-Sedeño et al., 2019) can make research more personal and intimate, while narrative inquiry and autoethnography can be an especially useful means to explore emotion. Our confessional tales show how recollection and reflection on lived experiences can be used to understand and appraise the emotions that arise during online learning and teaching. These emotions are not only worthy of research, but also have the potential to influence our teaching. Emotion online can be a pedagogic and epistemic tool.

The presence and absence of multimodal pragmatic conventions, such as textese and emojis, can also tell us something about how students may be feeling online. By paying more attention to these, as researchers and teachers, we may open up other ways of communicating and understanding emotions online. In particular, emotional interaction and engagement can be facilitated via personalisation, language play and storytelling by students and teachers. However, if too much urgency is felt, and anxiety is high, even these strategies can fail. In Toni's teaching story, synchronous interaction between teachers and students mediated feelings of intimacy and encouraged interaction, all of which gave rise to positive emotions being experienced by the teacher. In Maggie's teaching story, however, we can see the consequences of disrupted online synchronous contact and the constraints of time. Toni's teaching story illustrates the strong positive feelings and intimacy that can arise via personalised chat. It seems banter, play and small story telling mitigated against feelings of detachment and isolation that can arise in online contexts. However, it will be interesting to see if delivery of the unit in fully online mode next time will corroborate or question this initial experience. In contrast, Maggie's teaching story shows how negative feelings arose when there was urgency, low interaction leading to low intimacy and no time or opportunity for relationship building via banter, play and storying.

The teacher ecstasies, agonies, experiences and stories that were constructed in this emergency remote online situation helped us, as teacher-researchers, to construct a different form of knowledge through means other than surveys and interviews. This knowledge is essential if the new learning and teaching mode is here to stay. Australian universities have realised that they can capitalise on space and accompanying overheads by keeping courses online, or blended. Student numbers on Australian university campuses were diminishing even before the COVID-19 disruptions to face to face learning and teaching, probably due to the costs of parking, and students working more hours. This trend looks likely to continue. Slowing down and reflecting on emergency remote online experiences during this COVID-19 pandemic period, therefore, can provide insights into the emotional aspects of learning and teaching in both onshore and offshore online spaces in the future.

7   Food for Thought: Beyond ERT

On reflection, we, as teacher-researchers, need to pay much closer attention to teacher emotion, emotional experiences, the effect on learning and teaching that emotion has and vice versa. We should re-evaluate overemphasis on pedagogic tasks and learning design that leaves little consideration of emotion in human social interaction. Paying attention to the affective aspects of learning and teaching may even be more important in online learning than in face-to-face mode, especially when stress and urgency arise. Teachers can use their own, and students', emotional and relational meaning making, and teachers' capacity to understand the feelings of others, as pedagogic tools. Before advocating for technology as a vehicle for relationship building in online learning, we need to acknowledge the powerful impact of temporal, contextual and personal factors on emotion and learning.

Appendices

Appendix 1

Appendix 2

```
00:10:50.000 --> 00:10:50.900
<v student 1>do you have any requirements about the number of references, Maggie?

00:12:27.000 --> 00:12:27.900
<student 2>I am sorry, but is it possible for you to explain this statement "The report should include t

00:13:17.000 --> 00:13:17.900
<v Student 2>I think that, for example, if you use an interview, you must include the transcript of the

00:13:56.000 --> 00:13:56.900
<v student 3>Dear Dr. Maggie, the assignment folder I find on blackboard and the OU Unit Outline says A1

00:14:14.000 --> 00:14:14.900
<v Student 4>Do we have a specific outline for Assignment 1?

00:16:40.000 --> 00:16:40.900
<v student 3>Thank you

00:17:08.000 --> 00:17:08.900
<v student 5>So we get 50-50 for assignment 1 and 2, friends?
```

References

Agudo, J. D. M., & de Dios, J. (2018). Emotions in second language teaching: Theory, research and teacher education. *Springer*. https://doi.org/10.1007/978-3-319-75438-3.

Ahmed, S. (1998). Occupational segregation and caste-based discrimination in India. In M. Shah (Ed.), *Labour market segmentation in India* (pp. 67–92). Himalaya.

Akarasriworn, C., & Ku, H. Y. (2013). Graduate students' knowledge construction and attitudes toward online synchronous videoconferencing collaborative learning environments. *Quarterly Review of Distance Education, 14*(1), 35–48.

Allen, J., & Doherty, M. (2004). Learning through work, discourse and participation: Storied lives, self and social-changing cultures [online]. *Australian Journal of Adult Learning, 44*(2), 158–178.

Artino, A. R., & Jones, K. D. (2012). Exploring the complex relations between achievement emotions and self-regulated learning behaviors in online learning. *The Internet and Higher Education, 15*, 170–175.

Baldry, A. P., & Thibault, P. J. (2006). *Multimodal transcription and text*. Equinox.

Benesch, S. (2017). *Emotions and English language teaching: Exploring teachers' emotion labor*. Taylor & Francis.

Benesch, S. (2018). Emotions as agency: Feeling rules, emotion labor, and English language teachers' decision-making. *System, 79*, 60–69.

Boler, M. (1999). *Feeling power: Emotions and education*. Psychology Press.

Castro, M. Á. B., & Tenorio, E. H. (2020). Rethinking Martin & White's affect taxonomy: A psychologically inspired approach to the linguistic expression of emotion. In L. A. J. J. Mackenzie (Ed.), *Emotion in discourse* (pp. 301–332). John Benjamin.

Chen, J., & Dobinson, T. (2020). Digital communication in a virtual community of practice: Linguistic/paralinguistic behaviour in the multimodal context of blackboard collaborate. In S. Dovchin (Ed.), *Language, digital communication and society* (pp. 121–146).

Chen, K. C., & Jang, S. J. (2010). Motivation in online learning: Testing a model of self-determination theory. *Computers in Human Behavior, 26*(4), 741–752.

Cleveland-Innes, M., & Campbell, P. (2012). Emotional presence, learning, and the online learning environment. *The International Review of Research in Open and Distributed Learning, 13*(4), 269–292.

Cowie, N. (2011). Emotions that experienced English as a foreign language (EFL) teachers feel about their students, their colleagues and their work. *Teaching and Teacher Education, 27*(1), 235–242. https://doi.org/10.1016/j.tate.2010.08.006.

Cuéllar, L., & Oxford, R. L. (2018). Language teachers' emotions: Emerging from the shadows. In J. D. M. Agudo & J. de Dios (Eds.), *Emotions in second language teaching* (pp. 53–72). Springer.

Custer, J. (2014). Autoethnography as a transformative research method. *The Qualitative Report, 19*(37), 1–13.

Demetriou, H. (2018). *Empathy, emotion and education*. Springer.

Dixon, T. (2012). Emotion: The History of a keyword in crisis. *Emotion Review, 4*(4):338–344. https://doi.org/10.1177/1754073912445814.

Dörnyei, Z. (2020). *Innovations and challenges in language learning motivation*. Routledge.

Fortune & Mair. (2011). Notes from the sports club: Confessional tales of two researchers. *Journal of Contemporary Ethnography, 40*(4), 457–484.

Freeman, J. (2015). Trying not to lie…and failing: Auto-ethnography, memory, malleability. *The Qualitative Report, 20*(6), 918–929.

Garrison, D. R. (2009). Communities of inquiry in online learning. In P. L. Rogers (Ed.), *Encyclopedia of distance learning* (pp. 352–355). IGI Global.

Gedera, D., Williams, J., & Wright, N. (2015). Identifying factors influencing students' motivation and engagement in online courses. In C. Koh (Ed.), *Motivation, leadership and curriculum design: Engaging the next generation and 21ˢᵗ century learners* (pp. 13–23). Springer.

Gilmore, S., & Warren, S. (2007). Emotion online: Experiences of teaching in a virtual learning environment. *Human Relations, 60*(4), 581–608.

Gray, P. (2013). *Free to learn: Why unleashing the instinct to play will make our children happier, more self-reliant, and better prepared for life*. Basic Books.

Hammersley, M., & Atkinson, P. (2007). *Ethnography: Principles in practice*. Tavistock.

Hargreaves, A. (1998). The emotional practice of teaching. *Teaching and Teacher Education, 14*(8), 835–854. https://doi.org/10.1016/S0742-051X(98)00025-0.

Hawkins, A., Barbour, M. K., & Graham, C. R. (2012). "Everybody is their own island": Teacher disconnection in a virtual school. *The International Review of Research in Open and Distance Learning, 13*(2), 123–144.

Immordino-Yang, M. H., & Faeth, M. (2010). The role of emotion and skilled intuition in learning. In D. A. Sousa (Ed.), *Mind, brain and education: Neuroscience implications for the classroom* (pp. 1–23). Solution Tree Press.

Kim, J.-H. (2015). *Understanding narrative inquiry: The crafting and analysis of stories as research*. Sage.

Kress, G., & van Leeuwen, T. (2006). *Reading images: The grammar of visual design*. Routledge.

Lehtonen, M., Page, T., Miloseva, L., & Thorsteinsson, G. (2008). Development of social mediation and emotional regulation in virtual learning environment research. *i-Manager's Journal on Educational Psychology, 2*(1), 34–47.

Martin, J. R., & White, P. R. R. (2005). *The language of evaluation: Appraisal in English*. Palgrave Macmillan.

Martin, F., Sun, T., & Westine, C. D. (2020). A systematic review of research on online teaching and learning from 2009 to 2018. *Computers and Education, 159*, 104009. https://doi.org/10.1016/j.compedu.2020.104009.

McAlinden, M. (2014). Can teachers know learners' minds? Teacher empathy and learner body language in English language teaching. In K. Dunworth & G. Zhang (Eds.), *Critical perspectives on language education* (pp. 71–100). Springer.

McAlinden, M. (2018). English language teachers' conceptions of intercultural empathy and professional identity: A critical discourse analysis. *Australian Journal of Teacher Education, 43*(10), 41–59.

Nyanjom, J., & Naylor, D. (2020). Performing emotional labour while teaching online. *Educational Research*, 1–17. https://doi.org/10.1080/00131881.2020.1836989.

O'Halloran, K. (2004). Multimodal discourse analysis: Systemic functional perspectives. *Continuum*.

Ochs, E., & Capps, L. (2002). *Living narrative*. Harvard University Press.

Pérez-Sedeño, E., Almendros, L. S., Dauder, S. G., & Arjonilla, E. M. O. (2019). *Knowledges, practices and activism from feminist epistemologies*. Vernon Press.

Peters, H. (2004). The vocabulary of pain. In C. J. Kay & J. J. Smith (Eds.), *Categorisation in the history of English* (pp. 193–218). John Benjamins.

Richardson, L., & St Pierre, E. A. (2008). Writing: A method of inquiry. In N. K. Denzin & Y. S. Lincoln (Eds.), *Collecting and interpreting qualitative materials* (pp. 1410–1444). Sage.

Riordan, M. A. (2017). Emojis as tools for emotion work: Communicating affect in text messages. *Journal of Language and Social Psychology, 36*(5), 549–567. https://doi.org/10.1177/0261927x17704238.

Rudd, D. P., & Rudd, D. P. (2014). The value of video in online instruction. *Journal of Instructional Pedagogies, 13*, 1–7.

Salvatore, S., & Venuleo, C. (2008). Understanding the role of emotion in sense-making: A semiotic psychoanalytic oriented perspective. *Integrative Psychological and Behavioural Science, 42*, 32–46.

Sato, E., Chen, J. C., & Jourdain, S. (2017). Integrating digital technology in an intensive, fully online college course for Japanese beginning learners: A standards-based, performance-driven approach. *The Modern Language Journal, 101*(4), 756–775. https://doi.org/10.1111/modl.12432.

Scherer, K. R. (1999). Appraisal theory. In T. Dalgleish & M. J. Power (Eds.), *Handbook of cognition and emotion* (pp. 637–663). Wiley.

Shim, J. (2018). Problematic autoethnographic research: Researcher's failure in positioning. *The Qualitative Report, 23*(1), 1–11.

St Pierre, E. (2018). Writing post qualitative inquiry. *Qualitative Inquiry, 24*(9), 603–608. https://doi.org/10.1177/1077800417734567.

Takeuchi, M. A. (2016). Friendships and group work in linguistically diverse mathematics classrooms: Opportunities to learn for English language learners. *Journal of the Learning Sciences, 25*(3), 411–437.

Tanis, D.J. (2012). *Exploring play/playfulness and learning in the adult and higher education classroom*. [Unpublished Doctoral Dissertation]. Pennsylvania State University.

Turkle, S. (1995). *Life on the screen: Identity in the age of the internet*. Simon & Schuster.

Ugoretz, J. (2005). 'Two roads diverged in a wood': Productive digression in asynchronous discussion. *Innovate: Journal of Online Education 1*(3). https://www.learntechlib.org/p/107297/ Accessed 28 May 2020.

Uttamchandani, S. (2020). Educational intimacy: Learning, prefiguration, and relationships in an LGBTQ+ youth group's advocacy efforts. *Journal of the Learning Sciences, 30*(1), 52–75.

Van Maanen, J. (2011). *Tales of the field* (2nd ed.). University of Chicago Press.

Vu, P., & Fadde, P. J. (2013). When to talk, when to chat: Student interactions in live virtual classrooms. *Journal of Interactive Online Learning, 12*(2), 41–52.

White, C. J. (2018). The emotional turn in applied linguistics and TESOL: Significance, challenges and prospects. In J. D. M. Agudo & J. de Dios (Eds.), *Emotions in Second Language Teaching* (pp. 19–34). Springer.

Wiesner, A. (2020). Contemplating reflexivity as a practice of authenticity in autoethnographic research. *The Qualitative Report, 25*(3), 662–670.

Winnicott, D. W. (1971). *Play and reality*. Tavistock.

Yamagata-Lynch, L. C. (2014). Blending online asynchronous and synchronous learning. *International Review of Research in Open and Distance Learning, 15*(2), 189–212.

Zembylas, M. (2008). Adult learners' emotions in online learning. *Distance Education, 29*(1), 71–87.

How to Adapt in Crisis: An Autoethnographic Approach to (Re) Building Coursework

Katherine Morales, Gabriel Romaguera, and Edward Contreras

Highlights

We provide three separate ethnographic accounts on:

- The importance of autoethnographic methods for teaching – self-monitoring, writing, and keeping records of student progress.
- Transitioning to online teaching in an environment with unstable Internet access and electricity;
- Adopting flexibility in modes of assessment and teaching to meet the socioeconomic realities of the student population;
- Choosing a platform that matches our individual class objectives and teaching styles;
- Monitoring student wellness and academic success in emergency teaching;
- Maintaining healthy student-teacher communication in an asynchronous format.

1 Introduction

International news in February 2020 began to forecast that COVID-19 would likely derail the Spring 2020 semester. As university murmurs morphed into official memos, the semester that professors at our institution envisioned became one that needed to be rebuilt with little to no preparation. The success rate at which emergency remote teaching (ERT) would be carried out in a COVID-19 context would depend on a number of factors: faculty preparation for distance-modes of teaching, IT infrastructure or access to computer technology, and university funds, among others. However, an element that merits attention and is often excluded from

K. Morales (✉) · G. Romaguera · E. Contreras
University of Puerto Rico – Mayaguez, Mayagüez, Puerto Rico
e-mail: katherine.morales1@upr.edu; gabriel.romaguera@upr.edu; edward.contreras@upr.edu

© The Author(s), under exclusive license to Springer Nature
Switzerland AG 2021
J. Chen (ed.), *Emergency Remote Teaching and Beyond*,
https://doi.org/10.1007/978-3-030-84067-9_14

dominant discourse is the role of a reliable energy and Internet infrastructure; this, more than anything, is the lifeline that ensures communication and successful exchanges when teaching and learning remotely. Faculty members from our university have faced several challenges prior to COVID-19 ERT, which includes emergency teaching after Hurricane Maria (see Chansky et al., 2018). This event left thousands of islanders without power for almost a year (one of the "longest blackouts in U.S. history"[1]). Most recently, islanders faced a 6.4 magnitude earthquake with regular aftershocks for the first 3 months of 2020, a natural catastrophe that overlapped with the emergency of COVID-19 worldwide.

This chapter documents the experiences of three adjunct faculty (i.e., instructors hired on a contract basis) in the English Department of a Hispanic-serving institution. Through reflexive autoethnography, here defined as both a self-narrative and a method, we offer a layered participant-observer account of setbacks and progress in adopting ERT in Puerto Rico. We reflect on the diverse strategies adopted to meet course objectives in Linguistics, Film, Creative Writing, and Public Speaking classes. Some of these strategies include the transferal or preparation of class content to an online format, deciding on asynchronous vs. synchronous modes of teaching, reconfiguring assessment, and navigating the psychological distance of teacher-student relations. It is worth mentioning that several developing countries which are susceptible to environmental crises and financial instabilities could face similar difficulties in readjusting their educational practices during COVID-19 due to socioeconomic inequalities; in this way, the present chapter could serve as an example case for these communities. Public universities that cater to students encompassing varied cultural and economic backgrounds may also find utility in some of our reflections and recommendations.

2 Emergency Teaching Context of Our Institution

When it comes to unprecedented circumstances and emergency teaching, it seems that Puerto Rico faces a unique infrastructural disadvantage. Although a large majority of Puerto Ricans are dependent on Internet communication (UN Data statistics reported that 78.78% of PR residents used the Internet in 2014), only 56.2% had access to subscription-based Internet (U.S. Census Statistics, 2014–2018). Since 2017, a number of natural catastrophes have occurred which have left an unfortunate imprint on the island's power grid. Hurricane Maria, a Category 4 storm with sustained winds of 155 mph, left the island without power for much of 2017; it also left thousands of U.S. citizens living under blue tarps for months and years to follow. Already financially vulnerable with a government debt of $72 billion and a U.S. appointed financial oversight board (P.R.O.M.E.S.A.) imposing cut-throat

---

[1] Smith-Nomini, S. (2020). The Debt/Energy Nexus Behind Puerto Rico's long blackout: From Fossil Colonialism to New Energy Poverty. *Latin American Perspectives*.

austerity measures, Puerto Rico faced what many called a man-made "environmental injustice" (Garcia-Lopez, 2018).

Emergency teaching during this time consisted of finding a way to provide learning experiences amidst crisis, but it also became a much larger effort than that. Chansky, Contreras, and others (2018) report in an autoethnography transforming their efforts to transform individual classes to include autobiographical pedagogies. Chansky described this endeavor as a social justice effort led by professors at the southwestern university to provide the students with an outlet where they could come to understand their own emotions and experiences during Maria using English. In this sense, these educators combated negative ideologies attached to English on the island as the "colonizer language" or the "language of the elite" (Morales, 2019) by reimagining English as a tool we could use to construct an "us" and make sense of difficult experiences. These autobiographical pedagogies were also coupled with fieldtrips and charitable efforts to reach the hard-hit communities around the island as well as the collection of food and other resources for the island's most affected populations. Promoting empathy in times of emergency teaching is also present in COVID-19 ERT scholarship; practitioners encourage compassion and prioritizing needs, mindfulness, and "mak(ing) space for the difficulties and circumstances of others" (Shea, 2020, 8) (Fig. 1).

In January 2020, the island welcomed the second natural emergency since Maria when a 6.4 magnitude earthquake struck the southern coast of the island. This quake generated a "geological sequence" of daily aftershocks that have altered the living situations of thousands of islanders in both southern and southwestern coasts (Van Der Elst, Hardebeck, & Michael, 2020). The earthquakes delayed the start of the spring semester, typically held right after Epiphany (January 6th), until January

Fig. 1 Dr. Contreras and his students leading charitable efforts to provide aid to hard hit communities on the island (Photo source: Alexandra Jeanette, 2018) (Jeanette, A. (2018). Edward Contreras and the Brigada 3101. U.P.R.M. Department of English. https://www.uprm.edu/english/?p=6927)

27th 2020. The tremors of January and February worsened the state of electrical lines, poles, and power plants, which were key to ensuring technological communication for remote teaching (see Van Der Elst, Hardebeck, & Michael, 2020). Not long after, Puerto Ricans would join the rest of the world in taking precautionary methods to a pandemic through remote teaching practices (Fig. 2).

In mid-to-late February, the University of Puerto Rico started sending out preventative emails and posting flyers notifying student and academic populations of a "coronavirus" and the safety precautions to consider (see Fig. 3).

All of the campuses belonging to the university network (a total of 11) were instructed to make the shift to online teaching approximately 6 days after the World Health Organization (WHO) declared COVID-19 a pandemic and the first suspected case on the island was reported. Following this notice, a period of "academic recess" was declared for a week, in which academic staff received training on online teaching methods. Many questions arose during this time:

- What about those affected by the recent earthquakes?
- How could we ensure educational equity to a socioeconomically diverse population affected by recent natural disasters?
- How do we overcome the problem of Internet instability, a weakened electrical network, and people living in earthquake-prone regions?

Fig. 2 Electrical poles damaged by earthquakes in Guayanilla, Puerto Rico (Photo source: Katherine Morales, 2020)

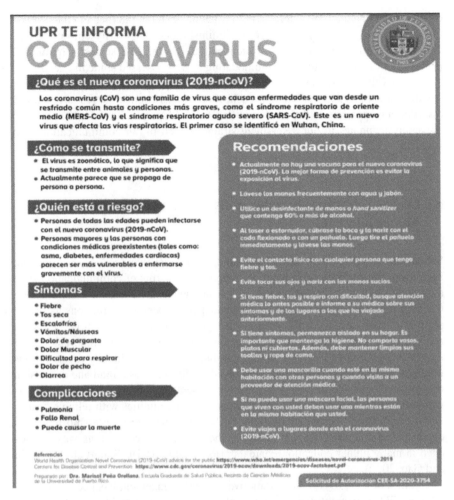

Fig. 3 COVID-19 Flyer distributed to the university community via email

Additionally, professors faced the challenge of having to become literate in digital teaching methods overnight. COVID-19 exposed the lack of literacy and preparedness in modes of online teaching around the world, a technical gap explored in world ERT literature (cf. Trust and Whalen, 2020).

During the initial stages of remote teaching, there were few mandates from the central university administration to faculty. The primary concern was adopting a more flexible approach to online teaching at initial stages. All classes had to be recorded, whether they were held live (synchronously) or pre-recorded (asynchronously). This flexibility allowed for synchronous delivery of class content at scheduled hours; however, should students face technical difficulties, they would have the opportunity to view the class on their own time. And yet, several students soon complained of their professors taking attendance, holding "live" classes off-schedule, demanding cameras "on," or having unstable Internet and thus "missing the lecture" or exam. In response, administrators temporarily enforced asynchronous teaching methods for the remainder of the Spring 2020 semester, reminding professors of their need to be accommodating as they assessed students' needs.

Collectively, the University's administrative efforts to adapt to our particular situation shaped our individual approaches to our classrooms: the resources at our disposal in responding to the pandemic (tablets and laptops), how we responded to university mandates in our assessment strategies, and in our communication with students.

3 Online Learning: Synchronous Vs Asynchronous Modes and ERT

Scholarship on e-learning has been around for at least two decades or more (see Hrastinski, 2008). With the advent of technological forms of communication such as mobile devices, computers, and tablets alongside the Internet, contemporary teaching practices are not uniquely dependent on in-person interactions as online platforms have surfaced throughout the years to facilitate remote learning. Asynchronous and synchronous teaching methods have formed an important part of the conversation in early 2000s work on at-distance modes, whereby asynchronous methods were deemed "traditional," involved media "such as e-mail and discussion boards," and provided flexibility to different student availabilities, and synchronous was seen as innovative and becoming popular in communities with reliable "bandwidth capabilities" (Hrastinski, 2008, 1). Some e-learning scholarship has been conducted in countries like China, where the use of blended learning was encouraged in many higher education contexts prior to COVID-19 (Sun et al. 2017; Lin and Gao, 2020).

In times of COVID-19, student motivation and engagement has been a pressing issue in ERT as content delivery is completely remote. Lin and Gao (2020) found that synchronous learning promotes "active interaction" and mimics classroom dynamics, such as immediate feedback and collaboration between peers, thus creating an "easy and fun" environment whilst preserving a sense of community or student identity (Lin and Gao, 2020,174). However, setbacks to this way of teaching include new distractions such as student "side chats"; furthermore, there is "an inability to control the learning pace" (ibid). For asynchronous teaching, the authors found that students were most likely to feel "socially isolated"; however, they were also more successful in learning as they could control their own learning pace and were less likely to be distracted by classmates (Lin and Gao, 2020, 172). Scholars conclude that the most engaging way to teach may be a blend of both, where both synchronous and asynchronous methods are adopted. While these methods have proved beneficial, they are tempered by the limitations of accessible Internet. In USA literature, Trust and Whalen (2020) report that among the many challenges of

ERT in Massachusetts school districts, Internet access (53%) is one of them. As such, one must consider the possibility of context obstructing certain modes of ERT.

The present Chapter reports on efforts of three professors to preserve a sense of "community" while engaging in ERT with unreliable Internet infrastructure. Additional considerations and vulnerabilities (mentioned in previous sections) were taken into account in order to decide upon a more reliable and equitable way of teaching that could promote student learning at-distance. Further, the present case is unique as it represents teachers' response to various emergencies (COVID-19, earthquakes, and vulnerable populations after Maria); as such, our considerations and reflections are shaped by a heightened sense of responsibility to deliver equitable and flexible teaching to already vulnerable communities.

4 Autoethnographies

In the process of ethnography, the researcher serves as the primary source about which others interpret and understand particular societal or cultural circumstances. They are the data providers – the insiders – concerned with getting down on the page their observations and experiences of outside practices, "reconstruct(ing) memories, prompted by jottings and headnotes, which privilege certain observational perspectives and certain members' experiences and voices over others" (Emerson, Fretz, Shaw, 2011, 2248). In contrast, autoethnography is described as a research method that "uses *personal* experience ('auto') to describe and interpret ('graphy') cultural texts, experiences, beliefs, and practices ('ethno')" (Adams, Ellis, Holman Jones, 2017, 1) with the ultimate goal of "figuring out what to do, how to live, and the meaning of... struggles" (Bochner and Ellis, 2006, 111). In autoethnographies, therefore, the core focus are the experiences and reflections of the participant-observer and their self-awareness and critical reflections of outside circumstances in order to arrive at a greater sense of purpose. Through personal experience, autoethnographers "provide alternatives to, dominant, taken-for-granted... stories" and "gaps in existing research" (Adams, Ellis, Holman Jones, 2017, 3).

In this process, we, as adjuncts at the University of Puerto Rico, serve a powerful role. We are the window through which our audiences will understand the challenges that arise in teaching English remotely in Puerto Rico. At the same time, we also represent a disadvantaged and often "muted" voice: that of the non-tenured faculty. Thus, a host of additional challenges face us, including the enduring reality that an adjunct's contract is subject to renewal based on student enrollment (necessity) and budget. As such, the pressure to perform as best we can is high.

4.1 Representation

The particulars of what we include in our narrative are therefore based around our realities as temporary faculty. Our self-reflections in this chapter allow us to learn how to become better educators. Our writings, therefore, offer insight into our experiences teaching in challenging contexts and our responses to these experiences. We hope that others may use our insights and reflection in their own professional practices.

In autoethnographies, issues of representation and choice may arise. Indeed, every lived experience offers one lens or one critical interpretation of lived realities. Our Chapter provides the autoethnographical reflections of three individuals through a series of essays on shared circumstances – listed below as "themes." A thematic analysis (through coding) of our individually written autoethnographies was conducted in order to detect universal themes and present a more accurate portrayal of our shared realities. As such, being able to cross-verify three autoethnographic stories makes our Chapter especially meaningful and valuable to the person coping with emergency teaching in a developing cultural context where other difficulties (beyond COVID) are simultaneously being addressed in teaching practices. Our representation of emergency teaching in Puerto Rico is further substantiated by use of polls, videos, informal student feedback, and images of classroom material.

Our diverse styles will be reflected in our individual accounts. Our responses to ERT are organized according to the following themes to grant our insights to readers and for ease of navigation:

- Transitioning to online (Sect. 4);
- Synchronous vs. asynchronous teaching (Sect. 5);
- Selection of platforms for teaching content (Sect. 6);
- Assessment (Sect. 7);
- Teacher-student relationship (Sect. 8).

4.2 Duration

We limit the temporal scope of our autoethnographical essays to the second half of the Spring 2020 semester in order to properly focus on that transitional time frame (March 2020 – May 2020). This decision helps in separating said moments from our current remote teaching experiences, which reflect more stabilized practices. This Chapter represents a summary of our lived experiences and individual circumstances and reflections.

4.3   Surveys and Informal Feedback

Our thematic reflections are coupled with short surveys as well as excerpts of conversations with students through e-mail, chat, and online platforms during synchronous teaching. The sample surveys were administered by Dr. Morales during the transitional period to monitor and ensure student wellness. Consent of the students was attained, assuring their right to abstain from participating in the poll as well as anonymity throughout the process.

5   Ethnographic Stories on Transitioning to Emergency Remote Teaching (ERT)

5.1   Prepping for a Whole New World (Dr. Romaguera)

The week before the major decision was made to shift to remote teaching, my students from both my Film and Creative Writing courses were concerned about the future and how we were to carry on with a swiftly encroaching pandemic. I naively tried to calm them down prior to class discussion. I assured them that things would calm down eventually and that, in the meantime, we would use an application like Discord[2] – an online group-chatting application popularized by the gaming community. At the time, this seemed like the ideal scenario: to host classes with the original schedule using a platform that allowed for "Live" dynamic discussions.

I categorize this moment as "naïve" because of the logistics of running my classes in a synchronous manner in Puerto Rico. Due to the logistical realities for myself and for my students, synchronous teaching would not be feasible since there could be different circumstances for all of us: i.e., differences in availabilities and responsibilities and/or poor bandwidth connections. By that Friday, administrators declared that there would be an academic recess of 1 week to give time to professors to accommodate and transfer their courses to be taught entirely through remote online platforms. Planning my class into a distance learning motif would be shaped by a prerogative linked to a shared time and space. To put it simply and to borrow from the legendary bard: *to synch or not to synch*?

---

[2] Discord is "a popular group-chatting app, was originally made to give gamers a place to build communities and talk. But since its launch in 2015, it has branched out to include communities from all over the internet, ranging from writers to artists to K-Pop stans" (See https://www.businessinsider.com/what-is-discord)

5.2   Dealing with COVID- 19 after Hurricane Maria and Tremors (Dr. Contreras)

Public Speaking was a performance class scheduled in the early evening from 5:00-6:15 PM on Tuesdays and Thursdays. Students would often ask me to end class at least 5 min early because they felt afraid to walk to their apartments given the dim illumination outside campus and the streetlights broken since Hurricane Maria in 2017. In-person classes back then involved considering the logistics of the time in which our class took place and ensuring student safety. At this time, I was also providing aid to students affected in earthquake zones on the island. I had contacted a community that was affected by the ongoing tremors and had organized a group of people to join me in bringing relief, food, clothes, and other necessities. Being a witness to my students' altered living situations caused me to reflect on whether they would be able to focus in class and whether they had the facilities – illumination in their communities, ceilings above their heads, a safe place to sleep – to even pursue university education at that time. Once COVID-19 became a public concern, I found myself preoccupied with these same communities and with how they would cope during a global health crisis in already vulnerable living circumstances (Fig. 4).

Fig. 4 Affected homes after earthquakes (Photo source: Katherine Morales, 2020)

Two weeks before going remote, I took the first minutes of class to discuss Reddit threads on how the pandemic was impacting countries around the world – like Italy and Spain – knowing that it was important to maintain a sense of awareness and collective empathy towards other countries struggling with different crises around the world.

The week before the island went on lockdown, I reviewed our online platform, let students know their grades thus far, and indicated that we would push forward in an asynchronous manner. During the week, I sent a questionnaire to inquire about their technological devices, access to the Internet, and comfort level with our online Canvas Instructure.

5.3   A Global Health Crisis amongst Earthquakes (Dr. Morales)

Prior to the university notice of going remote, all professors welcomed the new year with training on earthquake safety procedures and guidelines on flexibility during times of a geological earthquake sequence with no end in sight. I joined Dr. Contreras in his efforts to provide relief to those affected in early January. At the beginning of my classes, I took the first couple of minutes to survey those affected by the tremors. I assured them of the safety of our campus infrastructure – even if I, myself, experienced fear of teaching on the basement level of a multi-story building. I did not reveal my concerns because I wanted them to feel safe and focus on the lessons at hand, though my mind would wonder about possible escape plans should the worst occur. This mindset was verified when a colleague of mine shared with me her plans to break through a window should our door be insufficient to evacuate. Yet, I was emotionally prepared to teach in that class for the remainder of the semester. At the time, I never envisioned teaching during anything more severe. In February, I experienced a 5.0-magnitude earthquake while on the third floor of the Arts and Humanities building. I was alone at the time but took the necessary precautions to safely evacuate. I remember later using this experience as an anecdote to ease my students' worries with regards to the safety of our building.

Once COVID became a worry, I re-adopted a counseling approach and, much like Dr. Romaguera and Dr. Contreras, attempted to keep a calm environment where students could voice their concerns. In the lapse of time between COVID-19 being declared a pandemic and the university's decision to go remote, I advised my students to take care of themselves and those around them, to practice hygiene, and excuse themselves should they feel sick. I remember taking out my hand-sanitizer at the beginning of class one day and watching many students mimic my actions with their own purchased sanitizing items. During this stage, I also included safety procedures in my classroom material. For the earthquake safety procedures, I put a PowerPoint slide on measures to take in case of an earthquake. For COVID-19, I included a video from the BBC on how to wash one's hands safely. The week before going remote, I notified all students from my linguistics classes that we would be using Canvas Instructure and Zoom as primary platforms to host our classes. I also created WhatsApp groups with each of my classes to stay in touch more regularly. These measures helped me achieve a level of control in my coursework as the tide of uncertainty rose higher with each coming day.

6 Ethnographic Stories on Synchronous and Asynchronous Teaching

6.1 Synchronous Vs Asynchronous Internal Debate (Dr. Romaguera)

The synchronous teaching model seemed like the obvious answer when first considering teaching possibilities. My teaching style is dynamic[3] and highly dependent on student input. Depending on the interactions of the day, two sections of the same class would often have wildly different segments of class time based on how my students would react to varied questions and prompts. A former pupil of mine once said that the experience of taking one of my classes was familiar to a "one man improv comedy show": the enjoyment of the course was centered on the unexpected and witnessing how something apparently "chaotic" could all make sense at the end. My pedagogical approach is centered on the performative aspect of teaching, and a performance without an audience is essentially just rehearsal. Without the basis of a "live" performance, I honestly believed that my classes and my students would suffer greatly. Hence, a synchronous approach would best fit my style because I could gauge my students' reactions through the screens about as well as I could in the classroom.

6.2 Findings on Internet Access from a Student Poll (Dr. Morales)

In Mid-March, the university hosted a video tutorial on how to set a class up on Moodle as well as one on how to administer video calls via Google Meets. I logged in remotely from a different town – Ponce (on the south, hard-hit by earthquakes) – to watch this video that was being transmitted from Mayaguez (on the west side of

---

[3] According to Armour-Thomas and Gordon (2013): "Dynamic Pedagogy is a socio-cognitive approach to teaching in which assessment, curriculum and instructional processes are united in the service of student learning" (5). For this researcher, the dynamic aspects of teaching encompass the ability to assess students in real time and altering instructional methods as needed without straying too far from the heart of the curriculum.

the island). A pixelated image took up my screen of the instructor sharing his screen with over 180 faculty members logged in on this platform. This image was followed by his cut-off voice asking us to immediately "Mute" our microphones and "Turn off" our videos. I was logged in through the hotspot of my mobile device. It immediately felt dehumanizing; I wondered how that experience of being "muted" would translate over to a previously interactive language classroom, which awarded the student equal power and "voice" in seminar style teachings, and whether this would pose as a problem for the English language learner looking to improve their speaking and listening skills. I watched faculty members – already experiencing technological difficulties – dropping in and out of the meeting as their Internet cut off. If middle-class tenured professors experienced communicative breakdowns during a meeting, I feared the effect this would have on those islanders living in seismically-active regions where power plants were faltering and weakened electrical lines resulted in communicative disability. This was corroborated much later when I began teaching synchronously and quickly changed to asynchronous format after hearing things like "professor, I can't hear you" or "my electricity went out." I administered a poll of 13 items (*See Appendix I*) across all of my linguistics classes – English Grammar, Sociolinguistics, and World Englishes – for a total of 104 students; only 57 completed the poll. Although I would have been able to assess my students' situation more accurately had they all participated in the poll, the information I gathered was nonetheless insightful about their learning preferences and living circumstances. Qualitative feedback in open questions confirmed the need for better Internet access for some communities of the island:

> "Although I preferred live lectures, I may be unable to participate in the live lectures due to bad Internet connection." – *Student*

I asked students whether they preferred the "live" synchronous format over the asynchronous ready-made recording for them to watch at their own pace. Most of them positioned themselves against the "live" synchronous format as demonstrated by the pie chart below (Fig. 5) with 35.1% "disagreeing" against the synchronous live format and 29.8% "strongly disagreeing".

However, whether this preference for asynchronous learning was tied to poor bandwidth Internet connections remains unclear. When I asked students to disclose whether they were able to access the class content with home Internet, a total of 75.4% of respondents claimed not to experience significant issues with the Internet. Nevertheless, only 57 respondents out of 104 completed the poll. It is also worth mentioning that in rating the degree of satisfaction on of a scale of 1–5 (strongly disagree – strongly agree), the greater percentage of respondents marked "agree" rather than "strongly agree," demonstrating a level of hesitance towards complete satisfaction. This suggests that an asynchronous model would work more successfully for everyone, ensuring equitable access to content and different scheduling responsibilities (part-time jobs, care-taking responsibilities, etc.) (Fig. 6).

I wish the video lectures / classes were done "Live", using the old schedule.

57 responses

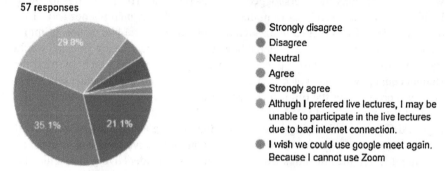

Fig. 5 Reported preferences of students in Advanced English regarding the scheduling of courses taught by Dr. Morales (57 respondents)

The class is accessible to me, I have reliable WiFi and a computer/smartphone device/other that I can go to to keep up with the material

57 responses

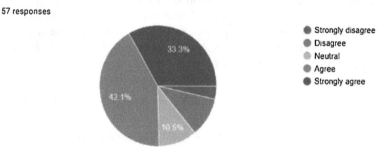

Fig. 6 Reported Internet access of students in Advanced English courses taught by Dr. Morales (57 respondents)

6.3   Public Speaking in Private Asynchronous Fashion (Dr. Contreras)

The Spring 2020 semester brought upon the following challenge: how could I turn an English class that relies on the spoken and the performative aspect of language to an online format? Surely, the obvious answer would rely on synchronous teaching. Much like my colleagues, I experimented with this style of teaching during the initial stages of ERT. However, following the many infrastructural challenges of the island and reports from my students – e.g., poor Internet connection, faulty microphones and/or video technology, and other living circumstances (such as shared family computers) – I considered that perhaps the more empathetic and equitable approach to teaching English to a socioeconomically diverse population would involve asynchronous teaching.

I experienced similar setbacks to Dr. Morales (above) in teaching synchronously. At the time, I opted to conduct my meetings through Zoom. For the first Zoom meeting on March 24th, most of my students attended, and we discussed their situations. It was then when I learnt of the sheer effort it took for some of them to even be present in that meeting with me: I had three students tell me that they were at a parking lot of a fast-food restaurant, "stealing" Wi-Fi; others reported being at a friend's house to "connect to class." I also remembered teaching after Hurricane Maria, where our students faced similar challenges in less-than-ideal circumstances. On several occasions during those first synchronous meetings, I recall having trouble understanding students over video, and I imagined the difficulty in assessing even a 2 min speech this way. In the following Zoom meeting, I made the authoritative decision to transfer class content to an asynchronous fashion. I later switched to a different online platform, Screencastify, to conduct my video recordings and have students conduct video responses.

My class became 100% asynchronous, which went against my traditional teaching style and made me rely solely on students completing their assignments on their own. This would require me to be available personally through phone if they faced technological difficulties. I would upload 20–30 min lectures on Tuesdays and then upload models of the speeches on Thursdays.

7   Ethnographies on Choosing an Online Platform

7.1   Digital Spaces for Film Discussion and Writing Workshops (Dr. Romaguera)

I was teaching two sections of Creative Writing and two sections of Film. For the latter, I did not need to reinvent the pedagogical wheel when it came to teaching the course. During ideal times, the students would convene in the classroom, and I would utilize the overhead projector and computer to show a film while highlighting different elements of cinematography and visual storytelling during the viewing. This was the class where I told my students that we would be using Discord so that we could all watch the movie together while listening to me; everyone else would be muted to avoid distractions. Upon further introspection, I realized that if my students were not able to say or do anything besides minor observations before and after the movie, then having them come together for class time would have no benefit in comparison to an asynchronous model. The model echoed that of on demand streaming services where students were free to watch the film when they so desired rather than the outdated Pay Per View movie style where the viewing experience was controlled by outside forces. Hence, I provided an audio recording with my commentary via the Moodle site of our course for students to start as they streamed the film through Netflix or other streaming services.

Creative writing is one of my favorite classes to teach, as it really allows students the freedom to tackle stories in a way that is unique to each of them. My own spin on the course was centered on the concept of fan fiction and would have students choose their favorite stories to recreate within different parameters throughout the semester. I had taught the class the previous semester and already had the mental model of how the course would ebb and flow with each coming week while still leaving room for student input on how certain aspects of storytelling would be explained/employed each class day. In class writing activities, group work, and peer review were the pillars of my pedagogical foundation for the course, and each of them would crumble as we went to a remote asynchronous model of teaching.

7.2   Digital Spaces for Asynchronous Linguistics (Dr. Morales)

During the Spring 2020 semester, I was preparing courses for English Grammar, Sociolinguistics, and World Englishes as a first-time professor at the university. This meant that on top of the logistics of my online platform, I was also planning the logistics behind every class and assessment (daily objectives, presentations, activities). My teaching style is heavily reliant on technology. I make use of PowerPoint slides and incorporate practice problems and discussion exercises in live classes. I have found that through slides, I get through more material, students are engaged, and students also possess an electronic version of class content in PDF form.

This meant that perhaps for my particular teaching style, the move to online platforms was less drastic than for those who use whiteboards or physical handouts in class or rely on immediate student feedback in dialectic performance (as does my colleague, Dr. Romaguera; see above). Where I chose to "Host" these classes and how I would "assess" would be my primary transitions. I chose Canvas Instructure (Canvas) for all of my linguistics classes. My choice was based on the layout of this platform, which contains a built-in syllabus option, announcements, files, quizzes, rubrics, user analytics; these were all neatly laid out in a left-hand menu while key files were on the right side. Furthermore, Canvas made it possible for me to transfer question pools from one course to another (see Fig. 7). I could also open each question to permit the JPEG (and other) submissions to be uploaded into a quiz – a useful technique in the event that a student is required to use phonetic notation or draw a syntax tree diagram but is unsure how to do this in the platform. Canvas also has a built-in video recording option, and Moodle did not at the time. In sum, I found the ready-made features of this platform more in alignment with my pedagogical needs for assessment. The students could also check out the grading feature and keep up-to-date with their scores in class.

After the central administration's mandate to move to asynchronous classes, I conducted most of my recordings through a different platform: Zoom. I made this change following recording problems with Canvas' BigBlueButton meeting feature (the video did not record after a one-hour lecture); I also enjoyed the multimodal features that Zoom offered: different backgrounds, Whiteboards, its closed

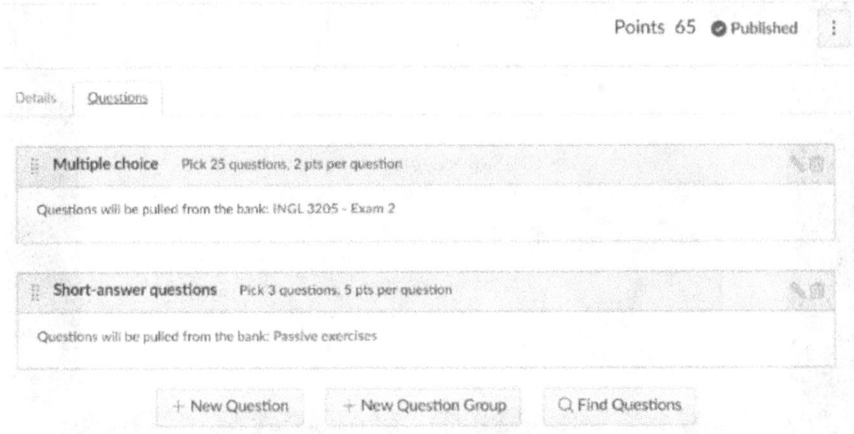

Points 65 ● Published ⋮

Details | Questions

⠿ **Multiple choice** Pick 25 questions, 2 pts per question

Questions will be pulled from the bank: INGL 3205 - Exam 2

⠿ **Short-answer questions** Pick 3 questions, 5 pts per question

Questions will be pulled from the bank: Passive exercises

+ New Question   + New Question Group   Q Find Questions

Fig. 7 Canvas Instructure "question pool" feature lends for randomization of test questions

captioning feature, recording into the Cloud and/or computer, etc. Towards the end of Spring semester, I was using 2 platforms: Zoom for recording my classes and sharing them and Canvas Instructure for assessing students.

Choosing Zoom for recording was a great choice for my personal teaching style, which relies on imagery and other multimodal effects. For my World Englishes course, I would often change my virtual background to match the World English country I was discussing that day. For the process of creating content, I used Microsoft PowerPoint and also turned on its "subtitle feature" for presentations (Fig. 7). My students would often comment on how grateful they were for the subtitles, especially in cases where the audio was unclear. I navigated Internet instability by making my videos 20–30 min long; in this way, they would be easier to upload and later watch. As evidenced by Fig. 8, I opted for simple presentations with a large font size, color coded terminology and information, and images to illustrate content. In this way, I opted to create a learning experience that would be attractive and stimulating both visually and orally. The core of my content was delivered orally; I would switch into my performative "teacher" voice by "paying attention to speech" (see Labov, 2006[4]) and delivering theatrical lectures by making use of rising and falling intonation, volume, code-switching into Spanish expressions such as "verdad" (right?), "algarete" (crazy), and translations of English definitions to encourage active listening and create cognitive linkages between second language content (English) and native language knowledge (Spanish). This latter linguistic method has been advocated in recent years in bilingualism and language

---

[4]*Attention paid to speech* is defined as altering one's speech adequately to match community norms of one's immediate addressee, environment, and context, typically from an informal style of speaking to a more formal style of speaking. More discussion of this phenomenon is found in:

Labov, W. (2006). *The social stratification of English in New York City*. Cambridge University Press.

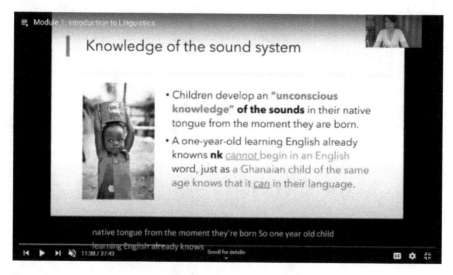

Fig. 8 Demonstration of PowerPoint lecture with automatic subtitles

teaching research under the label "translanguaging" (see Garcia & Wei, 2015). I would also encourage questions or comments in our WhatsApp group chats.

7.3 Online Platforms for Public Speaking and Communication (Dr. Contreras)

To make things simpler for students and myself, I recorded all of my lectures and modeling examples with a Google Chrome video editing software called *Screencastify*. This made my life easier and required almost little to no editing on my end. In addition, I could show my desktop and explain the examples from outlines, speaking techniques, and concepts. Screencastify is a Google Chrome Add-on; because of this, I would create my videos and upload them to a shared Google Drive. I would use that same folder to receive videos from students. It was practical to not use too many platforms for the teaching of this class, which already demanded that students create speeches in collaboration with me. I sent several tutorials so that students could educate themselves on using Google Drive and other mobile editing video applications. Most students recorded video assignments with their phones and uploaded them accordingly (a tutorial on how to use Screencastify can be found here: https://youtu.be/uuJ2lF9RkgE). I would send content twice a week: on Tuesdays, I sent 20–30 min lectures on public speaking techniques using Screencastify and on Thursdays, I uploaded models of speeches on the same platform (Fig. 9).

Fig. 9 Screencastify platform as alternative to creating video content

8 Assessment in Online Form

8.1 Remote "Writing Prompts" through Podcast (Dr. Romaguera)

When the semester restarted, the plan was to teach Creative Writing in a way akin to a podcast, wherein I would send my students audio recordings of me explaining the material for the day, provide writing prompts, and then use questions that I assumed would come up during the process and answer them accordingly. In my naivete, I believed that this plan would work wondrously and that students would be engaged in the writing process. However, without my students able to provide suggestions "live" (like in an improv show), my explanations fell flat, as I attempted to anticipate their prior knowledge and make connections in real time. In regular class times, these prompts were a way for students to participate and would allow for meaningful connections to the material, but with me giving the suggestions for them, it turned into a situation where they had to follow, rather than lead, discussion. The shift in dynamics was evident with the feedback that a handful of students were brave enough to send via email in the weeks after class had restarted. Without the ability to gauge my students' reactions through nonverbal cues in the classroom, I remained unaware until the feedback came in long after the faulty system was already in place.

Whenever I would give a writing prompt as part of the class, I actively decided to have that much time be part of the audio. Hence, if I asked students to write for 5 min, I would continue the recording for those 5 min; filling the silence along the way with gentle reminders of the instructions, how much time they had left, and extra information to consider as part of the thought process. The thought process behind this choice was centered on the idea that if I merely told students that they should pause the recording for 5 min, do the writing, and then come back, many would opt to ignore the prompt and the writing practice. I noticed that the atmosphere of uncertainty that pervaded the island and the world with the pandemic led to disassociating with their tasks at hand, even the ones they were actively being graded on. By placing the writing prompt as a feature of the class they should be participating in – rather than as an option they could easily ignore – engaging with the course became more streamlined. Students still had the option to fast forward the 5 min or to do nothing while the prompt countdown was at hand, but, at least from a personal standpoint, I knew I was doing my part to get them to engage actively with the material at hand.

8.2 Testing Linguistics through Built-in Quizzing Applications (Dr. Morales)

One of the main concerns in faculty meetings was assuring academic honesty during examination processes. Canvas Instructure and Moodle both have methods that allow for the randomization of questions and answers through the use of question pools. They also allow for timed examinations. Canvas Instructure, in particular, has an option for "locking" questions, such that once a question has been answered/submitted one could not "go back" to revise one's response after hitting "next" to move on to another question. I explored the use of this particular feature in initial testing stages, wishing to eliminate academic dishonesty – that is, students reporting the answers to one another via text messaging or phone and going back to mark the correct response. Unfortunately, I received several complaints from students who lost temporary connection to the Internet and feared their work was lost; although it was not, their anxiety made me rethink adopting the "lock questions" feature. The issues of plagiarism, cheating, and academic dishonesty are an outstanding concern for remote assessment. In some institutions, this is dealt with by demanding cameras to be "turned on" during examination processes, but a student's right to privacy was and still is protected by established ERT regulations.

My exams became largely multiple choice and timed to an hour and a half for 30 questions to lessen the anxiety of completing practice problems under strict "timed" deadlines. I gave students two attempts to complete exams for English Grammar. I gave "take-home style" analytical tests for my Sociolinguistics class. Essay style exercises were reduced in word count, and I demanded less of students and awarded extra time to complete work. I also incorporated more group activities where students could complete problems or exercises collectively, rather than individually, thus maintaining a classroom atmosphere. For instance, in my World Englishes class, the final assessment consisted of a classroom report of different non-native Englishes around the world. I also included "peer group" revisions for essay tasks in all of my classes. In this sense, I encouraged a learning community in an asynchronous format. I also made myself available via phone (WhatsApp) throughout assessment time.

8.3 Assessment in a Private "Public" Speaking Course (Dr. Contreras)

In English Public Speaking, students are assessed in terms of their ability to write and perform a variety of speeches ranging from elevator pitches to toasts to persuasive speeches. Some primary objectives of this course include the ability to "manage and overcome the fear of speaking English to an audience," "maintain appropriate eye contact and vocabulary delivery," and "respond to an audience in the appropriate fashion during a question-and-answer section" – all of which were made highly improbable to assess in asynchronous format. As mentioned earlier, students used Screencastify to deliver and edit their speeches. This gave students the ability to revise their performances and edit them rather than deliver a one-time performance to an immediate audience. My original objectives changed slightly to emphasize the preparation of a speech and less on students' ability to respond to an audience; more emphasis was paid to the anticipation of a hypothetical audience. In asynchronous classes, students could present through PowerPoint presentations, "share" their screens, or perform video demonstrations. Students were advised to look straight into the lens, limit external noise interference (mobile phones), and ensure their microphone was functioning, among other suggestions (Fig. 10).

Fig. 10 Google Drive with video speeches

9 Preserving a Sense of Student Identity

9.1 Encouraging a Collective Sense of Identity (Dr. Morales)

As a linguist and teacher, I am aware of the role of learner identity in language learning and motivation – particularly, how a positive sense of "L2" self can encourage successful acquisition of L2 (See Norton, 2013 for discussion). If the uncertain nature of lockdown restrains us from interacting with one another, relating to each other, and understanding our future selves, an important role of the language teacher then is to maintain student engagement and an active learning environment. The importance of community learner identity was highlighted in Lin and Gao's (2020) study of online teaching in Chinese universities. While they found that synchronous classes promoted a more "healthy" and "relaxed" environment, teachers at UPRM struggle with the anonymity of asynchronous modes of communication. How I would tap into this "sense of identity" with so much institutionalized red tape would require creative thinking on my end.

To lessen the psychological distance of teaching English linguistics remotely, I created WhatsApp group chats for all of my classes where students were free to ask questions in relation to video presentations, deadlines, or comments on class content. This platform allows for an almost three-dimensional classroom conversation between students, as it is multimodal: it relies on text messages and audio recordings or "voices," and students may also respond nonverbally through emojis, stickers, and GIFs. This mode of communication allowed my students to feel more engaged and part of a collective "classroom." Using WhatsApp may add what is otherwise lost in a "muted" and "invisible" Zoom call. It also allowed students to see me in a less threatening light as well as learn at their own pace.

In my poll, most students reported feeling satisfied with the platforms and strategies adopted in my classes. Some students admitted difficulty adjusting to online ways of teaching but thanked me for my efforts to keep them motivated. From this, I learned that using contemporary modes of communication that rely on informal use of symbols, emojis, memes, and stickers can establish positive rapport between students and myself.

10 Conclusion: Lessons from Emergency Remote Teaching in P.R

As adjunct professors, we are expected to fulfill the gaps in coursework that emerge in our department just before the start of an academic semester; hence, we anticipate changes to our class schedule and prepare to adjust our teaching tools as best we can. This degree of adaptability served us well in reshaping our courses in past and current times of crisis. As young professors, we are also well-adapted to technology and innovative ways of maintaining and engaging our students in our classes.

Throughout this chapter, we surveyed the many strategies we used to host our English content courses. These range from strategically choosing a "platform" that matches our course objectives – speech, writing, and linguistic theory – with Screencastify, podcast style writing prompts, and interactive PowerPoint presentations to adapting our teaching styles from dialectic (or involving student live feedback) to performative (developing a set of linguistic techniques to enhance solo delivery of content). We have also detailed how we adapted flexibility in assessment, from awarding additional time when necessary for assignment submission to changing to more qualitative style assessment to incorporating more group work. Our methods as autoethnographers involve active reflection, as learning occurs when we reflect on our experiences and not by simply living them. Our positive rapport with our students, flexibility, and feedback from conversations and polls have shaped the tools that we incorporate to deliver our classes.

11   Food for Thought

Our autoethnographies showcase the inner negotiations that took place to meet the new changes to university regulations and how students voiced their individual circumstances. While previous work suggest "asynchronous models" to be most traditional in online teaching and synchronous "live" methods as preferred, our current realities, which involve several "emergencies" (pandemic, natural disasters, vulnerable housing situations, income and wealth inequality, etc.), suggest that the most equitable and sustainable way to teach communities like Puerto Rico is by offering the "asynchronous" option or allowing students to watch content within a specific time frame (a week) and monitoring students' progress and participation through miniature assessments (shorter tests, essays) and frequent communication.

A potential area of research concerns whether our ERT teaching styles or the shift to remote learning will affect the success rate at which students learn or relate to English remotely. However, the linguistic impact of our current times is one that remains to be explored with time.

By regularly monitoring students' progress and needs via polls and emails, considering island infrastructure, and keeping up-to-date with university mandates, we were able to alter our teaching styles and course objectives to lessen the psychological anxiety of learning in this particular time in history. We urge our fellow educators to consider individual student circumstances to ensure equity in emergency remote teaching. Although our experiences as adjunct professors at our university are fairly unique, we believe that what we have learned from these experiences can apply to any and all educators despite the levels of crisis they are managing. Throughout our autoethnographies, we were able to reflect on our success and failures of teaching and assessment. A summary of our assessment strategies may be found below (Table 1).

Table 1 Summary table of ERT strategies per English content course

Content Course	Creative Writing	Film	Linguistics	Public Speaking
Linguistic skill	Writing	Listening	Theory	Speaking
Assessment platforms	Moodle	Moodle	Canvas Instructure	Canvas Instructure
Lectures	Podcast/audio uploaded to Moodle.	Podcast/audio uploaded to Moodle. Netflix streaming services	Zoom video lecture.	Asynchronous video sharing through Screencastify.
Activities	200-word weekly assignments/ reactions to writing prompts (30%); 4 writing assignments.	500-word weekly writing assignments (30%); 4 essay writing assignments.	2 multiple choice tests with 30 items and 2 possible attempts; with peer review component; final group report.	Preparing and writing speeches; editing videos of speeches. Total of 4 speeches.
Frequency of meetings	Recordings released twice a week	Recordings released twice a week	20 min videos released three times a week.	Videos released twice a week.

Acknowledgments Firstly, we would like to thank our students at our institution for staying motivated, asking questions, and for participating in our class surveys. Secondly, we would like to thank Dr. Julian Chen and the reviewers for the opportunity to collaborate on a meaningful project and their guidance and invaluable feedback during this process.

Appendix I

Content Course	Creative Writing	Film	Linguistics	Public Speaking
Linguistic Skill	Writing	Listening	Theory	Speaking
Assessment Platforms	Moodle	Moodle	Canvas Instructure	Canvas Instructure
Lectures	Podcast/Audio uploaded to Moodle.	Podcast/Audio uploaded to Moodle. Netflix Streaming services	Zoom video lecture.	Asynchronous video sharing through Screencastify.
Activities	200-word weekly assignments/reactions to writing prompts (30%); 4 writing assignments.	500-word weekly writing assignments (30%); 4 essay writing assignments.	2 multiple choice tests with 30 items and 2 possible attempts; with peer review component; final group report.	Preparing and writing speeches; editing videos of speeches. Total of 4 speeches.
Frequency of meetings	Recordings released twice a week	Recordings released twice a week	20-minute videos released three times a week.	Videos released twice a week.

References

Adams, T. E., Ellis, C., & Holman Jones, S. (2017). Autoethnography. In J. Matthes (Ed.), *The international encyclopedia of communication research methods*. John Wiley & Sons.

Armour-Thomas, E., & Gordon, E. W. (2013). *Toward an understanding of assessment as a dynamic component of pedagogy*. Princeton NJ: Gordon Commission.

Bochner, A. P., & Ellis, C. (2006). *Communication as...: Stances on theory* (pp. 13–21). Thousand Oaks, CA: Sage.

Chansky, R. A., Contreras Santiago, E. G., Correo Gonzalez, F., Denesiuk, M., Geliga Vargas, J., & Mazak, C. M. (2018). I is for Agency: Education, Social Justice, and Auto/Biographical Practices. *Revista Brasileira de Pesquisa (Auto) Biografica, Salvador, 03*, 416–440.

Emerson, R. M., Fretz, R. I., Shaw, L. L. (2011). *Writing ethnographic Fieldnotes, 2ˢᵗ edition* [Kindle version]. University of Chicago Press.

Garcia, O., & Wei, L. (2015). Translanguaging, bilingualism, and bilingual education. *The handbook of bilingual and multilingual education, 223*, 240.

Garcia-Lopez, G. A. (2018). The multiple layers of environmental injustice in contexts of (Un) natural disasters: The case of Puerto Rico post-hurricane Maria. *Environmental Justice, 11*(3).

Hrastinski, S. (2008). Asynchronous and synchronous e-learning. *Educause Quarterly, 31*(4), 51–55.

Labov, W. (2006). *The social stratification of English in New York City*. Cambridge University Press.

Lin, X., & Gao, L. (2020). Students' sense of community and perspectives of taking synchronous and asynchronous online courses. *Asian Journal of Distance Education, 15*(1), 169–179.

Morales Lugo, K. (2019). *Through the magnifying glass: An ethnographic account of the bilingual practices of adolescents in Puerto Rico*. (Doctoral dissertation, Trinity College Dublin, Ireland, 2019).

Norton, B. (2013). *Identity and language learning: Extending the conversation* (2nd ed.). Bristol, UK: Multilingual Matters.

Shea, L. M. (2020). No perfect syllabus for distance learning: DBT skills for deciding how to teach throughout uncertainty. *Pedagogy and the Human Sciences, 7*(1).

Smith-Nomini, S. (2020). The Debt/Energy Nexus behind Puerto Rico's long blackout: From fossil colonialism to new energy poverty. *Latin American Perspectives, 47*(232), 64–86.

Sun, Z., Liu, R., Luo, L., Wu, M., & Shi, C. (2017). Exploring collaborative learning effect in blended learning environments. *Journal of Computer Assisted Learning, 33*(6), 575–587.

Trust, T., & Whalen, J. (2020). Should teachers be trained in emergency remote teaching? Lessons learned from the COVID-19 pandemic. *Journal of Technology and Teacher Education, 28*(2), 189–199.

U.S. Census Bureau (2014 – 2018). QuickFacts Puerto Rico. Retrieved from [https://www.census.gov/quickfacts/fact/table/PR/POP815218#POP815218].

Van Der Elst, N., Hardebeck, J. L., & Michael, A. J. (2020). *Potential duration of aftershocks of the 2020 southwestern Puerto Rico earthquake* (No. 2020 – 1009). US Geological Survey.

"I Will Teach from the Heart": Teachers' Beliefs and Practices During an Emergency Remote Language Pedagogy in a Heritage Language School During the COVID-19 Lockdown

Anu Muhonen

Highlights

- Online ethnography allowed insights into teacher's beliefs and an investigation of why they think the way they do and what implications it has for their teaching practice.
- Teacher beliefs are based on personal experiences and previous experience with instruction. These beliefs drive practices; new practices can lead to changes in beliefs or create new beliefs.
- Remote learning offers children an opportunity to maintain their language skills, a sense of normality, and a continuing feeling of being part of their heritage community, even during a global pandemic.
- Remote teaching allowed new collaborations to take place; families gathered together to help children learn the heritage language.
- Folk linguistic theories are worthy of examination due to their impact on complementary heritage language teaching.

1 Introduction

Due to the unforeseen COVID-19 outbreak in spring 2020, many educators were suddenly asked to work remotely in an attempt to continue teaching during a time when there was a requirement to slow down the spread of the coronavirus through lockdowns and physical distancing. This meant a switch from face-to-face teaching in the classroom to virtual interaction in a remote learning space. Specifically, in Toronto, Canada, all public schools were suddenly required to move all instruction online to prevent the spread of coronavirus through physical distancing. These

A. Muhonen (✉)
University of Toronto, Toronto, Canada
e-mail: anu.muhonen@utoronto.ca

© The Author(s), under exclusive license to Springer Nature
Switzerland AG 2021
J. Chen (ed.), *Emergency Remote Teaching and Beyond*,
https://doi.org/10.1007/978-3-030-84067-9_15

regulations brought about changes in complementary and heritage language schools; they were also ordered to cease in-person gatherings for an unforeseeable future. In this chapter, I explore how the challenge was dealt with within a Finnish heritage language school in Toronto. I further discuss how teacher practices were impacted and what kinds of beliefs prevailed during this critical period. My role as a volunteer teacher, co-teacher, and administrative support for the teacher's online pedagogy allowed me to gain an insider perspective on these issues.

The Toronto Finnish Language School was established in 1960 and is the world's first Finnish language school outside of Finland. The school was founded by local immigrant communities to preserve the linguistic and cultural heritage of this community and their offspring. The language school offers instruction to preschool and school children for a few hours on weekends. It operates entirely with the support of volunteer work. In practice, teaching is conducted by parent-teachers, many of whom do not have teacher credentials.

When the City of Toronto went into the COVID-19 lockdown in March 2020, the Finnish school initially decided to suspend classes for the period of the mandatory provincial lockdown, which was preliminary and only planned to last 2 weeks after the school Easter break. Soon it became clear, however, that students would not be permitted to return to school before the fall. Thereafter, the teachers at the Finnish language schools began to discuss a switch to remote teaching, and after a short time-out, the school opened virtually again and began offering language and culture teaching remotely. During the time of the lockdown, the school had 61 registered students ranging from age 3 to 14, and 14 educators in the classrooms. None of the teachers had previous experience teaching children online.

In this ethnographic study, I take a discourse analytic approach (see Blommaert, 2005) to investigate the sudden switch to remote teaching in this community-run heritage language school and further explore the kinds of practices and beliefs the teachers, who mostly consisted of volunteers and parents, engaged in during an unexpected period of remote teaching. Beliefs form part of what teachers think about teaching and how they shape their pedagogy; in turn, their ways of thinking shape their pedagogy. Teachers' beliefs are often born from education-based or research-based principles, indicating that they gain their beliefs from learning principles of second language acquisition research or education (see Abdi & Asadi, 2015; Kindsvatter et al., 1988). In this case study, such beliefs did not implicitly occur, as the teachers at the Finnish language heritage school in Toronto did not have formal language teacher education. As none of the participants in this study had previous experience teaching heritage children online, this study of parent-teacher beliefs extends a folk linguistics study of teacher beliefs and practice. Folk linguistics generally refers to what ordinary people say about language (Preston, 1991, p. 584); they refer to "shortcuts, idealizations, and simplifying paradigms" (Keesing, 1987, p. 380). Folk linguistic statements, beliefs, and practices are not based on scientific knowledge or proven practices. The teachers who participated in this study—although being professionals in other fields—did not have formal education in language pedagogy, nor did they have schooling in virtual pedagogy or virtual language pedagogy. Therefore, this study of beliefs is closely connected to folk linguistic theories of (remote) learning (see Miller & Ginsberg, 1995).

A great deal of research has been conducted on beliefs in different contexts. In examining beliefs, it is relevant to explain how they differ from the concept of knowledge, and many scholars have differentiated between beliefs and knowledge (Alexander & Dochy, 1995; Pajares, 1992). Knowledge is often described as "learned," "agreed upon," "factual," and "experiential" in nature; knowledge is objective information that comes about as a result of formal learning. (Alexander & Dochy, 1995, p. 425). Beliefs depict memories and adjust our understanding of occurrences (Gilakjani & Sabouri, 2017, p. 78). However, they are sometimes called "a messy" construct (Pajares, 1992, p. 307). Definitions connected to beliefs are "subjective," "feelings," "idiosyncratic truth," and "personal" (Alexander & Dochy, 1995, p. 425). Wenden (1987) describes them as "metacognitive knowledge," which then also constitutes "theories of action" (p. 112). Other scholars have defined beliefs as social constructs born out of our experiences (see Freeman, 1991). Harvey (1986) defines belief as an individual's representation of reality that has enough validity, truth, or credibility to guide thought and behavior. Dewey (1933) describes belief as the third meaning of thought: "something beyond itself by which its value is tested; it makes an assertion about some matter of fact or some principle or law" (p. 6). Teachers' beliefs have a greater effect than the teachers' knowledge on planning their lessons, on the types of decisions they adopt, and on classroom practice (Gilakjani & Sabouri, 2017, p. 78). Nation and Macalister (2010) and Amiryousefi (2015) assert that what teachers do is identified by their beliefs. The distinguishing factor is that knowledge is often perceived as arising from experiences that have been formally constructed, as in the case of schooling, while beliefs are the outcomes of one's everyday encounters (Alexander & Dychy, 1995, p. 424).

In this study, beliefs are considered teachers' ideas, understandings, feelings, and sometimes subjective and personal ideas related to teaching and learning a heritage language. All the above-mentioned descriptions can relate to folk linguistic beliefs. Beliefs are described as a form of thought that covers all the matters of which we have no sure knowledge and yet of which we are sufficiently confident to act upon (Dewey, 1938, p. 6). According to Peacock (2001), beliefs are psychologically held appreciations, assumptions, or theorems about the world that are felt to be correct. They can also be described as synonyms for preconceived notions, myths, or even misconceptions. Both knowledge and beliefs arise from one's personal experiences. Teacher beliefs in educational settings have been investigated on a wide range of topics. Studies to elucidate volunteer-teacher beliefs in a complementary language school emergency virtual learning are scant.

2 Research Design, Aims, and Data

2.1 Ethnographic Method

This study applied sociolinguistic ethnographic methods in both data collection and in the analysis. A discourse-centered online ethnography makes use of ethnographic knowledge and observation as guidance in selecting, analyzing, and interpreting data among the participants within a particular (online) community (Androutsopoulos, 2008, p. 2). As the setting for this study was remote teaching, discourse-centered linguistic (online) ethnography was applied both in the data collection and as a method of the study. Online ethnography, also referred to as "virtual ethnography" (Hine, 2000), "netnography" (Kozinets, 2002), and "webnography" (Puri, 2007), is a virtual research method that adapts ethnographic methods to the study of the communities and discourse created through computer-mediated social interaction. In this study, I combined these methods and systematic observation of selected online discourse with direct contact where its social actors take place (Androutsopoulos, 2008, p. 2). Discourse practices are used as "a window" (see Blommaert, 2005, p. 66) through which teachers' practices and beliefs are explored. Different methods were combined to interpret teachers' beliefs in this time and space of the study.

Linguistic ethnography holds that language and social life are mutually shaping, and that close analysis of situated (language) practices can provide fundamental insights (Rampton, et al., 2004, p. 2; Creese, 2008, p. 229). As Heller (2008, p. 250) writes, ethnography illuminates social processes and generates explanations for why people do and think the way they do, and continues, "ethnographies allow us to get at things we would otherwise never be able to discover". Ethnography, as Van Maanen (1988, p. ix) writes, is "the peculiar practice of representing the social reality of others through the analysis of one's own experience in the world of these others". Conducting ethnographic research allows one to "tell a story of someone else's experience" (Heller, 2008, p. 250). When observing these lessons, my role as a co-teacher and administrator allowed me to participate as both an observer and a listener. My notes offered a method for capturing insights into these experiences, opening up these situated scenes and discourse (cf. "thick description" Geertz, 1973; "rich description" Erickson, 1985, p. 2). As this study asked teachers to reflect on their own teaching situation, this also included an aspect of self-ethnography (see Sakui & Gajes, 2003, p. 156). I consider these data collection methods a window to a multilayered narrative of teachers' beliefs. All of these form a core practice of sociolinguistic online ethnography, a method applied in this study.

The purpose of teacher research is not only to share knowledge with other researchers but also to share knowledge with fellow educators. Exploratory and inclusive in nature, this chapter not only contributes to research on blended learning, teaching, and its research trajectories, but it also explores how the sudden change in the trajectories changes the practices teachers engage in.

2.2 Research Aims and Data

In this chapter, I investigated teacher practices and beliefs in a Finnish language heritage school in Toronto, Canada, during the emergency switch from in-person teaching to remote teaching due to the COVID-19 pandemic lockdown. Students were not investigated. This study addresses the following research questions:

- Is there a change or shift in the focus of the practices when the pedagogical space changes?
- What kinds of beliefs and trajectories take place during this pedagogical emergency?

This chapter has a data-driven focus. The analysis was framed by the categories and themes that were found by exploring the ethnographic data, which were based on teachers' beliefs during this particular time and setting. As Heller (2008, p. 250) emphasizes, by applying ethnographic methods, one can explore how certain practices connect to the real conditions of people's lives and see how processes unfold and connect over time. Data-driven approach does not rely on any pre-existing theoretical frameworks.

The present study was based on data collected from Finnish language school online classes during 2020, selected by availability, comparability, and suitability for the research topic. Due to the situation created by the pandemic, the data collection was restricted to online only. The study used several virtual data collection methods. During the spring and fall of 2020, the school offered language classes for different age groups, as well as arts and crafts and book reading lessons. As a teacher-researcher, I had the opportunity to observe the teachers' discourse and practices by participating in classes.

Altogether, 11 parent-teachers participated in the study. All were females and mothers or grandmothers of children attending the school. All had a Finnish linguistic background and a native or near-native level in Finnish. Taru had been teaching the longest at the Finnish language school for more than 20 years. Armi had volunteered at the Finnish language school for 8 years; she was an educated primary school teacher. Kati joined the school in 2015. Outi, Sari, Raija, and Jonna had been volunteering since 2019, and Noora joined in 2018. Outi was also an educated preschool teacher. Eeva and Satu joined the school before the pandemic and did not have any previous teaching experience. Heli has been volunteering occasionally as a teacher assistant since 2013. All participants gave consent for this study. All the names have been changed. This study did not evaluate or judge teacher's practices and pedagogies.

The ethnographically framed data consisted of observers' (field) notes, teachers' written reflections, semi-structured interviews, and informal discussions with the teachers. The primary data consisted of field notes written based on online observations of 43 virtual classes (each 1 hour). A selection of the notes was rewritten into short vignettes. This enabled me to develop a "feel" for the discourses, emblems, and practices during the online classes. A selection of ethnographically informed written teacher reflections was collected. Written reflections were also collected via Padlet, which is a digital interactive notice board that can be made private (www.padlet.com). This gave the teachers an opportunity to participate anonymously. The data collected in the Padlet were included in its original form (see, for example, Fig. 1) to demonstrate the informal style of the reflective writing. The written Padlet reflections did not include comments from other participants. Questions triggered by the primary data were further triangulated in semi-structured teacher interviews. The different combinations of data enabled a triangulation process characteristic of an ethnography, and to arrive at a more faithful depiction of ongoing practices and circumstances. Because the data and methods were intertwined, they were dealt with in parallel throughout the present study.

All the teacher voices, other than my observations of the classes, were based on teachers' oral or written narratives. The combination of observations, interviews, and informal discussions offered a good way to gain insights to teachers' beliefs. Therefore, majority of the selected data for this study were excerpted from the reflections and interviews. Observations supported the selection process, and the themes that seemed to frequently occur based on my observations and that were reflected by the teachers were selected for this study. Teachers' reflections were written in Finnish or English, and translations were made by me. This chapter accepts the view that teachers' beliefs and practices are socially constructed, but it also acknowledges that my educational knowledge and beliefs—as a researcher— may have an impact on what I observed and what is reported as the research findings.

3 Teacher Practices and Beliefs during Emergency Remote Teaching

In the following section, I first explore the impact of the sudden switch from in-person learning to virtual learning on teaching and learning practices. Secondly, I reflect on how the teachers discuss these practices and what kind of beliefs and trajectories emerge due to this pedagogical emergency. In the end, I discuss the impact of this practice on the complementary heritage language school pedagogy.

3.1   Teaching and Learning Practices during Emergency Remote Teaching

Before the COVID-19 pandemic, the Finnish language school in Toronto had not offered classes online. Because personal contact and community involvement were considered central in the teaching and learning curriculum, classes were traditionally offered in-person. Before the spring of 2020, the teachers did not have previous experience in online teaching. As Outi reflected, "Switching online asked for braveness to try something that was new to me even if there was no promise of success, at least in the beginning" (*Opettajana tähän siirtyminen vaati minulta rohkeutta lähteä kokeilemaan itselle uutta, vaikka onnistumisesta varsinkaan heti alkuun ei ollut mitään takeita*). Further, some teachers did not even have much previous experience with teaching, as Sari reflected: "I had started as a teacher only a few months prior to COVID so my first reaction was, I cannot do this, it's scary!" (*Olin aloittanut opettajana vasta pari kuukautta ennen covidia joten ensireaktio oli etta "en osaa, hui!*). Some teachers had previous but somewhat negative personal experiences of remote learning as students, such as Satu, who said in an interview:

Data excerpt 1. Previous beliefs about remote learning

> I have always had negative beliefs about remote teaching based on my earlier experiences, teacher learner contact is suffering, especially if there are many students (Satu, interview)
>
> (*Olen aina ajatellut negatiivisesti etäopetuksesta, mitä olen ollut tekemisissä aikaisemmin ennen, opetuksessa kärsii opettajan ja oppilaan välinen kontakti, varsinkin jos on enemmän opiskelijoita.*)

Satu's personal experiences with remote learning relate to her beliefs about the possible advantages or disadvantages of the upcoming heritage language pedagogy. She indicates that "in remote learning, the student is not really present, becomes an outsider. In addition, it is very boring" (*etäopetuksessa ei ole oikeasti paikalla, jää ulkopuolelle ja se on lisäksi tylsää*). She believed that online learning is boring. As can be seen above, beliefs are generally shown to permeate individuals' perceptions of the world around them (see Abelson, 1986; Dooly & O'Dowd, 2018; Garner & Alexander, 1994). These teachers stepped into remote learning with many personal beliefs about it. Their beliefs were based on previous experiences of remote learning and teaching as a student, motivational ideas, and sometimes even feelings of fear and doubt.

Upon the COVID-19 emergency lockdown, teachers had no previous or scholarly framed knowledge of remote learning nor much time to reflect. As Riley (1994) emphasizes, "in ordinary life, people do not go around thinking or taking decisions on the basis of scientific reality, but on the basis of their reality" (p. 12). Teachers in this study switched online in a situation that was unprecedented and unfamiliar but deemed necessary. The initial decision the teachers made to proceed to remote teaching was made by good intention and variety of beliefs, according to which offering virtual classes was seen as challenging but also necessary for the needs of the school community and the young learners.

Richards and Rodgers (2001) assert that teachers' beliefs about language learning help them select certain practices they apply in their teaching, even when they may not have previous experience (see also Dooly & O'Dowd, 2018). Dewey (1938) writes that the importance of belief is crucial because "it covers all the matters of which we have no sure knowledge and yet which we are sufficiently confident of to act upon and also the matters that we now accept as certainly true, as knowledge, but which nevertheless may be questioned in the future" (p. 6). Echoing Armi's utterance before the first online class: "I don't quite know how to do this, but I will teach from the heart," the teachers jumped into teaching with their best intentions, with the belief that they will teach "from the heart" and attempt to do their best. Beliefs are evident in the way teachers define the learning environment or respond to instructional materials or approaches (see Anders & Evans, 1994; Borko et al., 1994). Some beliefs are based on personal experiences of the past (see, for example, Wenden, 1986), while others are based on the idea that with good motivation and dedication, one can overcome the challenges that remote teaching brings. As Williams and Burden (1997) declare, teachers' beliefs about learning languages will have a greater impact on their class activities than, for example, a specific methodology they are told to follow. Here, the teachers did not have many methodological frameworks but a great deal of beliefs about virtual teaching and learning that are embedded in this specific context: emergency teaching of heritage community children during a global pandemic.

3.1.1 Remote Learning Is Possible, Challenging, But Also Convenient

Once the sudden switch to the remote was achieved, there was not much time to plan. Based on the initial discussion between teachers, the fact that all participants had personal computers at home was crucial. One teacher wrote in Padlet (Fig. 1).

Fig. 1 Remote teaching is technically possible

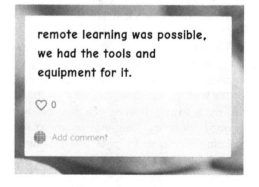

remote learning was possible, we had the tools and equipment for it.

♡ 0

Add comment

Fig. 2 Technical
challenges and unrealistic
parental expectations

Some technical challenges, and a few complaints from families. Emergent switch into remote mode teaching did not make us teachers technical experts over night and sometimes I felt that families did not understand that.

♡ 0

● Add comment

Well-functioning computers and the availability of the Zoom program, purchased by the Finnish language school, were a major motivator. The teachers who said that they did not have the hardware did not teach online. While technical availability was liberating, it also brought along somewhat new and unexpected technological challenges (Fig. 2).

Although many educators and families were suddenly facing technical challenges in the sudden lockdown of remote working, teaching, and learning, there were also expectations from the parents that the teachers were not always able to meet. Here, the teachers reflected a level of misunderstanding for the challenging situation of the somewhat unexperienced parent-teachers experienced. Remote teaching requires advanced technical skills, and teachers were not experienced in virtual pedagogy. Online teaching also brings upon other new challenges. As Armi wrote, "it was a lot of administration, much more than in the classroom." The preparations for the class, learning, and teaching material delivery and the new ways of communication needed for the virtual pedagogy are administratively time-consuming, as one teacher reflected (Fig. 3).

In an interview, she added that she feared that her internet would not work or that her family members would forget to be silent while she teaches. The parent-teachers did not necessarily have a private office space for working. Simultaneously, remote pedagogy brings about new ethical and internet safety-related issues. The teachers worried about how to create and manage safe virtual learning environments for the children. In a community-based complementary school, there was not much support for technological infrastructure, software, or internet security.

Fig. 3 Remote teaching at home sometimes challenging

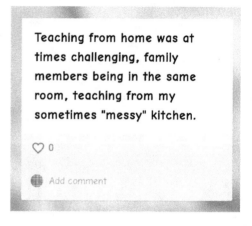

Teaching from home was at times challenging, family members being in the same room, teaching from my sometimes "messy" kitchen.

♡ 0

⬤ Add comment

Fig. 4 No need to commute is convenient

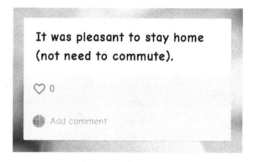

It was pleasant to stay home (not need to commute).

♡ 0

⬤ Add comment

All participants reflected that, regardless of unprecedented technical challenges, remote teaching was nevertheless convenient, practical, and motivating. Although the COVID-19 situation in general created challenges for families—they were suddenly ordered to work from home, children were not attending daycare or schools—remote teaching allowed the volunteer teachers to stay at home. The fact that one did not have to commute to the school was appreciated, as one teacher reflected (Fig. 4).

During the in-person school, the teachers travelled to the heritage school on weekends. Remote teaching at home enabled more time with family and work when weekend volunteering did not take as much time. For Eeva, who lived distant from the school, remote learning enabled more regular teaching to take place, as she writes: "For me personally, remote learning is practical because I live far away from the school; it is much easier to participate, and so is probably for students who live far." (Eeva, written reflection), (*Minulle henkilökohtaisesti etäisopettaminen on käytännöllistä, kun asun koulusta kaukana samoin kai myös oppilaille jotka asuvat kaukana, näin on paljon helpompi osallistua*). In a large metropolis such as Toronto, volunteering often means hours of commuting. Teaching from home was convenient and time-effective, and therefore was appreciated by the teachers.

3.1.2 Less Issues with Class Discipline

When teaching children, one is also responsible for keeping an order in the classroom. Several teachers reflected that teaching online brought about much less discipline-related issues and allowed them to concentrate on teaching more intensively. Sari wrote that "during normal times, a lot of time is spend helping the children stay on their seats" (*Normaaliaikoina on mennyt paljon aikaa siihen etta saa lapset istumaan paikoillaan*), and continued that during remote classes, if the participants stopped concentrating on the task and started disturbing others, one could simply mute their microphones. Tina, who taught very young children, commented similarly:

Data excerpt 2. Remote teaching keeps students in class.

We sometimes had challenges keeping the children in class, as they sometimes tried to run away to their parents. Remote learning does not have this challenge. (Tina, interview)

(Joidenkin lasten kanssa ongelmana se etteivat he meinanneet pysya luokassa vaan yrittivat karata vanhempien luo. Etakoulussa ei luonnollisesti ole sita ongelmaa.)

Because children were home and learning in the presence of their parents, responsibility for their classroom attendance and general safety relied on their parents. Teachers did not need to worry about the physical safety of the children, which allowed them to concentrate on the teaching practices. Raija reflected similarly in an interview: "I do not have the responsibility of their physical presence; if they run away, it is the parents' responsibility now." (Raija, interview), (*En ole vastuussa jos ne lähtee juoksemaan jonnekin, tavallaan mun ei tavallaan tarvitse hallita niiden fyysistä olemusta, jos ne karkaa ja on vanhempien vastuulla.*). Remote teaching means less disciplinary responsibility for the teachers. She confirmed that behind the screens, children who did not stay in class were the parents' responsibility. These reflections confirm that although beliefs are always subjective at one level, they are also based on experiences (see Alexander & Dychy, 1995; Freeman, 1991). When planning remote teaching, the teachers in this study did not think that some of the challenges they experience in in-person pedagogy would be absent in the remote mode. Folk linguistic theory can frame experience, supply interpretations of that experience, and provide goals for action (Quinn & Holland, 1987, p. 6). These observations came to the teachers as a positive surprise, and new beliefs and experiences emerged via authentic teaching experiences, proving that beliefs can develop over time. The teachers reflected that in remote learning, more time can be spent on teaching and less on taking care of the children.

3.1.3 Attendance and Participation

The COVID-19 outbreak and the transition to remote teaching had an impact on how actively the students were able to attend the virtual classes. The written reflections, interviews, and informal discussions with teachers all emphasized that the teachers observe differences in attention and participation. In general, about half of the school children opted out from participating in remote learning, while the rest of the families participated more regularly and enthusiastically. The teachers believed that it was convenient for families to find time to study when they did not need to leave their homes or commute. Participation partly increased because students who lived far away were now able to attend regularly. Remote learning was, for this reason, also appreciated by many.

The teachers felt that remote teaching allowed them to offer more time and attention to their students individually, as Heli wrote:

Data excerpt 3. More individual attention, keeping children's attention.

Children may get more individual attention during remote classes when, in the classroom, they need to wait for their turns. [...] I think one of the strengths of remote learning is that it is easier for me to get children's attention during the teaching because we are face-to-face all the time. (Heli, written reflection).

(Lapset saavat ehkä enemmän huomiota individuaalisesti, kun luokka tilanteessa ehkä saavat enemmän huomiota vuorotellen [...] Minusta opettajana etäkoulutuksen vahvuus on että on helpompi pitää lasten huomio opetus tilanteessa kun olemme kasvotusten koko ajan.)

The teachers considered remote mode time effective and personal. Remote teaching via camera offered a feeling that the teacher spoke directly to each of the children, whereas in the classroom, teachers moved around, and attention must be shared. Satu added that "real contact, imminent contact is important" (*Tärkeää on aito kontakti, välitön kontakti*); she indicated that "my own experiences of remote learning are that without the in-person contact and being there, something is missing, it is not even nearly the same" (*Mun oma kokemus aikaisemmasta etäopetuksesta on että ilman henkilökohtaista paikalla oloa, jotain jää puuttumaan, se ei ole lähellekään sama asia*). Sources of the teachers' beliefs were often the teachers' personal experience as language learners; the teachers have been previously learners themselves and remembered how they were taught (Abdi & Asadi, 2015; Kindsvatter et al., 1988). As seen here, Satu recalled her previous experiences, regardless of the somewhat positive experiences in the heritage language school context.

Attendance and participation were enhanced in other ways too. Heli reflected: "Children can perhaps concentrate better when there are no other children around disturbing" (*Lapset ehkä keskittyvät työhönsä paremmin kun ei ole muita lapsia ympärillä häiritsemässä*); but she added that "simultaneously they cannot communicate with their friends freely and develop friendships" (*mutta samalla eivät myöskään pysty kommunikoiman kaverien kanssa vapaasti ja kehittämään ystävyyssuhteita*). The fact that some students could concentrate on online learning was considered rewarding. Yet, although communication with other students during class time was sometimes considered disturbing, the positive outcome was in the friendships that were created and maintained. While remote teaching allowed for more individually targeted teaching, it also jeopardized the friendship bonds the children created when meeting in person. All these beliefs were, according to the teachers, part of successful heritage language teaching. The teachers also observed personal contact via screens to be challenging, as Sari wrote regarding challenges in addressing all the children:

Data excerpt 4. Challenges in addressing all the children.

It feels that personal contact with children is more difficult. We are trying our best to notice every child at the beginning of the class, address them by their names, and ask how they have been. This is easier in an in-person class. (Sari, written reflection)

(Tuntuu etta lapsiin on vaikeampi saada henkilokohtaista kontaktia etaopetuksessa. Yritamme parhaamme jokaisen tunnin aikana huomioida jokainen lapsi, kutsua nimella ja kysella kuulumisia. Fyysisessa koulussa tama on helpompaa.)

Satu believed that good teaching should include good personal contact with each student, and the online experience made this somewhat challenging. In addition, she stated that "it is important in teaching that the children listen" (*Opetuksessa on tärkeää, kuunteleeko nuo*). She considered teaching successful when she can capture the children undivided attention and maintain their attention. The teachers felt that face-to-face contact was important even in the remote space. For many, as observed here, beliefs play a role in what kind of actions and behaviours they apply in practice (see Alexander & Dochy, 1995, p. 424). The teachers reported that they work harder in their attempt to maintain a genuine connection. The importance of noticing every child and offering them individual attention made teaching practices feel successful and sometimes less comprehensive. When this was not always achieved, they felt less successful. The teachers' folk linguistic theories formed a bridge between their theories of how language is learned and actual teaching and learning practices.

Whereas issues related to attendance and participation sometimes went smoothly, the teachers occasionally reflected opposite experiences. Satu said, "sometimes students disappear, no connection, and they come back, no connection" (*Tunnilla joku häviää, yhteys katkeaa, tulee takaisin, ei saa ollenkaan yhteyttä*). It was challenging for the teachers to know what the students were doing behind the screens: "I do not know what they are doing there" (*En tiedä mitä ne oppilaat tekee siellä*). Some were seen as participating only partially, and the teachers thought that students were sometimes playing video games while attending classes. In addition to the students that seemed to disconnect, less active students requested more effort from the teacher, as a teacher reflected: "[They] do not participate all the time; one has to try to activate them all the time" (*Koko ajan eivät ole mukana, pitää enemmän aktiivisesti vetää mukaan*). The teachers also believed that because they could not, and did not have to, discipline the children in remote teaching in the same way they did in the classroom, they did not have control of what the student did behind the screens. Teachers' beliefs of language learning were heavily based on collaboration and interaction; active participation was considered very important and occasionally teachers' folk linguistic beliefs ignored the fact that perhaps passive listening was also part of language learning. Pajares (1992) writes that "beliefs are surrounded by emotional aura that dictates rightness and wrongness" (p. 312). Belief is based on evaluation and judgement. Here, teachers' beliefs about student behaviour and the practice it led to were based on feelings and experiences. Virtual teaching made contact both easy and challenging, which relates directly to teachers' beliefs and teaching practices.

All these experiences helped the teachers to become more aware of different kinds of learners, as Armi reflected: "Corona spring showed me that in some situations, for some children and youth, remote learning was even more effective than in-person teaching" (*Corona kevät osoitti minulle, että joissain tilanteissa etäopetus voi olla joillekin lapsille ja nuorille jopa tehokkaampaa oppimisen kannalta kuin lähiopetus*). Teachers felt that with remote learning, they could reach out differently to different kinds of learners and offer support in an individually designed manner and that remote learning offered tools to divide attention differently. Kati emphasized that this was "a practice we are not always able to do in the classroom". When the groups were small, it was easier to exercise communication and maintain interaction between students and teachers. This was especially beneficial for students who worked best in a more intimate environment, as one teacher reflected.

3.1.4 Collaborative Learning: Families Are Learning Together

When children attended the Finnish language school classes in the classroom, their parents dropped them off and picked them up after the class. Parents knew about their child's learning by talking to the teachers afterwards. One of the somewhat unexpected outcomes of remote learning is that while studying at home, children studied together with family members. Parents, siblings and sometimes even grandparents participated in the Zoom lessons. A teacher reflected on the following (Fig. 5).

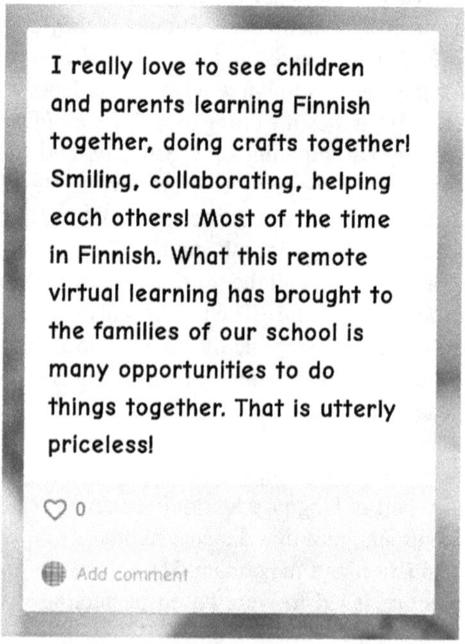

Fig. 5 New collaborative practices

I really love to see children and parents learning Finnish together, doing crafts together! Smiling, collaborating, helping each others! Most of the time in Finnish. What this remote virtual learning has brought to the families of our school is many opportunities to do things together. That is utterly priceless!

♡ 0

Add comment

Parental involvement was believed to have a positive impact on children's language learning. In the remote online space, learning suddenly turned into a collaborative encounter within and with the immediate family. Often siblings and parents gathered around the same table; sometimes even grandparents were seen participating. If the family had two children, sometimes I also observed two parents helping, one with each child. Sometimes, I observed parents joining the Finnish class and helping their children to write Finnish words. Perhaps since young children especially need technical support in navigating the online environment, many students relied on the presence of a parent. Parents might also be curious about the language school. As the reflection above shows, offering families opportunities to do things together was seen as priceless. "For heritage language learning, family support seems also important," Armi reflected in an interview. Collaborative learning was a major positive outcome of remote teaching practice. Taru welcomed parent involvement, especially to the learning practices of smaller children, and she continued: "I am sure the parents also got good advice/inspiration and the teaching can also continue at home during the week". Sometimes students asked the participating parent for help in finding words. The teachers seemed to unanimously agree about the importance of family involvement, which was related to teachers' beliefs about language learning and to the importance and significance of heritage language support even at home, as one teacher wrote in Padlet (Fig. 6).

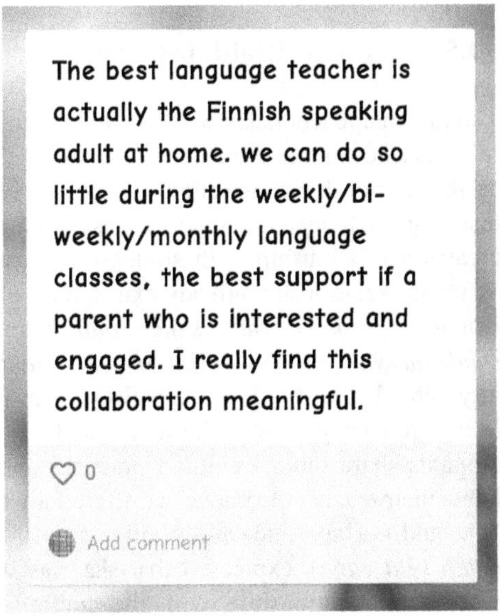

Fig. 6 Family members as co-teachers

The best language teacher is actually the Finnish speaking adult at home. we can do so little during the weekly/bi-weekly/monthly language classes, the best support if a parent who is interested and engaged. I really find this collaboration meaningful.

♡ 0

⊕ Add comment

The teachers felt that parents were supporting their work more in the online environment, and the responsibility of teaching the mutual heritage language was shared. Remote learning enabled new kinds of collaborative learning and teaching practices to emerge (see also Vaughan et al., 2013). All the teachers shared beliefs that collaborative learning was positive for the children's learning and wellbeing. It was the teachers' belief that good, and perhaps even far-reaching, things would come out of the collaborative language learning experiences. This proves that many of the beliefs the teachers express here, also considered folk linguistic theories, are not much different from known scholarly theories on language learning.

Although remote learning clearly enhanced collaboration within the families, the teachers' felt that collaboration with other students was, however, sometimes compromised, as Heli reflected: "It is challenging that the collaboration and interaction between children is minimal through the screen" (*haastavaa on mielestäni se että lasten yhteistoiminta jää aika pieneksi ruudun kautta*). What the students gained from the collaboration with the families at home may somewhat have a negative consequence on other learners. Natural contact with other young learners was challenging to arrange online. Although the parents were seen as a good support and resource, sometimes children lost some of their agency when relying on the help of the parent. In the remote learning environment, children did not always turn to their peers and teachers for support, which created feelings of disconnect. This response pattern explains why beliefs are possessions that individuals hold dear (see Abelson, 1986). The teachers believed that support at home was equally important as the interaction and collaboration with peers and teachers in the virtual classroom.

3.1.5   Authentic, Real-Life Contents

The fact that teachers knew their pupils beforehand was believed to be really meaningful. According to the teachers, knowing the children and their families involved aesthetic, moral, but also emotional connotations; this was related to their beliefs on teaching and to teaching practices, as Satu reflected in an interview: "With time, one creates a relationship with students, almost like a motherly caring relationship. When the relationship already exists, it also carries through online teaching" (*Ajan kanssa oppilaisiin syntyy suhde, äidillinen hoitosuhde, haluaa niille hyvää, kun suhde on syntynyt jo valmiiksi, se kantaa tähänkin*). In a heritage language community school, the relationship between teachers and children is sometimes close. Many are friends outside the school and belong to the same community where participants share mutual cultural practices and language. The fact that the students knew their teachers from earlier offered a well-needed continuity. Kati's utterance, "I would not agree teaching online to just anyone" (*En olisi valmis opettamaan etänä ketä vaan*), expressed that she was willing to teach online because of the established relationships with the community members; familiarity and earlier established relationships were motivating. The fact that the children knew each other was important for success. Teacher's identity emerged from the interplay of individuals' different identities, such as adult, parent member of a community, and former student (Sakui & Gaies, 2003, p. 155–156). Here, one can see different roles emerged. All the teachers believed that it was essential that everyone knew others; for children especially, familiarity is significant and meaningful. This proves itself correct in some unexpected teaching and learning practices upon which the teachers reflected.

The beliefs the teachers had guided them to practices that were intuitively and folk linguistically beneficial for students' learning and successful pedagogy. One of the positive outcomes of the remote teaching was that virtual classrooms offered participants visits to students' homes and provided teachers and students with glimpses of the lives of their peers (see also Combe & Codreanu, 2016, p. 123) (Fig. 7).

The teachers saw those beloved pets or favourite toys they have heard stories about. More importantly, language learning connected to the real-life environment of the children. When teachers asked questions about books the students were reading, the students could demonstrate by showing the actual book. Students came to virtual class with their favourite toys or had pets wandering around in the room. These objects became part of the virtual teaching and learning environment, and the teachers made use of the authentic home environment as tools for teaching and learning. For example, teachers in the groups aimed at younger students, asking the children to go to their rooms and "pick up something that is red, or something that begins with a letter 'a'", bringing a new dimension to the teaching. "There is an intimate and necessary relation between the processes of experience and education." (Dewey, 1938, p. 7). Language learning benefits from the real-life experiences. Such dimensions are beneficial for learning because these remote encounters offer new opportunities for learning. Blended learning, which is directed at enhancing engagement through the innovative adoption of purposeful online learning activities (Vaughan et al., 2013, p. 9), offers innovative ways to collaborate.

Fig. 7 Authentic teaching material

I have known the names of my students pets for many years now. Now I actually got to meet and greet them online!

♡ 0

Add comment

3.2   Teachers 'Beliefs

Teachers' beliefs became visible in the analysis demonstrated in the previous chapter, where I described and analyzed teachers' practices and beliefs that have led to them. In the following section, I describe some of the overarching beliefs that teachers validated during remote teaching. Among the teachers, there was a strong collective belief that the continuation of learning was beneficial for the students' learning and for their wellbeing; community contact was considered essential.

3.2.1   Maintaining Language Skills

When the sudden lockdown closed Toronto schools, free time activities, and workplaces, many families were left on their own to study and work in their homes. During that critical time, our teachers believed that families may had less time or effort to study and practice heritage language with their children (Fig. 8).

Language learning in the Finnish language school is complementary; there is often no homework. Parents do not always speak the heritage language at home or have time to study together, which the teacher above acknowledged. Therefore, she also believed that language learning is, at least partly, teachers' responsibility: teachers ought to make sure children do not forget their acquired language skills so that they can continue learning. Beliefs are psychologically held appreciations,

Fig. 8 Teachers'
responsibility in
maintaining language

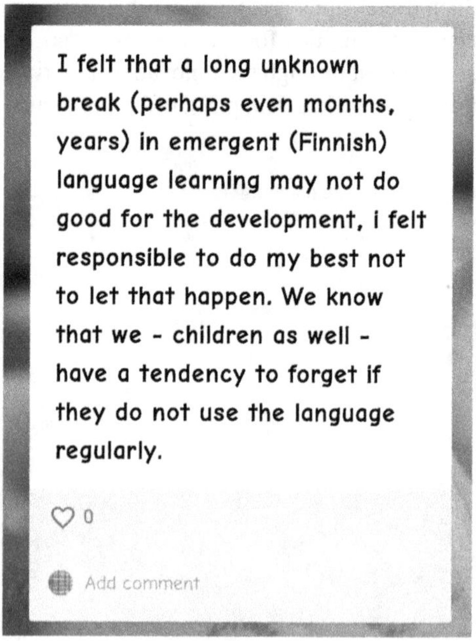

I felt that a long unknown break (perhaps even months, years) in emergent (Finnish) language learning may not do good for the development, i felt responsible to do my best not to let that happen. We know that we - children as well - have a tendency to forget if they do not use the language regularly.

♡ 0

● Add comment

assumptions, or theorems about the world that are felt to be correct (Peacock, 2001; see also Dweck, 1986). The teachers in this study believed that offering children a way to maintain their language skills was important during the time of the pandemic, as Armi further reflected: "Finnish language school functions as an important support network and motivator for families and children to use and learn language during the quarantine". The teachers shared a sense of responsibility toward the already achieved language skills and worry about the risk of losing it in case of a long interruption. As Taru wrote, "continuity in language teaching is essential from the perspective of children's language learning" (*Jatkuvuus opetuksessa on kielen kehityksen kannalta ehdoton*). In Garcia's (2009) words, this approach means bringing practices up, children up; it builds connections. Perhaps the fact that the teachers were also parents, they feel that this volunteering teaching assignment was important to them, as Satu reflected: "Finnish language school is important for me, I am very committed" (*Suomikoulu on mulle todella tärkeä asia, olen sitoutunut tähän*). Being a parent-teacher in a heritage language school is an important encounter. Families also worry that they were suddenly left alone in the support of heritage language learning; therefore, Outi uttered:

Data excerpt 5. Teacher's responsibility in maintaining social contact

I believe it is really important to contribute because through remote learning, it is possible to keep a connection to the Finnish language and to our community during this challenging time. (Outi, interview)

(Koen kuitenkin erittäin tärkeänä lähteä mukaan, sillä etäkoulun avulla on ollut mahdollista säilyttää lasten ja perheiden yhteys suomen kieleen ja suomikoulun yhteisöön tässä haastavassakin tilanteessa.)

Even here, the teachers experienced a feeling of responsibility. However, remote learning also brought about positive learning discoveries. The time at home and in remote learning was beneficial for some children's language learning path, as Armi reflects: "remote learning also allowed children to develop their skills in multilingual families where a parent spoke Finnish at least a little" (*etäopetusaika myös paransi monien lasten suomen kielen taitoa monikielisissä perheissä, joissa kotona toinen vanhemmista puhui lapsilleen suomea edes osittain*). Time together with families allowed more time for heritage language use; it also supported the work and efforts of the teachers. The practice in which parents participated in online classrooms was beneficial as they simultaneously became familiar with the curriculum.

3.2.2   Maintaining a Sense of Normality and a Feeling of Belonging

The teachers' beliefs were complex, closely related to their identities and often revealed through the metaphors they used in the narratives (see Sakui & Gajes, 2003, p. 167). Many teachers voiced that both continuation and routines were important, as Armi wrote: "Routines are important for children especially during exceptional times, social contacts during a time of virtual meetings seemed even more important"

(*Lapsille rutiinien jatkuminen on erityisen tärkeää poikkeusaikoina ja sosiaaliset kontaktit jopa etäopetuksen kautta tuntuivat entistä tärkeämmiltä*). Kati reinforced this with a commentary: "It felt important to offer children and parents continuity during a challenging time." To help families maintain a sense of normality also became a mutually shared belief, as Sari indicated: "everything closed down and Finnish language school gave an opportunity to hold on to something normal" (*Kaikki meni kiinni ja Suomi-koulu antoi tilaisuuden pitää edes jostain normaalista kiinni*). There was a shared collaborative feeling that the teachers played a role in maintaining some level of stability in the lives of the children. Teachers believed that they had the opportunity to support that in their roles as teachers. Teacher beliefs do not only deal with learning and cognition, but also the social environment in which they operate. Understanding somebody's beliefs also means understanding their world and identity (Barcelos, 2003, p. 8). The teachers' beliefs relate to the setting and environment in which the Finnish heritage school operated. By continuing to meet their students during a time of social distancing, the teachers hoped to offer a well-needed normality in the lives of the heritage school community.

Volunteer teachers were integral members of the community. They did not only address the importance of teaching a language; social contacts and community support were also important, as Taru reflected: "it is good to "see friends", get more impact, learn together" (*sosiaalisista syistä on hyvä 'nähdä' kavereita ja saada lisää vaikutteita, oppia yhdessä*). Heli wrote that "it was important that we continued teaching and being together also for the community feeling". Another teacher wrote in Padlet (Fig. 9).

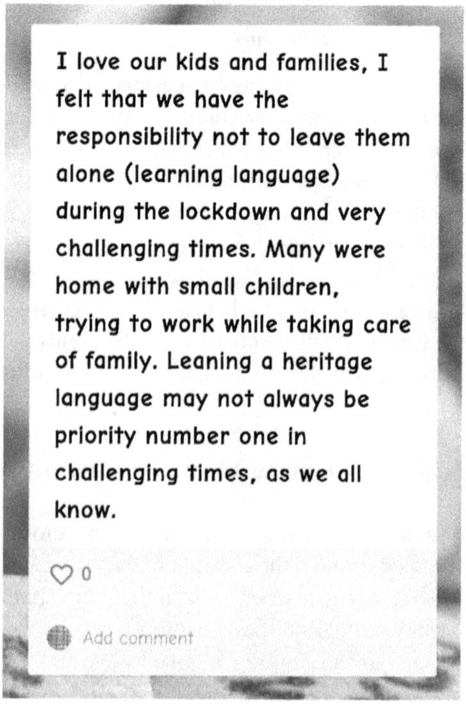

Fig. 9 Teachers' responsibility in supporting families

I love our kids and families, I felt that we have the responsibility not to leave them alone (learning language) during the lockdown and very challenging times. Many were home with small children, trying to work while taking care of family. Leaning a heritage language may not always be priority number one in challenging times, as we all know.

♡ 0

● Add comment

For many families, the school offered an important heritage language environment. Coming to school in person meant more than attending language education. The teachers reflected that virtual contact felt especially important when there were otherwise no opportunities to meet, when in-person contact is prohibited, and when children could not meet in their free time due to physical distancing regulations. Pajares (1992) writes that beliefs touching on an individual's identity or self are more connected, as are beliefs one shares with others (p. 318). This study showed that the teachers' beliefs had intimate connections to their role in the learning community. Many felt a shared responsibility to take care of the children and offer them moments of togetherness, as Kati reflected: "I know just these children, some random children would not get me involved" (*tunnen nämä lapset, satunnaiset uudet lapset eivät saisi mukaan*). Satu wrote that "these children are almost like cousins to us, almost family to me" (*Meillekin kuin serkkuja, melkein kuin sukua muille*). This emphasizes a mutual feeling of belonging to the heritage language community and the emotional connection created with it. Beliefs were based on participants' past and current interactions with the community; they are situationally specific and connected to relationships. Beliefs can be voiced out as attitudes, values, judgments, axioms, opinions, perceptions, personal theories, internal mental processes, action strategies, perspectives, and, for example, repertories of understanding (Pajares, 1992, p. 309). As this analysis showed, all these were reflected in teachers' beliefs, which originated from the fact that the teachers were also parents, friends, and members of the community.

Applying virtual pedagogy utilizes the internet in a way that capitalizes on its greatest asset: bringing people together in learning communities, where participants can interact and collaborate in a purposeful manner (Vaughan et al., 2013, p. 98). Remote education offers a way to create a sense of community among students and promote active participation (see also Petersen et al., 2009, p. 430). The teachers reported that families experienced a sudden feeling of isolation during the lockdown; however, remote learning allowed the continuation of social contact. Teaching remotely allowed our community participants to keep in touch, even during the pandemic.

4   Conclusions

In this chapter, I have discussed how parent-teachers in a Finnish heritage language school in Toronto dealt with the emergency-like switch to remote language pedagogy during a global COVID-19 pandemic, probably one of the most unprecedented and uncertain experiences in the school's 60-year-old history. In many complementary schools throughout the globe, language teaching is conducted by native speakers and parent-volunteers who, as Armi uttered, practice "from the heart". This study was conducted at a crossroads of the time when teachers did not have any experience in remote teaching but began gaining some as they kept teaching. Using online ethnographic methods turned out to be a feasible way to explore teachers' teaching practices and the beliefs related to them.

Remote teaching and blended learning pedagogy enabled communication and collaboration that would not have been available otherwise during the pandemic lockdown emergency. Remote teaching and learning practices took place in a time and space where participants were socially isolated but able to come together virtually and continue familiar teaching and learning practices. During the challenging times, not only were the teachers able to continue supporting their students, but the children were also able to keep meeting with their peers. The teachers were able to practice a pedagogy where more individual tutoring was possible. Remote teaching brought about fewer discipline-related issues and allowed teachers to concentrate on teaching more intensively. Remote pedagogy allowed teachers to address different kinds of learners. Families and generations came together in a new way to support children's language learning. A strong motivator for the emergent remote pedagogy was the teachers' loyalty and engagement with their heritage language school community. Remote learning offered the children an opportunity to maintain their language skills, a sense of normality, and a continuing feeling that they were a part of their heritage community even during a global pandemic. All this relates to different kinds of teachers' beliefs—beliefs about teaching.

Teacher beliefs are personal experiences and experiences with instruction (see also Richardson, 1996). Teacher beliefs are often stored in the form of stories, memories, or personal anecdotes. Beliefs are also closely related to teacher's various lived and learning experiences and multiple identities as well as different environmental affordances and constraints. Beliefs are based on participants' past and current interactions with the community; they are situationally specific and related to relationships. Teachers' beliefs can be changeable: teachers who initially thought remote learning cannot bring much good to the community due to, for example, the lack of important in-person contact, were able to revisit their beliefs in this unprecedented context and time and find many ways the remote learning brought positive things to the teaching, students, and families. In this completely unprecedented new situation, progressive changes in beliefs and new thinking and ideas are also welcomed. Not only do beliefs drive practices, but new practices also lead to changes in beliefs or even create new beliefs. Documenting teacher beliefs during the global pandemic and emergency switch to remote learning has also shown that beliefs can very much be fluid and evolving.

This study revealed the story of dedicated parent-teachers who did not want to let their community down during the most challenging times. It showed that strong folk linguistic beliefs can lead to good educational practice. The strong beliefs our teachers had about learning and teaching in a heritage language school provided an impeccable work ethic. Folk linguistic theories are worthy of examination due to their impact on complementary heritage language teaching. New knowledge can be based on folk linguistic explorations, and the beliefs of dedicated parent-teachers can bring relevant new knowledge to remote language pedagogy. During these unprecedented times, when a switch to emergency remote teaching was inevitable, teachers' practices and beliefs are central actors in this transformation. Therefore, this chapter offers both new perspectives for research on teacher beliefs and on the emergency remote language teaching of (heritage) children.

5   Food for Thought

Regardless of the fact that remote teaching and learning practices took place in a setting where participants were socially isolated, the participants in this study were able to come together virtually and continue familiar learning and teaching practices. During the challenging times, not only were the teachers able to continue supporting their students, but the children were also able to keep in touch with their heritage community. The teachers were able to practice a pedagogy in which individual tutoring was possible. Teaching online brought about much fewer discipline-related issues and allowed teachers to concentrate on teaching more intensively. Due to the remote teaching practice, families, and generations came together in a new way to support children's language learning. Using online ethnographic methods is a feasible way to explore teachers' beliefs and the teaching and learning practices related to them.

References

Abdi, H., & Asadi, B. (2015). A synopsis of research on teachers' and students' beliefs about language learning. *International Journal on Studies in English Language and Literature, 3*(4), 104–114.

Abelson, R. P. (1986). Beliefs are like possessions. *Journal for the Theory of Social Behavior, 16*, 223–250.

Alexander, P. A., & Dochy, F. J. R. C. (1995). Conceptions of knowledge and beliefs: A comparison across varying cultural and educational communities. *American Educational Research Journal, 32*(2), 413–442.

Amiryousefi, M. (2015). Iranian EFL teachers and learners' beliefs about vocabulary learning and teaching. *International journal of research studies in language learning, 4*(4), 29–40.

Anders, P. L., & Evans, K. S. (1994). Relationship between teachers' beliefs and their instructional practice in reading. In R. Garner & P. A. Alexander (Eds.), *Beliefs about text and instruction with text* (pp. 137–153). Hillsdale, NJ: Erlbaum.

Androutsopoulos, J. (2008). Potentials and limitations of discourse-centered online ethnography. *Language@Internet, 5*(9).

Barcelos, A. M. F. (2003). Researching beliefs about SLA: A critical review. In P. Kalaja & A. M. F. Barcelos (Eds.), *Beliefs about SLA: New research approaches* (pp. 7–33). The Netherlands: Kluwer Academic Publishers.

Blommaert, J. (2005). *Discourse*. Cambridge: Cambridge University Press.

Borko, H., Davinroy, R. H., Flory, M. D., & Hiebert, E. H. (1994). Teachers' knowledge and beliefs about summary as a component of reading. In R. Garner & P. A. Alexander (Eds.), *Beliefs about text and instruction with text* (pp. 155–182). Hillsdale, NJ: Erlbaum.

Combe, C., & Codreanu, T. (2016). Vlogging: A new channel for language learning and intercultural exchanges. In P.-S. Salomi, B. Linda, & T. Sylvie (Eds.), *CALL communities and culture – Short papers from EUROCALL 2016* (pp. 119–124). Dublin: Research-publishing.net.

Cortazzi, M., Pilcher, N., & Jin, L. (2011). Language choices and 'blind shadows': Investigating interviews with Chinese participants. *Qualitative Research, 11*(5), 505–535.

Creese, A. (2008). Linguistic ethnography. In N. H. Hornberger (Ed.), *Encyclopedia of language and education 10* (pp. 229–241). New York: Springer Science and Business Media.

Dewey, J. (1938). *Experience and education.* Macmillan: Collier Books.

Dooly, M., & O'Dowd, R. (2018). *In this together: Teachers' experiences with transnational, tele-collaborative language learning projects.* Peter Lang.

Dweck, C. S. (1986). Motivational processes affecting learning. *American Psychology, 10,* 1040–1048.

Erickson, F. (1985). *Qualitative methods in research on teaching.* Michigan State University, The Institute for Research on Teaching. Occasional Papers No. 81.

Freeman, D. (1991). "Mistaken constructs": Re-examining the nature and assumptions of language teacher education. In J. E. Alatis (Ed.), *Georgetown University round table on languages and linguistics 1991* (pp. 25–39). Georgetown University Press.

García, O. (2009). *Bilingual education in the 21ˢᵗ century: A global perspective.* Wiley-Blackwell.

Garner, R., & Alexander, P. A. (1994). *Beliefs about text and instruction with text.* Hillsdale, NJ: Erlbaum.

Geertz, C. (1973). *The interpretation of cultures. Selected essays (pp. 3–10).* New York: Basic Books.

Gilakjani, A. P., & Sabouri, N. B. (2017). Teachers' beliefs in English language teaching and learning: A review of the literature. *English Language Teaching, 10*(4), 78–86.

Harvey, O. J. (1986). Belief systems and attitudes toward the death penalty and other punishments. *Journal of Psychology, 54,* 143–159.

Heller, M. (2008). Doing ethnography. In L. Wei & M. G. Moyer (Eds.), *The Blackwell guide to research methods in bilingualism and multilingualism* (pp. 249–262). Oxford: Blackwell Publishing Ltd..

Hine, C. (2000). *Virtual ethnography.* London: Sage.

Keesing, R. M. (1987). Models, "folk" and "cultural": Paradigms regained? In D. Holland & N. Quinn (Eds.), *Cultural models in language and thought* (pp. 369–393). New York, Cambridge: University Press.

Kindsvatter, R., Willen, W., & Isher, M. (1988). *Dynamics of effective teaching.* New York: Longman.

Kozinets, R. V. (2002). The field behind the screen: Using netnography for marketing research in online communities. *Journal of Marketing Research, 39,* 61–72.

Miller, L., & Ginsberg, R. B. (1995). Folklinguistic theories of language learning. In F. F. Freed (Ed.), *Second language acquisition in a study abroad context* (pp. 293–315). Amsterdam: John Benjamins.

Nation, I. S. P., & Macalister, J. (2010). *Language curriculum design.* New York, NY: Routledge.

Pajares, M. F. (1992). Teachers' beliefs and educational research: Cleaning up a messy construct. *Review of Educational Research, 62*(3), 307–332.

Peacock, M. (2001). Pre-service teachers' beliefs about second language learning: A longitudinal study. *System, 29*(2001), 177–195. https://doi.org/10.1016/S0346-251X(01)00010-0.

Petersen, S. A., Divitini, M., & Chabert, G. (2009). Sense of community among mobile language learners, can blogs support this? *International Journal of Web Based Communities, 5*(3), 428–445.

Preston, D. (1991). Language teaching and learning. Folk linguistic perspectives. In J. E. Alatis (Ed.), *Georgetown university roundtable on languages and linguistics 1991* (pp. 583–603). Washington DC: Georgetown university press.

Puri, A. (2007). The web of insights. The art and practice of webnography. *International Journal of Market Research, 49*(3), 387–408.

Quinn, N., & Holland, D. (1987). Culture and cognition. In D. Holland & N. Quinn (Eds.), *Cultural models in language and thought* (pp. 3–40). New York: Cambridge University Press.

Rampton, B., Tusting, K., Maybin, J., Barwell, R., Creese, A., & Lytra, V. (2004): UK linguistic ethnography: A discussion paper. Accessed 24 Jan 2021.

Richards, J. C., & Rodgers, T. (2001). *Approaches and methods in language teaching*. Cambridge: Cambridge University Press. https://doi.org/10.1017/CBO9780511667305.

Richardson, V. (1996). The role of attitudes and beliefs in learning to teach. In J. Sikula, T. J. Buttery, & E. Guyton (Eds.), *Handbook of research in teacher education* (2nd ed., pp. 102–119). New York: Macmillan.

Riley, P. (1994). Aspects of learner discourse: Why listening to learners is so important. In E. Esch (Ed.), *Self-access and the adult language learner* (pp. 7–18). London: Centre for information on language teaching.

Sakui, K., & Gajes, S. J. (2003). A case study: Beliefs and metaphors of a Japanese teacher of English. In P. Kalaja & F. M. A. Barcelos (Eds.), *Beliefs about SLA: New research approaches* (pp. 153–170). The Netherlands: Springer.

Van Maanen, J. (1988). *Tales of the field. On writing ethnography* (2nd ed.). London: University of Chicago.

Vaughan, N. D., Cleveland-Innes, M., & Garrison, D. R. (2013). *Teaching in blended learning environments: Creating and sustaining communities of inquiry*. Athabasca University: Au Press.

Wenden, A. L. (1986). What do second-language learners know about their language learning? A second look at retrospective accounts. *Applied Linguistics, 7*(2), 186–205.

Wenden, A. L. (1987). How to be a successful language learner: Insights and prescriptions from 12 learners. In A. Wender & J. Rubin (Eds.), *Learner strategies in language learning* (pp. 103–117). London: Prentice Hall.

Williams, M., & Burden, R. (1997). *Psychology for language teachers*. Cambridge: Cambridge University Press.

Emergency Remote Teaching (ERT) or Surveillance? Panopticism and Higher Education in Bangladesh

Shaila Sultana

Highlights

1. The constant supervision through class attendance, systematic enforcement of assignments, quizzes and exams and a willing suspension of disbelief in students' miseries by the University authority during COVID-19 give the students a feeling of panopticism.
2. The sudden transition from face-to-face lessons to online lessons for ERT has caused anxiety, insecurity, frustration, and annoyance in students.
3. Students draw up rigorous plans to invent political technology and destabilise the mechanism of the perceived 'panopticon'.
4. While promoting technology-related resources and increasing information technology literacy among students and teachers, the university authority must give more attention to the preparatory stages and students' and teachers' mental readiness before they introduce the innovative intervention of ERT.

1 Introduction

Bangladesh, a densely populated and the seventh most populous country in the world, has been immensely affected by COVID-19. With 164,689,383 people and the current population density of 1,115,55 people per square kilometer, the Government of Bangladesh has found it impossible to enforce complete lockdown and social-distancing. With its limited resources, the Government of Bangladesh has tried to ensure the safety of people, but inadequate diagnostic facilities, health workers, resources such as hospital beds, intensive care units and ventilators in the

S. Sultana (✉)
University of Dhaka, Dhaka, Bangladesh
e-mail: shailasultana@du.ac.bd

hospitals, personal protective equipment, and little public awareness have become the major challenges for Bangladesh to tackle the situation effectively. Spatial distancing, isolation, and home quarantine have impacted on the economic sustainability of many (Bhuiyan et al., 2020). The economic instability has also affected the overall living standard. The capital market has sunk; the price hike of daily commodities has made life miserable (Alam et al., 2020). The severity of the crisis created by the economic recession, unemployment, poverty, and deaths in families has become the mediating force for worries, anxieties, depressions, panics, traumatic stresses, frustration, loneliness, and nervousness. Mental breakdowns have resulted in psychological comorbidities such as suicidal behaviors (Bhuiyan et al., 2020).

Amidst these contextual realities and uncertainties, the Government had to shut down the educational institutions on 18th March, 2020 to enforce social-distancing and ensure safety of students and teachers. ERT became the only way to foster learning during the unprecedented days of the pandemic. However, as expected, conducting online classes without much experience and training have baffled the entire higher education community in Bangladesh with a myriad of challenges. Amongst 46 public and 105 private universities along with 1500 colleges affiliated to National University, only a few private universities started ERT in March 2020 right after the Government declared the nation-wide lock down of the education institutions and public universities started functioning online for ERT in July, 2020. The private universities were quick in their action regarding ERT. On the one hand, these universities have the necessary technological affordances to offer the ERT. On the other hand, students and teachers, in general, come from affluent socio-economic conditions (Khan & Sultana, 2021; Sultana, 2018) and hence, have access to required gadgets, such as smartphones, laptops, and uninterrupted internet required for ERT. In addition, the financial obligations of the private universities are more compelling. The expenditures of private universities, including the salaries of teachers and staff, depend entirely on students' tuition fees. In order to minimise the possible financial crisis, the private universities are obliged to start online classes immediately after the nation-wide closure of educational institutions in Bangladesh. However, it should be mentioned that 'online teaching' as a term is more widely used in Bangladesh even though ERT and online teaching have distinctly different objectives in terms of learning (Hodges et al., 2020).

One of the very few universities in Bangladesh that transitioned to Emergency Remote Teaching (ERT) within the 7 days of the nation-wide lock-down is the University of Guardian Angels (UGA – pseudonym). The university authority and both teachers and students were technologically unprepared, fretted by various kinds of governmental interventions and administrative obstacles, and had little experience in on-line teaching and learning. Nevertheless, they plunged into ERT with utmost immediacy and sincerity. The sudden transition to ERT, however, may make students and teachers feel vulnerable. ERT, entirely dependent on technologies, has its own idiosyncrasies too. It is observed that online platforms do not always ensure optimal learning for students (Dumford & Miller, 2018). Its success is also determined by individual affordances, availability and accessibility and students' and teachers' mind-set and orientation with and training about technology (Tondeur et al., 2017). There are also reservations about the online environment, in general, since it is more prone to surveillance of authorities (Tondeur et al., 2017). Even though technologies are not always designed for surveillance, new technological developments (such as biometry, radio frequency identification, or GPS) support the surveillance system (Brivot & Gendron, 2011). In other words, ERT creates opportunities for an overt dependence on technology and consequently, develops more avenues for the authority to exert its power. Hence, an in-depth research with a specific focus on ERT seems pertinent. The research questions given below are addressed in the chapter:

- How do students in the higher education of Bangladesh discursively position themselves and the university authorities in relation to ERT (RQ 1)?
- What perceptions and attitudes do students have about ERT (RQ 2)?
- In what ways do students accept/resist ERT (RQ 3)?

With an understanding of online teaching practices within the contextual realities of Bangladesh and their effects on individual and collective student life, a more practical and theoretically viable solution for an effective implementation of ERT may be ensured for developing countries. It is also important to identify if the authorities of the higher education in Bangladesh are familiar with the differences between ERT and online teaching and learning – which are, even though not mutually exclusive, distinctly different from each other in ethos and objectives (Hodges et al., 2020).

2 Theoretical Framework

The metaphor of the panopticon is considered useful for researching the domain that thrives at the interphase of technology and human (Dupont, 2008) and the education system which depends on constant supervision and perpetual surveillance (Perryman, 2006). A symbolic representation of COVID-19 as the plague and a comparison between panopticism and ERT practices (which requires a structured and disciplined use of time and space and different gadgets and tools) at the metaphoric level may give an understanding of ERT. Consequently, a different kind of reality and truth may be unraveled about ERT in general and in Bangladesh in this chapter.

2.1 Panopticism – A Mechanism to Discipline and Surveil

"Panopticism" – dealt in a chapter of Michel's Foucault's book *Discipline and Punish: The Birth of the Prison* (1977) – refers to a whole set of historical measures, techniques and supervisions used for the ordering of docile, submissive, manageable, and controllable human masses and formation of a slavish disciplinary society in diverse regiments. It was developed based on Jeremy Bentham's architectural innovation, namely the 'panopticon' built for prisoners, a building with a tower at the center from which it is possible to see prisoners confined in each cell. The panopticon is the "strict spatial partitioning" of "segmented, immobile, frozen space" in which measures are taken by an authority of syndicate to keep people under surveillance, so that people remain visible and prohibited to move (Foucault, 1977, p. 195). The panopticon is a symbol of a "disciplinary society" visible and reflected even in the modern-day factory, prison, hospital, school, family (Deleuze, 1992, p. 3).

Foucault (1977) extended the idea of Bentham and identified the psychiatric asylum, the penitentiary, the reformatory, and the school as the symbol of the panopticon. According to him, the plague-infested seventeenth century Europe, the eighteenth century examination system in education, the modern twentieth century penal techniques, or the twenty-first century technologies are the modern-day examples of the old system of panopticism. A close analysis of the mechanism of panopticism in distinctly different times and spaces reveals a common feature – examination of students, workers, patients, or prisoners in order to train, subdue, and break them apart by the examination process. Thus Foucault (1977) provided the effective and efficient blueprint of the functioning of society executed by the disciplinary mechanisms of power.

The power in the panopticon may not be perceived as oppressive, however. The mechanism of the panopticon indicates an efficient operation of power by consent. Because of the presence of plague, chaos, or death, the disciplinary process in the panopticon becomes acceptable (Foucault, 1977). In addition, panopticism makes people productive – productive in completing different tasks broken down in pieces and allocated to them according to a hierarchical order. The continual completion and production create a sense of fulfilment and commitment to the deceptively independent and yet controlled tasks. For example, promises of a secured and tangible social and economic development or good grades ensuring a professional growth, fear of an unsecured career, visibility or punishment within a secured confinement of space, or an emancipation from a dire situation make it easier for the authority to enforce power.

2.2   Panopticism in Education

The top-down decision making and structured system in education may take away possibilities of creativity from teachers and students and turn the education system into a panopticon. Hence, the consequence of panopticism for the domain of education is appalling. Routinisation, monitoring, preoccupation with curriculum standard, state-controlled curriculum with teachers' minimal power and authority over it, carefully scripted controlled teacher-directed lesson, mandatory pedagogic protocol, standardised high-stake exams of students, disembodied presence of the authority in the form of instruction through school loud-speaker, and external scrutiny of teachers' performance ensure the "factorizing education" (Bushnell, 2003, p. 251). Both teachers and students become docile inmates. Hence, Bushnell (2003, p. 251), with reference to veteran school teachers in New York, stated that educational reformation with too much overt preoccupation with accountability sometimes reduces teachers' possibilities of achieving professional competence.

Teachers play a vital role for the execution of panopticism. On the one hand, teachers are under constant supervision and they go through an intense feeling of surveillance. Since they are observed throughout the year, teachers as well learn to behave according to the system of panopticism (Perryman, 2006). When they "construct their own spaces of practice within systems of surveillance", they become aware of their "own existence, and their own situation" and consequently, they manage to create their own meaning from it (Bushnell, 2003, p. 270). Hence, teachers are advised to "actively construct resistance", assuming a position of gracious submission (Bushnell, 2003, p. 270). On the other hand, teachers are "surveillant consumers" (Kumar et al., 2019, p. 145) who consider students' monitoring as teachers' responsibility. There are two configurations of monitoring in the classroom: tracking students' learning and keeping students on task.

The technology-mediated teaching techniques have become indispensable to education too. Learning management systems and monitoring tools have entered academia. However, the purpose of these technology platforms is sometimes dubious. While bringing efficiency or innovation into classrooms, they also offer greater capacities for surveillance" (Kumar et al., 2019, p. 145). Hence, the recent rise of surveillance in UK schools is labelled as "surveillance curriculum" (Hope, 2010 p. 319). With a dependence on technology, the covert curricula somewhat engage students in a discourse of control and teachers and students get into the 'culture of observation' and accept the "unremitting monitoring as a norm" (Hope, 2010, p. 319). With reference to teachers' orientation with technology platforms, Kumar et al. (2019, p. 145), hence, suggested a greater scrutiny of technology platforms.

2.3 Panopticism, Assessment and Conformity

Assessments are omnipresent in the education system across the world. Teachers seem to be the initiator of a discourse which predominantly promotes the ideologies of the panopticon. The endless assessment in a chain of systems called 360-degree assessment makes the teachers paranoid too. Hence, doubts have been expressed about the panoptic omniscient assessment and success of higher education. Hope (2010, p. 329) rhetorically asked, "Are the plethora of assessment practices within higher education actually designed to improve student academic experience, or are they instead mechanisms of surveillance intended to control, dominate and invoke paranoia among university workers?". The vicious circle of assessment continues within the organogram of the modern university in the name of accountability of curriculum and standardisation of the education system of higher education.

Even if there are agencies within the panopticon, these agencies are futile, as they are not addressed in the theoretical construct. With reference to teachers in a New York school, Bushnell (2003, p. 266) defined the teachers' resistance as the "water-cooler discourses - teachers complaining about their lack of autonomy, decision making, and authority—that did not evolve to action". Therefore, there is a necessity to explore the panopticon in relation to individual and collective agencies and resistances.

2.4   Panopticism and Resistance

The unidirectional top-down structure of the panopticon, as developed by Jeremy Bentham, is an idealized model, which, in reality, does not always exist. The static enforcement of power may activate an organic force of resistance. The activities in the panopticon may be considered the opposing force that makes the resistance possible. Because of the imposition of power from the top, panoptic may become the hub of transgression and resistance. The panopticism is, no doubt, conflicted with uncertainty, tension, anxiety, and resistances. There is ample evidence of resistance in any educational context.

The overt emphasis on the 'willing' subjection and conformity with the rules and authorities may tell a deterministic story of a polarised relationship between those who are the 'seers' and those who are 'seen'. This sort of polarised and unidirectional relationship ignores the fact that any kind of enforced submission consequences a certain level of resistance. A discrete form of resistance has been observed when Internet access was given to over 30,000 UK schools (Hope, 2005). While the authority adopted a variety of disciplinary policies, procedures and practices, such as physical observation and limited use of computer databases, students actively resisted surveillance through physical concealment. They played online games, read entertaining material, downloaded pornographic images, utilised chat-lines and opened sites, considered as 'undesirable' by staff. Three types of 'concealments were evident in students' surreptitious activities: physical concealment, virtual concealment and 'sousveillance'. While the word 'surveillance' in French means 'to watch from above', typically by a higher authority, the word 'sousveillance' in French means 'to watch from below' (Mann et al., 2003). In this form of 'inverse surveillance', people monitor the surveillors (Fernback, 2013).

Since ERT has been introduced to students without any prior notification and preparation, it is important to understand how they make sense of the knowledge. Since ERT is heavily dependent on technological devices, ERT may be explored through the theoretical framework of the panopticon. The interface of the computer screen, the automatic attendance, the systematic submission of assignments in the interface of Google Classroom, the enforced participation of students in Forum in the interface of Google Classroom, the automatic plagiarism checks by the Google Classroom and so on are critical to the understanding of the character of ERT. Specifically, when life is in turmoil with COVID-19, it is even more important to identify the possible politics involved in the surveillance and the 'willing participation of subjects', aka, students.

3 Research Design

Epistemologically the research is located within the critical tradition. The research is critical for three reasons. Firstly, as an educator at the tertiary level of education and with an experience of teaching during COVD-19, I had interests in broader power relationships between students and teachers/university authority as well as among students based on their role in ERT. I questioned the ideologies and critically evaluated whether there were any "hidden depths of exploitation, power, and disadvantage" (O'Reilly, 2009, p. 53). I also wanted to explore the use of students' languages (mixing of English – the compulsory foreign language, Bangla – the national language, and Hindi – the national language of the neighbouring country, India and one of the predominant languages of entertainment in Bangladesh) in order to identify the subjective or social dynamics that influenced their opinions and perceptions about ERT. Secondly, the findings of the research had implications for teaching and education policies, specifically during the time of COVID-19. Exploring the perceptions and attitudes of students regarding ERT, the research intended to contribute towards the betterment of pedagogic practices and education policies in higher education in general, and specifically in Bangladesh. In summary, my research enterprise was to critically evaluate ERT from students' perspectives and explore its efficacy in ensuring students' learning during COVID-19. Thirdly, I intended to problematise the *tacit assumptions about the universal validity* of ERT across the world inflicted by pandemic. ERT, similar to any pedagogic practice, is not a straightjacket appropriate for all students on board, as I personally observed as a teacher.

Because of the increased importance of the technologically mediated discourses in students' life during COVID-19, I chose 'virtual ethnography' or 'digital ethnography' as a research paradigm. The significant facet of my research was to observe participants in their digital environment and gain a deep understanding of the dynamics of their language practices within their digital spaces. For that I immersed myself in their digital spaces. By "getting close" to participants, I developed a "texture, an immediacy, and a depth of understanding" and saw their "experiences and involvements, their conflicts and their alliances, their perspectives, and their beliefs" (Grills, 1998, p. 16). I observed participants' digital environments, their use of English and Bangla or Hindi, any specific stylisation in the languages which had social symbolic significance, their interaction with each-others, expressions of solidarity or resentment, any practices of polarisation, and finally their use of various multimodal resources.

Because of ERT, computers, internet, mobile, and networking became indispensable in their life. In their own personal digital space which was not closely monitored by the authorities would create opportunities for them to share their opinions openly and unhesitatingly. I perceived digital space and their engagement with it a significant facet of their everyday life. An inclusion of the virtual site into the ethnographic research captured the complexity of students' life in a pandemic world and the versatility in experiences they were exposed to because of ERT. There was no way I could "delimit" the research "to traditional physical configuration" (Murthy, 2008, p. 849).

3.1   Sources of Data

I specifically focused on three Facebook (FB) pages for the sources of the data and these pages are run by anonymous groups of students of the UGA for the students of the UGA, in which they express their frustration, anger, and annoyance or preferences in and about education and love life in the University. Students' use of English and Bangla, manipulation of signs, symbols, and multimodal materials on three FB pages were observed. As in the 'guerrilla ethnography', following the footsteps of Androutsopoulos (2011), I surfed the walls of the FB pages and looked into the FB conversations about ERT, incorporating both micro and macro dimensions of the language: 1. the commonly accepted typical forms observable in digital discourse, which Crystal (2001) defined as 'netspeak'; 2. the idiosyncratic particular forms of language and *voices* and modes that were influenced by a variety of contextual parameters, emerging from the creative amalgamation of languages and modes of communication, which Sultana (2015, 2016, 2018) defined as 'transglossia' (cf. the section below).

Everyday 2 hours were spent on observing the FB pages. Observations were recorded using a systematic approach, analysing texts, photos, and topics of the texts/picture, and common themes that reflected individual and collective ideologies. The images and/or content were screen-grabbed, categorised, and archived. These subfolders were comprised of images and videos, accompanying notes describing the image and/or video, and the key categorizations. Since the discourses were available in public domains, no consent was needed for research ethics. However, in order to maintain any further complications and respect to the people, the names were replaced by pseudonyms and any sort of personal references were removed.

3.2   Epistemic Process and Data Analysis

In order to explore students' attitude and perception about ERT, their public posts on three public FB pages developed by the students of the university itself were collected and explored who wrote what in what ways in which situations from a critical point of view. Then the data were thematically organised, translated, and analysed through a *transglossic framework* (Sultana, 2015; Sultana, 2016; Sultana, 2018; Sultana et al., 2015; Sultana & Dovchin, 2015). They were explored for *contextual* (physical locations and participants), *pretextual* (historical trajectories of texts), *subtextual* (ideologies mobilised by texts), *intertextual* (meanings that occur across texts) references. The entextualisation and resemiotisation of linguistic and multi-modal resources were brought out to the fore, when the contextual and intertextual references were considered. Both these references unraveled the trajectories of linguistic and multi-modal resources from different locations, cultures, and changes in meanings that had been brought to them along with changes in their locations and purposes. *Pretextual* and *subtextual* references, in addition, disentangled the individual, political, social, and cultural values that influenced the choices of these resources. Seven threads of conversations from Facebook pages were selected based on the themes that reflected the ethos of the panopticon. Thus, the analysis ensured a rigorous and robust understanding of students' attitudes and perceptions about ERT. This process of making sense of the data reveals the *epistemic process* (Blommaert & Dong, 2010), i.e., the way I made sense of different bits of data, made connections, and interpreted them to come up with a newer kind of understanding about ERT.

3.3 Limitations of the Study

The admins of the FB pages maintained strict confidentiality. One of the admins of FB pages informed me on the messenger, *"Actually as it's a troll page, we have to use it anonymously. This is why our mail address and page names are this types so that people can't reach us easily. In our country, not everyone understands the sarcasm & that's why we have to do this.* " [*sic*]. Even the email ID was mysterious, the English translation of which stands something like this: 'namecantbe-shared@gmail.com'. Consequently, any information regarding students' life trajectories and the relationship between their experiences of life and their attitudes and perceptions about ERT could not be identified. Consequently, *post-textual references* (research participants' interpretation of their own data) could not be gathered.

4 Findings and Discussions

Based on the analysis of the data, the following sections show the discursive relationship that students negotiate with university authority (RQ 1), the perception they have about ERT (RQ 2) and the resistance they show towards ERT (RQ 3). It seems students consider ERT as a mechanism of surveillance that puts them in docile compromising positions. 'Panopticism' (Foucault, 1977) - as a metaphor, seems to uncover their interpretation of ERT appropriately.

4.1   Discursive Construction of the University and ERT

When the university authority considers online classes as a way to occupy students with constructive acts of learning, the students, by contrast, think of it as a thought-less top-down reinforcement of discipline and power by the authority, with little concern about students' physical and mental health.

In Extract 1, the unkind and insensitive stand of the University during COVID-19 (as perceived by the students) is depicted in 3 ways. Firstly, according to the students, the University is thoughtless and nonchalant about the deaths of people from COVID-19 across the country and in the neighbourhood of students (lines 1, 9, 20, 23, 24, & 28). Some parents also find the ERT irrelevant during the time of COVID-19, when death is looming large. Secondly, the University is shown as a Machiavellian force interested in ERT for money (line 10), without any concern about the mental state of students and parents (lines 2, 14, 15, 26, & 27) so much so that it has taken steps to fail students (lines 5 & 8), and punish them in the name of assignments (lines 8, 9, 12, 14, 16, 17, 18, 20, 25, & 26). Thirdly, the University plays pranks on the students in the name of ERT (line 3), considering them as 'sub-humans' (line 23) and docile beings ready to be subjugated (lines 11 & 17). Thus, all these statements *subtextually* refer to the University as a capitalist force against humanity, more interested in the money-making mechanism.

The University's financial dependence on students' tuition fees for its survival and existence during the COVD-19 pandemic seems to be misinterpreted by students. Students seem uncertain about the purposes of ERT and raise questions about the results of students who are unexpectedly receiving a Fail grade (lines 5 & 8). With *intertextual* reference to the discourses about the dubious act of manipulating students financially and ensuring their enrolment in the following semester given above, some of the students are, consequently, thinking of cancelling their enrol-ment in online classes (lines 6 & 7). Students, similar to the inmates in the panopti-con, present themselves as docile beings at the receiving end of the discipline and punishment. They define themselves as morons and donkeys (lines 11 & 13), with the repeated use of the word 'goru chagole'/cows and goats. With the imageries, they portray themselves as naïve and 'docile' beings (cf. Foucault, 1977) and *sub-textually* refer to the authorities as the executor of panopticism in the name of ERT.

The University is shown as the source of tension and anxiety as it transits to ERT during COVID-19. Hence, the repeated use of the word/s 'manoshik'(metal)/ 'manoshikota'(mentality)/mental, pressure, mentally sick, suffer, 'pagole hoye jai-tasi'/turning insane (lines 2, 14, 15, 26, & 27), all together, shows the outcome of discipline and punishment. Statements like 'asholei eishob pressure bhallagtese na'/ I really can't take the pressure anymore (line 2), 'mon manoshikota nai'/ I don't have any mentality to do classes and assignments (line 14), 'saradin bashai thheke atho pressure neoa asoley possible na'/ 'It's not possible to take such pressure stay-ing at home'(line 15), 'prai sobai mentally sick hoe gesi amar moto'/Almost every-one is sick just like me (line 15), 'depressed shobai'/all depressed (line 16), 'osojjo jontronay pore gesi'/experiencing extreme misery (line 25), 'bhai pagole hoye

Extract 1 Guide to language (regular font = Bangla; CAPITAL LETTERS= English; underlined=Hindi)

Line No	Name	FB status	Translation
1	Troll Page	গত পরশুদিন নতুন আক্রান্ত রোগীর সংখ্যা ছিল ৯/১০ জন, গতকাল সেটা গিয়ে দাঁড়িয়েছে ৩৬ জন, আজ ৭২+, কাল যে এই নতুন রোগীর সংখ্যা ৭২+ হবে না গ্যারান্টি কেউ দিতে পারব ?? সম্ভব কি এধরন (টেনশন, আতংকর মাঝে নিয়ে এই অনলাইন ক্লাস কনসানট্রেট করা সম্ভব ?? আমরা বলছি এই ক্লিপস কথাগুলা সবই শুনলেন ভালবাসা #প্রিয়	The number of newly infected patients was 9/10 the day before yesterday. Yesterday, it was 18 and the number is 36+ today. Can anyone GUARANTEE that this number won't be 72+ by tomorrow? Is it truly POSSIBLE to CONCENTRATE in ONLINE CLASS with this kind of TENSION and fear? Please listen to the [video] CLIP. Thank you. #Dear
2	Rakib Hasan	asholei r eshob pressure bhallagtesena Like · Reply · 11 w · Edited	I really can't take this PRESSURE anymore.
3	Asif Uz Zaman	Majak chal raha hainbhai majak Like · Reply · See translation · 11 w	Brother, we are being pranked here [Hindi].
4	Jakir Ahmed	oitai to bollam! Kono maanei hoyna eishob er ! Polapan re jor kore fail koraitese Like · Reply · 11 w	That's what I said. It doesn't make any sense. Students are being deliberately made to FAIL.
5	Zarif Hasan	Jataa obostha emne hoyni baal Like · Reply · 11 w	Very bad situation. Shit, is that so?
6	Tawhid Alam	online e course drop dey kemne Like · Reply · 11 w	How to DROP a COURSE ONLINE?
7	Saurav Ahmed	ami nijeo khujtesi Like · Reply · 11 w	I'm also searching.

(continued)

Extract 1 (continued)

Line No	Name	FB status	Translation
8	Afia Jahin	jor kore fail koraitese Like · Reply · 11 w	Students are being FAILED deliberately.
9	Ishtiak Hamid	Emon ki bashay o bole manush more jaitese ar varsity ekhon o ki bujhe class ney. Class ta bepar na but eto boro boro assignment, project tar upor 4 ta course. Emne possible na bhai.! Like · Reply · 11 w · Edited	And even our family said, "People are dying. Why is the VERSITY still taking the CLASSES? CLASSES are not a big deal but there are large ASSIGNMENTS, PROJECTS and most importantly, 4 COURSES. It's not POSSIBLE, brother.!
10	Raihan Hossain	Ora tou ase takar dhanda tey sobai koile hoite pare kisu 1 jon bolle hobe na.!	They are just thinking of money. If everyone speaks, something can happen. Nothing will happen with the request of a single student!
11	Shihab Mondal	hope kichu ekta hobe. Jodi tara student der goru chagol na mone kore.! Like Reply · 11 w	I think something will happen if they don't treat the STUDENTS as morons.
12	Samia Akhter	amdr ekhono 2000+ word er assignment dicche 😊 Like Reply · 11 w	Still, we are getting ASSIGNMENT with 2000+ WORD limit.
13	Jannat Zahan	amr tw goru chagol.! Like · Reply · 11 w	We are donkeys!

14	Shafiqul Islam	Bhai mon manoshikota nai r temon class assignment agula korar 1st a time mid samne chilo dekhe sobai try korse bt akhn r mon manoshikota nai	Brother, I don't have any mentality to do CLASSES and ASSIGNMENTS. At FIRST, we TRIED since the MIDTERM exam was knocking at the door. But now, we don't have the mentality to continue the academic activities.
15	Anika Mehrin	Saradin basay thke ato pressure neoa asoley possible na....Prai sobai mentally sick hoe gesi amr mote....apnar sathe akmot vai 🖤 Like Reply 11 w	It's not possible to take such PRESSURE staying at home all day.... In my view, almost everyone is MENTALLY SICK. …. I agree with you.
16	Sushmi Adhikary	Exactly.. Jader wifi nai tara ki korbe? Full lockdown emni depressed sobai tar upor 8 tai class 😡😡😡 Like Reply 11 w · Edited	EXACTLY. What will those who don't have WIFI? Everyone is DEPRESSED due to the FULL LOCKDOWN. To make it worse, there are CLASSES at 8 am.
17	Shoumik Bhuiyan	bhai i completely agree with this. shobai mile VC sir ar pro VC sir k mail korle hoito eta thik hobe . Ekta time fix kore shobar eta kora uchit so that they do realize the importance of stopping this pressure. Most of us are not able to cope up with this pressure along with the mental stress that is created due to this situation. 3-4 ta course er pora bashai boshe boshe kichu to bujha jai e na ulta or upor assignments and quiz diye bhora. Hope our authority would take a good decision keeping the current situation in mind.　⭕2 Like · Reply 11 w · Edited	BROTHER, I COMPLETELY AGREE TO THIS. If everyone MAILS to VC and Pro VC sir, it will be okay. We need to FIX a time to send email together so that THEY CAN REALIZE THE IMPORTANCE OF STOPPING THIS PRESSURE. MOST OF US ARE NOT ABLE TO COPE WITH THIS PRESSURE ALONG WITH THE MENTAL STRESS THAT HAS BEEN CREATED DUE TO THIS SITUATION. It's very difficult to get into 3/4 COURSES sitting at home. Moreover, there are many ASSIGNMENTS and QUIZZES. HOPE, OUR AUTHORITY WOULD TAKE A GOOD DECISION KEEPING THE CURRENT SITUATION IN MIND.
18	Imran Hossain	Hmm ai situation a class kora , assinment submit kora ,exam dauya konotai juktik na... Like Reply 11 w	Yeah, in this SITUATION, it's not logical to SUBMIT any ASSIGNMENT or to attend any EXAM.

(continued)

Extract 1 (continued)

Line No	Name	FB status	Translation
19	Sharar Shakib Dhrubo	Totally Agree with that. Ei obosthay online class, Assignment, Exam diya possible na. Like · Reply · 11 w	TOTALLY AGREE WITH THAT. In this situation, it's not possible to attend ONLINE CLASS, EXAM and to submit ASSIGNMENT.
20	Asmaul Husna	Ami mirpur 1 e thaki and now this is the most risky zone aisob voi niye asoleii oi mentality hoye uthena exam dewar Like · Reply · 11 w	I live in Mirpur 1. THIS IS THE RISKIEST ZONE NOW. With fear, it's hard to have the MENTALITY to attend exams.
21	Zakia Arefin	I do agree with you it's so hard to maintain all course together through online.Everyday we're giving exams,quiz,assignments in different course on this mental pressure.it sucks! Like · Reply · 11 w	I DO AGREE WITH YOU. IT'S VERY HARD TO MAINTAIN ALL THE COURSES TOGETHER ONLINE. EVERY DAY WE'RE GIVING EXAMS, QUIZ, ASSIGNMENTS IN DIFFERENT COURSES with THIS MENTAL PRESSURE. IT SUCKS!
22	Rocky Ahmed	Survived mid somehow pura panick attack kore exam disi But akhono iccha kore assigment extra hard korar kono mane hoyna Like · Reply · 11 w	I SURVIVED THE MIDTERM SOMEHOW. I attended the EXAMS with PANIC ATTACK. But there is no valid reason to make the ASSIGNMENT EXTRA HARD intentionally.
23	Shrijon Roy Chowdhury	I also agree they are doing too much. Amra ki manus na? Amader ki kono feelings nai? Eivabe kotodin? Manus bache thaka niye tention e mortese r unara semester ses korte chachhe.. Like · Reply : 11 w	I ALSO AGREE THAT THEY ARE DOING TOO MUCH. Aren't we human? Don't we have FEELINGS? How long will it go? People are struggling with their lives but they are busy with finishing the SEMESTER.

24	Nusaiba Binte Rahman	ki r bolbo koto r bolbo amr bashar pashei pawa gehe amr ki obostha kake bolbo Like · Reply · 11 w	Infected people have been found beside my home. Who will I tell my situation to?
25	Yasir Arafat	eke ten e jibon ses amader elakao log down korse tar upor abar verstyr pera cls,xm,quiz r tarupor assignment tao hard kore die dey etto pressure nie porasuna r assignment submit kora osojjo jontronay pore gesi…… Like · Reply · 11 w	Life is over. Our area is under LOCKDOWN. CLASS, EXAM, QUIZ makes my life painful. And even the ASSIGNMENTS are very HARD. Studying with such pressure is adding extreme misery to life.
26	Shamim Shikder	agree…. Evabe pera neya students der pokkhe asolei possible na.. Er cheye oi class a attend kora oita onk vlo…kiser relax kiser ki. Evabe aro beshi suffer korte hocche….. Like · Reply · 11 w	AGREE. It's not possible for the STUDENTS to continue with such pain. ATTENDING face to face class is far better than this. There is no relaxation. It causes more suffering.
27	Ahsanul Habib	Bhai pagol hoye jaitasi pura. r possible holtese na emne Like · Reply · 11 w	Brother, I am getting mad. It's not POSSIBLE to continue.
28	Shahed Khan	manush bache na..oi dik e online e class.amr ma bolce baba bari coila ay.onk pora lekha hoice..dhaka thakar r dorkar nai. Like · Reply · 14 w	People are struggling with their lives. On the other hand, we have to attend ONLINE CLASS. My mother said' 'Come back home. You have studied enough. There is no need to stay in Dhaka."

jaitesi pura'/I am turning mad (line 27) – indicate the role of ERT in pushing students to the verge of insanity (*cf.* Miller, 2020). The assignments are shown as a method to exert an authoritative power on students (lines 12, 18, 19, & 22). These statements refer to the mental state of students, reflecting the profound impact of the pandemic and ERT on students. These specific lexical items *pretextually* connect the present with the past, portrayed in Foucault's (1977) description of mental trauma induced by the punishment in the prison or treatment in the psychiatric department of a hospital.

In Line 3, ERT is compared with a prank and mockery. The use of Hindi is deliberate, since the use of Hindi (the language of entertainment from the neighbouring country in India) *pretextually* refers to the fact that it is associated with light-hearted buffoonery (Dovchin et al., 2018). However, students do not have power to change the situation because of the authoritative position of the University. The parents' reservation about ERT is irrelevant to the University authority too (lines 9 & 28). As their previous comments show, students are aware of the intensity of power held and exercised by the University authority in relation to the decisions of ERT and hence, they want to collectively write to the University authority (line 17). They expect that the authority will be respectful to their mental condition and take appropriate decision to reduce the level of stress they are experiencing (*cf.* the comments above made by the students).

When the University is promoting ERT with an apparent intention of supporting students in their ongoing education, students seem to have a different interpretation of their intention. They seem to consider the University as a capitalist functionary in the name of a self-centered neoliberal education (*cf.* Brown, 2015). ERT is associated with a profit based educational management that thrives in its preoccupation with an interest in education as a business venture. Thus, they indicate their frustration about the reinforced ERT, when the country is collapsing with the rapid spread of COVID-19.

Thus Extract 1 discursively constructs the University as a neoliberal capitalist space that is enforcing discipline and punishment in the name of ERT, deliberately ignoring the rampant invasion of COVID-19 into students' physical space and mental space, causing trauma, anxiety, and stress.

4.2   *Perception about and Attitude to ERT*

While Extracts 1 refers to the panopticism observable in the execution of power and instigation of mental stress and anxieties by the University authority, the following Extracts 2 and 3 indicate students' opinions about teachers' role and functions of assignments in ERT.

Standard Colloquial Bangla is usually used in the formal domains, such as education or administration – not on a troll page dedicated to fun, frolic, and laughter. In Extract 2, lines 1, 3, 4, 6 & 7, the use of the Standard Colloquial Bangla by students seems deliberate. Line 1 [One of our respectable faculty members told us to

Extract 2 Guide to language (regular font = Bangla; CAPITAL LETTERS = English)

Line No.	Name	FB conversation	Translation
1	Troll Page	আমাদের আত্মজ্ঞের একজন ক্যাকান্তি বলেছে আমকবোলে এসাইনমেন্ট তার ঠিকানায় পৌঁছে দিতে 🙂	One of our respectable FACULTY members told us to send the ASSIGNMENT to his home address by post.
2	Aminul Haque	ভাই.. সাথে একটু করিত-১৯ পাঠালে যায় না?? তুমি হয়ে আর কি 😊😊 উপহারস্বরূপ	Brother, can't we send a little bit of COVID-19?? Out of our happiness 😊 😊 as a gift
3	Shayan Rehman	একটা হাঁচির খাম হে যথেষ্ট	One envelope of sneeze is enough.
4		Eid r upohaar 🎁🎁🎁	Eid gift. 🎁🎁🎁
5	Troll Page	একজন আকাত্তি অনলাইন খাতা দেখে নাম প্রাক্তি করে এ আর তিনি আবার লেট প্রাক্তিও দেয় 🙄 #আ	In ONLINE, One FACULTY takes ATTENDANCE in the attendance copy book. Oh, he also keeps a record of students' LATE ATTENDANCE.
6	Zara Aynun Zabin	Kon Mohasoy tini? 🙄 Like · Reply · 11 w	Who is the gentleman?

(continued)

Extract 2 (continued)

Line No.	Name	FB conversation	Translation
7	Lyakot Hamid	এতো খারিহ ভয়াবহ রোগ 😊 Like · Reply · 11 w	It's such a terrible disease.
8	Rafiq Azad	FML -.- Like · Reply · 11 w	FUCK MY LIFE -.-
9	Traikul Islam Tarik	হোমওয়ার্ক কে কালেক্ট করে 😊 Like · Reply · 10 w	Who COLLECTS the HOMEWORK (referring to the Class Representative/CR)?
10	Nahian Hasnat	আমরা জন্যই ছোট বেলায় মাইর খাইছিলাম। Like · Reply · 10 w	When I was a child, I was beaten because of them (referring to the CR).
11	Gazi Raihan	Oray na maira kotha nai .mar shala ray .bainchod ra vab c****nor jaga pay na hala .desh ar j obostha ar majhay o salara home work chay Like · Reply · 10 w	There's no alternative to beating them (the CRs). Beat these brothers-in-law up. These sisters-fucker don't have any other place to show off and f***. These brothers-in-law ask for HOMEWORK when the country is in such a crisis.
12	Atif Aslam	vai re vai ogo hagay ki current. Like · Reply · 10 w	Oh.. Bro.. Their (CRs') shits are so full of high voltage CURRENT.

Extract 3 Guide to language (regular font = Bangla; CAPITAL LETTERS = English)

Line No	Name	FB conversation	Translation
1.	Troll Page		QUIZ, ASSIGNMENT EVERYWHERE!!
2.	Troll Page	Me trying to save my Grades this Semester.	ME TRYING TO SAVE MY GRADES THIS SEMESTER.
3.	Nishat Tasnim	পৃথিবীর সমস্ত মানুষ ভূত হয়ে যাক, তবুও আমরা এসাইনমেন্ট করবো, যা নাহলে আমার জীবন বৃথা যাবে 😊 আমরা এসাইনমেন্ট করে "কেমব্রিজ, হার্ভার্ড" এদের চেয়ে সেরা দেশ টেকনোলজিক্যাল মিশন জেতার মিশনকে কমপ্লিট করবো 😊👍👍 #wick	Let everyone in this country die and become zombies, but we'll do the ASSIGNMENTS. Otherwise, my life will be in vain. We will do assignments and we will COMPLETE the MISSION of defeating the TOP UNIVERSITIES such as Cambridge and Harvard. #wick

(continued)

Extract 3 (continued)

Line No	Name	FB conversation	Translation
4.	Ehsan Kabir	তাদের বলে দিয়ো আমরা এসাইনমেন্ট করতেছি। **DMP now seeking volunteers** Dhaka Metropolitan Police is set to go tougher on those who would roam aroun … thedailystar.net 👍😮 50 1 comment 5 shares	Tell them, we are doing our ASSIGNMENTS (embossed in the image).
5.	Md. Nasim Haque	When Shaitan can't irritate you, then He sends a project, assignment,presentation in your life 😜 👍😂 119 8 comments 21 shares 🙂😃😆	WHEN the devil CAN'T IRRITATE YOU, THEN HE SENDS A PROJECT, ASSIGNMENT, PRESENTATION IN YOUR LIFE 🙂😃😆

send the assignment to his home address by post.] is the double-voicing of a student who is sarcastic about the teacher's desire to receive the assignment by post. The formal linguistic features and lexical items are juxtaposed by the student's desire to send a little bit of COVID-19 in an envelope as an Eid gift (religious festival celebrated by Muslims). In line 3, it is mentioned that one envelope of sneeze is adequate for infecting the teacher with the Corona virus. Here the students seem so frustrated with the demands of the teachers about their assignments that they even want them to be infected by COVID-19. This also indicates how students want to challenge and resist the rules and regulations imposed in the panopticon.

Students are also hyper-critical about the effort of the teacher to control them, so that students are seemingly paranoid because of the surveillance. They show their surprise that the teacher has the energy to take attendance of the late-comers (line 5) which they define as a terrible disease (line 7) that other teachers should not get infected by it. Foucault (1977) mentioned that the panoptic discipline of constant potential surveillance may provoke paranoia in the population. He also identified the correspondence between the hegemonic capacity of constant surveillance and the creation of angst and anxiety. It seems that the panopticon created in the UGA has been successful in doing so (see all the extracts presented in the paper).

Students again critique the CRs. They are portrayed as the teachers' pet who engage in conversation with teachers, collect homework and assignments, arrange exams on behalf of the teachers. In this extract as well, the CRs are aligned with the authority and abused with strong swear words (line 11). The Colloquial Bangla in lines 11 & 12 put the CRs in a derogatory position too. The swearing carries *subtextual* meaning, referring to the teachers' failure in making the ERT acceptable. Bozkurt and Sharma (2020) mentioned that it is important to understand the ways teachers handle the ERT, how they interact with students and in what ways they use different media to ensure effective classes. The posts across all the pages indicate that teachers are failing in a great way to do so, specifically because of assignments and enforced assurance of attendance.

Students are over-burdened with assignments and quizzes in online teaching in absence of traditional summative examinations. In Extract 3, line 1, with reference to two characters of Toy Story, they indicate the differences in the level of enthusiasm about online assessments in students and teachers. With the depiction of Sheriff Woody, a 1950s old traditional pull-string cowboy doll, the students indicate themselves used to the traditional classroom with the regular practice of formative and summative assessments. By contrast, Buzz Lightyear, a symbolic representation of online teachers, is a modern Space-Ranger action figure with flashy white space suit which has features like retractable wings, transparent air helmet, a later 'weapon', sound effects, and various language options. As Buzz Lightyear has the false assumptions that he is a real Space Ranger and the super-heroic interplanetary trouble-shooter to win against space pirates, alien invaders, evil scientists, and other criminals, the teachers as well, falsely expect to ensure students' learning by online assignments and quizzes. They show their teachers' naivety in expecting assignments as an indicator of their learning.

The sudden shift to online classes has affected the grades of students too. Students are overburdened with assignments and they do not know how to maintain the grades they had in the previous semesters before the pandemic. Hence, the photo following line 1 depicts the futile attempt of students in maintaining their grades. The image shows the contrast between the amount of fire and water – the water is inadequate in extinguishing the fire as the amount of the effort is unable to secure good grades for students. This immense preoccupation with a narrow educational standard, based on purely quantitative testing of academic achievement, and call for accountability on the basis of a narrow range of outcomes is the reflection of a neo-liberal capitalist private education system (Brown, 2015). It seems that students in the UGA are preoccupied with CGP and CGPA. That is why line 2, with *a contextual reference* to the action happening in the image, shows students' situation with their grades which are being affected by COVID-19. It also implicitly refers to the consequences that may occur as an outcome of a panopticism.

In line 3, the double-voicing is obvious in the way the students use the image of themselves and the image of the University. By double-voicing, the student mocks at the mediocracy of his own university. Here *intertextually* the student refers to the global lists of top universities in local and global contexts and the implicit competitions in which private universities indulge in. He ridicules the attempt of the University, as it tries to change the status of UGA as a mediocre university to a better university, such as Cambridge and Harvard by making students complete the endless assignments, presentations, and quizzes. In line 4, it is also made clear with an *intertextual reference* to the news that the students of the UGA are not available for any humanitarian tasks asked by the Police force because of their assignments. In line 4, they compare the assignments, quizzes, and exams with the demonic forces directly sent by the evil when he cannot visit the students themselves. This, altogether, shows that the assignments are not associated with learning as such by the students. Instead, they consider it as the deliberate act to disempower and overburden them in order to fulfil their agenda of certain internationalisation and ranking. This practice reflects the ethos of the panopticon – disempowerment of citizens for the personal gain of the authority.

ERT is supposed to make students learn with a little preoccupation with assessment. However, all the extracts indicate that online teaching in private universities of Bangladesh has become immensely preoccupied with assessment. In other words, the ethos of ERT that ensures learning for students during the period of crisis has become another source of stress and anxiety for them. The preoccupation with marks-based learning also reflects yet another set of ideologies promoted by neoliberalism: individualism, meritocracy, and achievement for making better human capital (Brown, 2015). Even CORONA-19 cannot be a deterrent for it. The death by Corona and condition caused by assignments, students also indicate that the pedagogical goal of online teaching is no longer tied up with learning, but with individualistic success demonstrated in grades.

4.3 ERT as Surveillance and Resistance to Surveillance

Foucault's (1977) analysis of panoptic prison identified several features: a separation of spaces that ensures physical ordering of inmates; the architectural structure with an observation tower that ensures a clear vision of the inmates, and enforcement of hierarchical power on the 'observed' which, by dint of the asymmetrical relationship, is automatically created with the new economy of surveillance. In Extract 4, students refer to the surveillance mechanism of the University in the name of ERT.

ERT creates opportunities of surveillance of panopticism. The visibility of the names within the sidebars, the automatic record and depository of students' attendance create an opportunity for the teachers to observe the students, even when they are not willing to show their faces. They also confirm their attendance on the chat box. The shared link to the Google Meet makes the class accessible to the university authority. This also makes the teacher vulnerable to the surveillance of the university authority. Hence, hierarchical surveillance enables the sustenance of power of the authority. However, Extract 4 demonstrates how students challenge and show their resistance to the mechanism of panopticism.

Extract 4 refers to the practice of students using their photos as the 'blocking move' during the class and avoiding the surveillance and 'gaze' of the authority.

Extract 4 Guide to language

Line No.	Name	FB status	Translation
1	Troll page	*uff.. manusher je koto kaj thake!!* 😐 😐	uff [sound of impatience] ... people have so many tasks to finish!! ☹ ☹
2	Troll page	অনলাইন ক্লাস শেষ হওয়ার পরে, faculty যখন জিজ্ঞাসা করে "আজকে কি কি করেছো বল তো?"	When the FACULTY asks after the ONLINE CLASS, "What have you done today?"
3	Meena's voice on the video	chula jalaisi, jharu disi, pani ansi, kapore dhuisi, bashone majsi ...	I have kindled fire to cook, broomed, fetched water, washed clothes, and cleaned the dishes ...

regular font = Bangla; CAPITAL LETTERS = English

Preventing teachers seeing their faces, they also take the opportunity to engage in other pursuits of life, while teachers take online classes. With a *contextual reference* to their practice, thus, the photos allow the students to express their intentions to challenge the panopticon. In the video, the phenomenal well-known voice of Meena – the fictitious imaginary character in the South Asian children's television show launched by UNICEF– is dubbed into the voice of a young university adult. The intention of Meena is to educate children located in South Asian countries about gender, health, and social inequality through her stories in comic books, animated films. The show has been broadcast and widely popular in English, Bangla, Hindi, Nepali, and Urdu. Line 3 – *I have kindled fire to cook, broomed, fetched water, washed clothes, and cleaned the dishes* is famous for showing the amount of work that the girls require to do in a South Asian rural household. With *contextual* and *intertextual references* to the statement of Meena and by double-voicing (cf. Bakhtin, 1981), the student mocks the resistance at two levels: firstly, he mocks the teacher who may be fooled by their photos, showing that they are attending the class, when actually they have not had. On the other hand, they show resistance to online classes, indicating that they are engaged in household chores, not attending the classes and teachers have no clue about it. This reflects the practices of the participants in the research of Hope (2005), in which students were found engaged in three types of 'concealments: physical concealment, virtual concealment and 'sous-veillance' (*cf.* Section 2 above).

Similar practices have been observed in other research contexts too. With reference to the distributed structure of the Internet and the availability of observation technologies for surveillance in the modern era, Dupont (2008) showed that the democratisation of surveillance blurred the distinction between those who watched and those who were being watched; allowed marginalised individuals and groups to implement hi-tech surveillance technologies against the state or corporations and finally, encouraged the internet users to manipulate resistance strategies. They hid their online activities through blocking moves, such as the use of cryptography or masking moves. Showing the contested nature of relationship between employee and employer, Bain and Taylor (2000) showed that people are not passive; resistances are "possible or actual"; resistances are "circumscribed and individualised" (Bain & Taylor, 2000, p. 16).

Thus, this extract indicates that the panopticon is not static. It becomes volatile with moments of transgression by students. In the olden time, the panopticon represented restricted mobility within enclosed space whereas in the modern era, the mobility is dispersed and diffused, as shown in line 3. Similarly, in the olden time, the panopticon represented unilateral imposition of the supervisory power. However, these extracts given in the chapter show that students may demonstrate an opposing trend as well. A research study on the operation of an 'electronic panopticon' of a call centre indicates that there is no supervisory power that should be 'rendered perfect'. There are forms of resistance in emergence from employees (Bain & Taylor, 2000). Students may also come up with their own tactic of challenging the surveillance. Students are no less apt in challenging the enforcement of online classes. In the name of the internet inaccessibility, students turn their videos off and put their profile photos on. Some students also suggest that they do not have adequate balance to afford the internet data required to keep their videos on. Thus, when the panopticism of the ERT may enforce a conscious state of visibility to ensure the enforcement of power, students may easily counterfoil it with their innovative tactics.

5   Conclusion

The chapter shows that students seem unprepared and unwilling to accept online teaching which they perceive as the reinstatement of the normative model of education in Bangladesh. According to students, teachers transfer the traditional teaching approaches to the online platforms without any evolution in teaching methodologies. The sudden transition from face-to-face lessons to online lessons for ERT has also caused anxiety, insecurity, frustration, and annoyance in students. ERT is the reinstatement of the normative model of education in Bangladesh, according to students' perception. It is compared with an enclosed space – segmented, immobile, and frozen, ensuring a strict spatial partitioning of students from the reality of their life, distorted by the possibilities of death, loss, uncertainty and insecurity. ERT may also be perceived as the neoliberal marketisation of education that ensures the economic benefits and the capillary functioning of capitalism in the university (*cf.* Brown, 2015). The lexical items associated with pandemic and pandemic-related restrictions such as spatial distancing, isolation, lock-down, home quarantine, and the possible impacts of COVID-19 on mental health (e.g., depression, anxiety, panic, and traumatic stress) become sources of pun, sarcasm, and double-voicing – which in general, show students' reservation about ERT.

Students create resistance and express their subversion in yet another digital space which they consider as a counter force against the systematic teaching-learning endeavor. On these pages, they also share ways of subverting the constant surveillance of the teacher and authority. While the major effect of the panopticon is to induce a state of conscious and permanent visibility, students work out a way of hiding techniques. Students work out the map collectively to identify the strengths and weaknesses of the system, alter their behaviour and ensure their own victory avoiding physical confrontation with the authority. They draw up rigorous plans to counteract the hegemony of the authority. Consequently, they invent new mechanisms in their third space in order to identify political technology to survey the mechanisms of the panopticon. Teachers seem disorganised, but organised in overburdening students with systematic enforcements of assignments, quizzes and exams.

6   Food for Thought Regarding Teaching and Learning

The straight-jacket of online teaching and testing needs to be customised, considering the contextual realities of students and teachers. More innovative interventions and intensive preparatory stages for students and guardians are needed, so that they do not consider ERT as a disciplinary 'panoptic machine' generating tyranny. While promoting technology-related resources and increasing information technology literacy among students and teachers, the university authority must give more attention to students' and teachers' mental preparedness. Only then they may see ERT as a platform for intellectual freedom and effective engagement with the learning process.

Acknowledgement   The book chapter is based on a paper entitled "Emergency Remote Teaching or Surveillance? Panopticism and Higher Education in Bangladesh" presented by the author as an invited keynote speaker at the Department of English, Jahangirnagar University, Bangladesh on 5th December, 2020.

References

Alam, M. S., Alam, M. Z., Nazir, K. N. H., & Bhuiyan, M. A. B. (2020). The emergence of novel coronavirus disease (COVID-19) in Bangladesh: Present status, challenges, and future management. *Journal of Advanced Veterinary and Animal Research, 7*(2), 198–208.

Androutsopoulos, J. (2011). Introduction: Sociolinguistics and computer-mediated communication. *Journal of SocioLinguistics, 10*(4), 419–438.

Bain, P., & Taylor, P. (2000). Entrapped by the 'electronic panopticon'? Worker resistance in the call centre. *New Technology, Work and Employment, 15*(1), 2–18.

Bakhtin, M. (1981). *The dialogic imagination: Four essays* (C. Emerson & M. Holquist, Trans.). Austin: University of Texas.

Bhuiyan, A. I., Sakib, N., Pakpour, A. H., Griffiths, M. D., & Mamun, M. A. (2020). COVID-19-related suicides in Bangladesh due to lockdown and economic factors: Case study evidence from media reports. *International Journal of Mental Health and Addiction*, 1–6.

Blommaert, J., & Dong, J. (2010). *Ethnographic fieldwork: A beginner's guide*. Multilingual Matters.

Bozkurt, A., & Sharma, R. C. (2020). Emergency remote teaching in a time of global crisis due to Corona virus pandemic. *Asian Journal of Distance Education, 15*(1), 1–6.

Brivot, M., & Gendron, Y. (2011). Beyond panopticism: On the ramifications of surveillance in a contemporary proferssional setting. *Accounting, Organizations and Society, 36*(3), 135–155.

Brown, W. (2015). *Undoing the demos: Neoliberalism's stealth revolution*. MIT Press.

Bushnell, M. (2003). Teachers in the schoolhouse panopticon: Complicity and resistance. *Education and Urban Society, 35*(3), 251–272.

Crystal, D. (2001). *Language and the internet*. Cambridge University Press.

Deleuze, G. (1992). Postscript on the societies of control. *October, 59*, 3–7.

Dovchin, S., Pennycook, A., & Sultana, S. (2018). *A popular culture, voice and linguistic diversity - young adults on- and offline*. Palgrave Macmillan.

Dumford, A. D., & Miller, A. L. (2018). Online learning in higher education: Exploring advantages and disadvantages for engagement. *Journal of Computing in Higher Education, 30*, 452–465. https://doi.org/10.1007/s12528-018-9179-z

Dupont, B. (2008). Hacking the panopticon: Distributed online surveillance and resistance. *Surveillance and Governance: Sociology of Crime Law and Deviance, 10*, 257–278.

Fernback, J. (2013). Sousveillance: Communities of resistance to the surveillance environment. *Telematics and Informatics, 30*(1), 11–21.

Foucault, M. (1977). *Discipline and punish: The birth of the prison*. Pantheon.

Grills, S. (1998). *Doing ethnographic research: Fieldwork settings*. Sage Publications.

Hodges, C., Moore, S., Lockee, B., Trust, T., & Bond, A. (2020). The difference between emergency remote teaching and online learning. *Educause Review, 27.* https://er.educause.edu/articles/2020/3/the-difference-between-emergency-remote-teaching-and-online-learning

Hope, A. (2005). Panopticism, play and the resistance of surveillance: Case studies of the observation of student Internet use in UK schools. *British Journal of Sociology of Education, 26*(3), 359–373.

Hope, A. (2010). Student resistance to the surveillance curriculum. *International Studies in Sociology of Education, 20*(4), 319–334.

Khan, M. H., & Sultana, S. (2021). A critical exploration of private university students' approach toward English as a medium of instruction in Bangladesh. In *The Routledge handbook of English education in Bangladesh*. Routledge.

Kumar, P. C., Vitak, J., Chetty, M., & Clegg, T. L. (2019). The platformization of the classroom: Teachers as surveillant consumers. *Surveillance & Society, 17*(1/2), 145–152.

Mann, S., Nolan, J., & Wellman, B. (2003). Sousveillance: Inventing and using wearable computing devices for data collection in surveillance environments. *Surveillance & Society, 1*(3), 331–355.

Miller, E. D. (2020). The COVID-19 pandemic crisis: The loss and trauma event of our time. *Journal of Loss and Trauma, 25*(13), 1–13.

Murthy, D. (2008). Digital ethnography: An examination of the use of new technologies for social research. *Sociology, 42*(5), 837–855.

O'Reilly, K. (2009). *Key concepts in ethnography*. Sage Publication.

Perryman, J. (2006). Panoptic performativity and school inspection regimes: Disciplinary mechanisms and life under special measures. *Journal of Education Policy, 21*(2), 147–161.

Sultana, S. (2015). Transglossic language practices: Young adults transgressing language and identity in Bangladesh. *Translation and Translanguaging in Multilingual Contexts, 1*(2), 202–232.

Sultana, S. (2016). Language and identity in virtual space. *Journal of Asian Pacific Communication, 26*(2), 216–237.

Sultana, S. (2018). Language practices and performances of identity of young adults within spaces of a private university in Bangladesh. *Bangladesh English Language Teachers Association Journal, 2*, 1–28.

Sultana, S., & Dovchin, S. (2015). Popular culture in transglossic language practices of young adults. *International Multilingual Research Journal, 11*(2), 67–85.

Sultana, S., Dovchin, S., & Pennycook, A. (2015). Transglossic language practices of young adults in Bangladesh and Mongolia. *International Journal of Multilingualism, 12*(1), 93–108.

Tondeur, J., Van Braak, J., Ertmer, P. A., & Ottenbreit-Leftwich, A. (2017). Understanding the relationship between teachers' pedagogical beliefs and technology use in education: A systematic review of qualitative evidence. *Educational Technology Research and Development, 65*(3), 555–575.

Part VII
Researcher Corner: Social Media Research

The Generative Affects of Social Media Scroll-Back Interviews: In Conversation with Spanish as a World Language Teachers During the COVID-19 Lockdown in Australia

Danielle H. Heinrichs

Highlights

- Social media scroll-back method can work as a rapid rescoping method for research with world language educators during emergency remote teaching circumstances
- Incorporating social media into emergency remote teaching research with world language educators also invites alternative data beyond language/linguistics, thus, opening up the possibilities for exploring the personal/political/professional responses of world language educators to emergency remote teaching
- In conversation with Spanish as a world language teachers (SWLTs) during the COVID-19 pandemic in Australia, social media scroll-back generated insights into the ways in which the technology and repositioning of participants as researchers could affect agency, hesitation, avoidance, and shame.

1 In Search of Social Media in Emergency World Language Education Research

This chapter has emerged from the rapid rescoping of a project initially hoping to use action research to explore pedagogical approaches to response-able Spanish language practices in classrooms with Spanish as a world language teachers (SWLTs) in secondary schools in Queensland, Australia. The idea of response-able here refers to "the capacity to respond, response-ability" (Haraway, 2016, p. 78) and also acknowledges that "we are not all response-able in the same ways" (Haraway,

D. H. Heinrichs (✉)
University of Queensland, Brisbane, Australia
e-mail: d.jeffery@uq.net.au

J. Chen (ed.), *Emergency Remote Teaching and Beyond*,
https://doi.org/10.1007/978-3-030-84067-9_17

2016, p. 29). In March 2020, SWLTs', and my capacity to engage in action research was disrupted when a government mandate restricted research on school sites as teaching turned remote in response to the emergency circumstances of the COVID-19 pandemic. Thus, I turned my attention to rescoping the project by searching for a suitable method for working with SWLTs as part of emergency remote world language education (ER WLE) research; I began by exploring WLE methods more generally before digging into methods catering to emergency scenarios and finally, drilling down to the digital methods using social media that seemed most accessible at the time.

The search for method in WLE research is inherently complex given the interdisciplinary nature of the field. It is simultaneously entangled with both cognitive and social approaches from within and beyond the field (King et al., 2017). This is further complicated by debates about where to focus the data collection and analysis that guide the choice of method: at the macro or micro level? Yet the distinction between these the categories of macro and micro has been contested by Warriner (2012) who argues that these terms are not universally understood nor clear despite the presumption that macro approaches focus on broader societal issues and micro approaches on linguistic features (King et al., 2017). However, the recent sociolinguistic turn in WLE research acknowledges the need to develop methods which "bridge what is increasingly seen as a problematic and unproductive dichotomy between micro and macro" (King et al., 2017, p. xi). While much research has sought to attend to this call in recent years, the current context of COVID-19 in 2020 has highlighted the need to consider an additional layer of complexity in selecting method in WLE research: emergency and crisis situations that generate remote teaching responses. Here, remote teaching is broadly defined as methods of online and/or distance teaching and learning necessitated by emergency and crisis situations.

In the emerging field of emergency WLE, emergencies are defined as crisis circumstances (Hodges et al., 2020). While there is no singular or common definition of emergency in this context, a number of descriptions from the broader field of linguistics and education have emerged. One example surface from the field of crisis translation studies, in which crisis situations are extended beyond global pandemics. Drawing on the notion of "cascading disasters" from Pescaroli and Alexander (2015, p. 62), O'Brien and Federici (2019, p. 130) situate the notion of "crisis as a threatening condition with disasters as a triggering event of different magnitude and duration" in the linguistic arena. Looking at the UNESCO (2019) description of education in emergencies, there is further acknowledgement that pandemics, conflict, social unrest, and disasters caused by natural hazards warrant the need for emergency education. Additionally, the United Nations General Assembly Resolution (2010) on *The right to education in emergency situations* references additional emergency circumstances such as sexual violence, trafficking, and child labour; specifically in the Australian context, the Department of Foreign Affairs and Trade (2018) refers to emergencies situations as those arising from disasters including man-made disasters, drought, genocide and displacement. Taken together, these descriptions and definitions of emergency in the fields of linguistics and education point to a wide array of interconnected and complex factors that shape an emergency, suggesting that emergency WLE may take place in any one of these. What is less clear in the literature, however, is how (and if) researchers should and can approach WLE research in the midst of the aforementioned emergency circumstances. Given issues with access during such crises, digital means of research such as social media have become an increasingly popular avenue in WLE research.

Since the emergence of social media platforms over the past two decades, these platforms have continued to infiltrate users personal and professional lives. Social media users have increasingly turned to these platforms to make use of functions beyond the traditional social networking related to sharing photos, pictures and status updated. More recently, there has been a rise specifically in the use of social media for news sharing and fact-checking (Clayton et al., 2019; Dubois et al., 2020; Oeldorf-Hirsch et al., 2020), crisis communication (Maal & Wilson-North, 2019; Malecki et al., 2020; Xie et al., 2017; Xu, 2020) as well as a range of teaching and learning activities (Carpenter & Harvey, 2020; Manca, 2020; Xue & Churchill, 2020). Moreover, according to Statista (2020) there are currently 2.7 billion monthly users on Facebook. As a result, world language researchers have begun to question the possibilities social media in particular might hold as not only a source of data but also as a space/place for method.

Existing studies incorporating social media as method in world language research tend to frame social media as a source of data without specifically referencing its role as method. Commonly, studies have explored learner attitudes towards various social media sites using such as Facebook (Sirivedin et al., 2018), Twitter (Taskiran et al., 2018), as well as YouTube and Google+ (Villafuerte & Romero, 2017) using questionnaires. Social network analyses (SNA) of social media sites (in combination with surveys) have been conducted in a number of studies in attempts to map the complex social relationships that shape learning in the context of online networks. To illustrate, this approach has been applied to better understand peer-to-peer interactions (Peeters, 2019), or learners' grammatical accuracy (Paul & Friginal, 2019). Studies have also focused on the potential for social media sites in the development of learners' foreign language literacy skills through interactions with native speakers via thematic analysis of hashtags on Twitter (Solmaz, 2017). Whilst these studies have primarily been concerned with learners, other studies exploring the interaction of world language educators and social media generally explore professional development and reflective practice. The role of social media sites for building communities of practice and staying in touch after professional development sessions or as a form of engaging with the field on a regular basis for world language educators has also been explored (Carpenter & Krutka, 2015). For instance, reflective practice through the implementation of social media tools in WLE has been explored using traditional case study methodology (Xue & Churchill, 2020); however, the more recent poststructural/critical turn in world language research has also seen a keen interest in exploratory methods such as critical autoethnography combined with social media emerge. As one example, Kasparek and Turner (2020) incorporate Facebook messenger communication as part of reflective practice in a duoethnographic approach. Seemingly absent from these studies are suggestions for how to approach WLE research in times of crisis when additional ethical considerations around social distancing, the burden of participation, and access to participants must be taken into further consideration. Addressing response-able languaging is of particular relevance for SWLTs given the increasing demand for Spanish language skills worldwide combined with the underlying ethical issues associated with teaching and learning a colonial language in another colonial context (Heinrichs, 2020, 2021).

In this chapter, I propose a method for ER WLE research in an attempt to address some of the underlying restraints and situated ethical considerations for this context. In doing so, I explore social media scroll-back interviews through a diffractive reading highlighting the affects this method generates in a project exploring response-able Spanish languaging practices. In this paper, the term response-able refers to "the capacity to respond" (Haraway, 2016) in contrast to typical understandings of responsible as "morally responsible for one's behaviour" (Oxford Dictionary, 2021). It also is worth noting here that the understanding of affect I refer to moves beyond psychologised affect as specific feelings or emotions including motivation, grit, anxiety or confidence as commonly referred to in existing studies on online language education (Arnold, 2019; Besnier, 1990; Lee & Chen Hsieh, 2019; Reinders & Wattana, 2014; Tananuraksakul, 2015). Instead, I refer to the turn to affect in research which envisages a much broader notion of affect as the performative, bodily, personal encounters emerging from intra-actions of material-discursive, human and more-than—human (Ahmed, 2014; Haraway, 2016; Riley, 2005). Such a turn remains open to emotions and feelings and also invites examples such as fear, shame, disgust as entangled with embodied reactions/responses with agency and the more-than-human including technology. Hence, this approach serves the dual purpose of showcasing how social media data can diffract traditional discourse-based data and uncover the underexplored affective responses of SWLTs as an example of more ethico-onto-epistemological (Barad as cited in, Heinrichs, 2020) research during times of crisis.

2   Why Social Media in ER WLE Research Now?

More than just easing loneliness, such digital tools offer affordances for education in an emergency. As many K-12 schools rapidly transition to remote online forms of teaching and learning, further distancing students from classmates, friends, teachers and public life, social media offer benefits (Greenhow & Chapman, 2020, p. 342)

Approximately 80% of Australians between 16 and 64 years of age access Facebook on a monthly basis with those most likely to do so being females between 25 and 44 years of age (Hootsuite, 2020) who also constitute the largest cohort of WLEs in Australia (Weldon et al., 2014). Furthermore, use of social media such as Facebook has been shown to peak during crisis akin to the 2020 COVID-19 pandemic resulting in its use to engage students in civic participation and community building particularly of students engaged in remote education (Greenhow & Chapman, 2020). Given the additional complexities of misinformation or "fake news" during crises, the aforementioned skills seem particularly important. However, the responses of WLEs is largely ignored, possibly due to the perception that the informal language use and content on social media is not appropriate in educational spaces (Galvin & Greenhow, 2020). Research with social media such as Facebook seems even more relevant given the practical restraints on WLE researcher in 2020. This chapter outlines a project that took place during the first half of 2020 during the COVID-19 pandemic in Australia. This meant that while there were a number of activities I was interested in incorporating into the project, those available to me and those I was capable of responding to were situated in the unique circumstances of government lockdowns, social distancing laws and, as of March 31st, a mandate from the Queensland Department of Education that research "in state schools or other educational sites be postponed until further notice" (Queensland Government, 2020). The ease of accessibility of social media, therefore, provides an advantage in this situation.

These unique circumstances led me to wonder if the context of remote education during COVID-19 was increasing the engagement of our largest cohort of WLEs with Facebook, and if we are aware of the potential for this social media networking site to foster civic participation and community building, what might ER WLE research that taps into this look like? What kind of methods(ology/ies) might help ER WLE research address this? And in what ways might WL educators respond to ER WLE research with social media? These questions and concerns have guided the project beginning with a consideration of what this project might look like using diffracting as theory while allowing me to continue exploring response-able Spanish languaging practices.

3 A Guiding Light: Diffracting Data with Theory

Like the diffraction patterns illuminating the indefinite nature of boundaries—displaying shadows in 'light' regions and bright spots in 'dark' regions—the relation of the social and the scientific is a relation of 'exteriority within' (Barad, 2003, p. 803).

The above description of diffraction has guided my research in this project about response-able Spanish languaging practices and attempts to address my research questions here asking: What kind of methods(ology/ies) might help ER WLE research address the unique circumstances of COVID-19? An admittedly complex concept developed by feminist philosophers Donna Haraway and Karen Barad with backgrounds in primatology and quantum physics respectively, it may seem an unlikely companion in ER WLE research. Yet I saw the relation between the social and the scientific increasingly important for exploring the personal/professional lives of SWLTs during COVID-19 especially, so that I could avoid getting stuck in positivist approaches which sought to uncover patterns of sameness in data and were wary of differences. Hence, I found solace in Karen Barad (2007) and Donna Haraway's (2016) work on diffraction which encourages thinking about "patterns of difference and their entanglements with matter and meaning" (Barad, 2007, p. 29) and the "effects of these differences" (Haraway, 2016, p. 90). In other words, diffraction, as opposed to reflection/reflexivity which focuses on sameness and correction, attempts to map the interferences of multiple differences (Barad, 2007), but in doing so requires different ways of doing ER WLE research and different ways of thinking about what counts as valid ER WLE research data. For these reasons, this concept supports work that is open to more "inventive provocations" (Dolphijn & Tuin, 2012, p. 50) and transdisciplinary rather than interdisciplinary inquiry (Bozalek & Zembylas, 2017). This could include WLE from different languages working together or with those from other disciplines and looking beyond what is traditionally considered linguistic data.

Furthermore, allowing myself to be guided by the concept of diffraction has forced me to question "what counts as 'data'" (Benozzo & Gherardi, 2019, p. 45) and focus less on "what is and more on…what might be and what is coming into being" (St. Pierre, 2019, p. 4). Although it is impossible to name and list the specific types of alternative data that might emerge when guided by the concept of diffracting, I have found it helpful to refer to the prior research for inspiration and examples. Some of the earliest work in this regard relates to what St. Pierre (1997) refers to as "transgressive data"; she identifies these as: emotional data, dream data, sensual data and response data and explains how they are out-of-category in that they move beyond words and/or language. Further, transgressive data challenge the notion that data require words to be interpreted by looking for those data which escape language (St. Pierre, 1997).

More recently, scholars have added further suggestions to the pool of potential alternative data with similar more-than-language qualities. Benozzo and Gherardi (2019) conceptualise 'not-yet' data as those which appear in the shadows of research and may be described as illegible, wonderous, disorienting, hesitant and worn out. Mayes and Wolfe (2018) introduce shame-interest whereby educational researchers embrace their interest in shameful and/or shame inducing research as potential avenue for ethical research practice. This ties in with the affective turn in data promoted by feminist scholars such as Sara Ahmed (2004) which is continually being reimagined in various disciplines as everything from affective trouble (contradiction, disattachment, blame) in studies of social semiotics (Gafter & Milani, 2020) to embodied affect in gender studies (fear, loss, hope) (Fullagar & Pavlidis, 2020). I also see the discussion by Lupton et al. (2018) about the ways in which senses, space, affect, and affordances contextualise personal data generated by digital devices interact as useful for the ways in which personal data could potentially entangle emotion, affect and social media in ER WLE research. Considering the potential for diffraction to expose alternative data, I then needed a method for doing so that also took the lockdown context into consideration and provided opportunities for more-than-language data to emerge.

# 4	Diffracting Method: Social Media Scroll-Back Interviews

I started by thinking over the methods I had come across while studying, attending conferences and in my reading. Initially, I considered simply conducting online interviews via Zoom. Yet the more I considered this, the more I came to see how this method may not dig into the personal and professional examples of response-able Spanish languaging practices I hoped to explore. At this point, I thought back to December 2019, where at the Cultural Studies Association of Australasia Conference, a colleague suggested we attend a panel in which one of the presenters would be describing her Honours project using an innovative approach we had never heard of before: *scroll-back method*. We came to learn that scroll-back method was exactly what it sounded like: "a qualitative research method that works within interviews whereby a researcher and participant 'scroll back' through the social media history of the participant" (Robards & Lincoln, 2019, p. 1). Initially, I was unconvinced by the simplicity of scroll-back method; however, after seeing the Honours student present, where she combined the method with Instagram posts and new material theory in complex, innovative and provocative ways to explore relationality with/to social media, I was interested in exploring the potential ways that scroll-back method could highlight different data in my project (Kamberelis et al., 2018). However, it was not until March 2020 amidst the looming lock-down in Australia due to COVID-19, I became increasingly aware that I might need a suitable rapid research method given the emergency health situation for my project exploring response-able Spanish languaging practices from the perspective of SWLTs. Thus, the simplicity of social media scroll-back method became one its greatest strengths in this context. This was largely due to the method requiring very little training, being easily accessible from geographically diverse locations and a source of longitudinal and trans-semioticizing data as described by Wu and Lin (2019, p. 253) as "language as entangled with many other semiotics (e.g. visuals, gestures, bodily movement) in meaning-making...intimate multi-verbal/multi-modal/multisensory entanglement". At this point, I incorporated scroll-back method into my project through nine separate one-on-one interviews via Zoom during which SWLTs shared their screens and paused to narrate any posts related to response-able Spanish languaging practices. On average the interviews lasted 90 min, thus, we scrolled past innumerable posts. Therefore, for practical reasons, the number of posts was not tracked.

Although Robards and Lincoln (2019) outline a series of steps which can be followed to conduct scroll-back method interviews, I used their advice as a guide and began by contacting SWLTs through a language teachers' Facebook group as this ensured anyone I was interested in working with would have a Facebook account and would be able to take part in a one-on-one interview using this. After reaching out to SWLTs through the Facebook group, a number expressed interest in the one-on-one interviews but also concern that they did not have what I was looking for on their Facebook timeline, namely because they did not think they used Spanish on their timelines. They later explained that this was due to living in Australia, or for many, because it was not their first language and many of their Facebook friends did not understand Spanish, so they did not want to alienate anyone; although one SWLT, Alejandro,[1] proudly exclaimed, "it usually doesn't bother me if I'm posting in another language and it's like, yeah, if they can translate it or if it comes up translated then that's fine but if they – if it doesn't, too bad, yeah, too bad, that's so sad". However, mostly, it took some explanation to ensure SWLTs who were interested understood that I was not hoping to see *only* Spanish, but rather I was hoping for SWLTs to narrate examples of response-able Spanish languaging practice as they appeared on their Facebook timelines. These examples did not have to use Spanish and examples beyond their Facebook timelines were also welcomed. Additionally, SWLTs could choose to focus on posts related to language teaching, different uses of language or school related responsibilities, this was not explicitly the focus. Instead, I left it up to the SWLTs to decide which posts contained content of relevance to response-able Spanish languaging although I also asked them to stop on posts I considered relevant too. Figure 1 highlights examples from my own Facebook timeline of the types of posts that could be narrated including some related to alternative types of language usage such as translanguaging (using multiple linguistic and semiotic features (García & Wei, 2013)), Australian Sign language, British sign language as well as social and political issues pertaining to identity, sexuality, and corruption. The examples in Fig. 1 also indicate how posts might link to other social media platforms such as TikTok or YouTube in the hope of inviting transgressive and alternative data into our conversations and the project.

After convincing nine SWLTs that their timeline posts would be suitable, I was able to organize a time outside of school hours to have the one-on-one interviews using Zoom from the comfort of their homes. Given my interest in SWLT's conceptions of response-able languaging practices, the demographic data was of less interest. However, for those interested, I spoke with nine teachers across Queensland, New South Wales, and South Australia. The majority had learned Spanish later in life when at university although three grew up in Spanish speaking countries – Spain and El Salvador. Those who had not grown up in a Spanish speaking country, all spoke of extensive time spent abroad in Mexico, Argentina, or Spain. In addition, I

Fig. 1 Examples of response-able Spanish languaging from Facebook timeline

---

[1] All names of SWLTs in this chapter are pseudonyms

did not specifically collect information about the types of Spanish classes or year levels SWLTs as I was curious to see if this came up in conversation as something relevant to response-able Spanish languaging or not. It certainly did, and many mentioned their experience teaching all year levels in high school (in Australia this is year 7–12) in under the state curriculum before it turned into a national curriculum and three also noted teaching Spanish Ab Initio as part of the International Baccalaureate. Three also had experience teaching in Spanish immersion programs. Five teachers taught in public schools and four in private schools.

Many participated in the interviews with children in the background suggesting that this method may also afford further flexibility especially needed when conducting research in a majority female profession where many participants may be engaged in childcare. After a short discussion of their ability to scroll through their timeline and stop or skip posts they wanted to narrate, I also asked them not to mention the names, posts or comments shared by others for privacy reasons. I also did not record screens, but audio only for privacy reasons. Additionally, I chose not to record screens due to the risk of capturing private data about non-research participants and the impracticality of redacting this information. For example, many posts contained names and personal information of Facebook friends of the participants who had not given consent to take part in the project. At times, this meant posts that SWLTs may have deemed relevant were not included in the research as they were created and shared on the SWLTs Facebook timelines by someone else. However, this was rare and did not interrupt the flow of the conversation. Most times, SWLTs were able to find another post illustrating the point they wished to highlight from another user's post in something they had posted also. I discuss further ethical considerations that emerged as I spoke with SWLTs at the end of the chapter.

The SWLTs were excited and enthusiastic to begin after our brief introduction. I had explained that they were free to narrate any post they thought was relevant to response-able Spanish languaging whether or not the connection was immediately obvious. I would also ask SWLTs to pause on posts I thought might be relevant. Some SWLTs were on desktops, and others on mobile phones. Some had kids running around in the background while others hid in quiet places. Some scrolled linearly, and only made it back to 2019 whereas others jumped between years using the menu bar at the top of the page (See Fig. 1); some played the videos embedded on their pages and others took detours into stories about school, life and travels not mentioned on their Facebook timeline but prompted by a post, comment, or photo. Others sang along to music videos they had shared. I was also struck by their confidence in veering off course from my planned question which asked "Can you talk to me about any examples of response-able Spanish languaging on your Facebook timeline?". Before beginning the interviews, I spent time taking the SWLTs through a pre-prepared PowerPoint detailing the terms response-able and languaging making sure to check they understood that they could discuss more than their moral obligations and language/semiotic resources beyond Spanish. Out of the respect for the professionalism and intelligence of the SWLTS, I did not use layman's terms nor change the terminology here and instead engaged in conversation, invited questions, and broke down the terms with them before beginning the interview. The creativity of SWLTs responses was sparked by the posts resulting in a vast array of alternative data. Whilst I could have read and analysed the similarities in the language given this is a project in language education, I was struck by the differences in their responses particularly those that highlighted issues concerning ER WLE which is a topic I had not initially intended to explore but that arose from the politically motivated and situated posts due to conducting research during this time.

Having transcribed our conversations from the scroll-back interviews, I now present the findings from a diffracting analysis using individual examples that highlight what affects are generated by virtue of this method itself and in relation to ER. Firstly, I discuss the ways in which wonder generates interruptions to the agency of myself and SWLTs in this project as an example of how scroll-back method might affect the data highlighted in ER WLE research. I then explore the ways in which the various phenomena continue to interrupt agency with a particular focus on the agency of avoidance with an example pertinent to ER WLE by looking at hesitation as data. Finally, I elaborate on the ethical questions raised when researchers spot issues of interest, be they avoidance or shame, and offer some thoughts on how entangling ourselves with these uncomfortable affects generated by social media in ER WLE could help us (re)imagine response-able research practices.

5 Generative Affects Emerging from/with/Through Social Media Scroll-Back Interviews: Troubles for ER WLE

5.1 Wondrous Interruptions of Agency

Considering my final research question asking: IN what ways might WLE respond to ER WLE research with social media, I was initially drawn to the ways in which agency was interrupted in the interviews. While the control of the scrolling offered SWLTs "socioculturally mediated capacity to act" (Ahearn, 2001) emphasising their agency as participants and reducing mine as the researcher, my own wonder about the skipped over posts generated an interruption to this traditional notion of agency. The SWLTs scrolling-on and past particular posts sparked my interest and interrupted our focus on the initial research topic and search for themes. In one instance, I interrupted Flor's scrolling and asked her to explain the reasons behind sharing specific posts on climate issue and refugees (see Figs. 2 and 3). Instead of discussing response-able Spanish languaging explicitly, my curiosity-fuelled interruption encouraged Flor to describe her passion for climate related issues emerging from Central America and her personal and family history as a refugee from the region, thereby, (re)interrupting the direction of the research itself. Flor's narrations of these posts emphasise the situated, entangled, and complex personal sociopolitical histories underpinning SWLTs languaging practices, different to the personal/professional binaries which often encourage SWLTs to separate their

Fig. 2 Illustrative screenshot of climate issue Facebook post shared by Flor, SWLT (Evorevolución, 2020)

Amy Remeikis
@AmyRemeikis

Watching the panic buying, heightened tensions and me first attitude on display – and all before the pandemic actually hits - I get the fear. But once the dust settles, surely no one can look at a refugee again and wonder why they did what they had to do, to flee war or famine.

BRASS - Brisbane Refugee and Asylum Seeker Support Network
16 March

Fig. 3 Illustrative screenshot of a Facebook post about refugee issues during the pandemic shared by Flor, SWLT (BRASS – Brisbane Refugee and Asylum Seeker Support Network, 2020)

subjective positionings from objective pedagogical requirements. Despite, or perhaps even because of, the professional push for objectivity, during our conversation drawing on her Facebook posts Flor acknowledged that she "kind of put this out there to just, you know, throw it in their faces, really". I cautiously pondered whether my own interruption of Flor's scrolling spurred by my curiosity in posts blurring the personal/professional divide might be an example of what Maclure (2013) considers the "wonder that resides and radiates in data" (p.228), and that "is relational…and never completed within our control" (p.229).

The generative affects of interruption and (re)interruption emerging from Flor's embodied scrolling and storying as well as my own wonder counter many of the conventional discourses in WLE research that separate the agency of the researcher/ ed., the human/non-human, the social/scientific and the personal/professional. I refer to this using the adjectival form of wonder – wonderous – interruption of agency to highlight the entangled ways in which wonder inspires further wondering that is extraordinary in that we are moved beyond the ordinary research practices dictating teleology and objective data. Furthermore, this conceptualisation of agency embraces the ways in which social media scroll-back interviews entangle the human (researcher/ed) and non-human (wonder, technology) generate on-going agential intra-actions (Barad, 2007). Hence, the wonderous interruption and (re) interruption of scrolling posts and the research topic blur the boundaries of individual agency. On account of this, our conversation seems to acknowledge "the specificity of material entanglements in their agential becoming" (Barad, 2007, p. 72) performed in the context of social media research responding to a global pandemic.

5.2   Agency of Avoidance

Even with (re)configured, entangled agency in our conversations, SWLTs and their Facebooks timelines transgressed from my planned research focus on response-able Spanish languaging practices in unexpected ways. This suggested a particular way in which WLEs might respond to ER WLE research with social media. Whilst scrolling through her timeline, Ron spotted a post of a sunset photo she had taken (see Fig. 4) and then captioned. She comments "This one is about school, but there's no Spanish there either" before scrolling again and effectively avoiding any further discussion. In response to her attempt to avoid this post, I hastily responded with "Although I guess you've mentioned the online teaching there and how has that…" tentatively prompting Ron to go into more detail. My vague/imprecise comment stemmed from my hesitation to highlight a post that seemed off-topic and potentially off-limits. Ron's hasty response seemed to feed off my hesitation further as we only briefly diverted from the research topic as she described her affective response to moving teaching and learning online.

Ron: That was after the day one of the term. And I was just like my head was ready to explode, and I'd been crazy, and I'd gone for a run. That was my sunset. And I just shared it saying I made a bit softer. Sorry, after week one.

Danielle: Yeah. Was that week one this – this term?

Ron: Yeah. Where it was full online, no students at all. None in my classroom. And just yeah, that was sort of just seeing crisis mode like, the end of term one. This was, you know, after the first week of adaptation into remote learning and teaching.

The hesitation generated by Ron's attempted avoidance of a Facebook post she had likely forgotten about containing an emotional response to ER WLE but that put itself in our conversation reminded me of the ways in which a researcher hesitating to interpret such performativity "can open up surprisingly fruitful research spaces/

Fig. 4 Illustrative post of sunset photo post from Ron (Twelve Feet Wanderers, 2020)

possibilities" (Benozzo & Gherardi, 2019, p. 153). Ron's attempted avoidance also raises further questions about agency when the non-human (technology) intercepts our conversation with saved memories perhaps meant to be kept hidden, opening up the possibility for the researcher to draw these into the research. This concern is necessary for considering the ways in which we as WLE researchers are response-able for bringing context (COVID-19, ER WLE) into conversation whilst respecting the privacy of the SWLTs we might work with.

5.3   *Shame-Interest*

A final reminder of some of the ways in which WLEs might respond to ER WLE research with social media emerged in relation to shame-interest. This is also a further reminder of our response-abilities as WLE researchers that generated from my conversation with Rosalía (SWLT) about the emergency switch to online teaching and learning via Zoom:

> "even I hit the ceiling and there probably… here with me hitting the ceiling, because they did – they – I got to a post where I think I said "I'm looking at quitting" because I got so cranky that they kept on – the Department of Education. Every second day I'd go in and they have changed the settings on my Zoom so that I couldn't, you know, I couldn't record all of a sudden, or I couldn't get kids – kids couldn't log on because they needed to have their department email to log on. So, it's all to protect us, I get it. But it was like, you know, teachers aren't allowed to be on a Zoom with only one student. And I'm like, "Well, I've only got 16 in my year ten Spanish class and, you know, there's always going to be one of them who turns up before the others"

This particular complaint of Rosalía's is important for a number of reasons; first, due to the way in which she included an account of her emotive response to COVID-19 ER WLE. In doing so, she turns to matters of affect in educational research that may "disrupt patterns of disadvantage" (Mayes & Wolfe, 2018, p. 1) such as those departmental regulations that doubt the professionalism of SWLTs when attempting to work on-on-one with their students in ER WLE situations. This suspicion of SWLTs' lack the professional capacity to work safely with their students in ER WLE scenarios further unsettles my research topic exploring response-able languaging practices. On the one hand, this example showcases the ways in which SWLTs' hands are tied during ER WLE as they are legally shamed for being alone with students online. On the other hand, it raises questions about the types of emotional affects generated by EL WLE research and whether or not I as a research should "attempt to write shame as something of interest" as it "opens up the researcher to questions about whether she has breached ethical codes", thus, shaming me (Mayes & Wolfe, 2018, p. 3). However, (re)turning to Barad's (2007) notion of diffracting, I can see the potential for my interest in writing shame not as shameful but rather an opportunity for reconfiguring connection by generating an alternative ethics of ER WLE research. Rosalía's example can be seen as having the potential to disrupt the idea that the SWLTs shame is separate from mine my as the researcher, therefore, highlighting our co-constitutive affective states generated by our mutual interest and shame.

6   Conclusion

My attempt of diffracting the data generated from social media scroll-back interviews with SWLTs during COVID-19 points to some possible ways in which ER WLE research can be thought about and done differently in order to move beyond repetitive explorations of sameness whilst also offering an option for conducting research during lockdowns and other emergency situations that may limit access to school sites. In seeking out alternative or transgressive data rather than language and/or linguistic data, as might be expected in a project in WLE research, unexpected and surprising affects were generated. I came to realise that by diffracting rather than coding or thematically analysing my data, I could engage with more-than-language, but that this might also require more-than-human phenomena as part of the research project. By working with the difficulties of ER WLE, I was able to rescope the project in order to do this and explore some small examples of the generative affects of doing so. Most notably, I became keenly aware of the ways in which agency was entangled with researchers/participants and technology in ways that encouraged and disrupted the ability to avoid and engage with uncomfortable affects such as shame and hesitation generated by scrolling through a Facebook timeline together. I remain encouraged to undertake further research into how social media scroll-back method and diffractive analyses could open up qualitative research in ER WLE and see particular potential in the areas of pre-service and in-service teacher professional development and critical reflection where such an approach could be (re)imagined as a day-to-day tool for bridging the personal/professional, social-scientific and more.

7   Food for Thought

- The ethics of conducting online research in WLE using social media scroll-back method extend beyond questions of privacy and anonymity. The entanglement of technology, in this case Facebook timelines, in the research also generates interest on the part of the researcher in posts which SWLTs here may have highlighted shame or that they may have wished to avoid or. As a result, researchers in this space also need to consider their response-abilities to respond their own interest in affects of avoidance and/or shame.
- Given the potential for social media scroll-back method to focus on more-than-language data, it has the potential to be applied in a vast array of disciplines beyond WLE and in relation to a broad array of topics. However, one consideration is the fact that not all participants are comfortable sharing their social media in potentially public research and others may not have/use a social media account. In the case participants are not comfortable sharing their own personal account, there is scope to incorporate public accounts of government organisations or similar for them to narrate depending on the research focus or narrate the page of another educator – ethics permitting. These options could also work for those who do not have/use a social media page.
- In regard to future research, there seems to be significant potential for WLEs and educators in other disciplines to make use of social media scroll-back method as part of their reflective practice in novel ways. For instance, the more-than-linguistic data which may emerge through transemiotic posts as well as the affective responses to these posts provide opportunities for alternative analyses such as a diffractive analysis in the current project.

Acknowledgements I wish to thank A/Professor Liz MacKinlay and Dr. Adriana Díaz for their support in developing this methodology. I also wish to express my sincerest gratitude to the SWLTs who so enthusiastically worked with me in this project. *This research was supported by an Australian Government Research Training Program Scholarship.*

References

Ahearn, L. M. (2001). Language and agency. *Annual Review of Anthropology, 30*(1), 109–137. https://doi.org/10.1146/annurev.anthro.30.1.109

Ahmed, S. (2004). Affective economies. *Social Text, 22*(2), 117–139. https://www.muse.jhu.edu/article/55780

Ahmed, S. (2014). Conclusion just emotions. In *The cultural politics of emotion* (2nd ed., pp. 191–203). Edinburgh University Press. https://doi.org/10.3366/j.ctt1g09x4q.14

Arnold, J. (2019). The importance of affect in language learning. *Neofilolog, 52*, 11–14. https://doi.org/10.14746/n.2019.52.1.2

Australian Government Department of Foreign Affairs and Trade. (2018). *Education in emergencies.* https://www.dfat.gov.au/sites/default/files/foundation-education-in-emergencies.pdf

Barad, K. (2003). Posthumanist performativity: Toward an understanding of how matter comes to matter. *Signs, 28*(3), 801–831. https://doi.org/10.1086/345321

Barad, K. (2007). *Meeting the universe halfway quantum physics and the entanglement of matter and meaning.* Duke University Press. https://doi.org/10.1215/9780822388128

Benozzo, A., & Gherardi, S. (2019). Working within the shadow: What do we do with "not-yet" data? *Qualitative Research in Organizations and Management: An International Journal.* https://doi.org/10.1108/QROM-09-2018-1684

Besnier, N. (1990). Language and affect. *Annual Review of Anthropology, 19*(1), 419–451. https://doi.org/10.1146/annurev.an.19.100190.002223

Bozalek, V., & Zembylas, M. (2017). Diffraction or reflection? Sketching the contours of two methodologies in educational research. *International Journal of Qualitative Studies in Education (QSE), 30*(2), 111–127. https://doi.org/10.1080/09518398.2016.1201166

BRASS – Brisbane Refugee and Asylum Seeker Support Network. (2020). [Image attched] [Status update]. https://www.facebook.com/brassnetwork/photos/a.676105779096247/3793004544073006

Carpenter, J. P., & Harvey, S. (2020). Perceived benefits and challenges of physical educators' use of social media for professional development and learning. *Journal of Teaching in Physical Education, 1*, 1–11. https://doi.org/10.1123/jtpe.2020-0002

Carpenter, J. P., & Krutka, D. G. (2015). Engagement through microblogging: Educator professional development via Twitter. *Professional Development in Education, 41*(4), 707–728. https://doi.org/10.1080/19415257.2014.939294

Clayton, K., Blair, S., Busam, J. A., Forstner, S., Glance, J., Green, G., Kawata, A., Kovvuri, A., Martin, J., Morgan, E., Sandhu, M., Sang, R., Scholz-Bright, R., Welch, A. T., Wolff, A. G., Zhou, A., & Nyhan, B. (2019). Real solutions for fake news? Measuring the effectiveness of general warnings and fact-check tags in reducing belief in false stories on social media. *Political Behavior.* https://doi.org/10.1007/s11109-019-09533-0

Dolphijn, R., & Tuin, I. V. d. (2012). *New materialism: Interviews & cartographies.* Open Humanities Press. https://doi.org/10.3998/ohp.11515701.0001.001

Dubois, E., Minaeian, S., Paquet-Labelle, A., & Beaudry, S. (2020). Who to trust on social media: How opinion leaders and seekers avoid disinformation and echo chambers. *Social Media + Society, 6*(2), 2056305120913993. https://doi.org/10.1177/2056305120913993

Evorevolución. (2020, February 15). *#Evorevolución* [Image attached] [Status update]. Facebook. https://www.facebook.com/ecorevolucionoficial/photos/a.1784076738490518/2679766095588240/

Fullagar, S., & Pavlidis, A. (2021). Thinking through the disruptive effects and affects of the coronavirus with feminist new materialism. *Leisure sciences, 43*(1–2), 152–159. https://doi.org/1 0.1080/01490400.2020.1773996

Gafter, R. J., & Milani, T. M. (2020). Affective trouble: a Jewish/Palestinian heterosexual wedding threatening the Israeli nation-state?. *Social Semiotics*, 1–14. https://doi.org/10.1080/1035033 0.2020.1810555

Galvin, S., & Greenhow, C. (2020). Writing on social media: A review of research in the high school classroom. *TechTrends, 64*(1), 57–69. https://doi.org/10.1007/s11528-019-00428-9

García, O., & Wei, L. (2013). *Translanguaging: Language, bilingualism and education* (Vol. 63). Palgrave Macmillan. https://doi.org/10.1057/9781137385765

Greenhow, C., & Chapman, A. (2020). Social distancing meet social media: Digital tools for connecting students, teachers, and citizens in an emergency. *Information and Learning Science, 121*(5/6), 341–352. https://doi.org/10.1108/ILS-04-2020-0134

Haraway, D. J. (2016). *Staying with the trouble: Making kin in the Chthulucene.* Duke University Press. https://doi.org/10.1215/9780822373780

Heinrichs, D. H. (2020). Decoloniality, Spanish and Latin American studies in Australian universities: ¿es un mundo ch'ixi posible? *Third World Thematics: A TWQ Journal, 5*(01). https://doi.org/10.1080/23802014.2020.1798277

Heinrichs, D. H. (2021). 'Staying with the trouble' of response-able Spanish bilingualism. *Critical Inquiry in Languages Studies.* https://doi.org/10.1080/15427587.2021.1885296

Hodges, C., Moore, S., Lockee, B., Trust, T., & Bond, A. (2020). The difference between emergency remote teaching and online learning. *Educause Review, 27.* https://medicine.hofstra.edu/pdf/faculty/facdev/facdev-article.pdf

Hootsuite. (2020). *Digital 2020 July global statshot report.* https://hootsuite.com/pages/digital-2020

Kamberelis, G., Dimitriadis, G., & Welker, A. (2018). Focus group research and/in figured worlds. In *The SAGE handbook of qualitative research* (5th ed., pp. 692–716). Sage.

Kasparek, N., & Turner, M. W. (2020). Puzzling about special educational needs in EFL teacher development: A duoethnographic inquiry. In R. J. Lowe & L. Lawrence (Eds.), *Duoethnography in English language teaching: Research, reflection and classroom application.* Multilingual Matters. https://doi.org/10.21832/9781788927192

King, K. A., Lai, Y., & May, S. (2017). *Research methods in language and education* (3rd ed.). Springer International Publishing. https://doi.org/10.1007/978-3-319-02249-9

Lee, J. S., & Chen Hsieh, J. (2019). Affective variables and willingness to communicate of EFL learners in in-class, out-of-class, and digital contexts. *System, 82*, 63–73. https://doi.org/10.1016/j.system.2019.03.002

Lupton, D., Pink, S., Heyes LaBond, C., & Sumartojo, S. (2018). Digital traces in context: Personal data contexts, data sense, and self-tracking cycling. *International Journal of Communication, 12*, 647–665. http://ijoc.org

Maal, M., & Wilson-North, M. (2019). Social media in crisis communication – The "do's" and "don'ts". *International Journal of Disaster Resilience in the Built Environment, 10*(5), 379–391. https://doi.org/10.1108/IJDRBE-06-2014-0044

MacLure, M. (2013). The wonder of data. *Cultural Studies ↔ Critical Methodologies, 13*(4), 228–232. https://doi.org/10.1177/1532708613487863

Malecki, K. M. C., Keating, J. A., & Safdar, N. (2020). Crisis communication and public perception of COVID-19 risk in the era of social media. *Clinical Infectious Diseases.* https://doi.org/10.1093/cid/ciaa758

Manca, S. (2020). Snapping, pinning, liking or texting: Investigating social media in higher education beyond Facebook. *The Internet and Higher Education, 44*, 100707. https://doi.org/10.1016/j.iheduc.2019.100707

Mayes, E., & Wolfe, M. (2018). Shameful interest in educational research. *Critical Studies in Education*, 1–17. https://doi.org/10.1080/17508487.2018.1489871

O'Brien, S., & Federici, F. M. (2019). Crisis translation: Considering language needs in multilingual disaster settings. *Disaster Prevention and Management: An International Journal, 29*(2), 129–143. https://doi.org/10.1108/DPM-11-2018-0373

Oeldorf-Hirsch, A., Schmierbach, M., Appelman, A., & Boyle, M. P. (2020). The ineffectiveness of fact-checking labels on news memes and articles. *Mass Communication and Society, 23*(5), 682–704. https://doi.org/10.1080/15205436.2020.1733613

Paul, J. Z., & Friginal, E. (2019). The effects of symmetric and asymmetric social networks on second language communication. *Computer Assisted Language Learning, 32*(5–6), 587–618. https://doi.org/10.1080/09588221.2018.1527364

Peeters, W. (2019). The peer interaction process on Facebook: A social network analysis of learners' online conversations. *Education and Information Technologies, 24*(5), 3177–3204. https://doi.org/10.1007/s10639-019-09914-2

Pescaroli, G., & Alexander, D. (2015). A definition of cascading disasters and cascading effects: Going beyond the "toppling dominos" metaphor. *Planet@Risk, 3*(1), 58–67. http://citeseerx.ist.psu.edu/viewdoc/download?doi=10.1.1.874.4335&rep=rep1&type=pdf

Queensland Government. (2020). *Research services.* https://education.qld.gov.au/about-us/reporting-data-research/research

Reinders, H., & Wattana, S. (2014). Affect and willingness to communicate in digital game-based learning. *ReCALL, 27.* https://doi.org/10.1017/S0958344014000226

Riley, D. (2005). *Impersonal passion: Language as affect.* Duke University Press. https://doi.org/10.1215/9780822386780

Robards, B., & Lincoln, S. (2019). Social media scroll back method. In *Sage research methods: Foundations.* https://methods.sagepub.com/base/download/FoundationEntry/social-media-scroll-back-method

Sirivedin, P., Soopunyo, W., Srisuantang, S., & Wongsothorn, A. (2018). Effects of Facebook usage on English learning behavior of Thai English teachers. *Kasetsart Journal of Social Sciences, 39*(2), 183–189. https://doi.org/10.1016/j.kjss.2018.03.007

Solmaz, O. (2017). Autonomous language learning on Twitter: Performing affiliation with target language users through# hashtags. *Journal of Language and Linguistic Studies, 13*(2), 204–220. https://www.jlls.org

St. Pierre. E. A. (1997). Methodllogy in the fold and the irruption of transgressive data.*International Journal of Qualitative Studies in Education, 10*(2), 175–189. https://doi.org/10.1080/095183997237278

St. Pierre, E. A. (2019). Post qualitative inquiry, the refusal of method, and the risk of the new. *Qualitative Inquiry, 27*, 3–9. https://doi.org/10.1177/1077800419863005

Statista. (2020). *Number of monthly active Facebook users worldwide as of 2nd quarter 2020 (in millions).* https://www.statista.com/statistics/264810/number-of-monthly-active-facebook-users-worldwide/

Tananuraksakul, N. (2015). An investigation into the impact of Facebook group usage on students' affect in language learning in a Thai context. *International Journal of Teaching and Learning in Higher Education, 27*(2), 235–246.

Taskiran, A., Gumusoglu, E. K., & Aydin, B. (2018). Fostering foreign language learning with twitter: Reflections from English learners. *Turkish Online Journal of Distance Education, 19*(1), 100–116. https://eric.ed.gov/?id=EJ1165854

The right to education in emergency situations: resolution. (2010). https://digitallibrary.un.org/record/685964?ln=en

Twelve Feet Wanderers. (2020). [Image attached] [Status update]. Facebook. https://www.facebook.com/twelvefeetwanderers/posts/140206571135732

United Nations. (2019). *Education in emergencies.* https://en.unesco.org/themes/education-emergencies

Villafuerte, J., & Romero, A. (2017). Learners' attitudes toward foreign language practice on Social Network Sites. *Journal of Education and Learning, 6*(4), 145–158. https://doi.org/10.5539/jel.v6n4p145

Warriner, D. S. (2012). When the macro facilitates the micro: A study of regimentation and emergence in spoken interaction. *Anthropology & Education Quarterly, 43*(2), 173–191. https://doi.org/10.1111/j.1548-1492.2012.01168.x

Weldon, P., McMillan, J., Rowley, G., & McKenzie, P. (2014). *Profiles of teachers in selected curriculum areas: Further analyses of the Staff in Australia's Schools 2013 Survey.* https://docs.education.gov.au/system/files/doc/other/sias_2013_supplementary_report.pdf

Wu, Y., & Lin, A. M. (2019). Translanguaging and trans-semiotising in a CLIL biology class in Hong Kong: Whole-body sense-making in the flow of knowledge co-making. *Classroom Discourse, 10*(3–4), 252–273.

Xie, Y., Qiao, R., Shao, G., & Chen, H. (2017). Research on Chinese social media users' communication behaviors during public emergency events. *Telematics and Informatics, 34*(3), 740–754. https://doi.org/10.1016/j.tele.2016.05.023

Xu, J. (2020). Does the medium matter? A meta-analysis on using social media vs. traditional media in crisis communication. *Public Relations Review, 46*(4), 101947. https://doi.org/10.1016/j.pubrev.2020.101947

Xue, S., & Churchill, D. (2020). Educational affordances of mobile social media for language teaching and learning: A chinese teacher's perspective. *Computer Assisted Language Learning,* 1–30. https://doi.org/10.1080/09588221.2020.1765811

Peer Capacity Building in Emergency Remote Teaching: Informal Language Teacher Professional Development on Twitter

Highlights

- Peer professional learning during ERT focused on pragmatic aspects of the dominating topic of digital tools
- Participants of the online teacher community (OTC) empowered each other mainly on a practical level with little regard for emotional support
- The types of interaction were reflective of a crisis mode with few critical discussions and a dominating professional tone with few emotions-related references
- OTC during ERT are predominantly a venue for knowledge co-construction

1 Introduction

The Covid-19 pandemic has affected educational systems all over the world. A sudden need to use fully digital teaching during the time of school closures hit schools with insufficient infrastructure and teachers without pre-planned resources (Whittle et al., 2020). It resulted in an urgent need for effective and fast professional development activities in order for teachers to meet these challenges. Language teachers represented no exception to this and their situation was aggravated by the fact that foreign or second language functions as a medium and the content of instruction at the same time. In a foreign language classroom whose instructional practice is informed by the communicative approach to language teaching and learning (Vollmer & Vogt, 2021), emergency remote (foreign) language teaching adds the need to design appropriate online teaching environments that promote communication in the foreign or second language in the framework of an action-oriented

K. Vogt (✉)
University of Education Heidelberg, Heidelberg, Germany
e-mail: vogt@ph-heidelberg.de

© The Author(s), under exclusive license to Springer Nature
Switzerland AG 2021
J. Chen (ed.), *Emergency Remote Teaching and Beyond*,
https://doi.org/10.1007/978-3-030-84067-9_18

approach (Piccardo & North, 2019), often based on tasks (Ellis, 2018; Müller-Hartmann & Schocker-von Ditfurth, 2011). Transferring these teaching environments to a fully digital setting represents unchartered territory to many language teachers.

Before emergency remote teaching (term coined by Hodges et al., 2020), language teachers in the German context could be classified into a small number of digital teaching enthusiasts who would embed digital tools into their face-to-face teaching on a regular basis (often including systemic tasks like hosting or network management) and a majority of teachers who would use digital media only occasionally. In times of emergency remote teaching (henceforth ERT), more 'mainstream' teachers who would not consider themselves tech savvy have resorted to different online platforms and communities to seek peer support with technical questions, digital materials and methodological issues of online teaching. One of them is a community on Twitter which was originally frequented by teachers with more advanced digital teaching experience. Under lockdown and school closures, it has been increasingly used for peer capacity building often resulting in informal teacher professional development at school level. Twitter as a social media application is subsumed under informally-developed professional development by Lantz-Andersson et al. (2018), and the type of community that evolves in this type of professional development (PD) can be characterised as a community of practice (Wenger et al., 2002). The present study focuses on the dynamics of peer capacity building among foreign language teachers in an online teacher community happening on Twitter in the weeks following school closures due to Covid-19 in Germany (from mid-March 2020, depending on federal states). The results are supposed to provide insights into how the community functions as an online teacher community (OTC), with a focus on peer capacity building of foreign language teachers as part of an informal PD in an educational emergency.

2 The Context: Teaching (Foreign) Languages in Germany

In times of ERT, teachers in Germany had to resort to fully digital teaching. For foreign language teaching and learning, however, the vital role of communication has to be considered (Vollmer & Vogt, 2021), which had repercussions on the design and conception of digital teaching during school closures. The mainstream approach to EFL teaching, task-based language teaching as a form of communicative language teaching, is difficult to achieve in an asynchronous learning mode, which requires even more advanced resources and skills in order to design effective ERT environments conducive to language learning.

Although Germany is one of the richest countries in the world, many schools are behind in terms of digital transformation with insufficient infrastructure as basic as Wi-Fi networks at school, lacking hardware for teachers and learners and access to tools or software from individual applications to missing learning management systems or cloud solutions for schools, local educational authorities or entire federal states. Having said that, there are stark variations within the country and due to its decentralized educational system, this leads to different educational systems in the 16 federal states. Hence, there is variation in terms of resources, available infrastructure and access to e.g. professional development that has to be accounted for across and within federal states, local educational authorities, municipalities (who finance the school buildings) and down to individual schools (Edelstein, 2013). So available resources and educational policies in response to the Covid-19 crisis differ considerably. Regarding the foreign language (and other) teachers, the digital skills that teachers require for ERT were not fully developed on a broad scale in the German educational context. In a recent international study, only 25% of the German teachers who were surveyed confirmed that they had learned to use digital media during their initial teacher training, and their self-reported confidence levels regarding the use of digital media are below the international average, e.g. when it comes to making use of a learning management system or designing assessment in the digital mode (ICILS, Drossel et al., 2019). Therefore, it is no surprise that Germany-based teachers deploy digital media to a lesser extent (p. 220), clearly below the international average. Foreign language teachers represent no exception in the use of digital media in their foreign language teaching. In the same study, learners said that only 42.6% of their teachers used digital media in foreign language teaching, compared to an international average of 69.2%.

About a third of the surveyed teachers said that they had participated in professional development activities related to the integration of digital media in teaching in the previous two years, and informal co-operation among colleagues related to the use of digital media was significantly below the international average as well (Gerick et al., 2019). The figures on Germany-based teachers' PD levels in digital media have to be seen in light of their status and the requirements for PD activities. As the majority of Germany-based teachers are tenured civil servants with little opportunity for promotion, they have relatively secure jobs, which has to be seen in connection with the non-compulsory nature of PD. Moreover, the decentralised educational system leads to devolved responsibility in teacher development, which might account for varying availability of PD activities related to digital teaching. PD activities are pursued by teachers on a voluntary basis, and these factors might help to explain why foreign language teachers in Germany were not well-prepared overall and lacked the necessary digital skills for ERT in many cases.

3   Professional Development of (Language) Teachers

3.1   PD in Online Communities of Practice

Even before the global educational emergency, teachers had to meet the continuously changing demands in a dynamic and rapidly changing world and assure themselves of their professional competence to be up to this challenge. Professional development (PD) is defined by Fishman (2016, p. 14) as "learning activities related to the profession of teaching" and by Postholm (2012, p. 406) as "teachers' learning, how they learn to learn and how they apply their knowledge in practice to support pupil learning". Teachers' effective professional practice is determined by their instructional activities and activities aimed at improving their qualifications in the long term. Collaborative learning in groups of practitioners foregrounds joint reflection, exchange and learning opportunities that might engage participants in their professional growth (Göktürk Salam & Dikilitaş, 2020), forming a community of practice that Wenger et al. (2002, p. 34) define as "a group of people who interact, learn together, build relationships, and in the process develop a sense of belonging and mutual commitment". The affordances of digital technology can be beneficial for teachers as they can profit from access to online PD (characterised as "any internet-based form of learning or professional growth process that an educator can engage in", Elliott, 2017, p. 119) as it can transcend geographic and time constraints and thus might fit better into teachers' busy schedules. Online communities of practice for teacher development have therefore received a considerable amount of research attention (e.g. Greenhow & Askari, 2017; Hou, 2015; Macia & García, 2016; Trust & Horrocks, 2017). However, there is no standard form of online communities of practice although their common purpose is to support teacher learning. Lantz-Andersson et al. (2018), in their meta study of online teacher communities, make the distinction between formally-organised and informally-developed teacher communities, the latter defined as "bottom-up initiatives involving a group of practitioners who choose to come together to discuss, share information and work together "(p. 304). For informal PD purposes, various applications have been researched, e.g. Facebook (Kelly & Antonio, 2016; Ranieri et al., 2012), blogs (e.g. Carpenter & Krutka, 2015) or Twitter (e.g. Davis, 2015). The social media service Twitter seems to have received considerable attention lately in terms of its potential role as an informal learning space (Rehm & Notten, 2016) or its capacity building potential for certain groups of educators like K-12 teachers in the US (Visser et al., 2014).

3.2 Online Teacher Communities on Twitter

The potential benefits of online communities of practice can be adapted to social media apps like Twitter that engender informally developed online communities. They potentially reduce teacher isolation as they enable exchange and sharing of expertise as well as a sense of belonging. They develop and enhance teachers' reflective practice and empower teachers because rather than seeing reflection as a private endeavour, shared reflection practices are enhanced. Shared expertise and reflected practice might lead to mutual support and more collegial connection. Thus, Twitter spaces for informal online teacher communities could be characterised as venues of knowledge co-construction and enhanced professional practice on a cognitive level, and co-spaces of peer support, peer mentoring and enhanced teacher self-efficacy on a psychological-emotional level.[1] The specificities of Twitter as a social media application can function as a catalyst for co-operation. As a free app, Twitter is easily accessible on a variety of devices, particularly mobile devices, which enables fluid and rapid exchanges. It has a 280-character limit for tweets, which typically makes for brief exchanges. For longer contributions, more than one tweet can be published and successively numbered. While a focus on brief messages can help reduce inhibitions to contribute, messages might be superficial or extremely dense. Everybody who has a Twitter account can contribute and so the online teacher community can be classified as an informal teacher community that is based on members' following each other, which might include non-teachers. Hashtags such as #EFL are used for filtering information but also as a sign for belonging to an online community, e.g. #mfltwitterati for an international foreign language teacher community. Twitter communities are typically unmoderated but participants can directly address each other in their tweets (@xy), which makes it possible for key participants to be foregrounded or addressed. Critical points of online teacher communities concern e.g. a lack of criticality in a mainly pragmatic as well as a nonconflictual nature of exchange (Kelly & Antonio, 2016), the predominance of certain participants who might dominate the discussion (Macia & García, 2016) and thus establish or shift power relationships within a group meant to have a non-hierarchical structure. Active and time-consuming participation in an online teacher community with its continuous flows of information might become a burden on participants' time and overwhelm them (e.g. Davis, 2015).

In the German context, there is a paucity of research in online PD of language teachers in general and in social media applications used for informal PD or foreign language teacher capacity building in particular. More specifically, Lantz-Andersson et al. (2018) identify a need for studies that investigate teachers' interactions online, e.g. in social media environments such as Twitter. Moreover, the pandemic-related situation left teachers in an urgent need for immediate and effective capacity building particularly regarding issued around online (language) teaching. This unprecedented situation gives rise to a pressing need for research in this area. The present study is an attempt to address this need and provide insights into the dynamics of peer capacity building of language teachers taking place in an online teacher community (OTC) on Twitter in a German educational context during ERT in spring 2020. The research questions can be formulated as follows:

1. What are the affordances of a social media app like Twitter for participation of foreign language teachers in an online teacher community?
2. What roles do teachers take on in the process of peer capacity building as a form of online PD on Twitter during ERT?
3. What topics are prevalent in teacher interaction among foreign language teachers during ERT in the online teacher community? How can the types of foreign language teacher exchange be classified?

---

[1] Dellinger et al. (2008, p. 252) define teacher self-efficacy as "individuals' beliefs in capabilities to perform specific teaching tasks at a specified level of quality in a specific situation".

4. What dynamics can be observed from the contributions of foreign language teacher interaction in the OTC in terms of the development of an online teacher community during ERT?

4 Method

The study at hand can be characterised as part of social media research mainly using document analysis. Lundin et al. (2020) identify a growing interest in social media research relating to professional support of teachers. The qualitative nature of the study was to exploit the advantages of this type of research (Dörnyei, 2007, p. 38). The research took place in a natural setting which was one of several German-speaking online teacher communities on Twitter. No attempt was made to manipulate the situation under study, which was important because the focus is on organically developing communities in an educational emergency and the dynamics associated with it. The observation of the activities in the OTC went ahead without the researcher participating in it, so the research can be classified as passive social media research with no interaction with participants (Kotsios et al., 2019). Social media research involves ethical considerations. On the one hand, Twitter data is publicly available data, access is public and no intervention with individuals is required. On the other hand, the observational research was conducted with publicly available but identifiable information on participants, and privacy rights have to be protected. Many subject-specific codes of practice have not considered social media research yet, therefore, the following procedure was adopted for the present study. The observations were made in a natural setting with the public data used in an anonymised way to make collective observations. The name of the OTC, the user name of the participants and the publication date of the tweets were anonymised to make participants unidentifiable. In addition, since the OTC is mainly German-speaking, only a rough translation into English was used so that the person who published the tweets remained unidentifiable. For direct quotes that were deemed relevant for publication, the researcher approached the participants to obtain informed consent, applying the same procedures of anonymising their name and the name of the OTC and deleting the exact date of the publication of the tweet. An ethics application at the university was not necessary due to the public nature of the data.

Document analysis can be seen as an approach to research in a process of "evaluating documents in such a way that empirical knowledge is produced and understanding is developed" (Bowen, 2009, p. 33). The advantage of document analysis is that the data remain unchanged and can be read multiple times. Document analysis is therefore an important method in social media research.

The online teacher community (OTC) in the study is one of many and consisted mostly of teachers teaching in Germany in different federal states and in different school types. 255 tweets in 87 discussions (threads) were filtered out between 13 March, the time that most schools were closed across Germany, and 31 May 2020, the time when most schools had partly reopened at least for some students in the majority of German federal states. The tweets related to the OTC were filtered by way of hashtags with the name of the OTC, which was anonymised for ethical and data protection reasons. In addition, tweets were searched by using the key words "English", "English language teaching", foreign language teaching", "foreign language" in German. No Twitterscraper software, i.e. tools that are used to mine data from Twitter, e.g. complete profiles, was used in order to obtain the same results that a key word search by a teacher would yield. The search resulted in 255 tweets in 87 conversations/threads. A content analysis was carried out following a procedure adapted to Lamnek (1995). The data from tweets were content analysed using open and axial coding and categorization in an attempt to break down salient themes in the interactions and development of the OTC during ERT. Two researchers identified relevant passages or tweets, synthesised content into abstract units, which yielded a category system of recurring themes in the data (Appendix 1). Categories emerging this way were compared to deductive categories from the research questions and the theoretical framework. In order to control bias as a potential problem of document analysis, the two researchers underwent the coding process independently, which increases inter-coder reliability.

5   Results

5.1   *Affordances of Twitter as a Social Media App*

The results of the data analysis will be structured in accordance with the research questions. Regarding the affordances of Twitter as a social media app for participation in an OTC and therefore peer capacity building, the availability of the app to everyone with an account makes **access to the OTC** rather easy and accounts for accessibility of colleagues otherwise not available due to space constraints. Therefore the OTC can be characterised as informally developed in line with the classification of OTCs suggested by Lantz-Andersson et al. (2018). This makes lurking very easy, and although it was not possible in the study to establish how many teachers were following the exchanges without participating in them, one tweet by a teacher who introduces him/herself after having identified him/herself as an onlooker represents typical behaviour (Macia & García, 2016). S/he praises the benefits of lurking for him/herself (J, April), learning from the others' interactions.

Twitter's **retweeting function** maximises the scope of the tweet and also the audience and is systematically used in the data in explicit requests for retweets e.g. in a relatively general request for resources, namely apps for primary English language teaching in ERT that was posted by a colleague of the person who had the original query (F, March). The tweet was retweeted seven times and generated thirteen replies. Moreover, retweeting makes it possible to take an active part in the OTC without having to make a personal contribution. This way Twitter allows different degrees of participation and indeed of casual peer capacity building from lurking (passive capacity building) to controlling activity by starting threads frequently. Another feature, **direct addressing** (@xy) makes it possible to ask OTC participants directly for information, encourage them to comment or participate, or mention them in their tweets. Key participants might be foregrounded this way, e.g. by one key participant who shared a resource and mentioned another frequent poster:

"New TeachOz project uploaded: Going Places – a digital breakout for English language learners. Padlet https://bit.ly/39MwkOJ Thanks to @xy for the inspiration!   @teach_oz   (…)   #nameofOTC   #BreakoutEdu   @padlet   @ LearningAppsorg @yz".

This way, participants with key roles might address each other in order to raise their profile, which was evident in the present data, or to dominate the discussion in the OTC, which was not the case in the data.

5.2   Types and Roles of OTC Participants

In the online interaction in the OTC during ERT the different types and roles of OTC members become obvious. Their status seems to be directly linked to their online presence in the OTC. Since the data came from interactions on the OTC, it was only indirectly possible to obtain information about onlookers in the community, for example from participants who were contributing for the first time and introduced themselves as previous lurkers (e.g. J., April). **Lurkers** find themselves in the position of passive consumers of professional development as they typically do not contribute to discussions or practices of sharing resources or ideas but can still profit from them. It seemed to be common practice in the OTC under scrutiny for **new members** to introduce themselves to the other members of the community when contributing for the first time, e.g. one teacher (H., April) gave information on his/her federal state, which is important information due to the sixteen different school systems and their different Covid-19 regulations for ERT, his/her subjects and the areas of expertise and interests related to digital technology and the learning management system in use. Thus s/he positioned him/herself as a knowledgeable member regarding a particular learning management system. The responses can be classified into friendly welcome messages and gifs with or without a comment on the person's subject(s) or place of residence, and conversation aimed at networking along with tool-related acknowledgement. At other times new participants just post their tweets with requests, information etc. without a formal introduction to the community.

Active participants in the foreign language OTC attract varying attention with their tweets. When opening a thread or conversation topic, the participant cannot count on having created a conversation starter per se, e.g. T's (March) offer for collaboration on designing online learning activities for EFL that remained unanswered at the very beginning of the school closures. It has not been possible to discern a pattern in the data, and hence to attribute a certain kind of behaviour to certain types of participants who contribute to informal professional development. However, there seemed to be a tendency for participants to respond to requests (for information, ideas etc.) by actively contributing to the discussion thread, sharing and developing professional competence that way. They tended to respond differently (likes or, less often, retweets) to resources shared with them. The difference in responses was probably due to teachers' immediate needs of informal and real-time professional development needs in ERT, during which extreme time contraints merely allowed a quick reaction to other participants who had shared resources, without an explicitly formulated response. On the one hand, the behaviour patterns of active members of the OTC might reveal a "caring and sharing" attitude with the need to help others and (quickly) reward other participants who had provided professional support. They might also reflect the strain that ERT had put on teachers' already busy schedules. Davis (2015) maintains that some teachers in OTCs are overwhelmed by the flow of information in regular times, let alone in an educational emergency.

A special type of active participants on social media like Twitter who use "a self-presentation technique in which people view themselves as a public persona to be consumed by others" according to Marwick (2015, p. 333) are **micro-celebrity practitioners**. They strategically use content creation and dissemination to boost their online attention. In the present data, there are few members of the OTC in questions who could be characterised as micro-celebrities. Using the participatory culture the technology affords, they establish a stronger online presence than other, less regularly contributing members by their strong presence in the OTC. While these teachers do not share the features of e.g. YouTube influencers, they are likely to be better known within the community, their contributions might be liked and/or retweeted more often. Lantz-Andersson et al. (2018) highlight the importance of these key participants for online teacher communities and they maintain that these participants might dominate the discussions in the community and thus influence the type and prevalent topics of the professional development taking place there. In the present data, the mere presence of these micro-celebrity practitioners did foreground them, and even more so if key participants addressed each other by mentioning each other (@xy), e.g. for "advertising" someone's project or resources activity (e.g. C., April: "incredibly awesome project by @xy who combines #informatics & #English into intelligent #gamification. Here you can see everything that makes an excellent secondary school teacher: depth, wit, details galore, didactic finesse #schoolathome #nameofOTC", link to blog) or pointing out a formal professional development led by another micro-celebrity (B., May: "watch out for the webinar by @xy"). These participants had a comparatively higher online presence and some of them posted so frequently that they seemed ubiquitous. However, they did not dominate the topics of the conversation in the sense that they visibly manipulated topics. The need for real-time, interest-driven and immediate personal professional development centred around the application of digital tools in emergency remote foreign language teaching and there was no instance in the data of a key participant manipulating others.

5.3 Topics in the OTC During ERT

As mentioned above, the focus of the Twitter tweets in terms of topics during ERT clearly was on ideas, appropriate **tools and resources** that facilitate (or enable) digital foreign language teaching and thus help to survive ERT. The tweets hence constituted many instances of micro professional development, e.g. M. (March) sharing Padlet content and ideas for collaborative preparations for upcoming school-leaving exams or F. (March) requesting information on digital tools to be used for collaborative vocabulary lists. Some of this micro professional development concerns **methodological issues** such as the request by M., (May) for ideas and experience relating to an edu breakout, a gamified activity for EFL. Besides some ideas and resources suggested by other members, a participant mentions the formal professional development activity by a micro-celebrity practitioner. So while a discussion on reflective practice is missing, the hint at further professional development on the topic leads to the chance to pursue more formal, systematic types of professional development activities.

Overall, there are few **critical discussions** on general aspects of digital teaching such as assessment in ERT, which has raised concerns, has generated and heated debates in other circles. This finding might be indicative of teachers' tendency in the data to focus on aspects of immediate practical relevance, particularly in an educational emergency. In the data, a contribution by I. (March) that tentatively discusses the necessity of digital transformation and agency needed on the part of teachers is not followed up on. On another occasion, however, a simple request for a tool for designing digital vocabulary tests in the foreign language that comply with data protection regulations triggers a critical discussion of tests in ERT settings, about expectations of parents as important stakeholders and the difference between tests and diagnosis related to their respective purposes. **Advertisements** for commercial services or formal professional development activities are usually not commented in the data, with the exception of self-advertisements by micro-celebrity practitioners.

5.4 Types of Interaction

In the dataset, four main types of interaction in informal OTC could be identified (Table 1).

Six per cent of the interactions concern a **request for colleagues' experience** related to a tool or a resource, e.g. materials from a certain publishing house (C., April) or the use of a specific videoconferencing tool for use for international tandems for foreign language teaching (H., April). At times **requests for experience** are linked to requests for ideas or resources. Lantz-Andersson et al. (2018) maintain that some teachers seem to rely on the 'collective mind' of colleagues in order to save time rather than searching for information themselves. In the pandemic situation, teachers were even harder pressed for time than before and might have been

Table 1 Types of interaction

Type of interaction	Percentage
Experience requested	6%
Request for ideas, resources, tapping on the community's 'collective mind'	19%
Emotions related	8%
Resources, ideas, experience shared	47%
Other	20%

expected to rely on colleagues even more. However, only about 19% of the threads of foreign language teachers in the data were about e.g. asking colleagues for links or tools for teaching listening comprehension (A., March), podcasts (M., April) or film titles appropriate for a certain year group (E., May) for ELT. Most of the tweets in the data (47%) concern the **sharing of links, resources, and materials**, even down to showcasing learning tasks with digital tools, as is frequently done by key participants, e.g. the idea of a virtual museum for milestones of US history using a digital visualising tool (S., April).

Tweets sharing ideas, or resources, are often not commented on, possibly due to time constraints of the teachers who might take notice of the resource and save it but do not explicitly thank the poster (or even like the post). Given the nature of the data available, the reaction of the teachers to this kind of post would have to be explored by additional data sources such as follow-up interviews. Despite these limitations, it can be said that in times of ERT, there is no increased "smash-and-grab" attitude to be noticed in the data, on the contrary.

Discussions related to **emotions** make up only 8%. They do not often lead to lively discussions but often get many likes. Among the emotions related are pride, satisfaction and frustration, the latter expressed in rant tweets. An example of pride is provided in the data by O, April, who shares his/her pride in his/her learner who has made a podcast in English that the teacher cannot follow content-wise due to the complexity of the subject. H., April, shares his/her satisfaction with learners' excellent results of the video journals they submitted on a novel of their choice.

The rants are related to organisational constraints, e.g. when a teacher (F, April) is frustrated with the additional organisational effort they have to make when equipping rooms to prepare the listening comprehension part of the school leaving exams under Covid restrictions, which learners had to sit physically in some federal states. The emotions-related threads in the data might have the effect of reducing teacher isolation in ERT times with teachers satisfying their need to share their feelings or let off steam. In these cases, the OTC might be seen to substitute the role of colleagues because colleagues are less accessible in ERT times e.g. in physical staffrooms. Having said that, it is also obvious that the OTC cannot fully replace real interaction between trustworthy colleagues as only personal wins are related and failures are not openly discussed. The reason for this interaction pattern could be the participants' possible inhibition to reveal subjectively perceived weaknesses if they admit to a "failure" and a related wish for a positive representational image of their online persona (Marwick, 2015; Robson, 2018). The data available allow speculations only, however, and would have to be complemented by research instruments like follow-up interviews or think-aloud protocols.

5.5   Dynamics in the Development of the OTC

The dynamics in the development of the OTC in question is generally based on sharing practices on a pragmatic level, with **digital content and tools** for foreign language teaching in their assistive function clearly dominating the interactions. Participants with good practice examples or a knowledge edge regarding availability (e.g. free resources) or functionality lead the way as **driving forces** and help other community members to survive ERT. Regarding **power relationships**, key participants are generally better noticed, their tweets liked more often (though not always), but in the present data they do not moderate the overall discussion. Rather, they contribute on a regular basis and thus cement their online presence without manipulating or controlling professional development contents. The type of content the informal professional development activity provides is rather one-sided due to the ERT-related pressing need and lack of solid skills to design and implement fully digital foreign language teaching environments. Probably due to the aggravated time constraints teachers were facing during ERT, there was little off-topic discussion and a very **professional tone** prevailed, corroborating findings by Kelly and Antonio (2016). The focus of the conversations was entirely on practical and not on emotional support, with few exceptions when teachers transported emotions in their tweets – however, these tweets did get a response on the same level when colleagues liked them or commented using emojis or gifs. In the data, there was hardly any critical discussion, at times sarcasm was used to express criticism, e.g. when K., May, publishes an ironic tweet about social justice in education being restored when learners come back to face-to-face teaching on 2 days a week, including English.

> All classes come back to school before the holidays! All for 2, – TWO -, days each for lessons in German, English and Maths. It's a real weight off my mind. All problems of equal opportunities and care issues solved in one go. Thanks to everyone!

A discussion follows with similar sarcasm. Overall, there seems to be a **spirit of give-and-take** in a non-hierarchical informal network which might provide some sort of cohesion and a safety net of common knowledge to draw from during ERT. The tweets of more active members are more likely to get a response or be retweeted than those from less well-known members so that the role (and status) of the participants seem to influence the dynamics of the interaction in the OTC in some way, albeit not to the extent that Lantz-Andersson et al. (2018) point out in their study. There is in general little or no response to advertisements with the exception of (self-) ads of micro-celebrity practitioners addressed by other key participants. In general, key participants seem to be interacting more regularly with each other using the @mentioning function than less active community members.

6 Discussion

The data from 255 tweets published during ERT and more specifically the time of the school closures in Germany in 2020 provide interesting insights into the affordances of Twitter for peer capacity building among the foreign language teachers in an OTC, into the characteristics of OTCs that turned out differently in the data, the relationships and roles of participants and the dynamics of the peer capacity building in the OTC in the data.

The **affordances of Twitter** as a social media tool matched the needs of foreign language teachers in ERT because of the varying forms of engagement made possible by the technology, from lurking to retweeting, which avoids a contribution of "own" content, to repeated or regular own tweets. The possibility to fall back on the knowledge stock of and advice from the community might help them overcome isolation during school closures (cf. Krutka & Carpenter, 2016). The mentioning function @xy was used for foregrounding key participants, also when these addressed each other, using the function for networking or informal advertising purposes. However, in contrast to Lantz-Andersson et al. (2018), they did not dominate the discussion or control the type of professional development in the OTC. There was no negative impact on **power relationships** or an uneven distribution of power within the OTC that could be attributed to the behaviour of the key participants.

Different **roles of participants** with different functions could be discerned, from (outed) lurkers who contribute for the first time to the community to micro-celebrity practitioners (Marwick, 2015), who use the participatory culture the technology affords by establishing a strong online presence and use it for dissemination purposes when they share their ideas or resources. Tsiotakis and Jimoyiannis (2016) maintain that teachers use social media as a means of filtering information and by drawing on the 'collective mind' of other OTC members to get quick answers to immediate instructional problems as practical advice, in attempt to becoming informed without time-consuming research. During ERT in the OTC under study, a real sense of give and take was obvious with many teachers sharing their work down to showcasing it, leading to shared expertise as one characteristic of OTCs (Hou, 2015) which did remain on a pragmatic level most of the time, confirming Kelly and Antonio (2016) in their critical view. The pragmatic nature of the professional development activities was reflected in educational technology as a predominant topic during ERT, as was to be expected. The lack of diversity of topics, which has been highlighted by Marklund (2015), was obvious in the data but is understandable in an educational emergency and against the background of Germany-based teachers' comparatively underdeveloped digital experience (Drossel et al., 2019). **Shared reflection practices** as another characteristic of OTCs can be seen in the data to a limited extent only. The focus seems to be on shared digital resources and experience with digital tools and learning arrangements for ERT, on the exchange of very practical advice in order to survive the exceptional situation. The professional growth that results from it develops organically and is expressed in fast collaborative action like e.g. book sprints in which participants organise and publish a publication in very little time.

OTCs have been characterised as giving **emotional support** due to the supportive qualities of the communities of practice (Davis, 2015). In the data, the supportive qualities of the OTC during ERT mainly concerned pragmatic issues negotiated in a professional style of discourse, corroborating e.g. results by Krutka & Carpenter (2016), but emotionally distanced at the same time because very few tweets in which emotions were openly shared with the community were found. The emotional tweets that were related concerned only wins (e.g. pride in learners' achievement) while no failures were reported, thus contradicting findings by e.g. Trust et al. (2016, p. 24) who reported that OTCs helped teachers become more confident and more willing to take risks, make mistakes, and learn from failures. By contrast, the ERT situation is an exceptional situation which does not seem to call for overly emotional reactions. Rather, teachers might have felt that they needed to keep up a certain professionalism and make digital teaching work without much attention to their personal or emotional development by reflecting on risks taken or failures in the framework of the OTC. The supportive qualities of the informal learning network were definitely pragmatic in nature and foregrounded the OTC as venues of knowledge co-construction in ERT. The Twitter-based OTC in the data might have been seen as a **safety net of collective professional knowledge** that was tapped for peer capacity building in digital foreign language teaching. While this is one possible interpretation, more data (e.g. from teacher interviews) would be required to support it. One tweet from a participant in July 2020, after a temporary return to regular in-person schooling, might confirm one purpose of the OTC as giving direction in a difficult time (L., July): "In the crisis, the #(name of OTC) was to me compass, binoculars, radio, logbook, officers' mess, coffee and starry sky all at once. Ladies and gentlemen, it was – and still is – a privilege to work with you!"

The lack of criticality that Lantz-Andersson et al. (2018) find central in their study can be found in the present study as well. Non-conflicting and non-confrontational forms of discourse dominate even for controversial topics. The focus of the interactions is on collegial support with a fast turnaround for queries afforded by the social media tool. In addition, the supportive aspect is reflected in the data by the high percentage of tweets that share links, resources, tools or experience with digital tools. In this sense, the OTC under scrutiny did not seem to have the potential to enhance shared critical reflection practices due to its predominantly pragmatic approach.

A Twitter-based OTC like the one in the present study provides easy access, very informally developed capacity building and enables fast, fluid exchanges and multimodal sharing of resources. The accessibility and structure of the OTC makes for a potentially democratic approach to professional development (Ranieri et al., 2012) and peer capacity building, with teachers empowering each other. In the present data, the empowering function of the OTC worked on a pragmatic level, namely in dealing with digital tools to survive ERT all the while providing appropriate foreign language teaching under the circumstances, and less on a critical reflection level. During ERT as a time of crisis, teachers in the data, like so many other systemically relevant professional groups, seem to have been in survival mode, which affects the participation in, purposes and outcomes of the OTC.

7 Conclusion and Outlook

The present study has attempted to analyse the dynamics of peer capacity building as a form of informally-developed professional development in an OTC on Twitter during the time of school closures in Germany. The peer professional learning clearly focused on pragmatic aspects around the dominating topic of digital tools and foreign language learning environments for ERT, with little or no room for critical reflection or discussions. The participants of the OTC, even key participants with a micro-celebrity status, empowered each other on a practical rather than emotional level in a sort of survival mode that did not see an imbalance of power relationships or an increased 'smash-and-grab' attitude as could have been expected. The interactions were characterised by a very professional tone and by little to no off-topic discussion and few emotions-related tweets, which might underscore the crisis mode that teachers were subjected to.

The study certainly has limitations in that it is a small-scale study embedded in a specific educational context, which reduces its generalisability. Document analysis as the only data collection method did not allow for triangulation e.g. of methods. It could have been insightful to include the perspective of OTC participants themselves or of teachers in the function of lurkers to arrive at a thicker description of the dynamics of the peer capacity building. In addition, it was not possible to compare data with data from the OTC in "regular" times as the data collection period spanned the time of school closures from mid-March to the end of May.

In order to shed more light on informal professional development and the dynamics of OTC for professional development purposes using social media applications like Twitter, more empirical studies are needed that consider the affordances and challenges of the digital technology they are using. Longitudinal, multiperspective studies would help us better understand the interactions and longer-term development of professional competence in an informally-developed setting like Twitter. In this connection, ethical considerations must be made and integrated in e.g. foreign language research-specific codes of practice regarding appropriate procedures for safeguarding people's rights in social media research.

8 Food for Thought: Beyond ERT

The community spirit was remarkable in the online teacher community under scrutiny as the focus of the activity shifted. Previously smash-and-grab-style profiting from follower power and collective intelligence with the purpose of keeping abreast of professional knowledge and skills in a time-saving, effective way is reported as commonplace in the literature on online teacher communities. The focus of the activity during ERT was to share ideas, experiences and resources related to digital teaching in ERT with a view to pragmatic practical support. While in the first phase of ERT in spring 2020 teachers in the present study hardly discussed the affordances and challenges of digital teaching and digital transformation of foreign language teaching, this discussion is taking place on a bigger scale. The pandemic has turbo-charged digitisation in schools and now is the time to use the momentum to move digital foreign language teaching forward where it has proved beneficial and conducive to communication and learning progress in the foreign language. To do this, we need infrastructure and didactic concepts – infrastructure is a political decision, but didactic concepts are our responsibility.

Appendix 1: Category System After Coding

Category system	
Affordances of Twitter and impact on participation in OTC	
Role of participants	Lurkers
	Beginners
	Active participants
	Key participants/micro-celebrity practitioners
Types of interactions during ERT	Experience requested
	Collective mind/request for ideas and/or resources
	Emotions shared
	Experience and/or resources shared
Topics broached during ERT	Tools/ideas/resources for digital teaching
	Methodological discussions on ERT-related digital teaching
	Reflections and discussions on foreign language practice
	Announcements or advertisements of formal PD activities
Dynamics in the development of an online FL teacher community	Content development
	Driving forces and power relationships
	Professional tone
	Community spirit

References

Bowen, G. A. (2009). Document analysis as a qualitative research method. *Qualitative Research Journal, 9*(2), 27–40. https://doi.org/10.3316/QRJ0902027

Carpenter, J. P., & Krutka, D. G. (2015). Engagement through microblogging: Educator professional development via Twitter. *Professional Development in Education, 41*(4), 707–728. https://doi.org/10.1080/19415257.2014.939294

Davis, K. (2015). Teachers' perceptions of twitter for professional development. *Disability & Rehabilitation, 37*(17), 1551–1558. https://doi.org/10.3109/09638288.2015.1052576

Dellinger, A. B., Bobbett, J. J., Olivier, D. F., & Ellett, C. D. (2008). Measuring teachers' self-efficacy beliefs: Development and use of the TEBS-self. *Teaching and Teacher Education, 24*(3), 751–766. https://doi.org/10.1016/j.tate.2007.02.010

Dörnyei, Z. (2007). *Research methods in applied linguistics*. Oxford University Press.

Drossel, K., Eickelmann, B., Schaumburg, H., & Labusch, A. (2019). Nutzung digitaler Medien nd Prädikatoren aus der Perspektive der Lehrerinnen und Lehrer im internationalen Vergleich. In B. Eickelmann, W. Bos, J. Gerick, F. Goldhammer, H. Schaumburg, K. Schwippert, M. Senkbeil, & J. Vahrenholz (Eds.), *ICILS 2018 #Deutschland. Computer- und informationsbezogene Kompetenzen im Bereich Computational Thinking* (pp. 205–240). Waxmann.

Edelstein, D. (2013). *Das Bildungssystem in Deutschland*. Retrieved from https://bpb.de/gesellschaft/bildung/zukunft-bildung/163283/das-bildungssystem-in-deutschland

Elliott, J. C. (2017). The evolution from traditional to online professional development: A review. *Journal of Digital Learning in Teacher Education, 33*(3), 114–125. https://doi.org/10.1080/21532974.1305304

Ellis, R. (2018). *Reflections on task-based language teaching*. Multilingual Matters.

Fishman, B. (2016). Possible futures for online teacher professional development. In C. Dede, A. Eisenkraft, K. Frumin, & A. Hartley (Eds.), *Teacher learning in the digital age: Online professional development in STEM education* (pp. 13–30). Harvard University Press.

Gerick, J., Eickelmann, B., & Labuch, A. (2019). Schulische Prozesse als Lern- und Lehrbedingungen in den ICILS-Teilnehmerländern. In B. Eickelmann, W. Bos, J. Gerick, F. Goldhammer, H. Schaumburg, K. Schwippert, M. Senkbeil, & J. Vahrenhold (Eds.), *ICILS 2018 #Deutschland. Computer- und informationsbezogene Kompetenzen von Schülerinnen und Schülern im zweiten internationalen Vergleich und Kompetenzen im Bereich Computational Thinking* (pp. 172–203). Waxmann.

Göktürk Saglam, A. L., & Dikilitaş, K. (2020). Evaluating an online professional learning community as a context for professional development classroom-based research. *TESL-EJ, 24*(3), 17pp. Retrieved from: https://www.tesl-ej.org/wordpress/issues/volume24/ej95/ej95int/

Greenhow, C., & Askari, E. (2017). Learning and teaching with social network sites: A decade of research in education. *Education and Information Technologies, 22*(2), 623–645. https://doi.org/10.1007/s-10639-015-9446-9

Hodges, C., Moore, S., Lockee, B., Trust, T., & Bond, A. (2020). The difference between emergency remote teaching and online learning. *Educause Review, 27.03.2020*. Retrieved from https://er.educause.edu/articles/2020/3/the-difference-between-emergency-remote-teaching-and-online-learning.

Hou, H. (2015). What makes an online community of practice work? A situated study of Chinese student teachers' perceptions of online professional learning. *Teaching and Teacher Education, 46*, 6–16. https://doi.org/10.1016/j.tate.2014.10.005

Kelly, N., & Antonio, A. (2016). Teacher peer support in social network sites. *Teaching and Teacher Education, 56*, 138–149. https://doi.org/10.1016/j.tate.2016.02.007

Kotsios, A., Magnani, M., Rossi, R., Shklovski, I., & Vega, D. (2019). An analysis of the consequences of the general data protection regulation (GDPR) on social network research. *ACM Transactions on Social Commputing, 2*(3), 1–22. https://doi.org/10.1145/3365524

Krutka, D. G., & Carpenter, J. P. (2016). Participatory learning through social media: How and why social studies educators use Twitter. *Contemporary Issues in Technology and Teacher Education, 16*(1), 38–59.

Lamnek, S. (1995). *Qualitative Sozialforschung, Band 2: Methoden und Techniken* (3rd Ed.). Beltz.

Lantz-Andersson, A., Lundin, M., & Selwyn, S. (2018). Twenty years of online teacher communities: A systematic review of formally-organized and informally-developed professional learning groups. *Teaching and Teacher Education, 75*, 302–315. https://doi.org/10.1016/j.tate.2018.07.008

Lundin, M., Lantz-Andersson, A., & Hillman, T. (2020). Teachers' identity work in a professional Facebook group. *Journal of Information Technology Education: Research, 19*, 205–222. https://doi.org/10.28945/4540

Macia, M., & García, I. (2016). Informal online communities and networks as a source of teacher professional development. *Teaching and Teacher Education, 55*, 291–307. https://doi.org/10.1016/j.tate.2016.01.021

Marklund, L. (2015). Preschool teachers' informal online professional development in relation to educational use of tablets in Swedish preschools. *Professional Development in Education, 41*(2), 236–253. https://doi.org/10.1080/19415257

Marwick, A. (2015). You may know me from YouTube: (Micro)-celebrity in social media. In P. Marshall & S. Redmond (Eds.), *A companion to celebrity* (pp. 333–340). John Wiley.

Müller-Hartmann, A., & Schocker-von Ditfurth, M. (2011). *Task-supported language teaching*. U. Francke.

Piccardo, E., & North, B. (2019). *The action-oriented approach: A dynamic vision of language education*. Multilingual Matters.

Postholm, M. (2012). Teachers' professional development: A theoretical review. *Educational Research, 54*(4), 405–429. https://doi.org/10.1080/00131881.2012.734725

Ranieri, M., Manca, S., & Fini, A. (2012). Why (and how) do teachers engage in social networks? An exploratory study of professional use of Facebook and its implications for lifelong learning. *British Journal of Educational Technology, 43*(5), 754–769. https://doi.org/10.1111/j.1467-8535.2012.01356.x

Rehm, M., & Notten, A. (2016). Twitter as an informal learning space for teachers!? The role of social capital in twitter conversations among teachers. *Teaching and Teacher Education, 60*, 215–223. https://doi.org/10.1016/j.tate.2016.08.015

Robson, J. (2018). Performance, structure and ideal identity. *British Journal of Educational Technology, 49*(3), 439–450. https://doi.org/10.1111/bjet.12551

Trust, T., & Horrocks, B. (2017). 'I never feel alone in my classroom': Teacher professional growth within a blended community of practice. *Professional Development in Education, 43*(4), 645–665. https://doi.org/10.1080/19415257.2016.1233507

Trust, T., Krutka, D., & Carpenter, J. (2016). "Together we are better": Professional learning networks for teachers. *Computers and Education, 102*, 15–34. https://doi.org/10.1016/j.compedu.2016.06.007

Tsiotakis, P., & Jimoyiannis, A. (2016). Critical factors towards analysing teachers' presence in on-line learning communities. *Internet and Higher Education, 28*, 45–58. https://doi.org/10.1016/j.iheduc.2015.09.002

Visser, R. D., Evering, L. C., & Barrett, D. E. (2014). Twitter for teachers: The implications of Twitter as a self-directed professional development tool for K-12 teachers. *Journal of Research on Technology in Education, 46*(4), 396–413. https://doi.org/10.1080/15391523.2014.925694

Vollmer, H. J., & Vogt, K. (2021). Englischdidaktik. In M. Rothgangel, U. Abraham, H. Bayrhuber, V. Frederking, W. Jank, & H. J. Vollmer (Eds.), *Lernen im Fach und über das Fach hinaus. Bestandsaufnahmen und Forschungsperspektiven aus 17 Fachdidaktiken im Vergleich* (2nd ed., pp. 103–131). Waxmann.

Wenger, E., McDermott, R. A., & Snyder, W. M. (2002). *Cultivating communities of practice: A guide to managing knowledge*. Harvard Business School Press.

Whittle, C., Tiwari, S., Yan, S., & Williams, J. (2020). Emergency remote teaching environment: A conceptual framework for responsive online teaching in crises. *Information and Learning Sciences, 121*(5/6), 311–319. https://doi.org/10.1108/ILS-04-2020-0099

Part VIII
Researcher Corner: Case Study Research

Individual and Institutional Responses to the Exigency of Online Teaching: A Case Study from Qatar

Mick King and Sedigh (Sid) Mohammadi

Highlights

In the context of this case study:

- Institutions with prior experience in online education are more resilient to enforced adaptation to online teaching;
- Language teachers are flexible and willing to work collaboratively for the good of the institution;
- A combination of structured support and varied professional development options can prove to be an effective model for language teachers;
- Due to minimal time for a structured approach to a more robust online learning model, language teachers see the need for further training and development.

1   Introduction

Educational institutions in the State of Qatar had to make crucial decisions in early 2020 on how to respond to the transition from face-to-face (F2F) teaching in the wake of the rising COVID-19 pandemic (GCO, 2020). The Community College of Qatar (CCQ) was one such institution. So began a waiting period while government directives led us to understand what would happen and what our temporary (and maybe longer term) online teaching landscape would be. This period was one of uncertainty for all, with formal action required from the college administration and application of directives by both faculty and students. There was little time to reflect on these fast-paced changes.

M. King (✉) · S. (Sid). Mohammadi
Community College of Qatar, Doha, Qatar

© The Author(s), under exclusive license to Springer Nature
Switzerland AG 2021
J. Chen (ed.), *Emergency Remote Teaching and Beyond*,
https://doi.org/10.1007/978-3-030-84067-9_19

411

This case study, which was conducted 7 months after these tumultuous events, aims to address this absence of reflection. Its focus is on both language teachers and key members of the academic administration, whose decisions impacted on teaching and learning. As such, the study considers both individual and institutional lived experiences and responses to the urgency of online teaching. In particular, it seeks answers to the extent to which language teachers were prepared to teach online; the extent to which steps taken by the institution were effective; and the extent to which language teachers are prepared for future online teaching.

2 Background to the Study

CCQ provides tertiary education to Qatari nationals. It has a student body numbering around 5000 and comprises those who come from high school and those who are returning to education to upgrade their qualifications. Some students study in the foundation program in the English Language Center (ELC) to reach the requisite English level to enter college. At the time of this study there were 33 language teachers in the ELC. At the college level, the Department of Languages and Literature (DLL) offers courses in English academic writing, language, fiction, as well as second/foreign language courses in English, Spanish and French. The DLL language teachers numbered 23. Arabic is the students' first language and Arabic courses were delivered by a teaching team of 13. These 69 faculty members, alongside academic administrators, tasked with managing the transition, constituted the sample of this study.

Qatar is an Arabian Gulf State which has one of the world's highest per capita incomes, due mainly to its gas reserves (Anthony & Crystal, 2020). As part of its Qatar National Vision 2030, it invests heavily in education for its citizens (GSDP, 2008). Its wealth allows it to provide a high level of information technology access to its citizens and residents. This combination of wealth and technology makes an online learning environment a feasible option.

Prior to the COVID-19 pandemic, CCQ had already been using the Blackboard learning management system (LMS) for courses. Faculty and students all had a Microsoft Office 365 account including the Teams application, which was to become the videoconferencing platform for online teaching. The college had already started a hybrid learning project in which a number of language teachers were involved. In addition, its Teaching and Learning Center (TLC) had been providing faculty and students with training on how to use Blackboard effectively. This usage was tracked digitally for faculty as part of the annual performance appraisal.

Although usage varied among faculty, familiarity with EdTech was an integral part of recruitment decision-making, and ongoing training meant that faculty were expected to use it in their teaching. Some were more willing and able to make use of the EdTech tools than others. Usage among students was also evident, although faculty had expressed frustration at students' preference for social media over Blackboard. As a result, the TLC as well as the ELC EdTech Committee had been offering video tutorials and training sessions to support faculty and students. This was the contextual environment at CCQ when the decision was made to go online.

Once this transition started, the TLC moved its training focus to Teams and at the end of the Spring Semester, a professional development (PD) initiative called the 'Virtual Academy' (VA) was launched as a learning module on Blackboard, whereby all CCQ faculty were invited to upload self-developed online teaching modules and resources for use by their peers. Figure 1 below shows the content menu of the VA.

As can be seen, the Academy also provided discussion forums for immediate issues and concerns as well as responses to academic articles. Figures 2 and 3 show an example of a menu link to comment on a research article and an example snippet of a discussion forum respectively.

These discussion boards morphed into the Virtual Hub, an initiative of two language teachers, where up to 100 faculty members across disciplines logged on to a live discussion. These platforms were provided as optional PD. An example slide of one of the Hub discussion topics can be seen in Fig. 4. Most faculty actively engaged with the VA, but faculty were also encouraged to follow independent PD for online learning if they wished. It is the reflection on these training materials and PD experiences which form the basis of this case study.

Fig. 1 Virtual academy menu

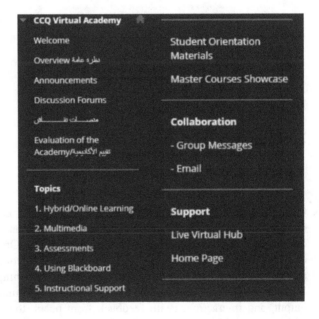

Fig. 2 Research article discussion link page

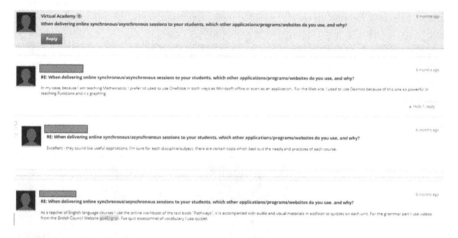

Fig. 3 Example discussion board

3 Literature Review

3.1 Finding a Suitable Model

Given its context, CCQ had various options in how to approach a move to learning online. As this study focuses on language teachers, the options reviewed here focus on language equivalents of more general approaches. Online Language Learning and Teaching (OLLT) requires a systematic process of course "planning, designing and determination of aims to create an effective learning ecology" (Bozkurt & Sharma, 2020, p. ii). In doing so, it should offer "opportunities for sufficient input, output, and interaction…with feedback from peers, the teacher, and technology with the possibility for individualization" (Gacs et al., 2020, p. 382) with "technology…facilitating pedagogy [and] not vice-versa." (McCarthy, 2016, p. 3). For Glick and Fang (2010, cited in Richards, 2015, p. 637), the success of an online language course depends on: a) a well-structured e-learning course design; b) a clearly defined role for e-tutors; c) training and orientation for e-tutors and students before the

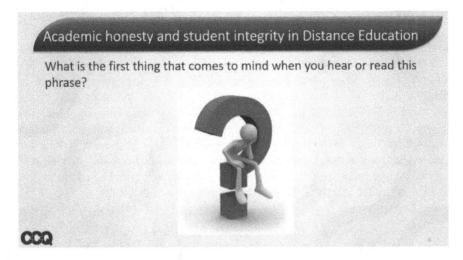

Fig. 4 Virtual hub question slide

course; d) regular assessment of tutors; and e) the interaction in the course of a range of automatic tools for assessment and self-learning. However, the urgency of action required by CCQ made such a systematic and planned option untenable.

The option of blended language learning (BLL) was a genuine possibility for CCQ as it was already planning to start hybrid courses the following academic year. BLL is "a course designed as a mix of face-to-face and distance learning, with both elements being an important part of the whole" (Sharma & Westbrook, 2016, p. 320). Some benefits of using this approach include improved pedagogy, increased access and flexibility, and increased cost-effectiveness (Graham, 2006). For CCQ students, many of whom work and study, there is a benefit in substituting travel time by time dedicated to study. From the institutional perspective, a reduction in usage of facilities can limit expenses and provide options to open up more courses.

According to Sharma and Westbrook (2016), BLL and OLLT both make use of synchronous and asynchronous learning. In the context of OLLT, Hockley (2015, p. 310) describes them thus:

> Students work fully online and mainly in asynchronous mode (that is, not in real time) to practice reading, writing, and listening; this is often complemented by regular synchronous (real time) speaking classes, for example via a videoconferencing platform.

Meskill and Anthony (2015) accentuate the importance of both, with asynchronous learning providing time for reflection on learning while synchronous learning allows for the demonstration of learning in real time. There was active debate at CCQ about whether classes should be fully asynchronous or not, with perceptions about students' ability to work independently, a common thread of conversation. Another concern was the effort required for fully synchronous online study in what would initially be the temporary approach; emergency remote teaching (ERT).

Emergency remote language teaching, (ERLT) is a hastily, forced, temporary, and (sometimes) haphazard shift to online delivery of an F2F language course in response to a circumstance such as COVID-19 (Gacs et al., 2020; Golden, 2020). The stakeholders are 'obliged' to switch to rapid, unsystematic online instruction; an unfamiliar territory which brings about challenges and resistance (Bozkurt & Sharma, 2020). While many elements of OLLT and BLL might be employed, it is questionable how effective they would be without systematic planning. Similarly, despite the many EdTech tools freely available to use, it is also questionable if broad use of them might overcomplicate learning when stakeholders were looking for calm in turbulent times. Given its background in Blackboard training for all and hybrid training for some, CCQ had the potential to move beyond ERLT. Its ability to do so depended greatly on the EdTech preparedness of its faculty.

3.2   EdTech Preparedness

CCQ faculty must have a minimum of 3 years' experience in the tertiary sector but the majority have more. The age range of the population is from the late 20s to early 60s with the more senior less likely to have received EdTech as part of pre-service teacher training. Yet EdTech is ubiquitous in the field of language teaching. Most introductory teaching methodology books cover it in their latest editions (e.g. Brown & Lee, 2015; Harmer, 2015; Scrivener, 2011). The myriad of options like Computer-Assisted Language Learning (CALL), Technology-enhanced Language Learning (TELL), BLL, and OLLT (for a complete overview, see Farr & Murray, 2016) is such that it can be challenging for practitioners to decide which is most appropriate for their context.

Some CCQ faculty had followed intensive pre-service language teacher training as part of their qualifications such as Cambridge CELTA, which focuses exclusively "on the delivery of a range of classroom survival techniques enabling the novice to approach the ELT classroom with a degree of confidence" (Brandt, 2006, p. 363). In addition, all language teachers have to have a Master's in language education. While such programs may include a module on EdTech, they tend to focus on the theoretical aspect of language teaching with little or no opportunity for teaching practice and practical application (Li and Tin, 2013; Mohammadi, 2018; Papageorgiou et al., 2019).

3.3   Institutional-Led and Self-directed PD

Assuming that a variance in preparedness exists, institutional action is needed to address this discrepancy. According to Leung (2009), professionalism in language teaching has two dimensions: institutional-led and self-directed. Institutional-led professionalism often takes the form of in-service training which primarily focuses on the immediate contextual needs of the institution (Richards & Farrell, 2005). Pre-service programs can be "of a fairly general nature, somewhat theoretical, and not directly relevant to their teaching assignments" (p.10), so in-service contextual training would be needed. However, such training is not always provided (Hobbs, 2013; Higginbotham, 2019), possibly due to restrictive budgets or a belief that the onus for development lies with the practitioner. As explained earlier, CCQ had provided faculty with broad EdTech training prior to the inception of online teaching. However, faculty may find such training too general for their teaching context. This is where self-directed PD can play an important role.

Self-directed PD can refer to teacher-initiated events, external PD, or any professional interactions with peers. CCQ language teachers had a history of providing contextual PD activities, often with an EdTech focus, as this proved more meaningful to teachers than generic institutional training. The ELC had its own dedicated EdTech Committee whose members also served as EdTech peer mentors. The VA gave opportunities to interact and reflect on experiences individually and in groups, allowing all to reflect on "their own values, beliefs and practices" (Richards, 2015, p. 705). While most teacher development of this kind takes place through a teacher's own personal initiative, collaboration and cooperation with colleagues "both enhances individual learning and serves the collective goals of an institution"(Richards & Farrell, 2005, p. 12). Studies have found that informal collaborative discussion and exchange of ideas in staff rooms is an effective support to teachers and productive in establishing affinity and identity among peers (Higginbotham, 2019; Mann & Tang, 2012). The effectiveness of this is due to "its democratic, collaborative, and reflective nature" (Richards, 2015, p. 400). Richards and Farrell (2005) endorse this type of informal learning where people work effectively together, and urge institutions to promote teamwork "because teaching is generally seen as an individual activity" (p. 12). Reinders (2009) maintains that although an institutional "formal [PD] approach is likely to lead to more consistent results across the board", informal learning networks should be supported by the institution, since teachers learn to use technology informally "out of enthusiasm for the medium and with help from colleagues" (p. 233). Such self-directed learning was the aim of the VA and its offshoot, the Virtual Hub. It was hoped the collaborative nature of the initiative would be a cornerstone for helping faculty maintain or build resilience in these exceptional circumstances.

3.4   Teacher Resilience

For Gu and Day (2013) teacher resilience is "the capacity to maintain equilibrium and a sense of commitment, agency and moral purpose in the everyday worlds in which teachers teach" (p. 26). Resilience can be tested in times of change and uncertainty, and there has been an emergence of research into teacher resilience in the times of COVID-19 (see, for example, Gao & Zhang, 2020; Macintyre et al., 2020). This psychological challenge is especially true for language teachers, many of whom may already perceive having less status than teachers of other subjects (Rádai et al., 2003). Boyd and Eckert (2001) further assert that one's ability to stay strong can be compromised when events happen which are out of a teacher's control. This can be caused at any time in the same place as institutions are non-static environments (Hernandez-Martinez & Williams, 2013), and can happen at any point in one's career (Mansfield et al., 2012). The move to online teaching was one such event that had the potential to test the resilience of language teachers at CCQ.

Teachers who were comfortable with EdTech were less likely to feel tested. However, there are other traits of resilient teachers which could also help as coping mechanisms. These include being vocationally and professionally committed (MacBeath, 2012), having self-confidence (Beltman et al., 2011) and being self-reflective (Mansfield et al., 2012). Relevant actions of resilient teachers in the CCQ context would include finding support networks (Gibbs & Miller, 2014; Meister & Ahrens, 2011), focusing on controllable aspects of the job (Howard & Johnson, 2004), and not worrying about perfectionism (Oxtoby, 2016). To do this, it was important for the institution to create an environment where patience was key, not too much was asked of faculty in relation to online teaching, and sufficient outlets were provided such as the VA to provide pedagogical, technical and peer support, and to give professional freedom to faculty in how they determined their way of conducting PD for their new teaching situation.

4   Methodology

This study was framed within an interpretivist paradigm (Cohen et al., 2018) as it aimed "to explore perspectives and shared meanings and to develop insights and a deeper understanding of phenomena occurring in the social world" (Burton et al., 2008, p. 60). It was also informed by aspects of pragmatism by focusing on "what works" (Teddlie & Tashakkori, 2009, p. 294), where "the methods used in research should be determined by the questions asked" (Punch, 2009, p. 290). Given the immediacy of the research theme, pragmatism informed decisions made on chosen data sources and instrument design to provide sufficient rich data as efficiently as possible.

4.1   *Research Questions*

The research sought to answer the following questions:

1. To what extent were CCQ language teachers prepared for online teaching?
2. To what extent were steps taken by language teachers and the institution to support online teaching effective?
3. To what extent are language teachers prepared for future online teaching?

4.2   Research Design

A case study approach was employed as the institution was bounded in a real-life context (Casanave, 2015). In such institutions "social action takes place, the boundaries of which may not be clear and are determined by the scope of the researcher's interests" (Hood, 2009, p. 68). The study was exploratory in nature (Boudah, 2020) as it sought to discover participants' views. It incorporated a multilevel element as it included different hierarchical social levels (management and faculty) within the educational establishment (Riazi, 2017). It also used an explanatory sequential design (Creswell & Plano Clark, 2018), whereby outcomes from one instrument informed the design of the next. The sample of the study was purposive (Wiersma & Jurs, 2009), as it comprised the 69 language teachers at CCQ as well as a number of colleagues tasked with providing the college response. Their specific roles in the study are elaborated on in Table 1, which describes data collection, participants and

Table 1 Documentary and primary data collection and analysis

Documents	Source	When	Thematic analysis details
Emails	From Vice President's Office	Over the 7-month period	79 relevant emails
ELC health check survey	ELC Department	After 1 month	21 qualitative responses
VA survey	Virtual Academy Coordination	After 3 months	Final report

Instrument	Participants	Selection	When	Design and thematic analysis details
Questionnaire part 1	32 CCQ language teachers	–	After 7 months	Likert scale agreement questions: 7 on initial efficacy and 7 on efficacy after 7 months. Comparative analysis of efficacy
Questionnaire part 2	32 CCQ language teachers	–	After 7 months	2 open questions on initial response and current efficacy
Faculty focus group	3 participants	Based on questionnaire responses	After 7 months	Participants represented strong resilience, growing resilience and continued uncertainty. Structured interview based on questionnaire findings
Management focus group	4 participants	Based on administrative involvement in college response	After 7 months	Participants represented one senior manager, 2 VA coordinators and one VH coordinator. Structured interview based on questionnaire findings

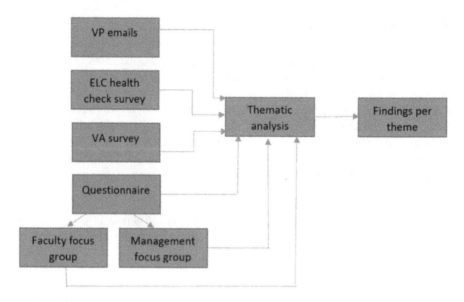

Fig. 5 Research process

analysis. The research process is shown in Fig. 5 and will be described below, incorporating instrument design.

At each stage of data collection, data were coded and tagged to a priori categories emanating from the literature review. These categories were: ability in EdTech, moving to online teaching, college response, ability to adapt, sense of worry, and peer support. Data were then transferred to a spreadsheet to aid thematic analysis (Creswell & Plano Clark, 2018). Documentary data comprised internal email directives from the VP Office, open question responses from an ELC health check survey conducted 1 month into online teaching, and a VA survey report compiled 2 months later. Primary data consisted of a questionnaire and two focus groups (see Table 1). The questionnaire sought Likert scale levels of agreement (Dörnyei & Taguchi, 2010) to compare language teacher views at the start of ERT and 7 months thereafter. Two additional open questions allowed respondents to elaborate on their feelings both at the start of online teaching and 7 months later. The online questionnaire can be found in Appendix 1.

After analyzing both quantitative and qualitative questionnaire responses and comparing levels of confidence at the two points in time, 3 participants of those who volunteered in the questionnaire were selected for the faculty focus group. They were chosen to provide a spectrum of perspectives ranging from resilience to uncertainty based on their questionnaire answers. The management focus group comprised those responsible for college directives, the VA and the Virtual Hub. On pragmatic grounds, focus group question design was structured based on findings in the questionnaire. The interviews were 1-h long. They were recorded and transcribed before being analyzed, coded and tagged to the a priori categories. Once all quantitative and qualitative data had been coded and tagged, a final phase of analysis looked to see if emergent categories were evident in the untagged codes. It was decided to add two categories not directly addressed in the literature review, due to their frequency of reference in the data and their relevance to this volume. The categories from the data analysis became the themes chosen for reporting results and discussion.

Ethical procedures were followed throughout in accordance with Dörnyei (2007). After receiving college consent to collect data and conduct the study, the case study questionnaire respondents and focus group participants were informed of their rights, the confidentiality measures, and data usage intentions. For focus groups, consent forms were signed, and post-analysis member-checking was conducted. In general terms, as access was granted, there were minimal limitations, the major one being time, given the immediate relevance of the case.

5   Results and Discussion

Given the thematic nature of the analysis, results will be shared and discussed per theme (considering two points in time for reflection: the start of ERT and the perspectives 7 months later). Thematic alignment with the research questions is shown in Table 2.

Both quantitative and qualitative data from the various sources are interwoven to highlight the concept of narrative participant voices. Documentary data is presented in summary format and is referred to as VP emails, ELC survey and VA survey. For primary data, respondents are referred to as per Table 3.

5.1   EdTech Preparedness

Questionnaire responses showed that 81% felt confident in their EdTech abilities at the onset of online learning and this rose to 100% 7 months later. This was echoed in the focus groups related to positivity in the team's ability (Ibrahim-VH) and belief in one's own ability (Harry-SR, Suzy-GR). Despite this, it appeared that the

Table 2 Theme-research question alignment

Theme	Research question
EdTech preparedness	1
College response	2
Self-efficacy	1, 2, 3
Collegiality	2
Students	–
Future directions	2

Table 3 Participant pseudonyms

Data source	Pseudonym	Description
Research questionnaire	R1, R2, R3 etc.	Questionnaire respondent
Faculty focus group	Harry-SR	SR denotes strong resilience
	Suzy-GR	GR denotes growing resilience
	Yara-CU	CU denotes continuing uncertainty
Management focus group	Ahmed-SM	SM denotes senior management
	Fred-VA	VA denotes VA coordinator
	Hind-VA	VA denotes VA coordinator
	Ibrahim-VH	VH denotes Virtual Hub coordinator

sense of the unknown made some a little unsure of their readiness. On the presumption that not all teachers receive sufficient EdTech training in their studies (Brandt, 2006), some respondents did feel that not all language teachers were ready. R2 said, "I knew that some colleagues were going to struggle and that worried me", while R11 felt "like we were walking into unknown territory". Fred-VA was worried about making this switch mid-semester and not knowing how teachers would fare, and Hind-VA felt that those who had not been involved in the hybrid project might struggle. Indeed, R30 admitted "I have no idea how I could use technology to my advantage" while R11 explained how difficult the adjustment was. This sense of uncertainty may be linked to the language teachers' inability to apply EdTech knowledge gained pre-service into practice (Mohammadi, 2018). Although all felt confident after 7 months, R15 felt that "staff and faculty [still] need to develop their technological skills".

5.2   College Response

Initial expectations about the level of college support varied among the sample. Ahmed-SM believed that an early decision to stick to the existing academic calendar and class schedules, and to choose Teams as the main platform to accompany Blackboard, brought a sense of stability. He added that the leveraging of the hybrid project, which bore the hallmarks of BLL (Sharma & Westbrook, 2016) was another key decision. As he said, "We capitalized on the resources we had". Harry-SR and Suzy-GR were both confident that training would be provided, given the amount of expertise among the team. However, contrary to McCarthy's (2016) assertion, early training centered on how to use the new technology rather than on how to apply it pedagogically, which led to some frustrations. Suzy-GR shared, "Initially I had no idea what I was doing", despite her following the prescribed training. Others were just not sure if the training would be effective, but were also knowledgeable of the in-house expertise, which eased their fears somewhat.

R13 did not have high expectations initially and feels that this belief was borne out. However, reflecting back, most respondents were very positive regarding training meeting the contextual needs of the college (Richards & Farrell, 2005). The most commonly coded responses showed a liking for the chosen platforms and the VA. The continued use of Blackboard and new use of Teams appeared to be strongly supported in the ELC survey, while the Academy was rated positively by over 80% of respondents in the VA survey. Ahmed-SM explained how the VA provided "an umbrella of skills...and gave the college administration a sense of comfort in this big challenge". In the questionnaire, 87% of respondents felt the college response met their expectations, with a number of them sharing that their initial concerns dissipated relatively quickly due to the college's prompt decision-making on platform choice and setting up of the VA.

A few respondents shared mixed-to-negative feelings on the college response, claiming insufficient practice opportunities (R11) and training (R16), and the need for a more standardized approach to course delivery (R19), as opposed to a more haphazard, temporary approach more typical of ERLT (Golden, 2020). Yara-CU felt that at the beginning there were signs of confusion about how to use the technology, finding training advice "ad hoc" at times. However, quantitative and coded analysis suggest that the majority were satisfied.

5.3 Self-efficacy

The faculty focus group participants shared their thoughts on self-efficacy at the start of online teaching. Harry-SR was ready to "use what we had at the beginning and then try to learn in the first few weeks or the first month how we would need to adapt our abilities to suit this new medium", seeing it as a chance to "learn something new and upskill". He did temper this enthusiasm by saying, "It's like being prepared for the sky to fall in on you", and Suzy-GR had mixed feelings, asking herself, "How am I going to do this?" Despite this concern, she also expressed liking a challenge, as did Yara-CU, who had briefly taught online before. However, Yara-CU did find it "overwhelming" citing various elements that concerned her such as not seeing students' faces (for cultural reasons, cameras were not switched on); working from home; and a perceived lack of clarity on the college response. Such events, which are beyond the control of a teacher, can negatively impact resilience (Boyd & Eckert, 2001). These concerns highlight that despite quantitative responses that indicated a good degree of self-efficacy among language teachers, some struggled at the beginning and still had concerns later.

Later reflection mostly indicated growing confidence for some, continued confident application for others, and the feeling that skills were being developed. 39% of questionnaire respondents indicated that they were more confident in general and 41% were less worried about online teaching. They spoke of growing awareness of expectations and being more comfortable using the prescribed tools. R30 shared, "[I was not] stripped of the ability to use the teaching techniques I was trained to use and comfortable within the face-to-face environment" and noted that "instructors...need not be IT whizzes in order to teach...online", mirroring Oxtoby's (2016) assertion that perfection should never be the ultimate goal. The questionnaire suggested that all who had initially indicated some level of confidence in EdTech usage either maintained or increased it, showing a resilience that comes from self-confidence (Beltman et al., 2011). From the ELC survey, the ease of transition was highlighted, and many felt they were developing new skills.

Yara-CU did feel that the VA may have been better served by focusing more on Teams mastery, and R2 said, "I feel I have improved but I am not the finished article". Various themes arose of the challenges faced in developing self-efficacy, the most common being IT issues and switched off student cameras. Most IT connectivity issues arose only in the ELC survey, so this suggests that they were resolved in the early stages of online teaching. Students not switching on cameras, which was mentioned mostly in the ELC survey, highlighted an inability to "read the room" by looking at students' facial expressions. Despite Howard and Johnson (2004) advising that one should only focus on what one can control, not all were able to do this. Yara-CU shared, "I personally struggle talking to a blank screen…I just keep trying different ways to see how I can possibly reach the students and… it's not pleasant". Class size was another issue raised as it was difficult to track student activity and, as Yara-CU said, "I can only get a few…in the class to respond…They don't answer at all so that part is hard".

5.4   Collegiality

In previous themes, although positive responses predominate, there are elements of concern. In relation to collegiality, coded responses suggested universal positivity, and this manifested itself primarily in the VA and its Virtual Hub. All management focus group members concurred in the success of the VA and it was representative of an institution creating a relatively informal learning network (Reinders, 2009). At the start Fred-VA felt that its development "was totally organic and I view this as a positive". Hind-VA explained, "We were trying to build a training system from faculty for faculty. Our message was that if you want support, we are here to support you", and she highlighted how faculty really wanted to be involved, with Ahmed-SM sharing, "The cooperative environment was very good. Many faculty members came with ideas and a willingness to take part". Such collaborative learning receives support in the literature (e.g., Richards, 2015; Richards & Farrell, 2005). Fred-VA was concerned that faculty would not submit contributions, but continued, "I affectionately began to call it a monster. Suddenly there was all this activity happening. It was very exciting as the torrent of material came in". 94% of questionnaire respondents showed initial confidence in being able to learn from their colleagues, with R11 saying, "I think we depend on each other the most", and continuing, "Our colleagues were the people in the same boat, so we could trust them for advice".

This initial positivity was borne out when reflecting back on their lived experiences. In general terms, language teachers sought out support networks to build resilience (Gibbs & Miller, 2014). R11 shared, "Our colleagues helped us a lot through the rough times", and R25 said, "I think having a community of faculty members who are always willing to help plays a significant role in adapting to the 'new normal' [and] having such a support group makes the transition smoother and less stressful". Harry-SR and Suzy-GR explained how they had become EdTech mentors for fellow faculty. However, most responses again referred to the VA. Yara-CU saw it as "an example of people really coming together", while Ibrahim-VH said, "It gave a chance to see what faculty from other departments were doing and a lot of it was very useful".

Most coded responses on collegiality were reserved for the Virtual Hub, which Ibrahim-VH had developed with another language teacher. He said, "It gave a chance for faculty to get a community spirit back after months of not coming on campus. It was [a] chance to reconnect", and Fred-VA felt that "people were craving communication", commenting on how "conversations involved people from various disciplines more easily than anything I have seen before". Both Ibrahim-VH and Hind-VA alluded to the Academy providing an outlet to discuss challenges and fears. Higginbotham (2019) extols the benefits of such informal discussion among peers. Harry-SR saw it as "a real eye-opener" and commented on how so many people logged in to participate. Yara-CU also mentioned its popularity, judging it as "amazing" and sharing, "I felt, you know, supported. I wasn't alone."

5.5 Students

As the focus of this case study is on language teachers, student response to ERLT was not considered when reviewing the literature. However, the frequency of reference to student abilities and reactions to the change indicates that this had some impact on language teachers' resilience and self-efficacy, and also played a role on language teacher views on future directions. Most related responses arose from the ELC survey, but there were also instances from the questionnaire, even though questions did not refer to students.

One ELC survey response stated that "the previous myth that teaching online courses - especially to our students – was impossible has been broken". From the same survey, it was shared that "abilities are flourishing out of need" and students became "increasingly self-aware of their own abilities and skills in terms of ICT and online platforms". Reinders (2018) proposes that an EdTech environment can promote autonomy, and another frequently coded response from the ELC survey did refer to students becoming more independent and more focused.

However, there were widespread negative experiences. The most coded were reluctance to interact and academic dishonesty. Regarding reticence, it was felt that it was easy for weak students to "hide" by claiming a broken microphone. Other respondents spoke of the teacher-student relationship being compromised, and the difficulty in gauging students' attention. Various faculty indicated frustration with the inability to track cheating, which is prevalent in e-learning environments (Chen et al., 2020). As one ELC teacher said, "When I give quizzes…there is no way of knowing whether students used their book or the assistance of a relative or tutor". Although some respondents had extolled the digital literacy abilities of students, a significant number of coded responses suggested that others were more critical. Other coded data explained how it was now more difficult to give feedback. In addition, it was highlighted how some students' lack of organizational skills and their initial sense of being lost and demotivated compromised the online teaching and learning process.

5.6 Future Directions

Despite generally very positive responses to current online teaching abilities as a result of the college response and language teachers' independent actions to develop professionally, advice on actions the institution and individuals could take to enhance online learning at CCQ was evident. The most prevalent advice was on the need for more training and PD on online teaching as opposed to ERT for both faculty and students. As an ELC teacher said, "Online learning is not 'slapping' classroom content online". As this need came predominantly from the ELC survey, it is possible that the VA, which was introduced later, may have addressed this to an extent. Indeed, Fred-VA and Ahmed-SM accentuated the need for the VA and Virtual Hub to continue. Other suggestions for EdTech training included sharing of best practice, further Teams training, further mentor support, and more video tutorials.

The second most frequently coded response was addressing academic dishonesty. Suggestions included looking at task design, using online interviews for assessment, and increasing the number of exam versions. A call was made to make camera use mandatory for assessments, although this would be difficult to mandate, given local cultural norms. It was also suggested to conduct first week placement interviews with each student in order to have a recording of their ability at the start which could be mapped against later assessment performance. Finally, the proposal for a more detailed 'honor code' was proposed to highlight the importance of academic integrity.

Linked to this 'honor code' concept was the need to set stricter standards as students were now used to online learning, so being flexible due to the transition was no longer needed. Standardization was also suggested in syllabus design to ensure an equitable learning experience. This does suggest that faculty were looking for a more sustainable and rigorous model such as Online Language Learning and Teaching (Bozkurt & Sharma, 2020) or Blended Language Learning (McCarthy, 2016). There was also a wish that students be obliged to use a suitable IT device and have the required bandwidth at home to ensure a smooth learning process.

6   Conclusion

This exploratory case study considered individual and institutional responses to the exigency of online teaching among language teachers at the Community College of Qatar. Of the data collected, only the data sources deemed most relevant were analyzed, as the timeframe for completion was short, given the time-bound relevance topic. Despite this potential limitation, data including emails, existing survey outcomes, discussion boards, a questionnaire and two focus groups proved sufficiently rich to produce pertinent themes. These were teacher preparedness, the college response, teacher self-efficacy, collegiality, students, and future directions. Research Question 1 considered the extent to which CCQ language teachers were prepared for online teaching. Results indicate that although there was a range of preparedness, most felt relatively comfortable with the transition or grew in confidence quite quickly. This was possibly due to existing Blackboard usage requirements in the college and familiarity of some faculty with hybrid models as part of the ongoing institutional hybrid project. Research Question 2 considered the personal and institutional measures taken to support faculty in online teaching. Although, there were a few cases of dissatisfaction, most respondents appeared to benefit from the dedicated platform training and the PD-oriented Virtual Academy, with its Virtual Hub element proving particularly popular. The Academy and Hub showed how faculty from all disciplines could work collaboratively to assist each other in coping with the transition to online. Research Question 3 considered the extent to which language teachers are prepared for future online teaching. While most indicated that they had definitely improved in their EdTech abilities, various suggestions were made to indicate how the institution could develop further in this regard.

One emergent theme from the data was the sense that the focus on emergency faculty development meant that some students had been left behind. Although some had coped admirably, others had not engaged in the change productively, which had the potential to limit their learning and challenge their teachers' resilience. Contextually, a study into student experiences at CCQ and their impact on the teaching and learning process to triangulate the study further may provide more impactful evidence of the way forward for the institution.

Food for Thought: Beyond ERT
The case of CCQ is most likely one that is familiar to many institutions where access to technology is available, so findings may be transferable to those contexts. Sterling efforts were made to adapt and take curriculum and practice beyond a survival strategy. However, the timing of the transition gave little opportunity to pursue a more systematic language teaching approach such as Online Language Learning and Teaching or Blended Language Learning before the summer break arrived and administrative planning for the Fall Semester took precedence. The uncertainty of what will happen in the future in times of a pandemic also complicates how to strategize, as it is unknown if it will be for the short- or the long-term. One option is to move operations completely online with requisite planning and technological investment. If budgets allow, various models of F2F, BLL or OLLT could be

employed on one site. Any of these options would provide certainty in uncertain times. If this happens, it is gratifying to know that even in the face of ongoing challenges, there is evidence at CCQ that language teachers, their colleagues from other disciplines, and students are quite resilient and adaptable to change. Faculty are willing to collaborate for personal professional development and for the benefit of their students and the institutions tasked with educating them. Almost all have indicated that they are more skilled in EdTech, with many eager for more training and more standardization of practice in online teaching and learning. Managing change is often complicated by a fear of the unknown. This unknown is now known. The ubiquitous 'we're all in this together' need no longer carry a hue of stoicism. Instead of surviving, we can focus on thriving.

Appendix 1

Online Questionnaire

Individual vs Institutional Responses to the Exigency of Online Teaching (V2)

This survey is one part of a case study designed to better understand CCQ language teacher responses and views on institutional responses to emergency remote teaching (ERT). All responses will be saved in a secure password-protected location and only the researchers will have access to the data. The survey does not collect any personal information unless you volunteer to be considered for a follow-up focus group. The survey should not take more than 10–15 min to complete fully. For Questions 1–6 and 8–13, choose the level of agreement response that most accurately reflects your level of agreement. If you feel you would have preferred to answer at a point between two levels of agreement, you can clarify this as part of your response to the qualitative questions, Questions 7 and 14. While there is no obligation to answer qualitative questions, rich responses to these questions will help us to more accurately understand your perspectives, so we encourage you to answer them. If you have any questions about this questionnaire or the study please feel free to contact the researchers at Michael.King@ccq.edu.qa or Sedigh. Mohammadi@ccq.edu.qa

Section 1

Initial response

   When emergency online teaching was announced:

1. I felt confident in my ability to use educational technology effectively (e.g. Blackboard tools, Office 365 apps, other web-based tools and platforms).

- Strongly agree
- Agree
- Disagree
- Strongly disagree

2. I felt comfortable about moving to teaching completely online.

- Strongly agree
- Agree
- Disagree
- Strongly disagree

3. I felt confident that the college would prepare me well for teaching online.

- Strongly agree
- Agree
- Disagree
- Strongly disagree

4. I felt I could easily adapt to changes related to online teaching.

- Strongly agree
- Agree
- Disagree
- Strongly disagree

5. I felt worried about the sudden change to online teaching.

- Strongly agree
- Agree
- Disagree
- Strongly disagree

6. I felt confident that I could rely on my colleagues for support when needed.

- Strongly agree
- Agree
- Disagree
- Strongly disagree

7. Please elaborate on your answers to Section 1 (Questions 1–6) – Initial Response

Enter your answer.

Section 2

Reflective response.
Now...

8. I feel more confident in my ability to use educational technology (e.g. Blackboard tools, Office 365 apps, other web-based tools and platforms).

   • Strongly agree
   • Agree
   • Disagree
   • Strongly disagree

9. I feel more comfortable about teaching completely online.

   • Strongly agree
   • Agree
   • Disagree
   • Strongly disagree

10. I feel that the college prepared me well for teaching online.

    • Strongly agree
    • Agree
    • Disagree
    • Strongly disagree

11. I feel that I easily adapted to changes related to online teaching.

    • Strongly agree
    • Agree
    • Disagree
    • Strongly disagree

12. I feel worried about online teaching.

    • Strongly agree
    • Agree
    • Disagree
    • Strongly disagree

13. I feel that I was well supported by my colleagues when needed.

    • Strongly agree
    • Agree
    • Disagree
    • Strongly disagree

14. Please elaborate on your answers to Section 2 (Questions 8 to 13) – Reflective Response.

Enter your answer

15. If you would be willing to participate in a follow-up focus group, please add your CCQ email below.

Enter your answer

References

Anthony, J. D., & Crystal, J. A. (2020). Qatar. In *Encyclopædia Britannica*. https://www.britannica.com/place/Qatar. Accessed 4 Dec 2020.

Beltman, S., Mansfield, C., & Price, A. (2011). Thriving not just surviving: A review of research on teacher resilience. *Educational Research Review, 6*(3), 185–207. https://doi.org/10.1016/j.edurev.2011.09.001

Boudah, D. J. (2020). *Conducting educational research: Guide to completing a thesis, dissertation, or action research project* (2nd ed.). SAGE Publications.

Boyd, J., & Eckert, P. (2001). *Creating resilient educators: A global learning communities manual*. Global Learning Communities and Julie Boyd.

Bozkurt, A., & Sharma, R. C. (2020). Emergency remote teaching in a time of global crisis due to CoronaVirus pandemic. *Asian Journal of Distance Education, 15*(1), i–vi. https://doi.org/10.5281/zenodo.3778083

Brandt, C. (2006). Allowing for practice: A critical issue in TESOL teacher preparation. *ELT Journal, 60*(4), 355–364. https://doi.org/10.1093/elt/ccl026

Brown, H. D., & Lee, H. (2015). Technology in language learning and teaching. In *Teaching by principles: An interactive approach to language pedagogy* (4th ed., pp. 237–256). Pearson Education.

Burton, N., Brundrett, M., & Jones, M. (2008). *Doing your education research project*. SAGE Publications.

Casanave, C. P. (2015). Case studies. In B. Paltridge & A. Phakiti (Eds.), *Research methods in applied linguistics: A practical resource* (2nd ed., pp. 119–136). Bloomsbury Academic.

Chen, C., Long, J., Liu, J., Wang, Z., Wang, L., & Zhang, J. (2020). Online academic dishonesty of college students: A review. In *Proceedings of the 2020 international conference on Advanced Education, Management and Social Science (AEMSS2020)* (pp. 156–161). Atlantis Press. https://doi.org/10.2991/assehr.k.200723.121

Cohen, L., Manion, L., & Morrison, K. (2018). *Research methods in education* (8th ed.). Routledge.

Creswell, J. W., & Plano Clark, V. L. (2018). *Designing and conducting mixed methods research* (3rd ed.). SAGE Publications, Inc.

Dörnyei, Z. (2007). *Research methods in applied linguistics: Quantitative, qualitative, and mixed methodologies*. Oxford University Press.

Dörnyei, Z., & Taguchi, T. (2010). *Questionnaires in second language research: Construction, administration, and processing* (2nd ed.). Routledge.

Farr, F., & Murray, L. (Eds.). (2016). *The Routledge handbook of language learning and technology*. Routledge.

Gacs, A., Goertler, S., & Spasova, S. (2020). Planned online language education versus crisis-prompted online language teaching: Lessons for the future. *Foreign Language Annals, 53*(2), 380–392. https://doi.org/10.1111/flan.12460

Gao, L. X., & Zhang, L. J. (2020). Teacher learning in difficult times: Examining foreign language teachers' cognitions about online teaching to tide over COVID-19. *Frontiers in Psychology, 11*, 549653. https://doi.org/10.3389/fpsyg.2020.549653

GCO. (2020). Qatar announces closure of schools, universities over coronavirus. *Government Communications Office of Qatar*. https://www.gco.gov.qa/en/2020/03/09/statement-on-the-suspension-of-public-and-private-schools-and-universities-for-all-students-until-further-notice-as-a-precautionary-measure-to-contain-the-spread-of-coronavirus/. Accessed 4 Dec 2020.

Gibbs, S., & Miller, A. (2014). Teachers' resilience and well-being: A role for educational psychology. *Teachers and Teaching, 20*(5), 609–621. https://doi.org/10.1080/13540602.2013.844408

Golden, C. (2020). Remote teaching: The glass half-full. *EDUCAUSE Review*. https://er.educause.edu/blogs/2020/3/remote-teaching-the-glass-half-full. Accessed 21 Nov 2020.

Graham, C. R. (2006). Blended learning systems: Definition, current trends, and future directions. In C. J. Bonk & C. R. Graham (Eds.), *Handbook of blended learning global perspectives local designs* (pp. 3–21). Pfeiffer Publishing.

GSDP. (2008). *Qatar national vision 2030*. Doha: General Secretariat for Development Planning (GSDP). https://www.gco.gov.qa/wp-content/uploads/2016/09/GCO-QNV-English.pdf. Accessed 4 Dec 2020.

Gu, Q., & Day, C. (2013). Challenges to teacher resilience: Conditions count. *British Educational Research Journal, 39*(1), 22–44.

Harmer, J. (2015). *The practice of English language teaching* (5th ed.). Pearson Education.

Hernandez-Martinez, P., & Williams, J. (2013). Against the odds: Resilience in mathematics students in transition. *British Educational Research Journal, 39*(1), 45–59. https://doi.org/10.108 0/01411926.2011.623153

Higginbotham, C. (2019). Professional development: Life or death after pre-service training? *ELT Journal, 73*(4), 396–408. https://doi.org/10.1093/elt/ccz021

Hobbs, V. (2013). 'A basic starter pack': The TESOL certificate as a course in survival. *ELT Journal, 67*(2), 163–174. https://doi.org/10.1093/elt/ccs078

Hockly, N. (2015). Developments in online language learning. *ELT Journal, 69*(3), 308–313. https://doi.org/10.1093/elt/ccv020

Hood, M. (2009). Case study. In J. Heigham & R. A. Croker (Eds.), *Qualitative research in applied linguistics: A practical introduction* (pp. 66–90). Palgrave Macmillan UK.

Howard, S., & Johnson, B. (2004). Resilient teachers: Resisting stress and burnout. *Social Psychology of Education, 7*(4), 399–420. https://doi.org/10.1007/s11218-004-0975-0

Leung, C. (2009). Second language teacher professionalism. In A. Burns & J. C. Richards (Eds.), *The Cambridge guide to second language teacher education* (pp. 49–58). Cambridge University Press.

Li, B., & Tin, T. B. (2013). Exploring the expectations and perceptions of non-native English speaking students in masters level TESOL programs. *New Zealand Studies in Applied Linguistics, 19*(2), 21–35. https://search.informit.com.au/documentSummary;dn=746681612779063; res=IELIND

MacBeath, J. (2012). *Future of the teaching profession*. Brussels, Belgium: Education International Research Institute. https://www.educ.cam.ac.uk/networks/lfl/about/events/pastlflsuppersemi-nars/PDFs/Future/of/teaching/Profession.pdf

MacIntyre, P. D., Gregersen, T., & Mercer, S. (2020). Language teachers' coping strategies during the Covid-19 conversion to online teaching: Correlations with stress, wellbeing and negative emotions. *System*. https://doi.org/10.1016/j.system.2020.102352

Mann, S., & Tang, E. H. H. (2012). The role of mentoring in supporting novice English language teachers in Hong Kong. *TESOL Quarterly, 46*(3), 472–495. https://doi.org/10.1002/tesq.38

Mansfield, C. F., Beltman, S., Price, A., & McConney, A. (2012). "Don't sweat the small stuff:" understanding teacher resilience at the chalkface. *Teaching and Teacher Education, 28*(3), 357–367. https://doi.org/10.1016/j.tate.2011.11.001

McCarthy, M. (2016). Blended learning. In M. McCarthy (Ed.), *The Cambridge guide to blended learning for language teaching* (pp. 1–3). Cambridge University Press.

Meister, D. G., & Ahrens, P. (2011). Resisting plateauing: Four veteran teachers' stories. *Teaching and Teacher Education, 27*(4), 770–778. https://doi.org/10.1016/j.tate.2011.01.002

Meskill, C., & Anthony, N. (2015). *Teaching languages online* (2nd ed.). Multilingual Matters.

Mohammadi, S. (2018). *Expectations and experiences of students on a Master level TESOL programme in the UK: A mixed methods study*. Unpublished Master's Dissertation. Faculty of Humanities. University of Southampton.

Oxtoby, K. (2016). Doctors' own mental health issues. *BMJ*, i1238. https://doi.org/10.1136/bmj.i1238

Papageorgiou, I., Copland, F., Viana, V., Bowker, D., & Moran, E. (2019). Teaching practice in UK ELT Master's programmes. *ELT Journal, 73*(2), 154–165. https://doi.org/10.1093/elt/ccy050

Punch, K. F. (2009). *Introduction to research methods in education*. SAGE Publications.

Rádai, P., Bernaus, M., Matei, G., Sassen, D., & Heyworth, F. (2003). *The status of language educators*. Council of Europe. http://archive.ecml.at/documents/pub211E2003Radai.pdf

Reinders, H. (2009). Technology and second language teacher education. In A. Burns & J. C. Richards (Eds.), *The Cambridge guide to second language teacher education* (pp. 230–238). Cambridge University Press.

Reinders, H. (2018). Technology and autonomy. In J. I. Liontas (Ed.), *The TESOL encyclopedia of English language teaching* (pp. 1–5). Wiley. https://doi.org/10.1002/9781118784235.eelt0433

Riazi, A. M. (2017). *Mixed methods research in language teaching and learning*. Equinox Publishing.

Richards, J. C. (2015). *Key issues in language teaching*. Cambridge University Press.

Richards, J. C., & Farrell, T. S. C. (2005). *Professional development for language teachers: Strategies for teacher learning*. Cambridge University Press. https://doi.org/10.1017/CBO9780511667237

Scrivener, J. (2011). *Learning teaching: The essential guide to English language teaching* (3rd ed.). Macmillan Education.

Sharma, P., & Westbrook, K. (2016). Online and blended language learning. In F. Farr & L. Murray (Eds.), *The Routledge handbook of language learning and technology* (pp. 320–333). Routledge.

Teddlie, C., & Tashakkori, A. (2009). *Foundations of mixed methods research: Integrating quantitative and qualitative approaches in the social and behavioral sciences*. SAGE Publications.

Wiersma, W., & Jurs, S. G. (2009). *Research methods in education: An introduction* (9th ed.). Pearson Education.

Pedagogical Insights into Emergency Remote Teaching: A Case Study of a Virtual Collaboration Project in the Turkish and Hungarian Pre-service Teacher Education Context

Işıl Günseli Kaçar and Imre Fekete

Highlights

- Thorough preparation and detail-mindedness based on informed pedagogical decisions and existing literature are the key necessities in the virtual exchange (VE) project implementation
- The part of the project that required most attention was learner pairing or teaming efforts, preferably accompanied by live online meeting sessions between project partners
- Project disruptions can easily be overcome by flexibility, open-mindedness, and constant instructor availability
- COVID-19 disrupted learners' everyday lives and learning environments in general in addition to disrupting this VE project
- The level of participant engagement in the VE project greatly affected project gains, as task-oriented participants disclosed little intercultural competence development as opposed to pairs or teams where communication was of utmost importance

1 Introduction

Emergency Remote Teaching (ERT), which started with the advent of the COVID-19 pandemic, has brought a vast array of unprecedented changes in English as a Foreign Language (EFL) teaching and teacher education. The sudden shift to online

I. G. Kaçar (✉)
Middle East Technical University, Ankara, Turkey
e-mail: isil@metu.edu.tr

I. Fekete
Pázmány Péter Catholic University, Budapest, Hungary
e-mail: fekete.imre@btk.ppke.hu

J. Chen (ed.), *Emergency Remote Teaching and Beyond*,
https://doi.org/10.1007/978-3-030-84067-9_20

teaching on a global scale has posed unsurmountable pedagogical and technological challenges to educators at all levels of education and in different teaching contexts. The educators felt a compelling need to consider how to adjust their face-to-face instructional strategies to effectively address the emergent learning needs of their students engaged in online teaching and how to align online pedagogies with contextual constraints in this turbulent, nebulous global educational landscape (Pelaez-Morales, 2020).

The exigencies resulting from an abrupt shift to fully online learning environments in the ERT era have raised issues for researchers as well as teacher educators engaged in virtual exchange projects. They were urged to make a considerable number of modifications in their research design, implementation, and evaluation procedures. Virtual exchange projects in the English as a Second Language (ESL)/EFL context are no exception. Although there has been a growing interest in VE for the past two decades, several gaps were identified in VE research (See The EVALUATE Group, 2019). The main gap is related to the methods utilized in the VE data analysis and their validity. Research on VE primarily focused on qualitative and/or descriptive case studies (Luo & Yang, 2018) which do not tend to be evidence-based or well-designed (The EVALUATE Group, 2019). Hence, taking into consideration the gaps in recent VE research, the current study is an evidence-based exploratory case study (Duff, 2012). It addresses the following research questions:

1. What were some key considerations of the instructors in the design, implementation, and evaluation in the virtual collaboration project?
2. In what ways did the COVID-19 pandemic impact the virtual collaboration project between pre-service Turkish and Hungarian EFL teachers?
3. What were the pedagogical, technological, and interactional challenges experienced by the pre-service Turkish and Hungarian EFL teachers in the virtual collaboration project and how were the participants able to cope with them?

2   Review of Literature

In today's turbulent world characterized by an erosion of boundaries, social and educational inequalities, political instability, increasingly growing linguistic and cultural diversity, there is an urgent call for global interconnectedness and more intense inter-cultural interactions (Çiftçi, & Savaş, 2018; Divéki, 2020; Kóris et al., 2020; Üzüm et al., 2019; Üzüm et al., 2020). In order to raise intercultural awareness and develop communicative competence among foreign language (FL) students by means of physical mobility, one of the most popular programs is the European Union's Erasmus programme (Rienties et al., 2020). ERASMUS is a funded international exchange framework aiming to promote international student and teacher/staff mobility in higher education, as well as offering academic, intercultural, and linguistic development opportunities in European countries (Barkhuizen

& Feryok, 2006). There is a plethora of evidence regarding the benefits of physical mobility regarding personal and professional skills and the competence development of prospective language teachers (Dolga et al., 2015). However, due to financial, socio-economic, and time constraints, mobility facilities are only limited to a small minority of the student population (O'Dowd, 2013). For the last two decades, there has been a growing emphasis on the virtual formats in the tertiary contexts from the perspectives on inclusive education, and transversal or soft skills development (Buiskool & Hudepohl, 2020). Nevertheless, neither face-to-face nor virtual formats are regarded as alternatives for one another as each form contributes to the enhancement of the instructional quality differently (Buiskool & Hudepohl, 2020). The integration of virtual forms of mobility into the curriculum along with the physical mobility option might pave the way for the development of intercultural and linguistic competencies as well as digital teamwork (EADTU, 2019).

2.1   Virtual Exchange: Affordances and Challenges

Virtual exchange (VE), or telecollaboration, can be defined as a process of sustained student engagement in online intercultural collaboration projects with partners from diverse cultural contexts or geographical locations as an integrated part of their academic studies under the guidance of teachers or trained facilitators (Dooly & Sadler, 2013; O'Dowd et al., 2020). Recently, virtual exchange has been acknowledged as a significant part of online approaches to international education with its student-centred, interactive, socio-constructive, negotiation-friendly, and collaborative features (Lewis & O'Dowd, 2016; The EVALUATE Group, 2019).

In FL education contexts, telecollaboration projects tend to be primarily informed by sociocultural and interactional theories of language acquisition to provide participants with an authentic interactional communication opportunity with speakers of other languages (Dooly, 2017). VE has been advocated as an ideal environment for FL competence within formal institutional contexts (The EVALUATE Group, 2019). Related literature has revealed that most participants regarded VE as a favourable learning experience (Antoniadou, 2011; Dooly & Sadler, 2013; Kohn & Hoffstaedter, 2017). Apart from enhancing the participants' FL competence, VE has been demonstrated to have the potential to promote intercultural competences (O'Dowd & Lewis, 2016) and skills for building a learner community (Dooly & Sadler, 2013; Kóris et al., 2020; Lee, 2009).

Despite the affordances that VE has, there are some challenges that it imposes on participants. These challenges can be categorized into four groups: individual, classroom-related, socio-institutional, and communication or interaction-related (O'Dowd, 2013). Regarding the socio-institutional challenges, the value participants assign to VE and the amount of effort they exert for the successful task completion in the project are related to the integration of VEs into the course syllabi and the credits students might be awarded via their participation in the VE activities (Chambers & Bax, 2006; O'Dowd, 2013). As O'Dowd (2013) argued, the institutional recognition of VE and its assessment is also a challenge in VE that is frequently cited. The integration of certain awareness-raising activities such as the application for quality awards, the announcements in the local media sources or mentions of the projects in publications or reports published by the local institution poses an important challenge regarding the prestige of the virtual exchange for the local institution (O'Dowd, 2013). The alignment of the virtual exchange activity with the learner needs and the institutional activities, as well as the achievement of the long-term stability of the partnership may also prove challenging in virtual exchange projects (O'Dowd, 2013).

In addition to the institutional recognition challenge, establishing a reliable and steady partnership and developing a professional relationship between partners based on negotiation and mutual trust constitute communication-related challenges for the partners. Flexibility and negotiation are the two key factors leading to an effective dialogue between partners that also prepare them for handling sudden emergencies effectively (Holló & Németh, 2009). It is equally important to address the interactional challenges as it is important to mentor the virtual exchange participants effectively while they are coping with the "linguistic, cultural, and digital" challenges of online intercultural collaboration (O'Dowd et al., 2020, p. 147) and with the negotiation of the "differences in social, cultural, political, and religious worldviews" (Kramsch, 2014, p. 305). The crucial role of the instructors' "pedagogical mentoring" (O'Dowd et al., 2020, p. 146) in the project initiation and development is highlighted in the literature.

In the facilitator-led model of virtual exchange, an approach to pedagogical mentoring, trained intercultural educators are in charge of opening the sessions, setting-up activities, and organizing synchronous interactions between students, thereby promoting the process of intercultural learning (O'Dowd et al., 2020). Facilitators are trained in facilitation skills such as "active listening, asking good questions, summarizing and reframing, as well as learning how to manage power dynamics and how to build a sense of safety in the virtual space and trust among participants" (O'Dowd et al., 2020, p. 150).

2.2   *Virtual Exchange and ESL/EFL Teacher Education*

Virtual Exchange projects and telecollaboration are increasingly incorporated into English as a Foreign Language (EFL) classes to promote intercultural exchanges between language learners of different cultures to enhance their language learning and intercultural awareness (e.g., Dooly, 2011; Kóris et al., 2020; Lee & Markey, 2014; O'Dowd, 2016), but it has only recently been integrated into teacher training (Antoniadou, 2011; Bueno-Alastuey & Kleban, 2016). In an increasingly interconnected world, it is necessary to offer students embedded contextualized learning opportunities reflecting how knowledge is co-constructed and shared, and help students internalize the "relevancy of what they are learning and how they are learning" (Dooly & Sadler, 2013, p. 8).

It is suggested that teachers need to develop their digital and pedagogical competencies to effectively relate them to their lesson objectives, teaching styles and curriculum design towards an integrated technology use (Dooly & Sadler, 2013). Apart from the joint knowledge construction through active participation, interaction, and reflection, telecollaboration facilitates "ownership of knowledge" (Dooly & Sadler, 2013, p. 5). There is also a need for "experiential modelling" in teacher education, emphasizing the importance of "exploratory teaching practice" (Dooly & Sadler, 2013, p. 5; see also Guichon, 2009; Hampel, 2009; Hampel & Stickler, 2005). Working in collaboration with more capable peers and enjoying the peer support in a technology-mediated virtual community of practice promote prospective teachers' critical thinking and reflection skills.

2.3   Virtual Exchange and the TPACK Skills Development of EFL/ESL Pre-service Teachers

Irrespective of the challenges students and pre-service teachers may encounter in VE, the previous VE literature has indicated the importance of VE in participants' technological pedagogical content knowledge (TPACK) skills development (Dooly & Sadler, 2013). The Technological Pedagogical Content Knowledge (TPACK) model, developed by Mishra and Koehler (2006), is the most widely used and validated framework (Graham, 2011; Rienties et al., 2020; Schmidt et al., 2009; Voogt et al., 2013). The TPACK model incorporates three knowledge sources: pedagogical knowledge (PK), content knowledge (CK), and technological knowledge (TK) (Voogt et al., 2013). The use and synthesis of these knowledge components together are likely to result in skilful and meaningful technology-inclusive lessons. The extant literature on TPACK revealed that being involved in technology-enhanced lessons and doing microteaching in a technology-equipped learning environment is reported to promote prospective teachers' TPACK. It is widely acknowledged that developing teachers' TPACK skills is of great importance to meet the demands of the twenty-first century (e.g., O'Dowd, 2013; Tondeur et al., 2012), as it is not possible to automatically transfer teachers' subject matter knowledge to knowledge of appropriate technology integration (Niess, 2011; Rienties et al., 2020). Hence, equipping pre-service teachers with digital competences is one of the main goals of pre-service teacher education programs (Kaçar, 2015; Seidel et al., 2013), as the ownership of digital devices does not entail using them skilfully for learning purposes (Fekete, 2020).

2.4 Emergency Remote Teaching and ESL/EFL Teacher Education

The COVID-19 pandemic has offered researchers and classroom practitioners the opportunity to reconsider new digital, online, and pedagogical possibilities (Peters et al., 2020). From the teacher's perspective, the need to redefine "the new normal" and revise our teaching styles, lesson planning, conduct, and assessment procedures in our classroom practices have echoed the characteristics of teachers in the post-method era in Kumaravedivelu's (2001) terms: being a practitioner who has internalized the principles of particularity (context-sensitive teaching), practicality (establishing a bridge between personal theories and professional theories), and possibility (raising one's awareness of the individual, social, and cultural factors in teaching). In fact, the pandemic brought to the attention of ESL/EFL teacher educators Kumaravadivelu's (2012) suggestions regarding the prerequisite knowledge for language teacher education in a global society (Sadler & Dooly, 2016). The pandemic has revealed the compelling need to revise the existing language teacher education programs in the 21st century in line with Kumaravadivelu's (2012) model for a global society (also known as KARDS), which aims to develop prospective and practicing teachers into strategic thinkers, exploratory researchers, and transformative teachers.

In the light of all the challenges and possibilities that the COVID-19 pandemic has brought to the TESOL practitioners as well as researchers, the integration of virtual exchange into the current educational practices on a global scale is of growing importance in the 21st century. As blended, hybrid, or fully online learning is becoming the new normal in contemporary TESOL education at different levels all over the world, virtual exchange or telecollaboration is likely to be regarded as an integral part of mainstream education soon.

3 Research Design

This study aims to provide emergent insights into the case of a virtual collaboration project by offering results based on several data sources. As the research questions concern the perceptions of students and instructors on a self-designed virtual collaboration project, a qualitative case study approach was selected to answer the proposed questions. It is hoped that many transferable implications can be formulated based on the rich data collected and that these implications prove to be of value outside the narrow focus in the study (Duff, 2012) by addressing relevant remote teaching, virtual collaboration, and online instructional design and implementation issues generally.

3.1 Participants

Participants of this study included 28 Turkish and 18 Hungarian undergraduate pre-service EFL teachers in their second (Turkish students), third and fourth year (Hungarian students) of studies (N = 46). Participants signalled their willingness to participate in the project by registering for an elective seminar advertised at both universities called *Designing and using digital materials for ELT* and *Elective seminar in language pedagogy: ICT in ELT* for Turkish and Hungarian participants, respectively. The Turkish students studied in one seminar group in which the sessions lasted for 100 min each, while the Hungarian students participated in two seminar groups (10 and 8 students, respectively) and each session lasted for 90 min. The project engaged students of both nations evenly for four months (February to May 2020), which is the length of the active teaching period of a university semester.

The prior English language teaching (ELT) methodology training of the participants was varied. By the time the project was launched, Turkish students had received training in information technologies and applications as well as digital instructional materials development, besides their training in ELT methodology and instructional principles and techniques. Hungarian students' ELT methodology background, apart from their general language development, literature, linguistics, culture, and history-related training, included ELT methodology classes related to activity and lesson planning, an academic English course and an ELT research seminar. For the collaboration, participants communicated with each other in English, which was the lingua franca between them. The approximate average level of English of both Turkish and Hungarian participants was IELTS 7.0/TOEFL IBT 110/CEFR C1.

Almost all the learners, except for two Hungarian students, granted their permission for their portfolio documents to be used for research purposes. Informants were ensured that their names would remain anonymous. There was also a Hungarian informant who decided not to continue his participation in the project mid-way; therefore, the findings of this study are based on a total number of 28 Turkish and 15 Hungarian student portfolios.

Besides the student participants, we, the two instructor-researchers, were also involved in the project. We contacted each other following a virtual exchange conference held in Autumn 2019. Our correspondence, memos and notes were also important data sources and contributed to the triangulation of the findings of this case study. We continuously exchanged ideas about the progress of the participants and were engaged in the decision-making process about how to change the direction of the project and how to accommodate the original project plan because of the emerging the COVID-19 related challenges.

Although funding for our project was not provided directly, we registered our collaboration as a UniCollaboration (https://www.unicollaboration.org/) Virtual Exchange project, thanks to which two online (via Zoom) facilitated sessions were held for students, each of which lasted for 90 min. The personal communication between the online facilitators and us was also a data source in this study. The facilitators provided us with their insights and perceptions of students as well as sharing the results of their post-session feedback questionnaire.

3.2 The Online Collaboration Project

This online collaboration project was designed by us, the two instructor-researchers, to best tailor the course to the needs of the students. To achieve this, the course content had been negotiated and finalised a month before the project was launched in February 2020. Because the participants were EFL teacher majors, the goal was to design a collaborative methodology course which provides them with the opportunities to learn about techno-inclusive language teaching and try their hands at designing techno-inclusive lessons using English as the sole medium of communication. We had also participated in an Erasmus+ online training programme for future facilitators of Virtual Exchange programmes and another online training program for developing virtual exchange projects in advance. We negotiated that the collaboration should have three main phases following the preparatory phase that was relevant for the students: (1) pairing and preparation (February–March 2020), (2) activity planning and socialization (March–April 2020), (3) portfolio submission and project evaluation (April–May 2020). Figure 1 summarises the online collaboration project by detailing its stages and the most important student and instructor responsibilities concerning each phase.

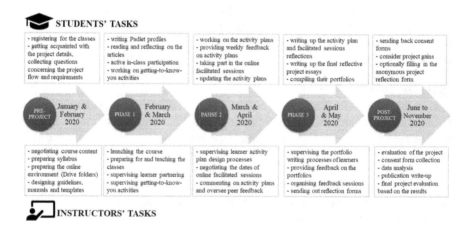

Fig. 1 A timeline summary of the project phases and the key student and instructor tasks

Because all participants had Gmail accounts, Google Drive was chosen to be the platform of online collaboration for sharing, storing, and creating collaborative content. Furthermore, many students later decided to carry out private conversations via WhatsApp or Messenger when designing their activity plans, yet each finalised document was required to be uploaded to the class' private Google Drive folder that was only accessible for the participants and the two instructors.

In the first phase (February–March 2020), pairing or teaming the students took place while using the classroom to discuss some relevant readings (literature reviews and research papers) on ICT inclusion possibilities in ELT. Pairing began by asking students to introduce themselves on a Padlet wall with guidelines provided for them regarding what to write about. Then, when pairs and teams were established, students were asked to work on a series of tasks to get better acquainted, such as identifying group members' strengths and weaknesses and establishing a group profile detailing who in the group could handle anticipated difficulties and how.

While the first phase of the project was carried out as it had originally been planned, university education moved entirely online at the same time when the second phase (March–April 2020) began. In the second phase, students had to design a 20-minute task-based ICT-inclusive EFL classroom activity in a way that supposed B1 learners were using ICT tools for learning some cultural issues (culture-specific, culture-general or intercultural interaction-based), vocabulary or grammar. For this, a task sheet template was provided. After the deadline scheduling, peers, and the instructors attached comments to the activity plans on Google Drive, and then the authors had to rework their activity plans following the comments. Thus, each week, two to four activity plans were created and commented on by the peers and the two instructors. Then, the activity plan had to be rewritten based on the provided commentary. Figure 2 features an activity plan with some learner and instructor comments.

SEQUENCING						
Timing	What the teacher says / does	What the students do	Organisation	Aim/Rationale	Materials needed	Comments
0 – 4	Welcome everybody to today's class. Last week we introduced the topic of environmental issues. And today we are going	Students open the website, type in the code and type in three keywords that come to	Frontal	To warm the students up to the activity, to revise previously	Projector, any type of ICT device for the students	Students might be reluctant to answer to the teacher's question

2020. ápr. 1.

I REALLY LIKE how you developed T's utterances into full sentences. This one, I think, is too technical for the learners. How about asking them if they remember? Asking them to recall some words?

2020. ápr. 1.

I find it great how you made a connection with the previous lesson but this part, especially brainstorming and answering will need more time.

Fig. 2 Part of an anonymized student-designed and commented activity plan

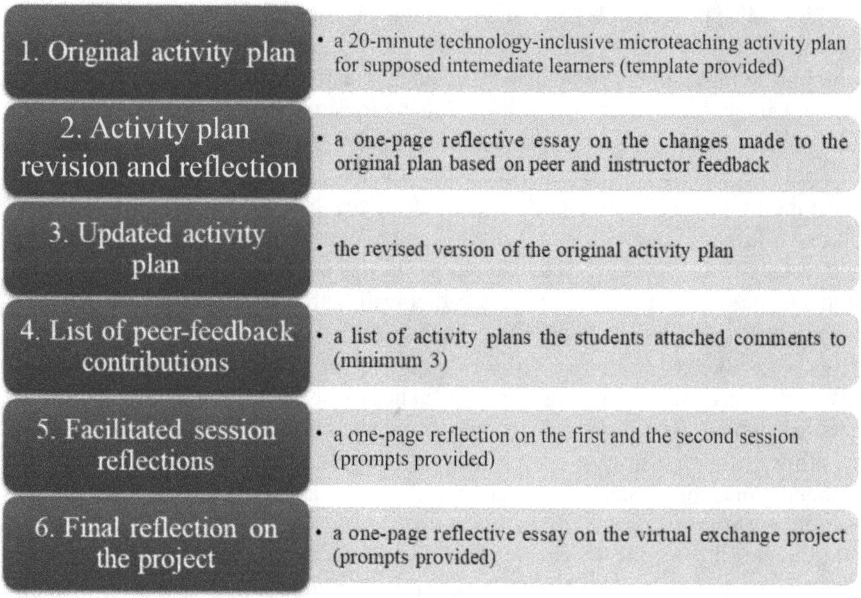

1. Original activity plan	• a 20-minute technology-inclusive microteaching activity plan for supposed intermediate learners (template provided)
2. Activity plan revision and reflection	• a one-page reflective essay on the changes made to the original plan based on peer and instructor feedback
3. Updated activity plan	• the revised version of the original activity plan
4. List of peer-feedback contributions	• a list of activity plans the students attached comments to (minimum 3)
5. Facilitated session reflections	• a one-page reflection on the first and the second session (prompts provided)
6. Final reflection on the project	• a one-page reflective essay on the virtual exchange project (prompts provided)

Fig. 3 Final portfolio contents

Two 90-minute facilitated Zoom sessions were provided free of charge for students by UNICollaboration. The two sessions were facilitated by multiple facilitators in groups of five to eight. The first session's topic was intercultural communication upon our request, and the second was information and communication technology inclusion in learning and teaching languages. As the sessions were facilitated by professionals, we did not participate in them, but the facilitators always provided us with some written feedback on the sessions later on. Additionally, the students were asked to write a one-page reflective essay on their facilitated sessions.

The third and last phase of the project (April–May 2020) required students to compile their individual final project portfolios. The portfolio contents are detailed in Fig. 3.

Students were also sent a final anonymous Google form link to elaborate on their project experiences online by answering open-ended questions. They were told that they could skip any questions if they like and they were encouraged to give detailed answers using their mother tongues if they preferred. The anonymous reflection sheet proved to be a valuable data source. The project areas surveyed are detailed in Fig. 4. Altogether 19 students (out of the 46) completed the anonymous form.

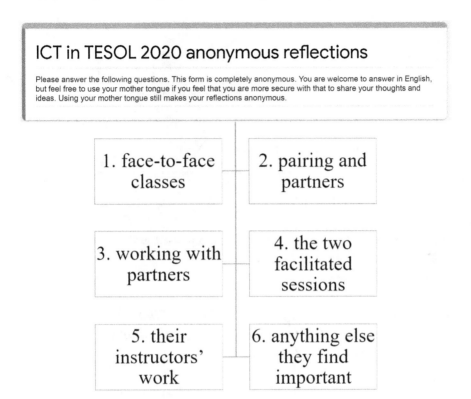

ICT in TESOL 2020 anonymous reflections

Please answer the following questions. This form is completely anonymous. You are welcome to answer in English, but feel free to use your mother tongue if you feel that you are more secure with that to share your thoughts and ideas. Using your mother tongue still makes your reflections anonymous.

1. face-to-face classes	2. pairing and partners
3. working with partners	4. the two facilitated sessions
5. their instructors' work	6. anything else they find important

Fig. 4 Anonymous reflection form contents

3.3 Methods of Data Collection and Analysis

To see what final data sources made up the data pool for this study, a table was created detailing the sources, type, and analysis of the data (Table 1). Table 1 also specifies, wherever possible, the quantity of the documents the researchers were granted permission to use as part of this study. The documents accumulated throughout this virtual collaboration project lent themselves to be the rich qualitative data sources of the present case study. The data pool was collected, and the data were analysed by identifying key themes considering the research questions. Then, the data were further analysed by linking the same content points together from different participants.

Table 1 An overview of data types and methods of analysis

Source	Data type	Method of data analysis
1	Students' portfolios (N = 43)	Thematic content analysis
2	Instructors' notes and personal communication (between January and June 2020)	
3	Instructors' notes about students' suggestions and feedback voiced throughout some online classes (Zoom, Skype)	
4	Students' anonymous feedback form answers (N = 19)	
5	Online session facilitators' feedback emails	

4 Results and Discussion

In this section, the findings are presented and discussed in line with the research questions.

4.1 What Were Some Key Considerations of the Instructors in the Design, Implementation and Evaluation in the Case of the Virtual Collaboration Project?

Before launching the project, the instructor-researchers did everything to design the project to the best of their abilities. It was decided that the following aspects had to be considered in detail before launching the project: (1) course preparation and planning, (2) integrating the project into students' syllabi, (3) transparency of the project (utilising Google Drive for storing and submitting all project-related documents), (4) initial pairing phase support, (5) providing continuous supervision and feedback, (6) taking care of the organisation of the online facilitated sessions, (7) providing students with some form of recognition for participating in the project and (8) sharing the project takeaways with instructors and researchers. The project consisted of three major stages: (1) pairing and preparation; (2) activity planning and interaction engagement within groups; and (3) portfolio submission and project evaluation. The first stage was preceded by a preparatory phase, while the last stage was followed by a post-project phase.

In the planning phase, the researchers based several decisions on the literature concerning VE projects. Previous studies conducted in similar contexts indicated that the socio-institutional challenges were referred to as a frequent source of challenge facing the instructors and students in the VE projects (Chambers & Bax, 2006; O'Dowd, 2013). Fortunately, in the current study, they did not constitute a challenge for the pre-service teachers. As the exchange was integrated into an existing course in both parties' syllabi and the project task evaluation was already incorporated into the course assessment, the pre-service teachers felt motivated to participate in the project.

Apart from the important role the facilitator-led sessions played in terms of alleviating or eliminating the pre-service teachers' interactional challenges, the course instructors also played a crucial role in monitoring the online interactions of the pre-service teachers through online Zoom meetings as well as through individual communication with them (O'Dowd et al., 2020). The instructors of the VE project were also engaged in negotiation regularly regarding the project flow and were monitoring the flow of interaction between the partners closely.

The instructors in the current study were actively involved in designing ice-breaking activities prior to the commencement of the virtual exchange project and some other interactive tasks which would help participants from different cultures establish interpersonal relationships and promote intercultural interactions (O'Dowd et al., 2020). The participants emphasized that their collaborative engagement with their partners in icebreakers prior to the joint technology-enhanced lesson plan preparation endeavour played an important role in reducing the potential interactional challenges in the VE.

> I believe that one of the reasons behind our good communication was the ice-breaker activities. Through those activities we had a chance to [get to] know each other more. We found our common personal characteristics. These activities helped us form a sound common ground for our collaboration in the project, ensuring a harmonious and smooth intercultural and interpersonal relationship and dialogic exchange among the group members. (Portfolio of Participant 12)

4.2   In What Ways Did the COVID-19 Pandemic Impact the Virtual Collaboration Project Between Pre-service Turkish and Hungarian EFL Teachers?

Regarding the second research question, we both reflected on the disruptive impact of the pandemic on the project. From our perspective, coping with the unprecedented circumstances beyond control such as the strict lockdown measures and the sudden shift to the fully online teaching following the university closures in both countries posed a considerable threat to the sustainability of the project management. The first hurdle we tackled was related to the realignment of the project design with the fully online teaching requirement. We had to change the original blended format of the project to a fully online version within a week.

Altering the existing project design involved a significant number of amendments in line with the requirements of fully online teaching. The classroom implementation component was omitted from the project. Additionally, the formative assessment (in the form of peer and teacher feedback to the first lesson plan drafts) component was revised. Apart from these changes, the submission dates of all tasks were revised and rescheduled within a week, following the shift to the fully online teaching, despite encountering a vast array of difficulties initially in terms of restructuring the project. Thanks to the transparent and open interpersonal communication dynamics established between us, the restructuring of the project went smoothly and swiftly. The adoption of an interactive and collaborative decision-making policy by the instructors facilitated the project flow (Lewis & O'Dowd, 2016; The EVALUATE Group, 2019).

With respect to the impact of the COVID-19 on pre-service teachers in the project, some participants reported having great difficulty adjusting themselves to the abrupt shift to the fully online format initially. The need for a quick adjustment to the changing deadlines and changing tasks promptly affected their level of engagement in the project unfavourably.

> I believe that students can work smoothly if a clear requirement is set in the very beginning. I know that we had an extreme circumstance this semester but changing the requirements several times made us totally confused and we lost the remaining motivation to follow the requirements. (Anonymous reflection form)

The pre-service teachers reported that due to the disruption of their face-to-face communication with the instructors and their peers, they felt demotivated in the project. They indicated that having whole class discussions about the project, asking for clarification and getting face-to-face feedback from their teachers regarding their lesson plans in the university setting and working together with their group members based on the project in face-to-face classes prior to the pandemic outbreak fostered their sense of commitment to and sense of ownership of the project. However, the discontinuation of their face-to-face contact with their instructions and their peers led them to feel disconnected. The frequent internet connection problems also exacerbated the emotional chaos. Due to these technological difficulties, students reported in their anonymous reflections that they failed to communicate with their foreign partners or had intermittent communication with them. This also caused them some problems concerning the timing of their collaborative work, which led them to late submissions.

> [Working together with my partner] was quite good except that our job responsibilities, examinations and other online classes could create some obstacles to meet. My foreign partner, from time to time, claimed that he hadn't been well informed about the schedule so afterwards I tried to keep him informed. (Anonymous reflection form)

> I feel that the partnership could have been better with face-to-face classes because at home we did not have the urge to complete the assignments in time. Also with real classes, the instructors had a chance to check on our progress. (Anonymous reflection form)

Some pre-service teachers also reported their difficulty understanding their peers' and instructors' online feedback on their lesson plans and expressed their need for more clarification regarding the feedback. However, in general, the pre-service teachers expressed their appreciation regarding the clear, detailed, and understandable feedback from their instructors and peers in their portfolio reflections. The following quote is quite revealing in this respect:

> Having taken a look at the first version of our activity plan, at some points we miscalculated things and the plan slipped away sometimes, although, we thought that we were really wise. Nonetheless, having received the teacher's and other fellow students' comments, it was really visible to us what we had to change. (Portfolio of Participant 13)

The participants also emphasized how the facilitated sessions played an important role in lessening the negative impacts of the COVID-19 pandemic on the participants in the project. These sessions were held by the facilitators in the UniCollaboration (https://www.unicollaboration.org/), who were "trained intercultural educators taking part in synchronous online discussions between students and facilitating the intercultural learning process" (O'Dowd, 2013, p. 150). The pre-service teachers emphasized that the two facilitated sessions that were held throughout the project helped them restore their disturbed affective states due to the pandemic-induced anxiety as well as building "a sense of safety in the virtual space and trust among the project participants" (O'Dowd, 2013, p. 150). They found the initial session quite useful as it was held just after the COVID-19 lockdown when they first encountered a disruption in communication with their partners. They emphasized that these sessions assisted in lowering their level of anxiety caused by the severe lockdown conditions. They felt much more connected to one another when they were informed that their partners were also trying to cope with the virus-related issues. These sessions helped create a bond of solidarity among the partners in the project. They also provided the project participants with an opportunity to contact their Turkish and Hungarian partners online. In these facilitated sessions, they also found a chance to improve their speaking skills in English and their intercultural communication skills by exchanging their ideas on a variety of issues including stereotypes, discrimination, and technology integration into education. The following quote by Participant 17 in the portfolio reflections illustrates this concisely:

> Thanks to the online session, I have concluded that technology integration is a necessity. In addition to this conclusion, I have also learnt that stereotypes are natural, and we have to overcome them. Lastly, I have found out that each culture is unique. When discussing cultural understanding, Hungarian friends gave a lot of examples that are a part of their culture but not ours. (Portfolio of Participant 17)

In spite of all the aforementioned unfavourable impacts of the COVID-19 pandemic on the project, the overwhelming majority of the pre-service teachers in the study were of the opinion that the instructors' flexibility contributed to the successful completion of the project in several ways. They expressed their appreciation of the latter's flexibility in terms of the following aspects in the project: the determination of their own topic choice, the design of their lesson plans, and the lesson plan submission dates in the project schedule. The participants also reported that they were content with the effective and open communication style of their instructors, in addition to the regular and constructive feedback provision. They also added that the regular Zoom project progress meetings as well as the proactive and problem-solving stance of their instructors reinforced their favourable perceptions of flexibility in the project. The following quotations from the anonymous reflections are quite significant in terms of the prospective teachers' ideas regarding flexibility in the project:

> My instructor has always been eager to help us both in class and online. We were always in touch during the project. (Portfolio of Participant 16)

> I have never felt lost in our classes about my assignments or the schedule and I always had a way to ask my questions or convey my messages through different channels. (Portfolio of Participant 30)

The participants also indicated that their engagement in collaborative knowledge construction, peer scaffolding and interaction in a technology-enhanced virtual community of practice fostered their Zone of Proximal Development as well as their critical thinking and reflective skills development (Dooly & Sadler, 2013), which is in line with the Kumaravadivelu's (2012) model of a global society, with an aim to develop prospective and practicing teachers into strategic thinkers, exploratory researchers, and transformative teachers. The prospective teachers in the study underlined that all the opportunities provided for them in the VE assisted them in tackling the pedagogical challenges in the study. From their reflections, it can be concluded that their project engagement equipped them with the characteristics of the 21st century teachers.

4.3   What Were the Pedagogical, Technological, and Interactional Challenges Experienced by the Pre-service Turkish and Hungarian EFL Teachers in the Virtual Collaboration Project and How Were They Able to Cope with Them?

With respect to the third research question, challenges the pre-service Turkish and Hungarian EFL teachers encountered throughout the virtual collaboration project could be classified into three main groups: pedagogical, technological and interactional.

Regarding the pedagogical challenges, both groups indicated that before the unexpected change in the task deadlines, the task descriptions and the project implementation right after the COVID-19 breakout and the advent of the pandemic, the project was originally designed to incorporate a microteaching component for both groups. However, due to the sudden shift from the face-to-face to fully online instruction at both universities, we decided to conduct the project in a fully online manner. The fully online instruction at university constituted a major challenge for the participants. Trying to catch up with all the online classes, exams and other job-commitments led some participants to miss the newly scheduled deadlines and to lose concentration on the project, which are reflected concisely in the following quotes by the participants in the anonymous reflections:

> Our job responsibilities, examinations, and other online classes created some obstacles for us. (Anonymous reflection form)

> The icebreaker task came as a surprise to me in the midst of craziness of the fully online instruction. I wasn't informed of it before. (Anonymous reflection form)

With respect to the TPACK development of the pre-service teachers, the analysis of the draft technology-enhanced lesson plans they prepared as well as the interim project progress Zoom meetings pointed towards a favourable contribution of the VE to their TPACK development in general, which confirmed the previous research findings in this field (e.g., Antoniadou, 2011; Bueno-Alastuey et al., 2016; Dooly & Sadler, 2013; Hauck et al., 2020). The findings of the current study indicated that the participants focused on the development of three sources of knowledge in the TPACK model during the VE: technological pedagogical knowledge, technological content knowledge, and pedagogical content knowledge.

> My professional takeaway from this project is that I have learnt how to use programmes, websites, applications for pedagogical purposes and it was exciting to design an activity plan based on ICT. (Anonymous reflection form)

As to the technological challenges, the participants mainly pointed out the instability or lack of internet connection. They indicated that due to these internet-related problems, they experienced certain disruptions in their online communication with their partners. They mentioned in their portfolio reflections that their participation in the VE helped them improve their pedagogical content knowledge, the intersection of the content and pedagogical knowledge, as well as technological content knowledge, the relationships and intersections among technologies and learning objectives. Nevertheless, they underscored in their portfolio reflections that due to the exclusion of the microteaching component from the project, they failed to improve their technological pedagogical knowledge which is concerned with the interactions between technological tools and specific pedagogical practices (see Mishra & Koehler, 2006).

> Thanks to this VE project, I have concluded that technology integration is a necessity. (Portfolio of Participant 23)

On the other hand, due to a lack of experiential learning opportunity to implement their technology-enhanced lesson plans in class, arising from the fully online teaching requirements at universities, they felt they did not develop a full understanding of the integration of the technological tools. In brief, as the pre-service teachers mentioned during the interim Zoom meetings, despite their active involvement in the preparation of technology-enhanced lessons, not having the opportunity to be engaged in teaching in a technology-rich environment prevented their full understanding of effective technology integration into teaching, which corroborates Voogt et al. (2013), who underlined the necessity of the pre-service teachers' engagement in technology-enhanced lessons where they are exposed to a model of how to teach in technology-enhanced learning environments to achieve effective technology integration into teaching.

Some participants pointed out the feedback challenge they encountered in the project. Some reported that they needed more specific and detailed feedback, particularly related to the first technology-enhanced lesson plan draft that they were supposed to submit right after the chaos that occurred at the start of the pandemic and the shift to the fully online instruction. The following quote from the portfolio reflections is representative in this respect:

> I think I needed a bit more guidance related to the first draft of my technology-enhanced lesson plan. It occurred to me that the first draft would have been much better with more detailed feedback. However, the other activities in the project were quite understandable and clear. (Portfolio of Participant 10)

However, most of the participants expressed their satisfaction with the teacher and peer feedback. They believed receiving feedback from both parties was a rewarding pedagogical experience for them in the project. The participants also seemed quite content with the online pedagogical mentoring they received during the project. They showed their appreciation for the course instructors' initiating, developing, and monitoring the virtual exchange project (O'Dowd et al., 2020).

The pre-service teachers in the current VE also underscored the amount of scaffolding their instructors provided for them while they were dealing with the pedagogical and digital challenges that the project posed to them, which is consistent with O'Dowd et al. (2020), stressing the importance of adopting effective mentoring strategies by instructors in charge of initiating, developing, and monitoring the VE projects. In fact, the following comment by one participant in the anonymous reflections is representative regarding the pedagogical mentoring strategies that her instructor displayed in the project:

> Our instructor worked so much to make this project work. Even though sometimes guidelines felt a bit vague, in general, everything turned out okay. Our communication with our instructor was more than enough for this course. (Portfolio of Participant 25)

The participants also reported some communication-related interactional challenges. These challenges revolved around the different communication styles of the partners or a lack of communication between partners. Some participants in the projects preferred to get engaged in an interactional exchange with their partners for task-related purposes. Some attributed the lack of communication with their partners to the latter's preoccupation with the task accomplishment and their relative unwillingness to establish an interpersonal relationship with someone from a different culture or to the psychological problems that they were having due to the COVID-19-related quarantine period. Some partners also appeared to be introverted and not very articulate as a personality characteristic.

> I did not get to know my partner very well, we focused on the activity plan only. I would have enjoyed facetiming with her instead of texting. (Portfolio of Participant 7)

The communication-related challenges the participants reported corroborate those revealed in previous research studies on social presence in computer-mediated learning contexts (e.g., Kehrwald, 2008), which indicated that the relational aspects (e.g., the degree of the affective bond between participants) may not be achieved due to different participant and contextual factors. The confinement of the interaction between partners to the task-related concerns in the project suggests that the instructors engaged in virtual exchange projects need to attach importance to the affective and relational aspects of the virtual exchange projects.

To address such intercultural and interactional challenges, two facilitated sessions were held in the project with the participation of all the participants, one in the middle and the other one at the end of the project. The first session focused on intercultural communication while the second one focused on digital cooperation and online professional development. The participants in the current project reported having benefited from these facilitated sessions that played an important role in raising their intercultural sensitivity and intercultural competence as well as developing their intercultural communication skills (O'Dowd et al. 2020), but they pointed out in both their portfolio reflections and in their anonymous reflections that the sessions should have been organized in such a way that enabled them to have a discussion with their project partners.

> The facilitated sessions that we participated in were quite effective and enjoyable, but I think it would have been much better if they had been held in the first two weeks of the project. (Anonymous reflection form)

> I must confess that the facilitated sessions were the best part of our class where I indeed felt like I was in an international environment and I liked these experiences. (Anonymous reflection form)

> I must admit that I had not thought that such sessions could have been that prolific and fun till I attended our facilitated sessions and my belief in online education consolidated considerably. (Anonymous reflection form)

5 Conclusions

The study concluded that while it is undeniable that COVID-19 resulted in certain project changes due to the sudden shift to online teaching, and the necessity to adjust to the new deadlines and project-related responsibilities, most participants still remarked that the project opened their eyes to the importance of techno-pedagogical knowledge development. Although adapting to changes due to certain project circumstances is not unheard of in the literature (for example Holló & Németh, 2009), a focal change, removing the microteaching sessions from the project, resulted in establishing a weaker link between participants' technological-pedagogical and pedagogical content knowledge components of TPACK. It is not surprising that pre-service teachers' perceived level of intercultural competence development depended on their willingness to focus on the project partners as opposed to remaining only task-oriented (Kehrwald, 2008). Those participants who managed to focus on each other while working on the icebreaker activities and were willing to communicate in speaking as opposed to texting developed more as far as their interactional and intercultural competences are concerned. Perhaps it could have been more effective if the project had involved some video-based icebreakers as opposed to the ones that require texting only. The participants gained experience in using several digital tools, which is summarized in Table 2 below.

Table 2 An overview of digital tools used in the project

Tools used by the pre-service teachers	Tools used by the instructors	Tools taught during the classes
Google Drive	Google Drive	Answergarden
Google Documents	Google Documents	Google Earth/Maps
Google Spreadsheets	Google	Kahoot
Zoom	Spreadsheets	Lyrics Training
Padlet for personal communication:	Zoom	Mentimeter
Discord, WhatsApp, Messenger	WhatsApp	Monolingual online dictionaries and thesaurus
		Padlet
		Quizlet
		Socrative
		Tricider
		Voicethread
		Worditout

All in all, despite the original project having been interrupted by COVID-19, most EFL pre-service teacher participants in the study reported certain gains regarding their pedagogical content knowledge and technological-pedagogical knowledge as well as their intercultural competences. Although designing and monitoring the project while having to cope with other teaching and research engagements required much invested effort from us, the instructor-researchers, we regarded pre-service teachers' collaboration as fruitful based on the data collected from them. The goal was to equip pre-service EFL teachers with relevant skills through a collaboration possibility backed up by UniCollaboration. Not only the students, but we also learned a lot about the nature of collaborations through our and the pre-service teachers' lenses. After all, based on the gains, planning, and implementing the project were well worth the effort.

6 Food for Thought: Beyond ERT

Based on the VE project conducted in the Turkish and Hungarian university contexts, several noteworthy conclusions can be drawn that might be transferable to other similar contexts.

First of all, the preparatory phase of online projects must be planned to the smallest detail that would provide learners with the greatest number of lifelines possible. These include the design of templates, guidelines, assessment grids, and sample documents. Even in this case, instructors should show maximum flexibility. Furthermore, the pairing process should be monitored by the instructors very intensively, as some participants of this study highlighted that their successful collaboration rested on the icebreaker tasks the instructors designed for them. How to establish the interpersonal and intercultural dynamics should be well-planned ahead of the project implementation. It is recommended that the instructors undertaking a virtual exchange project need to take into consideration the potential interaction-related issues at the design stage. For this purpose, it is strongly advisable to incorporate several online facilitated sessions in different stages of the project, preferably at the beginning of the project, right after the pairing process and icebreaker activities, in the middle and at the end of the project.

It was also of utmost importance for the instructors to ensure that the project participants get recognition, as it was suggested by previous VE reports (for example O'Dowd et al., 2020). The instructors in the project sought help from their departments to run the project as part of an elective seminar for which the students are awarded credits for and they enabled the participants to receive recognition badges from UniCollaboration upon their successful project completion. It was also important not to design an arbitrary course for the sake of participating in a VE project. It was the pre-service teachers' technological pedagogical development that remained in focus in the study.

References

Antoniadou, V. (2011). Using activity theory to understand the contradictions in an online transatlantic collaboration between student-teachers of English as a foreign language. *ReCALL, 23*(3), 233–251. https://doi.org/10.1017/S0958344011000164

Barkhuizen, G., & Feryok, A. (2006). Pre-service teachers' perceptions of a short-term international experience programme. *Asia-Pacific Journal of Teacher Education, 34*(1), 115–134. https://doi.org/10.1080/13598660500479904

Bueno-Alastuey, M. C., & Kleban, M. (2016). Matching linguistic and pedagogical objectives in a telecollaboration project: A case study. *Computer Assisted Language Learning, 29*(1), 148–166. https://doi.org/10.1080/09588221.2014.904360

Buiskool, B., & Hudepohl, M. (2020). *Virtual formats versus physical mobility.* European Union. https://doi.org/10.2861/588975

Chambers, A., & Bax, S. (2006). Making CALL work: Towards normalisation. *System, 34*, 465–479. https://doi.org/10.1016/j.system.2006.08.001

Çiftçi, E. Y., & Savaş, P. (2018). The role of telecollaboration in language and intercultural learning: A synthesis of studies published between 2010 and 2015. *ReCALL, 30*(3), 278–298. https://doi.org/10.1017/S0958344017000313

Divéki, R. (2020). Dealing with global, local and intercultural issues for global competence development in teacher training: A pilot study on the views of university tutors in Hungary. In K. Károly, I. Lázár, & C. Gall (Eds.), *Culture and intercultural communication: Research and education* (pp. 91–112). School of English and American Studies. https://core.ac.uk/download/pdf/322824082.pdf

Dolga, L., Filipescu, H., Popescu-Mitroi, M. M., & Mazilescu, C. A. (2015). Erasmus mobility impact on professional training and personal development of students' beneficiaries. *Procedia – Social and Behavioral Sciences, 191*, 1006–1013. https://doi.org/10.1016/j.sbspro.2015.04.235

Dooly, M. (2017). Telecollaboration. In C. A. Chapelle & S. Sauro (Eds.), *The handbook of technology and second language teaching and learning* (pp. 169–183). Wiley-Blackwell.

Dooly, M. A. (2011). Crossing the intercultural borders into 3rd space culture(s): Implications for teacher education in the twenty-first century. *Language and Intercultural Communication, 11*(4), 319–337. https://doi.org/10.1080/14708477.2011.599390

Dooly, M., & Sadler, R. (2013). Filling in the gaps: Linking theory and practice through telecollaboration in teacher education. *ReCALL, 25*(1), 4–29. https://doi.org/10.1017/S0958344012000237

Duff, P. (2012). How to carry out case study research. In A. Mackey & S. M. Gass (Eds.), *Research methods in second language acquisition: A practical guide* (pp. 95–116). Wiley-Blackwell.

European Association of Distance Teaching Universities (EADTU). (2019). *Innovative models for collaboration and student mobility in Europe: Results of EADTU's task force and peer learning activity on virtual mobility*. European Association of Distance Teaching Universities. http://openaccess.uoc.edu/webapps/o2/bitstream/10609/93586/1/Innovative%20Models%20for%20 Collaboration%20and%20Student%20Mobility%20in%20Europe.pdf

Fekete, I. (2020). Information and communications technology use of Hungarian English majors: A large-scale questionnaire study. *Journal of Foreign Language Education and Technology, 5*(2), 251–275. http://jflet.com/jflet/index.php/jflet/article/view/209/279

Graham, C. R. (2011). Theoretical considerations for understanding technological pedagogical content knowledge (TPACK). *Computers & Education, 57*, 1953–1960. https://doi.org/10.1016/j.compedu.2011.04.010

Guichon, N. (2009). Training future language teachers to develop online tutors' competence through reflective analysis. *ReCALL, 21*(2), 166–185. https://doi.org/10.1017/S0958344009000214

Hampel, R. (2009). Training teachers for the multimedia age: Developing teacher expertise to enhance online learner interaction and collaboration. *International Journal of Innovation in Language Learning and Teaching, 3*(1), 35–50. https://doi.org/10.1080/17501220802655425

Hampel, R., & Stickler, U. (2005). New skills for new classrooms: Training tutors to teach languages online. *Computer Assisted Language Learning, 18*(4), 311–326. https://doi.org/10.1080/09588220500335455

Hauck, M., Müller-Hartmann, A., Rienties, B., & Rogaten, J. (2020). Approaches to researching digital-pedagogical competence development in VE-based teacher education. *Journal of Virtual Exchange, 3*(SI), 5–35. https://doi.org/10.21827/jve.3.36082

Holló, D., & Németh, N. (2009). Ten years on: Applying the lessons of a research project in thinking about the practicalities of research design. *Working Papers in Language Pedagogy, 3*, 114–139. http://langped.elte.hu/WoPaLParticles/W3Hollo_Nemeth.pdf

Kaçar, I. G. (2015). Turkish EFL pre-service teachers' attitudes towards multi-media enhanced wiki-mediated blended learning environments: A case study. In V. Turel (Ed.), *Intelligent design of interactive multimedia listening software* (pp. 357–404). IGI Global.

Kehrwald, B. (2008). Understanding social presence in text-based online learning environments. *Distance Education, 29*(1), 89–106. https://doi.org/10.1080/01587910802004860

Kohn, K., & Hoffstaedter, P. (2017). Learner agency and non-native speaker identity in pedagogical lingua franca conversations: Insights from intercultural telecollaboration in foreign language education. *Computer Assisted Language Learning, 30*(5), 351–367. https://doi.org/10.1080/09588221.2017.1304966

Kóris, R., Oswal, S. K., & Palmer, Z. B. (2020). Internationalizing the communication classroom via technology and curricular strategy: Pedagogical takeaways from a three-way online collaboration project. In P. K. Turner, S. Bardhan, T. Q. Holden, & E. M. Mutua (Eds.), *Internationalizing the communication curriculum in an age of globalisation* (pp. 235–242). Routledge.

Kramsch, C. (2014). Teaching foreign languages in an era of globalization: Introduction. *The Modern Language Journal, 98*(1), 296–310. https://doi.org/10.1111/j.1540-4781.2014.12057.x

Kumaravadivelu, B. (2001). Toward a postmethod pedagogy. *TESOL Quarterly, 35*(4), 537–560.

Kumaravadivelu, B. (2012). *Language teacher education for a global society: A modular model for knowing, analyzing, recognizing, doing, and seeing*. Routledge.

Lee, L. (2009). Promoting intercultural exchanges with blogs and podcasting: A study of Spanish-American telecollaboration. *Computer Assisted Language Learning, 22*(5), 425–443. https://doi.org/10.1080/09588220903345184

Lee, L., & Markey, A. (2014). A study of learners' perceptions of online intercultural exchange through Web 2.0 technologies. *ReCALL, 26*(3), 281–297. https://doi.org/10.1017/S0958344014000111

Lewis, T., & O'Dowd, R. (2016). Online intercultural exchange and foreign language learning: A systematic review. In R. O'Dowd & T. Lewis (Eds.), *Online intercultural exchange: Policy, pedagogy, practice* (pp. 21–60). Routledge.

Luo, H., & Yang, C. (2018). Twenty years of telecollaborative practice: Implications for teaching Chinese as a foreign language. *Computer Assisted Language Learning, 31*(5–6), 546–571. https://doi.org/10.1080/09588221.2017.1420083

Mishra, P., & Koehler, M. J. (2006). Technological pedagogical content knowledge: A framework for teacher knowledge. *Teachers College Record, 108*(6), 1017–1054.

Niess, M. L. (2011). Investigating TPACK: Knowledge growth in teaching with technology. *Journal of Educational Computing Research, 44*(3), 299–317. https://doi.org/10.2190/EC.44.3.c

O'Dowd, R. (2013). Telecollaborative networks in university education: Overcoming barriers to integration. *Internet and Higher Education, 18*, 47–53. https://doi.org/10.1016/j.iheduc.2013.02.001

O'Dowd, R. (2016). Emerging trends and new directions in telecollaborative learning. *Calico Journal, 33*(3), 291–310. https://doi.org/10.1558/cj.v33i3.30747

O'Dowd, R., & Lewis, T. (2016). *Online intercultural exchange: Policy, pedagogy, practice.* Routledge.

O'Dowd, R., Sauro, S., & Spector-Cohen, E. (2020). The role of pedagogical mentoring in virtual exchange. *TESOL Quarterly, 54*(1), 146–172. https://doi.org/10.1002/tesq.543

Pelaez-Morales, C. (2020). Experiential learning in the COVID-19 era: Challenges and opportunities for ESOL teacher educators. *Teaching/Writing: The Journal of Writing Teacher Education, 9*(1), 1–5. https://scholarworks.wmich.edu/wte/vol9/iss1/12

Peters, M. A., Rizvi, F., Gibbs, P., Gorur, R., Hong, M., Hwang, Y., Zipin, L., Brennan, M., Robertson, S., Quay, J., Malbon, J., Taglietti, D., Barnett, R., Chengbing, W., McLaren, P., Apple, R., Papastephanou, M., Burbules, N., Jackson, L., ... Misiaszek, L. (2020). Reimagining the new pedagogical possibilities for universities post-Covid-19. *Educational Philosophy and Theory*, 1–44. https://doi.org/10.1080/00131857.2020.1777655

Rienties, B., Lewis, T., O'Dowd, R., Rets, I., & Rogaten, J. (2020). The impact of virtual exchange on TPACK and foreign language competence: Reviewing a large-scale implementation across 23 virtual exchanges. *Computer Assisted Language Learning*, 1–28. https://doi.org/10.1080/09588221.2020.1737546

Schmidt, D. A, Baran, E., Thompson, A. D., Mishra, P., Koehler, M. J., & Shin, T. (2009). Technological pedagogical content knowledge (TPACK): The development and validation of an assessment instrument for preservice teachers. *Journal of Research on Technology in Education, 42*(2), 123–149. https://doi.org/10.1080/15391523.2009.10782544

Sadler, R., & Dooly, M. (2016). Twelve years of telecollaboration: What we have learnt. *ELT Journal, 70*(4), 401–413. https://doi.org/10.1093/elt/ccw041

Seidel, T., Blomberg, G., & Renkl, A. (2013). Instructional strategies for using video in teacher education. *Teaching and Teacher Education, 34*, 56–65. https://doi.org/10.1016/j.tate.2013.03.004

The EVALUATE Group. (2019). *Evaluating the impact of virtual exchange on initial teacher education: A European policy experiment.* Research-publishing.net. https://doi.org/10.14705/rpnet.2019.29.9782490057337

Tondeur, J., van Braak, J., Sang, G., Voogt, J., Fisser, P., & Ottenbreit-Leftwich, A. (2012). Preparing pre-service teachers to integrate technology in education: A synthesis of qualitative evidence. *Computers & Education, 59*(1), 134–144. https://doi.org/10.1016/j.compedu.2011.10.009

Üzüm, B., Akayoglu, S., & Yazan, B. (2020). Using telecollaboration to promote intercultural competence in teacher training classrooms in Turkey and the USA. *ReCALL, 32*(2), 162–177. https://doi.org/10.1017/S0958344019000235

Üzüm, B., Yazan, B., Avineri, N., & Akayoğlu, S. (2019). Preservice teachers' discursive constructions of cultural practices in a multicultural telecollaboration. *International Journal of Multicultural Education, 21*(1), 82–104. https://doi.org/10.18251/ijme.v21i1.1777

Voogt, J., Fisser, P., Pareja Roblin, N., Tondeur, J., & van Braak, J. (2013). Technological pedagogical content knowledge – A review of the literature. *Journal of Computer Assisted Learning, 29*(2), 109–121. https://doi.org/10.1111/j.1365-2729.2012.00487.x

A Multi-Case Study of English Language Teachers in Vietnam in Emergency Remote Teaching Mediated by Technologies: A Sociocultural Perspective

Hanh Dinh and Thu Dao

Highlights

- The abrupt transition from face-to-face classrooms to online teaching in the COVID-19 lockdown posed various challenges to teachers and students in Vietnamese contexts, highlighting a lack of knowledge about technological applications and ineffectiveness in retaining teacher-centered norms of teaching in online teaching settings.
- ERT provided a unique opportunity for self-regulated teachers to actively construct knowledge from the emergent situation, reframe content, and rethink traditional teaching methodologies.
- Despite the lack of institutional support and pedagogical preparation, the metacognitive transformation from teacher-centered norms to student-centered and harmonious coordination between synchronous and asynchronous technological platforms facilitates teachers' instructional strategies to manipulate those tools.
- The evolution of methodologies mediated by technologies and teachers' adaptability to provide students with learning skills in ERT could be systematized and classified into three phases: disorganized teaching, adaptive teaching, and optimal teaching.
- The sociocultural framework of how teachers acquire new knowledge for applying technology in teaching and management in ERT provides a foundation for future teacher education programs and training even when the pandemic is over.

H. Dinh (✉)
Department of Educational Theory and Practice, School of Education, State University of New York, Albany, NY, USA
e-mail: mdinh@albany.edu

T. Dao
English Department, Ho Chi Minh City University of Education, Ho Chi Minh City, Vietnam

© The Author(s), under exclusive license to Springer Nature Switzerland AG 2021
J. Chen (ed.), *Emergency Remote Teaching and Beyond*,
https://doi.org/10.1007/978-3-030-84067-9_21

459

1   Introduction

The first known case of the Novel Coronavirus (COVID-19) in Vietnam was reported on January 23rd, 2020. At the beginning of February 2020, the Vietnamese Ministry of Education and Training (MOET, 2020) ordered the suspension of all school activities across the country as a part of quarantine measures against the spread of the virus and issued a guide for modifying teaching plans accordingly. It was one of the first Asian countries to switch to online teaching platforms. Many other countries worldwide also decided to temporarily discontinue in-person teaching when the rapid and unpredictable spread of the virus hit their countries. Even after the curve of COVID-19 cases has been flattened, several universities might continue online learning formats.[1]

Emergency remote teaching (ERT), according to Hodges et al. (2020), indicates an urgent and mandatory online education implemented during a temporary shutdown of face-to-face educational instruction. Hence, for ERT, both the teachers and students must improvise quickly in less-than-ideal circumstances to switch their learning to online communicative platforms, while receiving limited administrative support. The sole reliance on online connection poses a constant pressure of dealing with emergent technical problems. Teachers need to navigate their syllabus and lesson plans under a higher level of stress and uncertainty. There is an urgent, unprecedented need in educational research to understand how teachers handle ERT and how they interact with students by using different media to design effective lessons (Bozkurt & Sharma, 2020). Such understanding is necessary since it would be uncertain whether normal teaching could resume anytime, or if new expected norms would be established. Nevertheless, there is little research on how different teachers deal with emerging issues in their sociocultural teaching context so that a contextualized insight into preparing similar types of teaching in crisis can be understood.

This chapter's central purpose is to fill that literature gap in ERT by presenting the Vietnamese context, focusing on the English language classroom teachers' views of their roles and their instructional strategies using technologies in ERT. A multi-case study was adopted since it allows us to create more convincing theoretical insights grounded in plentiful evidence, such as understanding the differences and the similarities between the cases and analyzing the data both within each situation as well as across situations (Yin, 2003). Therefore, the aim of this multi-case study is twofold: firstly, we attempt to provide an enriched picture of how English as a foreign language (EFL) teachers in Vietnam employ instructional strategies and classroom activities to deliver lesson content, interact with their students, and accommodate individual student's learning needs in ERT. Secondly, the study

---

[1] The COVID-19 pandemic in Vietnam is part of the worldwide pandemic of coronavirus disease, which has severely disrupted the schools' schedules nationwide. As of May 30, 2021, fourth waves of high infection have been recorded, forcing an estimation of 21.2 million children nationwide to switch to some forms of emergent remote learning during local or national lockdowns.

examines what EFL teachers know, believe, and think about the digital future of teaching in ERT and online teaching.

The chapter summarizes the empirical studies related to ERT English language teaching and introduces the mediation theory embedded in the sociocultural theory (SCT) that guided the data analysis. A multi-case study on how teachers mediate English language teaching for Vietnamese university students using online technologies is presented. Subsequently, the thematic analysis and an ecological, sociocultural framework are proposed to conceptualize technologies-mediated L2 teaching during ERT, followed by a discussion of several key findings and recommendations for digital language teaching post-COVID-19.

2   Literature Review

2.1   Technological Uses in English Language Teaching in ERT

Empirical studies investigating the implementation of technology-based practices in language classrooms during the pandemic have recently emerged (Ferdig et al., 2020; Hebebci et al., 2020). Such an approach demonstrates various technological applications and pedagogical considerations for using different Internet-based devices (e.g., smartphones, laptops, etc.) and online platforms (e.g., YouTube, Zoom videoconferencing, Google Slides, Google Classroom, etc.). The main modes of delivery in ERT are in either synchronous or asynchronous environments, or the combination of both.

The synchronous teaching environment is structured because teachers conduct live teaching sessions via videoconferencing with real-time interactions. Synchronous language teaching has long been praised for its high level of interaction, simulation, and collaboration, in which teachers can maximize an interactive environment for students to use the English language (Kohnke & Moorhouse, 2020). English language teachers in ERT still explain the target linguistic features (vocabulary, morphology, syntax, and grammar) (Basilaia et al., 2020), give instant feedback and immediate accommodation to students' questions and concerns (Liguori & Winkler, 2020), facilitate online discussion and social cohesion (Gruber & Bauer, 2020; Rinekso & Muslim, 2020), and provide students with stimulating digital content with authentic language input and hands-on assessment (Fansury et al., 2020).

On the other hand, asynchronous learning environments are structured in a way that allows English language learners to self-regulate their learning pace with materials made available online, participate in offline forums to consolidate and review English vocabulary, get access to recorded teacher talks for deep learning, and organize e-learning portfolios, exercises, and revisions (Okmawati, 2020). Asynchronous English language learning can also be used with embedded multimedia, such as audio feedback, to provide detailed, differentiated feedback on each student's writing (Fitzpatrick et al., 2020).

2.2 Teacher-Initiated Experiences in ERT

Qualitative studies that garner teachers' perceptions of their specific technological applications during the pandemic are scarce. Even before the pandemic outbreak, teaching online was challenging for university teachers due to their lack of pedagogical foundations to facilitate meaningful online learning experiences and complex administrative aspects (e.g., tracking class attendance, managing class assignments and materials, grading, organizing workflows) (Kali et al., 2011). Rapanta et al. (2020) reported teachers' experiences navigating ERT after conducting expert interviews in online teaching. Specifically, teachers are aware that they need to fine-tune their activities design to retain students' lengthened time in front of computer screens. The study categorizes teachers in ERT into "non-expert online teachers" and "expert online teachers." Non-expert online teachers can be overwhelmed, while expert online teachers have fewer expectations and lean on situated pedagogy, facilitating students' learning ownership to take the initiative in their learning. However, a rigid dichotomy between two types of teachers may not be effective to reflect the complexity of teachers' navigation strategies in different instructional contexts.

Zhang (2020) conducted a questionnaire survey among university teachers in Denmark and detailed their profiles of technology use in ERT. The results revealed that teachers' beliefs, educational conceptions, and self-perceptions encompass three key elements that play a crucial role in their ERT competence: awareness, attitude, and ability (3 As). Furthermore, Rapanta et al. (2020), focusing on university teachers' pedagogical preparedness in ERT, claimed that teachers hold a different yet more demanding cognitive expectation for students: students need to self-regulate learning to manage their learning processes to be systematically oriented to achieve goals.

In summary, the studies of ERT in English teaching in both asynchronous and synchronous settings have focused on how technology-based tools and devices could be used in lesson delivery to maximize the learning experiences. Such studies predominantly depict the availability and convenience of physical tools (Zhao, 2020). Alternatively, qualitative studies about teacher-initiated ERT experiences tend to focus only on the teachers' opinions towards online teaching in general. Notwithstanding, no study has been done to fully demonstrate the relationship between their own beliefs and their instructional materials, while taking into account the contextual factors (i.e. the awareness of instructional techniques and strategies, knowledge about students, and the engagement strategies in the technology-mediated situation).

Consequently, Egbert (2020) called for a more detailed, enriched understanding of teachers' perspectives and practices regarding their personalized ERT experience. Thus, the current multi-case study focuses on both the tools and resources for English language instruction and the teachers' psychology and intention underlying such utilization. The following are two guiding research questions: (1) Which tools have the EFL teachers been using in ERT to mediate students' English language learning? (2) How do English language teachers perceive their instructional roles during ERT, and how does such conceptualization affect their mediation of students' learning in ERT?

2.3 Theoretical Framework

We adopted the sociocultural theory (SCT) (Dendrinos, 2006; Lantolf & Thorne, 2007) to analyze the English language teachers' experiences with ERT because it affords a holistic description of fundamental components and the interrelations of an activity system. This theory draws on Vygotsky's developmental psychology, emphasizing that an individual's human mind is mediated. In other words, a human's mental functioning is fundamentally a mediated process governed by their interactions with sociocultural artifacts, activities, and concepts (Engeström, 2001; Ratner, 2002). A person does not "establish a direct relationship with the world, but this relationship is mediated through the use of *tools*" (Guerrero Nieto, 2007, p. 215). Tools can be either external (physical, technical) such as artifacts, instruments, and machines, or internal (psychological) signs, methods, procedures, and languages.

SCT has recently become popular in foreign language education (Storch, 2017; Swain et al., 2015), providing a culturally and socially contextualized account of how linguistic knowledge can be delivered in a classroom setting. The notion of tools is the key to understanding mediation in language teaching. First, tools include any kind of *physical tools and teaching materials*. For example, technologies have long been regarded as crucial physical mediating tools for English teaching (Gánem-Gutiérrez, 2006; Sahragard & Meihami, 2017; Thorne, 2008). Furthermore, physical tools are integrative to instructional activities. Such frequent use of physical tools in English language instruction helps diversify students' learning experience and connect them with other agents (e.g., peers), along with other accessible, inexhaustible, authentic materials (e.g., search engines, online dictionaries, multimedia resources, online articles, and magazines) (Lantolf et al., 2018).

Second, tools are also *psychological or mental tools* because English language teachers not only undergo a collection of cognitive processes, but they are also involved in a complex interaction with the world directed to the process of living and its sociocultural context. Psychological tools are ways to approach, understand, and engage students, such as intentional self-positioning and beliefs about teaching sequence, dialogue process, and their expertise on task management and interactivity in the teaching process. The third type of tools, also speaking metaphorically, refers to *scaffolding and assistance (tools)*, which are the learning tasks provided by teachers that help the learner reach their zone of proximal development or initiate language learning progress. This third type of tool can be comprehensible language input, instructional language, explanation about the lesson content, task scaffolding, and feedback.

What matters most in SCT is the reciprocal relationship between physical tools and resources and the underlying conceptual constructs of psychological and

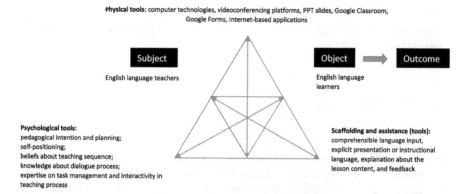

Fig. 1 The sociocultural framework for the mediational effect of using technologies in English language teaching

cognitive resources in a sociocultural context (see Fig. 1). For instance, if the teacher's pedagogical goal is to use group work as a scaffolding tool to enhance students' speaking skills, they are motivated to look for the appropriate technology to enhance this process. When observing the students' discussion while using this technology, the teacher is aware that students' familiarity with technology affects their participation. Hence, the teacher utilizes the students' needs analysis as a psychological tool to provide some individual students with sentence stems to extend their talk time. ERT English language teaching pedagogy, a higher-level psychological tool, must be studied in its natural surroundings where teachers interact with emerging salient social and cultural artifacts. Such technological applications and virtual interactions cannot be separated from how the teachers psychologically situate themselves under the influence of personal, rational, situational, and sociocultural factors, and shape their instruction (Cross, 2010; Ohta, 2017). The psychological tools and scaffolding/assistance tools help dig deeper into the teachers' experience and affect how they utilize the physical tools (Vitanova et al., 2015).

3 Methods

3.1 Participants Recruitment and Contextual Information

Purposive sampling was adopted for this multi-case study. It allows the researchers to carefully select cases of participants, examine similar results across cases, and predict contrasting results to gather in-depth investigation and informative data (Neuman, 2009). Specifically, we decided to choose teachers who had received some training and had some experience integrating technology into English language teaching. We contacted VNE University (a pseudonym, as are all other names), located in an urban area in the Southern part of Vietnam, where one of us had conducted professional workshops related to English teaching before COVID-19. When the university was closed during the lockdown, we sent a recruitment flyer to the English Department and kindly asked eight teachers (four are Vietnamese teachers teaching English, and four are English native-speaking teachers) who used to participate in our previous workshops. Hence, the 'site' here would be understood as the virtual university's institution, not the school's physical site, as we got access to and finished the data collection with the teachers via Zoom video-conferencing and online platforms (e.g., emails, Google Drive).

The instructional context has similar characteristics across cases, making the comparison possible. The university prepares its students for the International English Language Testing System (IELTS). The score students must achieve is the level B2 (Upper-intermediate) in the Common European Framework of Reference for Languages (CEFR). This graduation benchmark aligns with the National Foreign Languages Project 2020 (Pham & Bui, 2019). Their English courses are designated for first-year students who are enrolled in a preparation program before they commence their official university course for their selected majors. Students enroll in English Language classes and receive training in four language modalities, which are Reading, Listening, Writing, and Speaking. There are two teachers per class for each proficiency level, of whom one is a native English speaker, and the other is Vietnamese. The native teachers teach Listening and Speaking skills, whereas the Vietnamese teachers teach Reading and Writing skills courses. Treating each teacher as a unique case, we want to reveal that their teaching practices during ERT are examined along with their subject matter and teaching profiles, such as their assigned language skill, student population, years of teaching experience, age, and language skills they taught. The cohort of participants in this study represents a varied study background (see Table 1).

Table 1 Participant information

Participant	Gender	Age	Origin	Years of experience	Skills	Students' proficiency level
Uyen	Female	30	Vietnam	7	Reading & writing	Lower-intermediate
Thuy	Female	28	Vietnam	5	Reading & writing	Intermediate
Tim	Male	29	England	6	Listening & speaking	Intermediate
Alex	Male	39	England	14	Listening & speaking	Intermediate
Mike	Male	35	US	8	Listening & speaking	Lower-intermediate
Rob	Male	35	US	9	Listening & speaking	Upper-intermediate
Vi	Female	29	Vietnam	6	Reading & writing	Upper-intermediate
Trail	Female	27	Vietnam	4	Reading & writing	Lower-intermediate

3.2 Data Collection and Coding Analysis

The fundamental principle underlying a "multiple or collective case study" method is that researchers need to adopt a discovery-oriented approach grounded in data (Arghode & Wang, 2016; Hong & Cross Francis, 2020; Kleining & Witt, 2001). In other words, the "multiple or collective case study" addresses not only questions of "how" but also "why", focusing on a contemporary phenomenon within real-life contexts (Yin, 2003). Hence, the research data were a triangulation of a two-hour semi-structured interview with each teacher via Zoom and their teaching artifacts.

Each interview was divided into three parts: (1) background information of the teachers regarding their lives during ERT; (2) the specific tools and resources used in their online instruction; (3) the reflections, perceived positioning, and interpretations of some representative instructional episodes and circumstances during ERT. Before the interview, the teachers had agreed to submit samples and screenshots of notes, lesson plans, exercises, teaching slides, website links, apps, and software that they used for instruction. Those teaching artifacts would be used for research purposes and would not be shared without the teachers' permission. Teachers also completed a report tracking the frequency of tools and resources, the language skills they focused on, and the instructional phases when they engaged particular tools in the week before and after the interview (10 sessions in total per teacher). Teachers also provided a brief explanation about how those technologies help with their teaching and the learning objectives.

The interviews were audiotaped, transcribed, and put into the NVIVO 12 software. We followed Strauss and Corbin's (1998) open coding system to explore the data inductively, including the axial and selective coding process of departmentalizing, examining, and conceptualizing data. The codes helped to ground the analysis thoroughly and identify and challenge any preconceived assumptions. Next, using Stemler's (2001) taxonomic analysis and theoretical framework as a lens, we developed a list of codes and separated them into categories, including technological uses, psychological tools, and scaffolding tools, along with their sub-categories.

Data from the interview are triangulated with the teaching artifacts (lesson plans, teaching tools, teaching memos, etc.). For example, Ms. Vi noticed that students switched their cameras off and remained silent during the Reading session, so she encouraged participation by capturing the text from the coursebook, pasting it into the PowerPoint slide, and asking students to take turns reading it aloud. We analyzed the screenshots' data informed by SCT in this way: the teacher replaced the physical tool in face-to-face sessions, the coursebook, with the digital text by using the combination of both the Zoom videoconferencing platform and PowerPoint. That technological deployment affirmed the teacher's authoritative role and ensured the students' engagement in the activity without invading their privacy (revealing their faces and showing evidence of reading activity):

> The teacher must make sure the students are learning, although I could not see their faces. Reading aloud is more than a learning activity. It is a method for me to manage the class and feel assured that everyone works. (interview, 05/20/2020)

When the interviews supported the teaching content data, we added them to the categories' matrix. We checked all codes and categories that illuminated the teachers' physical tools, psychological tools, scaffolding, and assistance tools. An inter-encoder agreement of 80% was achieved after resolving disputed categories. We used a two-stage analysis of Merriam (1998): within-case analysis and cross-case analysis. During within-case analysis of each teacher, we considered the cases of the teachers individually, focusing on their views of their roles and teaching practices using technologies. After that, the cross-case analysis was conducted to compare any similarities or differences in similar aspects, and generalize patterns or key themes representing the eight teachers' cases. Finally, all data from different sources were assembled as a matrix according to themes and subthemes to facilitate cross-checking and triangulation.

4 Results and Discussion

4.1 Diversity in Technological Tools and Resources Used by English Language Teachers' Language Teaching

For the first research question, *"Which tools have the EFL teachers been using in ERT to mediate students' English language learning?",* all participants reported using various e-tools and e-resources during ERT. A comprehensive summary of those resulted in categories about their functions and cognition types (see Table 2 for the details).

Several observations can be made from Table 2. First, technological tools and their employment are inherently different between ERT and other online learning forms. Tools and resources in ERT were used at different rates in the English language classrooms. Specifically, videoconferencing, presentation software, and asynchronous platforms (Google Classroom) are the overarching categories of technologies and need to be deployed to retain the instructional process. Half of English language teachers in this study adopted the technologies in a somewhat hybrid way. Thus, those platforms and tools are called "essential technologies for ERT" in this study because they play an indispensable role in providing a virtual space to sustain teacher-student communication. Those "essential technologies" were channels that ensure teacher-student communication and the delivery of English language knowledge to students. They align with the pedagogical focus of the examination-oriented approach (Le, 2017; Tavakoli & Baniasad-Azad, 2017) since the knowledge is used to transmit information from the main sources of knowledge (teachers, materials) to students via the platforms. Five out of eight teachers used asynchronous tools to post lecture notes and academic materials, homework assignments, reminders, and grading. On the contrary, technologies intentionally used for enhancing learning such as collaborative learning and e-templates for learning games, stimulating learning autonomy, or resulting from learner decisions were occasionally found.

Table 2 Categories of e-tools and e-resources used by the English language teachers

	Categories	Frequency of use	Instructional functions	Interactional patterns	Examples
Essential Technologies for ERT	Videoconferencing	80	Creating a virtual context where learning can take place, helping to organize the class into small groups (Zoom and BigBlueButton only), screen-sharing	Teacher's monologue, groupwork in virtual Zoom's "break-out" rooms, individual communication via Zoom chatbox	Zoom, Google Meet, Microsoft Teams, BigBlueButton
	Presentation program	80	Presenting vocabulary and grammar, annotating key information, modeling language production or skills	Teacher's monologue	Microsoft PowerPoint, Google Docs, Google Slides
	Asynchronous platform	40	Organizing self-regulating study resources, assigning homework, uploading materials and discussion questions, delivering class announcement, recording students' learning progress (grading)	Teacher's monologue and personalized feedback on student performance and progress	Google Classroom

(continued)

Table 2 (continued)

	Categories	Frequency of use	Instructional functions	Interactional patterns	Examples
Complimentary technologies for ERT	Collaborative web-based app	35	Organizing in-class writing, quizing or surveying the students' opinions, treating it as an online workbook for peer-feedback and peer-correction	Teacher's monologue, group writing, teacher's feedback on individual student writing	Google forms, Google Slides, Google Docs
	E-learning and mobile-based apps	22	Organizing vocabulary practice at individual or whole-class pace, increasing learning motivation, reviewing vocabulary, facilitating game-based learning and assessment, differentiated learning for students	Teacher-student communication	Kahoot, Quizlet, online learning dictionary, Rachel's English website
	E-resources with special sound and visual effects	13	Creating lead-in introduction, stimulating students' participation.	Teacher-student communication	Wheel of Fortune, Who Wants to be Millionaire? Trivial Game,
	Multimedia	11	Presenting new words, eliciting ideas for writing topics,	Teacher's monologue	YouTube videos
	Emergency contact	10	Keeping in touch with students for technical support	Individual communication	Facebook Messenger, Facebook group, Google Classroom "Stream", email

They are put in the secondary categories called "complementary technologies in ERT."

Second, the teachers' technological adoptions in ERT reveal the harsh reality of converting face-to-face into computerized online instruction. Online courses or technology-assisted language teaching suggested by instructional designers and educational software developers demonstrate a systematic, meaningful, and seamless manner. The tools are strategically applied to optimize the pedagogical process for teachers. However, during ERT in Vietnam, teachers were compelled to commit to the approved in-person curriculum before the pandemic. While the curriculum remained the same, they had to manually digitalize instructional materials, such as transferring the printed content to digital platforms using scanning, typing, photographing etc., to carry forward without severely disrupting their teaching. All the process of transferring and creating teaching materials for online classes was contingent, and all teachers only received an announcement about the national lockdown and moved to ERT the day after that. Hence, the complimentary technologies were not abundantly and strategically used.

Third, some features available in videoconference platforms are not user-friendly and time is needed to learn how to use them well (Stafford, 2020). According to the university policy, students did not need to reveal their faces via webcams due to privacy issues and lack of technical preparation. Such administrative requirements cause additional psychological stress for teachers about the class discourse, especially for English language teaching, where human communications play a critical role in developing communicative competences. Due to those changes, teachers felt unprepared and disconnected from the sense of authentic teaching while navigating new instructional platforms. Thus, Mike explained that he struggled to convert all printed instructional materials into PowerPoint slides, operate each feature on Zoom (e.g., screen-sharing, breakout rooms, sharing files), and simultaneously monitor students' completion of tasks without seeing them. Such logistical tasks consumed a considerably longer time and more cognitive processing to accomplish, so he did not have time and energy for relevant YouTube videos to contextualize his vocabulary teaching or to create an interactive mobile-based learning game using Kahoot.

4.2 Psychological Tools and Scaffolding Tools in English Language Teachers' Technology-Mediated Teaching

For the second research question, *"How do English language teachers perceive their instructional roles during ERT and how does such conceptualization affect their mediation of students' learning in ERT?"*, three broad themes emerged from the results: the disorganized ERT, the adaptive ERT, and the optimal ERT. Those themes represent the hypothetical development of teachers' perceptions of technologies-mediated instruction during ERT. Despite the similar patterns found across cases, there are personalized features associated with each individual. A teacher could find themselves in the disorganized ERT throughout his teaching experience, while another could transform themselves from the disorganized ERT to the optimal ERT within a short amount of time.

Disorganized ERT

Disorganized ERT indicates the stage when teachers are unwilling yet forced to use technological tools and resources. Their perceptions of ERT are shaped in the context of social amplification of uncertainty in responding to the emergency (e.g., COVID-19). Those perceptions stemmed from an inadequate amount of time to mediate teaching practice using unfamiliar technological employment. Thus, even when teachers adopt positive perceptions towards online teaching in ERT, the lack of pedagogical support for online teaching makes them less competent and confident in navigating online instruction. Rob recalled his experience being as if he were "thrown into the water and told to swim without any scaffolding."

The psychological tool that teachers in Vietnam want to maintain is professional and organized instruction in front of students. This psychological tool reflects the Confucian heritage culture in Asian countries to maintain the master or teacher professional image so as not to lose "face" in front of students (Park & Kim, 2008). Tim expressed the expected portrayal of teachers:

> We would not want students to see the side of us that we have no ideas how to use the technologies. It affects our image as teachers, so I was insecure about conducting an online class. I do not know what to do if something goes wrong. Ironically, that made me feel uncomfortable to try new technological tools. (interview, 05/22/2020)

Another teacher, Tran, said she endured tremendous pressure to appear to be a resourceful and calm teacher, which resulted in intensive 10–12 h in front of the computer to conduct extensive research and finalize teaching ideas. However, such self-investment did not guarantee that teachers could retain the traditional roles found in face-to-face teaching as they expected. For example, students turned off the webcams. Thus, when teachers shared a YouTube video to help students generate ideas for a writing or listening task, teachers could not observe students' facial expressions to accommodate their needs for clarification. Furthermore, teachers in the exam-oriented approach, who want to control students' experience, yet have little or no experience with online teaching, are pedagogically unprepared to effectively operate an online instructional task since there are uncontrollable aspects. When Tran asked her students to complete mock tests using Google Forms, most of her students consulted the Internet for answer keys. Thuy wanted to continue calling on students by name to answer multiple-choice reading comprehension questions, yet there was no way to check if the student just carelessly chose an option. Such incidents prove that the psychological tool of teacher-centered positioning does not help with grasping the complexity of human variability in ERT. Thus, contradictory to Rapanta et al. (2020), students were not automatically capable of self-regulated learning. Teachers must first modify their presence in online learning situations, embracing a more facilitatory discourse to direct instruction rather than control learning activities.

Paradoxically, teachers in "disorganized ERT" would continue to reinforce their power and employ additional disciplinary methods to control the class's dynamism. Such psychological tools intensified the dissonance between their expected instructional planning and teaching practice reality. Alex randomly joined different breakout rooms, where students were expected to work with their teammates, in order to detect uncooperative students. If a student did not pay attention or neglected the group work, his performance score would be deducted:

> [I]n face-to-face class, I am more supportive and offer students rewards. Whereas online, I offer more threats just to make sure they study for real. But I do not think my students like those threats and truly want to engage. (interview, 05/19/2020)

According to SCT, the psychological mechanism affects the selection of scaffolding tools (Kozulin, 2003). Teachers in "disorganized ERT" provide little flexibility or modification and resist exploring the new online setting's technological possibilities. Uyen stated that she did not know how Zoom features and e-resources could be used alongside instructional activities, so she was very hesitant to try the group work using "breakout rooms," polls, or emoticons on Zoom. Five out of eight teachers who kept their teacher-centered instruction to a certain extent during ERT repeated their scaffolding and assistance tools as if they were in the face-to-face classes. They also did not allow students to open any other browsers or e-lexical tools, classifying those tools as distractions rather than learning aids.

Adaptive ERT

Adaptive ERT indicates a gradual construction of metacognitive awareness between ERT and face-to-face teaching. Teachers learn to evaluate the technologies' new instructional features and how those features must require modifications to align with individual's teaching methodologies. Alex elaborated on the inherent difference between remote teaching and face-to-face teaching:

> If you only talk, students may or may not listen to you – that cannot be good. In an online class, it requires different sets of skills to operate the tasks effectively. Students must do something with you. That was when they must listen to you and each other. (05/19/2020)

ERT is construed as a dual goal: (1) selecting the tools that ameliorate the online teaching effects (e.g., long hours sitting still in front of the computers) on students' learning and (2) generating a learner-centered atmosphere to retain students' attention. In this view, ERT is a unique professional development opportunity to reflect on current teaching methods and enhance their adaptability, so teachers' anxiety is replaced with the excitement to explore e-materials and e-tools. Thuy commented:

> The willingness to welcome new ways and be open to new options and the willingness to adapt shall be the motto. ERT urges me to (re)think in a more structured and micro way to conduct my teaching while motivating me to be more creative in my content delivery. Using technologies is not for presenting knowledge but engaging students. (interview, 05/23/2020)

She asked students to imagine as if English was their "voice" to create a digital storytelling script using the YouTube studio. Without the pandemic, she would not have recognized her passion for taking both the role of an English instructor and an innovative content creator.

The adaptive ERT witnessed teachers' attempts to employ a student-centered approach as a psychological tool to organize their classroom interactions and conduct trial-and-error experiments with technologies using appropriate scaffolding tools. For instance, Vi could articulate the assimilation of face-to-face teaching into online teaching:

> Online teaching is a type of reality where the teacher-student connection is the key to its success (or failure). I observed that students learn differently. They lost attention quickly in the online setting. Thus, I know that I need to have a different mindset to teach online, so I divide my lesson into smaller sections with more varied, problem-solving tasks to engage them. (interview, 05/31/2020)

The psychological tools teachers employ include reflective teaching, a resourceful staging of online instructional techniques, genuine accommodation to engage students, and willingness to deal with spontaneous technical issues.

Optimal ERT

Optimal ERT indicates the stage where teachers seamlessly integrate technological uses with instruction. Unlike the "adaptive ERT," where teachers are testing out ideas and learning to integrate technologies into teaching in a meaningful way, teachers who achieve optimal ERT have already worked out concrete instructional strategies and solidified the principles for accommodating their students' needs, manipulating both technological tools and pedagogical tools.

Teachers boost students' engagement in a technological context, reflect on the qualities of their work, and use that information for adjusting future teaching (Hill & McNamara, 2012), which resonates with the characteristics of teachers in optimal ERT. For instance, Tran found that she could synthesize different scaffolding techniques to stimulate group work while simultaneously track individual student's learning progress using Google Slides. She assigned specific and clear responsibilities for them with meaningful, specific, goal-oriented feedback throughout the learning process's small phases.

Tran "[went] beyond students' answering questions" by organizing activities using "complementary technologies" that "at least involved a game atmosphere" and emphasized students' voices. First, she divided the students into pairs in breakout rooms. Each pair was then assigned a slide number to compile a reading comprehension question for the opponent group (Fig. 2). Once all reading questions were prepared, the pair who solved the given question correctly in the shortest amount of time would win. After group work in the breakout rooms, all students came back to the whole class discussion. Each pair needed to explain the strategies that helped them solve the type of reading question, by sharing a screenshot of them using Zoom annotations to reach a mutual agreement. Tran offered scaffolding guidance if they encounter difficult questions. She modeled the essential reading strategies again. Sometimes, if the knowledge was too abstract, she would show a YouTube video to demonstrate the skill in question. The library of questions and answers was uploaded on Quizlet for later review. Zoom provides an opportunity for differentiated learning when reserved and introverted students can provide the answers (e.g., via the Zoom chat box or polls) without being dominated by more active students.

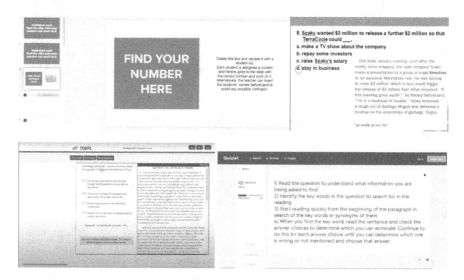

Fig. 2 Technological tools for an English reading activity in Tran's class

Addressing the interactional challenges, Rob flexibly navigated assistance tools to shift to a student-centered atmosphere:

> I used anonymous writing on Google Docs to let students practice English journaling and feedback as an attentive and sympathetic peer reviewer. That helped my students become the center of learning, and our interactions were bettered even when I could not see their faces. The interactions between us become real once trusting connections are established. (interview, 06/01/2020)

This stage, therefore, demonstrates teachers' improved command of using technologies for both pedagogical purposes. They have a clear vision of combining scaffolding and assistance tools with physical tools in a coherent, meaningful way. Even after ERT, Rob has retained the technologies-mediated teaching since "it helps build a stronger rapport with students, set deadlines for homework in an organized way, and motivates teachers to share resources for self-study." He established more optional communicative platforms using social media tools, which helped his students build social, emotional capital and practice English naturally outside class time. Such insight is promising since technologies-mediated teaching in ERT is no longer a last resort. It has become a valuable solution that is worth considering.

5 A Sociocultural Framework for Technologies-Mediated English Language Teaching in ERT

The findings that have emerged from this study demonstrate distinct features indicative of both English native-speaking teachers and local teachers in language teaching experience during ERT. A holistic framework is constructed to summarize sociocultural key agents and their interplay that determine the technological

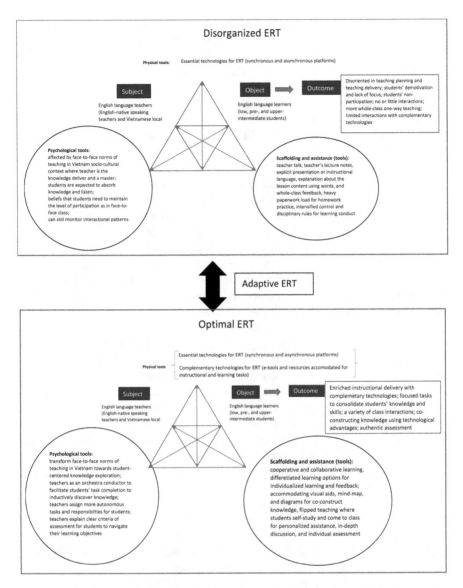

Fig. 3 The mediational phases of technologies-mediated English language teaching from the sociocultural framework

mediation in ERT instruction (Fig. 3). The agents include the teachers, the students, physical tools, psychological tools, scaffolding, and assistance tools.

This study found that videoconferencing, Google classroom, and PowerPoint slides have become leading technological tools that dominate language instruction in the Vietnamese sociocultural context. However, they do not necessarily result in ubiquitous, innovative teaching methods since both English-native and local teachers are familiar with teacher-centered teaching. Although richer technological repositories for instruction are made possible for the students in diverse geographic locations (Yoon, 2019), ERT teaching poses several concerns for all teachers regarding the ineffectiveness of teaching delivery and frustrations regarding assessments and classroom management. Such findings align with Peeraer & Van Petegem (2015) that Vietnam exhibits a slow uptake of technological applications and mostly integrates technologies that mainly replace traditional lecture-based teaching practice, rather than regular, innovative use in support of student learning. Hence, Vietnam would require significant reforms and changes that have more to do with pedagogy and curriculum instead of the mere provision of fancy technological devices (Nykvist et al., 2003).

There are specific subtle disparities between Vietnamese and English-native-speaking teachers, although both groups demonstrate similar characteristics throughout the three phases of ERT teaching described above. When ERT started, at first English-native speaking teachers tended to be more mentally prepared. They were able to predict the switch from face-to-face to e-teaching since the worsening COVID-19 scenarios in their home countries had already enforced the idea of closing schools earlier than Vietnam. Thus, they seemed to have a faster speed of familiarizing themselves with the new teaching environment. However, Vietnamese teachers were quick technology learners, despite the fact that all of them claimed to have limited official training with CALL.[2] They invested considerably more time and effort in lesson planning and gathering new teaching ideas and resources, while also exchanging ideas with the native English teachers during virtual faculty meetings. Despite those minor differences in their reactions, both teachers' groups complemented each other. The Vietnamese teachers learned from the English native-speaking teachers to adopt a more game-based and visual approach. In contrast, the English native-speaking teachers became more aware of maintaining a disciplined and austere environment to ensure that the students were engaged. They demonstrated resilience in the face of regulatory hurdles and lack of Internet access in Vietnam, as promoting e-learning in Vietnam had stalled for years.

The study also unfolds some cases where teachers start to go beyond the current prevailing predicaments of technological integration and make meaningful contributions to students' learning during the pandemic. ERT provides a unique experiential environment for practitioners to become more flexible, competent, and creative in their pedagogies. Adaptive ERT demonstrates teachers' efforts to begin adopting more complementary technologies by creating a virtual learning environment with socio-affective benefits such as collaborative instructional tasks. Indeed, it is not a linear trial-and-error process: whether it results in failure or success depends on internal factors, including teacher agency, teacher motivation, teacher perception towards ERT, as well as external factors, including flexibility in program administration, supportive network from colleagues, and the cooperation of students. Thus, the study affirmed Zhao (2020) that the combination of critical awareness, attitude, and abilities are critical for constructing ERT pedagogies that work for a specific student population.

---

[2] Computer-assisted language learning.

Optimal ERT describes the highest metacognitive awareness is when teachers know how to stay reflective on ERT experience and formulate core practices that can be transferred in any teaching context in which the learning is situated. In the case of Vietnam, teachers' technological applications follow a design-based approach where teachers observe how students respond to more student-centered activities and modify their teaching accordingly. Teachers can pinpoint the differences between face-to-face teaching and ERT teaching and transform instruction, ranging from organizing tasks to establishing personal relationships. In that view, instead of placing teachers in a dichotomy of "non-expert online teachers" and "expert online teachers" (cf. Rapanta et al., 2020), a varying degree is found in maneuvering related sociocultural factors to leverage teachers' professional development during their "adaptive" stage.

6   Conclusion and Future Research

Based on the SCT and the mediation theory, the current multi-case study provides a multidimensional scenario of English language teachers' teaching-mediated instruction in ERT. This study has illustrated teachers' abilities to navigate ERT by cultivating their critical awareness of teaching across contexts and their openness in exploring how to integrate technological tools into instructional methods to increase students' involvement. The instructional norms in Vietnam, flexibility in instructional mindsets, and technological updates further underscore teachers' navigation to facilitate instruction in and beyond ERT. Future studies may investigate whether these phases of instructional transformation are found in other contexts of online education. Second, more data sources can be used for teachers in different countries, program settings, or levels of language proficiency levels. Years of experience, age, educational background, and prior experience with technological integration into teaching might impact teachers' performances. The learning outcomes need to be statistically analyzed to evaluate the effectiveness of instructional modifications in ERT.

7   Food for Thought

There are specific implications that help practitioners across disciplines transform physical, psychological, and scaffolding tools to new teaching norms during and beyond ERT.

Maintain students' motivation and attention

Teachers can design tasks that can successfully engage students and help them avoid being distracted by external factors, such as background noise or notifications on their phones (Christenson et al., 2012). Diverse, short, but coherent lesson content and a clear explanation of learning objectives would help keep students' attention (Major et al., 2016). Also, interactive instructions to promote two-way communication can help students complete the tasks and to give them a sense of confidence and competence (Ryan & Deci, 2000). Teachers must explicitly inform students of the tasks and activities' purposes and criteria for assessment.

Give personalized feedback

Modeling and giving formative feedback to students' working process rather than summative feedback are highly recommended. Teachers can create a codebook for common comments. They can also organize online workbooks by using Google Slides or Google Sheets for some peer review activities. This enables students to be more responsible and eager to learn from each other. Students can view their friends' assignments uploaded on the platform or responses to discussions in an open forum.

Promote different patterns of interaction in and out of "class."

Another concern about online teaching is that the teacher's talking time far exceeds students' talking time. A possible solution to this is to add more variety to communication patterns between class members. Teachers can facilitate Zoom breakout rooms by putting students into information gap or jigsaw activities, and allow them to do flipped classrooms. Students should be encouraged to study the materials in advance and then visually share their ideas or present them by sharing their screens and asking the teacher and their classmates questions during synchronous class. Activities that are project-based and task-based should be promoted; to complete them, interaction among students is a must. After class, social network sites and messaging apps, such as Facebook, Twitter, Viber, WhatsApp, etc., are useful in facilitating interactions.

Be resourceful about class activities and materials.

Below is a list of resources English teachers to maintain students' attention and interest and encourage their creativity (Table 3).

Table 3 Resources for English teachers

Source	Materials	Link
Cambridge University Press	A webinar series to online teaching and learning while social distancing on their YouTube channel	https://www.youtube.com/channel/ UCKKTzzdnA1VBvlpixxaI0Ow
British Council	A separate site for Covid-19 support	http://learnenglish.britishcouncil.org/ covid-19-learning-support
Oxford University Press	A wide array of resources for both teachers and learners	https://elt.oup.com/feature/global/learnatho me/?cc=vn&selLanguage=en
National Geographic	Free e-books and webinars readily available for teachers to use	https://eltngl.com/assets/html/ digital-resources/

Acknowledgments We would like to express our gratitude to Dr. Julian Chen, the reviewers, and Deanna Bennett for their valuable proofreading and feedback on our manuscript. We also want to sincerely thank the eight participants and the institution willing to share their ERT experiences in this critical time.

Resources

Arghode, V., & Wang, J. (2016). Exploring trainers' engaging instructional practices: A collective case study. *European Journal of Training and Development, 40*(2), 111–127. https://doi.org/10.1108/EJTD-04-2015-0033

Basilaia, G., Dgebuadze, M., Kantaria, M., & Chokhonelidze, G. (2020). Replacing the classic learning form at universities as an immediate response to the COVID-19 virus infection in Georgia. *International Journal for Research in Applied Science and Engineering Technology, 8*(3), 101–108.

Bozkurt, A., & Sharma, R. C. (2020). Emergency remote teaching in a time of global crisis due to CoronaVirus pandemic. *Asian Journal of Distance Education, 15*(1), i–vi.

Christenson, S. L., Reschly, A. L., & Wylie, C. (Eds.). (2012). *Handbook of research on student engagement.* Springer.

Cross, R. (2010). Language teaching as sociocultural activity: Rethinking language teacher practice. *The Modern Language Journal, 94*(3), 434–452.

Dendrinos, B. (2006). Mediation in communication, language teaching and testing. *Journal of Applied Linguistics, 22*, 9–35.

Egbert, J. (2020). The new normal?: A pandemic of task engagement in language learning. *Foreign Language Annals, 53*(2), 314–319.

Engeström, Y. (2001). Expansive learning at work: Toward an activity theoretical reconceptualization. *Journal of eEducation and Work, 14*(1), 133–156.

Fansury, A. H., Januarty, R., & Ali Wira Rahman, S. (2020). Digital content for millennial generations: Teaching the English foreign language learner on COVID-19 pandemic. *Journal of Southwest Jiaotong University, 55*(3), 1–12.

Ferdig, R. E., Baumgartner, E., Hartshorne, R., Kaplan-Rakowski, R., & Mouza, C. (2020). *Teaching, technology, and teacher education during the COVID-19 pandemic: Stories from the field.* Association for the Advancement of Computing in Education (AACE).

Fitzpatrick, E., Mckeown, D., & Schrodt, K. (2020). Asynchronous audio feedback: Time- and space-flexible writing instruction. In *Teaching, technology, and teacher education during the COVID-19 pandemic: Stories from the field* (pp. 717–725). Association for the Advancement of Computing in Education.

Gánem-Gutiérrez, G. A. (2006). Sociocultural theory and its application to CALL: A study of the computer and its relevance as a mediational tool in the processes of collaborative activity. *Essex Reseach Reports in Linguistics, 52*, 1–39.

Guerrero Nieto, C. H. (2007). Applications of Vygotskyan concept of mediation in SLA. *Colombian Applied Linguistics Journal, 9*, 213–228.

Gruber, A., & Bauer, E. (2020). Fostering interaction in synchronous online class sessions with foreign language learners. In *Teaching, technology, and teacher education during the COVID-19 pandemic: Stories from the field* (pp. 175–178). Association for the Advancement of Computing in Education.

Hebebci, M. T., Bertiz, Y., & Alan, S. (2020). Investigation of views of students and teachers on distance education practices during the Coronavirus (COVID-19) Pandemic. *International Journal of Technology in Education and Science (IJTES), 4*(4), 267–282.

Hill, K., & McNamara, T. (2012). Developing a comprehensive, empirically based research framework for classroom-based assessment. *Language Testing, 29*(3), 395–420.

Hodges, C., Moore, S., Lockee, B., Trust, T., & Bond, A. (2020). The difference between emergency remote teaching and online learning. *Educause Review, 27,* 1–12. Retrieved online at https://er.educause.edu/articles/2020/3/the-difference-between-emergency-remote-teaching-and-online-learning

Hong, J., & Cross Francis, D. (2020). Unpacking complex phenomena through qualitative inquiry: The case of teacher identity research. *Educational Psychologist, 55*(4), 208–219.

Kali, Y., Goodyear, P., & Markauskaite, L. (2011). Researching design practices and design cognition: Contexts, experiences and pedagogical knowledge-in-pieces. *Learning, Media, and Technology, 36*(2), 129–149. https://doi.org/10.1080/17439884.2011.553621

Kleining, G., & Witt, H. (2001, February). Discovery as basic methodology of qualitative and quantitative research. *Forum Qualitative Sozialforschung/Forum: Qualitative Social Research, 2*(1), 1–26.

Kohnke, L., & Moorhouse, B. L. (2020). Facilitating synchronous online language learning through zoom. *RELC Journal.* https://doi.org/10.1177/0033688220937235

Kozulin, A. (2003). Psychological tools and mediated learning. *Vygotsky's educational theory in cultural context, 4*(6), 15–38.

Lantolf, J. P., & Thorne, S. L. (2007). Sociocultural theory and second language learning. In B. VanPatten & J. Williams (Eds.), *Theories in second language acquisition* (pp. 201–224). Lawrence Erlbaum.

Lantolf, J. P., Poehner, M. E., & Swain, M. (Eds.). (2018). *The Routledge handbook of sociocultural theory and second language development.* Routledge. https://doi.org/10.4324/9781315624747

Le, V. C. (2017). English language education in universities: National benchmarking in practice. In E. S. Park & B. Spolsky (Eds.), *English education at tertiary level in Asia: From theory to practice.* Routledge.

Liguori, E. W., & Winkler, C. (2020). From offline to online: Challenges and opportunities for entrepreneurship education following the COVID-19 pandemic. *Entrepreneurship Education and Pedagogy.* https://doi.org/10.1177/2515127420916738

Major, C. H., Harris, M. S., & Zakrajsek, T. (2016). *Teaching for learning: 101 intentionally designd educational activities to put students on the path to success.* Routledge.

Merriam, S. B. (1998). *Qualitative research and case study applications in education. Revised and expanded from "case study research in education".* Jossey-Bass Publishers.

Ministry of Education and Training (Vietnam). (2020, March 31). Bộ GDĐT hướng dẫn điều chỉnh nội dung dạy học kì II năm học 2019–2020 đối với cấp THCS, THPT. *moet.gov.vn* (in Vietnamese). Archived from the original on 3 April 2020. Retrieved 21 May 2020.

Neuman, W. L. (2009). *Social research methods: Qualitative and quantitative approaches.* Pearson/Allyn & Bacon.

Nykvist, S., Lloyd, M., & Vui, T. (2003). ICT education in Vietnam: Diving into the second wave. In *The second wave of ICT education-from facilitating teaching and learning to engendering education reform: Proceedings of the international conference on computers in education 2003* (pp. 138–141). Association for the Advancement of Computing in Education.

Ohta, A. S. (2017). Sociocultural theory and second/foreign language education. *Second and foreign language education. Encyclopedia of language and education, 4,* 57–68.

Okmawati, M. (2020). The use of Google classroom during pandemic. *Journal of English Language Teaching, 9*(2), 438–443.

Park, Y. S., & Kim, B. S. (2008). Asian and European American cultural values and communication styles among Asian American and European American college students. *Cultural Diversity and Ethnic Minority Psychology, 14*(1), 47–56.

Peeraer, J., & Van Petegem, P. (2015). Integration or transformation? Looking in the future of Information and Communication Technology in education in Vietnam. *Evaluation and Program Planning, 48,* 47–56.

Pham, T. N., & Bui, L. T. P. (2019). An exploration of students' voices on the English graduation benchmark policy across Northern, Central and Southern Vietnam. *Language Testing in Asia, 9*(1), 1–20.

Rapanta, C., Botturi, L., Goodyear, P., Guàrdia, L., & Koole, M. (2020). Online university teaching during and after the Covid-19 crisis: Refocusing teacher presence and learning activity. *Postdigital Science and Education, 2*(3), 923–945.

Ratner, C. (2002). *Cultural psychology: Theory and method.* Kluwer/Plenum.

Rinekso, A. B., & Muslim, A. B. (2020). Synchronous online discussion: Teaching English in higher education amidst the COVID-19 pandemic. *JEES (Journal of English Educators Society), 5*(2), 155–162.

Ryan, R. M., & Deci, E. L. (2000). Self-determination theory and the facilitation of intrinsic motivation, social development, and well-being. *American Psychologist, 55*(1), 68–78.

Sahragard, R., & Meihami, H. (2017). A sociocultural perspective into intercultural competence and computer-assisted language learning: Intercultural competence and computer-assisted language learning. In *Multiculturalism and technology-enhanced language learning* (pp. 130–141). IGI Global.

Stafford, V. (2020). Tech review: Teaching through Zoom–what we've learned as new online educators. *Journal of Applied Learning and Teaching, 3*(2), 150–153.

Stemler, S. (2001). An overview of content analysis. *Practical Assessment, Research & Evaluation, 7*, 137–146.

Strauss, A., & Corbin, J. (1998). *Basics of qualitative research.* Sage Publications.

Storch, N. (2017). Sociocultural theory in the L2 classroom. In S. Loewen & M. Sato (Eds.), *The Routledge handbook of instructed second language acquisition* (1st edition, pp. 69-83). Routledge.

Swain, M., Kinnear, P., & Steinman, L. (2015). *Sociocultural theory in second language education: An introduction through narratives* (Vol. 11). Multilingual matters.

Tavakoli, M., & Baniasad-Azad, S. (2017). Teachers' conceptions of effective teaching and their teaching practices: A mixed-method approach. *Teachers and Teaching, 23*(6), 674–688.

Thorne, S. L. (2008). Mediating technologies and second language learning. In J. Coiro, M. Knobel, C. Lankshear, & D. Leu (Eds.), *Handbook of research on new literacies* (pp. 417–450). Lawrence Erlbaum.

Vitanova, G., Miller, E. R., Gao, X., & Deters, P. (2015). Introduction to theorizing and analyzing agency in second language learning: Interdisciplinary approaches. In P. Deters, X. Gao, E. R. Miller, & G. Vitanova (Eds.), *Theorizing and analyzing agency in second language learning: Interdisciplinary approaches* (pp. 1–13). Multilingual Matters.

Yin, R. K. (2003). *Case study research: Design and methods.* Sage.

Yoon, H. (2019). An online college near me: Exploring the institutional factors of E-learners' local orientation. *The International Review of Research in Open and Distance Learning, 20*(5), 64–84.

Zhang, C. (2020). From face-to-face to screen-to-screen: CFL teachers' beliefs about digital teaching competence during the pandemic. *International Journal of Chinese Language Teaching, 2020*, 31–52.

Zhao, Y. (2020). Tofu is not cheese: Rethinking education amid the COVID-19 pandemic. *ECNU Review of Education, 3*(2), 189–203. https://doi.org/10.1177/2096531120928082

Part IX
Researcher Corner: Mixed Methods Research

Exploring EFL Teachers' Technological Pedagogical Content Knowledge and Student Engagement in an Emergency Remote Teaching Context

Dian N. Marissa and Wedad Allahji

Highlights

- Teacher's Technological Pedagogical Content Knowledge (TPACK) predicts 20.8% variation in Student Engagement (SE).
- On reflexivity: Throughout the emergency period, competent teachers engaged in active internal dialogue about their own beliefs, knowledge, and contextual constraints.
- On adaptability: Despite the range of technological choices available to them, competent teachers were mindful of adapting their teaching to meet the demands of their unique classroom contexts.
- On responsiveness: Competent teachers were also perceptive of their students' problems and responded to their individual and instructional needs on a moment-by-moment basis.

1 Introduction

The year 2020 will be remembered as the year in which the long-standing tradition of face-to-face (f2f), in-person education was disrupted. With the spread of COVID-19 worldwide, many English language providers have been forced to move their courses online. Although online education in this unprecedented time has allowed many institutions to continue the teaching and learning process, the speed at which this transition occurred presents a set of challenges for many teachers (Hodges et al., 2020). In a study of the global impact of COVID-19 on higher education institutions, Marinoni et al. (2020) cited teachers' lack of pedagogical competence as one of the main challenges in transitioning to emergency remote teaching

D. N. Marissa (✉) · W. Allahji
Yanbu English Language Institute, Yanbu Al-Sinaiyah, Saudi Arabia
e-mail: marissadi@rcyci.edu.sa

J. Chen (ed.), *Emergency Remote Teaching and Beyond*,
https://doi.org/10.1007/978-3-030-84067-9_22

(ERT). From the student perspective, Read (2020) also found that a sense of disconnection impacted learners' engagement in online classes.

Although these two variables—lack of teachers' pedagogical competence and lack of student engagement (SE)—have been regarded as two of the major hurdles in ERT, their relationship remains unclear. A recent study in the field of chemical education seems to suggest a positive correlation between the two. Researchers believe that the existing strong student–teacher relationship, which is rooted in teachers' pedagogical competence, contributes to high SE (Gares et al., 2020). Expanding on this investigation among EFL teachers in Saudi Arabia, this explanatory sequential mixed methods study aims to examine the role of teachers' pedagogical competence in predicting SE during ERT.

2 Theoretical Framework

2.1 Technological Pedagogical Content Knowledge (TPACK) and Pedagogical Competence

TPACK, as a theoretical framework, originated 15 years ago with a call to understand the complex relationships between teaching, learning, and technology integration (Mishra & Koehler, 2006). With the rapid development of digital technology at the turn of the twenty-first century, there has been increased pressure on teachers to learn new ways of incorporating technology into their teaching (Mishra et al., 2011). The use of the term *knowledge* (i.e. the 'K' in TPACK) to capture teachers' competence is grounded in teacher education research, which views teacher knowledge as a set of repertoires that consist of a variety of techniques, skills, and approaches that teachers have at their disposal (Feiman-Nemser, 2001; Wasley et al., 1997). Therefore, teacher competence is the manifestation of the teacher's knowledge base in three interrelated areas: pedagogy, content, and technology (Koehler et al., 2013; Mishra & Koehler, 2006).

These three core areas interact in important ways (Fig. 1). Traditionally, good teaching requires knowledge of what teaching approaches fit the content and how elements of the content can be arranged for better teaching (*pedagogical content knowledge*) (Shulman, 1987). With technology integration, good teaching also requires an understanding of what makes concepts difficult or easy to learn, and how technology can help redress some of the problems that students face (*technological content knowledge*). Good teaching also means that teachers understand how various technologies can be used in teaching and learning or how teaching and learning might change as a result of using particular technologies (*technological pedagogical knowledge*) (Koehler et al., 2013; Mishra & Koehler, 2006). From this perspective, competent teachers are defined by their abilities to critically synthesise the complex relationships between technology, pedagogy, and content, and to use this understanding to address their specific, unique contexts (Mishra et al., 2011).

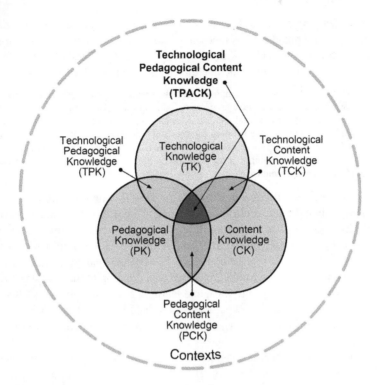

Fig. 1 TPACK framework. (Source: http://tpack.org/)

We chose TPACK as a theoretical lens to investigate teachers' pedagogical competence in an ERT context for two reasons: First, the three core areas of knowledge, and their intersections, provided us with a comprehensive framework for examining how competent teachers integrated technology as they transitioned to ERT. Second, the framework highlighted the socioculturally situated nature of teaching and learning with technology. Despite the many barriers to technology integration (Keengwe et al., 2008), which were exacerbated during the pandemic (Hodges et al., 2020), it was useful to think of technology integration—or the lack thereof—in terms of its connection, interaction, affordances, and constraints in relation to the content, pedagogy, and context. Thus, in our exploration of teachers' practices, we aimed to explore this complex dynamic.

2.2 Student Engagement (SE)

Like TPACK, SE as a theoretical framework has also witnessed significant development with the growing role of technology in education. Several studies have explored the interplay between SE and educational technology in different settings, including grade schools (Bond, 2019), higher education (Redmond et al., 2018), and informal learning contexts (Joksimović et al., 2018). Despite the ongoing debate about the depth and breadth of its theorising and its operationalization in empirical research (Fredricks et al., 2004; Kahn, 2014; Zepke, 2014), Bond et al. (2020) synthesised SE as a socioculturally mediated metaconstruct and defined it as:

> the energy and effort that students employ within their learning community, observable via any number of behavioral, cognitive or affective indicators across a continuum. It is shaped by a range of structural and internal influences, including the complex interplay of relationships, learning activities and the learning environment. The more students are engaged and empowered within their learning community, the more likely they are to channel that energy back into their learning, leading to a range of short and long term outcomes that can likewise fuel further engagement (p. 3).

Similar to the theoretical conceptualisation of TPACK, the definition above provides a glimpse into the sociocultural positioning of SE. From a sociocultural standpoint, SE does not occur in a vacuum. It is influenced by many contextual factors. Therefore, as Bond and Bedenlier (2019) assert, these contextual influences need to be considered when exploring the construct. With the unique contextual backdrop of ERT, we aimed to explore how SE changed as a function of the complex dynamics of relationships, learning activities, and learning environments that shifted suddenly due to the pandemic. We specifically examined how teachers' technological/pedagogical choices influenced SE, as they observed the following indicators presented in Table 1.

The term 'indicators' here is understood as the manifestation of SE that is observable through cognitive, affective, and behavioural actions or reactions. We selected this list of indicators from a larger list outlined in Bond and Bedenlier (2019) based on our inter-rater agreement on the most prevalent indicators in our context. Although we did not measure these indicators directly from the students' perspective, we relied on the teachers' observations of their students' engagement.

2.3   Research Questions

Informed by the two theoretical frameworks, we posed the following research questions:

Table 1 Indicators of SE (Bond & Bedenlier, 2019)

Cognitive engagement	Affective engagement	Behavioural engagement
Self-regulation	Enthusiasm	Attendance
Effort to understand	Sense of connectedness	Homework completion
Focus/concentration	Positive attitude about learning	Participation
Doing extra to learn more	Satisfaction	Asking teacher or peers for help
Integrating ideas	Feeling appreciated	Assuming responsibility
Positive self-efficacy	Enjoyment	Action/initiation
Purposeful	Pride	Attempting

Quantitative Research Question

   1. Does teachers' TPACK predict SE in ERT contexts?

Qualitative Research Question

   2. If so, how do teachers with high TPACK sustain SE throughout the transition period?

Mixed Methods Research Question

   3. How can the results that emerge from quantitative and qualitative analyses provide a deeper understanding of pedagogical competence?

3 Methods

3.1 Research Design

The study used an explanatory sequential mixed methods design, wherein a quantitative research was first conducted and analysed, followed by qualitative research to explain the quantitative results in more detail (Creswell, 2014). A mixed methods design is based on the pragmatic worldview which assumes that collecting diverse types of data provides a more complete understanding of a research problem than a quantitative or qualitative design alone (Greene, 2007; Greene & Caracelli, 1997; Tashakkori & Teddlie, 2010). Rather than simply exploring whether a relationship existed between TPACK and SE, or whether one predicted the other, we also sought to investigate *how* the former helped sustain the latter in this unprecedented time.

   Following the common mixed methods notation (Creswell, 2014; Morse, 1991), Fig. 2 shows the procedures used in this study.

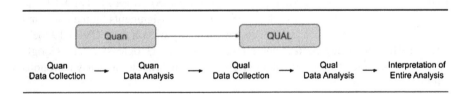

Fig. 2 Mixed methods procedures

3.2   Participants

Participants in the quantitative study were 53 faculty members who taught preparatory-year English at a small university in Saudi Arabia ($N = 53$). From this cohort, we purposefully sampled seven teachers who scored high on our TPACK and SE scales to participate in the follow-up qualitative case study. Participation in both the quantitative and qualitative studies was voluntary, and all participants signed a consent form before the surveys and interviews. The focal participants included three male and four female teachers. These seven teachers shared few other characteristics, including age (all above 30), qualification (all had a degree or training in applied linguistics/TEFL), and teaching experience (all above 10 years with the exception of one teacher). To maintain the focal participants' anonymity, all names were changed to pseudonyms. By choosing this teacher cohort, we hoped to highlight the pedagogical strategies that these teachers utilised to sustain their students' engagement throughout the transition period and therefore help other teachers in developing these practices in their own teaching.

3.3   The Course

Preparatory-year English was a 16-week, 8-credit course offered to high school graduates who were enrolled at the university before declaring their college majors. The course had two levels that were designed for different proficiency levels: (a) basic level (starting at A1 on Common European Framework (CEFR)) for first-semester students and (b) pre-intermediate level (starting at A2 on CEFR) for second-semester students. The course met for four hours, five days a week, and followed an integrated approach in teaching listening, speaking, reading, and writing. The course used a unified curriculum with standardised contents, pacing schedules, and assessment schemes and was divided into 21 parallel sections with varying class sizes (i.e. between 20 and 30 students in each section). Google Classroom was used as the official Learning Management System (LMS) prior to COVID-19, and all students were required to join the LMS to receive assignments, homework, and other updates from their teachers. When the university was on the COVID-19 lockdown, the four-hour/day contact hours migrated online. Google Meet and Google Classroom became the two main platforms for synchronous and asynchronous activities.

3.4   Quantitative Data Collection and Analysis

Sampling The 53 participants in the quantitative study were sampled using a convenience sampling strategy. Sample size was determined using G*Power (Faul et al., 2007), considering the desired effect size (correlation value) of 0.4, α error probability of 0.05, and statistical power of 0.95.

Instruments We devised two sets of surveys: (a) the TPACK scale based on a systematic review of existing TPACK measurements (Koehler et al., 2012; Koehler et al., 2013; Valtonen et al., 2017) and (b) the SE scale based on the SE framework developed by Bond and Bedenlier (2019). SE was measured indirectly through teachers' perceptions of SE. Our choice to develop the instruments, rather than utilising existing TPACK and SE surveys, was guided by the goal of uncovering the specific dynamics of the teaching and learning of English during the emergency transition period (Appendix 1). To ensure the construct validity of both instruments, we mapped each survey item to its operational definitions and behavioural indicators. We used some negatively worded or reversed items to improve the scale validity. Although the use of reversed items has been debated in survey literature (e.g. Feifei & Tanner, 2013), it can help correct for acquiescence (Weijters & Baumgartner, 2012) and serves as cognitive 'speed bumps' because it causes a slower, more careful reading (Józsa & Morgan, 2017). To ensure the instruments' reliability, we piloted both scales to get the internal consistency scores (item-rest correlations set at 0.30 and above and Cronbach's α at .80 and above) and revised the items based on these scores (Creswell, 2014). The final instruments were sent as one Google Form questionnaire through the teachers' mailing list.

Data Analysis We treated the Likert scale data from the TPACK and SE questionnaires as continuous variables, following the argument that ordinal variables with five or more categories can be used as an approximation of a continuous variable without any harm to the analysis (Norman, 2010; Sullivan & Artino Jr, 2013). Therefore, simple linear regression was used to investigate the relationship between TPACK and SE, and to determine how much variation in SE was predicted by TPACK. We ran four assumption tests (normality, linearity, homoscedasticity, and residual errors) to ensure the appropriateness of using this statistical analysis. Descriptive statistics were also used to categorise the responses on each scale into five categories (i.e. low, moderately low, average, moderately high, and high) based on the mean and standard deviation scores. Based on this categorization, we purposely sampled seven participants who scored moderately high to high on both scales to participate in the qualitative study (i.e. competent teachers). All statistical analyses were performed using the free statistical software JASP.

3.5 Qualitative Data Collection and Analysis

Design We used an exploratory case study design (Marshall & Rossman, 2011; Yin, 2006) to unpack the teaching and learning dynamics during the emergency transition, including how the teachers' TPACK influenced their teaching strategies to sustain SE. In this case study, the unit of analysis was the group (Creswell, 2014), that is, the teacher cohort with high TPACK and high SE. Therefore, the case was bounded by the characteristics of the participants as well as the ERT context. Yet, as Yin (2006) argued, though bounded, the use of case study is relevant to expand the theoretical propositions of TPACK and SE in other dynamic, volatile contexts that define twenty-first century education.

Data Collection There were two main data sources for the qualitative study: (a) semi-structured interviews with the seven teachers and (b) artifacts of six weeks' worth of activities on Google Classroom. All interviews were conducted online via Zoom and recorded for transcription. Each interview lasted between 30 and 60 minutes, totalling up to five and a half hours. The interviews focused on exploring teachers' experiences during the emergency transition and how they used technology to sustain SE (Appendix 2). All teachers used Google Classroom as the LMS, as per the preparatory-year program's regulation. We were given access to their online courses and took relevant screenshots of various strategies that the teachers used to sustain engagement. The interviews and artifacts were collected sequentially to allow emerging insights from the interview to guide our observation of the archived online classroom. In this sense, the artifacts served as our secondary data, confirming the teachers' reports on their classroom practices.

Data Analysis Teacher interviews were analysed using typical procedures for coding and developing themes (Creswell, 2014; Miles & Huberman, 1994). Both of us transcribed the online interviews verbatim and later reviewed the transcriptions. For the coding procedures, we used a combination of theoretical and in vivo coding (Richards, 2009) to allow new ideas to emerge from the teachers' experience. The main theoretical codes for TPACK were (a) pedagogical content knowledge, (b) technological content knowledge, (c) technological pedagogical knowledge, and (d) technological pedagogical content knowledge. The main theoretical codes for SE were (a) cognitive engagement, (b) affective engagement, and (c) behavioural engagement. The TPACK and SE codes were not always mutually exclusive in that a particular interview excerpt could be coded at multiple codes at the same time if it represented different underlying phenomena (Richards, 2009). Codes were continually added and refined, as new insights emerged. These insights were later grouped into broader categories and themes. Each theme was discussed and clarified, as we revisited them until a final set of three socially mediated pedagogical practices that positively impacted SE was determined. To assist with the coding and thematization of data, we used a mixed methods data analysis software called Dedoose. Once our coding had been refined, emerging patterns were investigated further using

Dedoose's analytic features, such as coding frequency across individual interviews, coding co-occurrence (e.g. data points coded at 'TPACK' and 'SE'; data points coded at 'challenges' and 'SE'), as well as memo links across datasets to check for negative cases from the emerging themes. Finally, we triangulated the themes emerging from the interviews using Google Classroom data. When analysing the artifacts from Google Classroom, we collected screenshots of pedagogical practices that were consistent with the teachers' own descriptions of their strategies.

4 Findings

4.1 RQ1: TPACK's Contribution in Predicting SE

A simple linear regression was calculated to predict SE based on teachers' TPACK. The hypothesis being tested (H_0) was that there was no predictive relationship between the two variables. If there was no relationship, the intercept of the model (i.e. the slope of the correlation) was equal to zero. If there was a significant relationship, we rejected the H_0 and provided an alternative hypothesis (i.e. H_1). Based on the statistical analysis (Tables 2 and 3), a significant regression equation was found ($F(1,51) = 13.362$, $p < 0.001$).

Despite the low correlation between the two variables, the results in Table 2 indicate that the teacher's pedagogical competence as measured in TPACK was a significant predictor of SE and explained 20.8% of its variance (R^2 of 0.208). Furthermore, Table 3 indicates that the regression model predicted the dependent variable significantly well.

In other words, the p-value (significant at $<.001$) in Table 3 demonstrates that overall, the regression model statistically significantly predicted the outcome variable (i.e. it was a good fit for the data). Additionally, the predictive model showed that teachers' ratings on the SE scale increased by 0.468 for each unit difference in the TPACK scale (Table 4).

4.2 RQ2: How TPACK Afforded Opportunities to Sustain SE

Early Transition Challenges The sudden shift to ERT created three challenges that directly affected SE: (1) poor or no internet connection, (2) absence of f2f interaction, and (3) limited choices of synchronous interactive activities. Although

Table 2 Correlation coefficient

Model summary				
Model	R	R^2	Adjusted R^2	RMSE
H_1	0.456	0.208	0.192	5.875

Table 3 Model fit

ANOVA						
Model		Sum of Squares	df	Mean Square	F	p
H₁	Regression	461.133	1	461.133	13.362	< .001
	Residual	1759.999	51	34.510		
	Total	2221.132	52			

Table 4 Predictive model

Coefficients						
Model		Unstandardized	Standard error	Standardized	t	p
H₁	(Intercept)	10.039	7.271		1.381	0.173
	TPACK	0.468	0.128	0.456	3.655	< .001

Internet connectivity issues were not related to teachers' pedagogical competence per se, all the focal teachers noted that they negatively impacted online classroom dynamics. In some cases, students who lived in remote areas or in areas heavily affected by the outbreak did not have Internet access. In other cases, the teachers faced connection problems. Overall, poor connectivity disrupted the flow of the class.

Second, in the absence of f2f interaction, the teachers were faced with the sudden loss of the interactional dynamics that were naturally afforded in the in-person classroom. One such dynamic was the teacher's ability to 'read' their students' faces as a gauge of their attention, interest, and understanding. Another dynamic that was lost was simultaneous and organic conversations among students and between the teacher and the students:

> It wasn't the same because in the class ... the discussion is going on seamlessly but [with] online you have to wait for one response and it takes time and then all of them can't participate at the same time (Mr. Ibrahim).

In the case of male teachers teaching male students, although they had encouraged their students to turn on the cameras to make up for these lost interactional clues, some teachers still found it initially difficult to maintain their students' engagement:

> With online (class), ... they can just 'show up' for participation, but they can mute their audio, they can turn off their video, and they can leave. But you can't see them. So, I always try to call out their names to get their attention (Mr. Ryan).

This difficulty was even more noticeable in female teachers teaching female students. Because of the conservative nature of Saudi Arabian culture, activating cameras during synchronous sessions was not considered a common practice. One female teacher noted:

> When teaching online, because of the cultural dynamics here, I can't ask them to turn their videos on. I can't always see who's really there [and who] is paying attention. So, that's the biggest difference: Not being able to really see who was mentally present and listening or paying attention, and not being able to monitor the work that is being done (Ms. Maliha).

As a natural consequence of the absence of f2f interaction, all the focal teachers acknowledged that the types of online activities they could engage with the students initially became restricted. For example, the use of games and other interactive group activities that language teachers normally rely on to promote and maintain SE was very difficult:

> In the classroom, I played Kahoot. Even online I played, but it was not so practical because the students would need two devices to play. So, if they have it, they can play (Mr. Ryan).

This restriction was particularly pronounced in the teaching of writing. On the one hand, marking student drafts and giving feedback online required more time and effort by the teacher. On the other hand, it also required sufficient sense-making to utilise the feedback tools, both by the teacher and the students. This challenge, in turn, affected SE in the writing task:

> Writing was gruelling, especially in giving feedback. When you give feedback on a para-graph, if you're in class, the students can ask, 'What do you mean by that, Miss?' or 'What do I do, Miss?' And of course, you can't do that online. It's very limited. I cannot do a one-on-one orally; I had 24 students. So, I give oral feedback for the general class. Then, I do individual feedback on Google Classroom, and not just once. So, for one paragraph, for example, it would be like three or four sets of feedback for one student. They cannot get it in the beginning, because when the teacher writes feedback, it's different from when the teacher explains the feedback in front of the students (Ms. Jessa).

As all the focal teachers attested to, the early transition to ERT disrupted the class-room dynamics that had already been established in the first six weeks of class. As a result, the teachers had to think strategically to navigate their way through transi-tion and 'recalibrate the equilibrium' that they had achieved in the in-person class-room before. However, a consistent pattern emerged from the focal teachers, as they reflected on their experiences. Although they faced the same set of challenges that most language teachers had during the transition period, they were able to bounce back and improve their students' engagement through three distinct pedagogical practices: *reflexivity*, *adaptability*, and *responsiveness*. The discussion of each of these practices is elaborated in the following sections.

Reflexivity Reflexivity is defined in the educational literature as an internal dia-logue that leads to action for transformative practices in the classroom (Archer, 2010; Feucht et al., 2017). It stems from Dewey's philosophy (1933) which involves active, persistent, and careful consideration of the teacher's own beliefs that serve as the basis for the changes in their practice (Schön, 1983). The initial TPACK frame-work (Mishra & Koehler, 2006) alluded to teachers' reflexivity in technology inte-gration in terms of 'essential tension' (Kuhn, 1977). As the authors mentioned, the incorporation of a new technology sometimes forces teachers to confront basic pedagogical or content issues because the technology disrupts and eventually recon-structs the dynamic equilibrium of their knowledge. More recently, the framework incorporated the construct of reflexivity in the form of teachers' critical thinking and problem-solving skills (Mishra et al., 2011; Valtonen et al., 2017).

Our data revealed that reflexivity was prominent in focal teachers' reflections. First, the results showed that the teachers developed cautious restraint on experimenting and overburdening their students with new tasks, tools, or activities, as described by one teacher below:

> We were given so many options on what we could use, but I really did not expand on what I was already doing. I just kind of stuck to what they did know, because we were in the middle of the semester. We had already established a certain dynamic, and I didn't want to really rain things on them. You know, like Google Classroom, iTools, PowerPoints.... It should be minimalistic and should really serve a certain purpose and not just random bombardment of information on different resources (Ms. Maliha).

Second, their cautious restraint was coupled with deep awareness that teaching and learning would change given the particular technological affordances and constraints that came with ERT. In the case of games, for example, although some of the teachers acknowledged the constraint of using the same technologically mediated games that they used to play in an f2f classroom, they were able to choose other alternatives or modify the use of the technological tools so they could still afford the same level of interactivity without adding the unnecessary cognitive overload that came with working with multiple pages or screens. One teacher showcased such awareness when he noted:

> The point is, if at the beginning of (the transition) you know that you have to go online, then definitely mentally, as well as in terms of your materials, you should be ready. This would make it easier for you (Mr. Ali).

In the process of reflecting, questioning, and modifying their strategies, the focal teachers were able to transform the teaching and learning process to meet the demands of the moment. This transformation is discussed in the following section.

Adaptability The second pedagogical practice that we found relevant in mediating SE was adaptability. Mishra and Koehler (2006) addressed the importance of teacher adaptability in the context of technological content knowledge (TCK) and technological pedagogical knowledge (TPK). As the authors have noted, teachers need to know how the subject matter can be changed by the application of technology. Teachers also need to understand that a range of technological tools exists for a particular task. Teachers' ability to use tools based on their affordances is part of their pedagogical adaptation.

Our data revealed that when the focal teachers observed a drop in SE at the outset of the transition, they strategically modified their teaching practice to align with the nature of online interaction. For instance, upon the early realisation that the quality of the online classroom interaction was hampered, some of the teachers adapted their teaching strategy by incorporating routine asynchronous online discussion to ensure that their students could participate outside of the synchronous class (Fig. 3). In so doing, the teachers were able to encourage the participation of most of their students. This adaptation demonstrates technological pedagogical knowledge in maintaining SE.

Fig. 3 Google classroom asynchronous online discussion in maintaining SE

Other focal teachers demonstrated technological content knowledge when they adapted their online teaching strategies to help students learn language skills more effectively. One of the most prominent strategies used by the teachers was the use of other technological tools besides the Google Classroom ecosystem. Ms. Nayla, for example, used online games to teach grammar and motivate them to participate actively. Ms. Maliha, on the other hand, frequently used WhatsApp for speaking tasks. As she recalled:

> We also used WhatsApp for things like speaking tasks, because they could send me their recordings and I'd give them feedback. It was easier for them to do that than upload it to Google Classroom because it gets kind of complicated for them to figure out how to do that (Ms. Maliha).

Or, as Ms. Jessa demonstrated in her Google Classroom post below (Fig. 4).

One thing was notable in the pedagogical strategies that the focal teachers used. Despite the choices that were available, these teachers were mindful in selecting the technological tools that best addressed the unique constraints they faced in their

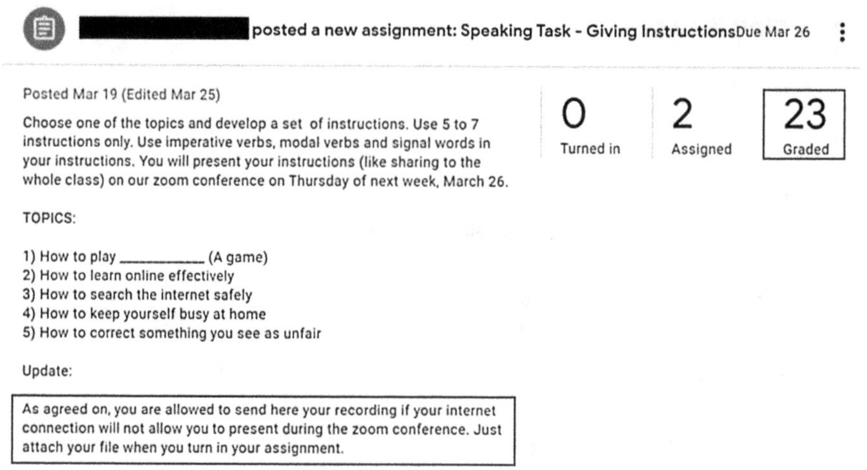

📄 ████████████ **posted a new assignment: Speaking Task - Giving Instructions**Due Mar 26 ⋮

Posted Mar 19 (Edited Mar 25)

Choose one of the topics and develop a set of instructions. Use 5 to 7 instructions only. Use imperative verbs, modal verbs and signal words in your instructions. You will present your instructions (like sharing to the whole class) on our zoom conference on Thursday of next week, March 26.

0	**2**	**23**
Turned in	Assigned	Graded

TOPICS:

1) How to play _____ (A game)
2) How to learn online effectively
3) How to search the internet safely
4) How to keep yourself busy at home
5) How to correct something you see as unfair

Update:

> As agreed on, you are allowed to send here your recording if your internet connection will not allow you to present during the zoom conference. Just attach your file when you turn in your assignment.

Fig. 4 Promoting SE in a speaking task

classrooms. We saw this in the different routes that the two teachers took to encourage students' participation in speaking. While Ms. Jessa instructed her students to send their speaking recordings *within* the Google Classroom ecosystem, Ms. Maliha chose to do it *in lieu of* the main online platform. However, both teachers skilfully found alternative ways to encourage participation despite the initial SE challenge. As Koehler et al. (2013) and others have pointed out (see Collie & Martin, 2016; Corno, 2008), this example highlighted that competent teachers understood the socioculturally situated nature of technology integration, especially in contexts with high uncertainty, such as ERT.

Responsiveness The third pedagogical practice that emerged from the qualitative data was teacher responsiveness. This pedagogical practice was distinct from the previous two categories in that it encompassed an affective rather than a cognitive component of teaching. Upon closer examination of TPACK literature, we found that this affective component was not included in the existing TPACK framework, perhaps because it was a cognitive-oriented framework (Mishra & Koehler, 2006) (i.e. knowing 'what' and knowing 'how to' as cognitive indices of the technological pedagogical content knowledge).

To fill this conceptual gap, we turned to the responsive teaching literature. Responsiveness, according to Sherman (2004) and others (see van Manen, 2002), is a professional disposition grounded in teachers' ability to grasp their students' idiosyncratic conditions and respond to their particular instructional needs. It is an attitudinal quality where teachers feel responsible and care for the success and well-being of their students and are attentive to their needs in distinctive ways. Responsiveness is an act of encouragement, support, and suggestions that are spontaneous and moment-by-moment (Hansen, 2001).

One common manifestation of responsiveness among our focal teachers was the practice of 'walking the extra mile' to reach out to students when they faced difficulties with the materials or with the online learning experience in general. As the two teachers reflected:

> If there are cases where they don't understand, they can send me a message on WhatsApp, which some did. They ask me about things that they couldn't understand from Google Classroom. So, I explain to them on WhatsApp. But before this, I generally explain things orally in class in the Google Meet session. Then, I give individual feedback on the work that they submit. And they have to reply. Some do it thrice. The good thing is, they all did it. At the end, they were able to follow (Ms. Jessa).

> I was trying to keep the momentum. For example, 2–3 students did not submit (their online work). Other students lived in remote villages. Like one student, for example, he came from a remote village, so he went home, but because the connection there was very bad, he came back to his apartment and he continued here for the semester. As I said before, I was really behind them to support them (Mr. Ryan).

Another form of responsiveness was to build positive relationships with students. All the focal teachers understood the value of building positive relationships with students, especially when they could not see them in person:

> When you have this good relationship with the students, they will tell you about their problems. They will tell you about what is difficult for them and how they manage them. You can help them solve these problems. So, I think being close to them is one of the things I really feel positive about (Ms. Wardah).

As seen in this example, the focal teachers were perceptive of their students' problems and idiosyncrasies and tried to adapt their teaching to meet their needs. They actively incorporated the affective components such as caring and being attentive to students' emotional well-being as part of their pedagogical strategies.

4.3   RQ3: Is There More to Teachers' Pedagogical Competence?

Our simple linear regression analysis demonstrates that there is a significant relationship between teachers' pedagogical competence and SE. Teachers' pedagogical competence explains 20.8% of the variance in SE. The low *variance explained* indicates that other predictors may explain the degree of variability in SE, such as students' self-efficacy, perceived stress, learning strategies, or belief systems (Bedard et al., 2010). These other predictors can be studied in future research to determine the unique contribution of each individual predictor. Nevertheless, at this juncture, our quantitative data show that pedagogical competence still plays a significant role in influencing SE.

On a practical level, since we know that teachers' pedagogical competence influences SE, teachers might ask the question: How can we develop our pedagogical competence, especially in contexts with high novelty and uncertainty? The qualitative data revealed that competent teachers have highly organised systems of fundamental knowledge not only of English as a subject matter (i.e. the 'C'), but also of how students think and learn (i.e. the 'P') and how to integrate appropriate technology as part of the teaching and learning process (the 'T' in TPACK). The fruits of this knowledge, as observed through the lens of the focal teachers, are the three pedagogical practices discussed in the previous section: reflexivity, adaptability, and responsiveness.

Going back to the concept of teacher knowledge, we mentioned before that TPACK defines teacher knowledge in terms of a repertoire that consists of a variety of techniques, skills, and approaches that teachers have at their disposal (Feiman-Nemser, 2001; Wasley et al., 1997). This repertoire was developed through formal education and sustained practical experience. Alternatively, to use Cochran-Smith and Lytle's (1999) terms, we can speak of TPACK in terms of the three types of knowledge that teachers amassed over time: (a) knowledge *for* practice, (b) knowledge *in* practice, and (c) knowledge *of* practice. While the first type concerns the basic domains of knowledge that teachers receive in their teacher education program, the second and third types of knowledge are acquired through experience and deliberative inquiry as teachers problematize and transform their teaching. Teachers' pedagogical competence, therefore, is a manifestation of the teacher's knowledge base *in* and *of* practice.

Despite TPACK's theoretical appeal in describing, developing, and measuring teaching and teachers' effectiveness in the digital age (Abbitt, 2011; Graham, 2011), we want to add one cautionary note about inferring pedagogical competence from teacher knowledge alone. The TPACK framework, as acknowledged by its proponents, is a cognitive framework. Mishra and Koehler (2006), for example, characterise 'teaching as a complex cognitive skill…' (p. 1020). Yet, as our data has shown, and as critics have argued (see Brantley-Dias & Ertmer, 2013), pedagogical competence encompasses more than just knowledge. In fact, pedagogical competence is manifested in the triadic relationships of cognitive, behavioural, and affective/attitudinal qualities that are reflected in the focal teachers' reflexive, adaptive, and responsive practices. Although these three practices are closely related in that they all involve changes in the way the teacher approaches technology integration, they encompass distinct psychological processes.

As depicted in Fig. 5, adaptability can be seen as the observed behavioural changes in teachers' instructional practices that result from both the reflexive cognitive process and responsive attitudinal qualities. This model is consistent with the literature which considers knowledge, skills, and dispositions as the three main components of teacher competence (Danielson, 2007; NCATE, 2008; Parsons & Vaughn, 2016). In other words, we believe that teachers' pedagogical competence lies in the teacher's holistic ability to adapt their teaching based on a strong knowledge base of content, pedagogy, and technology, as well as a sense of professional disposition to serve the best interest of their students.

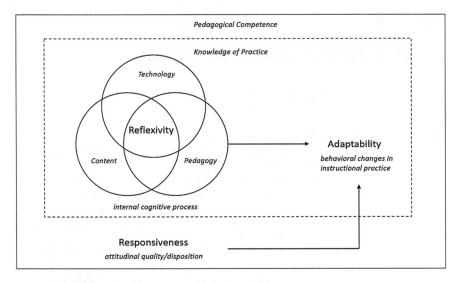

Fig. 5 Moving beyond the cognitive approach to pedagogical competence

5 Food for Thought: Beyond Emergency Remote Teaching

Although this small study is situated in the context of COVID-19's emergency teaching response, we hope it can provide some insights beyond the pandemic for researchers and teachers alike. First, we hope that this study informs teacher-researchers of alternative ways to conduct collaborative research in a fully online setting. With the affordances of online technology and tools, we have shown that data collection and analysis are within the realms of realities for many teacher-researchers, even those separated by geographical distance. The free and inexpensive tools that we have utilised (e.g. Zoom video interview/recording, G*Power, JASP, and Dedoose) can be used to produce robust research despite all contextual constraints. More information on these tools can be found in Appendix 3.

Finally, as twenty-first century teachers, we know that change, novelty, and uncertainty are part of our daily reality. To help navigate the demands of work, we must engage in active reflection on our own teaching. We need to continue to expand our knowledge base through evidence-based practice. Yet, to truly transform the teaching and learning experience, we believe that teachers must inculcate values, commitments, and professional ethics to engage with students in a supportive manner. Finally, for teachers who are incorporating online learning into their class (ourselves included), we believe it is helpful to incorporate reflexivity, adaptability, and responsiveness into our teaching practices.

Appendices

Appendix 1: ERT Questionnaire Sample Questions

1 = strongly disagree   5 = strongly agree

Scale	Component	Sample questions
TPACK	PCK	I clearly convey expectations, standards, and rules of engagements in my class to my students.
		I often do not understand why some students are confused with a concept that I explained or an activity that I design.*
	TCK	I utilized different technologies to teach different components of English (i.e. listening, speaking, reading, writing, vocabulary, and grammar).
	TPK	It was difficult to modify my regular lesson plan to fit the demands of the online course.*
		I used a variety of assessment strategies for my online course.
	TPCK	I was underprepared to teach new concepts/skills since the course was moved online.*
		I have enough technological skills to make the teaching of new skills effective in the new online setting.
SE	Cognitive Engagement	Most of my students showed efforts to try to understand new materials that I presented online.
		Most of my students did not do extra work on their own initiative other than what I had assigned to them online.*
	Affective Engagement	Despite the challenge of not meeting face-to-face, I was able to maintain a sense of connectedness with most of my students.
		The enthusiasm of many of my students decreased when the course was moved online.*
	Behavioural Engagement	Most of my students asked me or their friends questions if they did not understand a material or task that they had to do online.
		Student attendance dropped when the course was moved online.*

reversed items

Appendix 2: Interview Questions

1. Tell us what you think about your online teaching experience last semester.
2. Tell us about how you transitioned from face-to-face (f2f) to fully online classes.
3. Tell us about some of the challenges that you faced throughout the process.
4. You indicated in the questionnaire that you were generally able to handle the transition from f2f to online classes quite well. What do you think contributed to this relative ease?

5. Tell us about some of the innovative things you did with technology that helped improve your students' online learning experience.
6. Talk about how you maintain students' positive attitudes and participation in this unique circumstance.
7. Share your reflection on the assessments of the course.

Appendix 3: Summary of Research Tools

Tool	Feature	External link
G*Power	• Free and open-source application • Sample and effect size analyses • Power calculation for a wide variety of statistical tests (t-tests, F-tests, chi-square-tests, etc.)	https://www.psychologie.hhu.de/arbeitsgruppen/allgemeine-psychologie-und-arbeitspsychologie/gpower.html
JASP	• Free and open-source application • Quantitative data analyses (Correlation, regression, t-tests, variance analyses, factor analyses, SEM, binomial, multinomial, meta-analysis, etc.)	https://jasp-stats.org/
Dedoose	• Monthly subscription, web-based • Collaborative platform • Qualitative and mixed methods data analysis • Visualization and analytics	https://www.dedoose.com/
Zoom	• Free web-based video conferencing • Online interview recordings • Online discussion platform for researchers	https://zoom.us/

References

Abbitt, J. T. (2011). Measuring technological pedagogical content knowledge in preservice teacher education: A review of current methods and instruments. *Journal of Research on Technology in Education, 43*(4), 281–300.

Archer, M. (2010). Introduction: The reflexive re-turn. In M. Archer (Ed.), *Conversations about reflexivity* (pp. 1–14). Routledge.

Bedard, D., Lison, C., Dalle, D., & Boutin, N. (2010). Predictors of student's engagement and persistence in an innovative PBL curriculum. Applications for engineering education. *Journal of Engineering Education, 26*(3), 1–12.

Bond, M. (2019). Flipped learning and parent engagement in secondary schools: A South Australian case study. *British Journal of Educational Technology, 50*(3), 1294–1319. https://doi.org/10.1111/bjet.12765

Bond, M., & Bedenlier, S. (2019). Facilitating student engagement through educational technology: Toward a conceptual framework. *Journal of Interactive Media in Education, 11*(1), 1–14. https://doi.org/10.5334/jime.528

Bond, M., Buntins, K., Bedenlier, S., Zawacki-Richter, O., & Kerres, M. (2020). Mapping research in student engagement and educational technology in higher education: A systematic evidence map. *International Journal of Educational Technology in Higher Education, 17*(1), 1–30. https://doi.org/10.1186/s41239-019-0176-8

Brantley-Dias, L., & Ertmer, P. A. (2013). Goldilocks and TPACK: Is the construct "just right?". *Journal of Research on Technology in Education, 46*(2), 103–128.

Cochran-Smith, M., & Lytle, S. (1999). Relationship of knowledge and practice: Teacher learning in communities. *Review of Research in Education, 24*, 249–305.

Collie, R. J., & Martin, A. J. (2016). Adaptability: An important capacity for effective teachers. *Educational Practice & Theory, 38*(1), 27–39.

Corno, L. (2008). On teaching adaptively. *Educational Psychologist, 43*(3), 161–173. https://doi.org/10.1080/00461520802178466

Creswell, J. W. (2014). *Research design: Qualitative, quantitative, and mixed methods approaches* (4th ed.). Sage.

Danielson, C. (2007). *Enhancing professional practice: A framework for teaching* (2nd ed.). ACSD.

Dewey, J. (1933). *How we think: A restatement of the relation of reflective thinking to the educative process*. Heath & Co..

Faul, F., Erdfelder, E., Lang, A. G., & Buchner, A. (2007). G*Power 3: A flexible statistical power analysis program for the social, behavioral, and biomedical sciences. *Behavior Research Methods, 39*(2), 175–191.

Feifei, Y., & Tanner, L. W. (2013). Psychological sense of school membership scale: Method effects associated with negatively worded items. *Journal of Psychoeducational Assessment, 32*(3), 202–215.

Feiman-Nemser, S. (2001). From preparation to practice: Designing a continuum to strengthen and sustain teaching. *Teachers College Record. Teachers College Record, 103*(6), 1013–1055.

Feucht, F. C., Lunn Brownlee, J., & Schraw, G. (2017). Moving beyond reflection: Reflexivity and epistemic cognition in teaching and teacher education. *Educational Psychologist, 52*(4), 234–241. https://doi.org/10.1080/00461520.2017.1350180

Fredricks, J. A., Blumenfeld, P. C., & Paris, A. H. (2004). School engagement: Potential of the concept, state of the evidence. *Review of Educational Research, 74*(1), 59–109. https://doi.org/10.3102/00346543074001059

Gares, S. L., Kariuki, J. K., & Rempel, B. P. (2020). Community matters: Student-instructor relationships foster student motivation and engagement in an emergency remote teaching environment. *Journal of Chemical Education, 97*(9), 3332–3335. https://doi.org/10.1021/acs.jchemed.0c00635

Graham, C. R. (2011). Theoretical considerations for understanding technological pedagogical content knowledge (TPACK). *Computers & Education, 57*(3), 1953–1960.

Greene, J. C. (2007). *Mixed methods in social inquiry*. Jossey-Bass.

Greene, J. C., & Caracelli, V. J. (Eds.). (1997). *Advances in mixed-method evaluation: The challenges and benefits of integrating diverse paradigms* (New Directions for Evaluation, No. 74). Jossey-Bass.

Hansen, D. T. (2001). Teaching as a moral activity. In V. Richardson (Ed.), *Handbook of research on teaching* (4th ed., pp. 826–857). American Educational Research Association.

Hodges, C. M., Lockee, S., Trust, B., & Bond, A. (2020). The difference between emergency remote teaching and online learning. *Educause Review*. Retrieved from: https://er.educause.edu/articles/2020/3/the-difference-between-emergency-remote-teachingand-online-learning. Accessed 7 Sept 2020.

Joksimović, S., Poquet, O., Kovanović, V., Dowell, N., Mills, C., Gašević, D., Dawson, S., Graesser, A. C., & Brooks, C. (2018). How do we model learning at scale? A systematic review of research on MOOCs. *Review of Educational Research, 88*(1), 43–86. https://doi.org/10.3102/0034654317740335

Józsa, K., & Morgan, G. A. (2017). Reversed items in Likert scales: Filtering out invalid responders. *Journal of Psychological & Educational Research, 25*(1), 7–25.

Kahn, P. E. (2014). Theorising student engagement in higher education. *British Educational Research Journal, 40*(6), 1005–1018. https://doi.org/10.1002/berj.3121

Keengwe, J., Onchwari, G., & Wachira, P. (2008). Computer technology integration and student learning: Barriers and promise. *Journal of Science Education & Technology, 17*(6), 560–565.

Koehler, M. J., Mishra, P., & Cain, W. (2013). What is technological pedagogical content knowledge (TPACK)? *Journal of Education, 193*(3), 13–19.

Koehler, M. J., Shin, T. S., & Mishra, P. (2012). How do we measure TPACK? Let me count the ways. In R. N. Ronau, C. R. Rakes, & M. L. Niess (Eds.), *Educational technology, teacher knowledge, and classroom impact: A research handbook on frameworks and approaches* (pp. 16–31). Information Science Reference (IGI Global).

Kuhn, T. (1977). *The essential tension.* University of Chicago Press.

Marinoni, G., Land, H. V., & Jensen, T. (2020). The impact of COVID-19 on higher education around the world: International Association of Universities Global Survey Report. Retrieved from: https://www.iau-aiu.net/IMG/pdf/iau_covid19_and_he_survey_report_final_may_2020.pdf. Accessed 10 June 2020.

Marshall, C. & Rossman, G. B. (2011). Designing qualitative research (5th ed). Sage.

Miles, M. B., & Huberman, A. M. (1994). *Qualitative data analysis: An expanded sourcebook* (2nd ed.). Sage.

Mishra, P., & Koehler, M. J. (2006). Technological pedagogical content knowledge: A new framework for teacher knowledge. *Teachers College Record, 108*(6), 1017–1054.

Mishra, P., Koehler, M. J., & Henriksen, D. (2011). The 7 transdisciplinary habits of mind: Extending the TPACK framework towards 21st-century learning. *Educational Technology, 51*(2), 22–28.

Morse, J. M. (1991). Approaches to qualitative-quantitative methodological triangulation. *Nursing Research, 40*(2), 120–123.

NCATE. (2008). Professional standards for the accreditation of teacher education institutions. Retrieved from: https://bit.ly/3naa9sV. Accessed 10 Oct 2020.

Norman, G. (2010). Likert scales, levels of measurement and the "laws" of statistics. *Advances in Health Sciences Education: Theory & Practice, 15*(5), 625-632. Retrieved from: https://link.springer.com/article/10.1007%2Fs10459-010-9222-y#citeas. Accessed 12 Aug 2020.

Read, D. L. (2020). A drift in a pandemic: Survey of 3,809 students finds uncertainty about returning to college. Retrieved from: https://tophat.com/press-releases/adrift-in-a-pandemic-survey/. Accessed 10 June 2020.

Redmond, P., Heffernan, A., Abawi, L., Brown, A., & Henderson, R. (2018). An online engagement framework for higher education. *Online Learning, 22*(1), 183–204. https://doi.org/10.24059/olj.v22i1.1175

Richards, L. (2009). *Handling qualitative data: A practical guide* (2nd ed.). Sage.

Schön, D. (1983). *The reflective practitioner.* Basic Books.

Sherman, S. (2004). Responsiveness in teaching: Responsibility in its most particular sense. *The Educational Forum, 68*(2), 115–124.

Shulman, L. S. (1987). Knowledge and teaching: Foundations of the new reform. *Harvard Educational Review, 57*(1), 1–23.

Sullivan, G. M., & Artino, A. R., Jr. (2013). Analyzing and interpreting data from Likert-type scales. *Journal of Graduate Medical Education, 5*(4), 541–542.

Tashakkori, A., & Teddlie, C. (Eds.). (2010). *SAGE handbook of mixed methods in social and behavioral research* (2nd ed.). Sage.

Valtonen, T., Sointu, E., Kukkonen, J., Kontkanen, S., Lambert, M. C., & Mäkitalo-Siegl, K. (2017). TPACK updated to measure pre-service teachers' twenty-first century skills. *Australasian Journal of Educational Technology, 33*(3), 15–31.

van Manen, M. (2002). *The tone of teaching: The language of pedagogy* (2nd ed.). Althouse. Press.

Parsons, S. A., & Vaughn, M. (2016). Toward adaptability: Where to from here? *Theory into Practice, 55*(3), 267–274. https://doi.org/10.1080/00405841.2016.1173998

Wasley, P., Hampel, R., & Clark, R. (1997). *Kids and school reform.* Jossey-Bass.

Weijters, B., & Baumgartner, H. (2012). Misresponse to reversed and negated items in surveys: A review. *Journal of Marketing Research, 49*(5), 737–747.

Yin, R. (2006). Case study methods. In J. L. Green, G. Camili, & P. B. Elmore (Eds.), *Handbook of complementary methods in education research* (pp. 111–122). Erlbaum.

Zepke, N. (2014). Student engagement research in higher education: Questioning an academic orthodoxy. *Teaching in Higher Education, 19*(6), 697–708. https://doi.org/10.1080/1356251 7.2014.901956

Listening to Student Voice to Improve the Quality of Emergency Remote Teaching

Olga Yashenkova

Highlights

- Students should be afforded opportunities to influence change in education.
- Student voice is an effective tool to collect information about the teaching-learning process.
- Students meet the minimum requirements for e-learning but lack digital and soft skills, and need teacher support.
- In emergency remote teaching, students prefer practical interactive classes and are willing to try something new.

1 Introduction

To prevent the spread of COVID-19, the Ukrainian government introduced stringent quarantine measures on March 12, 2020 (Cabinet of Ministers of Ukraine, 2020). All educational institutions in Ukraine were forced to halt in-person classes and move to fully remote teaching as the only way to ensure the continuity of education. Such teaching, known as *distance education* or *distance learning*, meant a physical separation of teachers from students and required the facilitation of learning through technology.

Remote or distance learning in Ukraine is mostly internet-based and may be referred to as *online education*, *online learning* or *e-learning*. In the context of COVID-19, it is necessary to differentiate between well-planned online learning experiences and *emergency remote teaching* (ERT) that aims "to provide a

O. Yashenkova (✉)
Taras Shevchenko National University of Kyiv, Kyiv, Ukraine

J. Chen (ed.), *Emergency Remote Teaching and Beyond*,
https://doi.org/10.1007/978-3-030-84067-9_23

temporary access to instruction and instructional supports in a manner that is quick to set up and is reliably available during an emergency or crisis" (Hodges et al., 2020).

Although distance learning as a form of remote education and online teaching practice has been implemented in Ukrainian universities for more than twenty years, the abrupt transition to a fully e-learning environment turned to be an unbearable burden for certain educational units (Sakalo, 2020). As language training in Ukraine before the pandemic was predominantly offline, a significant number of language teachers had no prior experience in organizing online courses and were not aware of distance learning technologies. The speed with which they had to adapt to the new reality and make fundamental changes to course design, delivery, and assessment was unprecedented. Many decisions on creating virtual classrooms were made in a hurry without student involvement and consultation. The main purpose was to make classes run and give students a chance to complete their courses.

Today, as we are still facing the COVID-19 challenges and have to continue remote teaching, we can be more thoughtful and invite students as important stakeholders to work close together and discuss how to improve ERT and deliver high quality distance education in Ukraine. Gathering students' words is essential because students know what is pertinent for them to succeed. Ukrainian students who have always played an active role in the development of higher education (Rusnak, 2016) are often willing to raise issues that teachers and administrators may not see or avoid. Student voice is an untapped resource for universities in search of the best ERT solutions.

This chapter attempts to address the need to empower students and ensure that student voice is heard. Of particular importance in this study is the voice of the individual student by which every individual is able to express their opinions, suggestions and concerns which relate directly to teaching and learning during the COVID-19 pandemic.

2   Student Voice

The concept of student voice is not new and goes mainstream, representing a significant movement in education (Brunauer, 2019; Mitra, 2004). The concept is widely discussed in the literature and described by different terms, such as student perceptions (Simpson, 2012), student perspectives (Ropeti, 2015), student evaluations (Loveland, 2007), student participation (Bergmark & Westman, 2018), students' involvement (Põld & Kangro, 2019), student engagement (Zyngier, 2007), student consultation (Downes, 2016), student partnership (Monico & Kupatadze, 2020) and many others. All these terms may overlap or be interchangeable, acknowledging the right of students to have a say and construct their learning. However, *student voice* is most commonly chosen and has gained increasing credence as an umbrella term that signals a range of efforts to reposition students in educational research and reform (Cook-Sather, 2006; Coutts, 2020).

Student voice acquires various shades of meaning based on how and why the concept is used. It may be theorized within sociocultural, social constructionist or post-structural frames (Fleming, 2015), encompassing all possible ways of engaging students in the design of educational programs and learning experiences, in the governance and decision-making processes in school, or in the civic life of their community (Rennie Center for Education Research & Policy, 2019, 2021). At its core, student voice is profoundly student-centered as it deals with the visions and needs of the students themselves, and is largely oriented to action, participation and change (Toshalis & Nakkula, 2012). Student voice, seen as any expression of learners about any education matters, takes a variety of forms (Fig. 1). It can be student or teacher driven and put into practice in the school community, in and outside the classroom. It stretches from informal situations in which students share opinions with their peers and teachers to participation in democratic structures, such as student parliaments and school policy committees. Students may approach these opportunities on their own or as a group.

Experts use a continuum to illustrate roles and levels of student agency (Fig. 2) that may increase as students assume more leadership and have more rights and responsibilities (Mansfield et al., 2018; Mitra & Gross, 2009; Toshalis & Nakkula, 2012). At the basic level (expression), educators can collect and use students' opinions to inform change; students are passive recipients or data sources. At the highest level (leadership), students take on governance roles and responsibilities: they convene meetings, direct actions, write proposals and make decisions. The middle areas are where students are recognized as stakeholders and provided opportunities to collaborate with educators to achieve some specific goals, but they cannot act as independent researchers and leaders of change yet.

Researchers have found that allowing students to have a voice, even at the basic level, fosters the development of civic habits that are essential to democracy (Mansfield et al., 2018). They argue that student voice opportunities lead youth to

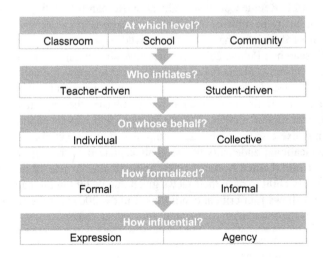

Fig. 1 Types of student voice

Students articulating ◄ - - - - - -● Students involved as stakeholders ●- - - - - -► Students directing
their perspectives   collective activities

Students as data ◄- - - - - - - - -● Students as collaborators ●- - - - - - - - ►
sources   Students as leaders
                                                                                        of change

Expression	Consultation	Participation	Partnership	Activism	Leadership
Volunteering opinions, complaining, praising, objecting	Asked for opinions, providing feedback, serving on focus groups, completing surveys	Attending and preferably playing an active role in meetings	Formalized role in decision-making	Identifying problems, generating solutions, and advocating their adoption	(Co-) Planning, making decisions and accepting significant responsibility for outcomes

●- ►

Fig. 2 Continuum of student voice oriented activities (*Note.* Adapted from Toshalis & Nakkula (2012))

an awareness of being included and valued as community members (Toshalis & Nakkula, 2012), cultivate trust and respect, and increase attachment to schools, which in turn correlates with academic success (Mitra, 2004), improved student satisfaction, and well-being (Halliday et al., 2019). A large body of research documents that inviting students to co-construct the teaching-learning dynamic helps increase curricular relevance and improve classroom practice, strengthens teacher-student and peer relations, builds collective responsibility for academic outcomes, and develops a better understanding of learning that eventually keeps motivation and engagement high (Bergmark & Westman, 2018; Brunauer, 2019; Downes, 2016; Mitra, 2021; Rennie Center for Education Research & Policy, 2019).

Despite the many benefits of student voice, there is evidence that students are often left out of decisions that affect their lived experiences (Rennie Center for Education Research & Policy, 2021). Studies have shown that when student voice is ignored or tokenistic, students may feel alienated, disempowered and have reduced self-concept. Such students exhibit lower academic achievement and higher dropout rates (Mitra, 2018). In this respect, educators emphasize the importance of extending practices that support students to form opinions and provide genuine opportunities for them to exercise their influence and power (Finneran et al., 2021).

Recent educational endeavors fit the goals espoused in the *Convention on the Rights of the Child* (United Nations, 1989), in particular, Article 12 that establishes the right of every child to have their views given due weight in all matters affecting them. Figure 3 shows four critical conditions (Lundy, 2007) for the full realization of Article 12 as the foundation for meaningful student voice:

- Space: Students must be given the opportunity to express a view.
- Voice: Students must be facilitated to express their views.

Fig. 3 Conditions for Student Voice Success. (*Note.* Adapted from Lundy (2007))

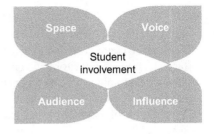

- Audience: The view must be listened to.
- Influence: The view must be acted upon, as appropriate.

Thus, student voice is much more than just saying something; it is about having the power to influence change. There must also be duty bearers (educators or policy makers) to listen, value, elevate, and respond to students' voices inclusively and respectfully.

This study shares the belief that "young people have unique perspectives on learning, teaching, and schooling, that their insights warrant not only the attention but also the responses of adults, and that they should be afforded opportunities to actively shape their education" (Cook-Sather, 2006, p. 28). Students are seen as partners and co-constructors of educational discourse who share responsibilities for its effectiveness. Student voice is defined as an active opportunity for all students to express their opinions, attitudes, and ideas about ERT, and collaborate with educators regarding its implementation and evaluation.

3   Research Aim and Questions

A body of literature has emerged to study the teaching-leaning process during COVID-19 from various perspectives and in multiple contexts. In particular, researchers have examined the difference between ERT and planned online learning (Hodges et al., 2020), strengths, weaknesses, opportunities, and challenges of e-learning modes in the time of crisis (Bedenlier et al., 2020) and changing trends in distance learning (Wotto, 2020). Some studies have focused on educational design for transition during an emergency (Green et al., 2020; O'Keefe et al., 2020), innovative ways to deliver student-driven education (Zhao, 2020) and best practices for ERT to benefit students and ensure equity (Morgan, 2020).

Although extensive research has been conducted on moving to distance education during COVID-19, there is hardly any study devoted to the incorporation of student voice into ERT in the Ukrainian context. The present study aimed to explore student perspectives on the implementation of ERT in a leading Ukrainian university in order to create an effective learning environment for every student.

The following research questions guided the study:

1. Are Ukrainian students ready to switch to e-learning?
2. What are Ukrainian students' perspectives on e-learning regarding types of distance learning, course formats, interaction patters, and technologies?
3. How do Ukrainian students prefer to communicate with teachers and peers? Do students feel their voices are heard during ERT?
4. What forms of assessment and feedback do Ukrainian students find most useful in ERT?
5. How do Ukrainian students evaluate their ERT? What concerns do they have?

4   Method

4.1   Setting and Participants

The setting of this study included the Institute of Philology at Taras Shevchenko National University of Kyiv (KNU), a classic university with a distinct research profile, ranked #33 in QS EECA University Rankins 2021. With almost 3000 students, the Institute of Philology is the largest KNU unit composing 24 academic departments and 22 language centers. It offers a variety of BA, MA and PhD programs in Linguistics, Literary Studies, Language Teaching and Translation. The language of instruction depends on students' specialization, and all teaching is commonly on-campus.

The study participants were 549 BA and MA students, majoring in Western or Eastern European languages and literatures. They were from various parts of Ukraine, and ranged in age from 18 to 23. The participants had to take remote classes taught by Ukrainian teachers due to COVID-19 during the spring and fall semesters in 2020. They had no previous experience in e-learning.

4.2   Study Design

To obtain more complete and corroborated results, and involve participants in the study, a mixed-methods approach was applied to sampling, data collection and analysis. Taking into account the research aim and specific research questions, the study was implemented as a convergent design (Creswell & Clark, 2018), in which two separate data bases – quantitative and qualitative – were collected and analyzed and then merged for the purpose of comparing or combining the results (Fig. 4). A nested sampling (Collins et al., 2006) was used, i.e. the sample members selected for one phase of the study represented a subset of those chosen for the other component of the research (e.g., the BA students who were interviewed also participated in the survey on e-learning).

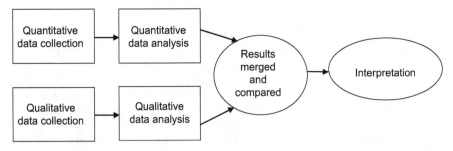

Fig. 4 The convergent design. (*Note.* Adapted from Creswell & Clark (2018))

The intent of the convergent design was to bring together the strengths and weaknesses of quantitative and qualitative research (quantitatively, a large sample, objective measures, trends, and generalization combined with, qualitatively, a small sample, subjective interpretation, details, and depth) and obtain rich data to better understand student voices in ERT. Mixing methods made several types of triangulation (Hastings, 2012) possible, which boosted the credibility of the study. First, data triangulation involved collecting data over different times (e.g., student voices in ERT were studied during the spring and fall semesters in 2020) and from different sources (e.g., to investigate students' readiness for e-learning, interviews with second-year BA students, majoring in English, were compared and cross-checked with surveys among BA and MA students from various departments). Second, investigator triangulation allowed for the auditing of data consistency and reduced the potential bias inherent in employing only one investigator (e.g., forty-six students as co-researchers participated in the authentic task to explore students' concerns about distance learning). Third, methodological triangulation engaged multiple methods to study the research problem (e.g., to investigate students' preferences in distance learning, course feedback, and survey questionnaires, containing a mixture of open-ended and closed-ended questions, were used, giving the opportunity to obtain complementary data, compare and illustrate quantitative results with quotes from respondents, and deepen the understanding of the research question).

4.3   Data Collection

The quantitative and qualitative data were collected via questionnaires, interviews, an authentic task, course feedback, and institutional survey reports from May to December 2020 (Table 1). During the fall semester the participants were involved in the study not only as data sources or consultants but also as co-inquirers and co-researchers.

Table 1 Data collection instruments

Instrument	Spring 2020	Fall 2020	Participant role
Questionnaires	*E-Learning Survey*	*E-Learning Survey*	Data sauces
		Your Communication Style and Preferences	Consultants
		Student voice survey	Active respondents
Course feedback	*Business English (BE) Course Feedback*	*Communication Theory Course Feedback*	Evaluators and consultants
Institutional survey reports	*Distance Learning Survey 1*	*Distance Learning Survey 2*	Evaluators
Interviews	*Readiness for E-Learning*		Active respondents
Authentic task		*Exploring ERT at the Institute of Philology*	Co-inquirers and co-researchers

4.3.1 Questionnaires

Using Google forms, online self-report questionnaires were developed. They contained closed-ended (multiple-choice, checkboxes, rating and Likert scale) and open-ended questions, and were available in English. The links were posted in Google Classrooms and sent to students by email. The convenience sampling strategy was used. As a teacher of BE and Communication Theory, I had access to second-year BA students, majoring in English. Additionally, being responsible for the organization of the English Exit Exam, I had access to fourth-year BA and second-year MA students, majoring in Eastern European languages and literatures. Student participation was voluntary and anonymous. To address different research questions, there were created three questionnaires: *E-Learning Survey* (June, September 2020; 92 respondents), *Your Communication Style and Preferences* (October 2020; 74 respondents) and *Student Voice Survey* (December 2020; 57 respondents).

4.3.2 Course Feedback

Some data about students' perspectives on distance learning were gained when collecting feedback on the online courses I taught to second-year BA students during the spring and fall semesters in 2020: *BE Course Feedback* (June 2020; 11 respondents) and *Communication Theory Course Feedback* (December 2020; 63 respondents). The students could give anonymous course feedback through Google forms.

4.3.3 Institutional Survey Reports

The data about the quality of ERT at the Institute of Philology were collected from two institutional survey reports. The reports presented the results of *Distance Learning Survey 1* (April–May 2020; 226 respondents) and *Distance Learning Survey 2* (November 2020; 212 respondents), which were conducted online, using Google forms. The surveys were anonymous and voluntary. Any student from the Institute of Philology could participate.

4.3.4 Interviews

Individual semi-structured interviews were conducted during the spoken part of the BE exam that was held in Zoom in June 2020. As a teacher of BE and examiner, I interviewed 11 second-year BA students who were purposefully selected, considering their diversity in terms of location (rural/urban), socioeconomic backgrounds, and academic performance. The aim was to explore students' diverse perspectives on the transition to distance learning. The interview questions (Appendix B) were specified but could be reworded in any sequence based on the situation. Each interview lasted up to ten minutes, was video-recorded, and transcribed. The students gave their consent to use the video recordings for research and educational purposes. To keep their responses confidential, the interviewees' names were changed.

4.3.5 Authentic Task

An authentic task (Appendix D) was designed for the second-year BA students enrolled in the Communication Theory course for the fall semester 2020. After attending the online lecture on the strategies of effective interviewing, the students were asked to complete the task *Exploring ERT at the Institute of Philology*. The task goals were to actively engage students as co-inquires and co-researchers and get them to practice a range of soft skills. The participants acted as members of the working group aimed to improve ERT. They worked in pairs to conduct a ten-minute interview to elicit students' concerns about e-learning and suggest solutions. I received 42 video-recoded interviews and ERT action plans. The students gave their consent to use the video recordings and papers for research and educational purposes. In the study, their names were changed.

4.4 Data Analysis

The collected data were examined thoroughly, summarized, and organized according to the research questions. Both qualitative and quantitative data analyses were conducted. The quantitative data obtained through the closed-ended items of the online questionnaires, course feedback, and institutional survey reports were analyzed using descriptive statistics on frequencies and percentages. The qualitative data were derived from the video-recorded interviews and authentic task, answers to open-ended questions and comments written by the participants in the questionnaires/course feedback. The qualitative data analysis was carried out descriptively and through thematic analyses of text. The content of data was analyzed to generate and categorize recurring themes. Relevant themes and categories were selected and coded. Some qualitative data (collected through the authentic task and open-ended survey items) were quantitized. The data obtained during the spring and fall semesters 2020 were compared, contrasted, synthesized, and merged.

5   Results and Discussion

5.1   Student Readiness for Distance Education

Readiness is a significant input for online teaching and learning. It includes not only technical matters, such as equipment availability and access to the internet and e-resources, but also human perceptions about technologies, computer and internet self-efficacy, and a number of skills to participate in distance learning. The data concerning students' readiness for e-learning were gained through closed-ended (multiple choice) questions 1–4 of the online survey questionnaire (Appendix A) and Zoom interview questions, which were mostly open-ended (Appendix B).

The survey takers could select one multiple answer from the list of choices. Table 2 indicates 38% positively perceived e-learning, while the rest were neutral (39.1%) or could not decide (12%). The vast majority had the necessary equipment (95.7%) and a good internet connection (80.2%), but only a bit more than half (54.3%) were completely confident in their digital skills.

Based on the interviews, it was not easy for students to adapt to a new learning environment, especially for those with low or moderate confidence in the use of technology. "Oksana" (BA student) confessed:

> You know, it was a bit hard to change this … first of all, work place, study place, to start working from the computer, from these technical sources, resources … Also, I had some problems with recording my video presentation. I spent three hours on it. I just spent three hours in front of my telephone, recording, recording, recording … it was quite challenging.

"Olena" (BA student) emphasized the importance to be open for change and develop a number of competencies to enhance e-learning:

> I suppose that most of us have to improve our … our information and IT literacy so that all of us will be confident with using different information technology … because as for me I had some problems during this term because I am not that techy… so it was quite hard. And I suppose that flexibility and openness to change is also very important because as, as I have mentioned everything is changing and we have to be open for new, open to gain some new knowledge, some new areas …

Table 2 Student readiness for E-Learning

Questionnaire item	Frequency N = 92	Percent 100%
Perception of e-learning		
Positive	35	38
Neutral	36	39.1
Negative	10	10.9
Undecided	11	12
Having the equipment for e-learning		
Yes	88	95.7
No	4	4.3
Having a good internet connection		
Yes	74	80.4
No	18	19.6
Confidence in using digital technologies		
Completely	50	54.3
Moderately	37	40.2
Slightly	4	4.4
Not at all	1	1.1

Although many students experienced difficulties due to the lack of technology-related knowledge and skills, they accepted changes and were optimistic. Overall, students met the minimum technological requirements and were psychologically ready to switch to e-learning but needed teacher support.

5.2   Students' Perspectives on Distance Learning

While distance education provides a variety of options in terms of course structure and offers the possibility to learn from anywhere, anytime, and with any means, the KNU teachers were requested to hold online sessions in real time according to the traditional study timetable, and use free digital tools and platforms. Specifically, Zoom, Google Classroom and other Google products were recommended to use. It was interesting to hear student voices about synchronous (live lectures or classes with opportunities for social interaction in real time) and asynchronous (self-paced without instant feedback) learning, and preferred features of online course design. The data were obtained through questions 5–8 of the online survey questionnaire (Appendix A). The respondents could choose one or multiple options from the list of possible answers to the questions about course formats, tools and technologies, and write their own answers or comments.

Table 3 shows that almost equal percentage of the respondents chose synchronous (16.3%) or asynchronous (18.5%) e-learning, and about two thirds (65.2%) did not give preference to any of these. Most respondents reported the best use of

Table 3 Students' preferred types of e-learning, course formats and technologies

Questionnaire item	Frequency N = 92	Percent 100%
Type of e-learning that suits you		
Synchronous	15	16.3
Asynchronous	17	18.5
Any	35	38
Undecided	25	27.2
Best use of e-learning for you		
Self-study	59	64.1
Lectures	63	68.5
Seminars	28	30.4
Practical classes	41	44.6
Research	28	30.4
Project work	37	40.2
Tests	54	58.7
Technologies you prefer to use in e-learning		
Zoom	79	85.9
Goggle classroom	83	90.2
Google docs	47	51.1
MOOCs	15	16.3
Forums (not in real time)	21	23.8
Other	2	2.2

e-learning for lectures (68.5%), self-study (64.1%) and tests (58.7%). As to e-learning tools and technologies, the vast majority preferred Goggle Classroom (90.2%) and Zoom (85.9%), and a little more than half (51.1%) mentioned Google docs.

To create supportive e-learning environments, it was also necessary to know student perspectives on interaction patterns (if they preferred to work online individually, in pairs or in groups). The data were gathered from BE/Communication Theory course feedback given by second-year BA students. The students could rate the usefulness of certain interaction patterns for e-learning on a scale from 1 (*least useful*) to 4 (*very useful*) and make comments. Table 4 shows that over 70% positively accepted four types of interaction patterns, but more people rated individual (64.9%) and pair (54.1%) work as very useful.

Based on the course feedback comments, the biggest students' concern was how to make online sessions more interactive and engaging. The students were willing to share their ideas, such as "I suggest to increase the number of academic hours to discuss some issues deeper, enhance interaction doing online lectures, do more projects in small groups", or

> I like projects which we had to complete in pairs; online courses on the FutureLearn platform and, of course, our lectures during which I got much information and details about specific topics (I have already started applying the acquired skills and knowledge).

Table 4 Student perspectives on interaction patterns in e-learning

Questionnaire item	Students N = 74	Percent 100%
Individual work		
Very useful	48	64.9
Useful	22	29.7
Somewhat useful	4	5.4
Least useful	0	0
Pair work		
Very useful	40	54.1
Useful	28	37.8
Somewhat useful	6	8.1
Least useful	0	0
Small group work		
Very useful	26	35.1
Useful	35	47.3
Somewhat useful	12	16.2
Least useful	1	1.4
Whole class work		
Very useful	23	31.1
Useful	29	39.2
Somewhat useful	15	20.3
Least useful	7	9.5

Other students' suggestions included: "decrease usage of google forms", "collaborate actively in discussion forums: post reviews, comments, 'likes' etc.", "more videos from TedTalks", and "more practical lessons, more interactive tasks and maybe, some games…".

Thus, the students did not insist on a certain form of e-learning but wanted more dynamic and practical online courses regardless of their modes, formats or interaction patterns. They emphasized the importance of enhancing e-learning through active discussions, teamwork and collaboration, role play, project work, task- and problem-based learning, visualization, and gamification.

5.3   Communication and Listening to Student Voice

Student-teacher and student-student communication is critical to successful distance learning and humanizing online courses. Regular interactions can help bridge the communication gap created when classes are moved online. Online teacher presence, genuine connection and communication with students become even more important in ERT, being the only way to provide expert guidance of the learning process and help keep students on track. In this context, it is required to select the right channel and medium to convey information and maintain effective communication. Students may not necessarily interact with the teacher in real time in the online environment, but options and opportunities should be provided.

The data on students' communication preferences were obtained through closed-ended and open-ended questions of the questionnaire (Appendix C) that was sent to second-year BA students enrolled in the Communication Theory course for the fall semester 2020. As Table 5 shows, the majority (85.9%) could maintain constant communication with teachers who used different communication media to send them study materials, sometimes giving preference to Google Classroom (36.6%). The students could contact their teachers through messaging apps (28.2%) or Google Classroom (21.1%), but over half (50.7%) chose email.

The comments from the questionnaire explained the students' choices:

> If I want to obtain information from my teachers, I usually write them emails, because I understand that they are very busy people. If I do not get their answer, I may try to contact them on Viber,[1] Telegram,[2] Google class. And if it is possible, I may call them, if they do not mind, because for me it is the quickest way to get information.

Table 5 Communication preferences in ERT

Questionnaire item	Frequency (N = 71)	Percent (100%)
Regular communication with your teacher		
Yes	61	85.9
No	10	14.1
Best way to communicate with your teacher		
Email	36	50.7
Messaging apps	20	28.2
Google classroom	15	21.1
Common way to receive study materials from teachers		
Email	23	32.4
Messaging apps	22	31
Google classroom	26	36.6
Common way to communicate with other students		
Email	1	1.4
Phone	4	5.6
Videoconferencing	5	7
Messaging apps	36	50.7
Social media	25	35.2
Necessity to introduce online classroom etiquette		
Yes	66	93
No	5	7

---

[1] It is a calling and messaging app that allows users to make free calls, send texts, pictures and video messages to other Viber users, see https://www.viber.com/en/

[2] It is a cloud-based mobile and desktop messaging app with a focus on security and speed, see https://telegram.org/

One student noted that the teacher was supposed to decide upon the communication medium and inform the students:

> I can't say for sure, maybe mail or telegrams. I think that here a more convenient way should be chosen by the teacher and told where it is more convenient for him to see our messages and where he can answer as quickly as possible.

In peer communication, most participants (85.9%) gave priority to social media and messaging apps, especially to Telegram and Instagram (Fig. 5). Some students wrote: "In order to obtain information from my group mates I prefer to use the social networks I use in my daily life. They are a convenient and fast way to communicate", or "If I want to obtain information from my group mates, I usually write them in Telegram or Instagram or somewhere else in order to get information. If it doesn't work, I can call them."

Many students mentioned their ability to adjust to a new situation: "if my motivation is to obtain the information I would choose any possible way to obtain it, thus preferences are not relevant." Thus, the students were flexible and ready to switch from one communication channel or medium to another in order to achieve their intended goals. However, 93% indicated the necessity to introduce an online etiquette.

To clarify how effective teacher-student communication was, another Google form questionnaire was sent to the same group of students. They were asked to rate their level of agreement to two statements on a five-point Likert scale and make comments; 57 responses were received (Table 6). Over 80% reported they could feel their voices were heard and valued, and agreed or strongly agreed their teachers listened to all students and attended to their needs. Over 77% made comments.

The respondents shared their positive learning experiences, showing appreciation, such as "Collaboration in my group positively changes my views. University teachers do their best in teaching students and imparting knowledge. I appreciate their work", or

> What I really love about our university is that here, unlike the school I was in, we can actually express our opinion, the teachers don't focus on just one student who is their "favourite" and work with everyone who is willing to work.

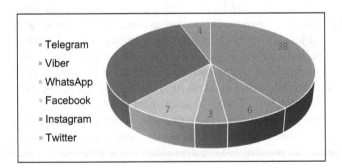

Fig. 5 Student preferences for social media and messaging apps

Table 6 Student voice survey results

Questionnaire item	Frequency (N = 57)	Percent (100%)
I am heard and feel my views are valued in my classroom.		
Strongly agree	33	56.9
Agree	17	29.8
Undecided	6	10.5
Disagree	0	0
Strongly disagree	1	1.8
My teachers pay attention to the needs of all students.		
Strongly agree	32	56.1
Agree	17	29.8
Undecided	5	8.8
Disagree	2	3.5
Strongly disagree	1	1.8
Comments if any		
Students' comments	44	77.2%
No comment	13	22.8%

There were a few comments that contained concerns, such as "sometimes teachers are more likely to address to the needs of more successful students and it becomes harder to catch up with them." Thus, teachers should pay more attention to individual learner differences, needs and concerns, and think how to give every student a sense of achievement.

5.4 Assessment and Feedback in Distance Learning

The pandemic is forcing educators to rethink traditional student assessment, which may not work properly in ERT, and look for alternative approaches to measuring learning outcomes. This study captures the rich views of assessment as a continuous teaching-learning cycle jointly projected by teachers and students, which is not only for grading purposes, but may involve multiple assessments, including assessment as learning. The participants were invited to share their opinions about types of assessment and teacher feedback through BE/Communication Theory course feedback. The data were gained from answers to closed-ended questions and written comments. The feedback results indicated the highest percentage of the students (70.3%) rated teacher assessment as very useful, although the large majority reported the usefulness of all types of assessment (Table 7).

The students' comments highlighted the value of self-assessment, such as "firstly, an opportunity to assess myself independently made me to look at me more sober and clear seeing all positive and negative sides, that actually helped me to become

Table 7 Student perspectives on types of assessment

Questionnaire item	Frequency (N = 74)	Percent (100%)
Self-assessment		
Very useful	30	40.5
Useful	36	48.6
Somewhat useful	7	9.5
Least useful	1	1.4
Peer assessment		
Very useful	27	36.5
Useful	37	50
Somewhat useful	10	13.5
Least useful	0	0
Teacher assessment		
Very useful	52	70.3
Useful	18	24.3
Somewhat useful	3	4.1
Least useful	1	1.4

Table 8 Student preferences for teacher feedback

Questionnaire item	Frequency (N = 74)	Percent (100%)
Communication code		
Verbal oral	33	45.1
Verbal written	22	29.4
Nonverbal (score)	19	25.5
Time		
Immediate	20	27.5
Delayed	3	3.9
Any	51	68.6

better interlocutor...", or included suggestions about peer assessment of task-based performance:

> Projects, lectures, feedbacks. Maybe, it would be interesting to discuss the dialogues and videos we made all together in class, practice learnt material in some practical assignments (situations) in class and discuss them to see your thoughts and thoughts of your peers...

Although the students understood the importance of developing peer and self-assessment skills, they relied more on traditional assessment and wanted teacher guidance.

Table 8 shows that only a little more than a third (25.5%) were satisfied with just getting a score. Many participants needed "more of a feedback from a professor", i.e. descriptive feedback on student performance. Almost half of the participants (45.1%) preferred verbal oral feedback, and over a third expected immediate feedback from the teacher. However, the large percentage of the participants (68.6%) were flexible concerning the mode of teacher feedback.

In their written comments, the students appreciated timely teacher feedback on task performance, such as "I especially liked that we were engaged in different kinds of activity and always gained feedback on completed tasks." They considered feedback as a two-way process and an opportunity to be heard and valued, such as "useful practical classes, the teacher's will to communicate with us and take our feedback in consideration…", or "I like feedback (because it shows that the teacher appreciates our opinion)."

Thus, the students wanted to be involved in the process of assessment/feedback in any form, but needed more teacher assessment and teacher feedback.

5.5   Student Concerns and Evaluation of ERT

Given the critical importance of student voices concerning the quality of education, there were conducted institutional surveys on distance learning in spring and fall 2020. Students from different departments could evaluate their ERT overall and measure improvements in the educational process at the Institute of Philology. The survey results, taken from the institutional reports, were analyzed and compared. Table 9 indicates that 16% of the participants did not notice any changes in ERT, a little less than half (43.4%) could see some, and 34% reported moderate improvements. Only several students (6.6%) thought ERT improved considerably in fall 2020.

The participants also were asked to rate ERT from 1 (*poor*) to 4 (*very good*) and make comments. Figure 6 shows the percentage of the students who rated ERT as very good increased considerably from 18.1% to 42.5%, while the percentage of those who rated ERT as fair decreased by almost a third (31%). The percentage of students who considered ERT good almost did not change, and those who rated it as bad decreased by 4.3% in fall 2020.

The respondents' comments included entirely opposite opinions about distance learning. Some students were satisfied with the quality of online courses, such as "All is great, the teacher is very responsible and responsive, what is significant, English classes are the best organized among other subjects", or "This semester

Table 9 Students' Perceptions of ERT improvements

Questionnaire item	Frequency (N = 212)	Percent (100%)
Do you think ERT improved compared to spring 2020?		
Considerably	14	6.6
Moderately	72	34
Somewhat	92	43.4
Not at all	34	16

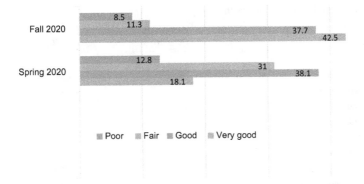

Fig. 6 Student rating of ERT

distance learning is better and quite effective, spares time and energy." Others were disappointed and shared their concerns, such as "Ridiculous how tutors don't take lessons seriously. All we do is listen to the professor speak and that's pretty much it", or:

> Too much homework. Studying online is more overloaded than when we went to university. Unfortunately, all homework in various subjects should be done online. That is, you need to be 24/7 in front of a computer screen. It's hard, I have a headache every day!

Overall, more students liked their online classes and evaluated ERT as good or very good. However, they could not see significant improvements in fall 2020; there were still a lot of problems to be solved. More research was needed to understand student perspectives on the quality of ERT.

To be able to improve ERT at the Institute of Philology, it was necessary to be aware of students' problems and concerns. The data were obtained through the authentic task offered to second-year BA students enrolled in the Communication Theory course in fall 2020 (Appendix D). Through the interview, the participants could elicit students' concerns about e-learning. Forty-six interviews were conducted, video-recoded and analyzed thematically. The themes were counted to know students' biggest concerns.

As seen in Table 10, there were identified seven main problem areas dealing with technical, organizational, communication, skills, teaching, mental, and psychological issues. The main technical problem was a bad internet connection (56.5%), although some students confessed that was not always true. The biggest organizational issue was a frequently changing and inconvenient study timetable, which was one of the reasons for sitting at the computer all day (21.7%). The students were struggling with email overload (30.4%) and did not know how to deal with a big amount of information they received. Further, they mentioned too much homework (19.6%), sometimes with poor instructions (10.9%) and insufficient teacher support (13%). The students (13%) wanted better communication with teachers. Over 30% could not concentrate on their studies because of external or internal distractions (family, job, thoughts, emotions, etc.). Some students confessed they procrastinated

Table 10 Students' problems or concerns in ERL

Issue/Problem	Frequency (N = 46)	Percent (100%)
Technical issues		
Bad internet connection	26	56.5
Lie about bad internet	3	6.5
Poor equipment	4	8.7
Organizational issues		
Bad timetable	6	13
Changing timetable	7	15.2
Sitting at the computer all day	10	21.7
Inappropriate learning environment	5	10.9
Communication		
Email overload	14	30.4
Bad teacher-student communication	6	13
Lack of skills		
Adaptability	5	10.9
Digital skills	3	6.5
Big data skills	14	30.4
Time-management	16	34.8
Self-organization	15	32.6
Teaching		
Poor instructions	5	10.9
Too much homework	9	19.6
Insufficient teacher support	6	13
Mental and psychological issues		
Lack of concentration	14	30.4
Procrastination	5	10.9
Distractions	14	30.4
Lack of motivation	6	13
Feeling of isolation	2	4.3
Missing live communication	12	26.1

(10.9%), and had no motivation (13%) to study from home. More than half thought they could not study effectively due to lack of time-management (34/8%), self-organization (32.6%) and big data (30.4%) skills. Almost a third (26.1%) missed live communication. Table 11 illustrates some students' concerns mentioned above.

During the interviews, the participants were sincere and open to discuss their concerns, and often suggested to work closely together with teachers to tackle the problems related to ERT, such as "discuss the topic with your teachers, maybe they could provide you with non-simultaneous education or record session for students who face problems with technological aspect", or

> I would talk to all the teachers and ask them to sort their emails and to provide better feedback. And students should wait for some time for the answer, because things happen, but if

Table 11 Student problem illustrations from interviews

Problem/Concern	Example quote
Bad internet connection	"It's difficult to find a good internet provider." (Sophia, BA student)
Poor equipment	"Poor devices, low quality of video and audio. When watching, the sound can disappear." (Iryna, BA student)
Inappropriate learning environment	"Family members do not always understand that you are busy and learning at home." (Olena, BA student)
Distractions	"It's difficult to find a place for studies to avoid distractions." (Petro, BA student)
Lack of concentration	"Harder to concentrate on the study when we study at home…" (Roman, BA student)
Changing timetable	"Teachers know they can work these hours later…" (Svitlana, BA student)
Too much homework	"No free time as we have to do homework from morning till night…" (Ivanna, BA student)
Sitting at the computer all day	"Too much time spent sitting in front of the screen, frequent eye-sore…" (Kateryna, BA student)
Missing live communication	"Online chats cannot replace live communication" (Julia, BA student)

they don't receive a response then I'd recommend to write to teachers, but they should be concise and write only if it is necessary. (Alyona, BA student)

It may be too early to say how students and teachers will cope with ERT but using student voice is sure to contribute to positive changes in education.

6   Conclusion

The study aimed to explore student perspectives on ERT. The findings show that involving students in various forms of collaboration, including consultations, discussions, course evaluations, and research, may help educators reveal and understand many challenges students experience in ERT.

Based on student voice, most Ukrainian students meet the minimum requirements for online education. They are flexible concerning the types of ERT, course formats, interaction patterns, and communication modes, and use the e-platforms and tools recommended by teachers. What they are worried about is the way of the content delivery. They prefer practical interactive classes and are willing to experiment, take risk and try something new. They need teacher guidance and support, want to be in constant communication with teachers and receive a descriptive teacher feedback. Many students have positive e-learning experiences, but cannot see significant improvements in ERT. There are still some problems to be solved, such as a bad internet connection, an inconvenient timetable, sitting at the computer for hours, email overload, too much homework, poor instructions, insufficient teacher support, distractions and lack of concentration.

Students are open to discuss their challenges and eager to work together to find solutions. They can feel their voices are heard and valued, but want their teachers to pay more attention to individual learner differences, needs, and concerns.

7   Food for Thought

As human beings, we need face-to-face live contacts, but have to admit digitalization is inevitable. My big concern is how to integrate online activities and resources into academic courses to meet the needs and expectations of every student. What should we change in our teaching practices? Should we give up our long-standing values and beliefs about learning and teaching?

There is no doubt that we are transitioning into a phase of big changes. ERT has revealed the week points of the existing education, and made us think about new ways of course delivery, involving students in close collaboration. I strongly believe we have to extend the scope of ERT and give up the strict scenario of offline classes and exams. To improve language education in emergencies, it is essential to change teachers' and students' views, attitudes, and perceptions of distance education, which can be realized through fundamental changes in the teaching practices. Students' feedback, judgments, and comments are a valuable source to inform change and make decisions. Online interactive classes in the form of collaborative problem-solving or task-based activities, a free choice of course formats, interaction patterns, and types of distance learning can ensure that each student is inclusive and equitable, and give all students an opportunity for creativity and self-realization. Providing multiple options for communication and encouraging a continuous teacher-student dialogue will make students feel they are heard and valued.

Acknowledgements I wish to express my appreciation to Dr. Julian Chen for his valuable guidance, support and assistance with this chapter, and to anonymous reviewers for their constructive feedback. I also wish to express my thanks to the students of the Institute of Philology, KNU, for their openness and sincere answers to survey and interview questions, and willingness to collaborate to improve ERT.

Appendices

Appendix A

E-Leaning Survey

Dear student:

Thank you for agreeing to participate in this survey, which aims to improve the educational process at the Institute of Philology, Taras Shevchenko National

University of Kyiv. Your thoughtful and objective responses to questions are highly appreciated. Your responses will remain confidential and anonymous.

For each question, please choose the relevant circle/s or write a short comment.

1. How do you feel about e-learning?

   - Positive
   - Neutral
   - Negative
   - Undecided

2. Do you have the necessary equipment for e-learning?

   - Yes
   - No

3. Do you have a good internet connection?

   - Yes
   - No

4. How confident are you in the use of technology to learn online?

   - Completely
   - Moderately
   - Slightly
   - Not at all

5. Which type of e-learning do you think suits you?

   - Synchronous
   - Asynchronous
   - Any
   - Undecided

6. What do you think is the best use of e-learning?

   - Self-study
   - Lectures
   - Seminars
   - Practical classes
   - Research
   - Project work
   - Tests
   - Other_____

7. Which technologies do you prefer to use in e-learning?

   - Zoom
   - Goggle Classroom
   - Google docs
   - MOOCs

- Forums (not in real time)
- Other _____

8. Do you have any other comments? If yes, specify. _____

Appendix B

Interview Questions

1. What do you think about moving your classes online?
2. Was it easy or difficult for you to switch to distance learning?
3. Did you face any problems when you started to learn online? Which?
4. What was the biggest challenge for you in e-learning? Were you able to overcome it? How?
5. Do you think you can study and work effectively online? Why or why not?

Appendix C

Your Communication Style and Preferences

(extract from the online questionnaire)

Are you in constant communication with your teacher?

- Yes
- No

Which is the best way to communicate with your teacher?

- Email
- Google Classroom
- Messaging apps
- Other _____

How do your teachers commonly give you study materials?

- Email
- Google Classroom
- Messaging apps
- Other _____

How do you commonly communicate with other students during the COVID-19 pandemic? Please specify. _____

What messaging apps and social media platforms do you mostly use? Please specify. _____

Is it necessary to introduce online classroom etiquette?

- Yes
- No

Appendix D

Exploring ERT at the Institute of Philology

Dear students:
    You are going to work in pairs.

Student A: You are a member of the working group aimed to improve emergency remote teaching at the Institute of Philology. Talk to a student to learn about at least two problems/concerns about their online learning. Ask a variety of questions to elicit as much information as you can. Think what you can recommend to solve the problems and make online learning more effective.

Student B: You have to be open and sincere, and eager to improve your online learning. Share your concerns/problems with the interviewer and ask for advice or recommendations.

The interview should be no more than ten minutes. Video record the interview, analyze/reflect on it and write an action plan.

Action Plan: Think what could be done to improve online learning and teaching. Remember to be SMART (specific, measurable, achievable, relevant, and timely). Based on the interview you have conducted, complete the table below. Then send your action plan to the interviewee who should decide how useful your recommendations are.

What problems or concerns does the interviewee have?	Why do you think these problems occur?	What suggestions do you have that could prevent or reduce problems?	*The interviewee's comments*

References

Bedenlier, S., Wunder, I., Gläser-Zikuda, M., Kammerl, R., Kopp, B., Ziegler, A., & Händel, M. (2020). *"Generation invisible"*. *Higher education students' (non)use of webcams in synchronous*. PsyArXiv. https://doi.org/10.31234/osf.io/7brp6.

Bergmark, U., & Westman, S. (2018). Student participation within teacher education: Emphasising democratic values, engagement and learning for a future profession. *Higher Education Research & Development, 37*(7), 1352–1365. https://doi.org/10.1080/07294360.2018.1484708.

Brunauer, A. H. (Ed.) (2019). *Student voice in education. CIDREE yearbook 2019*. National Education Institute Slovenia.

Cabinet of Ministers of Ukraine (2020, March 11). *Pro zapobihannya poshyrennyu na tery-toriyi Ukrayiny koronavirusu COVID-19* [On prevention of the spread of COVID-19 on the territory of Ukraine]. Governmental portal. https://www.kmu.gov.ua/npas/pro-zapobigannya-poshim110320rennyu-na-teritoriyi-ukrayini-koronavirusu-covid-19

Cook-Sather, A. (2006). Sound, presence, and power: "Student voice" in educational research and reform. *Curriculum Inquiry, 36*(4), 359–390. https://doi.org/10.1111/j.1467-873X.2006.00363.x.

Collins, K. M. T., Onwuegbuzie, A. J., & Jiao, Q. G. (2006). Prevalence of mixed-methods sampling designs in social science research. *Evaluation & Research in Education, 19*(2), 83–101. https://doi.org/10.2167/eri421.0.

Coutts, N. (2020). Student voice, choice, agency, partnerships and participation. *Connect, 241,* 14–15. https://research.acer.edu.au/connect/vol2020/iss241/1/.

Creswell, J. W., & Clark, V. L. P. (2018). *Designing and conducting mixed methods research* (3rd ed.). Sage.

Downes, J. M. (2016). *Middle grades students as teacher educators: Consulting with students in professional development* [Doctoral dissertation, University of Vermont]. Graduate College Dissertations and Theses. 544. https://scholarworks.uvm.edu/graddis/544

Finneran, R., Mayes, E., & Black, R. (2021). Pride and privilege: The affective dissonance of student voice. *Pedagogy, Culture & Society*. https://doi.org/10.1080/14681366.2021.1876158.

Fleming, D. (2015). Student voice: An emerging discourse in Irish education policy. *International Electronic Journal of Elementary Education, 8*(2), 223–242. https://files.eric.ed.gov/fulltext/EJ1085872.pdf.

Green, J. K., Burrow, M. S., & Carvalho, L. (2020). Designing for transition: Supporting teachers and students cope with emergency remote education. *Postdigital Science and Education, 2*(3), 906–922. https://doi.org/10.1007/s42438-020-00185-6.

Halliday, A. J., Kernb, M. L., Garrettc, D. K., & Turnbulla, D. A. (2019). The student voice in well-being: A case study of participatory action research in positive education. *Educational Action Research, 27*(2), 173–196. https://doi.org/10.1080/09650792.2018.1436079.

Hastings, S. L. (2012). Triangulation. In N. J. Salkind (Ed.), *Encyclopedia of research design* (pp. 1538–1540). https://doi.org/10.4135/9781412961288

Hodges, C., Moore, S., Lockee, B., Trust, T., & Bond, A. (2020, March 27). The difference between emergency remote teaching and online learning. *EDUCAUSE Review.* https://er.educause.edu/articles/2020/3/the-differencebetween-emergency-remote-teaching-and-online-learning

Loveland, K. A. (2007). Student evaluation of teaching (SET) in web-based classes: Preliminary findings and a call for further research. *The Journal of Educators Online, 4*(2), 1–18.

Lundy, L. (2007). Voice is not enough: Conceptualizing article 12 of the United Nations convention on the rights of the child. *British Educational Research Journal, 33*(6), 927–942.

Mansfield, K. C., Welton, A., & Halx, M. (2018). Listening to student voice: Toward a more holistic approach to school leadership. *Journal of Ethical Educational Leadership, Special Issue, 1,* 10–27.

Mitra, D. L. (2004). The significance of students: Can increasing "student voice" in schools lead to gains in youth development? *Teachers College Record, 106*(4), 651–688. https://doi.org/10.1111/j.1467-9620.2004.00354.x.

Mitra, D. (2018). Student voice in secondary schools: The possibility for deeper change. *Journal of Educational Administration, 56*(5), 473–487. https://doi.org/10.1108/JEA-01-2018-0007.

Mitra, D. (2021). Secrets to a more successful partnership between students and teachers. In J. S. Brooks & A. Heffernan (Eds.), *The school leadership survival guide: What to do when things go wrong, how to learn from mistakes, and why you should prepare for the worst* (pp. 3–16). Information Age Publishing.

Mitra, D. L., & Gross, S. J. (2009). Increasing student voice in high school reform: Building partnerships, improving outcomes. *Educational Management Administration & Leadership, 37*(4), 522–543. https://doi.org/10.1177/1741143209334577.

Monico, C., & Kupatadze, K. (2020). Developing meaningful and practical global experiences through student-faculty-community partnerships. *International Journal for Students as Partners, 4*(2), 9–27. https://doi.org/10.15173/ijsap.v4i2.4002.

Morgan, H. (2020). Best practices for implementing remote learning during a pandemic. *The Clearing House: A Journal of Educational Strategies, Issues and Ideas, 93*(3), 135–141. https://doi.org/10.1080/00098655.2020.1751480.

O'Keefe, L., Rafferty, J., Gunder, A., & Vignare, K. (2020). *Delivering high-quality instruction online in response to COVID-19: Faculty playbook.* Every Learner Everywhere. http://www.everylearnereverywhere.org/resources

Põld, P.-K, & Kangro, M. (2019). Students' involvement in improving school environment in Estonia. In A. H. Brunauer (Ed.), *Student voice in education. CIDREE yearbook 2019* (pp. 103–113). National Education Institute Slovenia.

Rennie Center for Education Research & Policy. (2019). *Student voice: How young people can shape the future of education.* Rennie Center for Education Research & Policy. https://www.renniecenter.org/condition-education/action-guide-2019

Rennie Center for Education Research & Policy (2021). *Community-school connections: Shaping the future of learning through collaboration.* Rennie Center for Education Research & Policy. https://www.renniecenter.org/condition-education/action-guide

Ropeti, S. (2015). *Student perspectives regarding school failure at the American Samoa Community College* [Doctoral dissertation, Walden University]. Walden Dissertations and Doctoral Studies. 190. https://scholarworks.waldenu.edu/dissertations/190

Rusnak, O. (2016, May 27). Student agents of change – shaping higher education. *University World News.* https://www.universityworldnews.com/post.php?story=20160527124250828

Sakalo, Y. (2020, May 16). *Vyklyk, yakoho ne mozhna ne pryjnyaty* [The challenge that cannot be ignored]. *ZN,UA.* https://zn.ua/ukr/EDUCATION/viklik-yakogo-ne-mozhna-ne-priynyati-347904_.html

Simpson, J. M. (2012). *Student perceptions of quality and satisfaction in online education* [Doctoral dissertation, The University of Alabama]. UA Institutional Repository. https://ir.ua.edu/handle/123456789/1571

Toshalis, E., & Nakkula, M. J. (2012). Motivation, engagement, and student voice. *Job for the Future.* https://studentsatthecenterhub.org/resource/motivation-engagement-and-student-voice/

United Nations. (1989). *Convention on the rights of the child.* United Nations, Human Rights Office of the Higher Commissioner. https://www.ohchr.org/en/professionalinterest/pages/crc.aspx

Wotto, M. (2020). The future high education distance learning in Canada, the United States, and France: Insights from before COVID-19 secondary data analysis. *Journal of Educational Technology Systems, 49*(2), 262–281. https://doi.org/10.1177/0047239520940624.

Zhao, Y. (2020). COVID-19 as a catalyst for educational change. *Prospects, 49*, 29–33. https://doi.org/10.1007/s11125-020-09477-y.

Zyngier, D. (2007). Listening to teachers-listening to students: Substantive conversations about resistance, empowerment and engagement. *Teachers and Teaching, 13*(4), 327–347. https://doi.org/10.1080/13540600701391903.

LSP Teacher Perspectives on Alternative Assessment Practices at European Universities Amid the COVID-19 Crisis and Beyond

Ágnes Pál ⓘ **and Rita Koris** ⓘ

Highlights

- Failure of traditional assessment methods during ERT calls for alternative assessment in teaching LSP.
- Tasks developing students' HOTs prove to be a more effective means of assessment.
- ERT may have a long-term impact on the widespread application of formative assessment methods in the post-COVID era.
- Possible transition to blended LSP teaching and learning may be foreseen in the post-COVID era.

1 Introduction

Over nearly three decades, studies (Broadfoot et al., 1999; Brown, 2005; Knight, 1995; O'Sullivan, 2012; Rea-Dickins, 2007) have shed light on the pitfalls of a number of traditional assessment methods. The applicability of in-class examinations used for summative assessment has been questioned in the transition to emergency remote teaching (ERT) (Hodges et al., 2020) due to the COVID-19 pandemic. Between March and June 2020, European higher education institutions (HEIs) introduced emergency measures and new regulations to not only prevent the disruption of teaching but also lay down the conditions of remote teaching and ensure that students could follow and finish their university courses online. These regulations often included evaluation guidelines that educators had to comply with as well as reference to the required application of specific online tools for assessment.

Á. Pál (✉) · R. Koris
Budapest Business School, Budapest, Hungary
e-mail: pal.agnes@uni-bge.hu; koris.rita@uni-bge.hu

© The Author(s), under exclusive license to Springer Nature
Switzerland AG 2021
J. Chen (ed.), *Emergency Remote Teaching and Beyond*,
https://doi.org/10.1007/978-3-030-84067-9_24

535

Assessing students' language learning in times of ERT has posed great challenges to Languages for Specific Purposes (LSP) teachers. In European HEIs, wide use of traditional forms of assessment (e.g. in-class tests, in-class writing assignments, in-class oral presentations and closed-book exams) in the LSP classroom no longer seems effective in the context of online teaching. Alternative solutions for assessment needed to be designed and built into the university training programmes to accommodate the changed educational environment. This required revisiting assessment practices and pedagogical approaches so that good practices of alternative assessment could be identified for a broader spectrum of university course curriculum.

2   Alternative Assessment in LSP Teaching

In contrast to Language for General Purposes (LGP), teaching LSP aims at developing foreign language competence in accordance with the diverse and specific communication needs related to a particular academic or professional field such as business, technology, tourism, natural sciences or law (Hutchinson & Waters, 1987; Laurence, 2018; Woodrow, 2018). Besides generic classroom activities (e.g. drills, gap-fill, role-play, simulation, games) also found in the context of general communicative language courses, LSP teaching usually involves contextualised tasks using authentic materials to develop linguistic and communicative skills which provide context for the professional discourse and genre in a given area.

In the ERT teaching context, technology supports LSP learning through the inclusion of online learning applications, the integration of language and content as well as the use of critical academic skills, online communication, and collaboration (Bárcena et al., 2014; Bates, 2015). Under previous conditions, this would have been the choice of the teachers, who would learn and comfortably integrate these effective strategies when and how they saw fit. However, due to the global phenomenon of the restrictions introduced during the COVID-19 pandemic, university teachers were obliged to take on the challenge of remote assessment, which shed light on some limitations of traditional assessment methods, such as academic dishonesty, lack of infrastructure and technical difficulties (Guangul et al., 2020). The period of ERT can thus be considered as a timely call for change and innovation in LSP assessment approaches and a clear opportunity for moving away from traditional towards alternative assessment practice.

There is a long tradition in the field of drawing distinctions between traditional and alternative assessment and contrasting the definitions of summative and formative assessment (Barbero, 2012; Bloom et al., 1971; Brown, 2005; Broadfoot et al., 1999; Crisp, 2012; Dixson & Worrell, 2016; Harlen & Gardner, 2010; Knight, 1995; Rust, 2002; Stiggins, 1994; Wiggins, 1998). Traditional summative assessment, or assessment *of* learning, consists of "standardized tests and exams taken at the end of courses of study to check progression through the curriculum" (Barbero, 2012,

p. 39). Although milestones are important in the learning process, conventional summative feedback provides only "judgements about students' progression and completion" (Brown, 2005, p. 84). In contrast, formative assessment, or assessment *for* learning, goes beyond judgement to place learning and development at the centre of student assessment (Black & Wiliam, 1998; Broadfoot et al., 1999; Brown, 2005; Stiggins, 1994; Zhang et al., 2020). As Brown (2005) explains, feedback as a component of formative assessment "needs to be detailed, comprehensive, meaningful to the individual, fair, challenging and supportive" (p. 85). Ideally, formative and summative assessment complement one another, serving different purposes in LSP course design. Summative assessment often tends to outweigh formative assessment in university course curricula, while the latter may only appear as an informal activity in the classroom rather than as an integral part of the course (Birenbaum et al., 2015).

With the advent of various forms of distance and online courses at HEIs, the term "e-assessment" has emerged to refer to a great number of technology-enabled assessment-related activities performed online, posing new challenges for teachers and students alike (Alruwais et al., 2018; Baleni, 2015; Boitshwarelo et al., 2017; James, 2016; Crisp et al., 2016; Romeu Fontanillas et al., 2016). According to Guàrdia et al. (2017), most current e-assessment tasks can be considered traditional summative assessment as they "do not consider the adoption of user-centred approaches with the potential to engage students in authentic assessment tasks", nor do they "aim at testing higher order capabilities since students typically have to recall information to complete the assessment" (p. 37). Nevertheless, innovative assessment approaches (Boud & Soler, 2016; Cano & Ion, 2017; Hidri, 2020) and convincing e-assessment examples in the literature (Alruwais et al., 2018; Crisp et al., 2016; Gikandi et al., 2011; Nicol, 2007; Pachler et al., 2010) argue for the successful application of formative assessment techniques, such as e-portfolios, self-test quiz tools, discussion forums, in the online teaching and learning space.

3 Theoretical Framework and Research Questions

The conceptual framework of this study is based on Bloom's revised taxonomy of educational objectives put forward by Anderson and Krathwohl (2001). Their hierarchical model categorizes levels of learning and progress, which are meant to reflect stages of the development of critical thinking (Zapalska et al., 2018), to determine whether the focus of an activity targets the development of lower- or higher-order thinking skills (Bloom et al., 1971). According to Anderson and Krathwohl (2001), tasks aiming at remembering, understanding, and applying knowledge build on lower-order thinking skills, while student assignments that require analysing, evaluating and creating content are appropriate to develop higher-order thinking skills (HOTs). When students are asked to perform real-world tasks and demonstrate the meaningful application of complex knowledge and skills, the effective assessment strategy needs to be "practice-orientated" (Brown, 2005, p. 82). This is particularly true in the case of assessing students LSP competence, and practice-orientated assessment can be achieved by testing students' HOTs (Crisp, 2012).

LSP teachers can use various assignments to assess student HOTs. Based on Bloom's revised taxonomy, LSP tasks can be classified under the six categories according to their main objectives. Some assignments may prove to serve different learning objectives and therefore can be assigned to more categories. Table 1 summarizes the most frequently used tasks to assess LSP students' competence.

Our study focuses on the assessment-related experiences of LSP teachers and aims to explore LSP teachers' experiences with alternative assessment practices applied during ERT. Based on the classification of tasks in Table 1, the study was designed to provide insight into the perceptions of university LSP teachers on the effectiveness of these assessment tasks, the extent of integration of innovative assessment into their teaching approaches, and the eventual application of these alternative assessment tasks in the post-COVID era. Therefore, our study seeks to answer the following research questions:

RQ1: What perceptions do LSP teachers have related to the effectiveness of assessment tasks in normal teaching mode and during ERT, and what tasks gained more emphasis in teachers' pedagogical thinking as a consequence of ERT?

RQ2: What challenges do LSP teachers face in adopting their assessment practice to ERT?

RQ3: What potential consequences do LSP teachers perceive ERT to have on future assessment practices in the LSP classroom and innovations in LSP pedagogy for the post-COVID era?

Table 1 Classification of tasks under the six learning objective categories (Based on Anderson & Krathwohl, 2001)

Learning objective	Types of assignments/tasks
Creating	Blog, case-study, telecollaborative task, mediation, portfolio, project task, learning journal, simulation
Evaluating	Persuasive essay, presentation, poster presentation, open-book exam
Analysing	Argumentative essay, presentation, poster presentation, topic discussion
Applying	Narrative/descriptive essay, guided writing, oral/written summary, role-play, topic discussion, translation
Understanding	Reading/listening comprehension test, matching, sequencing task
Remembering	Closed-book exam, cloze-test, multiple-choice test, true/false task

4   Research Design and Procedures

Our research followed a mixed methods approach, integrating both qualitative and quantitative data collection and analysis in a single study (Cohen et al., 2018; Creswell & Plano Clark, 2018; Johnson & Onwuegbuzie, 2004). Multiple data sources were used to confirm and cross-validate findings of the two parallel investigations with a final integration of the results for overall interpretation in a research strategy referred to as "convergent design" (Creswell & Plano Clark, 2018, p. 122). Combining the results of the analysis of the two data sets is designed to offer a deeper insight into the assessment practices of LSP teachers. Data were collected quantitatively through an online survey and qualitatively from in-depth personal interviews that targeted LSP practitioners teaching at European HEIs.

The initial preparation and design of the instrument occurred between May and July 2020, leaving a limited time for data collection between September and October 2020. The online survey was designed to register perceptions on the effectiveness of various tasks and activities used by LSP teachers with their students. 29 tasks frequently used for assessment purposes in LSP teaching were selected based on the results of an international project (Incollab Project, 2021). Survey participants were asked to rate the effectiveness of all the tasks out of these 29 that they have used in class before both in normal teaching mode and during ERT. Tasks were rated on a 6-point Likert scale from 1 to 6 (Taherdoost, 2019), where 1 stands for *very ineffective* and 6 means *very effective* for assessing students' LSP learning. The participants were asked to leave the tasks that they have not had experience with before unrated. The list of 29 tasks can be found in Appendix A. Quantitative data were analysed in SPSS 25.0 for Windows by using frequencies and descriptive statistics to report and interpret the data. Subsequently, paired sample t-tests were run to compare means to reveal any statistically significant differences between the categories of assessment tasks based on Bloom's revised taxonomy (Anderson & Krathwohl, 2001). The statistical significance level was set to $p < 0.05$ for all statistical analyses of the study (Craparo, 2007).

To gain insight into their views and attitudes, in-depth semi-structured interviews were conducted with the participants (Galletta, 2013). After initial contact, they were informed about the aims of the study and the interview procedures. Their consent was obtained for recording the interviews, including their agreement to participate in our research on a voluntary basis. The interview guide approach (Cohen et al., 2018; Galletta, 2013), which uses a set of questions and guiding prompts to drive the discussion, assured a comfortable flow of discussion. The recordings were then transcribed using an online transcription application tool. The transcripts were examined for a final correction before being scanned for recurring themes and patterns following the constant comparative method (Creswell, 2013). To increase the trustworthiness of data collection and analysis, the concept of Lincoln and Guba's (1985) taxonomy of quality criteria was followed. The findings of the two data sets were merged to arrive at a more comprehensive interpretation via the synthesized results.

4.1 Survey Participants

The survey was sent to the international offices and language departments of more than 200 partner universities in Europe. Overall, the online questionnaire obtained responses from 177 university educators, all of whom were teaching LSP courses at European universities during the COVID-19 pandemic. The participants represented 41 European universities in 21 European countries. Most of the respondents ($n=129$; 72.9%) were teachers of English, while the remaining 27.1% ($n=48$) were teaching other languages. Nearly half ($n=86$; 48.6%) of the respondents were running some forms of specialized business language courses, while others were teaching LSP courses like language for media and public relations (PR) ($n=12$; 6.8%), health sciences ($n=10$; 5.6%), tourism ($n=7$; 4%), engineering ($n=6$; 3.4%), cultural studies ($n=6$; 3.4%), political science ($n=6$; 3.4%), and other LSP fields ($n=44$; 24.9%). Before the pandemic, participants reported that most of the courses had run as face-to-face seminars ($n=120$; 67.8%) or lectures (13.6%; $n=24$), while some courses ($n=20$; 11.3%) had been blended, combining both face-to-face and online teaching modes.

The gender distribution of the participants is irregular, with more females ($n=125$; 70.6%) than males ($n=36$; 20.3%) and less than 10 percent ($n=16$; 9.1%) who did not specify. Most teachers were aged between 40 and 60 ($n=118$; 66.7%) followed by those between the age of 20 and 40 ($n=34$; 19.3%), and the smallest group over 60 years of age ($n=25$; 14.1%). Just over half of the sample ($n=93$; 52.5%) had more than 20 years of teaching experience in HEIs, while the remaining experience was expressed as 10–20 years ($n=58$; 32.7%), 6–10 years ($n=13$; 7.3%) and less than 5 years ($n=13$; 7.3%). Nearly two-thirds of the teachers had only begun teaching online in the last year ($n=111$; 62.7%), and the remaining teachers ($n=66$; 37.3%) were more experienced with online space.

4.2 Interview Participants

The qualitative strand of our study involved interviews with university educators who were teaching LSP courses at European HEIs during the COVID-19 pandemic. The interviewees were selected using a purposive sampling procedure to include four different priorities: 1) a large variety of European countries; 2) different LSP teaching focuses; 3) a wealth of experience in terms of number of years taught at HEIs; and 4) individuals having implemented international collaboration projects. Participants ($N=12$) were teaching in ten countries, were affiliated to 12 HEIs located in Europe and were teaching different LSP courses focusing on subjects that ranged from business to sciences and engineering. All interviewees had extensive teaching experience. The overview of participants can be found in Table 2.

Table 2 Overview of interview participants

Participant	Gender	Country	LSP focus	Teaching experience (years)
Participant 1	female	Italy	Natural Sciences;Teacher Education	30+
Participant 2	female	Poland	Business and Tourism	16–20
Participant 3	female	France	Human and Health Sciences	11–15
Participant 4	male	Belgium	Business	40+
Participant 5	female	Finland	Business Writing;Language for Professional Life	20+
Participant 6	female	Finland	Business and marketing communication	16–20
Participant 7	female	Portugal	Business; Office management	20+
Participant 8	female	Portugal	Technology and Engineering	30+
Participant 9	female	Czech Republic	Business	20+
Participant 10	female	Hungary	Special needs education	20+
Participant 11	female	Slovakia	Business	20+
Participant 12	female	Germany	Business	11–15

Table 3 Overall reliability of the quantitative study

Cronbach's alpha normal teaching mode (n1 – n29)	Cronbach's alpha Online/ERT (o1 – o29)	Number of items
0.910	0.936	29

5 Results

Following the convergent design approach, the results of the quantitative and qualitative data collection of the study are presented separately in the order of the research questions (RQ1–3).

5.1 Results of the Quantitative Data Analysis

The results presented in this section correspond to the consolidated statistical summary of the findings obtained from the quantitative data analysis. The overall reliability of the study was calculated for both normal (pre-COVID) teaching mode and ERT responses, and the corresponding values of the Cronbach's alpha coefficients for the 29 items of the survey are shown in Table 3. The high internal consistency of the items implies that the study can be considered highly reliable (Cohen et al., 2018).

5.1.1 Innovative Assessment Practices and their Perceived Effectiveness Before and During ERT

In the survey, 29 items corresponding to various assessment tasks were listed, and the respondents were asked to rate the effectiveness of each item on a 6-point Likert scale both in normal teaching mode and during ERT. Descriptive statistics revealed (Table 4) that in normal teaching mode, the assessment tasks that received the highest mean average values were those identified as 'presentation' (*M=5.3, SD=0.92*), 'dialogue' (*M=5.24, SD=1.15*), 'oral summary' (*M=5.06, SD=1.2*), 'topic discussion' (*M=5.03, SD=1.22*), 'project task' (*M=4.96, SD=1.26*) and 'role-play' (*M=4.93, SD=1.35*). These results for the six assessment tasks show that, in normal teaching mode, teachers considered oral tasks that are usually performed face-to-face in the classroom the most effective ways of assessing students' performance.

In the case of ERT, however, teachers selected not only oral tasks but also written and collaborative tasks as the most effective means of assessment (Table 5). The mean average values of 'presentation' (*M=4.59, SD=1.25*) and 'project task' (*M=4.55, SD=1.42*) were the highest, while 'written summary' (*M=4.45, SD=1.55*), 'oral summary' (*M=4.44, SD=1.48*), 'portfolio' (*M=4.43, SD=1.55*) and 'telecollaborative task' (*M=4.42, SD=1.58*) were also considered effective by the respondents.

5.1.2 Shift in Emphasis of Tasks in ERT

A further aim of the statistical analyses was to identify those task types, which indicated a shift in emphasis; the difference between the mean average values assigned in normal teaching mode and the one in ERT was calculated to identify this change. Table 6 summarizes the tasks with the largest increase in their perceived effectiveness and those tasks considered to be more effective in ERT, which require students' self-reflection on their own learning process ('blog', 'learning journal'), collaborative engagement ('blog', 'telecollaborative task'), or synthesized and critical thinking ('video', 'open book exam').

The opposite can be observed in Table 7, where items of decreasing mean average values are listed. Tasks with the largest decrease in their perceived effectiveness

Table 4 Mean average values – effectiveness of assessment tasks (Normal teaching mode)

Assessment tasks scored highest on effectiveness scale (normal)		Mean	SD
n20	Presentation	5.3012	0.9242
n8	Dialogue	5.2403	1.1550
n15	Oral summary	5.0662	1.2092
n26	Topic discussion	5.0392	1.2294
n21	Project task	4.9638	1.2638
n24	Role-play	4.9379	1.3500

Table 5 Mean average values – Effectiveness of assessment tasks (ERT)

Assessment tasks scored highest on effectiveness scale (ERT)		Mean	SD
o20	Presentation	4.5939	1.2537
o21	Project task	4.5556	1.4229
o16	Written summary	4.4551	1.5506
o15	Oral summary	4.4430	1.4813
o17	Portfolio	4.4375	1.5509
o10	Telecollaborative task	4.4298	1.5802

Table 6 Comparison of mean average values – tasks with a positive shift in the perceived effectiveness from normal to ERT

Assessment tasks with positive shift in effectiveness		Normal		ERT	
		Mean	SD	Mean	SD
n3/o3	Blog	3.4365	1.54659	4.1000	1.56933
n10/o10	Telecollaborative task	3.9512	1.67358	4.4298	1.5802
n28/o28	Video	3.9063	1.62867	4.2266	1.62275
n6/o6	Open book exam	4.1702	1.40894	4.3776	1.46703
n23/o23	Learning journal	3.8125	1.66864	3.9298	1.71778

Table 7 Comparison of mean average values – tasks with a negative shift in the perceived effectiveness from normal to ERT

Assessment tasks with major shift in effectiveness		Normal		ERT	
		Mean	SD	Mean	SD
n5/o5	Closed book exam	4.8221	1.34679	2.9114	1.72793
n24/o24	Role-play	4.9379	1.35000	3.2867	1.55926
n25/o25	Simulation	4.7023	1.49200	3.6202	1.64504
n8/o8	Dialogue	5.2403	1.15501	4.2614	1.54226
n11/o11	Listening comprehension	4.8153	1.35789	3.8750	1.75791

include activities that are based on face-to-face communication using speaking or listening skills ('role play', 'simulation', 'dialogue', "listening comprehension'), or standardized testing ('closed book exam').

5.1.3 LSP Teachers' Perceptions on the Overall Effectiveness of Each Task Category

The last part of the statistical analyses aimed to group the 29 items and define constructs corresponding to the task categories identified in Bloom's revised taxonomy. The definition of the constructs, the allocation of the items to the constructs and the reliability of the constructs can be found in Table 8. The Cronbach's alpha values of

Table 8 Reliability and construct validity of the quantitative study

Constructs	Variables	Cronbach's alpha	Number of items
Remembering/Understanding (Online/ERT)	o5, o7, o11, o12, o14, o22, o29	0.860	7
Applying (Online/ERT)	o2, o8, o9, o15, o16, o24, o27	0.834	7
Creating/Evaluating/ Analysing (Online/ERT)	o1, o3, o4, o6, o10, o13, o17, o18, o20, o21, o23, o25, o26, o28	0.895	14

Table 9 Mean average values of the constructs (ERT)

Constructs	Mean	SD
Remembering/Understanding (Online/ERT)	3.6804	1.2641
Applying (Online/ERT)	4.1787	1.0136
Creating/Evaluating/Analysing (Online/ ERT)	4.2883	0.9965

Table 10 Differences between rated effectiveness of task categories in ERT (Paired Samples t-Test)

Constructs	N	Mean differences	Sig. (2-tailed)*
Pair 1 (Remembering/Understanding – Applying)	172	–0.57438	.000
Pair 2 (Remembering/Understanding – Creating/ Evaluating/Analysing)	172	–0.68184	.000
Pair 3 (Applying – Creating/Evaluating/Analysing)	174	–0.11150	.013

Note. *Significant at the $p < .05$ level

all three constructs turned out to be high, all of which were beyond the minimum threshold of .60 and therefore can be considered reliable (Cohen et al., 2018).

To reveal the perceived effectiveness of different assessment tasks based on the Bloom's taxonomy learning objectives, t-tests were run on their paired samples. The results of the paired sample t-tests indicate a significant difference between the construct "Remembering/Understanding" and the two other constructs ($Sig=0.00$; $p<0.05$) (Table 9).

The mean average value of the construct "Remembering/Understanding" is significantly lower than that of the constructs "Applying" and "Creating/ Evaluating/Analysing" (Table 9). Accordingly, using tasks for assessment which follow "Applying" and "Creating/Evaluating/Analysing" approaches are perceived to be significantly more effective in ERT than tasks from the "Remembering/ Understanding" category. A statistically significant difference is also manifest between the constructs "Applying" and "Creating/Evaluating/Analysing" (Table 10).

5.2 Findings of the Qualitative Data Analysis

The first part of the semi-structured interviews focused on teachers' institutional background, teaching context, pedagogical views, assessment practices and instructors' freedom and possibilities for innovation in assessment in 'normal' teaching mode. In the second part of the interviews, participants gave a detailed account of their teaching experience during ERT, the assessment practices they applied, the challenges they faced, and reflected on the possible effect of ERT on their future assessment strategy.

5.2.1 Innovative Assessment Practices and Their Perceived Effectiveness Before and During ERT

First, we asked interviewees to reflect on their own LSP teaching pedagogy and most interviewees associated good teaching with the ability to adapt to change and to innovate, and they considered these abilities were crucial in their own teaching practice. Participants 2 and 7 elaborated on the evolution of good teaching pedagogies in time. As Participant 7 put it, "what I considered to be very good teaching in the past, I do not consider it to be effective with my students anymore". The innovativeness might be linked to the fact that most interviewees have been involved in European projects focusing on methodological innovation in the following areas: digital storytelling, design-thinking, telecollaboration/virtual exchange, autonomous learning, intercultural communication, CLIL.

The interviews revealed that the participants could rely on and develop further their innovative assessment practices introduced before the ERT, including a strong focus on continuous assessment (Participants 1, 2, 6, 7, 9, 10, 11, 12), the use of portfolios (Participants 4, 6, 10, 12), reflection journal (Participants 1, 3, 6), or telecollaboration (Participants 2, 3, 4, 5, 7, 8, 9) for assessment. All the interviewees reflected on the importance of student-centred, formative assessment in their teaching practice, both before and during ERT, as illustrated by the following quotes:

> To measure students' progress, I try to use this mixture of summative and continuous assessment (...) I'm more inclined to having this formative way of evaluating my students, because this is about self-learning. (Participant 12)

> I like that type of assessment when students can be trusted (...) and I need their trust in my system of assessment. (...) So, I am less a teacher and more a coach. (Participant 4)

Only very few participants had previous experience with completely online and blended teaching. Participants 2, 4, 12 provided examples of their own teaching practice when they did not need to revise assessment tasks at the transition to ERT. As Participant 6 explained her good classroom practice that she had introduced several years before. Her students pursue real marketing tasks for companies simulating a client-provider relationship. Following a project-based teaching approach, students work on authentic tasks in small groups and present their final assignment at the end of the course. In her case, ERT did not imply any alteration to the assessment. Peer-evaluation and formative feedback on individual and team-work were used both before and after the transition to ERT. Among the interviewees, Participants 1, 2 and 6 claimed that they were using peer- and self-assessment practices in their courses and considered these approaches to be effective forms of assessment.

5.2.2   Shift in Emphasis of Tasks in ERT

For most participants, the transition to ERT occurred in the middle of their ongoing semester and they opted for different ways of adapting their courses to the sudden shift to remote teaching. Four interview participants (Participants 4, 7, 11, 12) reported high flexibility and freedom in their course design and assessment methods, indicating that they could modify their assessment practice. Others (Participants 2 and 3) claimed to have limited freedom in terms of changing course syllabus and assessment methods, and they must comply with university rules and regulations in place, which often regulate assessment. As the interviews occurred in September and October 2020, some participants reflected on their plans for the following semester. For example, Participant 12 specified some changes she would introduce: "The exam for the final grade is worth 75 percent depending on the course. I'm thinking of reducing it to 40 percent".

While most universities consider summative final exams to be a key for standardization, thus highly important, all interviewees questioned its relevance as it can be traced in the quotes below:

> An end of the term exam just reflects a given situation, at a given point. (Participant 12)

> I think that students can be more motivated when I can put aside all the stressful elements from learning, such as the final exam. (Participant 11)

> My authorities decided to have online exams at the end of the term and to make it as close to real-life classroom exams as possible (…), which was a silly decision to make, because you cannot create such conditions. (Participant 2)

> It is important to move away from this type of assessment (summative), (…) I have always found that so terribly unfair. (Participant 1)

One of the main problems perceived by some interviewees related to computer-based tests in an online environment was the possibility of students' dishonest academic behaviour: "I think that doing tests online in the Moodle environment is useless because I cannot control who is doing the tests". Therefore, 7 of the 12 respondents (Participants 1, 2, 3, 5, 7, 8, 12) explained that they have reduced the weight of the summative assessment in ERT to place more emphasis on formative assessment, while Participant 11 contemplated on the need to reduce it in the future. Three respondents (Participants 2, 5, 9) modified their course description and announced a slightly revised version of the syllabus, which included changes in the assessment criteria and course completion requirements. However, Participant 2 explained that teachers at their institution must comply with university regulations that do not allow them to modify the syllabus and course requirements in the middle of the course. Therefore, she had to find ways of ensuring adequate assessment during ERT in compliance with institutional regulations. As Participant 2 had to administer an end-course test online, she decided to change the questions and included tasks instead that required creative thinking and composition. In the case of Participant 9, students were given individual written tasks they could choose from and compile their work in a portfolio, which implied a new way of assessment. Others (Participants 7, 8, 10, 11) moved their face-to-face courses to online platforms, and "gave extra points" as a reward to students' continuous work (Participant 11), or simply cancelled their final written exams to replace them with a more complex online oral exam. As Participant 7 admitted, "when it came to the final exam, I decided I would not do any written test". Participant 12 reported that her summer semester began only in April, so she could consider that courses would be held remotely and thus adapted her syllabus before the start of the semester. Her newly designed online course consisted of five complex authentic tasks, with formative feedback from the teacher at the end of each. Transition to ERT and e-assessment was not demanding for Participant 4 who runs blended courses and uses formative assessment methods to measure performance and provide feedback.

5.2.3 Challenges Faced by LSP Teachers in Adopting New Assessment Approach in ERT

Global challenges resulting from the use of virtual platforms were manifold: interviewees indicated initial technical difficulties related to internet connection and lack of experience using videoconferencing tools and reported screen fatigue. Nevertheless, the interviewees had different perceptions of delivering classes face-to-face or on an online platform. While Participant 11 expressed her opinion that she had not noticed any major differences between teaching online and offline, the reduction of the interpersonal dimension in classroom communication online was felt by Participants 2, 5, 8 as a loss. Participant 8 highlighted the importance of the facial expression or the eye contact in classroom interactions. Participant 4 explained that similar personal relationship can be also created online by "making a lot of efforts just to be able to communicate and re-establish a human relationship when we are online, but it is worth the effort."

Beyond the technical difficulties, our interviews have clearly revealed that many challenges of remote teaching coincided with previously existing problems, such as students' lack of motivation or interest, mixed ability groups and diverse foreign language competence, or the genuine need to focus on transversal skills in LSP classes. All interviewees reported an increase in their workload and screen-time during ERT compared to face-to-face classes. Continuous formative assessment takes more time and increases the workload of the teacher. Administrative tasks to set up the courses, upload materials, assign tasks, review students' work and communicate with them offline are all time-consuming.

Participants emphasised a shift in their own attitude towards students during ERT. As Participant 7 mentioned, "I think I was a little bit more motherly to my students than I usually am", and explained "I realized I needed to go into a little bit more of intimacy to get them some kind of emotional support". Participant 3 highlighted that she had to "do a lot of handholding" and addressing the needs of mixed-ability students on an individual basis. To characterize their attitude towards students, Participant 12 emphasised the need for *scaffolding* during ERT, Participants 4 and 6 highlighted the effectiveness of *coaching* methods, and Participant 11 argued that students needed to get extra support.

However, in case of complex assessment tasks in which students had to create content individually (Participant 9) or in the group (Participant 12), cheating and plagiarism issues were also reported. Participant 9 pointed out that in some cases dishonesty was difficult to control, while it was rather obvious in some other tasks. For example, students simply copied entirely or partially their peer's ideas from a blog. Participant 12 stated that she had made it clear at the beginning of the semester that she would not tolerate cheating and plagiarism. However, she tried considering the difficult situation everybody was in, and instead of notifying the student about course failure, she explained the problem to the student giving them a second chance. Participant 4 explained that it is not possible to prevent students from cheating online, so teachers should find alternative ways for assessment (e.g. case study, oral exam) to eliminate the "cheat factor".

5.2.4 Potential Impact of ERT on LSP Teachers' Future Assessment Practices and Innovations in Their Pedagogy

Participants without exception express their view that the consequences of ERT should drive major change and innovation in university assessment practices across the globe. They believe that formative assessment practices will become the most preferred forms of assessment, they will form an integral part of the student learning process and will be a formal complement to summative assessment methods. Interviewees also welcome these long-waited developments in assessment pedagogies, which they believe will be accelerated by ERT. Participants will incorporate newly acquired alternative assessment practices and pedagogies of ERT into their LSP classrooms of the post-COVID era. As Participant 12 stated, "I started using an e-portfolio (…) that's something I'm going to use again." Also, the possible transition to blended LSP teaching is expected. As Participant 12 put it, "we probably won't go back to the way things were before (…) once you realise, things are possible, whether we like it or not (…) maybe we can somehow have more blended learning".

Participant 4, being also an advisor at the Pedagogical Department of his university, believes that the biggest challenge is to convince their colleagues to change their teaching attitude, including their assessment practice. With ERT, teachers were forced to turn digital and realised that they cannot continue teaching and assessment practices traditionally. In the future, the focus of the assessment should change from assessing students' knowledge to assessing their skills. As Participant 4 questioned, "It is easy to check if they (*students*) know things, but what can they do with everything they know?" Consequently, teaching peda-gogies and assessment practices should follow these trends and focus on students' ability and creativity to apply what they have learned. Participant 4 summarises his hopes for the future as ERT has opened a space for everybody to learn and "my hope is that this space is going to exist in the future and people will learn to do things better".

6 Discussion

The findings of this mixed-method study are combined, and synthesized results are discussed here following the order of the research questions.

6.1 RQ1: What perceptions do LSP teachers have related to the effectiveness of assessment tasks in normal teaching mode and during ERT, and what tasks gained more emphasis in teachers' pedagogical thinking as a consequence of ERT?

The underlying aim of this chapter goes beyond the exploration of how educators solved an emergency, but rather it reveals their perceptions based on their first-hand experiences. Consequently, in our quantitative part of our study focussed on the methods LSP teachers would find effective when teaching online and in traditional settings, based on their comparable experience during ERT. During the semi-structured interviews we asked the participants how the transition to ERT affected assessment in their LSP courses.

Findings of the survey and interviews reveal that the relevance of summative end-of-term exams in LSP courses can be questioned beyond the ERT situation. Teachers identified creative and collaborative tasks (e.g. telecollaboration or project work) and tasks aimed at developing students' autonomous learning skills (e.g. open-book exam, portfolio, learning journal) as tools being effective to assess students' LSP competence. Survey results indicate that respondents perceived that 'blogs', 'telecollaborative tasks', 'videos', 'open-book exams' and 'reflection journals' assessed students' learning more effectively in a remote setting compared to normal teaching mode. The opposite can be seen in the case of 'closed-book exams', 'role-plays', 'simulation', 'dialogue', and 'listening tasks', as these are considered to be less effective in ERT.

Teachers' perceptions on effective tasks are consistent with students' preferences for remote assessment methods reported by Guangul et al. (2020). In their recent study on remote assessment during ERT, Guangul et al. (2020) found that 68% of the university students taking part in their survey preferred assignment-based and project-based assessment to question-based summative assessment; ranking report, open-book assignment and presentation among the most preferred methods of assessment. Our statistical analyses revealed that tasks that target the development of students' HOTs are significantly more effective in ERT than tasks employing lower-order thinking skills. Qualitative data analysis confirms these results and allows for the conclusion that more complex tasks, which reinforce students' creative language use should be placed in the focus of LSP assessment. Our findings go beyond previous reports that argue for the applicability and effectiveness of online formative assessment methods (Baleni, 2015; Dermo, 2011; Gikandi et al., 2011; Pachler et al., 2010; Romeu Fontanillas et al., 2016). Contrary to previous research into online summative assessment that argued for the possible efficiency of online examinations (Alruwais et al., 2018; Boitshwarelo et al., 2017; James, 2016; Nicol, 2007), our findings could not confirm the validity of using summative assessment methods in the ERT setting.

6.2   RQ2: What challenges do LSP teachers face in adopting their assessment practice to ERT?

Interviewees had the opportunity to experiment with various forms of assessment during ERT and are in the position to suggest innovation and change in institutional assessment practice. However, classroom innovations are subject to institutional support and approval. Formative assessment is based on the idea of teacher-student partnership, and it is also crucial that teachers are regarded as partners by university management in institutional-level pedagogical innovations, hence bottom-up teacher initiatives are supported.

One of the biggest challenges of teaching and assessing students' performance during ERT was the increased workload. Although technology-enabled assessment may reduce teachers' marking time (Romeu Fontanillas et al., 2016), our findings confirm that online formative assessment during ERT was a time-consuming burden on the teachers (Brown, 2005), which calls for recognition by university management. Another challenging factor of ERT according to LSP teachers was related to technology use, which is in line with previous literature reporting on teachers' lack of digital competence (Alruwais et al., 2018; Amhag et al., 2019; Hodges et al., 2020; Mirete et al., 2020). The need for teachers to develop higher-level of digital literacy should be in accordance with the development of pedagogical methods, which should be introduced in academic development programs in post-COVID times. Tackling problems with academic dishonesty and plagiarism was also perceived as a major challenge and also reported in previous studies (Boitshwarelo et al., 2017; Guangul et al., 2020; James, 2016), but the institutionalization of formative assessment could provide a possible solution.

6.3   RQ3: What potential consequences may ERT have on future assessment practices in the LSP classroom and innovations in LSP pedagogy for the post-COVID-19 era, as perceived by LSP teachers?

When we started to work on our research, we assumed that traditional assessment methods could not be used effectively in LSP teaching during ERT, and believed that this global pandemic shed light on the limitations of traditional assessment methods and called for change and innovation. Results indicate that the teachers realised how difficult it was to measure students' real development by using only traditional forms of assessment. Interviews account for teachers' adaptation techniques to the ERT landscape by reimagining the assessment activities set for students, very often reducing the weight of summative tests, for example multiple choice questions. Hence, a shift in teachers' pedagogical mindset can be witnessed as they tend to move away from traditional assessment methods. Our findings echo the results of the report published by an Irish independent state agency, Quality and Qualifications Ireland (QQI), revealing that "the crisis stimulated assessment innovation" (QQI, 2020, p. 8), which may have long-term consequences for the post-COVID era.

7   Conclusion

Our European-wide survey and the interviews conducted with academics generated rich data on LSP teachers' perceptions of how ERT, introduced as a direct conse-quence of the COVID-19 pandemic, shaped their pedagogical thinking and assess-ment. The challenges of traditional assessment methods during ERT call for learner-centred assessment practices and innovative solutions that make assessment accountable, fair, and reliable in the digital learning environment. Results of this study allow for the conclusion that tasks targeting the development of students' HOTs prove to be a more effective means of assessment during ERT and beyond. The inclusion of innovative ideas and pedagogic approaches, applied in the ERT context, into the LSP classroom is a promising trend for the future, and the potential impact of ERT on the widespread application of formative assessment methods may be projected in the post-COVID era.

8   Food for Thought

Formative assessment places the LSP teacher in a new role as they should become practitioners of coaching-oriented teaching, and work very closely with the students to guide their learning with constructive, student-centred feedback. As coaching-oriented teaching requires a higher-level commitment from teachers, it can work to the educator's advantage as it promotes learner autonomy, higher student engage-ment and self-reflection on their own learning process. Assuming a new teacher role can fully-support students' development through innovative pedagogies and assessment practices, therefore it contributes to the success of LSP teaching in the post-COVID era.

Appendix A: 29 Tasks to Be Rated for Effective Assessment of Students' LSP Learning (Extract from the Online Survey)

In your opinion, how effective are the following assessment activities in NORMAL teaching AND in ONLINE teaching mode to assess students' LSP learning? Please mark the effectiveness of each activity on a 6-point scale as follows: 1=Very ineffective, 2=Ineffective, 3=Slightly ineffective, 4=Slightly effective, 5=Effective, 6=Very effective

Assessment tasks	Normal teaching (pre-COVID-19)	Online teaching/ERT[*]
1. Argumentative/persuasive essay	1 2 3 4 5 6	1 2 3 4 5 6
2. Narrative/descriptive essay	1 2 3 4 5 6	1 2 3 4 5 6
3. Blog	1 2 3 4 5 6	1 2 3 4 5 6
4. Case study	1 2 3 4 5 6	1 2 3 4 5 6
5. Closed-book exam	1 2 3 4 5 6	1 2 3 4 5 6
6. Open-book exam	1 2 3 4 5 6	1 2 3 4 5 6
7. Cloze test (students fill in the gaps)	1 2 3 4 5 6	1 2 3 4 5 6
8. Dialogue	1 2 3 4 5 6	1 2 3 4 5 6
9. Guided writing	1 2 3 4 5 6	1 2 3 4 5 6
10. Telecollaboration (online projects based on students' cooperation from different universities)	1 2 3 4 5 6	1 2 3 4 5 6
11. Listening comprehension test	1 2 3 4 5 6	1 2 3 4 5 6
12. Matching, sequencing task	1 2 3 4 5 6	1 2 3 4 5 6
13. Mediation task	1 2 3 4 5 6	1 2 3 4 5 6
14. Multiple-choice test	1 2 3 4 5 6	1 2 3 4 5 6
15. Oral summary	1 2 3 4 5 6	1 2 3 4 5 6
16. Written summary	1 2 3 4 5 6	1 2 3 4 5 6
17. Portfolio	1 2 3 4 5 6	1 2 3 4 5 6
18. Poster presentation	1 2 3 4 5 6	1 2 3 4 5 6
19. Pre- and post-questionnaire	1 2 3 4 5 6	1 2 3 4 5 6
20. Presentation	1 2 3 4 5 6	1 2 3 4 5 6
21. Project task	1 2 3 4 5 6	1 2 3 4 5 6
22. Reading comprehension test	1 2 3 4 5 6	1 2 3 4 5 6
23. Learning journal	1 2 3 4 5 6	1 2 3 4 5 6
24. Role-play	1 2 3 4 5 6	1 2 3 4 5 6
25. Simulation	1 2 3 4 5 6	1 2 3 4 5 6
26. Topic discussion	1 2 3 4 5 6	1 2 3 4 5 6
27. Translation	1 2 3 4 5 6	1 2 3 4 5 6
28. Video creation	1 2 3 4 5 6	1 2 3 4 5 6
29. True or false task	1 2 3 4 5 6	1 2 3 4 5 6

[*]The answers in this column referring to normal teaching (pre-COVID) were coded as n1-n29
[**] The answers in this column referring to online teaching/ERT were coded as o1-o29

References

Alruwais, N., Wills, G., & Wald, M. (2018). Advantages and challenges of using e-assessment. *International Journal of Information and Education Technology, 8*(1), 34–37. https://doi.org/10.18178/ijiet.2018.8.1.1008

Amhag, L., Hellström, L., & Stigmar, M. (2019). Teacher educators' use of digital tools and needs for digital competence in higher education. *Journal of Digital Learning in Teacher Education, 35*(4), 203–220. https://doi.org/10.1080/21532974.2019.1646169

Anderson, L. W., & Krathwohl, D. R. (Eds.). (2001). *A taxonomy for learning, teaching, and assessing: A revision of Bloom's taxonomy of educational objectives.* Longman.

Baleni, Z. G. (2015). Online formative assessment in higher education: Its pros and cons. *Electronic Journal of e-Learning, 13*(4), 228–236.

Barbero, T. (2012). Assessment practices and tools in CLIL. In F. Quartapelle (Ed.), *Assessment and evaluation in CLIL* (pp. 38–56). Ibis.

Bárcena, E., Read, T., & Arus, J. (Eds.). (2014). *Languages for specific purposes in the digital era.* Springer.

Bates, A. W. (2015). *Teaching in a digital age: Guidelines for designing teaching and learning for a digital age.* BCcampus.

Birenbaum, M., Deluca, C., Earl, L., Heritage, M., Klenowski, V., Looney, A., Smith, K., Timperley, H., Volante, L., & Wyatt-Smith, C. (2015). International trends in the implementation of assessment for learning: Implications for policy and practice. *Policy Futures in Education, 13*(1), 117–140. https://doi.org/10.1177/1478210314566733

Black, P., & Wiliam, D. (1998). Inside the black box: Raising standards through classroom assessment. *Phi Delta Kappan, 80*(2).

Bloom, B. S., Madaus, G. F., & Hastings, J. T. (1971). *Handbook on formative and summative evaluation of student learning.* McGraw-Hill.

Boitshwarelo, B., Reedy, A. K., & Billany, T. (2016). Envisioning the use of online tests in assessing twenty-first century learning: A literature review. *Research and Practice in Technology Enhanced Learning, 12*, 16. https://doi.org/10.1186/s41039-017-0055-7

Boud, D., & Soler, R. (2016). Sustainable assessment revisited. *Assessment and Evaluation in Higher Education, 41*(3), 400–413. https://doi.org/10.1080/02602938.2015.1018133

Broadfoot, P., Daugherty, R., Gardner, J., Gipps, C., Harlen, W., James, M., & Stobart, G. (1999). *Assessment for learning: Beyond the black box.* University of Cambridge.

Brown, S. (2005). Assessment for learning. *Learning and Teaching in Higher Education, 1*, 81–89.

Cano, E., & Ion, G. (Eds.). (2017). *Innovative practices for higher education assessment and measurement.* IGI Global.

Cohen, L., Manion, L., & Morrison, K. (Eds.). (2018). *Research methods in education* (8th ed.). Routledge.

Craparo, R. M. (2007). Significance level. In N. J. Salkind (Ed.), *Encyclopaedia of measurement and statistics* (pp. 889–891). SAGE.

Creswell, J. V. (2013). *Qualitative inquiry and research design: Choosing among five approaches.* SAGE.

Creswell, J. V., & Plano Clark, V. L. (2018). *Designing and conducting mixed methods research* (3rd ed.). SAGE.

Crisp, G. T. (2012). Integrative assessment: Reframing assessment practice for current and future learning. *Assessment & Evaluation in Higher Education, 37*(1), 33–43. https://doi.org/10.1080/02602938.2010.494234

Crisp, G., Guàrdia, L., & Hillier, M. (2016). Using e-assessment to enhance student learning and evidence learning outcomes. *International Journal of Educational Technology in Higher Education, 13*, 18. https://doi.org/10.1186/s41239-016-0020-3

Dermo, J. (2011). Technology enhanced assessment for learning: Case studies and best practice. *HEA Academy Evidence Net Briefing Paper.* Retrieved from: http://www.heacademy.ac.uk/assets/documents/learningandtech/Bradford_Briefing_Report_8_Dec_2010.pdf

Dixson, D. D., & Worrell, F. C. (2016). Formative and summative assessment in the classroom. *Theory into Practice, 55*(2), 153–159. https://doi.org/10.1080/00405841.2016.1148989

Galletta, A. (2013). *Qualitative studies in psychology. Mastering the semi-structured interview and beyond: From research design to analysis and publication.* https://doi.org/10.18574/nyu/9780814732939.001.0001. New York University Press.

Gikandi, J. W., Morrow, D., & Davis, N. E. (2011). Online formative assessment in higher education: A review of literature. *Computers & Education, 57*(4), 2333–2351. https://doi.org/10.1016/j.compedu.2011.06.004

Guangul, F. M., Suhail, A. H., Khalit, M. I., & Khidhir, B. A. (2020). Challenges of remote assessment in higher education in the context of COVID-19: A case study of Middle East College. *Educational Assessment, Evaluation and Accountability.* https://doi.org/10.1007/s11092-020-09340-w

Guàrdia, L., Crisp, G., & Alsina, I. (2017). Trends and challenges of e-assessment to enhance student learning in higher education. In E. Cano & G. Ion (Eds.), *Innovative practices for higher education assessment and measurement* (pp. 36–55). IGI Global.

Harlen, W., & Gardner, J. (2010). Assessment to support learning. In J. Gardner, W. Harlen, L. Hayward, G. Stobart, & M. Montgomery (Eds.), *Developing teacher assessment* (pp. 15–28). Open University Press.

Hidri, S. (Ed.). (2020). *Perspectives on language assessment literacy: Challenges for improved student learning.* Routledge.

Hodges, C., Moore, S., Locke, B., Trust, T., & Bond, A. (2020, March 27). The difference between emergency remote teaching and online learning. *EDUCAUSEReview.* https://er.educause.edu/articles/2020/3/the-difference-between-emergency-remote-teaching-and-online-learning.

Hutchinson, T., & Waters, A. (1987). *English for Specific Purposes.* Cambridge University Press.

Incollab Project. (2021). *Assessment framework for innovative online modules.* https://incollabeu.wixsite.com/project/outputs

James, R. (2016). Tertiary student attitudes to invigilated, online summative examinations. *International Journal of Educational Technology in Higher Education, 13*, 19. https://doi.org/10.1186/s41239-016-0015-0

Johnson, R. B., & Onwuegbuzie, A. J. (2004). Mixed methods research: A research paradigm whose time has come. *Educational Researcher, 33*(7), 14–26.

Knight, P. (1995). *Assessment for learning in higher education.* Kogan Page.

Laurence, A. (2018). *Introducing English for specific purposes.* Routledge.

Lincoln, Y. S., & Guba, E. G. (1985). *Naturalistic inquiry.* Sage.

Mirete, A. B., Maquilón, J. J., Mirete, L., & Rodríguez, R. A. (2020). Digital competence and university teachers' conceptions about teaching: A structural causal model. *Sustainability, 12*, 4842. https://doi.org/10.3390/su12124842

Nicol, D. (2007). E-assessment by design: Using multiple-choice tests to good effect. *Journal of Further and Higher Education, 31*(1), 53–64. https://doi.org/10.1080/03098770601167922

O'Sullivan, B. (2012). Assessment issues in languages for specific purposes. *The Modern Language Journal, 96*, 71–88. https://doi.org/10.1111/j.1540-4781.2012.01298.x

Pachler, N., Daly, C., Mor, Y., & Mellar, H. (2010). Formative e-assessment: Practitioner cases. *Computers & Education, 54*(3), 715–721. https://doi.org/10.1016/j.compedu.2009.09.032

Quality and Qualifications Ireland (QQI). (2020). *The impact of COVID-19 modifications to teaching, learning and assessment in Irish Further Education and Training and Higher Education.* https://www.qqi.ie/Articles/Pages/COVID-19%2D%2D-Updates-from-QQI.aspx

Rea-Dickins, P. (2007). Classroom-based assessment: Possibilities and pitfalls. In J. Cummins & C. Davison (Eds.), *International handbook of English language teaching* (pp. 505–520). Springer.

Romeu Fontanillas, T., Romero Carbonell, M., & Guitert Catasús, M. (2016). E-assessment process: Giving a voice to online learners. *International Journal of Educational Technology in Higher Education, 13*, 20. https://doi.org/10.1186/s41239-016-0019-9

Rust, C. (2002). The impact of assessment on student learning: How can the research literature practically help to inform the development of departmental assessment strategies and learner-centred assessment practices? *Active Learning in Higher Education, 3*(2), 145–158. https://doi.org/10.1177/1469787402003002004

Stiggins, R. J. (1994). *Student-centered classroom assessment*. Merrill.

Taherdoost, H. (2019). What is the best response scale for survey and questionnaire design: Review of different lengths of rating scale/attitude scale/Likert scale. *International Journal of Academic Research in Management, 8*. https://hal.archives-ouvertes.fr/hal-02557308/document

Wiggins, G. P. (1998). *Educative assessment: Designing assessment to inform and improve student performance*. Jossey-Bass.

Woodrow, L. (2018). *Introducing course design in English for specific purposes*. Routledge.

Zapalska, A. M., McCarty, M. D., Young-McLear, K., & White, J. (2018). Design of assignments using the 21st century bloom's revised taxonomy model for development of critical thinking skills. *Problems and Perspectives in Management, 16*(2), 291–305. https://doi.org/10.21511/ppm.16(2).2018.27

Zhang, H., Yan, Y., & Gronseth, S. (2020). Adding flexibility to curriculum: A practical guide for students directed assessment. In R. E. Ferdig, E. Baumgartner, R. Hartshorne, R. Kapan-Rakowski & C. Mouza (Eds.), *Teaching, technology, and teacher education during the COVID-19 pandemic: Stories from the field* (pp. 113–117). Association for the Advancement of Computing in Education (AACE). https://www.learntechlib.org/p/216903/